TOPS®
The IBM®/Macintosh® Connection

Applied Networking Series

TOPS®
The IBM®/Macintosh® Connection

Stephen Cobb
Marty Jost

W WINDCREST

TOPS® is a registered trademark of Sun Microsystems.
IBM® is a registered trademark of International Business Machines.
Macintosh® is a registered trademark of Apple Computer, Inc.

Published by **Windcrest Books**
FIRST EDITION/FIRST PRINTING

© 1990 by **Windcrest Books.** Reproduction or publication of the content in any manner, without express permission of the publisher is prohibited. The publisher takes no responsibility for the use of any of the materials or methods described in this book, or for the products thereof. Printed in the United States of America.

Library of Congress Cataloging-in-Publication Data

Cobb, Stephen, 1952-
    TOPS: the IBM/Macintosh connection/by Stephen Cobb and Marty Jost.

      p. cm.
    Includes index.

    ISBN 0-8306-3210-7 (P)   ISBN 0-8306-3410-X
    1. Local area networks (Computer networks) 2. IBM microcomputers.
3. Macintosh (Computer)   I. Jost, Marty. II. Title.
TK5105.7.C63   1989
004.6—dc20   89-35636
                                                                                 CIP

TAB BOOKS Inc. offers software for sale. For information and a catalog, please contact TAB Software Department, Blue Ridge Summit, PA 17294-0850.

Questions regarding the content of this book should be addressed to:

**Windcrest Books
Division of TAB BOOKS Inc.
Blue Ridge Summit, PA 17294-0850**

Director of Acquisitions: Ron Powers
Technical Editor: Sandra L. Johnson
Production: Barry Brown
Book Design: Jaclyn B. Saunders

Contents

About This Book ix

1 About Networks 1

The network difference *1*
What is a LAN? *2*
Why do we have LANs? *5*
Network organization *10*
Local area networks today *12*
The question of speed *14*
Along came TOPS *14*

2 About TOPS 17

Basic TOPS vocabulary *17*
The TOPS products *20*
About the TOPS software *22*
The features *23*
The TOPS possibilities *26*
The requirements of TOPS *29*
Network actions *30*
Security on TOPS *33*
Multi-user applications on TOPS *33*
TOPS network etiquette *34*
File compatibility across systems *34*

3 Connecting TOPS 37

Basic connectors *37*
The cable standards *40*
Twisted pair cabling systems *42*
Expanding the bus for large networks *45*
Some practical advice *45*
Coaxial cabling and the Ethernet bus *48*
Combining the benefits of twisted pair and Ethernet *49*
The star topology *50*

4 Installing TOPS 52

A question of versions *52*
Installing TOPS/Macintosh *53*
Installing TOPS/DOS *58*

TOPS/DOS *72*
TOPS/DOS special cases *76*
Dedicating a TOPS server *77*
Clients and dedicated servers *78*
Handling upgrades *78*

5 Using TOPS/Macintosh *81*

Using TOPS for networking *82*
The TOPS window *82*
Getting started with commands *84*
Multiple network access to a published volume *86*
Optional commands *86*
Using an MS-DOS computer as a server *90*
File management on DOS servers *92*
TOPS on a floppy disk only system *93*
TOPS icons *95*

6 TOPS/DOS by the Menus *97*

Loading TOPS/DOS *97*
About the TOPS menu *99*
Loading the TOPS menu *100*
Server utilities *101*
Client utilities *105*
The remember option *107*

7 General Printing with TOPS *110*

The PostScript factor *110*
About network printing *111*
TOPS Spool *116*

8 The DOS Side of Sharing Printers *128*

Possible printers *128*
Publishing and mounting printers *129*
Using TPRINT *134*
Printing with TOPS NetPrint *140*

9 Commanding TOPS/DOS and the Utilities *159*

About DOS commands *159*
The TOPS command format *164*
TOPS utilities *172*
TOPS batch files *179*
A system of batch files *184*

10 Word Processing and Translating — 189

Why things are as they are *189*
Word processing at work *191*
The translation alternatives *195*
Using TOPS Translators *195*
Other translation sources *214*
A translation application *223*
A word processing strategy *228*

11 Spreadsheets and Databases — 231

A legal disclaimer *231*
A spreadsheet example: Excel *232*
Excel and Multiplan *243*
Limits to Excel file exchange *244*
Unlisted programs *245*
TOPS Translators and Spreadsheets *247*
TOPS Translators and Databases *247*
FileMaker—a Macintosh database *248*
Running Excel across TOPS *255*
Running other spreadsheets across TOPS *259*
Running Filemaker on TOPS *259*
Running other databases across TOPS *262*

12 Graphics and Desktop Publishing — 264

A graphical world *264*
Types of graphics *266*
Sharing graphics *280*
Converters and translators *282*
Bringing it all together: desktop publishing *297*

13 Mail and Communications — 302

Electronic messages *302*
Electronic Mail with TOPS In Box *304*
Another look at cable connections *318*
Network troubleshooting *328*
Connecting to minicomputers and super micros *329*
Remote access *333*
Bridging TOPS networks to remote sites *334*
Network modems, FAXES, and so forth *337*

14 Tips and Tricks and Other Connections — 339

Tips for TOPS gateways *339*
Some special situations *349*
RAM-cram: The PC memory problem *358*

Dealing with RAM-cram: outside TOPS   *364*
Dealing with RAM-cram: within TOPS   *372*
TOPS tips   *373*
Future developments   *379*

Appendix A   TOPS Error Messages   *381*

Appendix B   TOPS-Related Product Directory   *399*

Appendix C   The Basics of PC and Mac Operation   *405*

Appendix D   Installing and Configuring FlashCards   *410*

Glossary   *418*

Index   *423*

About This Book

We have written this book to help you evaluate, install, use, maintain, and benefit from, the powerful technology of TOPS. The TOPS technology allows computers to communicate with each other, sharing information, programs, and peripherals, such as printers. The focus of this book is the connection of microcomputers into a local area network, with particular attention paid to the linking of Apple Macintosh and IBM PC compatible computers.

WHO IS THIS BOOK FOR?

Anyone who has computers to connect should find this book readable, even enjoyable. Despite the fact that the subject of computers and local area networks is littered with acronyms and terms of art that strike the uninitiated as unintelligible, we think we have done a good job of leading you through the subject, explaining acronyms like LAN (local area network) when they first appear, and providing an extensive glossary at the end of the book for reference purposes. However, we have tried to avoid bogging the experienced computer user down with unnecessary preambles. When there is a shortcut to the nuts and bolts, we tell you.

This book was written to serve the needs of several different groups of users. This book is for you if:

- You need to connect several Macintosh computers.
  The book shows you how to share programs, data, and LaserWriter printers with TOPS.
- You need to connect Macintoshes and IBM PCs.
  The book addresses the issues of compatibility and file transfer between systems, as well as how to utilize LaserWriters from the IBM.
- You are considering a Local Area Network.
  The book discusses the evolution of local area networks, where TOPS stands in relationship to other networks, and some of the key factors in network design.
- You are already using TOPS.
  The book will help you use your network more efficiently and hopefully expand your understanding of its capabilities.

HOW THIS BOOK CAME TO BE

This book was a project waiting to happen. Several years ago, we worked for the same computer training company, teaching business applications and installing networks. Marty went on to work for TOPS, and Stephen took to writing books. Marty racked up some impressive hours in technical support for TOPS and used his teaching experience to develop effective explanations of networking concepts. Stephen found himself using both Macs and PCs in his own office and decided to network them with TOPS. The more TOPS increased its installed base, the more logical a joint project became.

HOW THIS BOOK IS ARRANGED

The approach we have taken is to start with the basics and build up from there. If you are already familiar with networks and how they have developed, you may feel like skipping the first chapter. If you have already installed TOPS you can probably skip the first few chapters, although you may want to peruse them anyway, just to make sure that you have not missed anything. The material is arranged as follows:

1. About Networks
2. About TOPS
3. Connecting TOPS
4. Installing TOPS
5. Using TOPS/Macintosh
6. TOPS/DOS by the Menus
7. General Printing with TOPS
8. The DOS Side of Sharing Printers
9. Commanding TOPS/DOS and the Utilities
10. Word Processing and Translating
11. Spreadsheets and Databases
12. Graphics and Desktop Publishing
13. Mail and Communications
14. Tips and Tricks and Other Connections

Appendices:
A   TOPS Error Messages
B   TOPS-Related Product Summary
C   The Basics of PC and Mac Operation
D   Installing and Configuring FlashCards

In writing this book, we have tried to keep technical jargon to a minimum and to make sure that technical terms are explained the first time they are used. There are some terms that are explained each time they appear. This does not imply a low estimate of your ability to retain what you have read; such repetition is for the benefit of some readers who prefer to dip into parts of the book rather than read it from cover-to-cover. A glossary is provided at the back of the book to make sure that all jargon is covered one way or another.

We have endeavored to make the material in this book as accessible as possible. In some cases, we may have failed those with technophobia by leaving out some of the basics. In other cases, we may have skimmed over subjects about which the more technically advanced reader would have preferred more detail. If anything, we have tried to lean in favor of the new user. We ask that you let us know, by mail in care of Windcrest books, what you think. There will eventually be a new edition of this book and any suggestions from readers that are acted upon will be acknowledged therein.

1
About Networks

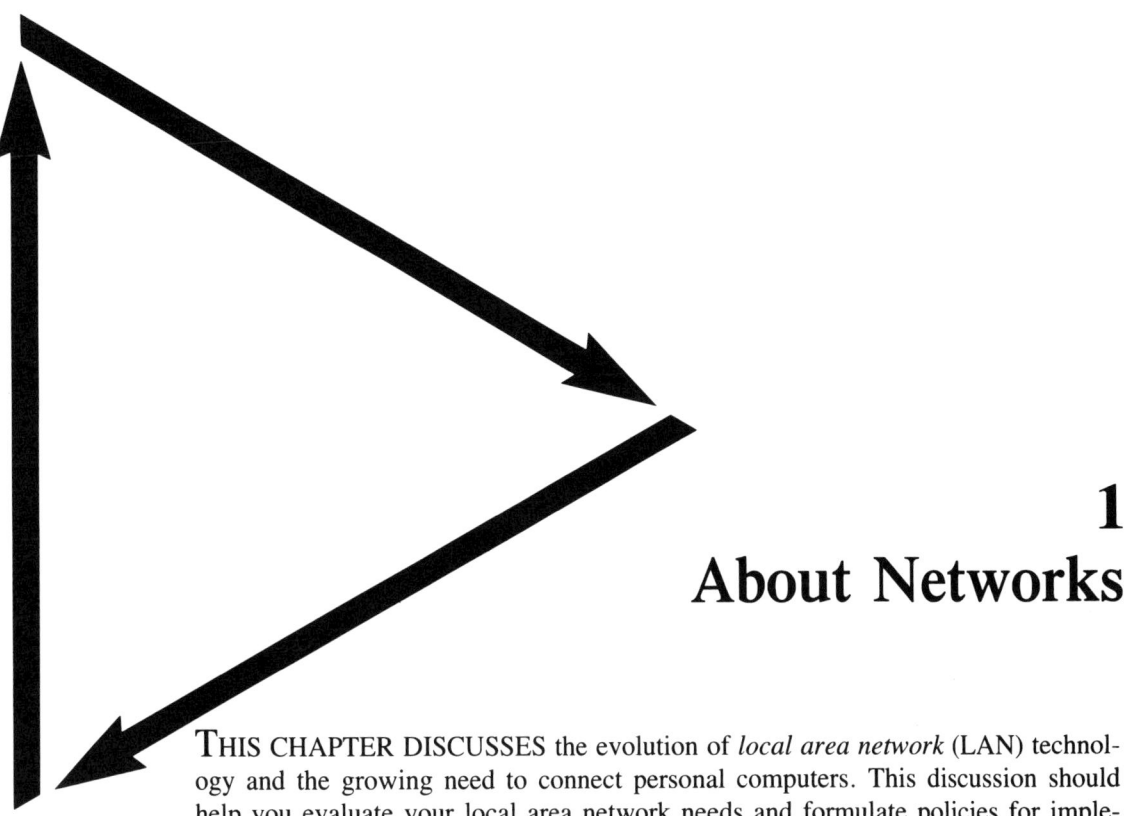

THIS CHAPTER DISCUSSES the evolution of *local area network* (LAN) technology and the growing need to connect personal computers. This discussion should help you evaluate your local area network needs and formulate policies for implementing network strategies in your office. Knowing why there are networks and how network technology is developing will help to put your use of a network product like TOPS into perspective.

We should point out that you can probably install and run a TOPS network without being aware of the content of this chapter. This means that if you are in a hurry to get "up and running," you can skip to Chapter 2. However, we recommend that you read this chapter at some point, as it will provide a context for what you are doing with TOPS.

THE NETWORK DIFFERENCE

At this point, you might be thinking about more immediate concerns than strategies and perspectives. Nevertheless, it is important to recognize one significant difference between TOPS and other software/hardware you might have installed or used on your personal computer. TOPS is about connections, and that means more than one computer, which means more than one user. When dealing with networking and sharing resources, matters are inherently more complex than when handling single-user applications on a single-user system. You will need to cooperate with others to set up and run the network. For the network to improve productivity, all users of the network will need to show consideration to their fellow networkers.

The TOPS network provides a degree of network control to each worker that many users find more consistent with "personal" computing than the restrictions imposed by other networking systems. However, there must be consensus among network users on certain procedures, as well as adherence to some basic rules and we will return to this subject in later chapters.

WHAT IS A LAN?

A local area network is formed when two or more computers in the same area are connected in order to share resources. The resources that are shared can be either hardware, such as mass storage devices (such as hard disks), output devices (such as printers and plotters), or software, such as data files or programs. A typical LAN is diagrammed in Fig. 1-1.

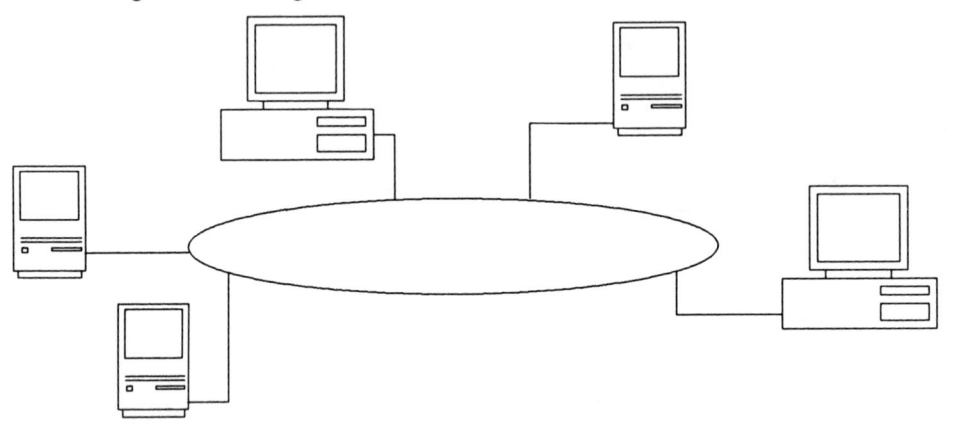

Fig. 1-1. A simple LAN ring.

Note that the arrangement of machines is essentially a circle, usually referred to as a *ring configuration*. Another typical LAN arrangement, this time a *star configuration*, is diagrammed in Fig. 1-2.

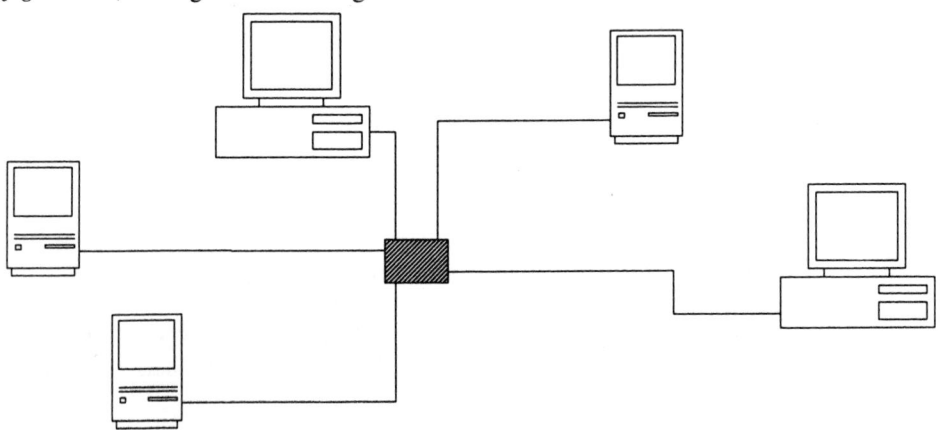

Fig. 1-2. A simple Lan star.

The definition of *same area* is what distinguishes a local area network (LAN) from a *wide area network* (WAN). Typically, same area means same office, same department, or same building. In other words, any area in which computers can be directly connected without resorting to long distance telephone lines, satellite links, or microwave transmissions. A typical wide area network is shown in Fig. 1-3.

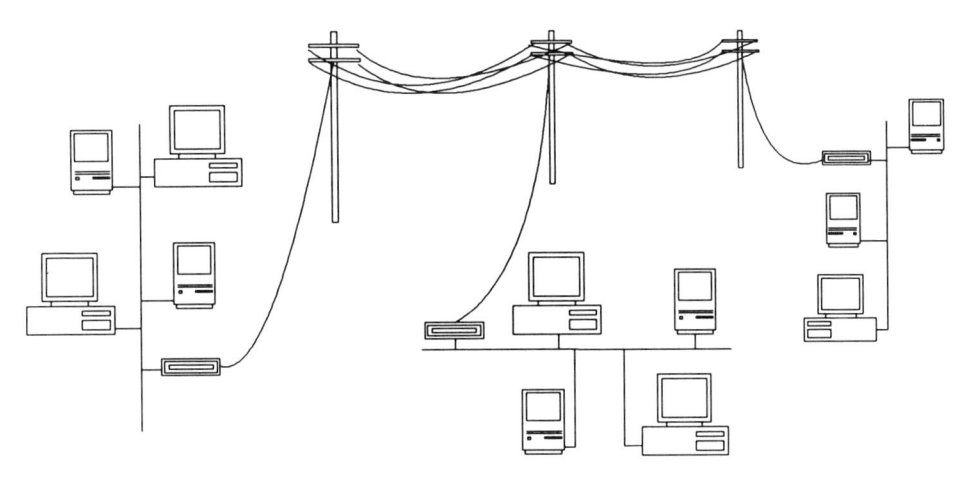

Fig. 1-3. A wide area network (WAN).

Note that the distinction between a WAN and LAN is one of convenience rather than exactitude. The distinction gets increasingly blurred as communications technology grows more sophisticated. For example, users on a TOPS LAN can connect to remote computers through a network modem, as described in Chapter 13.

The physical size of a local area can be extended significantly through the use of *bridges* and *gateways*. A bridge is a combination of hardware and software that enables you to connect one LAN to another and communicate across the connection as though it was a complete entity. The LANs being connected can be of the same kind, for example, two TOPS LANs, or they can be two different types of LAN. You can see a bridge diagrammed in Fig. 1-4.

A gateway provides a network with a high-speed communication to a large computer. By means of the gateway, which is usually a combination of hardware and software, users on the network can access data and software on the large computer, just as though they were directly linked to it as a terminal. You can see a gateway in the arrangement shown in Fig. 1-5.

Local area networks with bridges and gateways are at the upper end of the scale. In its simplest form, a LAN is just a piece of cable and a set of commands. The cable wires the computers together. The commands control the communications between the computers. Commands that control communications are often referred to as *protocols*. Thus software commands that are supposed to work across a network must conform to the appropriate network protocols.

A TOPS LAN

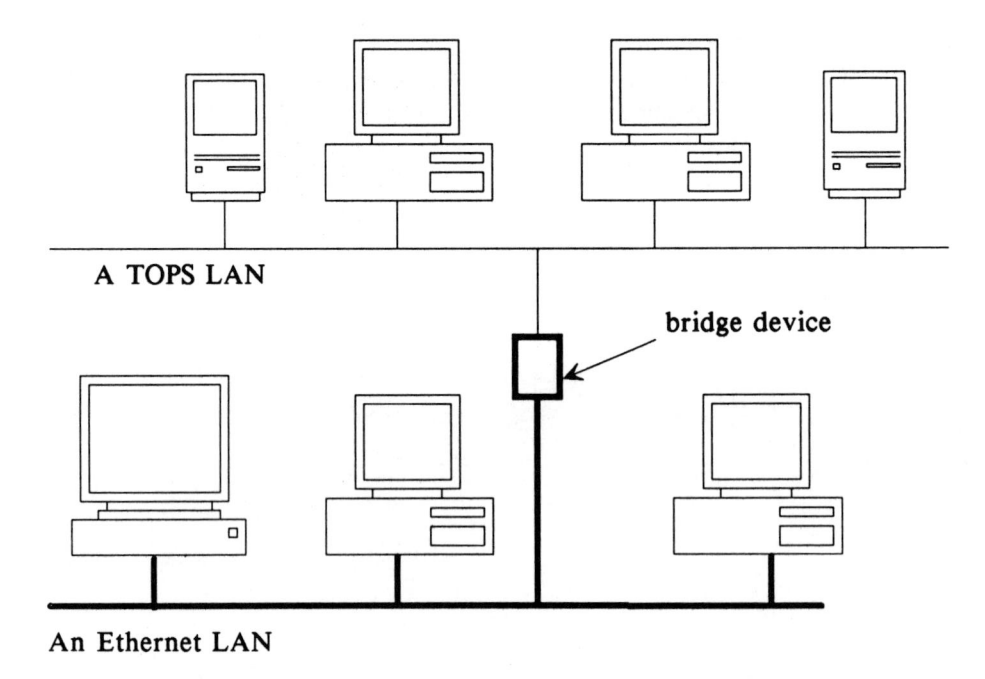

An Ethernet LAN

bridge device

Fig. 1-4. A LAN bridge.

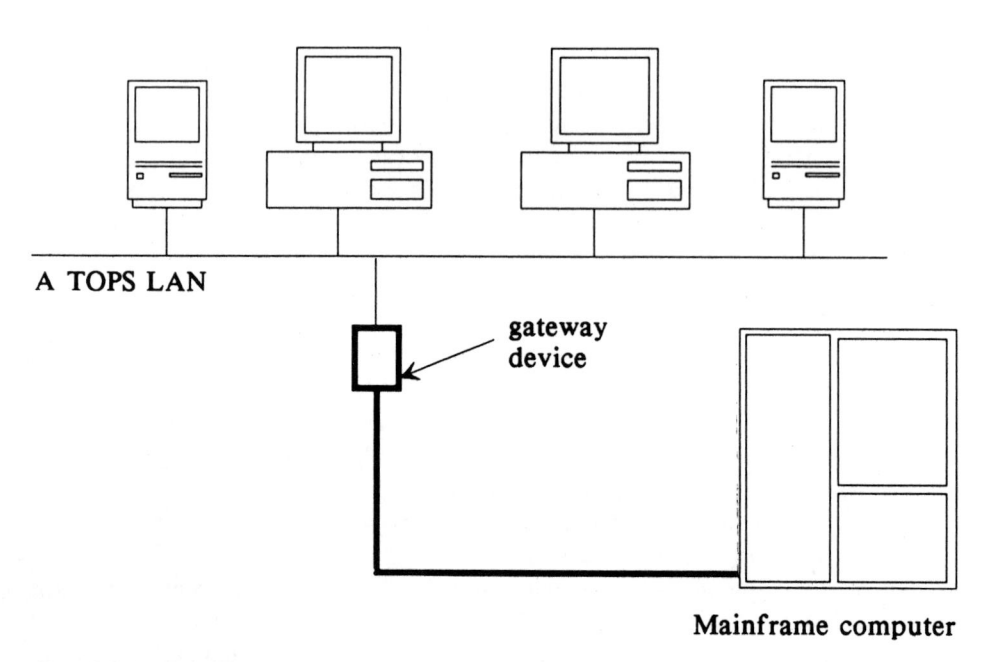

A TOPS LAN

gateway device

Mainframe computer

Fig. 1-5. A LAN gateway.

WHY DO WE HAVE LANS?

Having defined what a LAN is, let's look at why we need them. After all, successfully installing and mastering even a simple LAN takes considerable effort. A clear grasp of the purpose of the LAN will help direct that effort effectively.

Some Computer History

To understand the merits of LANs relative to other approaches to computing, you need to look at the history of the small computer. If you define a computer as a data processing device that has facilities for data input, storage, and output, as shown in Fig. 1-6, then the first "personal" computers were those developed in the mid-seventies by such companies as MITS, which marketed the Altair, and later Apple, which put out the Apple 1 in 1976.

Input, processing, storage, and output

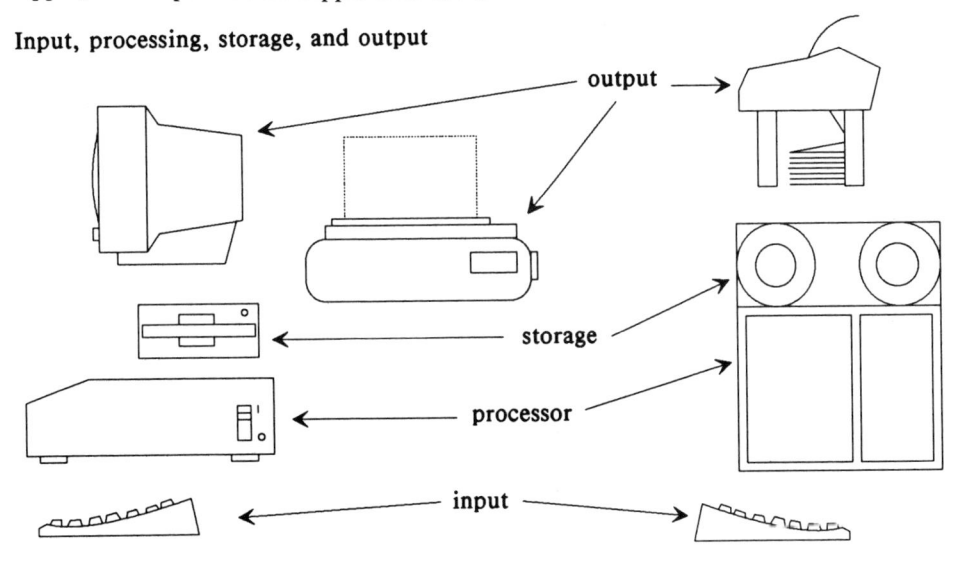

Fig. 1-6. Elements of a computer system.

These computers were personal in that the four essential elements (input, storage, processing, and output) were self-contained in one unit, capable of being grouped together on one person's desktop. This was quite a break from previous systems which were centrally located and provided storage and processing to a number of different users. You can see a diagram of this distinction in Fig. 1-7.

These large "central" computers were referred to as *mainframes* because they consisted of numerous components assembled in a large framework, one that might occupy a whole room specially designed to accommodate it.

The mainframe computer, with its centralized storage and multiple users who shared its processing power, was a natural evolution from the early days of computing. The first computers only came into being through the combined efforts of teams of scientists and engineers. In order to make these machines economically feasible,

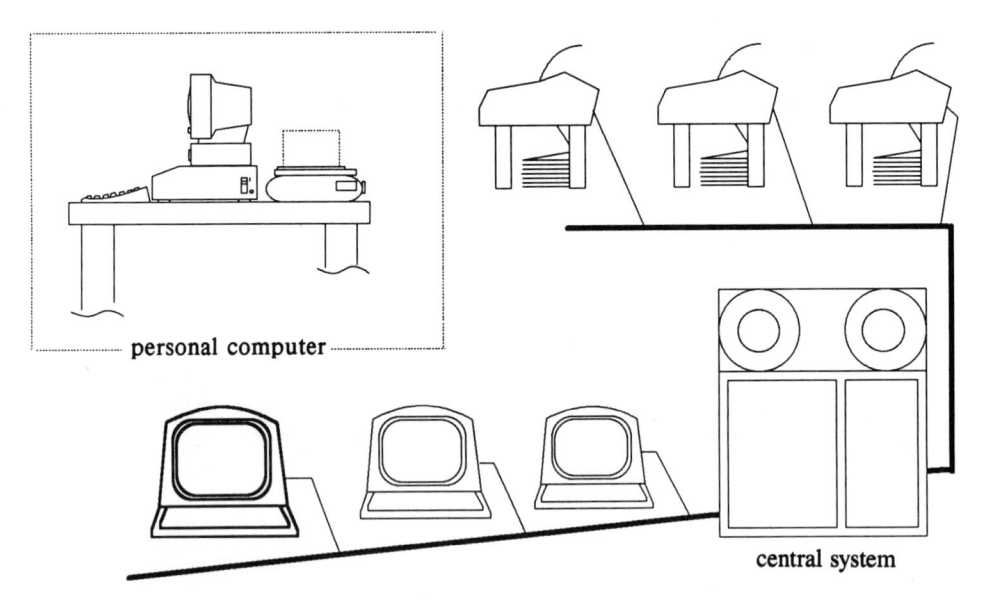

Fig. 1-7. Personal computer vs. central system.

their power was shared. Computing time was parcelled out around the clock. Because not everyone who needed computer power could afford the great expense of building one, connections were made from the central computer to remote terminals to allow access.

While the advent of computer power was welcomed by many companies and government institutions, the original centralized, multiple-user systems had several disadvantages. They imposed a need for coordination between the different users. Sometimes this meant scheduling of work for certain times of the day. Often it meant uniform procedures that were centrally imposed. Making changes to improve programs required consensus, followed by lengthy programming efforts to achieve changes that were often outdated before they could be implemented. Individuals eager to apply computer power to their specific tasks found this restrictive.

The Personal Computer Arrives

When the personal computer appeared, it promised to free computer users from central authority and restrictions. Individuals could set their own work timetable and no longer had to wait for a free terminal. Users who were willing to learn how to run the personal computer could organize their data in a way that made sense to them, and make immediate changes to system design and procedures rather than submit changes to lengthy approval and implementation processes.

However, the early models of personal computer were limited in their storage capacity and this seriously hampered their ability to cope with tasks such as database management. In the early eighties the advent of hard disks that worked with small computers offered increased storage and opened up new applications. Yet these disks were perceived as expensive. For example, in 1983 you had to pay one and a half times as much for a hard disk drive as you did for the computer itself. At this price point, the idea of sharing a disk between computers made sense.

The Network Idea

In addition to the savings that it offered, the idea of sharing a hard disk appealed to some systems managers because this is the way earlier computers had worked, sharing large storage devices between many users. Thus early attempts to connect personal computers into a network had both economic and philosophic justification. Although there was clearly going to be a cost involved in connecting computers, it was thought that this would be offset by the sharing of hard drive costs. One of the first personal computer networks was Omninet from Corvus, introduced in 1981, and designed primarily to provide multiple-user access to a central hard disk drive.

The cost of networking could be further offset by the savings from additional printers. In the early eighties, a good letter quality printer could cost you more than a computer system. Because nobody is printing all the time, people sought ways to make greater use of printers shared between workers. Thus several personal computers with floppy disks networked together and sharing a common printer and a hard disk were seen as an economic alternative to everybody having their own hard disk and printer.

There were other reasons for wanting to network users together. Almost as soon as individuals found uses for the personal computer, they had need to share the data between several people. Consider a simple database of clients. The person who designed the database might want someone else to type in the existing client list. Typically this meant giving up the computer so that the typist could enter the information. The alternative was to have the data entry done on another computer and transferred back to the original by means of copying to and from floppy disks. Thus was born the infamous "SneakerNet" that saw people swapping disks from machine to machine. When the clients have been entered into the database, several people might want to sort the list and print out their own copies: more SneakerNet as copies of the database proliferated to different computers. The benefits of wiring everybody together quickly became apparent.

A further reason for wiring personal computers together was the need to transfer data between dissimilar machines. Early personal computers for business came from several different companies, each with their own system of managing files. The way data is arranged on a disk is called the *disk format*. The way data is arranged in a file on the disk is called the *file format*. Even today, competing companies use different disk and file formats. Early users of personal computers saw the potential of a network of computers to overcome the problem of data stored onto disk by one company's computer not being readable by another company's system. There were also hopes that networks would facilitate access to data stored on large computers. If users of small computers could share a single link to a large computer, it would increase the cost effectiveness of such a link.

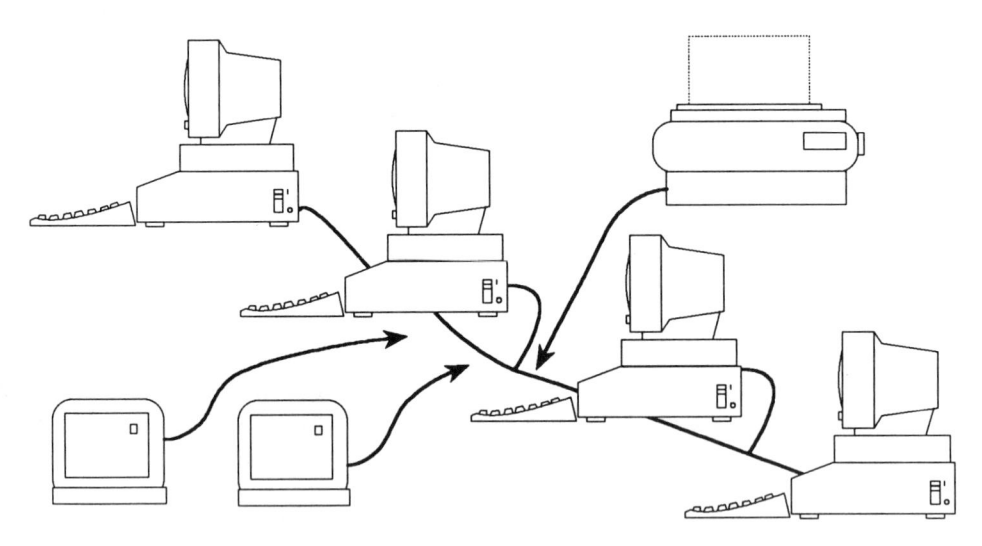

Fig. 1-8. Early perceptions of network benefits—sharing hard disks and printer.

The Continuing Need To Share

The circumstances which gave rise to the desire to network personal computers together have changed somewhat since the early mid eighties. As you can see from Fig. 1-9, the price of letter quality printers and hard disks has declined significantly.

This means that it is more feasible for everyone to have a hard disk, and some form of printer. However, the economics of sharing devices have not gone away.

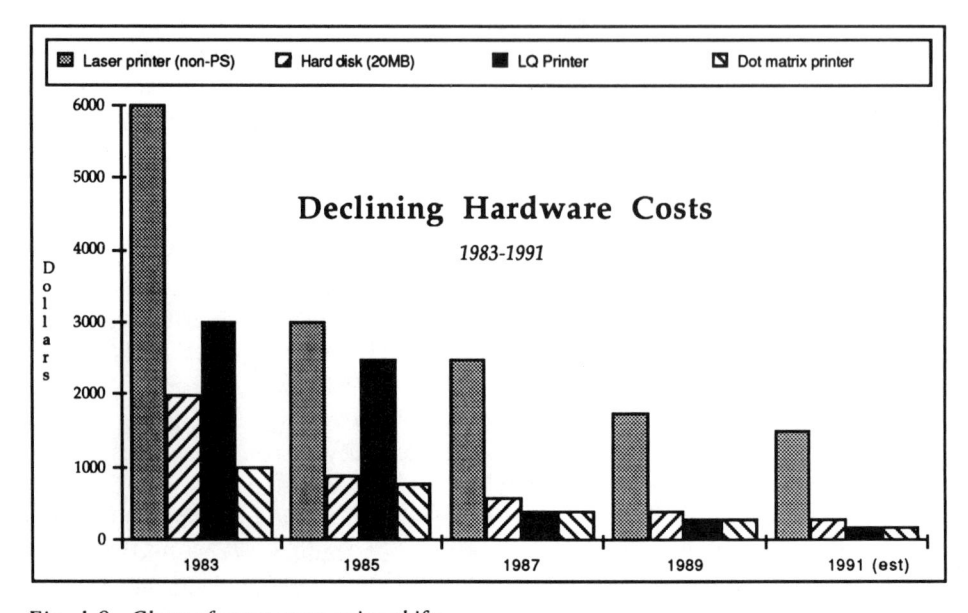

Fig. 1-9. Chart of component price shifts.

Some printers, such as those like the Apple LaserWriter that support PostScript, remain relatively expensive. There is an economic argument for sharing these printers. Plus there are new peripheral devices, such as typesetters, slide makers, CD-ROM drives and scanners, which need to be factored into the equation, as seen in Fig. 1-10.

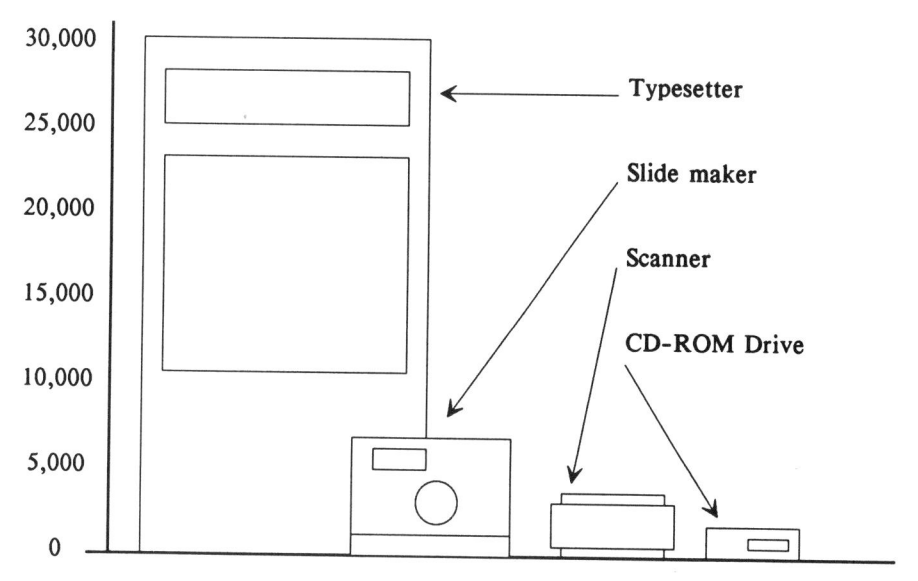

Fig. 1-10. New peripherals represent added costs to be shared across multiple users.

Although the relative cost of some equipment has changed, today's networks are still based on the idea of sharing. They allow users of single computer system to share with others three elements: storage space, data, and peripherals. In many ways, the need to share is greater now than it was when personal computers first entered the office.

The extreme diversity of systems in the early years of personal computers has given way to increasing standardization; however, today's offices have to contend with at least two standards: that derived from the IBM PC, and that used by the Apple Macintosh. (NOTE that we refer to computers based on the Apple Macintosh standard as Macs; we use the term PC to refer to any personal computer that runs PC-DOS or MS-DOS, distinct from the term personal computer which refers to any computer used primarily by a single person, and which includes both Macs and PCs.)

The existence of multiple standards means that there is an ongoing need for techniques and tools that facilitate the exchange of data between the two worlds. TOPS is a leading product in this arena.

Several aspects of data sharing have recently increased in importance. One of these is electronic mail. This is a means of distributing messages and documents to different users on a network. As the percentage of workers with computers on their desks approaches one hundred, electronic mail becomes increasingly practical as a means of communication and sharing specific data with specific individuals.

Another way in which the sharing of data is becoming more important arises from the snowball effect of computerization: the more people who have computers, the more data there is on computers that needs to be shared. Users now want to connect to mainframes, the large centralized systems that many companies and government institutions still use to accumulate data. There is also a need to connect networks with other networks. In this area, TOPS offers several advantages.

NETWORK ORGANIZATION

When the first networks were designed, the traditional paradigm of the central computer was still very influential. Early systems envisioned one particularly powerful personal computer supporting a number of less powerful machines. The powerful computer would have the expensive hard disk and would be the centralized storage for the network, dubbed the *file server*, as seen in Fig. 1-11.

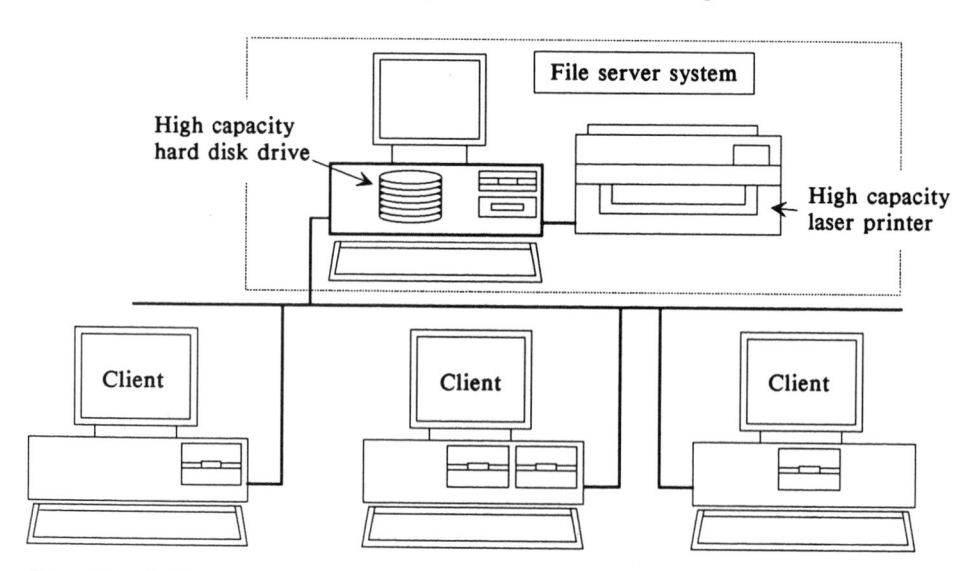

Fig. 1-11. A file server system.

In the early networks, this file server could not be used for anything but serving and was called a dedicated network server or dedicated file server. Omninet and Novell's NetWare follow this pattern. Networks such as Apple's AppleShare, IBM's PC Network, and TOPS, can also be configured with file servers, but they can also be arranged in ways that dilute the relative importance of the file server.

A personal computer that is attached to a network to use the storage and computing power of a server is called a *client*. As you can see from Fig. 1-12, a typical client computer might consist of a keyboard, monitor, system unit with single floppy disk drive, and network interface.

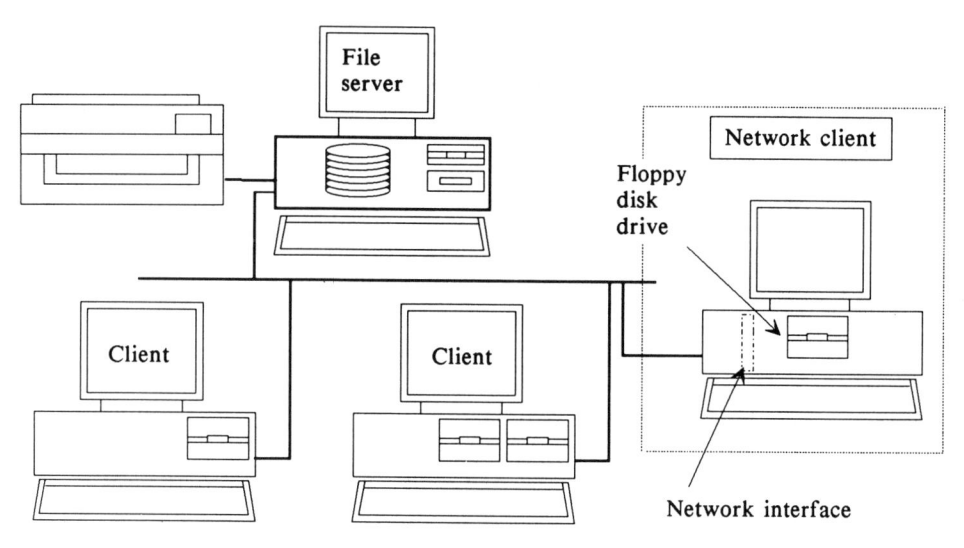

Fig. 1-12. A network client.

This client has limited storage of its own, but it can write data to its own floppy disk. The floppy disk is also used when the computer is turned on. A disk containing the programs that connect the server to the network, or *sign on* is placed in the drive. This is sometimes referred to as a *boot disk* (as in pulling the system up by its own bootstraps, not kicking it). For some networks, you can buy client computers without disk drives. These are sometimes referred to as *diskless workstations* and they have their sign-on procedures stored in ROM (read only memory). A diskless client computer or workstation has no data storage facilities of its own. This distinction is diagrammed in Fig. 1-13.

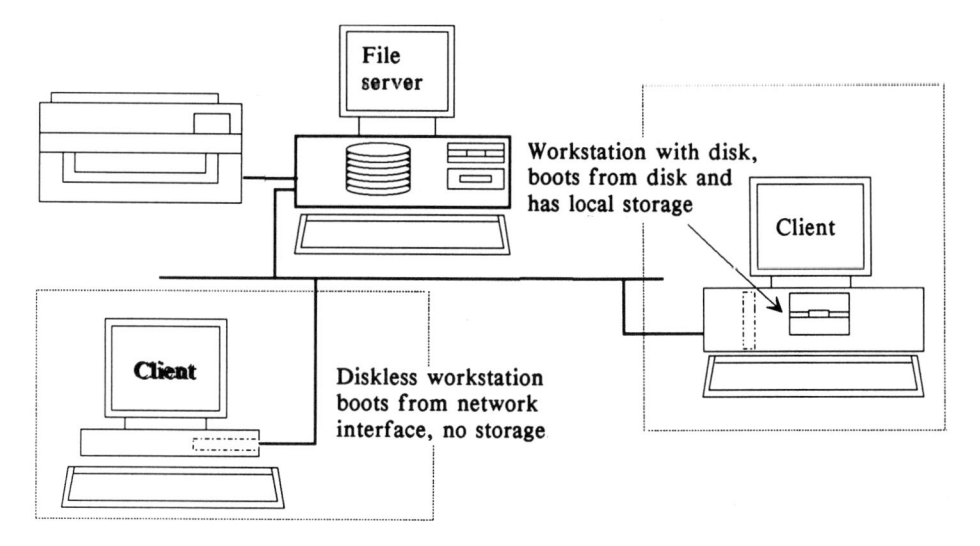

Fig. 1-13. Disks and diskless workstations.

You might wonder what distinguishes a simple client computer or workstation from a computer *terminal*. The usual distinction involves the processing power of the client. Although a diskless client does not have storage facilities, it does have computing power, which a terminal does not. When performing a task, the client might use both programs and data that are stored on a file server, as shown in Fig. 1-14, but the processing of data is done on the client, by the client's *CPU*, (central processing unit), or chip, that is at the heart of every personal computer.

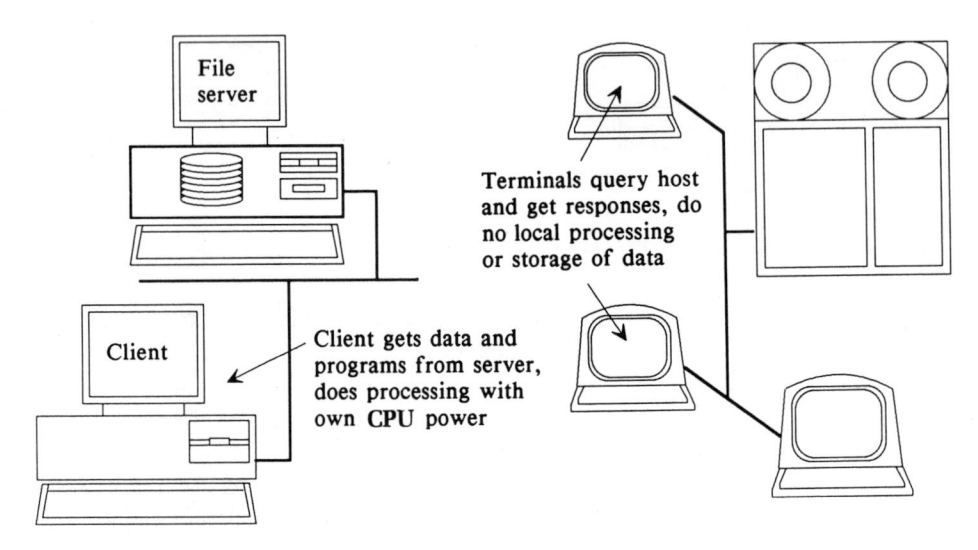

Fig. 1-14. The client and the terminal.

Communication between users and computers usually follow one of three models. The early model is the dumb terminal connected to a powerful central computer. The second model, the *client/server* network model, has intelligent terminals, machines that have their own computer power, borrowing storage and other resources from the server, a computer that is usually more powerful than the clients it serves. The third model is peer-to-peer communications, in which each computer has client and server capability. This is sometimes referred to as a *distributed network architecture*, which is what TOPS uses.

LOCAL AREA NETWORKS TODAY

Writing about the current state of affairs in LAN technology is a bit like trying to sketch a wave. Every week, new products are announced that alter the overall picture. However, some standards have emerged in the last few years, and, although these will doubtless continue to evolve and change, the basic descriptions here will hold true for some time.

Fundamental Protocols

In the world of networking, it is important to distinguish between specific products and underlying technology. This is true in other hi-tech fields such as video cassette recorders. You might have a VCR and it might be VHS, it might also be a Toshyo Super-Search Digital X100. The underlying technology is called VHS, specific product is the Toshyo Super-Search Digital X100. In networks, some sets of protocols have names that sound like specific product names, when in fact they refer to a general technology rather than a single piece of hardware or software. Some of the major players in networking are reviewed here so that their names will not be new to you when they appear in later discussions of TOPS.

ARCnet. Datapoint's ARCnet was originally developed in the seventies as a network for *minicomputers*, computers that are between mainframes and personal computers in terms of power and number of users supported. Many vendor companies have licensed the ARCnet technology, and many brand names of ARCnet are now available for personal computers.

Ethernet. One of the most popular network systems is Ethernet which originated in a joint project of Digital Equipment Corp. (DEC), Intel Corp., and Xerox Corp. Most major computer companies offer Ethernet-based networks (although IBM has long been a hold-out in this field). Ethernet was not originally developed as a personal computer network, but in 1983 the 3COM company introduced its EtherSeries network for personal computers. In simplest form, Ethernet is a standard method of connecting computers, and TOPS will run on networks that follow this standard. To connect PCs or Macintoshes to Ethernet cabling requires an Ethernet adapter or interface card and Ethernet driver software. In the case of TOPS running on Ethernet, the driver is referred to as EtherTalk because it is an adaptation of the AppleTalk protocols to the Ethernet cabling system. Unix-based computers often come with a built-in Ethernet interface but require EtherTalk drivers to run on a TOPS network.

IBM Networks. There are three elements to consider when discussing networks and IBM. The IBM technology referred to as *Systems Network Architecture* (SNA) is not a network for personal computers, but rather a system for connecting to larger computers, as well as an overall strategy for distributing data. In 1983 IBM announced a wiring system for networks called the *token-ring* standard. However, the IBM PC Network that was released in 1984 used technology from a company called Sytek and did not follow token ring standards. IBM did agree with Microsoft to incorporate network support in version 3.1 of the IBM PC operating system (called PC-DOS if you buy the IBM brand, MS-DOS if you buy the generic offering from Microsoft). All subsequent versions of DOS have maintained this network support. IBM's first actual token ring network products were released in 1985, and networks based on this standard are now quite widespread. Both the IBM PC Network and the token ring support a set of protocols called *NETBIOS* and so you will see some network products advertised as NETBIOS compatible; indeed, TOPS is NETBIOS compatible.

Apple's Network. The Macintosh computer from Apple comes with a hardware interface to *LocalTalk*, a low-cost cabling system. Apple uses LocalTalk to connect LaserWriters to Macintoshes and the software that drives communications over LocalTalk cabling is built into the Macintosh system software. The LocalTalk driver is referred to as *AppleTalk*, more formally, the AppleTalk Network System (ANS). AppleTalk's seven-layer architecture is similar to the Open Systems Interconnect (OSI) model established by the International Standards Organization (ISO). AppleTalk supports peer-to-peer communications between networked devices. However, the network software that Apple sells, called *AppleShare*, adopts the dedicated network file server model in which one Macintosh is used to run the network, a network that can include PCs as well as Macintoshes. Basically, AppleShare is a network product that uses LocalTalk cabling and AppleTalk protocols.

By building network support into the Macintosh, Apple gave a big boost to the whole idea of networking in the office, preparing for the day when all manner of computer resources would be tied together for greater productivity. Indeed, although the LocalTalk connection is built into Macintoshes, the AppleTalk protocol can run on other media. Technically defined, LocalTalk is shielded twisted pair wiring. AppleTalk will also run on unshielded twisted pair, such as Farallon Computing's PhoneNet, on Fiber-Optic LAN from DuPont Connector Systems, and on Ethernet coaxial cabling.

THE QUESTION OF SPEED

The distinctions between different network systems involve more than the question of network architecture. There is also the question of speed, how fast information is transferred across the network. On a network raw speed is measured in terms of the number of units of information that can be transmitted in one second. The unit of information used is normally one bit. One bit per second is sometimes referred to as one *baud*. When you use a modem to dial up an information service such as CompuServe you can communicate at 300, 1200, or 2400 baud, or bits per second. Networks communicate considerably faster. The standard speed of AppleTalk is 230,000 bits per second, or 230 kilobits per second (230 kbps). You could also refer to this as 230 kilobaud. This is about the speed at which data is retrieved from a floppy disk.

Relative to other networks, AppleTalk's 230 kilobits per second is not fast. Both ARCnet and IBM PC Network can handle 1000 kbps or 1 megabit per second (Mbps). Ethernet can run at 10 Mbps. Of course, speed is not everything. Productivity also depends upon how much the network is used, the level of network traffic, and how well users get along with the network. The TOPS network offers ease of use, and a range of speeds, from 230 kbps to 10 Mbps, depending upon the hardware you use.

ALONG CAME TOPS

One of the best-selling local area network systems is TOPS, a product of Sun Microsystems. TOPS began life as the Web, a low cost network for CP/M machines. The Web was put together in the early eighties by Nat Goldhaber who saw a need to connect the new personal computers. He diverged from the classic central computer paradigm in thinking that a network of personal computers would work best if it was decentralized.

The Web was one of those great products that seem doomed to disappear in a morass of negotiations and then later emerge, reincarnated. After the decline of CP/M and limited discussions with Tandy, the maker of Radio Shack computers, the Web gained a new lease of life when Goldhaber saw a golden opportunity in the Apple Macintosh. Like such pioneering computers as the Acorn, the Macintosh was built with a network interface in every model. However, Apple did not at first provide network software with the Macintosh. To provide that software, Goldhaber founded Centram and called his network product for the Macintosh the Transcendental OPerating System (TOPS).

The guiding principle of TOPS is that it transcends boundaries between operating systems, providing what is referred to as *inter operability*. This means that computers which are themselves controlled by different operating systems can deal with each other as though they had the same operating system. This makes for greater ease of use and a smaller learning curve for users. Furthermore, with the TOPS network, users transcend the need for technical autocrats who rule the network because they know more about it. This means that TOPS is simple to use, shielding the user from complex network commands, but at the same time powerful enough to empower each user.

To get slightly more technical, when TOPS is loaded in your computer, it catches all the commands addressed to the operating system that you give, either DOS on the PC or OS on the Macintosh. TOPS examines the command and passes it on to local equipment or to remote systems, as shown in Fig. 1-15.

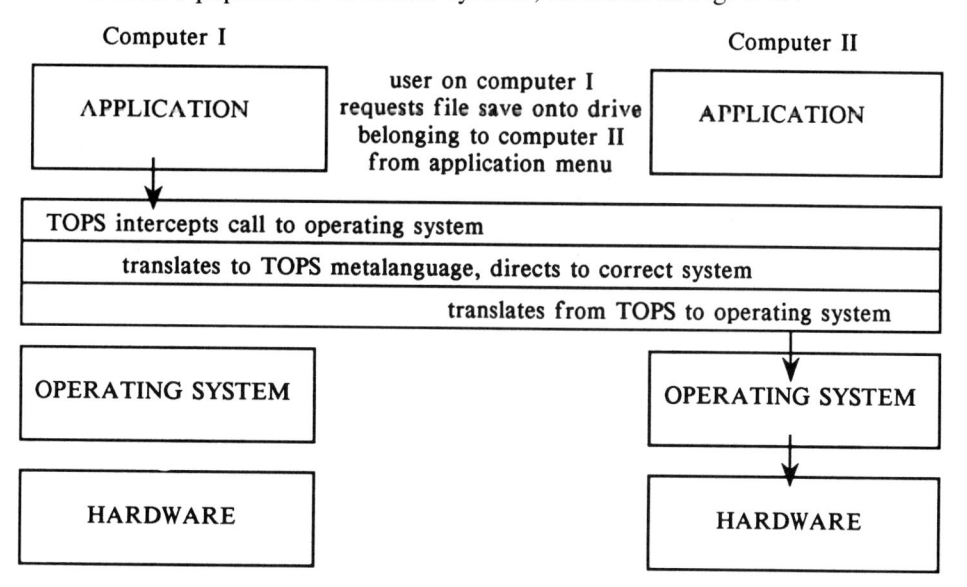

Fig. 1-15. How TOPS works.

For example, if you are using a PC and you issue a command to open a file that is on a remote Macintosh, TOPS takes the DOS command to open a file and translates it to a Macintosh operating system command that means the same thing. As a user, you see none of this activity; after all, TOPS is a transcendent operating system.

To accomplish its goals of power and ease of use, TOPS employs the decentralized concept of distributed servers. TOPS allows each user to be both server and client, as is described in the next chapter. This provides much greater flexibility and user control and promotes sharing of the responsibility for the network, rather than concentrating it in the hands of an administrator.

TOPS originally ran on Macintoshes and was most commonly connected using the LocalTalk ports and cabling of unshielded twisted pair telephone wire, with simple RJ-11 telephone jacks for connections. TOPS also worked over Apple's proprietary-shielded cabling. Later, TOPS developed the LocalTalk driver called Flash-Talk to operate at 770 kbps versus the 230 kbps of Apple's LocalTalk.

The speed 770 kbps is closer to the speed at which data is retrieved from a hard disk, as opposed to the floppy-disk-like speed of 230 kbps. The higher-speed Flash-Talk was first implemented on the FlashCard, an interface card for the IBM PC that allowed the PC to run TOPS network software and print to LocalTalk printers such as the Apple LaserWriter. The TOPS FlashBox, a connector for the Macintosh that enabled FlashTalk's higher speeds for Macintoshes on a TOPS network came later. More recently TOPS has introduced drivers for Ethernet networks so that TOPS users can take advantage of the higher speed of the Ethernet system and still have the ease of use of the TOPS network software.

CONCLUSION

When TOPS was introduced in the summer of 1986, it was one of the first products to confront directly the growing problem of integrating Macintoshes and PCs in the same office. This was perhaps the product's primary appeal and a feature that will be dealt with extensively in later chapters. However, TOPS also appeared at a time when the true dimensions of PC networking were beginning to emerge. What had sounded like a simple prospect, wiring together PCs to share data and devices, had turned into a morass of confusion, partly because IBM's first network product did not follow the token ring standards that IBM had previously laid down for networks. Questions of cabling, compatibility, and responsibility took a back seat to the race to install the fastest network hardware, resulting in many delays as the ensuing confusion was resolved. Meanwhile some people saw that a simple solution, while not the performance leader, might make a lot of sense if people could use it right away. TOPS offered such a simple solution.

2
About TOPS

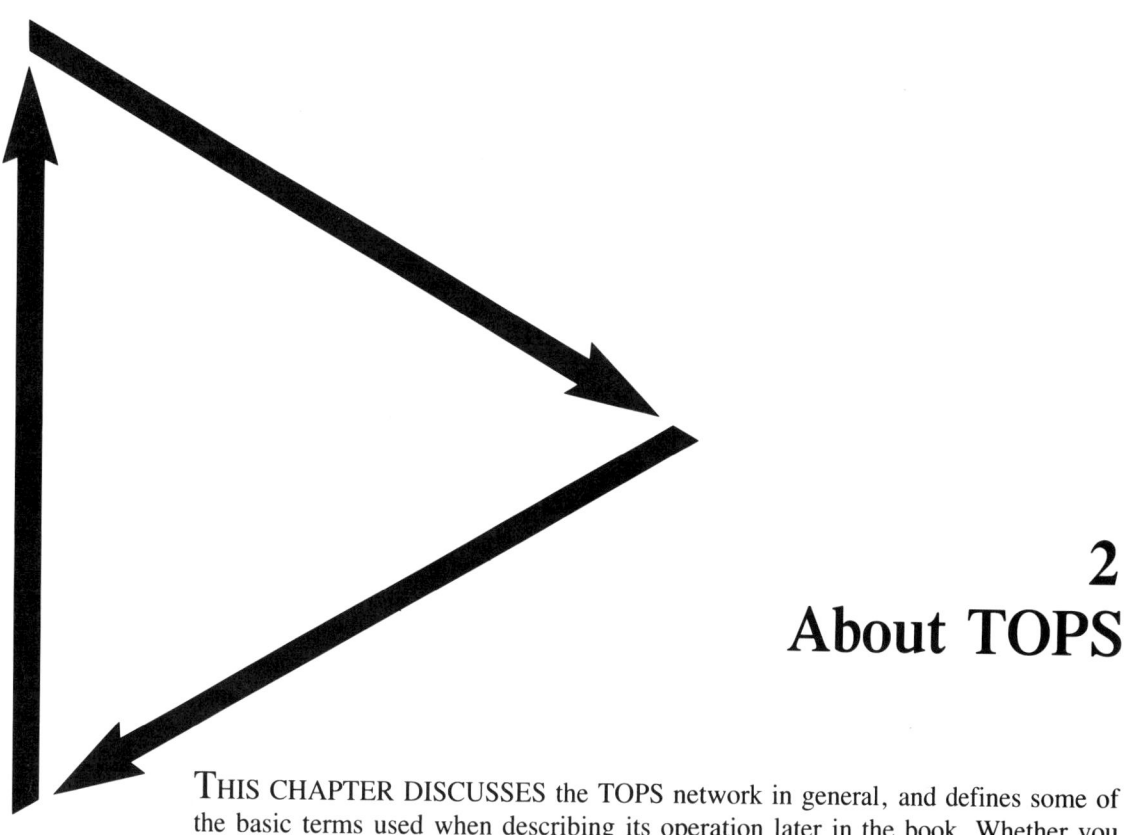

THIS CHAPTER DISCUSSES the TOPS network in general, and defines some of the basic terms used when describing its operation later in the book. Whether you will be using all Macs or all PCs on your TOPS network, many of the basic operating principles are identical. Any user of any machine that runs TOPS software, regardless of whether a Macintosh or an MS-DOS computer, should be familiar with these principles.

The notable characteristics of the TOPS network are the ability to link computers running under different operating systems, the ability to run on a variety of cabling systems, including LocalTalk and Ethernet, and the fact that it is a distributed server type of network. This chapter discusses each of these aspects of TOPS after a look at some basic vocabulary.

BASIC TOPS VOCABULARY

One of the obstacles to smooth installation and operation of network systems is the extensive new vocabulary that is required to understand manuals, menus, and procedures. The following sections present some of the basic terms with which you will find it useful to be conversant when working with TOPS.

Stations, Workstations, and Nodes

From this point on, we use the term *station* to refer to any computer connected to a TOPS network. This is not to be confused with the term workstation. By station, we mean connected computers generically, rather than as either Macs or

IBM PC-compatibles. However, there is one particular product that is very closely associated with the term workstation and which deserves a special mention. The company that makes TOPS, Sun Microsystems, is also a leading maker of technical workstations, high-performance computers that are used for such demanding tasks as computer-aided design (CAD). A typical Sun workstation consists of a high-resolution screen, a keyboard and mouse, and a connection to a storage system shared by several other workstations. Sun workstations can be connected to a TOPS network, using TOPS/Sun, as described in Chapter 13.

While the word *station* refers to computers attached to the network, computers are not the only equipment that a TOPS network supports. For example, you can attach a LaserWriter printer to the network for everyone to use. The term for each item attached to the network is a *node*. You can see these terms explained in Fig. 2-1.

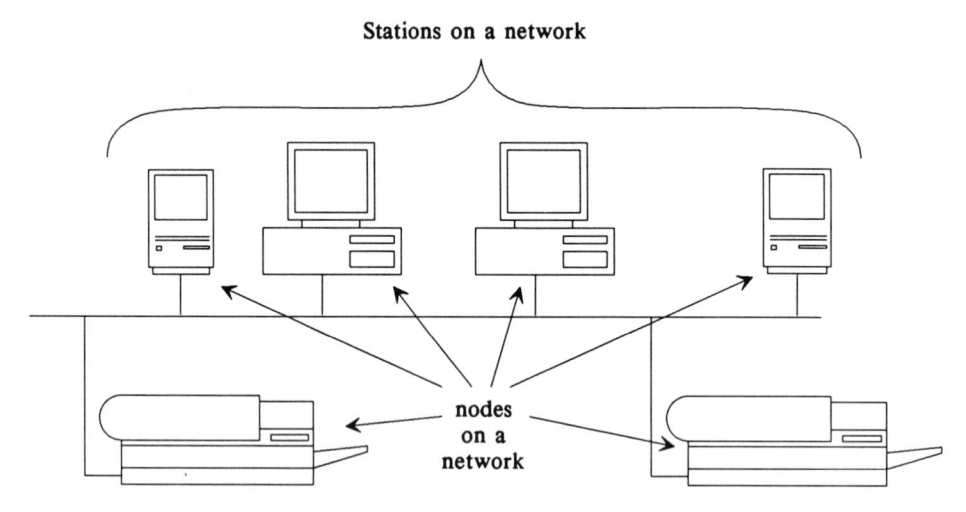

Fig. 2-1. Network terms.

More specifically, a node can be defined as any intelligent network device, a term that is discussed next.

Network Devices

You might think that some people who work with computers spend a lot of time thinking up new uses for old words. For example, the word *default* is used by computer people to refer to "what the computer does unless you tell it to do otherwise," which is something of a stretch from what happens if you do not make your mortgage payments. Another example is the word *device*, which is used to refer to any component part of a computer system. Thus both monitors and printers are output devices while keyboards and mice are input devices. A hard disk and a floppy disk are both storage devices.

In network terminology, pieces of equipment that are attached as nodes to the network are referred to as *network devices*. Computers or workstations often share the network with devices such as printers, modems, CD Rom Disks, and others. Some of these devices, such as LaserWriters, are referred to as *intelligent devices* because they have microprocessors of their own which control them. Such devices have communication abilities built into them and are attached directly to the network. Other kinds of devices are not intelligent and must be attached to an individual station, as seen in Fig. 2-2.

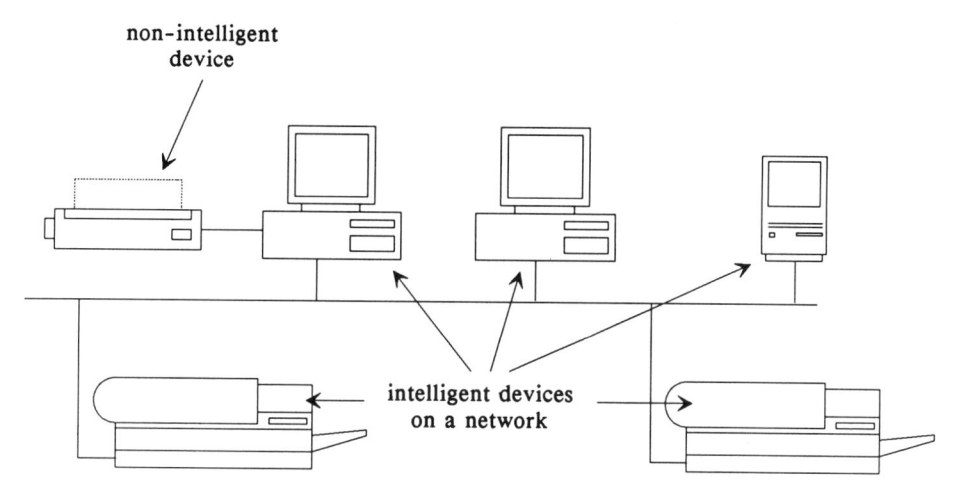

Fig. 2-2. Intelligent devices.

Access to nonintelligent devices is controlled by the computer to which these devices are attached. As we said earlier, intelligent devices, whether computers or printers, can be directly attached to the network and accessed directly.

Local and Remote

In the network context, the non-intelligent devices and disks that are attached to a specific computer are said to be *local*. Your own hard disk, in this terminology, would be your local disk. Disks and devices that belong to another computer are referred to as *remote* devices. Once again, devices such as the LaserWriter that are directly attached to the network are referred to as network devices. You can see these terms diagrammed in Fig. 2-3.

As an example of using these terms, if you are printing a document on a printer that is attached directly to your machine, you are printing it to a local printer, as opposed to a remote printer (attached to someone else's computer), or a network printer, such as a LaserWriter directly attached to the network.

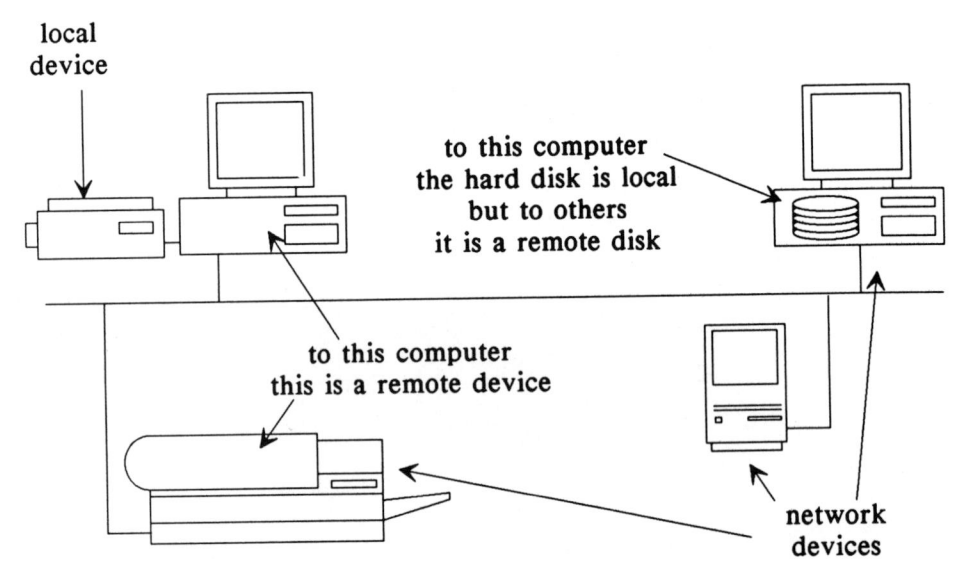

Fig. 2-3. More network terminology.

THE TOPS PRODUCTS

The last chapter described a network as a set of cables and commands, a combination of hardware and software. When we talk about the TOPS network, it is important to realize that we are referring to a range of products rather than a single package.

TOPS/Macintosh

This is the software that enables TOPS networking on a Macintosh. Because TOPS runs on the LocalTalk cabling interface that is built into Macintoshes, you can connect two Macs through their LocalTalk ports, load a copy of TOPS/Macintosh into each one, and begin networking.

TOPS/Macintosh includes a product called TOPS Spool which handles printing to a LaserWriter that is attached to the network. With TOPS Spool and a hard disk, you can send a lengthy document to be printed and return to your work almost immediately, without having to wait for the printing to be completed. TOPS Spool will store the document on disk and feed it to the printer while you continue to work. Alternatively, it will store the document on disk to be printed at a later time. If someone else is using the printer, TOPS Spool will hold your document until the printer is free. You do not have to have a full-blown network to use or appreciate TOPS Spool. A single Macintosh connected to a LaserWriter can benefit from this software.

Also included with TOPS/Macintosh is software known as TOPS Translators. This program overcomes some of the incompatibilities between file formats used on PC and Macintosh software. TOPS Translators lets you translate files from WordStar, Multimate, WordPerfect, and dBASE III to popular Macintosh formats. This increases your ability to load files from PC applications into Macintosh applications.

TOPS/DOS

This is the software that controls a DOS-PC running on the TOPS network. TOPS/DOS consists of several modules, including ALAP, PSTACK, TOPSTALK, and TOPSKRNL. These are memory resident programs, meaning that once loaded they remain in memory as an extension of DOS. The program ALAP is the basic LocalTalk driver, which is usually loaded first (a different program module is used if you are running on Ethernet). The PSTACK program provides higher protocol functions. The TOPSTALK program provides the TOPS system protocols, while TOPSKRNL is the actual TOPS system software. A further program, TOPSPRTR is used when publishing printers.

Note that some versions of TOPS/DOS before 2.1 used an entry in the CONFIG.SYS file to load the same driver information handled by the ALAP program. By removing the driver from the CONFIG.SYS, TOPS allows you more complete control over the loading and unloading of TOPS. With ALAP, you can unload the entire TOPS system from memory without rebooting. This ability alone is a good reason to upgrade to the latest version of TOPS/DOS.

When you want to issue instructions to TOPS to make a set of files available on the network, you can use a program called TOPSMENU. This lets you send commands to TOPS by making choices from a menu. Alternatively you can issue commands at the DOS prompt, or command line, with TOPS.EXE, the TOPS Command Interpreter Software. These commands can also be incorporated into batch files.

Because TOPS/DOS sometimes has to relate to the very different file structure of the Macintosh, several utilities come with TOPS/DOS to help maintain the data integrity of files and disks. The TOPS System Utilities are TDEL, TDIR, XDIR, XDEL, and XSYNC.

TOPS NetPrint

Basic printing to a network printer from a DOS machine is supported by TOPS/DOS. However, for full control of printing from DOS machines to LocalTalk printers such as the LaserWriter, TOPS provides a separate product, TOPS NetPrint. This software allows you to print directly to the LaserWriter from within an application such as Excel. You also get spooling of print task to disk so as to free up your application while printing is taking place, and queuing of print jobs waiting for the printer to become available. A PostScript translator is also provided for those DOS-based applications that do not yet support PostScript.

TOPS FlashCard

This is the adapter card that fits into a PC and provides it with a high speed LocalTalk port capable of communicating at 770 kbps under TOPS FlashTalk software.

TOPS/Sun

This is the software that enables Sun workstations to operate on a TOPS network. TOPS/Sun provides both file server functions and print server capability.

TOPS Repeater

When you need to extend the total length of a TOPS network beyond the normal limits, which are discussed in the next chapter, you can extend the network with a TOPS Repeater. This device also allows you to create branches from the main network, as described in the next chapter.

LocalTalk Connector

A LocalTalk connector is used to connect LocalTalk ports on Macintoshes, LaserWriters, and FlashCards to the actual network wiring. The TeleConnector is more fully described in the next chapter.

TOPS FlashBox

TOPS FlashBox is used to connect LocalTalk ports on Macintoshes to the actual network wiring while at the same time implementing the higher speed of Flash-Talk.

In-Box

In-Box is an electronic mail program that provides message transfer between computers on a TOPS network. This software is described in Chapter 13.

ABOUT THE TOPS SOFTWARE

Each station that is to communicate via the TOPS network must have its own copy of the TOPS software. If you are connecting an MS/PC-DOS based computer then you must have a copy of TOPS/DOS. If you are connecting a Macintosh, you must have a copy of TOPS/Macintosh, as diagrammed in Fig. 2-4.

The TOPS software is not copy protected. This means that you can copy the disk on which the program is distributed. Indeed, you should do this as soon as you open the package, placing the original distribution disk in a safe place and using the copy for actual installation work.

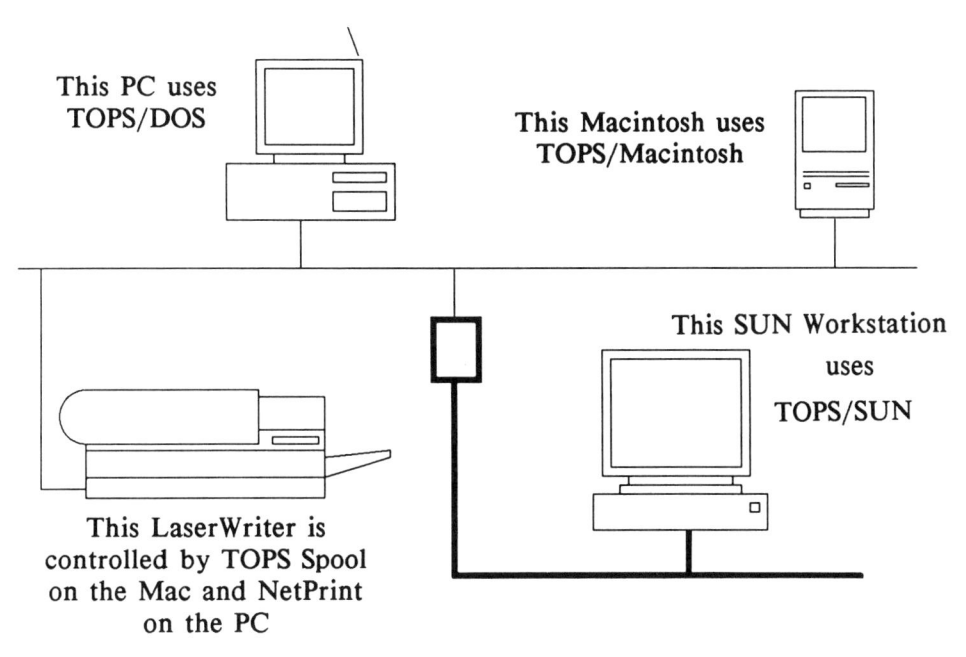

Fig. 2-4. The TOPS software.

Although TOPS is not copy protected, this does not mean that you can buy one TOPS software package and make one copy for each of the stations on the network. The TOPS licensing agreement requires that you buy a copy of the software for each station. Each software package has a serial number which identifies the station on which the program is installed. If a station with the same number as one that is already on the network attempts to connect to the network, TOPS denies network access. The problem of preserving serial numbers is discussed in the next chapter.

Note that there is essentially no limit to the number of machines or stations that can be on a TOPS network. However, each computer system will have a different serial number. If your network grows beyond about 30 nodes, you should refer to the next chapter for cabling solutions to maximize the network's efficiency.

THE FEATURES

The features that set TOPS apart from other networks are reviewed here. This will give you a better grasp of what TOPS can, and cannot, do.

Mixing Operating Systems

TOPS was designed as a "transcendental operating system," one that transcends the limitations of one particular operating system. An *operating system* is software that controls the running of a computer, managing the flow of information between the component parts. For example, a request to store information onto disk is handled by the operating system. You can issue the save command for a file from a menu within an application, such as Excel or WordPerfect, but the application passes the request on to the operating system which actually carries it out. Exactly how the task is executed varies from one operating system to another, but all operating systems perform much the same kinds of tasks. In this sense operating systems are like languages, using different words and syntax to communicate the same meaning.

Prior to TOPS, it was possible to network computers of the same make or type, running the same operating system. But TOPS was the first LAN designed to translate operating system commands into a common language that is understood across the network and can be translated to other operating systems. In simplified terms, what happens when you issue an instruction to open a file is that TOPS intercepts the request as it is being passed from the application you are using to the operating system of your computer. If the request involves a file on a remote computer, the command is translated by TOPS into "TOPS-ese" which is then passed over the network to the remote computer. At the remote computer, which is also running TOPS, the TOPS-ese is translated and passed on to the operating system of that computer, which executes the command. A diagram of this process can be seen in Fig. 2-5.

A more technical description of this is that TOPS uses a metalanguage, a set of commands that can be used to describe any type of operating system activity. This language can then be used to describe commands to any operating system. This is a very sophisticated system, and the programmers at TOPS have compressed this capability into a surprisingly small program.

To perform in this way with such diverse operating systems as DOS, Unix, and Macintosh, the core technology of TOPS was made to be adaptable to a variety of

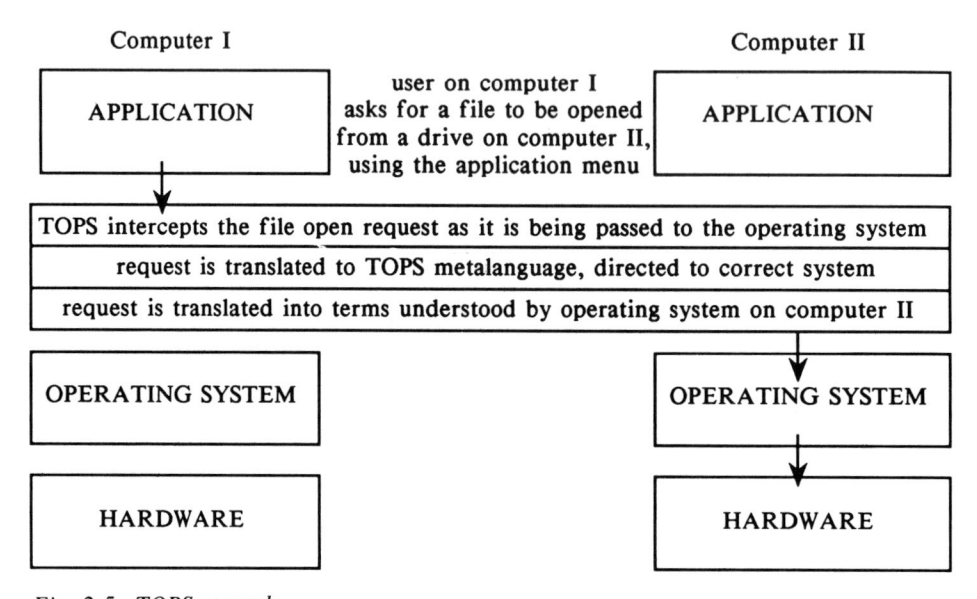

Fig. 2-5. TOPS at work.

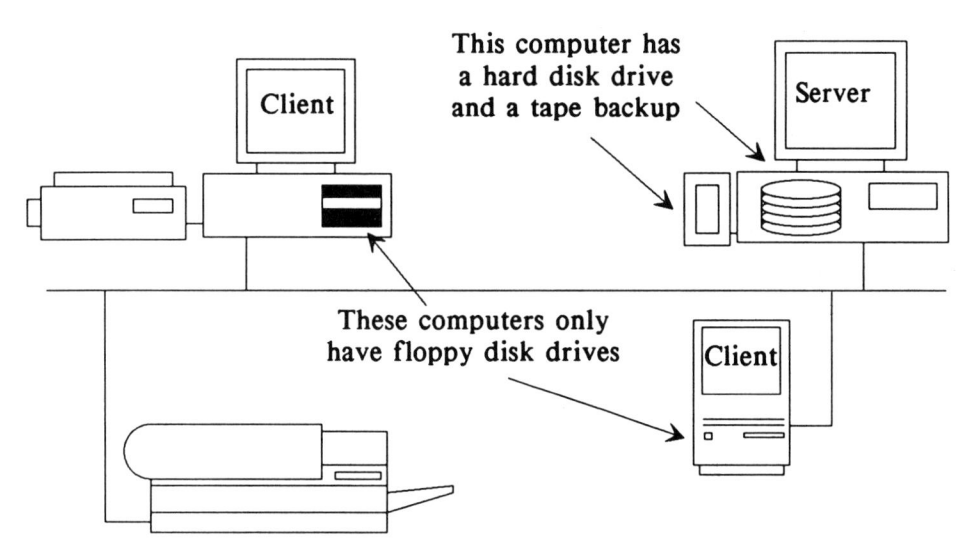

Fig. 2-6. Server network.

hardware and software environments. Furthermore, this translation is not evident to the user, it takes place "in the background." However, amazing as the TOPS technology is, it does not extend to background translation of data file formats. There are simply too many application specific formats that are used for storing data. Instead of providing file format translation within TOPS, a separate application called TOPS Translators is provided, as described in Chapter 7.

Distributed Services

TOPS allows each computer on the network to be both client and server. This means that the total workload of computing performed by the network as a whole can be assigned in a variety of ways. This ability to distribute network activity, particularly the role of file server, across the network, provides a great deal of flexibility in network design and expansion. The fact that TOPS does not require computers acting as servers to dedicate themselves to the task means that every computer can be used at once.

As an example of this flexibility, consider the arrangement of resources shown in Fig. 2-6.

Here you can see that one computer has significantly greater resources than the two others and so acts as a server while the other two systems act as clients. As the needs of the company expand another system is added to the network. In Fig. 2-7, you can see how the same network is reoriented, simply by changing the roles of the computers.

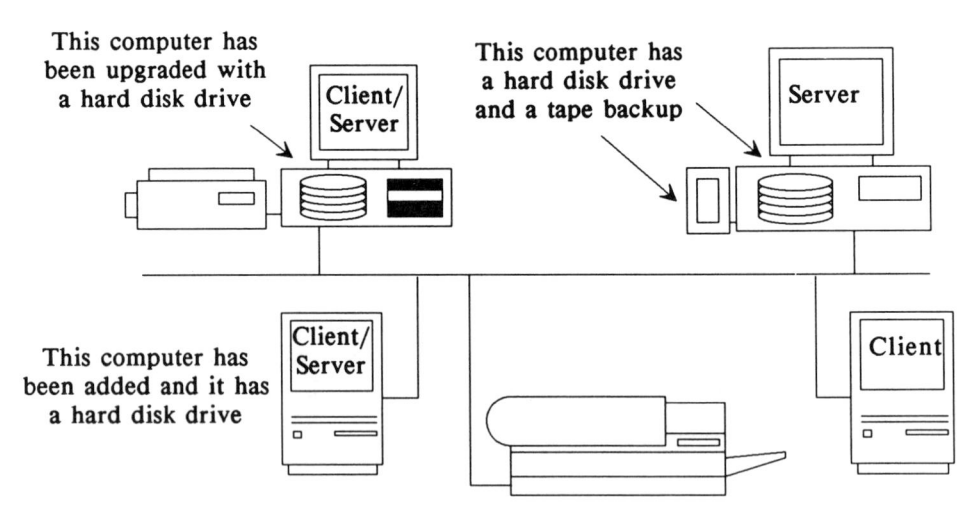

Fig. 2-7. Reoriented network.

THE TOPS POSSIBILITIES

In addition to allowing flexibility between the roles of server and client, TOPS allows flexibility between operating systems. A TOPS network can be made up of a variety of product mixes. Following the "open computing" philosophy of Sun MicroSystems, deciding to use TOPS for your network does not lock you into any particular brand of computing hardware.

PC-Only Networks

You can run TOPS as an all PC network. Because the TOPS/FlashCard allows a data transfer speed of 770 kbps, an all PC network will have respectable, if not blazing, performance. The slower speed is compensated for by added flexibility and ease of use relative to network systems that offer greater speed.

While you can operate an all PC network without having hard disks in any of the PCs, you would probably not want to do this. We suggest that you have at least one hard disk on the network. If you have just one computer with a hard disk, this disk will probably be the repository of most data stored on the network, and the computer with the hard disk will act as a file server. An 80286 system such as the IBM PC AT or Compaq 286 is adequate as a server for a small network and can also be used as an active workstation as well. When you have more than one PC with a hard disk on the network, each of them has the potential to act as a server, although a central file server arrangement might be preferred (see Chapter 6 for more discussion of different network arrangements or network topology).

Because TOPS provides compatibility with DOS 3.1, the networking version of DOS, multi-user applications which use the features of DOS 3.1 will work over TOPS. We have used TOPS successfully with DOS 3.3 and it should work with

DOS version 4.0 and later, but the greater RAM requirements of successive versions makes them less attractive as a basis for TOPS.

We have found that TOPS works fine with a wide range of personal computers known as IBM-compatibles. You can mix and match any combination of "plain vanilla PC" models including those of the XT and AT type as well as models based on the 80386 processor. If the computer runs MS-DOS 3.1 or later, it will probably run on a TOPS Network if fitted with an AppleTalk board, TOPS software and AppleTalk connectors and cables. At any time you can expand an all PC network to include Macintoshes and Unix-based computers, although these computers require their own TOPS software and/or hardware packages.

Networks with Both Macs and PCs

A TOPS network that combines Macs and PCs allows files created on a Mac to be stored on a PC's hard disk or vice versa. You have access to any published file from any computer on the network, regardless of the types of computers involved. (We return to the term "published" in a moment.)

To a PC on the network, a remote volume or group of files that has been published through TOPS is used as a PC drive. Thus the Excel folder on a remote Macintosh might be available as drive J: on your PC. Even when a PC accesses a volume that is stored on a Mac, it looks and acts just like a local PC drive; for example, as seen in Fig. 2-8, you can use the DOS command DIR to list the files on the Mac.

```
Thu   4-26-1990  C:\>DIR F:

Volume in drive F is PageMaker
Directory of   F:\

ALDUS_PR           25770    6-08-88    9:43a
PAGEMAKE 01            0    7-18-88   10:02a
PM_CHRON TXT        1449    2-06-40    6:28a
%APDS           <DIR>       3-27-89   12:51a
%CHEY'S_        <DIR>       3-26-89    4:48p
%HELP           <DIR>       3-26-89    4:49p
%HYPHENA        <DIR>       3-27-89   12:51a
       7 File(s)   41840640 bytes free

Thu   4-26-1990  C:\>
```

Fig. 2-8. Using DIR to view Mac files.

A Mac user sees PC volumes as disk icons, just as if they were on the internal floppy drive of the Mac. You can see this in Fig. 2-9, where a PC drive is displayed.

To a Mac user, a file created on a PC looks like a generic document icon, a piece of paper with no design. Files created by a Mac but stored on a PC still appear

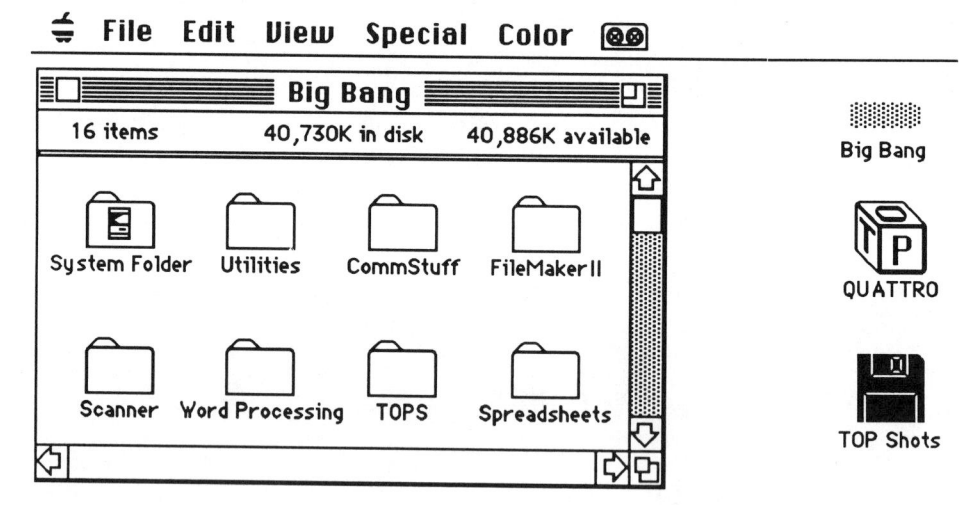

Fig. 2-9. A PC drive seen on a Mac.

to the Mac user as regular Mac icons filled in with appropriate application motif. Mac applications can access data stored on networked Mac drives or disks in PC drives.

Many users find that, because TOPS works in the background and presents network resources in the same form as its host operating system, they quickly become comfortable with TOPS, avoiding the need to become familiar with a new operating environment. DOS users can use the same DOS or application commands as usual. Mac users can click and point as usual.

Note that if you are reading files from a Mac using the older *Macintosh File System* (MFS) that Mac's files and applications will appear in one directory. This is because MFS is a flat filing system, not a hierarchical one like DOS. While the Mac's Finder can "see" these older folders and use them for organizing work, TOPS cannot. However, most Macs use the newer *Hierarchical File System* (HFS). When you mount an HFS disk with TOPS/DOS, all folders appear as DOS subdirectories.

Networks with Other Systems

Beyond PCs and Macintoshes, TOPS can connect computers running Unix. There are many different makes of Unix computers, and several different versions of Unix. A typical Unix-based computer is the Sun workstation. These workstations consist of monitor, keyboard, mouse, and a certain amount of memory and computing power. Sometimes, a Sun workstation does not have local storage. The Unix operating system is then used to control a central computing unit and its communication with diskless workstations. Sun systems have built-in Ethernet connections and so can be attached directly to a TOPS network running on Ethernet. Alternatively, if the TOPS network is running on LocalTalk, then a LocalTalk/Ethernet gateway can be fitted to the network. For more on connecting to Unix systems, see Chapter 13.

THE REQUIREMENTS OF TOPS

In order to set up a TOPS network, you need certain minimums of equipment. These are described here.

Basic Requirements for TOPS/DOS

For best results, TOPS should be run on a PC which has at least 512K of memory. TOPS is a memory resident program that occupies about 120K to 200K, depending on the way it is configured. Thus, depending on the resident memory requirements of DOS and other applications, you might need more than 512K free to run TOPS. Many users running PC spreadsheet or database applications find they need the full 640K recognized by DOS. The amount of memory used by TOPS can be adjusted by adjusting values in the TOPSKRNL.DAT file, as explained in Chapter 4.

You need to be running MS-DOS or PC-DOS version 2.1 or higher in order to run TOPS. We recommend, however, that you use DOS 3.1 or higher in order to get the most networking capabilities.

To run TOPS/DOS over LocalTalk, you need to have an AppleTalk card and its driver software in your computer. We recommend the TOPS FlashCard due to its faster communications, although any AppleTalk card will do. The AppleTalk driver is included in the TOPS/DOS software and runs as a program, not a configuration file.

To run TOPS/DOS over an Ethernet system, you need an Ethernet adapter card and the Ethernet driver that comes with TOPS/DOS.

TOPS can work with many different hardware setups. The standard TOPS configuration is a PC with one or two floppy drives and a hard disk. If your configuration is different from this (for example, if you have a RAM disk), you might need to change the file called TOPSKRNL.DAT after you install TOPS. This procedure is described in Chapter 4.

Basic Requirements for TOPS/Macintosh

You need a Macintosh 512K or later, such as the 512KE, Plus, SE, SE30, II, IIx, and IIxc. The latest versions of the System file and Finder should be used although you can use Version 3.2 or higher of the System, and Version 5.3 or higher of the Finder.

Make sure that each Macintosh station uses the same version of the Laser-Writer and Laser Prep files. Versions since 3.1, except 5.1, are acceptable. Again, the latest version is usually preferred.

You need to have 65K of memory available and 40K of disk space free. To use the spooler feature, you should have around 100K of free disk space for temporary spooler files. You need a free Desk Accessory slot out of the 15 available.

NETWORK ACTIONS

Because TOPS is designed to perform in the background, TOPS can be used with relatively few actions. The following sections describe what the basic actions do, while later chapters will elaborate on how these actions are performed in specific situations.

Access to Files

The two basic states of computers on a network are servers and clients. On a TOPS network, any computer user who chooses to do so can make the computer a server by issuing the appropriate commands. Likewise, any other computer that has been given permission to access the server can become a client by similarly appropriate steps.

Two commands, *publish* and *mount*, are the keys to server and client activities. These two commands, and the concepts they represent, are common to all the machines on TOPS, whether Macintosh, MS-DOS, or some other. In TOPS parlance, to become a server you make something public, or publish. To become a client, you mount what has been published by the server.

To be more specific about publishing, you need to know what you can publish. You can publish an entire disk or only a selected folder/directory (the term directory on a PC equates to folder on the Mac). Because these mounted items are of differing size, TOPS refers to the resources that you publish or mount as *volumes*. A volume can be either an entire disk or just a folder or directory. You can see these terms diagrammed in Fig. 2-10.

Note that it is the disks, and directories that are published or mounted, and not the files themselves. Volumes are containers in which files are stored.

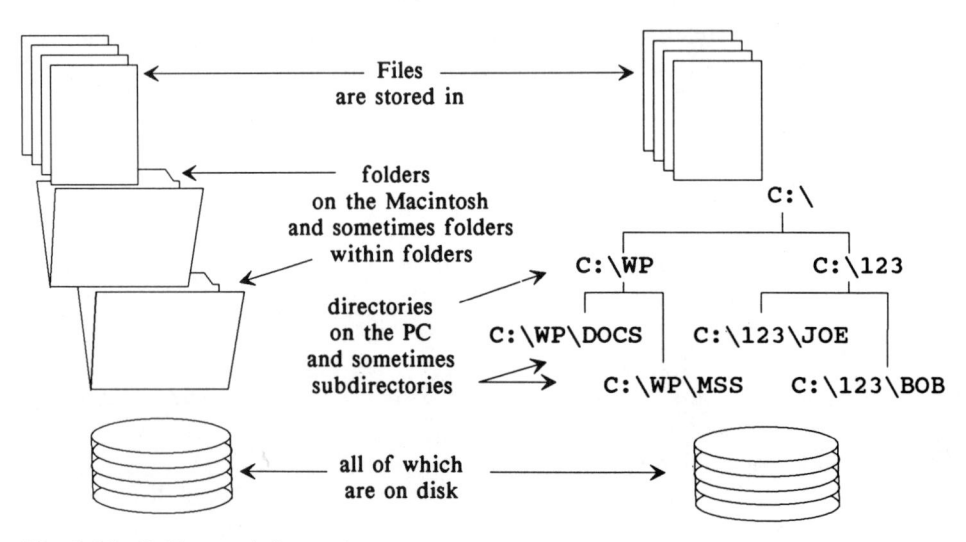

Fig. 2-10. Folders and directories.

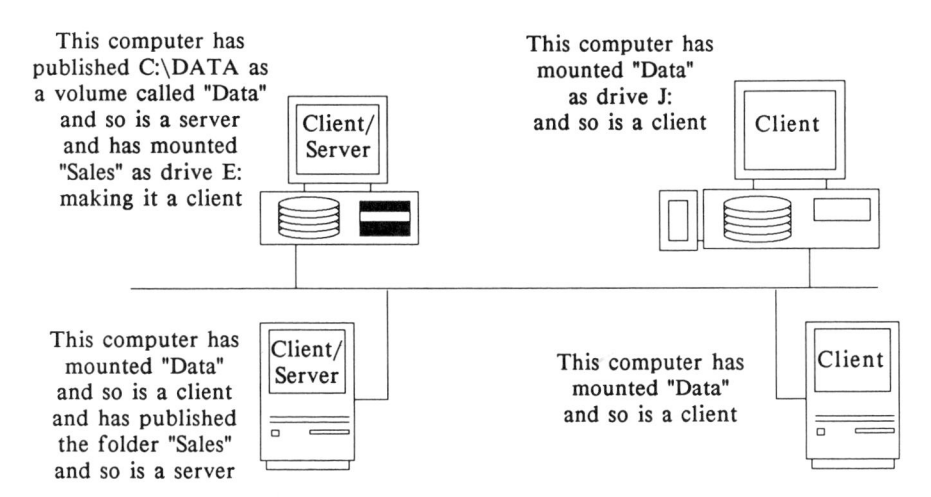

Fig. 2-11. Being both client and server.

If you choose to publish a folder or directory or an entire disk, and therefore become a server, that does not prevent you from also mounting something published by another user. Nor are you restricted to publishing or mounting only one volume. A station on a TOPS network can be both a client and a server at the same time. You can see this diagrammed in Fig. 2-11.

Procedural Considerations

Some applications might need a particular volume to always be published. TOPS accommodates this need with automatic publishing features that can publish a specified volume at the time the server boots. Mounting can also be automated; however, timing becomes important when automounting. The server needs to be allowed to start first and finish publishing before the client automounts.

Users whose experience is limited to just one kind of machine like the Macintosh, but not MS-DOS, or vice versa, need not be deterred from mounting volumes on the other machines. The user who mounts a volume over the network will see and use the volume as they would any other disk on their own machine. To an MS-DOS user the mounted volumes appears as a drive D or E or J, and so on. For example, in Fig. 2-12, you can see a directory listing from a PC, showing some of the contents of a Macintosh system folder.

To a Mac user, the drive appears as another icon on the desktop, as seen in Fig. 2-13, which shows a directory of DOS files as seen on a Macintosh.

You can see that the PC drive appears as a Macintosh drive icon even though the server to which the volume belongs is a different kind of machine.

With the above choices of publishing and mounting, users control what they want to do on the network. It is a form of computer communication not so different from human communication by the telephone or intercom network in any office. The network works the way that people work. Via the network, any computer can

32   Chapter 2

```
Directory of  G:\

CAPTURE              0   9-12-88  10:56a
COLOR                0   8-26-88  12:00p
FINDER               0   4-13-89   4:42p
FONTS                0   4-13-89   4:11p
GENERAL              0   8-26-88  12:00p
GENERAL  APD     11508   2-21-88  11:14p
KEYBOARD             0   8-26-88  12:00p
KOLOR                0   7-13-87   4:07a
MACROS               0   4-26-89   1:12p
MAP                  0   4-30-88  12:00p
MONITORS             0   8-26-88  12:00p
MOUSE                0   8-26-88  12:00p
PMUSUSER OLD       118   2-18-89  10:49a
PMUSUSER TXT       118  10-13-87  11:44a
SOFTTALK             0  11-16-88   4:25p
SOUND                0   8-26-88  12:00p
SPOOL                0   4-26-89  10:30a
(SYSTEM)           758   4-26-89   1:12p
TOPS                 0  11-16-88   4:25p
UPDOC1   SND         0   1-14-89   3:49p
       20 File(s)   41857024 bytes free

Thu  4-26-1990 C:\>
```

Fig. 2-12. Mac files seen on a PC.

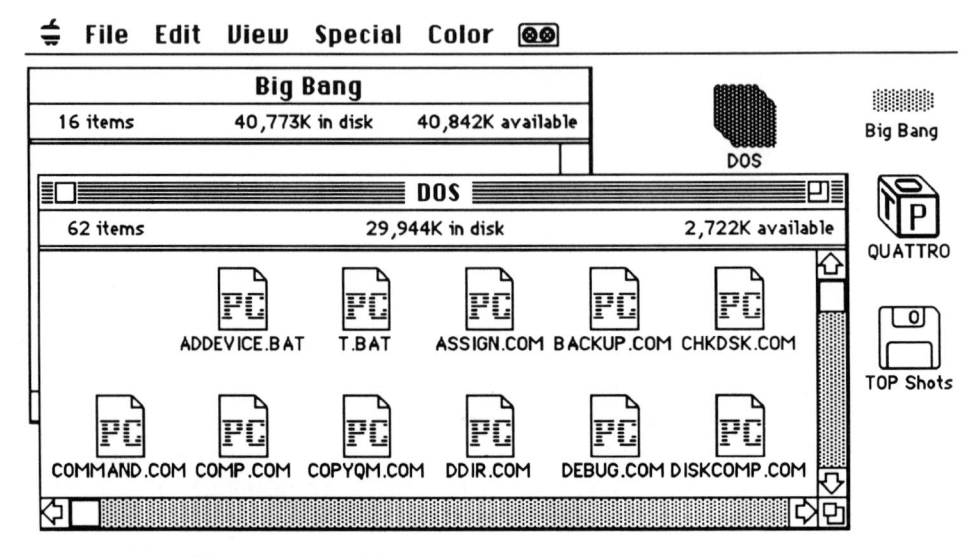

Fig. 2-13. PC files seen on a a Mac.

exchange information with any other. Users possessing information that others need to share can publish that information, and those others have access to it. There is no need to copy data to floppy disks to share it, and there is no particular need to store data on a central server.

SECURITY ON TOPS

As soon as you connect your computer to another, the issue of security raises its head. Can other users get at your stuff? Will your data be damaged? Questions like these might smack of paranoia, but the first time you loose files or find some of your personal data in someone else's hands, you will realize that security is a very real issue in networking.

The simplest rule for security on a TOPS network is that you should not publish data that you don't want other users to access. When you publish a directory on your hard drive, other users are only allowed access to that directory (and its subdirectories). Other users cannot log onto your published directory and explore other parts of your system or tell your system to make other areas available. What they can access is entirely in your control.

Beyond this basic security of controlled access, TOPS provides additional security. A TOPS menu option allows the server to publish a volume with a password, so it can be mounted and access only by those users who know the password.

Another useful security option is the ability to publish volumes that clients can read files from, but not write files to. This prevents inadvertent overwriting of your files by clients who access your published volumes. Files within volumes that are published as *read-only* cannot be erased by a user who mounts that volume. If a user at a remote station reads one of the files from your read-only volume into an application, modifies it and then needs to save the modified version, they can only save it to a different, non-write protected drive or volume (either local or remote).

You will find further details on the security aspects of TOPS in Chapter 7. If you are responsible for supporting a number of computer users and network users and are concerned about security issues, you might want to consult a book devoted to security, such as *Stephen Cobb's Complete Guide to PC and LAN Security* (Windcrest book No. 3280).

MULTI-USER APPLICATIONS ON TOPS

Write access and write protection are very important concerns in environments that require multiple accesses to the same data. In accounting or database applications for example, it is very important that two users are not allowed to open the same file with the same ability to write to the file. In other words, the file, or records in the file, need to be locked so that the changes to the file made by one user are not negated when the file is saved by the second user. Most multi-user applications have this file or record locking written into them. Most single user applications do not. TOPS supports standard DOS file and record locking for MS-DOS applications. Standard Macintosh file and record locking is also supported. However, TOPS does not do anything in itself to lock files.

From the TOPS perspective, it is the application that should provide the file locking protection. True multi-user programs generally do provide this. Publishing as read only is the only way to protect your data if your program does not have file or record locking.

Some software developers have created multi-user database programs that share and lock the same files across Macintosh and DOS boundaries. This is a little trickier to implement than strictly DOS or Mac only programs, but several companies have products which have done this, and several others are working on it. Implementations of this feature can be network dependent so if you are shopping, make sure to check with the manufacturer whether they are TOPS compatible. See Appendix B for further details.

TOPS NETWORK ETIQUETTE

For those used to operating in a computing environment consisting of only single user, stand-alone personal computer, the TOPS network requires some new rules of etiquette. This is because you are now networking with others and no longer have just yourself to consider. For example, if you make your computer a server on TOPS and you have an active client, you don't want to power off your machine until your client has a chance to unmount. Your failure to give that client that chance at minimum will cause them inconvenience, and perhaps, much worse, loss of data.

To prevent inadvertently causing this situation, TOPS has supplied commands for users to unpublish and unmount volumes. For example, a server should always unpublish before shutting down. If a server has active clients when the unpublish command is issued, TOPS will notify the server. Proper etiquette as a client is to unmount volumes when finished with them, so as not to inconvenience the server that wants to shut down.

A few activities should not be done while you are a server on the network. Bear in mind that the TOPS software is running in the background while you use your computer. Therefore you should not run programs or commands that tend to dominate the computers microprocessor and deny its use to TOPS. These activities would include formatting disks and other system intensive tasks. While programs like these run, the CPU is not able to react to the needs of the clients, and it will appear to the clients that the server has shut down.

FILE COMPATIBILITY ACROSS SYSTEMS

TOPS allows users to share data between PCs and Macs. However, several questions of file compatibility need to be considered.

File Translation

While TOPS communicates between different operating systems, it does not automatically translate your data files between applications that normally are not compatible. Just because you can connect a Macintosh to a PC does not mean that a MacWrite document can be edited in WordStar on the PC. That task is left for the application program you are using or to special translation utilities such as the TOPS Translators application supplied with TOPS for the Macintosh. Other translation programs deal with specific formats, and these are described in later chapters.

Multiple Versions

Several major software companies, like Microsoft, WordPerfect, and Ashton-Tate, sell application programs that come in both Macintosh and MS-DOS versions. dBASE, for example, is available for both MS-DOS computers and Macintoshes. With products like these, users on one kind of machine are able to use the same files created by a user on the other type. It's a wonderful ability, but it requires a few operational guidelines which will be discussed in later chapters.

Filename Conventions

For networks that have a mix of both Macintoshes and MS-DOS machines, there are some important considerations for file naming and handling. On Macintoshes, the names of files can be up to 32 characters and can contain spaces. MS-DOS files, on the other hand, are a maximum of 8 characters, with an optional 3 character extension. While it is an easy task for the Macintosh to read the shorter MS-DOS filenames, MS-DOS cannot read the longer Mac names, which appear truncated. While TOPS has the ability to retain the long name, and thus preserve the unique identity of the file, DOS applications and commands, like COPY, simply ignore the long version of the name. Therefore, when working in environments where PC applications will read Mac files, it is usually advisable to have users on the Mac conform to the DOS limitations, even for the Mac's files. In Table 2-1, you can see the rules for DOS filenames.

File Structure

In addition, the basic file structure differs between systems. A Macintosh file actually consists of two parts. These parts are called *forks*, and the user only sees a fork called the *data* fork. The other fork, called the *resource* fork, is invisible but essential to the Mac. If a Mac file is being transferred over the network, it is usually best done by a Macintosh. The Macintosh Finder will automatically handle each file's hidden resource fork. If the MS-DOS Copy command is used on a Macintosh

Table 2-1. File naming rules.

DOS Rules

- Filenames follow the format FILENAME.EXT
- Up to 8 characters, no spaces, optionally followed by a period and up to 3 more characters.
- Allowed characters are the numbers 0–9 and the letters A–Z, plus the following special characters:

    ~ ! @ # $ % ^ & ( ) – __ { } '

- You cannot use the following as filenames:

AUX	COM1	CON	LPT2	NUL
CLOCK$	COM2	LPT1	LPT3	PRN

- The following extensions have special meaning to DOS and should not be used for documents:

    COM   EXE   BAT   SYS   BAS

Macintosh Rules

- Up to 31 characters, blank spaces acceptable, no colons, all other special characters acceptable.

Unix Rules

- Up to 256 characters, blank spaces acceptable, and should avoid using:

    / $ ' * ? ! # { } [ ] ( )

---

file, it will copy only the data fork, and not the resource fork, because DOS files do not have two parts. We return to the question of handling file forks in Chapter 5.

Aside from these differences, TOPS allows you to ignore, for the most part, what kind of machine is acting as your server. In general, a published volume is accessible to either a Macintosh or an MS-DOS client with equal ease. The volume appears like just another disk drive for you to use. The files on this drive look just like files on any other drive on your system.

CONCLUSION

As you can see, there are really just a few key concepts to grasp in order to use and understand the TOPS network. Using the concepts described in this chapter, move on to review in the next chapter the techniques used to connect computers to the TOPS network.

3
Connecting TOPS

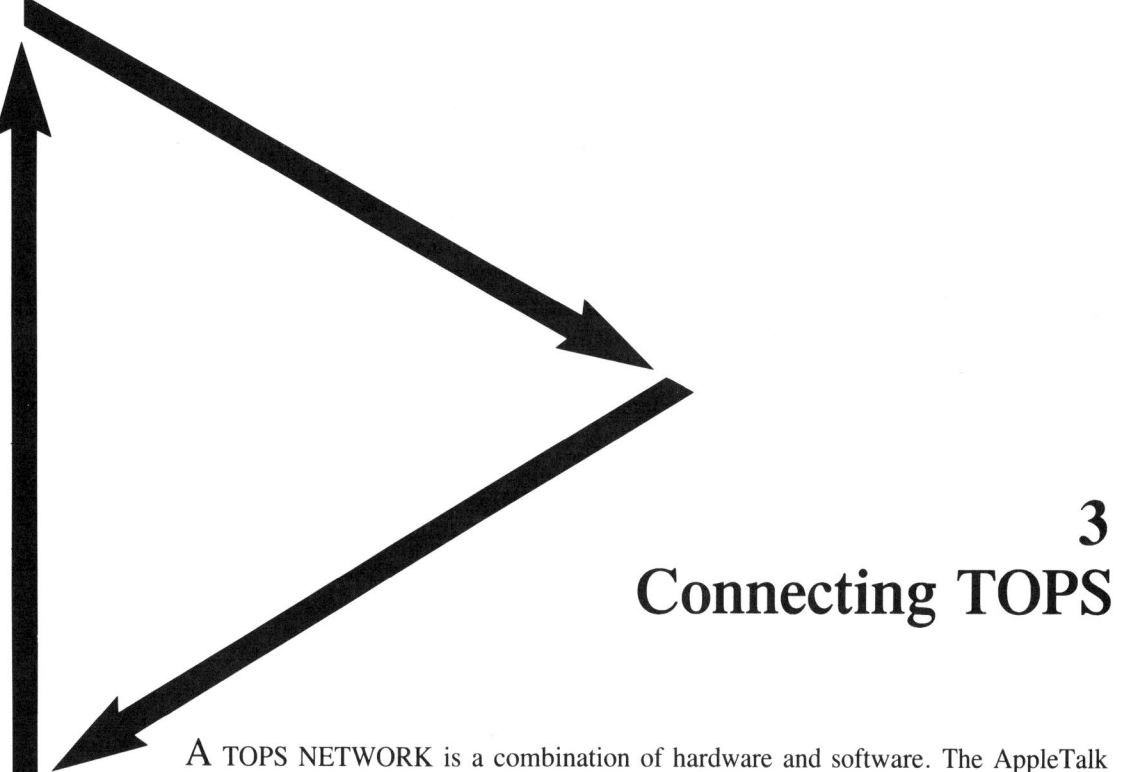

A TOPS NETWORK is a combination of hardware and software. The AppleTalk and Ethernet protocols, used by TOPS, are formats for how the machines on a network talk to each other, and how the data that passes through the network wires is structured. The wires themselves, however, can be many different types. This chapter discusses the possibilities as far as the physical connection of the TOPS network is concerned. This chapter begins with a look at the basic connectors used in a normal TOPS network.

BASIC CONNECTORS

In this section, we review the items needed to connect together a simple network of PCs and Macs using standard equipment. If your cabling needs go beyond this to the more exotic connections, see the later sections.

The Mac Connectors

In Fig. 3-1, you can see two examples of TOPS TeleConnectors. These are the pieces of equipment that go between the network wiring and AppleTalk ports on Macintosh devices.

TeleConnectors get their name from the fact that they connect to standard telephone wire, the kind that you probably have between the wall socket of your home phone and the phone itself. Each TeleConnector consists of a box with two sockets in it and a piece of cable that terminates in a plug. The sockets accept modular phone plugs, the type that are standard in the U.S.A.

38   Chapter 3

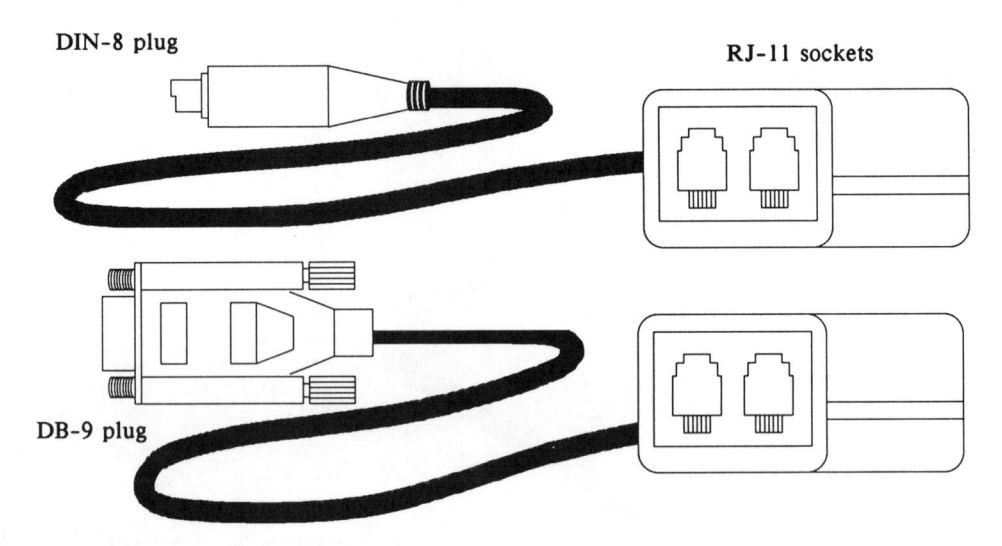

Fig. 3-1. Macintosh TeleConnectors.

Figure 3-1 shows two types of plug for TeleConnectors. This is because there are two types of AppleTalk port. These are described as DIN-8 and DB-9 respectively. The round DIN-8 port is found on the Macintosh Plus, the SE, the II, the Apple IIe and IIGS, the ImageWriter II with AppleTalk option, the LaserWriter IINT, and so on. The DIN-8 plug can handle up to eight wires and is a round connector; however, it only fits into the socket if it is lined up correctly. When you make a DIN-8 connection, make sure that the groove in the metal part of the plug is lined up with the slot in the socket.

The larger, rectangular plug type is the DB-9 used on older Apple LaserWriters, some models of the Macintosh 512K, and on the TOPS Repeater. The DB-9 connector gets its name from the fact that it can connect up to nine wires and has a D shape that prevents it from being plugged in the wrong way round.

TOPS is not the only company that markets TeleConnector type equipment. You can use similar connectors from Farallon Computing and other vendors, as described in Appendix B. All of these support the standard AppleTalk communication speed of 230 kbps.

In Fig. 3-2, you can see the TOPS FlashBox. FlashBox is a specialized TeleConnector that supports faster than standard AppleTalk communication.

As mentioned in the last chapter, TOPS FlashCards can run AppleTalk at 770 kbps. By using a FlashBox instead of a standard TeleConnector to connect Macintoshes to the network, you can speed up network operations considerably. The FlashBox looks much like a TeleConnector but has special wiring inside that enables the higher communication speed. While FlashBoxes cost a little more than regular TeleConnectors, the increase in network throughput might well be worth the investment. However, before you rush to replace TeleConnectors with FlashBoxes, note that there are two caveats. First, you do not need FlashBoxes for ImageWriter or

LaserWriter printers, because these printers cannot go any faster. Second, you will not maximize the gains from FlashBoxes if you mix "TeleConnected" Macintoshes with "FlashBoxed" Macintoshes. This is because TOPS has to convert the higher speed data coming from a FlashBox down to slower speed when it encounters a TeleConnector. This conversion adds to network overhead and performance degradation. The best way to upgrade a TOPS network to "Flash" speed is make sure you connect each Macintosh computer with a FlashBox while using TeleConnectors for printers and PCs.

The PC Connection

Connecting a PC to a TOPS network is a two-step process. First you must equip the PC with a network adapter. This step is done by inserting a circuit board into PC, the practical aspects of which are described in Appendix D. The next step is to cable the port on the network card to the network.

The network adapter can either be AppleTalk or Ethernet. If you are using Ethernet as the basis of your network, refer to Chapter 13. As far as AppleTalk network cards for PCs are concerned, there are several from which to choose. The FlashCard, made by TOPS, offers AppleTalk support at a higher speed than the AppleTalk standard of 770 kbps. The speed of operation provided by the FlashCard for PCs is the same as that offered by the FlashBox for the Macintosh.

Once you have a FlashCard in your PC, you can cable it to the network with a TeleConnectors. In Fig. 3-3, you can see the TOPS TeleConnector used for PC devices.

This connector has a DB-9 plug like those used for serial ports on the IBM PC AT and other DOS machines. The DB-9 connection is also used for AppleTalk on older Apple LaserWriters as well as the TOPS FlashCard and Repeater. The D

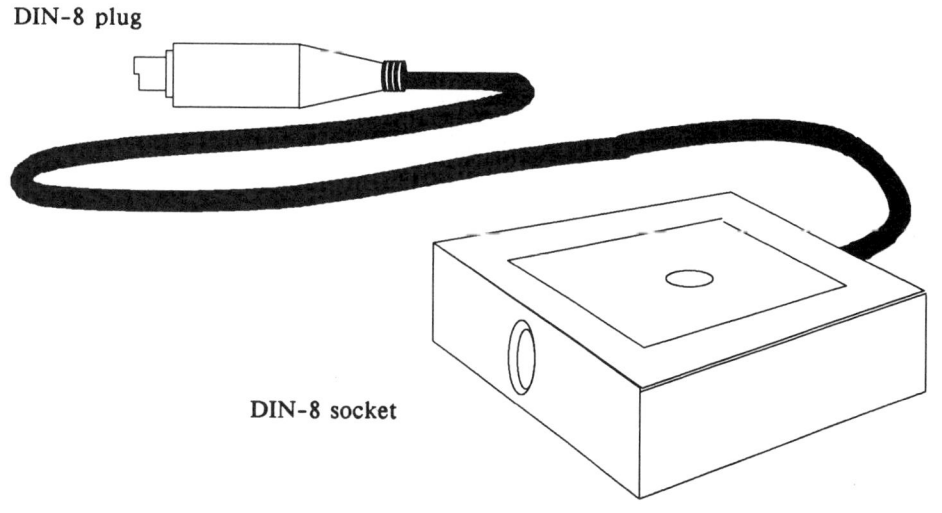

Fig. 3-2. TOPS FlashBox.

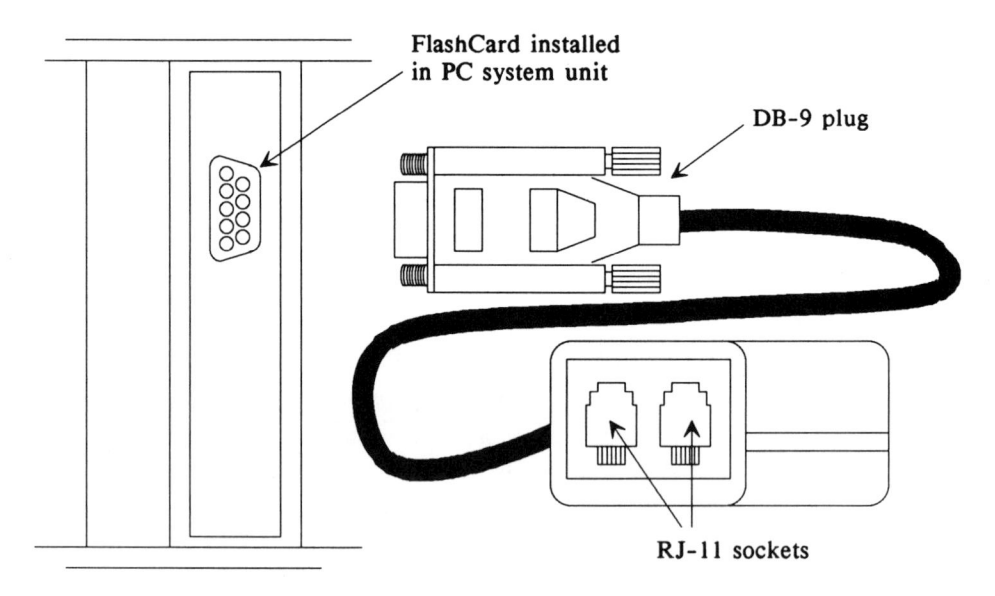

Fig. 3-3. TOPS TeleConnector for DOS.

shape prevents it from being plugged in the wrong way, however, this does not prevent it from being plugged into the wrong socket: Always make sure you are connecting TOPS to the AppleTalk port and not to a serial port.)

The Cable

When you have put TOPS TeleConnectors on the AppleTalk ports of your equipment, you can proceed to connect the TeleConnectors. If a network is a system of cables and commands, what kind of cabling does TOPS require? The normal method of cabling TOPS workstations together is thin wire like that used to connect ordinary telephones to wall sockets. This wire is known as *twisted pair* and is about the least expensive form of network cabling. The usual connector for this cable is called an RJ-11, familiar to users of modular phones, as seen in Fig. 3-4.

You get a length of this cable in each TeleConnector package. This allows you to proceed with a network connection immediately, as seen in Fig. 3-5.

However, there are several other factors to consider when cabling a network, and they are discussed next.

THE CABLE STANDARDS

The three basic types of cabling standards supported by TOPS networks are twisted pair, coaxial, and fiberoptic. Twisted pair and coaxial wiring seem to be the most common and are used in many everyday electronic applications. Twisted pair wiring is the kind used in phone systems. Coaxial is commonly used for cable TV and some kinds of computer communications. Fiberoptic is a newer technology that

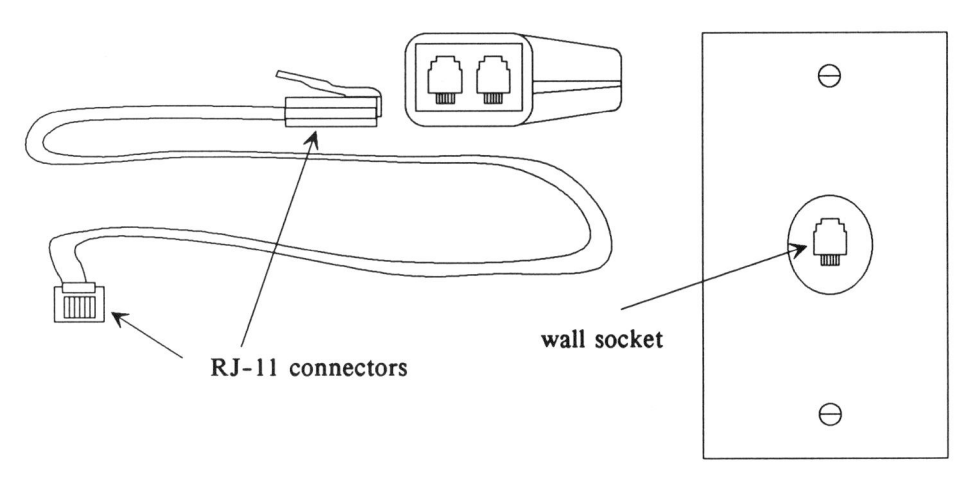

Fig. 3-4. Twisted pair cable and connector.

converts data to light, and it is being used in newer long distance phone lines. Each system has advantages and disadvantages. The table below shows a brief summary of each type's relative merits.

Twisted Pair	**Coaxial**	**Fiberoptic**
Low cost	Medium cost	High cost
Low speed	High speed	High speed
High noise	Medium noise	No noise

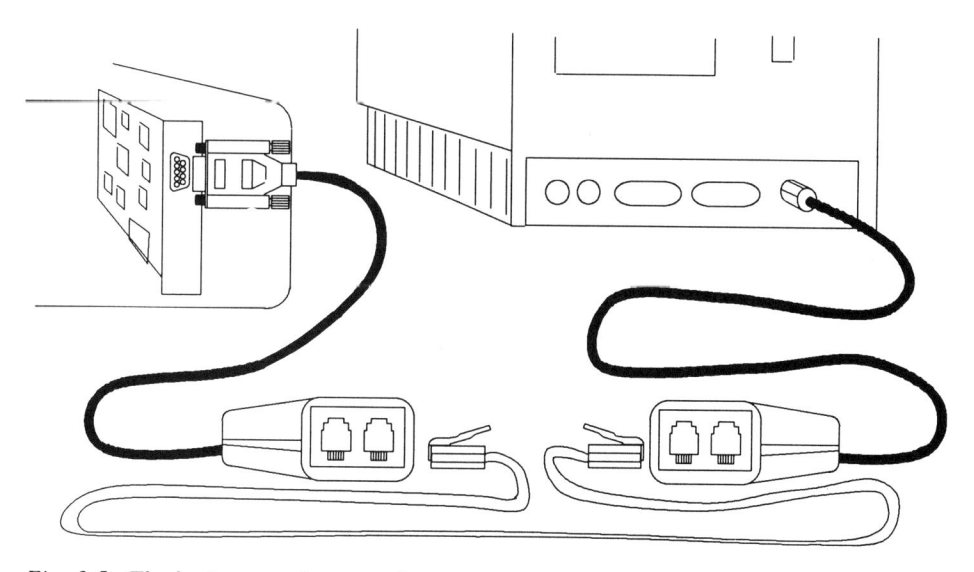

Fig. 3-5. The basic network connection.

While this table oversimplifies matters somewhat, it at least gives a few factors for comparison if you are not yet committed to a certain type of wiring. Each type of cabling is reviewed in greater depth in the following sections.

TWISTED PAIR CABLING SYSTEMS

Twisted pair is the medium that generally requires the least setup cost. The transmission speed of networks using twisted pair, as defined by AppleTalk is 230 kbps. In the world of local area networks, this is regarded as slow. The slow speed is a tradeoff for the low cost. The perception of speed, however, is a subjective one. For many applications, 230K baud is adequate. Average access to a remote network hard drive at this rate is usually as fast as access to a local floppy disk.

FlashTalk

Although some users find AppleTalk acceptable in terms of speed, TOPS has enhanced the Apple standard with FlashTalk in the interest of better performance. Like AppleTalk, FlashTalk runs over twisted pair wiring. The TOPS FlashCard for the PC and FlashBox for the Macintosh will transmit at roughly three times the speed of AppleTalk. The FlashTalk data rate is 770 kbps. If the conditions are right, FlashTalk connections can significantly improve the performance of TOPS networks. However, on a TOPS network, it is better to run all FlashTalk than to mix speeds.

One condition for successful use of FlashTalk is quality cabling. The cable can be twisted pair, but the quality must be good and all connections securely made. Another prerequisite for the network to reach these higher performance levels is that all of the network stations should be FlashTalk capable. If they are not, the network spends a lot of time trying to figure out which are and which aren't, and the performance increase is compromised.

Some types of twisted pair cabling systems use the same kind of wire used for the telephone. TOPS TeleConnectors and Farallon PhoneNet fall into this category. These cables end with the same RJ-11 adapter as your telephone, as seen in Fig. 3-6.

Under the right circumstances these connectors make it possible for the network to use the same wires running through your walls that your phone system does. Other systems, such as Apple's LocalTalk, use a less common three-pin DIN adapter.

Twisted Pair Topologies

Twisted pair cabling can be implemented in two topologies, the *bus* and the *star*. Large networks are sometimes a combination of the two. The bus topology is basically a trunk (straight line), with one computer connected to the other like a line

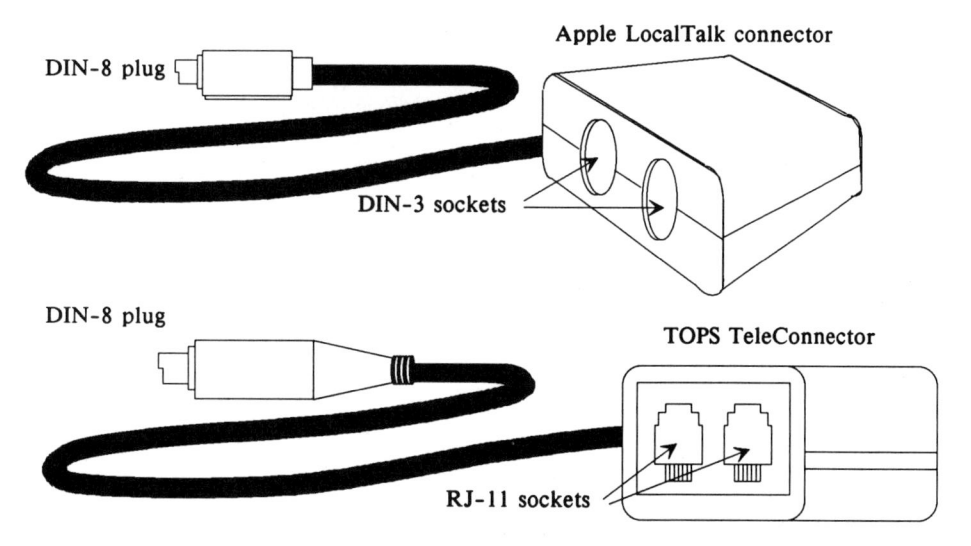

Fig. 3-6. Connectors using RJ-11 plugs.

of people holding hands. The star, on the other hand, revolves around a central hub, like the roundhouse of a railroad system. Both systems are pictured in Fig. 3-7.

Each node on the network, whether a computer, a printer, or some other type of device, uses a special connector to drop off from the network wire. If the device is IBM PC compatible, the connector has an oblong fitting on the end called a DB-9. If the device is a Macintosh, the fitting is a round DIN-8. The connector has two sockets to receive network connections. One socket is incoming, the other outgoing, which is how the network passes through the node. Consequently, the network is electronically continuous, even when some of the nodes are not turned on.

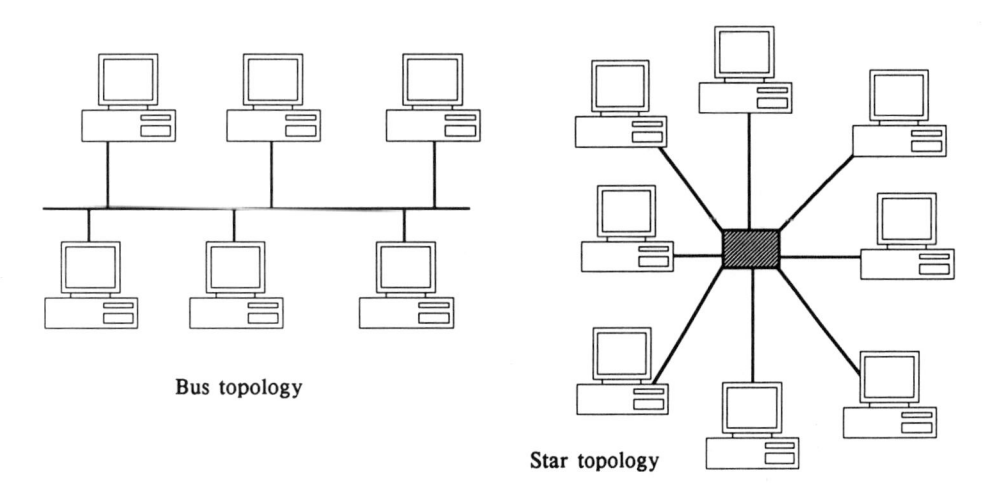

Fig. 3-7. Star and bus topologies.

Bus Topology

The bus or trunk topology is a simple one to implement. It is a chain with cable going from one machine to the next. The only rules are that the length of the cable (end to end) should not exceed 1000 feet and that the bus should not contain more than 32 nodes. At least, these are the Apple specifications for Apple LocalTalk cabling. TOPS TeleConnectors and PhoneNet connectors can usually exceed these limits.

The ends of the bus must be electronically terminated. With LocalTalk connectors, this termination is built in. With TOPS TeleConnectors and PhoneNet connectors, a small plastic item, called a resistor, must be placed in the open socket of the last connectors. The resistor is supplied in the connector package.

The above specifications are results of the electronic limits inherent in the twisted pair type of cabling being used. Exceeding these limits will probably increase the likelihood that the network will suffer from bad connections. It is generally wise to stay within the limits, even though in some cases things will still work if you don't.

The network bus's electronic limits can be extended with the aid of a signal strengthening device, called a *repeater*. If the length of the bus for a given network needs to exceed 1000 feet, a repeater is the solution. Repeaters filter noise out of a network signal and pass it along at a boosted level. Consequently the signal can carry for another 1000 feet. In fact, a repeater actually creates an entirely new electronic bus on the other side. So in addition to allowing another 1000 feet of cable, another 32 nodes can be placed on the newly created bus. Naturally, each bus would need to be terminated at its ends, as shown in Fig. 3-8.

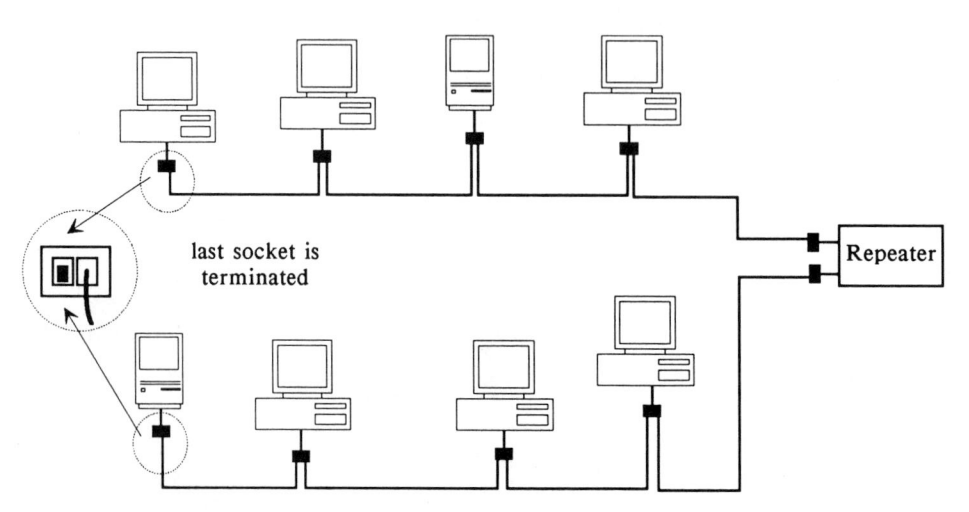

Fig. 3-8. Using a repeater.

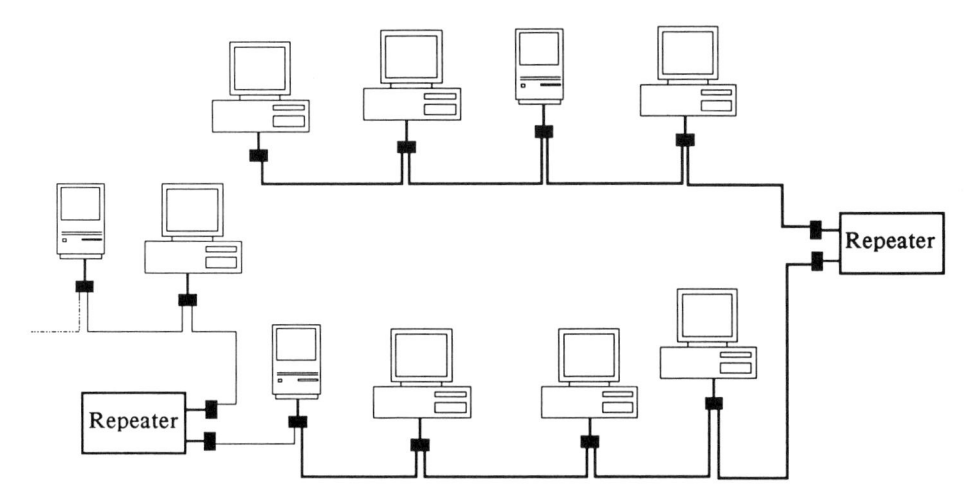

Fig. 3-9. Adding a new bus.

The network would then consist of two individual, but joined, electronic buses, each of which can contain up to 32 nodes. If the network grew beyond those numbers, another repeater could be added, which would again create another new bus, as shown in Fig. 3-9.

This pattern could be carried on until the network grows to a maximum of 255 nodes (the limit for a FlashTalk or AppleTalk network, unless you are using the new AppleTalk 2.0).

EXPANDING THE BUS FOR LARGE NETWORKS

Repeaters can also be used to create drops off of a trunk, as illustrated in Fig. 3-10.

If circumstances dictated that more than 255 nodes needed to be joined, the network would need to add a device called a bridge. A bridge, shown in Fig. 3-11, is like a repeater, in that it creates a new electronic bus, but it is also much more. The bridge actually runs software which separates (or joins as the case may be) two different networks.

Each side of the bridge could then be a series of buses, and each side could theoretically contain 255 nodes. The software is downloaded into the bridge from one of the computers on the network.

SOME PRACTICAL ADVICE

The previous discussion was meant to explain the theoretical specifications, both electrical and protocol, for FlashTalk or AppleTalk networks. Some recommended maximums were mentioned. In practice however, many users have no need for networks anywhere near the 32-node limit per bus, let alone the 255-node limit overall.

Using Repeaters

There are good reasons for even small networks to use repeaters. For example, a common practice for many installed FlashTalk and AppleTalk networks is to use existing phone lines in a building, or to install new wires in the walls that enter the room through a telephone jack. Wires can then run right from the jacks in the wall to the connector attached to the computer. It is a very nice way to keep things tidy. As with many electrical phenomenon, however, sometimes the runs of wire seem to work great in some rooms, but not in others. It is often a result of some hard to trace factor that dissipates the signal somewhere along the line. Repeaters centrally placed within the building will often solve the problem, because they boost the weakened signal.

When networks are medium or large, users often find that they need to put repeaters in more often than 1000 feet, have less than 32 nodes in a bus, or have far fewer than 255 nodes on one side of a bridge. For example, if the network receives heavy use or the cabling is subjected to sources of electrical interference, performance will suffer unless a different physical scheme is followed. There is nothing wrong with placing repeaters more often than the maximums dictate.

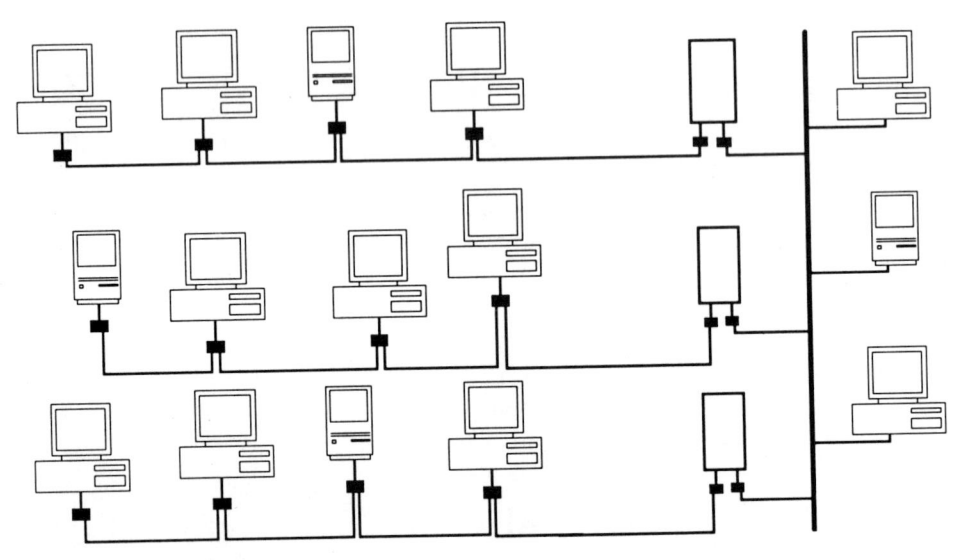

Fig. 3-10. Drop off from a trunk.

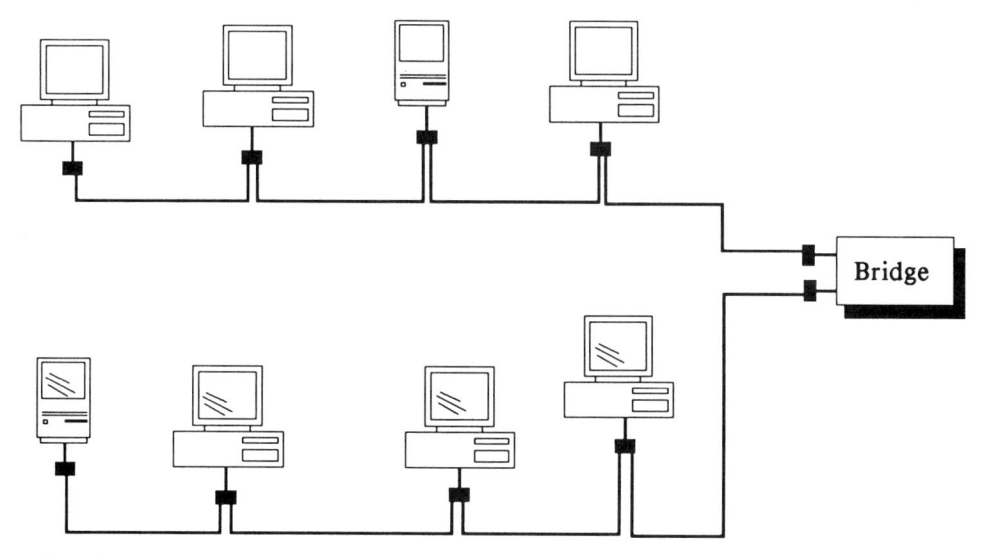

Fig. 3-11. Using a network bridge.

Using Bridges

In addition to added repeaters, some networks can benefit by the strategic placement of bridges in places they are technically not required. The result is a logical separation of large groups of users, into smaller departmental or workgroup configurations. In a heavily used network, the number of users can be broken into smaller groups by placing bridges, rather than repeaters, in the proper locations.

The benefit of using a bridge is that the software in the bridge can be configured to segregate most of the network traffic within each workgroup. Users can communicate through the bridge to another workgroup when they need to, but this way intergroup activity on either side of the bridge will not interfere with the other group. The areas on either side of the bridge are referred to as *zones* as illustrated in Fig. 3-12.

Because most communication and network traffic happens on one side of the bridge, within the *local zone*, there is usually a large gain in network efficiency. Somewhere around 20-25 users within a zone might be the most you would want if the network is a busy one.

Another practical application of a bridge is the ability to tie together two remote networks. The networks might be across town or even in two different cities. With the use of a modem, and a bridge at each of the two sites, the network can be connected over the telephone lines. Users can then send mail or print jobs back and forth over the remote bridge, as illustrated in Fig. 3-13.

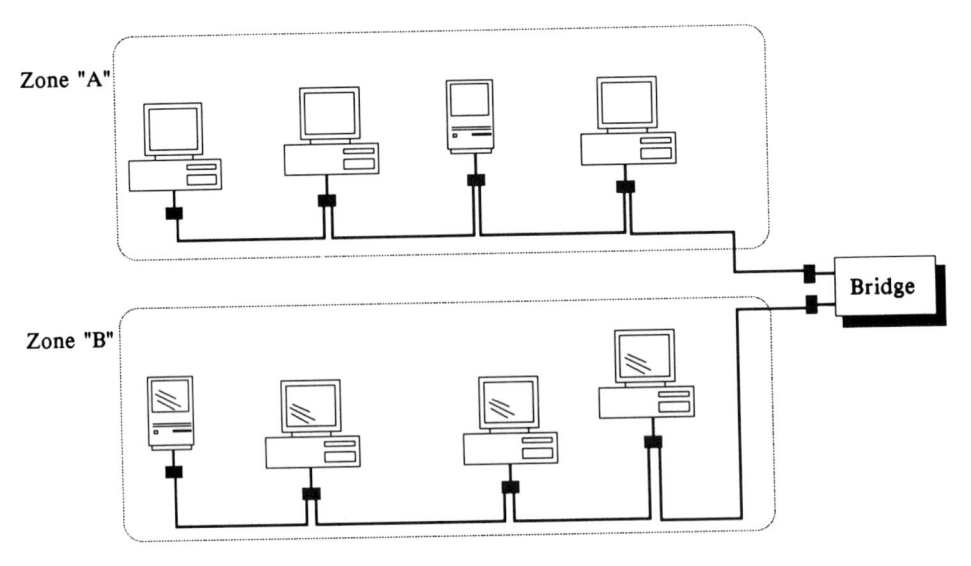

Fig. 3-12. Zones created by bridges.

COAXIAL CABLING AND THE ETHERNET BUS

Ethernet, like LocalTalk, TOPS TeleConnectors, and PhoneNet, also consists of an electronic bus. Ethernet however, does not use twisted pair wiring. Instead Ethernet uses a higher quality shielded coaxial cable. Coaxial cable is the kind used in your home for cable TV. It is shielded to reduce interference, and generally provides a high quality signal. This cable comes in two flavors.

The first is called Thick Ethernet, which is fairly expensive because of high cable density and an extremely heavy shield. The second is called Thin Ethernet, which is more modestly built and much less expensive.

The data transmission rate of Ethernet is dramatically greater than that of twisted pair. Ethernet signals are rated at 10 megabits per second. This doesn't mean that you will see performance 40 times the speed of AppleTalk, because there are some nonprotocol limitations to network performance such as disk speed, but the greater bandwidth of Ethernet does make a big difference. It also makes it less likely that network traffic will measurably slow performance.

Ethernet buses are not subject to the same electronic limits as twisted pair buses. For one thing a Thin Ethernet bus can be much longer before requiring a repeating device. Ethernet has historically been the standard of choice for large networks. However, it is quite a bit more expensive when compared to twisted pair, because each computer must be supplied with an Ethernet interface device whereas the Macintosh has the interface built in for FlashTalk or AppleTalk.

COMBINING THE BENEFITS OF TWISTED PAIR AND ETHERNET

It is sometimes possible to have the best of both the twisted pair and Ethernet worlds. Various cabling methods and products are available that can either increase twisted pair data rates to Ethernet speeds or bridge twisted pair cabling into Ethernet.

For example, sometimes a company will use a combination of coaxial Ethernet and twisted pair AppleTalk wiring layouts. Twisted pair wiring is often adequate within workgroups, but to connect workgroups, the twisted pair wiring is bridged to an Ethernet backbone. The Ethernet serves as a high bandwidth trunk to connect the segregated workgroups. One such AppleTalk/Ethernet bridge is called the Fastpath (see Appendix B for more detailed product information).

A different kind of solution, Lattice Net, from a company called Synoptics, is a system that allows 10 megabit per second speed over twisted pair wires. The Lattice Net system replaces the LocalTalk style connectors with a proprietary Lattice Net connector. The network also is fitted with a special signal condenser. The combination of condenser and Lattice Net connector zip the data along the wire at a much accelerated pace. A system such as Lattice Net is a nice way to get higher performance in a building already wired for twisted pair without having to rewire.

One other common scenario in many business and educational settings is a need to integrate Macintoshes and IBM compatibles with larger systems such as DEC VAX computers, and Hewlett Packard and Sun workstations. Typically the

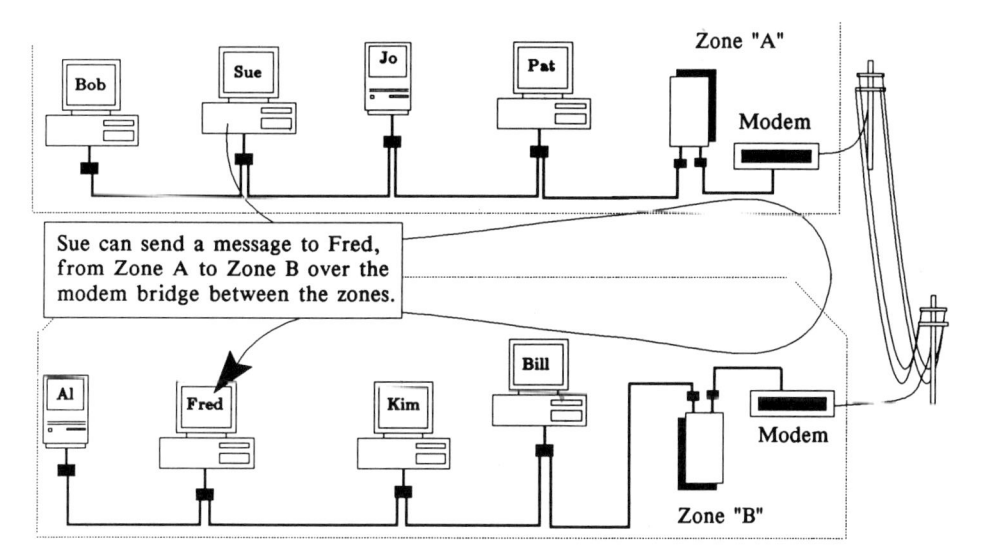

Fig. 3-13. Bridging via modem.

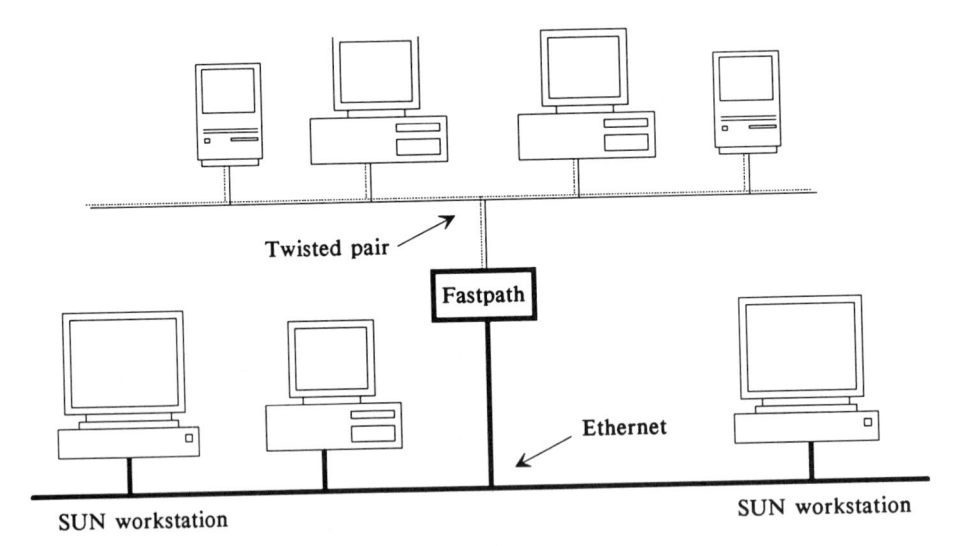

Fig. 3-14. Combined networks.

larger systems are configured to run on Ethernet, so in this case the Ethernet is more than just a backbone, it is an extension of the FlashTalk or AppleTalk network. With the same AppleTalk to Ethernet bridge (the Fastpath) mentioned earlier, the cabling systems can be joined together. The result is that Macintoshes and IBM compatibles which use TOPS on twisted pair wiring can share the network, and communicate with the more powerful systems on Ethernet, as diagrammed in Fig. 3-14.

Here the Fastpath acts as a gateway, converting AppleTalk protocols to Ethernet and vice versa. The Fastpath is an intelligent box, much like the bridge discussed earlier in this chapter. The gateway has two connection ports on the back, one for AppleTalk cabling and one for Ethernet (Thick and/or Thin). Depending on which side you stand on, the gateway has Ethernet or AppleTalk coming in and the other going out.

Like a bridge, a gateway runs software that tells it how to do its work. The difference between the gateway and the bridge is that the gateway software is sophisticated enough to convert the data that passes through it. This is necessary because the data structure of Ethernet information is slightly different from that used by TOPS on the twisted pair side (under either the FlashTalk or AppleTalk protocols).

THE STAR TOPOLOGY

The star topology is a configuration that can be supported by twisted pair, but not by Ethernet. In Fig. 3-15, you can see what a star topology looks like.

In prewired buildings, the hub is usually a telephone closet into which all the separate runs converge. At the center of the star is a signal managing piece of hardware called a *star controller*. A popular brand is one manufactured by Farallon computing, the same company that makes PhoneNet cabling.

Although it is sometimes possible to create a star network without using a star controller, it is not recommended. A star controller is essentially a multiple port repeater. It maintains a quality signal down all of the star's branches. Passive stars, ones that don't use repeaters, can't guarantee the same signal quality. Passive stars are notorious for problems.

One caveat is in order, even to sites considering implementing an active star (one with a star controller). The wiring task is significant and probably should be attempted only with the help of professionals competent in cable installations. Choose your cabling contractor with care.

CONCLUSION

While the question of cabling can get very technical, most issues are resolved when the network is first set up. In the case of large networks, changes after initial installation are best dealt with by discussion among the more technical users. Most individual users need not worry about how they are connected, just that the connection works. Having looked at how you make connections to a TOPS network, we move on to the installation of TOPS software.

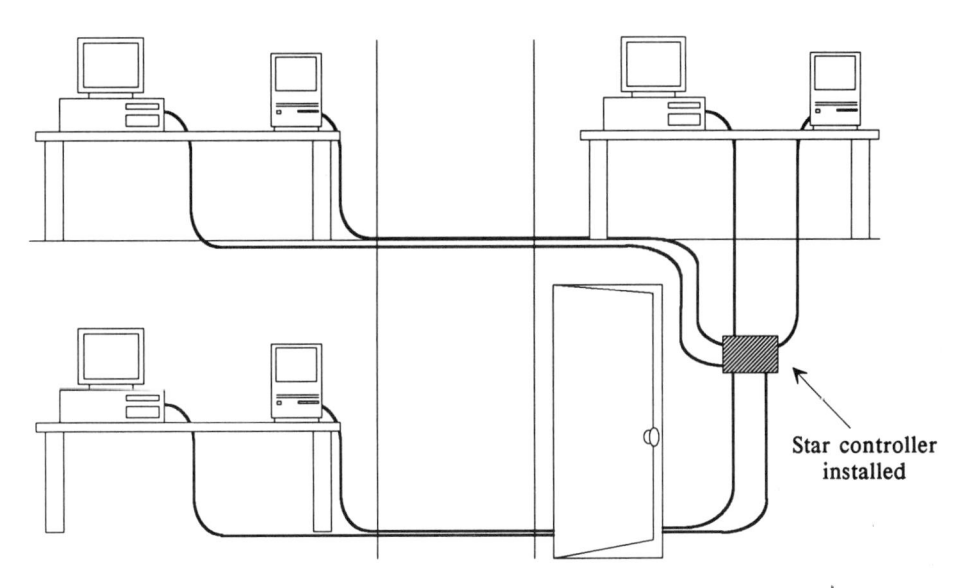

Fig. 3-15. Star topology installed.

4
Installing TOPS

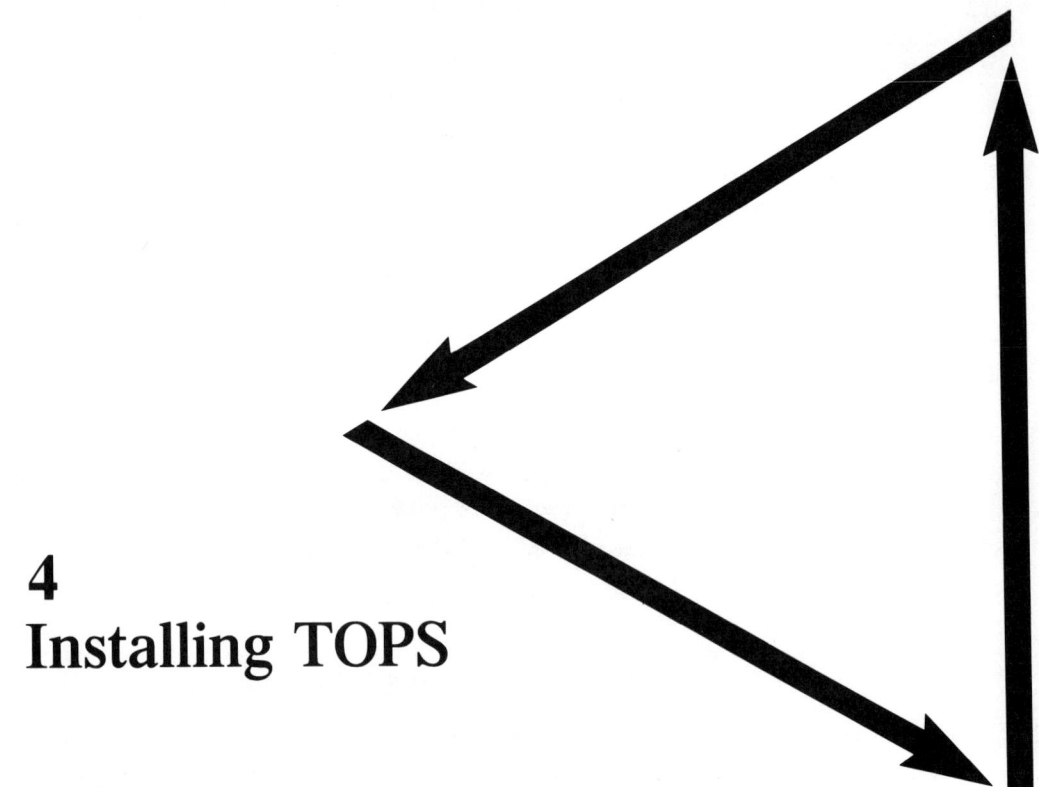

THIS CHAPTER DISCUSSES how to set up TOPS software on both a PC and a Macintosh. We assume that you have connected the computers to the network as described in the last chapter. Basic software installation is very straightforward and well described in the TOPS manuals. However, we discuss some special cases which might present problems, and describe some techniques that might save you some time and effort. We deal with TOPS/Macintosh software first, as this is generally easier to set up than TOPS/DOS.

A QUESTION OF VERSIONS

Before getting to specifics, a word about versions. As you probably know, just about every piece of software published is an exercise in compromise. The main compromise is between the desire to include every possible feature, and the desire to finalize a product that is useful enough to be sold. A successful compromise means that the first version of a program is rarely the last. Even before one version is on the shelves, programmers are busy enhancing it, improving it, until marketing says it is time for the next version to be released.

When a new version of a program comes out, users of what is now the old version have a decision to make: upgrade to the new or stick with the old. In most cases, the best course of action is to upgrade, and this is certainly the case with TOPS. This book is based on version 2.1 of TOPS/DOS and TOPS/Macintosh.

If there are users on your network who are using version 1 of TOPS/DOS (which was called TOPS for the PC version 1) and you use TOPS/DOS version 2, you will not be able to communicate with them, although they will continue to be able to communicate with other version 1 users. As far as TOPS/Macintosh is concerned, we recommend that you upgrade all users to the same version. This is the best way to prevent confusion between users limited by earlier versions.

If you have already got TOPS installed on a system and need to upgrade it, see the section on upgrading later in this chapter. The mechanics of upgrading are fairly simple and it only takes a few moments.

INSTALLING TOPS/MACINTOSH

For the experienced Macintosh user, installation is simply a matter of copying the TOPS files, installing the TOPS Desk Accessory, and restarting system. (These steps are detailed below.) However, TOPS does provide an automated installation procedure the use of which is also described. Before proceeding with the installation process it is a good idea to learn what files make up the TOPS/Macintosh package. See Table 4-1 for a list of the various modules in TOPS/Macintosh and for what they are used.

Table 4-1. TOPS software modules.

TOPS File	What the file does
SoftTalk	TOPS network communication module.
TOPS	The main part of the TOPS system module.
TOPS Key	Holds the serial number.
TOPS DA	The TOPS Desk Accessory module.
TOPS Prep	Holds station name and information about automatic publishing and mounting on startup.
Start TOPS	Module that loads TOPS when it is not loaded at startup.
Interbase	Translates Macintosh filenames to network names that can be accessed by a PC.
TOPS Help	The tutorial help text for the TOPS Desk Accessory. Non-tutorial help works without this module.
PC Icon	Provides a Finder Icon for PC documents.
Unix Icon	Provides a Finder Icon for Unix documents.
VMS Icon	Provides a Finder Icon for VMS documents.

You should not install TOPS while MultiFinder, Switcher, or Suitcase are active. If you use these programs, deactivate them before continuing with the installation. In the case of MultiFinder, this means selecting Set Startup from the Special menu and picking Finder, then using the Restart option on the Special menu to reboot the system. To deactivate Suitcase, simply drag the Suitcase file from the System folder and place it elsewhere on the desktop, then restart.

Getting Connected

In the last chapter, we covered the basics of connecting your Macintosh to a TOPS compatible cabling system. Basically, there are two such systems, LocalTalk and Ethernet. Because the TOPS software cannot work unless you are properly connected, we suggest you check your connections before proceeding with the installation.

LocalTalk. If you are connecting with LocalTalk cabling, you should make sure your Mac is plugged in to the network via the AppleTalk or printer port on the back of the system unit. You can see this diagrammed for both a Mac SE and a Mac II in Fig. 4-1.

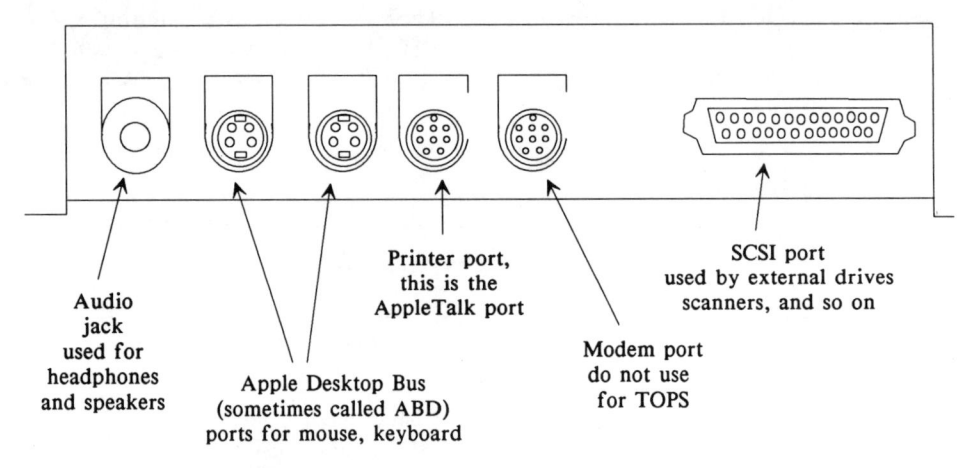

Fig. 4-1. The AppleTalk/printer port.

On some machines, it is possible to confuse the AppleTalk port with the modem port. Don't do this or TOPS will definitely get confused.

One other step is necessary when connecting to the AppleTalk port: you must activate AppleTalk. This part of the System is not always active, so you should make sure it is turned on by picking the Chooser from the Desk Accessory menu. In the lower right of the Chooser dialog box, you will see a pair of AppleTalk buttons, as seen in Fig. 4-2.

Make sure that you click Active. You should also enter a user name. This is a courtesy to other users on the network so they will know who is using shared resources. For example, if you enter Fred's Mac II as the user name and sent a job to the printer, others who are waiting for the printer will be able to see the name Fred's Mac II in the print queue.

Ethernet. Because there are several ways of connecting a Mac to an Ethernet network, we cannot provide detailed instructions here. You can be connected by a plug-in card that provides an Ethernet port for your Mac or you can be connected via a network gateway. Both cards and gateways should come with the necessary software and instructions on how to perform the installation. A plug-in Ethernet card will probably give you an Ethernet option in the Control Panel under an icon for Network, as seen in Fig. 4-3.

You can change the setting to Ethernet from Built-in (AppleTalk) or back to Built-in if you are going off Ethernet and back to AppleTalk. In order for a change to Network to become effective, you must restart your Mac.

TOPS/Macintosh Expert Installation

The following steps assume you know how to perform standard Macintosh operations and have made backup copies of your TOPS program disks.

1. Place TOPS Disk 1 in a floppy drive and drag all the files into the System folder on your hard disk or startup disk. (These should be the files listed in Table 4-1.)
2. Run the Font/DA Mover and click the Desk Accessory button. Now hold down the Option key and click Open on the right side of the window. Next click on Drive and select the TOPS disk. Pick the TOPS DA file.
3. Note the «Copy» button in the Font/DA Mover window. Click on this button to install the TOPS Desk Accessory into the System file. You can pick Quit when the cursor turns back to an arrow.
4. From the Special menu pick Restart. You will see the TOPS icon appear as the system boots.

You should now be able to use TOPS from the Desk Accessory menu. Click on the Apple icon in the top left of the menu bar and pull down the menu. TOPS should be near the top, as seen in Fig. 4-4.

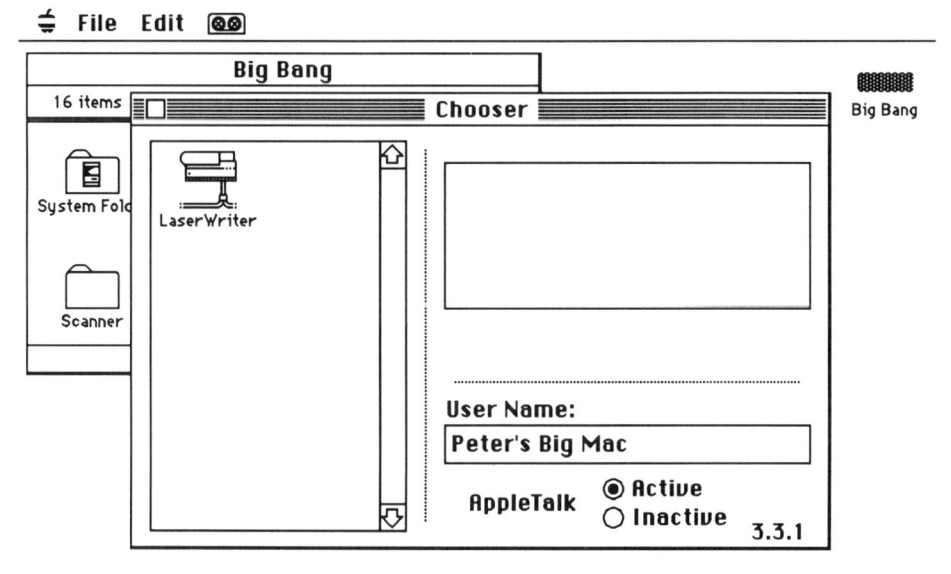

Fig. 4-2. The Chooser.

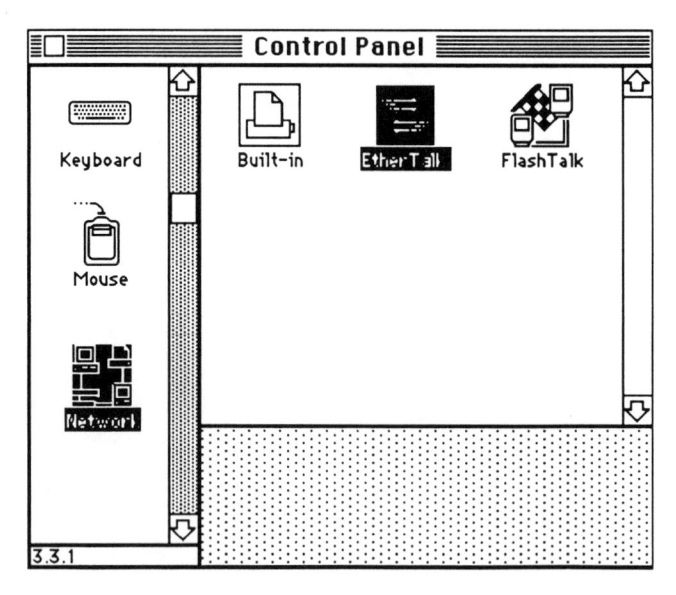

Fig. 4-3. Control Panel.

If you have moved Suitcase out of the System folder, you can now move it back in and restart. TOPS does not conflict with the operation of Suitcase. Remember that the TOPS DA file must remain in the System folder for you to be able to access TOPS as a DA. If TOPS does not appear as a DA after following the above steps, try the automated procedure described next.

Note that the above steps do not install the TOPS Spool program. Installation of the Spool program is covered in a later section. TOPS Spool provides a DA to control print operations on LaserWriters connected to the network.

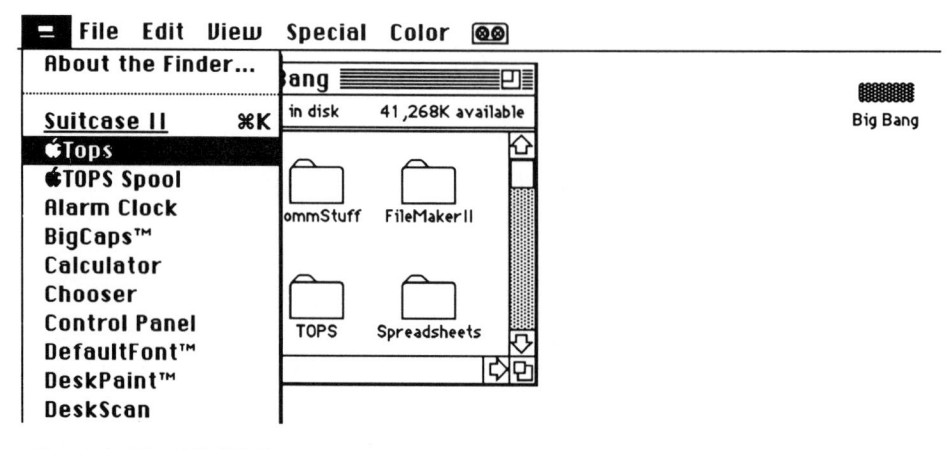

Fig. 4-4. The TOPS DA.

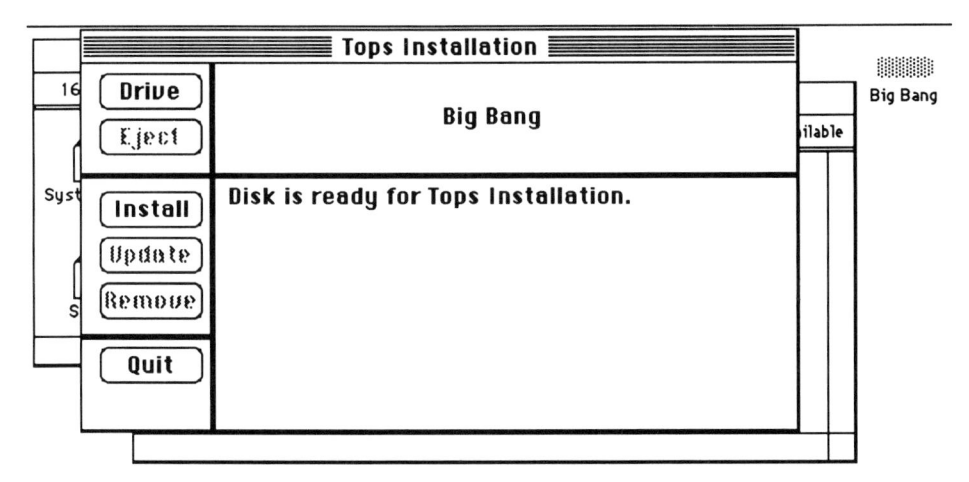

Fig. 4-5. Tops installation window.

The TOPS/Macintosh Installer

To use the menu-driven installation procedure for TOPS, follow these instructions. First insert the TOPS Disk 1 in a floppy drive and open it. Double click on the file called Installer. You will be presented with the screen seen in Fig. 4-5.

Click on Drive until the disk onto which you want to install TOPS is selected. Now click on Install. You will see several status messages as the installation program reports on what it is doing, then you will see the dialog box shown in Fig. 4-6.

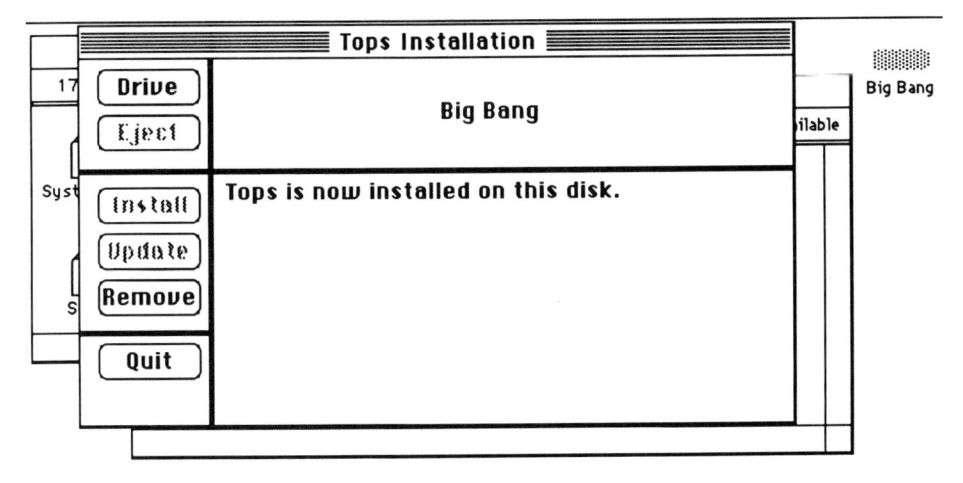

Fig. 4-6. Completed TOPS installation.

If you click on Restart, your system will reboot and you should see the TOPS icon appear as the system starts up. If you pick the Continue button, your system will not reboot. This allows you to perform other housekeeping, like putting Suitcase back in the System folder; however, bear in mind that TOPS will not be active until you do restart. One task you might want to tackle right away is the installation on TOPS Spool, as discussed in the next section.

Installing TOPS Spool

To install TOPS Spool, first copy the files Spool and Spool Installer from TOPS Disk 1 to the System folder on your hard disk or System disk. Then you can double click on Spool Installer. In a moment, you will get a choice between Install, Remove, Update, or Quit. Install is selected if the machine currently does not have TOPS Spool installed already. When the procedure is complete, you see the dialog box shown in Fig. 4-7.

> **TOPS** TOPS Spool has been installed, but will not be active until you restart your Macintosh.
>
> [OK]

Fig. 4-7. TOPS Spool installation completed.

Simply click on OK to return to the Desktop where you can pick Restart from the Special menu. Unless you restart your Mac, the newly installed TOPS Spool DA is not active. See Chapter 7 for more on using TOPS Spool.

Installing TOPS Translators

The TOPS Translators help you convert files from one file format to another, allowing the exchange of documents between popular word processing and database format. Installing the TOPS Translators is merely a matter of copying the appropriate files from TOPS Disk 2 to a folder on your Macintosh. For example, on a hard disk you can create a new folder called TOPS and drag the files there, as seen in Fig. 4-8.

You do not access TOPS Translators from the DA menu. Instead you run TOPS Translators as a regular program, double clicking on the TOPS Translator icon. Details of how to use TOPS Translators can be found in Chapter 8.

INSTALLING TOPS/DOS

If you have some experience with computer hardware and local-area networking, you can get up and running quickly by using the steps outlined in the Running

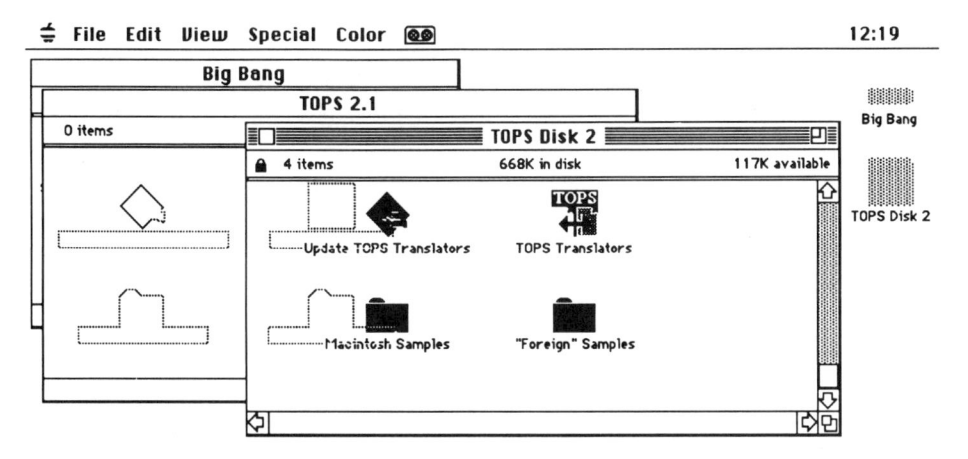

Fig. 4-8. Copying TOPS Translator files.

Start section. Otherwise you will find more detailed instructions in the Automated Installation section.

TOPS/DOS Running Start

These are the basic steps involved in getting TOPS up and running on a DOS machine. They assume that you have installed an AppleTalk board (such as TOPS FlashCard) in one of the system's expansion slots and attached AppleTalk or AppleTalk-compatible cables (such as TOPS TeleConnectors) to the connector on the back of the AppleTalk card, as shown in Fig. 4-9.

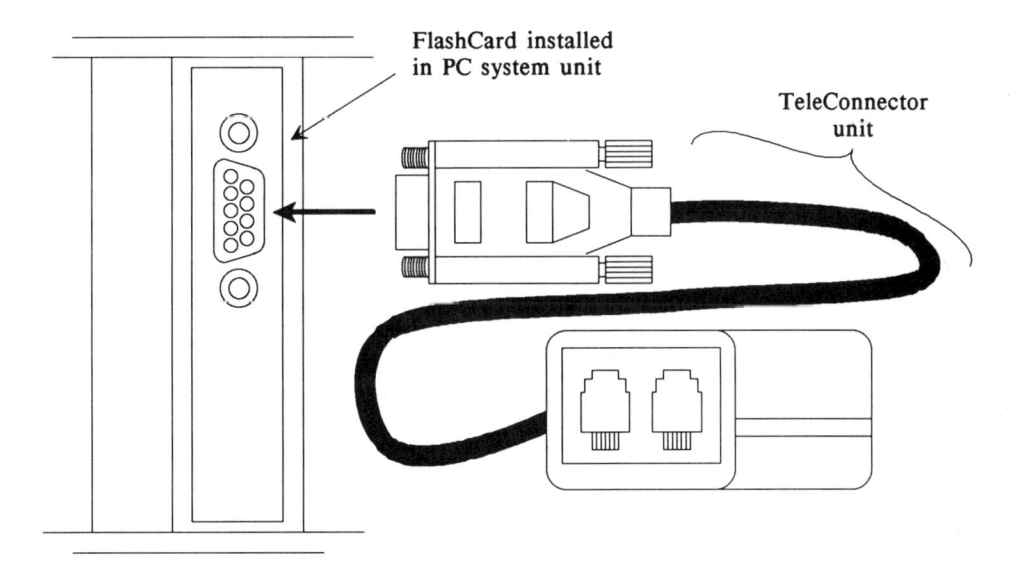

Fig. 4-9. The TOPS FlashCard connection.

60   Chapter 4

The steps are as follows:

1. Make backup copies of the two TOPS program disks, making sure that you label the copies with the serial number from the program disk. Place the original disks in a safe place.
2. Put the working copy of TOPS Disk 1 in drive A. Change to drive A and type SETUP, then press the Enter key.
3. Answer the questions as they are displayed on the screen. Change to TOPS Disk 2 when prompted.
4. If the Setup program has modified your AUTOEXEC.BAT or CONFIG.SYS files, reboot your system.

You are now ready to load TOPS. You can do this by entering LOADTOPS at the DOS prompt. If you do this and get an error message, consult the more detailed description of the installation process that follows. Note that entering LOADTOPS loads the necessary program modules into memory, but it does not present you with a menu. The correct result of LOADTOPS is a smooth return to the DOS prompt, as seen in Fig. 4-10 which shows the screen display during a typical loading operation.

Note that details of this display might be different on your system due to differences in configuration.

```
Mon 4-29-1991 C:\>loadtops
Mon 4-29-1991 C:\>ALAP

TOPS FlashCard FlashTalk Driver, Version LAP 2.102 Installed: Flash = E
Board Address = 398, Board Interrupt = 2, Board DMA = 1, Access Interrupt = 5C

Copyright (c) 1987 Sun Microsystems, Inc.
All Rights Reserved.

Mon 4-29-1991 C:\>pstack
TOPS AppleTalk Protocol Stack, Version TSR 2.102 Installed:

Copyright (c) 1988 Sun Microsystems, Inc.
All Rights Reserved.

Mon 4-29-1991 C:\>topstalk
TOPSTalk - SoftTalk Module for TOPS/DOS Version 2
Copyright (C) Sun Microsystems, Inc. 1987, 1988 . All rights reserved.
TOPSTalk           Version 2 .10        10/17/88
TOPSTALK loaded.

Mon 4-29-1991 C: \>topskrnl
TOPS/DOS Version 2
Copyright (C) Sun Microsystems, Inc. 1987, 1988. All rights reserved.
TOPSKRNL           Version 2 .10        10/17/88

TOPSKRNL Serial Number: P200005729
Reading TOPSKRNL.DAT file....
Initializing network name: Fred's XT ...

Mon 4-29-1991 C: \>echo off
Mon 4-29-1991 C:\>
```

Fig. 4-10. DOS session loading TOPS.

You are now ready to learn the TOPS/DOS commands, described in Chapter 6. If you have problems with the above procedure or need to customize your installation, continue with this chapter.

Automated TOPS/DOS Installation

The TOPS distribution disks contain a program called SETUP which performs all the steps necessary to install the TOPS software on your hard disk. This section describes how to use the Install option of the Setup program. The Setup program offers two other options besides Install, Update, and Configure. The question of updating TOPS/DOS is discussed toward the end of this chapter. The Configure option is used to match the network driver software to your network hardware and is also discussed later in this chapter.

Making backup copies. Regardless of whether you are using a hard disk or floppy disks, you should begin the installation process by making backup copies of your original TOPS disks. To do this, follow these steps if you have a PC with two floppy disk drives and no hard drive:

1. Place your DOS system disk in drive A and at the DOS prompt type DISK-COPY A: B: and press Enter.

2. You will be prompted to place the SOURCE disk in drive A and the TARGET disk in drive B. Remove your DOS disk from drive A and replace it with your TOPS Disk 1. Place a blank disk or one that contains data you no longer need (formatted or unformatted) in drive B. Then press any key.

3. When DOS reports that the copy is complete, it will ask: Copy another disk (Y/N) ? Type Y for yes because you need to repeat the process for Disk 2, the second TOPS master disk.

4. Remove the diskettes from both drives. Label the disk from drive B as TOPS/DOS Disk 1 - Working Copy.

5. Put the TOPS Disk 2 in drive A and a blank disk in drive B and press any key to start the copy process.

6. When the copying is done, type N for no more copies and remove both disks. Mark the disk from drive B as TOPS/DOS Disk 2-Working Copy. Proceed to the section called After Backup.

If your system has a hard disk plus a single floppy disk drive, you can still use the command DISKCOPY A: B: from the DOS prompt. You do not need to log on to drive A, you can issue this command from the C prompt. You will be prompted to insert the SOURCE disk in drive A which means you will place the TOPS Disk 1 there. After pressing any key to commence the copy process and waiting a few moments, you will be asked to insert the TARGET disk in drive B. This means take TOPS Disk 1 out of drive A and replace it with the blank disk that will become the working copy. Your system will think of drive A as though it were drive B until the copying process is completed. Just watch the screen and carefully read the messages to switch disks during the rest of the process. When the copy is complete, enter Y to make another copy and repeat the process with Disk 2. Enter N for no more copies after the second disk has been copied. Proceed to the section called After Backup.

If your system has only one floppy disk, you will need to place the DOS disk in drive A, then issue the command DISKCOPY A: B: and press Enter. You will then be prompted to insert the SOURCE disk. This means you take out the DOS disk, replace it with TOPS Disk 1, and then press any key to continue. When prompted for the TARGET disk, take out the TOPS Disk 1 and insert the blank disk that will become the working copy. Press any key to continue and carefully read any screen messages about further disk swapping. When the copy is complete, enter Y to make another copy and repeat the process with Disk 2. Enter N for no more copies after the second disk has been copied. Proceed to the next section.

After backup. When you have made working copies of the program disks, write the serial number from the master disks on the copies. This is very important because a multiple PC network can quickly generate lots of backup copies and you will need to distinguish them according to the unique serial number on each TOPS package. Now you can put the TOPS master disks away and perform the installation with the copies. If your backup disks ever fail, you can use the TOPS master disks to make a new copy following the previous steps. Remember that you cannot use the copies to install TOPS on more than one station because each package has a unique serial number and two stations with the same serial number cannot log on to the same network.

Running the TOPS Installer. The Install option of the TOPS Setup program automatically copies all TOPS files to their proper locations on hard or floppy disks. The program will ask you some questions and will guide you through the installation process. You will be told what is happening and given the option to skip certain parts of the installation. You will also have a chance to confirm the information you enter at each step of the installation procedure. If for some reason you want to stop the installation procedure before it is complete, simply press the Escape key. This will abort the installation at any time except during the automated process of copying the files from the TOPS distribution disk. Of course, if you do not let the Installer complete all of the installation procedures, you might not be able to run TOPS properly.

For the technically-minded, here is a rundown of what the Installer does:

1. Creates a TOPS subdirectory on the drive you specify to hold TOPS files.
2. Copies the files from TOPS Disk 1 to the TOPS subdirectory. Then asks you to insert Disk 2.
3. Copies files from TOPS Disk 2 to the TOPS subdirectory.
4. Creates or modifies a file called CONFIG.SYS on your boot disk to include Files = 20 and Buffers = 20.
5. Creates or modifies a file called AUTOEXEC.BAT on your hard disk to include the TOPS subdirectory in your DOS search path.
6. Asks you to reinsert TOPS Disk 1.

The following sections explain in detail what is happening during each phase of the installation and what the options mean. We suggest that you follow this installation guide step-by-step as you answer the questions asked by the TOPS Installer program.

CONFIG and AUTOEXEC. Two files particularly important in the installation process are AUTOEXEC.BAT and CONFIG.SYS. These files control what DOS does right after your system is turned on and what DOS knows about your hardware. Typically these files are created by using an editor like EDLIN. Your system might already have these files created. In Table 4-2, you can see an annotated listing of a typical CONFIG.SYS and AUTOEXEC.BAT. TOPS will need to fine-tune a couple of entries in order to work properly on your system. The Files and Buffers settings are the only ones in CONFIG.SYS that TOPS might need to adjust. TOPS will want to adjust the PATH entry in AUTOEXEC.BAT to make sure that it includes the drive/directory in which you store the TOPS program files.

Table 4-2. Annotated CONFIG.SYS and AUTOEXEC.BAT

CONFIG.SYS		AUTOEXEC.BAT	
BUFFERS = 20	Sets size of memory used for temporary storage	DATE	Reads computer clock date into memory
FILES = 20	Sets number of files that can be open at once	TIME	Reads clock time into memory
DEVICE = RD.SYS	A driver for a nonstandard device	PROMPT DP$G	Sets prompt to read date and path

TOPS takes great pains to preserve the existing settings of these files, and even the last lot of settings. You see, each time you use an editor like EDLIN to alter an existing file, say the one called AUTOEXEC.BAT, a backup file, called AUTOEXEC.BAK is created that contains the pre-edited version. This file overwrites the previous BAK file. Hence, TOPS reminds you to rename the old BAK files if you think they might be important later.

Installing TOPS on a Hard Disk

This section describes the installation from the TOPS distribution disks in drive A to a hard disk designated as drive C. If you usually boot from the hard disk but would like to create a separate TOPS boot disk, read the later section on boot disks.

If your PC has an IBM color/graphics board and a monochrome monitor, you might need to use the DOS command MODE BW80 before using the Installer. Otherwise, you might find the screen instructions difficult to read.

```
┌─────────────────────────────────────────────────────────────┐
│        TOPS/DOS 2.1 Software Installation and Configuration v1.02        │
└─────────────────────────────────────────────────────────────┘

            Welcome to TOPS/DOS 2.1 installation and configuration!

        Press:   [ I ]    to install TOPS/DOS 2.1

                 [ U ]    to update TOPS/DOS 2.0 to TOPS/DOS 2.1

                 [ C ]    to configure driver for network card


              Press <ESC> to abort TOPS Installation/Configuration
```

Fig. 4-11. The TOPS/DOS Setup menu.

To install TOPS on a hard disk with the automated Setup program:

1. Place the backup copy of the original TOPS Disk 1 in drive A and type A: and press Enter.
2. Type SETUP and press Enter. You will see the menu shown in Fig. 4-11.
3. You can use the second option of this menu if you just need to update an older version of TOPS. The third option is used to coordinate the settings of the network card in your PC with the TOPS driver software. You will have a chance to use this option after you pick the first option, to install. You can also use the configure option if later hardware chances require adjustment of the configuration. At this point, you will want to type i to install TOPS/DOS. You will then see the screen shown in Fig. 4-12.
4. The warning seen in Fig. 4-12 might be important if you have recently edited your AUTOEXEC.BAT and CONFIG.SYS files.

Press Escape to leave the installation process and do the renaming, after which you can begin the Setup program again. Press any other key to continue the installation. You will come to the Software Transfer menu shown in Fig. 4-13.

5. You need to say in which directory you want the TOPS files stored, the so-called TOPS Path. You can see that C:\TOPS is the default suggestion. Unless you have a burning desire to be different, we suggest you go with TOPS as the directory. Press Enter to confirm the selection of TOPS or type an alternative, making sure that the drive as well as the directory is included. If a directory does not already exist, one is created by the Setup program.
6. The Startup Drive field becomes active when you press Enter at the TOPS Path, and the Status/Help message changes to Specify the disk drive from

Installing TOPS 65

```
┌─────────────────────────────────────────────────────────────┐
│     TOPS/DOS 2.1 Software Installation and Configuration v1.02     │
└─────────────────────────────────────────────────────────────┘
```

WARNING!

The SETUP program will modify your existing AUTOEXEC.BAT and CONFIG.SYS files.

· If your disk has backup files (AUTOEXEC.BAK or CONFIG.BAK) and you want to save them, rename them.

Press <ESC> to abort TOPS Installation/Configuration.
Press any other key to continue.

Fig. 4-12. TOPS/DOS installation.

which the system is booted. Make sure that the entry in this field is correct and press Enter.

7. At this point, you get a chance to reconfirm your entries or change them. Press Y for Yes or N to reenter the data. You can press Escape to abort the installation process. When you type Y, the program proceeds to the next phase.

8. The program now begins copying files from Disk 1. You will be prompted to insert Disk 2, and press any key to continue. There is more copying from Disk 2, and then you are prompted to reinsert TOPS Disk 1.

```
┌─────────────────────────────────────────────────────────────┐
│     TOPS/DOS 2.1 Software Installation and Configuration v1.02     │
└─────────────────────────────────────────────────────────────┘
┌─────────────────────────Software Transfer─────────────────────┐
│ TOPS Path      C:\TOPS                                         │
│ Startup Drive  C:                                              │
│                                                                │
└────────────────────────────────────────────────────────────────┘



┌─Status/Help───────────────────────────────────────────────────┐
│ Specify the drive and directory on which to copy TOPS files.  │
│ This directory will be created if it does not exist.          │
└───────────────────────────────────────────────────────────────┘
```

Enter value. Press ↑↓ or <ENTER> to record value.

Fig. 4-13. Software transfer menu.

66   Chapter 4

```
┌─Status/Help─────────────────────────────────────────────┐
│ Do you want to append "C:\TOPS" to the PATH in your AUTOEXEC.BAT? │
│ (AUTOEXEC.BAT will first be copied to AUTOEXEC.BAK.)    │
│                                                         │
│ Y = Yes,  N = No                                        │
└─────────────────────────────────────────────────────────┘
         Press <ESC> to abort TOPS Installation/Configuration
```

Fig. 4-14. Changing AUTOEXEC.BAT.

9. When you return Disk 1 to the floppy drive, you will see the message in Fig. 4-14.

10. Type Y if you want the TOPS directory to be added to the DOS search path in your AUTOEXEC.BAT file. We advise doing this because it will make using TOPS commands easier, eliminating the step of switching to the TOPS directory first. Note that if you already have an existing AUTOEXEC.BAT file, the Setup program will save a backup copy of it for you under the name AUTOEXEC.BAK before the modifications are made. If the file AUTOEXEC.BAK doesn't exist in the root directory of the disk in the boot drive, this might cause a problem if you have been telling DOS to find AUTOEXEC.BAT in another directory. If you have done this, we assume you know how to alter your startup file to include the TOPS path. Type N if you do not want Setup to create or modify your AUTOEXEC.BAT file.

11. The next question will be the one seen in Fig. 4-15.
    Your CONFIG.SYS file will be changed to include these parameters: Files =

```
┌─Status/Help─────────────────────────────────────────────┐
│ TOPS needs a CONFIG.SYS file with a minimum of 20 buffers.  The current │
│ value of buffers = 4  . Modify the buffers line in CONFIG.SYS? │
│ (CONFIG.SYS will first be copied to CONFIG.BAK.)        │
│ Y = Yes,  N = No                                        │
└─────────────────────────────────────────────────────────┘
         Press <ESC> to abort TOPS Installation/Configuration
```

Fig. 4-15. Changing CONFIG.SYS.

20 Buffers = 20. Your old CONFIG.SYS file is stored in CONFIG.BAK. This number of files and buffers is recommended for the average network station, although your needs might vary. If your CONFIG.SYS file already has values of 20 or greater for these commands, they are not changed. The current settings are shown in the Status/Help message. Enter Y to modify the CONFIG.SYS file. (If it doesn't exist, Setup creates it; if the file does already exist, it is renamed CONFIG.BAK before the modified file is created.) Nothing in your CONFIG.SYS file is changed except the Files and Buffers statements. Enter N if you do not want the CONFIG.SYS file created or modified. (Note that if you decide to run your system without a CON-

Installing TOPS 67

FIG.SYS file, DOS assigns default values to the files and buffers settings and these will probably not be sufficient to operate TOPS efficiently.)

12. After Setup has carried out your wishes as far as AUTOEXEC.BAT and CONFIG.SYS are concerned, you are asked if you want to configure your network interface card, as seen in Fig. 4-16.

```
┌Status/Help═══════════════════════════════════════════════════╗
│                                                              ║
│ Do you want to configure the driver for your network interface card?
│                                                              ║
│ Y = Yes,  N = No                                             ║
╚══════════════════════════════════════════════════════════════╝
         Press <ESC> to abort TOPS Installation/Configuration
```

Fig. 4-16. Configuring interface card.

You only need to answer Yes if you have altered any of the settings on the card from their defaults. See Appendix D on configuring network cards for details of this process. When you have completed configuration, or if you should not choose to configure at this time, you are shown the completion message seen in Fig. 4-17.

```
                    TOPS/DOS 2.1 Installation is done !

              Please restart your computer before loading TOPS.
              After you restart your computer, type:

       ▶    LOADTOPS    to load TOPS 2.1 server and client software.

       ▶    LOADCLNT    to load TOPS 2.1 client-only software.
```

Fig. 4-17. Install completed.

Now that TOPS is installed on your hard disk, you can skip the following section about TOPS on a floppy disk and move to loading TOPS, described in the next chapter.

Booting TOPS/DOS from Floppy Disks

These days the word floppy disk refers to a variety of devices with different storage capacities. We give you the procedure for installing TOPS on three different sizes of disk. Booting from a floppy drive means loading DOS from a floppy disk, a lengthier process than booting from a hard disk, but even if you have a hard disk system, you might want to consider using a floppy boot disk for TOPS.

As you probably know, a hard disk PC will boot from drive A if you insert a disk with the DOS system files in the drive and close the drive door before powering up the system or resetting it. If you have a PC that does not always need to be on the network, you can insert a floppy boot disk in drive A only on those occasions when you want to access the network. Reset you machine, and you can load TOPS automatically. If you reboot without a floppy in drive A, your normal configuration is in effect. This system can also provide a level of network access control because the network boot disk can be locked away.

Users of early versions of TOPS should note that TOPS no longer needs the DEVICE=ATALK.SYS entry in CONFIG.SYS because the ALAP and PSTACK programs provide this information. Thus TOPS can be completely unloaded and does not require a radically different CONFIG.SYS file. However, the floppy boot disk is still a useful option of your need to slim down the CONFIG.SYS and AUTOEXEC.BAT to conserve RAM. Other options to achieve this end are discussed in Chapter 11.

The High Density Installation

If your drive A is a 1.2MB or 1.44MB drive, then you can make a TOPS boot disk by creating a formatted system disk (FORMAT with the /S option) and copying all of the TOPS files to a directory called TOPS on this disk. To make a directory called TOPS use the command MD \TOPS. Make sure that this floppy contains a CONFIG.SYS file with the settings Files = 20 and Buffers = 20. The disk should also have an AUTOEXEC.BAT file that contains the line PATH=A:\;A:\TOPS together with any other directories required for your work. If you plan to load applications from a remote system you should edit the TOPSKRNL.DAT file as described in the Special Cases section later in this chapter. In Table 4-3, you can see the files that will be on a high-capacity boot disk. If you need help editing files, such as AUTOEXEC.BAT and CONFIG.SYS, please see Appendix B.

The 720K Installation

If you have a system with one or more 720K disks (in the 3.5 inch size such as some popular lap top computers use), you can install TOPS on a single floppy disk. However, you will need to leave a few files off the disk if you are using a recent version of DOS. In Table 4-4, you can see a list of files for a 720K boot disk. The floppy should be created with the FORMAT /S option to transfer the system files to it, then a directory called TOPS should be created with the command MD \TOPS. The path setting in the AUTOEXEC.BAT should reflect the directory A:\TOPS. If you plan to load applications from a remote system, you should edit the TOPSKRNL.DAT file as described under Special Cases later in this chapter. If you need help editing files such as AUTOEXEC.BAT and CONFIG.SYS, please see Appendix B.

Table 4-3. High capacity book disk (1.2 or 1.4 megabyte).

The entire suite of TOPS/DOS files will fit onto a high capacity disk with DOS and room to spare for other files such as device drivers and favorite utilities.

```
Volume in drive A is TOPS BOOT
Directory of  A:\

ALAP      EXE     17156   10-17-88    2:10a
ALAP      CFG      1330   10-17-88    2:10a
ELAP503   CFG      1001   10-17-88    2:10a
ELAP503   EXE     22794   11-03-88   12:34p
ELAP523   CFG       308   10-17-88    2:10a
ELAP523   EXE     20874   11-03-88   12:35p
FILELIST  IN2       223   10-17-88    2:10a
FILELIST  IN1       262   10-17-88    2:10a
INITPRIN  EXE     11742   10-17-88    2:10a
LOADCLNT  BAT       119   10-17-88    2:10a
LOADTOPS  BAT       119   10-17-88    2:10a
PSTACK    EXE     28352   10-17-88    2:10a
README    DOC      2455   10-17-88    2:10a
SETUP     EXE     89957   10-31-88   12:43p
TCOPY     EXE     26776   10-17-88    2:10a
TDEL      EXE      8056   10-17-88    2:10a
TDIR      EXE      8446   10-17-88    2:10a
TEXTEND   EXE      4005   11-03-88    2:45p
TNETBIOS  EXE     17170   10-17-88    2:10a
TOPS      EXE     64840   10-17-88    2:10a
TOPS2D1   UPD       113   10-17-88    2:10a
TOPS2D2   UPD        25   10-17-88    2:10a
TOPSCLNT  UPD     45926   11-03-88    2:16p
TOPSEXEC  COM       142   10-17-88    2:10a
TOPSKRNL  DAT       678   10-17-88    2:10a
TOPSKRNL  UPD     74256   11-03-88    2:15p
TOPSMENU  EXE     66984   10-17-88    2:10a
TOPSPRTR  EXE     16139   10-17-88    2:10a
TOPSPRTR  DAT       349   10-17-88    2:10a
TOPSTALC  EXE     13875   10-17-88    2:10a
TOPSTALK  EXE     19985   10-17-88    2:10a
TPRINT    EXE     36815   10-17-88    2:10a
TUPDATE   EXE     10936   10-17-88    2:10a
TWINDOVL  EXE     13076   10-17-88    2:10a
XDEL      EXE     18332   10-17-88    2:10a
XDIR      EXE     11008   10-17-88    2:10a
XSYNC     EXE     20262   10-17-88    2:10a

37 Files - bytes free depends on disk capacity
```

If you need more room you can remove UPD files, and either ELAP or ALAP files that are not needed (remove ELAP files if you are not going to use Ethernet, remove ALAP files if you are not going to use an AppleTalk network adapter).

Table 4-4. TOPS/DOS files for 720K boot disk.

All of the important files will fit on a 720K boot disk. Your directory should look something like this:

```
Volume in drive A is TOPS720BOOT
Directory of  A:\

    ALAP     CFG      1330  10-17-88   2:10a
    ALAP     EXE     17156  10-17-88   2:10a
    AUTOEXEC BAT       268  10-30-89  12:00p
    COMMAND  COM     26268  10-26-88  12:00p
    CONFIG   SYS       297  10-30-89  12:00p
    INITPRIN EXE     11742  10-17-88   2:10a
    LOADCLNT BAT       119  10-17-88   2:10a
    LOADTOPS BAT       119  10-17-88   2:10a
    PSTACK   EXE     28352  10-17-88   2:10a
    SETUP    EXE     89957  10-31-88  12:43p
    TCOPY    EXE     26776  10-17-88   2:10a
    TDEL     EXE      8056  10-17-88   2:10a
    TDIR     EXE      8446  10-17-88   2:10a
    TEXTEND  EXE      4005  11-03-88   2:45p
    TNETBIOS EXE     17170  10-17-88   2:10a
    TOPS     EXE     64840  10-17-88   2:10a
    TOPSEXEC COM       142  10-17-88   2:10a
    TOPSKRNL DAT       678  10-17-88   2:10a
    TOPSMENU EXE     66984  10-17-88   2:10a
    TOPSPRTR EXE     16139  10-17-88   2:10a
    TOPSPRTR DAT       349  10-17-88   2:10a
    TOPSTALC EXE     13875  10-17-88   2:10a
    TOPSTALK EXE     19985  10-17-88   2:10a
    TPRINT   EXE     36815  10-17-88   2:10a
    TUPDATE  EXE     10936  10-17-88   2:10a
    TWINDOVL EXE     13076  10-17-88   2:10a
    XDEL     EXE     18332  10-17-88   2:10a
    XDIR     EXE     11008  10-17-88   2:10a
    XSYNC    EXE     20262  10-17-88   2:10a
         29 File(s)      132555 bytes free
```

Substitute appropriate ELAP file for ALAP if you need to boot on an Ethernet card.

The 360K Floppy Installation

To install TOPS/DOS on 360K floppy disks with a dual floppy machine, first boot up your system with the DOS disk in drive A. Then perform the following steps:

1. Insert your DOS system disk in drive A and a blank disk in drive A.
2. Type A: and then press Enter to make sure you are logged on to drive A.
3. Format the blank disk by typing FORMAT B: and then pressing Enter.

4. After the disk is formatted, type N when DOS asks about formatting another disk. Then remove the formatted disk from drive B, label it Disk 2, and then place another blank disk in B.
5. To format a system disk, type FORMAT B: /S and press Enter.
6. After the disk is formatted, type N when DOS asks about formatting another disk. Then remove the DOS disk from drive A, replacing it with your backup copy of TOPS Disk 1, leaving your newly formatted system disk in drive B.
7. Copy the files listed in Table 4-5 from the program disk to the copy, using the command COPY A:FILENAME.EXT B:
8. Create an AUTOEXEC.BAT file on the disk on drive B that contains the line PATH=B:\TOPS and any other settings/commands you normally use. If you need help editing files such as AUTOEXEC.BAT and CONFIG.SYS, please see Appendix B.
9. Create a CONFIG.SYS file on the disk in drive B with the settings Files = 20, Buffers = 20, and any other settings you normally use.
10. If you plan to load applications from a remote system, you should edit the TOPSKRNL.DAT file as described under Special Cases later in this chapter. Now remove the disk from drive B and label it, "TOPS Boot Disk" with the serial number.
11. Now place the second formatted to the floppy disk in drive B. Copy the files listed in Table 4-6 to this disk.

When you are done, the first disk is your TOPS boot disk, and the second disk is your TOPS working disk. When you have installed TOPS onto floppy disks, we suggest that you make a backup copy of your new TOPS disks using the DISKCOPY command described earlier in this chapter. Remember to write the serial number from the original TOPS program disks on the working copies.

Loading TOPS/DOS Software

Once your TOPS software has been properly installed on your hard or floppy disks, the next step is to activate the software by loading it into your computer's memory. Note that your network adapter card and its driver software must be installed before you start this procedure, which is described in detail in Chapter 6.

Nonstandard Configurations

Many TOPS users have a hardware configuration other than the TOPS default configuration of one or two floppy drives and one hard drive. For example, you might have no hard drive, a multiple-partition hard drive, an external floppy drive, a Bernoulli backup unit, and so on. In these cases the TOPSKRNL.DAT file must be edited to reflect your nonstandard configuration. The TOPSKRNL.DAT file is located in your TOPS subdirectory or wherever your TOPS files reside. See the next section for more information on adjusting your TOPS/DOS configuration.

FINE-TUNING TOPS/DOS

If you are running TOPS on a nonstandard system you will probably need to modify the default configuration used by both TOPSKRNL.EXE and TOPSCLNT.EXE. You can also modify these settings if you wish to optimize TOPS performance or to minimize memory requirements. This section discusses some of the options.

Table 4-5. TOPS/DOS files for 360K boot disk 1.

Use this disk as the boot disk placed in drive A when you turn on your system. Your directory should look something like this:

```
Volume in drive A is TOPS BOOT1
Directory of  A:\

ALAP     EXE    17156   10-17-88    2:10a
ALAP     CFG     1330   10-17-88    2:10a
AUTOEXEC BAT      268   10-30-89   12:00p
COMMAND  COM    26268   10-26-88   12:00p
CONFIG   SYS      297   10-30-89   12:00p
INITPRIN EXE    11742   10-17-88    2:10a
LOADTOPS BAT      119   10-17-88    2:10a
LOADCLNT BAT      119   10-17-88    2:10a
PSTACK   EXE    28352   10-17-88    2:10a
TEXTEND  EXE     4005   11-03-88    2:45p
TNETBIOS EXE    17170   10-17-88    2:10a
TOPSKRNL DAT      678   10-17-88    2:10a
TOPSPRTR EXE    16139   10-17-88    2:10a
TOPSPRTR DAT      349   10-17-88    2:10a
TOPSTALC EXE    13875   10-17-88    2:10a
TOPSTALK EXE    19985   10-17-88    2:10a
TWINDOVL EXE    13076   10-17-88    2:10a
       16 File(s)     132555 bytes free
```

NOTES:

1. Have your AUTOEXEC.BAT file call LOADTOPS.BAT or LOADCLNT.BAT, as in:
   DATE
   TIME
   PROMPT DP$G
   LOADTOPS

   This will load all of the essential memory resident parts of TOPS/DOS.

2. Substitute the appropriate ELAP program for ALAP.EXE if you are using an Ethernet board.

3. You may not need TNETBIOS.EXE, used by some multi-user applications, or TEXTEND.EXE which is used by dBASE III Plus.

4. After loading DOS and TOPS from this disk, switch to disk 2 when you need TOPS commands or menu system.

The TOPSKRNL.DAT File

The way that TOPS stores its configuration information is in a text file called TOPSKRNL.DAT. As TOPS loads, it reads the information in TOPSKRNL.DAT. For this to work, however, one of the following two conditions must be true:

1. The TOPSKRNL.DAT file is in a subdirectory called TOPS.
2. The TOPSKRNL.DAT file is in the same subdirectory that TOPS is being loaded from.

Otherwise if TOPS does not find TOPSKRNL.DAT, it uses internal defaults and ignores your configuration changes. It is important to be aware of these conditions if you make modifications to TOPSKRNL.DAT or if you have stored TOPS files in different subdirectories.

In Table 4-7 is a listing of the original, default TOPSKRNL.DAT that comes on the TOPS distribution diskette. The TOPS manual includes a line-by-line description of the items. This section discusses the parameters which most commonly need to be modified. To modify these parameters, edit the DAT file using a text editor such as EDLIN, which is described in your DOS manual.

Line 2 Station name. Before you can issue commands across the network, you must give your station a name. TOPS does not automatically store this name

Table 4-6. TOPS/DOS files for 360K boot disk 2.

Your directory should look something like this:

```
           Volume in drive A is TOPS BOOT2
           Directory of  A:\

           AUTOEXEC BAT       268   10-30-89   12:00p
           COMMAND  COM     26268   10-26-88   12:00p
           CONFIG   SYS       297   10-30-89   12:00p
           LOADTOPS BAT       119   10-17-88    2:10a
           LOADCLNT BAT       119   10-17-88    2:10a
           TCOPY    EXE     26776   10-17-88    2:10a
           TDEL     EXE      8056   10-17-88    2:10a
           TDIR     EXE      8446   10-17-88    2:10a
           TOPS     EXE     64840   10-17-88    2:10a
           TOPSEXEC COM       142   10-17-88    2:10a
           TOPSMENU EXE     66984   10-17-88    2:10a
           TPRINT   EXE     36815   10-17-88    2:10a
           XDEL     EXE     18332   10-17-88    2:10a
           XDIR     EXE     11008   10-17-88    2:10a
           XSYNC    EXE     20262   10-17-88    2:10a
                  12 File(s)       14995 bytes free
```

This disk provides access to TOPSMENU, all the main TOPS commands and utilities, as well as room for DOS, allowing you to leave this disk in drive A and avoid those "Insert disk with COMMAND.COM in drive A" messages.

because you might want to change it from time to time. However, if you want TOPS to know your station name whenever TOPS is loaded and you want to avoid having to enter it manually, you can put your station name here on line 2. Maximum length for station names is 15 characters, and spaces are allowed. For example, the entry

    Station Name (15 chars): Fred's AT

will name the station Fred's AT whenever TOPS is loaded.

Line 4 Printer redirection timeout. If you are printing with TOPSPRTR and TPRINT, as described in Chapter 7, you might need to increase this setting if documents are not printing in their entirety. The usual cause of incomplete document printing is that there are pauses in the flow of characters going to the printer, and the print handler is interpreting those pauses as the end of the current document. Increasing the wait time will make the print redirector wait longer before assuming the page is ended.

Line 6 TOPSEXEC.COM path. TOPS uses a file called TOPSEXEC.COM to permit launching of remote programs. If you are working on a floppy-only machine and launching applications from a server, you should change this to the drive letter that designates your floppy drive.

Table 4-7. Default TOPSKRNL.DAT.

TOPSKRNL Version 2.10
Station Name (15 chars):
Client
Printer redirection time-out, in seconds (20 - 60): 40
Flush printer redirection buffer on exit (Y/N): Y
TOPSEXEC.COM Path (66 chars): C:\TOPS
No. Servers (1 - 10): 5
No. Remote Volumes (1 - 10): 5
No. Remote Files (5 - 40): 20
No. FCBs (2 -20): 8
Last Logical Drive (C - Z): J
Drive Map (F=floppy, H=hard disk (or ram disk), U=unused): FFHUUUUUUU
Server
No. Clients (0 - 20): 10
No. Published Volumes (0 - 10): 5
No. Open Volumes (0 - 20): 10
No. Files (0 - 100): 30
No. Locks (0 - 100): 30
No. Directories (0 - 30): 20
Buffer Size, K Bytes (4 - 16): 12
No. Handles reserved for Server (0 - 8): 3

Line 7 No. servers. This setting specifies how many servers are simultaneously accessed. If you are in a dedicated server environment, you can change it to 1. Your memory gain is less than 1K for just this item, but if you changed all the associated settings to the minimums permissible in your network environment, you could probably cut 15K from the size of TOPSKRNL (the gain would be slightly less from TOPSCLNT). If you are in a tight squeeze as far as memory is concerned, that amount can make the difference between running or not running an important application.

Line 8 No. of remote volumes. The maximum number of volumes that you can simultaneously mount is determined by this setting. Again, if memory constraints are a problem, you could squeeze the size of TOPS a little by reducing this and other parameters to some practical minimum.

Line 9 No. of remote files. This setting specifies maximum number of files that can be simultaneously opened. Some applications have multiple files open, but it is unlikely many would exceed 30. Most likely, you would receive a relevant error message from your application if you encounter a problem where you need to increase this setting. So it makes sense to decrease this number to whatever is in your CONFIG.SYS under the Files = setting.

Line 11 Last logical drive. This setting specifies what TOPS recognizes for the purposes of publishing and/or mounting. Memory gains or losses for changes made here are not large. If you do change this, however, you must modify the drive map on line 13 accordingly.

Line 13 FFHUUUUUUU. This is called a *drive map*. The two Fs represent physical drives A and B respectively. The F stands for floppy. The H, stands for a hard disk, which is assumed to be drive C. The position in the line is significant. The first character in the line represents A, the second B, and so on. The Us indicate that the remaining drive letters are unused, and can thus be chosen for mounted drives. If your system included a physical drive D, such as an additional hard disk, you would need to change the first U to an H, otherwise TOPS would not recognize the drive (the message Invalid drive specification will be returned when you try to access the drive). Note that there are ten drives represented when your last logical drive is J. If you increase the last logical drive to L, you will need to assign two more Us to the drive map.

Line 15 No. clients. After the drive map comes a list of settings for the server. Again, you can save some memory on the server if you minimize some of the server related variables in the TOPSKRNL.DAT file. If you have a server that needs more memory to run a particular application program and you know you will never need the 20 client default, you can decrease this value to save some more memory.

Line 16 No. published volumes. The same theory applies here as above. Reduce this setting if possible when you need to conserve memory.

Line 21 Buffer size. Here is one value in particular that you should be careful about changing. While decreasing this value will result in a small memory gain, reducing buffer size on a fairly busy server will definitely degrade performance.

The TOPSPRTR.DAT File

If your server is publishing a printer (see next section for explanation), you should be aware that the TOPSPRTR.EXE program loads a configuration file in the same way the TOPSKRNL.EXE does. That file, TOPSPRTR.DAT is displayed in Table 4-8. The most likely changes you might make to this file follow.

Line 3 No. clients. You might want to increase the number of clients that can use your published printer. This specification controls how many of the clients can mount the same printer at the same time.

Line 8 Calls per print attempt. If printing on the server is unacceptably slow, decreasing this might help. A decrease in this number decreases contention for CPU time during print jobs.

Line 9 Characters per print attempt. If print jobs are only partially printing, TOPSPRTR may be interpreting pauses in the output as the end of a document. Increasing this value might solve the problem.

One important point must be made about changing any of the previous configuration values of TOPSKRNL.DAT or TOPSPRTR.DAT. The need to make changes and the results of the changes are very situation specific. Different hardware and different user conditions create a huge number of variables. It is hard to predict how effective or, in some cases, detrimental any one change will be. So a commonsense rule to follow is to make changes only if you must. The defaults that were selected by the TOPS programmers are pretty good general choices. If everything is working OK, the best course of action might be to leave it alone. However, you should not copy the DAT files from one network PC to another because each machine needs a slightly different DAT file if only to account for the individual station name.

TOPS/DOS SPECIAL CASES:
Floppy Booting and Added Drives

On line 6 of the TOPSKRNL.DAT file is the TOPSEXEC.COM path. Typically this is C:\TOPS. TOPS uses the TOPSEXEC.COM program to permit launch-

Table 4-8. Default TOPSPRTR.DAT.

TOPSPRTR Version 2.10
Server Information
No. Clients (0 - 20):   2
No. Files in Spool Queue (0 - 100):   30
Delete Spool files after printing (Y/N):   Y
Printer Information
LPT port for local printing (1 - 3):   1
Calls per print attempt (1 - 1000):   80
Characters per print attempt (1 - 80):   30
Time-out (seconds) for local printing (5 - 120):   20

ing of remote programs. If you are working from a floppy boot disk and plan on launching applications from a server, you should change this entry from the default of C:\TOPS to A:\ or possibly B:\TOPS, depending on where the TOPSEXEC.COM program will be located in your drive arrangement.

As mentioned in the previous section, the drive map in TOPSKRNL.DAT might need to be altered to accommodate for additional drives. A common example is the logical drive D that is often created when a hard drive of more than 30 megabytes capacity is installed. Because many versions of DOS cannot properly recognize drives larger than 32MB, most drives of larger size than this are installed as two drives. Although there is one physical drive, software such as Speedstor is used to make it appear to DOS as though there are two "logical" drives. Typically, the first drive is C and the second is D. TOPS needs to be told about D by editing line 13 of TOPSKRNL.DAT. Here is what a map for a system with two floppy drives and two hard drives would look like:

    FFHHUUUUUU

The two Fs represent physical drives A and B respectively. The F stands for floppy. The H stands for hard disks C and D. The Us indicate that the remaining drive letters are unused and can thus be chosen for mounting as drives those volumes of information that have been published by other users on the network. Note that there are ten drives represented when your last logical drive is J. If you increase the last logical drive to L, you need to assign two more Us to the drive map.

If you have a Bernoulli Box on your system, you need to assign it an H in the drive map. For example, this is what the drive map looks like for a system with one floppy drive, one hard disk, and a single Bernoulli Box:

FHHUUUUUUU

Note that TOPS requires that a cartridge be present in the Bernoulli Box while TOPS is loading. Defining the Bernoulli Box as a floppy drive does not eliminate this problem. However, if you have a recent version of DOS, you can load TOPS without inserting a cartridge. DOS will give you the error message "Abort, Retry, Fail?" as TOPS is loading and you can press F for Fail. This gets you past the error message, and you can still use the Bernoulli drive later on.

If you use a RAM drive on your system and want to use it while TOPS is active, you need to define it on the drive map, using H to identify it.

DEDICATING A TOPS SERVER

The distributed architecture of TOPS does not require that a server be dedicated to being nothing but a server. This design allows TOPS to enable a user to publish files for the use of others, and, even while others are accessing those files, allow the server continue to work on entirely separate tasks.

However, several practical factors can constrain how much can be expected of a machine that is acting as a TOPS server. One of them is the available RAM memory in the server. In the 640K world of MS-DOS, depending on what parts of TOPS are loaded, a server might not have much memory left for running applications.

For example, the file server portion of TOPS (TOPSKRNL) together with drivers (ALAP and PSTACK) takes approximately 185K of RAM. If you add to that about 60K used by DOS 3.1 (the number is higher for subsequent versions) then about 245K of the computer's available 640K is full. That leaves almost 400K for application programs. Then if your server publishes a printer, you need to load TOPSPRTR, which takes about 40K more. Some of today's larger programs will not run on the server under those conditions. There isn't enough memory for them.

The memory problems can sometimes be overcome with relatively little expense through the aid of some third-party products that extend the memory addressing abilities of DOS. Although TOPS will not run in extended memory, there are some solutions for machines that run the Intel 80386 microprocessor. The products, sometimes called DOS extenders, allow DOS to address regions of memory above 640K but below 1 megabyte. For a discussion of memory problems and potential solutions see Chapter 14.

Another constraint is that some LAN versions of software are not able to run on anything but a dedicated server because that is the way they were written. Additionally, if the server is not a pretty fast machine with a pretty fast hard disk, and there are to be more than a few clients frequently accessing the server's disk, and possibly a published printer as well, it is unrealistic to expect the server to be able to handle this load without significant slowing down of local application use.

CLIENTS AND DEDICATED SERVERS

The result of the above-mentioned factors such as memory constraints and performance degradation is that sometimes the network environment will require that a server be dedicated. In other words, the server is not used for running application software. TOPS gives you this option and works fine in this fashion. There is nothing special to do in this case; just load TOPS and don't use the server for anything else while the network is active. In a dedicated server situation, you might want to organize the other PC users with client-only status to minimize their use of memory.

To run TOPS/DOS in client mode, you load TOPS with the command LOADCLNT. This runs the batch file LOADCLNT.BAT which loads TOPSTALC.EXE instead of TOPSTALK.EXE and uses TOPSCLNT.EXE instead of TOPSKRNL.EXE. These alternative files use less memory because they do not incorporate the server functions.

HANDLING UPGRADES

As we mentioned at the beginning of this chapter, the need to upgrade TOPS software from one version to another is likely to arise from time to time as the software is improved, enhanced, and refined. When you already have TOPS installed and receive an update, there should be instructions included with the package. Typically, these instructions tell you how to run an automated installation program that performs the upgrade. This is one situation where it is best to take the easy route. Use the automated procedure rather than trying to perform the upgrade manually.

Upgrading TOPS/Macintosh

Though future upgrades might alter this procedure slightly, you will probably be safe doing the following:

1. Start your Mac with the Finder, not Multi-Finder.
2. Insert the TOPS upgrade disk in a floppy drive and open the disk. Double click on the Installer.
3. Click on Update to execute the upgrade, then pick Quit and select Restart from the Special menu.

All users on the network should be updated at the same time because mixing versions is simply not good practice and can lead to communication problems between users of differing versions. You can upgrade Macintoshes over the network if you like. If you copy the contents of the upgrade disk to a new folder called Upgrade and then publish it, you can mount this volume on any networked Macintosh and execute the Installer. Be sure you select the correct drive on the local machine using the Drive button before telling the Installer to Update.

Bear in mind that one copy of the latest version of TOPS can be used to update multiple older versions. TOPS preserves the serial numbers of each station during the update process. However, you should not choose the Installer's Remove option or trash TOPS files unless you have the correctly numbered TOPS package handy. You risk loosing the serial number, which requires buying a new package.

Upgrading the Macintosh System

One upgrade situation that Macintosh users face is presented by new versions of the Macintosh System software, which Apple seems to issue every six months or so. This arrangement, in which Apple periodically distributes improved operating system programs to dealers and users at no extra charge, is somewhat confusing to IBM users, who have to wait longer for DOS upgrades, and usually have to pay for them.

The situation can also be confusing for TOPS/Macintosh users. We have found that it is sometimes necessary to reinstall TOPS after upgrading the System files.

Upgrading TOPS/DOS

The SETUP program that comes with TOPS/DOS has an UPDATE option that can be used to update existing older versions. Bear in mind that one copy of the latest version of TOPS/DOS can be used to update multiple older versions. TOPS preserves the serial numbers of each station during the update process. However, you should not delete any TOPS files yourself unless you have the correctly numbered TOPS package handy. You risk loosing the serial number, which requires buying a new package.

CONCLUSION

If you have read this chapter and are still experiencing difficulty getting TOPS running on a particular system, then you should check Appendix A where error messages and further tips can be found. If you have TOPS running on a Macintosh then you can move on to the next chapter where TOPS/Macintosh commands are discussed. Go to Chapter 6 if you are ready to learn TOPS/DOS commands.

5
Using TOPS/Macintosh

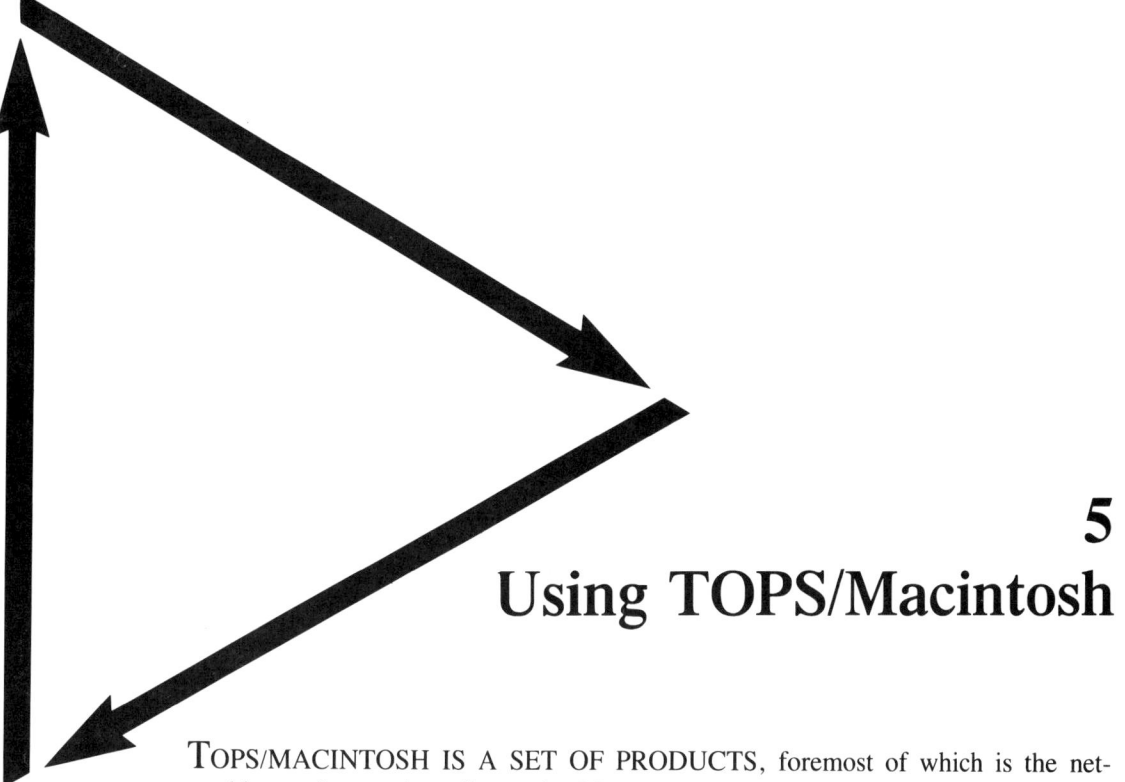

TOPS/MACINTOSH IS A SET OF PRODUCTS, foremost of which is the networking software that allows the Mac to communicate with MS-DOS and other types of computers. In addition, TOPS provides a print spooler (TOPS Spool), which eliminates the inconvenience of a busy LaserWriter, and a set of document translators (TOPS Translators) that can convert documents created in MS-DOS applications into those that Macintosh applications can read. The use of these programs will be discussed in this chapter. This chapter assumes that you are familiar with basic Macintosh commands. If you are not, you might want to refer to Appendix C, which presents the basics of Macintosh operation.

Both the spooler, and the translators are very complimentary additions to a network environment. As the number of users who share a LaserWriter increase, productivity generally suffers as users must wait while somebody else's document finishes printing. Anyone who has ever waited out the completion of a long document knows the frustration. The spooler, which temporarily stores the document on disk while the LaserWriter is busy, gives the user back the use of the program long before the Mac ordinarily would.

TOPS translators fill an important need in offices with a mixture of Macintosh and MS-DOS users. Documents created on an IBM PC or compatible with applications such as WordStar, Multimate, WordPerfect, and others can easily be translated into something Mac programs can read. Think about that project, such as a newsletter, that you need to get done. Those PC users in the office who don't use the Macintosh can become major contributors because they can do their work on their PC, and then you can translate it for final editing and layout on the Mac.

USING TOPS FOR NETWORKING

When it has been installed on your Macintosh, TOPS will start every time you boot your computer (turn it on, or pick Restart from the Special menu). The exception to this rule is booting while you hold the Option key down. This gives you the option not to load TOPS.

Once your Macintosh has finished booting, you access TOPS through the Desk Accessory (DA) under the Apple logo, as seen in Fig. 5-1.

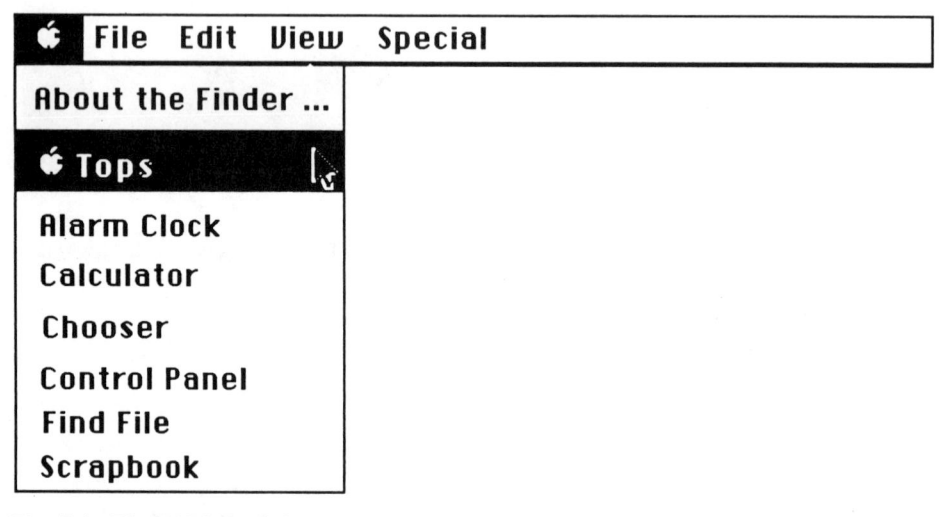

Fig. 5-1. The TOPS Desk Accessory.

Because TOPS is a DA, it means you can control the network even while working in an application program. If you need to mount a volume to access files on another machine, just pull down the TOPS Desk Accessory (DA).

THE TOPS WINDOW

The TOPS DA Window is like a picture of the network. On the left-hand side, you see at the top the name of your station, as it appears to the rest of the network. Below you see the resources (disks) of your own computer, as seen in Fig. 5-2.

If you are going to publish something, you open these disks and select the volumes to publish. On the right-hand side are the servers currently on the network (in the local zone).

You can change the network name of your station by clicking on its icon, which is at the Top left-hand side of the window, and then dragging down on the Open button. Be careful when you change the name however, because if you have clients that automount, then their mounts will no longer work because your server name has changed. So if you do change the name, notify your clients, so they can redo their automount instructions.

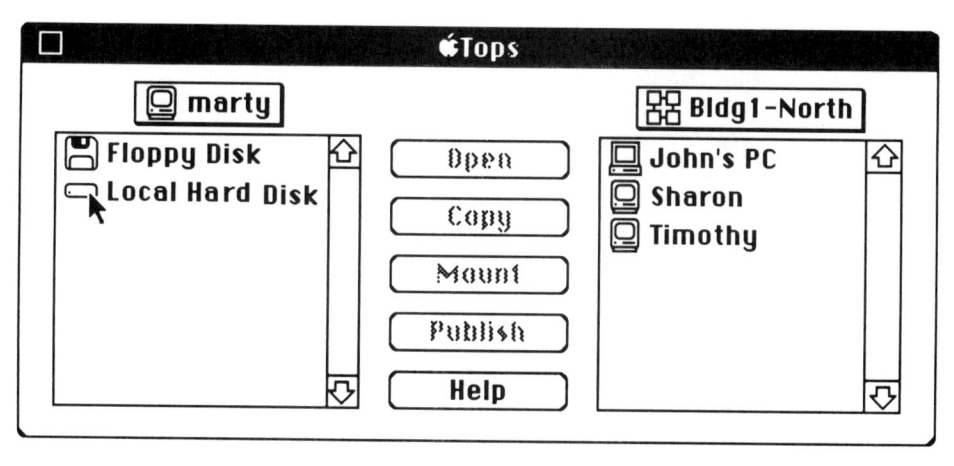

Fig. 5-2. The TOPS window. The local window is on the left, and the server window is on the right.

Only stations that have published something will show up in the right-hand window. If you have not published anything, you are not a server, though you can still mount the published volumes of users who are servers. These servers can be other Macintoshes or MS-DOS machines, and as you can see from the figure, the icons will differ according to machine type. If your network is large enough that you have multiple zones, the other zones can be accessed by pulling down on the name of the local zone, for which an icon appears above the window. (Zones are created by placing special hardware bridges in the network; if you don't have this you won't see any zones and the icon at the tops will just say File Servers.) When you change zones, the window on the right shows the servers in that other zone.

As you can see from Fig. 5-3, in the center of the TOPS window are the TOPS commands.

You should have a handle on the meanings of Publish and Mount from their discussion in the previous chapter. Open and Copy will be introduced here.

Publish, you recall, means making a volume available to the network. Mount is used to access the volumes on a TOPS server, and in a sense, make them yours. Open should be a familiar term in Mac windows, and means the same thing here as

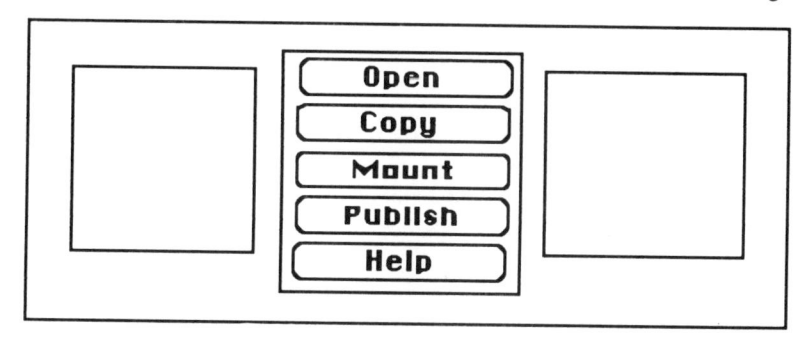

Fig. 5-3. The TOPS commands.

elsewhere in Mac programs. You would use it if you intend to publish a particular folder. First select the appropriate disk and then click Open to get into the disk and see the folder. As usual in Mac applications, double clicking an icon accomplishes the same thing as Open.

The Copy command in the TOPS window can be used for a quick file transfer from a server to your local disk. This can be done without actually mounting the server and therefore can save a few steps in some cases. It can also be used as a text filter to eliminate untranslatable DOS characters. More will be said about the Copy command in later sections.

GETTING STARTED WITH COMMANDS

When the TOPS window is first opened, all of the commands are grayed out. As selections are made, these commands will become active as appropriate. To publish something and become a server, you work in the left-hand side of the TOPS window. This window shows the resources of your own computer. As you click on a disk, both the Open and Publish commands will darken to indicate they are active. To view the contents of the disk, click Open and the files and folders of the disk will become visible, as seen in Fig. 5-4.

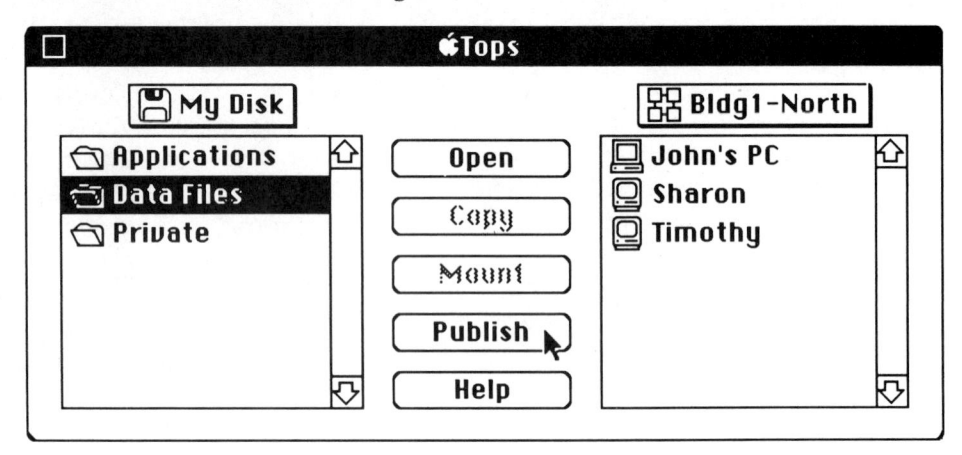

Fig. 5-4. Viewing disk contents to Publish a volume (in this case a folder).

The Publish Command

When traversing through the disk folder hierarchy, the icon at the top of the window becomes the folder or disk that was just opened. You can go backwards by pulling down the icon that appears at the top. To proceed with publishing, select a folder you want to make available, and then click Publish. When you publish, you will see the icon change to indicate that it is now a network volume. If there is a second folder that you want published, do the same thing for it.

Note that all other folders within the one published are also published. This fact has considerable strategic value. It can be used to your advantage. If you organize

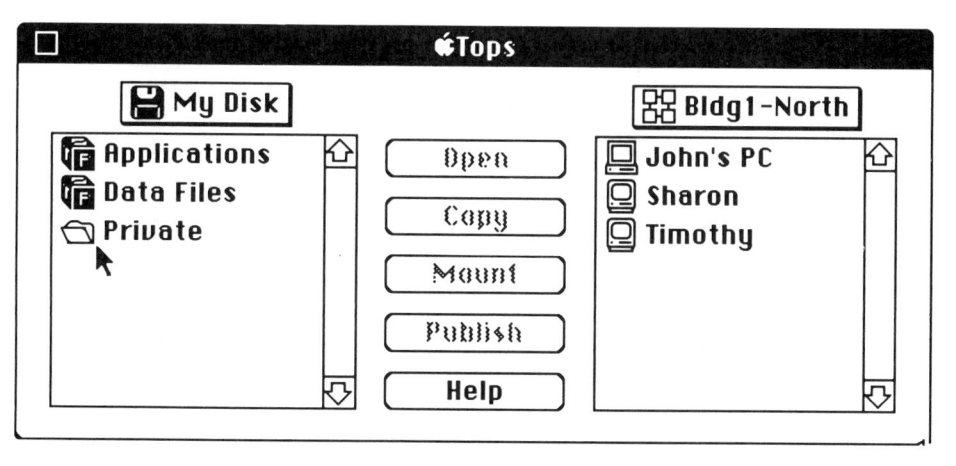

Fig. 5-5. Keep files that you don't want others to access out of published folders.

things properly, you can simplify your publishing requirements. By creating folders within the one you publish, you could publish them all in one step. Conversely, if you don't want a folder published, don't keep it within a folder you do want published, as shown in Fig. 5-5.

The Mount Command

After publishing something, your station will show up as a server in the right-hand side of other users' TOPS windows. Likewise, that is how the stations of those other users became visible in the right-hand side of yours. To mount something from one of those servers, pick the server whose volume(s) you want to access, and open it (double click or use the Open button). Only the published volumes will be visible. When one is selected (click once), the Mount button becomes active, as seen in Fig. 5-6.

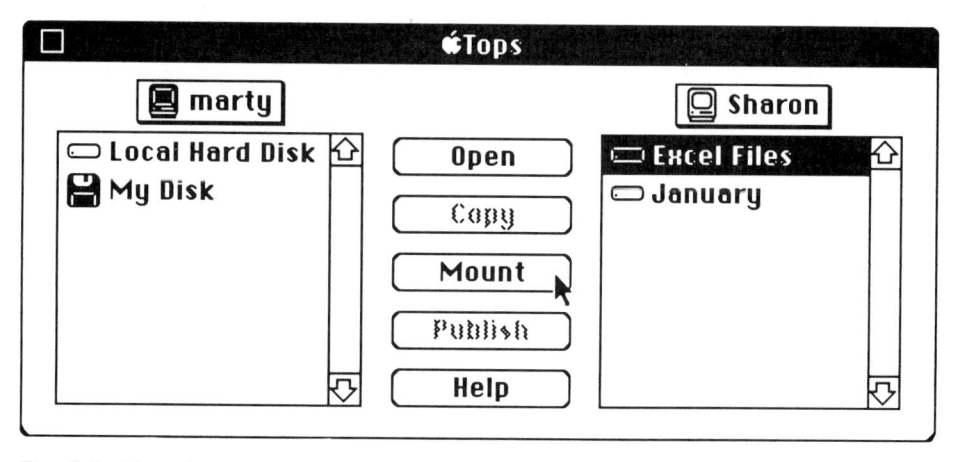

Fig. 5-6. Mounting a server.

Fig. 5-7. A mounted volume on the Macintosh Desktop.

Click the Mount button and the action is performed. Once again, the icon will change to indicate that it is now a network volume.

After a network drive is mounted, an icon for it will appear on your Macintosh desktop, as seen in Fig. 5-7. This mounted TOPS volume can be used just like any local disk. When finished with the volume, it can be unmounted by dragging the icon into the trash.

MULTIPLE NETWORK ACCESS TO A PUBLISHED VOLUME

TOPS tends to make assumptions on the side of safety, when it comes to publishing. It automatically restricts a volume to allow only the first user that mounts it to write to it. This is a good protection against two users trying to modify the same file, only the first user can save it. You can override this if you want to give all potential users write access, or you want to prevent even the first user from writing, and make the volume read-only. Most of the commands in the TOPS window have optional choices like this.

OPTIONAL COMMANDS

Pulling down on any of the active buttons in the TOPS window will produce a new button with the same command, followed by a three dot ellipse. In Fig. 5-8, you can see how this looks with the Publish button.

These optional commands summon secondary windows that allow the user to redefine the assumptions TOPS would normally make, such as publishing so that only the first user who mounts the volume can write to it. All of the buttons have this pull-down feature, as well as some additional options.

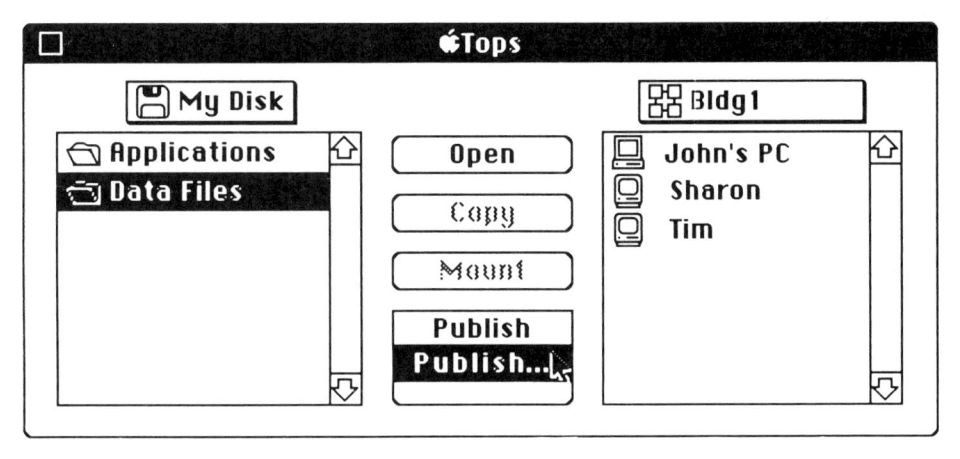

Fig. 5-8. Pulling down the Publish button for the optional Publish command.

Mount and Publish Options

The optional choices for Publish and Mount are shown in Fig. 5-9.

In the case of Publish, the optional command permits publishing with a password, changing the write permissions, and even a way to have the publish command remembered (this means autopublish whenever you start your computer). A corresponding second level appears by pulling down on Mount, which allows mounting as read only, and automounting by Remember. Note that the Mount and Publish commands are closely linked. You can only mount things that have been published, and you can only mount something as Read/Write if it was published that way.

To unremember published or mounted volumes, once again pull down the dotted command, and click the Remember button off.

When a volume is mounted by a Macintosh, the Macintosh Finder writes a file to that volume called the Desktop file. Among other things, the Desktop file is what allows the Mac to remember window and icon placement. Consequently, if the Finder is to use a volume, the first time that volume is published it cannot be

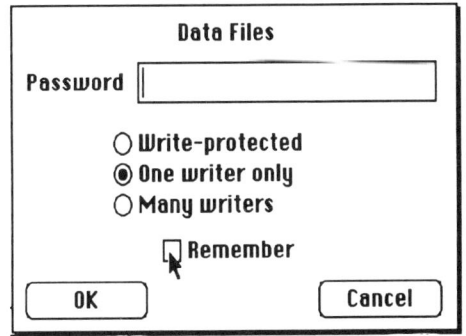

Fig. 5-9. Publish and Mount options.

published read-only. If it were, when the mounting user's Finder tried to write the Desktop file, the write would fail and the Finder would reject the volume after returning the message Unable to write Desktop file. In mounts subsequent to the first mount, when a Desktop file already exists, the Finder will use the existing Desktop file. So in other words, don't publish a volume as read-only until after it has been mounted at least one time.

Automated Actions

Having described the Remember option that provides the automount and autopublish capability in TOPS/Macintosh, some tips on its use are in order. A typical scenario in which autopublishing works well is the following. Your Macintosh has a high-capacity hard disk which is used to store sales reports sent in from regional offices. The reports are stored in Excel, the Macintosh version. Several users on the network need regular access to these reports. Therefore you use the TOPS DA to publish the Reports folder that is within the Excel folder. You drag down on the Publish command and check the Remember box. From now on this folder will be published whenever you boot up your system.

At a Macintosh station on the network that wants regular access to the Reports folder, you might be tempted to use the Remember option when mounting Reports with the TOPS DA. However, you need to bear in mind that if you use this option then booting your system will always cause it to look for the published Reports folder. If the system on which the reports reside is not already booted itself, TOPS cannot mount the Reports volume, and indeed, can become confused. You might want to use the TOPS DA to mount the Reports volume if you cannot always be sure that the server will be on when you boot your system.

In some situations, such as networks that are left on all the time, this limitation of automounting is not so much of a problem. One situation in which automounting is valuable is the floppy disk Macintosh which does not have the TOPS DA installed, a condition described later in this chapter. In this case automounting helps ensure that desired resources are available prior to launching applications.

The Copy Command

The optional Copy command, briefly mentioned earlier in this chapter, was designed as a text transfer/filtering tool. It literally lets you make a copy from a file on a remote disk to one of your local disks. The copied file will have the same name as the original. We suggest that you use this command sparingly, because duplicate files on different disks can cause confusion as to which is the latest version. In fact, if you work in a mixed Macintosh and PC environment, and your Mac and PC programs will import the other's file types, or you have files that the TOPS Translators will convert, you really don't need the Copy command.

However, the Copy button can be handy for the transfer and conversion of ASCII text files, if your programs don't have this ability. The text in ASCII files,

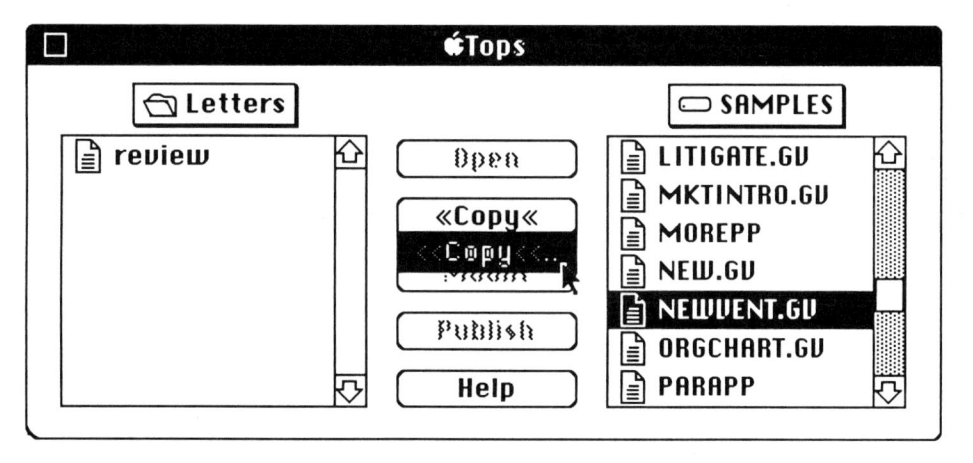

Fig. 5-10. Using the optional Copy command from the TOPS window.

short for American Standard Code for Information Interchange, is basically the same on any kind of computer. You create an ASCII file on the Macintosh by saving it as text. Most MS-DOS applications also have this ability, however the ASCII used by DOS has characters that Macintosh ASCII doesn't (such as line feeds). When programs on the Macintosh read DOS ASCII, those characters for whom the Mac has no equivalent show up as boxes or other strange symbols. These characters can be removed from the text by using the TOPS DA's Optional Copy, seen in Fig. 5-10.

To use Copy in this way, open the folder on the local disk where you want the duplicate file copied. Then open the volume on the published remote disk and select the file you want copied. The Copy button will become active and display arrows indicating the direction you are copying. When you pull down the second level Copy command, a dialog box appears which allows you to Copy Text Only, as seen in Fig. 5-11.

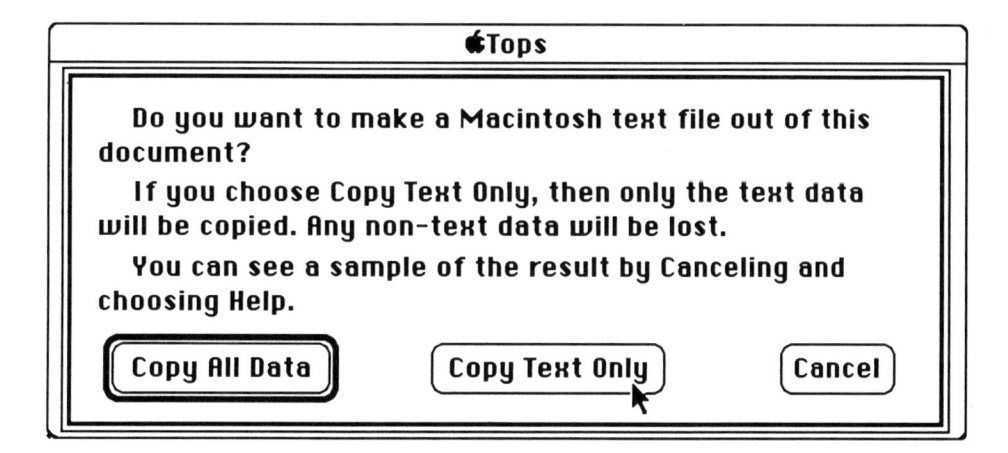

Fig. 5-11. Filtering ASCII by copying text only.

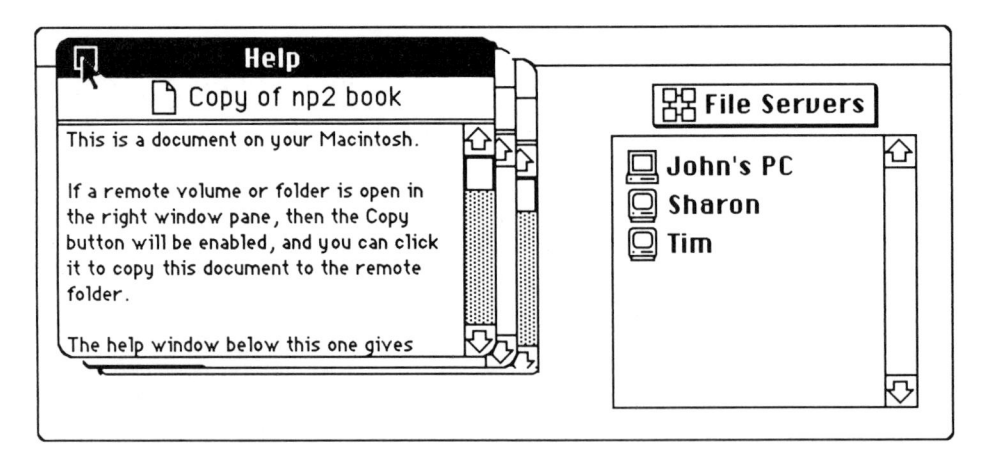

Fig. 5-12. Using Help to browse through a file.

Note that once this file gets to the Macintosh, it doesn't belong to any specific Macintosh program. Therefore, it is not a document you can double click and launch. To open the file you must first open the application you want to use (MacWrite for example), and then give the File-Open command from the menu line. For a further explanation of using MS-DOS files on a Macintosh, reference the section later in this chapter on using an MS-DOS computer as a server.

The Help Command

Among the options for the Help command in the TOPS window is the ability to have a peek at the text inside the file. To use this feature, first open the volume that contains the file you want to work with, select the file itself, and then pull down the optional Help. Three stacked windows will appear, and the third one down will contain a peek inside the file, as seen in Fig. 5-12.

It can be extremely useful for the Mac user to browse through the files on a DOS server, whose eight-character names can be a bit cryptic, to find the right file, and thereby make sure of mounting the right volume. It is also useful to browse through your own local volumes to make sure that you are publishing the right thing.

When running single-user applications, run them from local floppy disks, or your own local hard disk if possible. Use the server to store the data files, but not to store and start all your application programs. Application programs are large files, usually several hundred kilobytes, and launching them over the wires adds a tremendous traffic burden to the network. In addition, it taxes the server more than is necessary. That increases the likelihood that other users will have to wait while the server's disk is busy. Running the applications off of local disks and using the server's disks to store and access only the data files will keep the network running much smoother and more efficiently.

USING AN MS-DOS COMPUTER AS A SERVER

The procedures for a Macintosh to mount a volume that is on an MS-DOS server is no different than for mounting volumes on a Macintosh server. A DOS volume will appear on the clients desktop exactly the same as any other. The Macintosh client can drag files on and off the volume with the Finder, and save files to the volume from within their application programs just like any other Macintosh disk. There are, however, some subtle differences that are worth mentioning. The differences are primarily in the structure of the files systems. This was mentioned briefly in earlier discussions but is important enough to repeat here.

No HFS on TOPS/DOS

In the first place, MS-DOS has a different type of hierarchy than the Macintosh. The Macintosh's system of folders within folders is analogous to the branching subdirectories of DOS, but it is not the same. The designers of TOPS chose not to try to merge them. The result is that the Macintosh does not see an MS-DOS volume as HFS. If there are DOS subdirectories inside a volume that gets published on a PC, the Mac will not have access to them. Another DOS machine will, but the Mac won't. The DOS server must publish the specific subdirectory that has the files.

File Structure Differences

In addition, DOS files are structured a little differently than Mac files. Mac files have two forks to them; one is called the data fork, another called the resource fork. Some of the file is in each fork, though the proportions depend on the application program that creates the file, as you can see in Fig. 5-13.

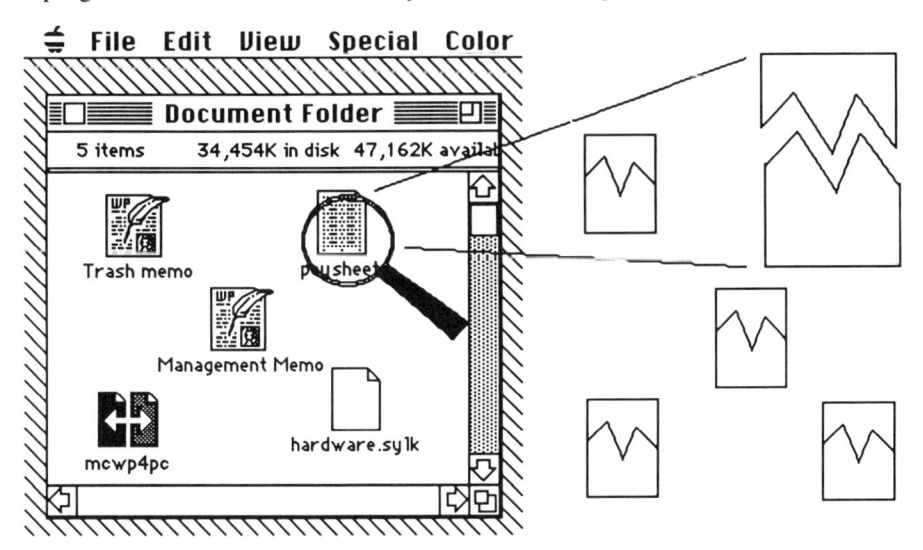

Fig. 5-13. File forks.

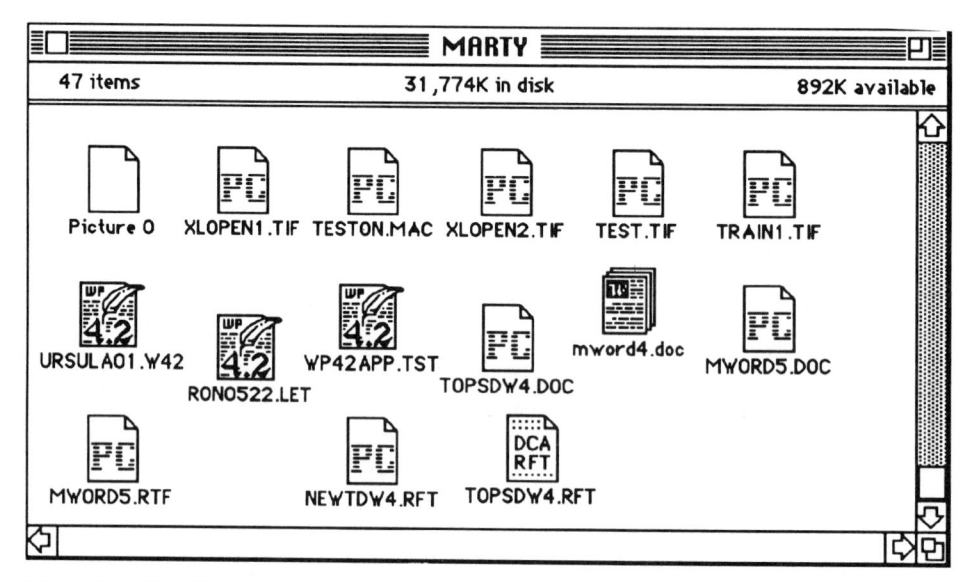

Fig. 5-14. Mac files on a DOS server.

One of the benefits of this two-fork system is the Macintosh's ability to double click on a file, and have the file load itself and the application that it came from. DOS does not have this ability, and its files are all one piece. Consequently if a file on an MS-DOS server was created by a DOS application program, the Macintosh won't retrieve the file when you double click on it. So even though Mac programs like Microsoft Excel can read Lotus 1-2-3 files, you must first start Microsoft Excel, and then use the Open command from the File menu to retrieve them.

You can always tell which files are Mac files, and which are PC files by their icons. TOPS will show the PC files with a generic PC icon, which you can see in Fig. 5-14. So that the Macintosh finder will recognize the file, TOPS creates a hidden resource fork for the PC files. The resource file is empty, but present. As you can also see from Fig. 5-14, Mac files stored on the DOS server will appear to the finder as their normal Macintosh icons.

FILE MANAGEMENT ON DOS SERVERS

Macintosh files on a DOS server must be handled with consideration for their dual fork structure. If it is a Mac file it is best to manipulate the file, if it must be copied or deleted, with the Mac Finder. The Finder will automatically handle both of the file's forks. Never copy a Mac file with the DOS COPY command, as DOS commands will only handle the data fork.

If you want to do file management of Macintosh files with DOS commands, use the special set of TOPS Utilities (TCOPY, TDEL, and so on) which were written to take the dual fork structure of Mac files into account and to keep the two forks together. To do back-ups of a DOS volume from the DOS machine itself, when that volume stores Macintosh files, TCOPY works quite nicely. It will copy both forks of all the files. TCOPY is a lot like the DOS command XCOPY in that it can copy across multiple disks. This means that when one disk fills up, it will prompt you to put in a new disk. For a Macintosh acting as a server to an MS-DOS machine, the file differences don't really matter. DOS files only have one piece.

TOPS ON A FLOPPY DISK ONLY SYSTEM

Running TOPS on a floppy disk only Macintosh requires a few minor adjustments because as the Macintosh's system has grown to be more sophisticated, it also has grown larger. Because most Macintosh floppy drives still only handle 800K, there isn't enough space for the system and TOPS on the same disk. Newer floppy drives that hold more data promise to alleviate the problem in the future.

Single Floppy Systems

The last version of the System which was small enough to permit TOPS to reside on the same disk with it, was System 4.1 with Finder 5.5. However, even back then there was little room for anything else, including printer and screen fonts.

There are two solutions to this dilemma. One is to omit TOPS on the startup disk, and launch TOPS from a separate floppy. This method works fine, but you will find yourself wanting to add a second floppy disk drive because it does involve frequent disk swapping.

The other solution is to use the older system versions (4.1 System and 5.5 Finder) on the floppy disk system, along with a tool that allows you to access screen fonts on the server, via the network. Note that there are costs if you mix system versions on your network. If you are printing to a LaserWriter, the printer will need to be reinitialized between jobs when the user's computer has a different version of LaserWriter resources (the LaserWriter and LaserPrep files in the system folder) from that of the previous user.

Launching TOPS from a Floppy Disk

If, in addition to the startup drive, you have a second floppy disk drive, it is reasonably practical to leave TOPS off the startup disk and launch it from a disk inserted into your second drive. The space on your startup disk left after the system, finder, and other options can be used for the printer fonts or screen fonts you need for your documents.

After the Mac is started and the system is loaded from the TOPS-less startup disk, TOPS can be started by opening up the disk containing the TOPS files, and double clicking the icon called Start TOPS. When this procedure finishes, the TOPS window can be accessed by double clicking the TOPS DA file. TOPS will still have full functionality, and you can publish and mount just like on any hard disk system with TOPS. What you do lose, however, is the ability to use TOPS as a DA within an application. You can only publish and mount volumes through double clicking the DA file from the Finder.

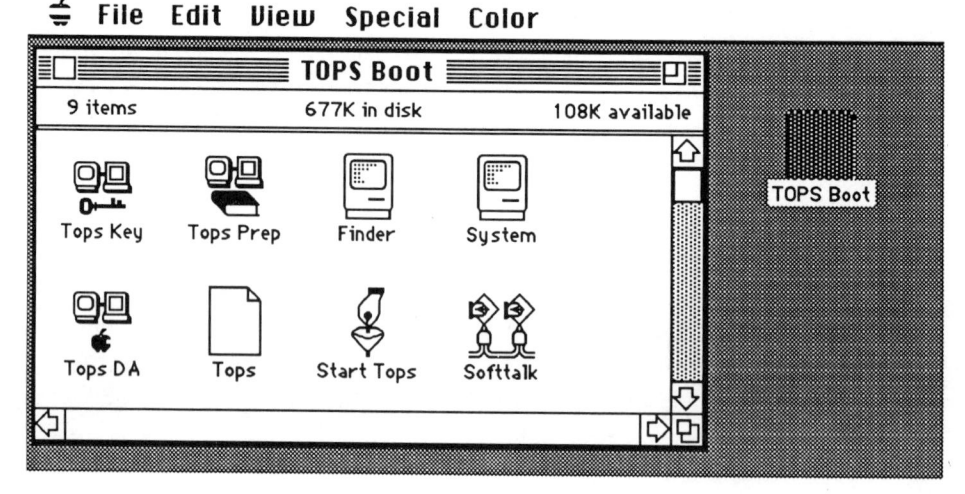

Fig. 5-15. Files essential to running TOPS.

If the decision is to use System 4.1 and Finder 5.5 so that TOPS will fit on the startup disk, your startup disk will have room for little more than essential system files, and the essential TOPS files. If you are not sure, use Fig. 5-15 to help you figure out what is essential.

Note that two TOPS files, TOPS Help and Interbase, have been omitted. In this situation, Help is something you will have to do without and Interbase is something you can do without if your client will not use an MS-DOS computer as a server.

Using Server Screen Fonts

A little more space can be saved on the startup disk for printer fonts, by keeping the screen fonts in your system file to a minimum, and using tools to access screen fonts stored on a server. One such tool is a utility called Suitcase. Suitcase can link the startup disk's system to screen fonts stored in remote files, accessed through TOPS. The server can publish a folder containing these font files, which the floppy only clients can mount and open with Suitcase. This kind of procedure is an ideal use for TOPS' autopublish/mount features when the users find daily mounting of these font volumes to be a burden.

To set up the server so that clients can use remote screen fonts:

- Create a folder which will contain the font files and can be easily published.
- Use Apple's Font/DA mover to create a New file (Fig. 5-9) inside the above folder.
- Open the file containing the fonts you want to put in your new file, which you eventually will publish.
- Copy the fonts into the new file. You can have many fonts in one large file, or create different files for different families of fonts.

To access the fonts remotely, as a client:

- Mount the servers published font volume.
- Assuming Suitcase is installed on the clients startup disk, select it from the DA menu (the apple).
- Click the Open Font/DA ... button.
- In the dialog box that appears, click the drive button until the server's volume with the fonts appears, and select the file with the fonts you want.

TOPS ICONS

One of the most distinctive features of the Macintosh is the use of icons. When it comes to icons, TOPS/Macintosh really goes to town, providing more than a dozen images that help users navigate the otherwise unfriendly world of networking. In Fig. 5-16 you can see all of the icons, together with their meaning.

Some of these icons are fairly rare; for example, the tortoise only appears if TOPS detects a particularly slow PC on the network. If you encounter the tortoise icon instead of a regular PC station icon, then you might want to check that the PC is functioning properly. In some situations, the tortoise will disappear if you unmount and then remount the PC.

When you are using the TOPS DA menu, clicking on the file server label on either the left or right side of the menu takes you into a multi-level set of icons. These represent the hierarchical relationship between the zones, servers, volumes, and files that you can manipulate with TOPS.

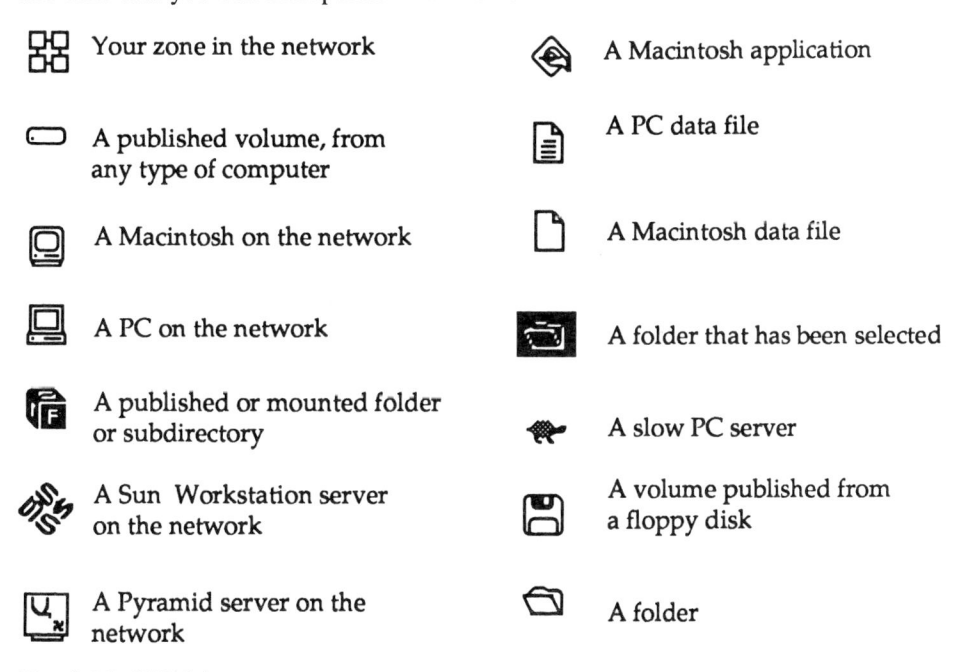

▦	Your zone in the network	◈	A Macintosh application
⊂⊃	A published volume, from any type of computer	🗎	A PC data file
▢	A Macintosh on the network	🗋	A Macintosh data file
▯	A PC on the network	📁	A folder that has been selected
	A published or mounted folder or subdirectory	🐢	A slow PC server
	A Sun Workstation server on the network	💾	A volume published from a floppy disk
	A Pyramid server on the network	📂	A folder

Fig. 5-16. TOPS icons.

CONCLUSION

This chapter should give you a good idea of how the basic TOPS commands work on the Macintosh. For more information about how these commands are applied in specific situations, see the appropriate later chapters: Chapter 10 for text applications, Chapter 11 for data applications, and Chapter 12 for graphics and desktop publishing applications. To learn how the TOPS commands work on DOS machines, see the next chapter. To learn more about TOPS Spool see Chapter 7. The use of TOPS Translators on the Macintosh is covered in Chapter 10.

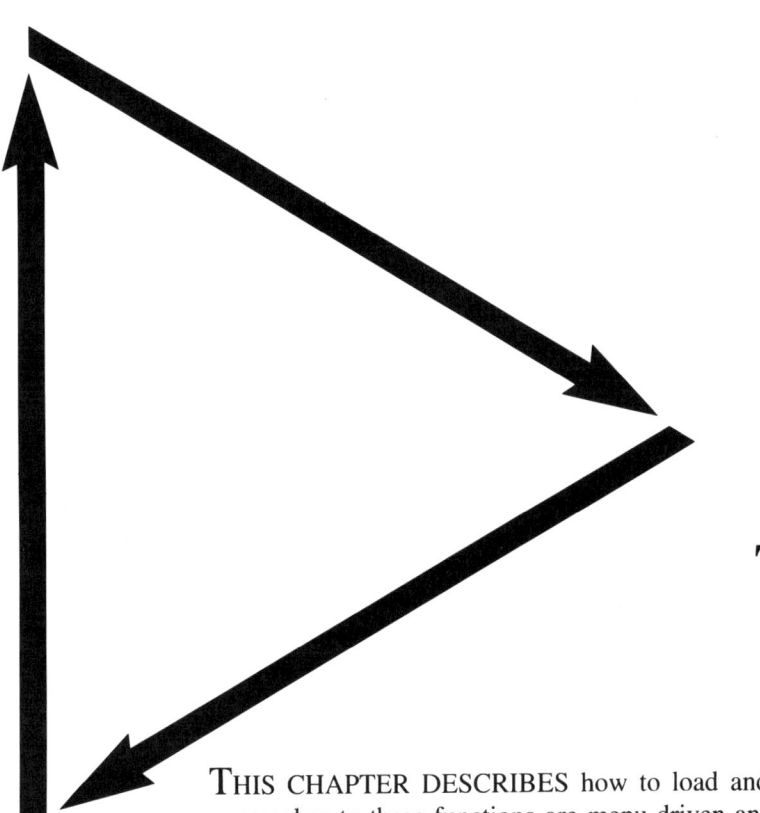

6
TOPS/DOS by the Menus

THIS CHAPTER DESCRIBES how to load and run TOPS/DOS. The two basic approaches to these functions are menu driven and the command line, which correspond to automatic and manual. The automatic approach is easier for the novice to use, but expert users might prefer the power and flexibility of the manual approach. The latter is described in Chapter 9. This chapter caters to the less experienced PC user, but should be read by all who are planning to use the DOS side of a TOPS network.

LOADING TOPS/DOS

The simple answer to the question, "How do I load TOPS/DOS?" is to type LOADTOPS at the DOS prompt, then press Enter. The simple answer to the question, "How do I run TOPS/DOS?" is to type TOPSMENU and press Enter. However, you might need a little help before you get to the point where you think that this is a simple answer.

Right after Installation

If you have just installed TOPS on your PC, you must first reboot your computer in order to have DOS load the two files that the Setup program modified (CONFIG.SYS and AUTOEXEC.BAT). For floppy disk users, this means inserting the TOPS boot disk in drive A. For users of both floppy disk and hard disk PC systems, rebooting means holding down the Ctrl and Alt keys and then pressing the Delete key. After clearing everything from memory, DOS will then read the necessary File and Buffers statements from the CONFIG.SYS as well as the TOPS path statement in the AUTOEXEC.BAT file.

When the DOS prompt reappears, you can type LOADTOPS and press Enter. This step runs a batch file called LOADTOPS.BAT that was copied onto your startup disk by the Setup program. LOADTOPS loads four programs: ALAP.EXE—the AppleTalk driver; PSTACK.EXE—the protocol stack driver; TOPSTALK.EXE—the TOPS SoftTalk system protocols; and TOPSKRNL.EXE—the TOPS network software. If you want to share your printer, type TOPSPRTR and press Enter. If you are a floppy disk user with a boot disk like the one we described in Chapter 4, you can boot DOS and load TOPS from the same floppy disk.

Once these programs have been run, they stay in your computer's memory, managing communication between computers on the network. Although you just loaded these programs via a batch file, they could also be loaded from the DOS command line, by typing:

ALAP	then press Enter
PSTACK	then press Enter
TOPSTALK	then press Enter
TOPSKRNL	then press Enter
TOPSPRTR	then press Enter

The approach you use for loading TOPS is up to you, but you can see that a stand-alone batch file like LOADTOPS.BAT saves quite a bit of typing. Of course, you can add these command lines to your AUTOEXEC.BAT file to make loading of TOPS automatic when you start up your computer. The TOPSMENU program (explained in detail later in the chapter) can also be run from the DOS command line as well as from a batch file.

When the ATALK, PSTACK, TOPSTALK, and TOPSKRNL programs are loaded, the AppleTalk board installed in your PC is initialized and the TOPS version number and serial number are displayed. While these are the only programs you have to load to use TOPS, TOPSKRNL will look for two other files called TOPSKRNL.DAT and TOPSEXEC.COM. TOPSKRNL.DAT contains configuration data about your TOPS system, telling TOPS such things as how many disk drives your system has. Included on your distribution disks is a sample TOPSKRNL.DAT file. The configuration parameters provided in this file are the same as the default configurations that take effect if no TOPSKRNL.DAT file is found by TOPSKRNL. You might have to modify this file, as described in Chapter 4, to properly configure TOPS for your system. TOPS looks in the current drive and directory for this file. If not found there, TOPS looks in the TOPS subdirectory.

The second file that TOPSKRNL looks for is TOPSEXEC.COM. TOPSEXEC.COM is used by TOPS to run applications that are stored on a remote computer. If you only intend to store data files (rather than application files) on remote disk drives, this file need not be accessed. However, it must be present in either the current directory or the directory defined on line 6 of TOPSKRNL.DAT if you plan to run applications stored remotely.

About TOPS and Other Memory-Resident Software

TOPS is compatible with a great majority of popular RAM-resident software available today. However TOPSKRNL, being a RAM-resident program itself, can conflict with other such programs if they are loaded in the wrong order with respect to TOPSKRNL. In general, TOPSKRNL should be loaded *before* other RAM-resident software. The only exceptions are programs like RAM disks, disk caching software, keyboard buffers, PC-LAN software, or clock devices that extend the basic services of DOS or the BIOS. These should be loaded before TOPSTALK and TOPSKRNL. A good rule of thumb is to determine if the memory-resident program uses data files stored on disk. If it does, then it should be loaded after TOPSTALK and TOPSKRNL. If a program does not use DOS, you can probably load it safely before TOPSKRNL. If in doubt you can always try it both ways and see which way works the best. In Table 6-1, you can see a list of popular programs and when they should be loaded with respect to TOPS.

ABOUT THE TOPS MENU

TOPS for DOS was written with the novice DOS user in mind, and so has features to make it easy to use. Publishing and mounting with TOPS for DOS can be done through a menu that TOPS provides, and which makes DOS all but invisible. The TOPS menu is by far the easiest way to work with TOPS/DOS. It only takes a few short steps to be up and running. The menu can even be made to remember published and mounted volumes so that the next time you start up, it happens automatically.

Table 6-1. Loading software with respect to TOPS.

The following should be loaded after TOPS:

Sidekick	INSET
ProKey	Grafplus
Superkey	Software Carousel
SmartKey	Turbo Lightning
Microsoft Windows	Note-It
SmartNotes	DESQview

Note that memory resident programs loaded after TOPS must be removed before TOPS can be unloaded.

The following can be loaded before TOPS:

Mouse drivers
Screen blankers
ANSWER (Complete Answering Machine)
INSET

Power and flexibility are still there for the advanced user or administrator. TOPS for DOS also has an entire command language that can come in handy for troubleshooting. If you are knowledgeable about DOS, the language will also allow you to write batch files that can significantly automate startup, shutdown, printing, and other procedures. Chapter 9 discusses the TOPS/DOS command language and provides some practical examples of how to use it.

The assumption made in this chapter is that the server you are using has a hard disk and TOPS is installed on the hard disk. Many of your clients might also have hard disks. Some of your clients, however, might have only floppy disks and no hard disks. In that case, the hard disk can be the server for these clients.

LOADING THE TOPS MENU

To summon the menu for TOPS the command is TOPSMENU. This must be issued at the DOS prompt after TOPS has been loaded. If TOPS has been loaded in client-only mode, then only the client options will be available and the Server Utilities has a different shading to show this item cannot be selected.

Issue the command TOPSMENU at the DOS prompt, and the menu system starts to load. If your station does not have a name included in the TOPSKRNL.DAT file, as described in Chapter 4, then you need to enter one. This can be up to 16 characters; spaces are allowed. After you have given a name for your station you will come to the list of choices seen in Fig. 6-1.

The menu consists of a list of items on the right-hand side, and on the left-hand side is an explanation of the meaning of the item that is currently highlighted by the cursor bar. A set of menu instructions, telling you how to move the cursor bar, and

```
┌─────────────────────────────────────────────────────────────────┐
│ Fred's XT            Welcome to TOPS            Main            │
├─────────────────────────────────────────────────────────────────┤
│  Main Menu                                                      │
│    Lists all Servers on the network and      Client Utilities   │
│    the Volumes and Printers available on     Server Utilities   │
│    each.  You may Mount remote Volumes and   Remember           │
│    remote Printers for 'local' use.          Quit               │
│                                                                 │
│                                                                 │
└─────────────────────────────────────────────────────────────────┘



┌─────────────────────────────────────────────────────────────────┐
│ MENU INSTRUCTIONS                                               │
│   Select a Command using the space bar, up arrow, down arrow or first │
│      letter of the Command.                                     │
│   <ENTER>- Invoke a selected command.                           │
│                                                                 │
│   <ESCAPE>- Return to the previous window.   <CNTRL-Q>- Exit to DOS. │
│                                                                 │
└─────────────────────────────────────────────────────────────────┘
```

Fig. 6-1. The TOPS menu.

a list of key combinations or function keys always appears in the menu's bottom panel. A less obvious, but very handy, feature of the menu is that you can move quickly to a choice by typing its first letter.

The item labeled Client Utilities is the choice for mounting server volumes or printers that other TOPS users have published. Server Utilities is the choice you use to publish resources for use by others. Remember is an item that is used after publishing and mounting, to automate the tasks for future convenience.

SERVER UTILITIES

The server menu that appears depends on whether or not TOPSPRTR is used. TOPSPRTR is a software module that does not need to be loaded in situations where printers are not published. If printers are to be published, TOPSPRTR must be run. In Fig. 6-2, you can see the menu as it appears when TOPSPRTR is not loaded.

In Fig. 6-3, you can see how the menu differs when the additional TOPSPRTR software is loaded.

The choices for printer serving are mirrors of the choices for file serving. Printer publishing is discussed in the next chapter. This section concentrates on the publishing of disk volumes.

Server Rules

The options for a server are fairly straightforward and follow three basic rules.

1. The server can publish any disk, subdirectory of a disk, or any locally attached printer.

```
Fred's XT                      TOPS : Server Utilities    Server Utilities

Server Utilities Menu
  Publish a Volume to allow network access.      Publish a Volume
  You will be prompted for the full              Volumes Published
  pathname. You must choose an                   File Clients
  alias, mode and password.                      Show Name
```

```
MENU INSTRUCTIONS
  Select a Command using the space bar, up arrow, down arrow or first
    letter of the Command.
  <ENTER>- Invoke a selected command.

  <ESCAPE>- Return to the previous window.      <CNTRL-Q>- Exit to DOS.
```

Fig. 6-2. The Server Utilities menu, without printers.

```
┌─────────────────────────────────────────────────────────────────┐
│ Fred's XT              TOPS : Server Utilities   Server Utilities │
├─────────────────────────────────────────────────────────────────┤
│  Server Utilities Menu                      ▐Publish a Volume▌  │
│    Publish a Volume to allow network access. Volumes Published  │
│    You will be prompted for the full        File Clients        │
│    pathname.  You must choose an            Show Name           │
│    alias, mode and password.                Publish a Printer   │
│                                             List Published Printer│
│                                             My Printer Clients  │
└─────────────────────────────────────────────────────────────────┘


┌─────────────────────────────────────────────────────────────────┐
│ MENU INSTRUCTIONS                                               │
│   Select a Command using the space bar, up arrow, down arrow or first│
│     letter of the Command.                                      │
│   <ENTER>- Invoke a selected command.                           │
│                                                                 │
│   <ESCAPE>- Return to the previous window.    <CNTRL-Q>- Exit to DOS.│
└─────────────────────────────────────────────────────────────────┘
```

Fig. 6-3. The Server Utilities menu, with printers.

2. Data security is achieved by publishing with passwords or by publishing the volume as read-only or read-write.
3. Any volume that is published, should be unpublished before powering down the machine. (Always remember to notify clients before you shutdown.)

The commands in the menu simply support these procedures.

Publishing a Volume

To publish a volume means to publish a disk or subdirectory. Selecting Publish a Volume from the TOPS menu brings up the screen seen in Fig. 6-4.

This screen prompts for the path of the volume. For one of your floppy disks, you need only type in the name of the drive. If the volume you intend to publish is a subdirectory of a hard disk, you need to specify the whole path. As the menu instructions in the bottom of the screen indicate, the F1 function key is a browse feature that can list the disk's subdirectories and let you choose the one you want via a cursor bar. It is a quicker and more accurate alternative than trying to remember the correct spelling of a subdirectory name.

As a rule, it is best not to publish an entire hard disk. First, there is the question of security or control: everybody has access to anything when you publish the whole disk, whereas they have access to only a specific subdirectory if that is all you publish. Second, there are the mechanics of TOPS. So that non-DOS computers like the Macintosh, which have a different file structure, can read the DOS disk, TOPS builds its own file table of the volumes that you publish. If you publish the whole disk, TOPS has a lot more work to do to build the table. This slows down the publishing operation and means that other computers take longer to read the server's directory. It is more efficient to publish appropriate subdirectories, rather than an entire hard disk.

After the path is specified, the menu prompts for an alias. The alias is what network users see as the name of the volume. The menu assumes you will use the same name as the actual name of the directory, but this is not required. Sometimes your subdirectory might have a name that is meaningless to other users. With the alias command, you have the chance to publish it as something meaningful, and you can use up to 16 characters. You can even put spaces in an alias name. The volume in Fig. 6-5 is a good example of the use of an alias.

The actual subdirectory name of wp was published under the alias of Word Processing, so that users had a clearer idea of what the volume contained.

When you have entered an alias, you need to enter your choice for security modes. If you type in a password, clients who attempt to mount this volume are required to enter the same password. If they don't know the password, they are not able to complete the mount. Note that the password is visible in the publish screen, so that you can visually verify what you are typing. Obviously, you want to be sure that those who should not see the password, do not.

The last specification of the publish command is Access mode. The menu defaults to read-only, represented by R. This means users can read the files and copy them, but no files, new or old, can be written to the volume. To allow writing to the volume, just type a W, which follows the R, which appears automatically. Read-only is the best method of data protection you have when using an application program that does not do file locking. The Read-only restriction does not pertain to

```
┌─────────────────────────────────────────────────────────────────────────┐
│ Fred's XT                    TOPS : Server Utilities    Publish a Volume │
│ Publish a Volume                                                         │
│     Path:                                                                │
│                                                                          │
│                                                                          │
│                                                                          │
│                                                                          │
│                                                                          │
│                                                                          │
└─────────────────────────────────────────────────────────────────────────┘

┌─────────────────────────────────────────────────────────────────────────┐
│ MENU INSTRUCTIONS                                                        │
│   Type each item as requested and press <ENTER>:                         │
│     Full path including drive specification.                             │
│                                                                          │
│   <F1>- List directories on a local drive.                               │
│   <ESCAPE>- Return to the previous window.    <CNTRL-Q>- Exit to DOS.    │
└─────────────────────────────────────────────────────────────────────────┘
```

Fig. 6-4. Publishing a volume.

specific files, but rather to the entire subdirectory. Of course, under these conditions, users of your files cannot make changes and save them back to your volume. The only true solution if you need to do this is to use a multi-user application that does lock files to protect against concurrent writes.

When a Macintosh mounts a PC volume, the Macintosh Finder (often referred to as the Desktop) needs to write a file called the Desktop file to the volume it mounts. The Mac does this so that it can show icons for the volume on its screen. If your volumes are accessed by Macs, let a Macintosh do this once before you publish as read-only or the Desktop file never gets created and the Mac Finder will keep rejecting the volume. Once that Desktop file is created, the Mac has no subsequent troubles.

When the publishing of a volume is finished, your screen choices disappear in anticipation of the next publishing operation. If no other volumes are to be published, the menu instructions in the bottom panel permit either Ctrl–Q to drop out of the menu to DOS, or Escape to return to the Server Utilities Menu (shown in Fig. 6-2) which preceded the publish screen.

Volumes Published

Other commands in the Server Utilities Menu, such as Volumes Published, allow you to change the passwords or alias of the published volumes, or even unpublish them. As you can see in Fig. 6-6, you can perform any of these operations by using the keys designated in the menu instructions at the bottom menu panel.

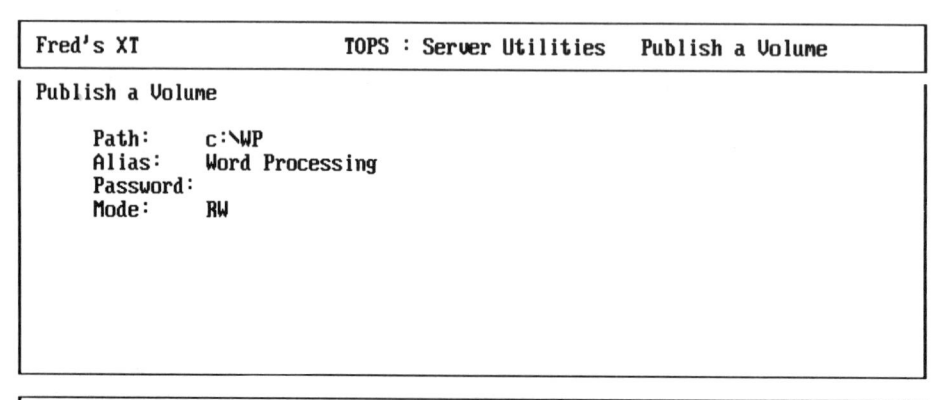

```
Fred's XT                       TOPS : Server Utilities    Publish a Volume
Publish a Volume

    Path:       c:\WP
    Alias:      Word Processing
    Password:
    Mode:       RW




MENU INSTRUCTIONS
   Type each item as requested and press <ENTER>:
      1-16 character alias by which you want this Volume known on the network.
      0-31 character password with which you wish to secure access.
      1 or 2 character mode: R- Read Only; RW- Read/Write.
   <ESCAPE>- Start over.                         <CNTRL-Q>- Exit to DOS.
```

Fig. 6-5. Using an alias.

The File Clients Command

Remember that it is important to unpublish before you shut down your system. If you have active clients when you try to unpublish, the menu notifies you. The File Clients option in the Server Utilities menu tells you who those clients are.

There is another way to accomplish both the listing of active clients and the unpublishing of volumes that some users find more convenient. Two TOPS commands that can be given from the DOS prompt, TOPS CSTAT and TOPS SHUTDOWN, does the same thing as the menu commands, but a lot faster. Refer to Chapter 9 on the TOPS command language for details.

The Hide Name Command

The Hide Name command is an interesting security option. If you choose this command, your volumes remain published, but other PC users do not see your station in their menu. Also, Mac users will not see your station when they pull down the TOPS Desk Accessory. Note that after issuing the Hide Name command, any clients who previously mounted the now invisible server remain active, but the existence of the server is unadvertised.

CLIENT UTILITIES

In order to keep this description brief, only the mounting of disk volumes is discussed. The mounting of printers is covered in the next chapter.

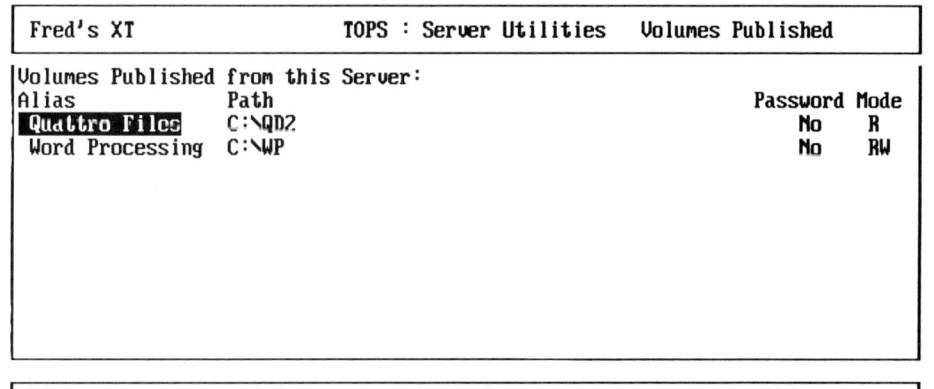

```
┌─────────────────────────────────────────────────────────────────────┐
│ Fred's XT                    TOPS : Server Utilities   Volumes Published │
├─────────────────────────────────────────────────────────────────────┤
│ Volumes Published from this Server:                                 │
│ Alias           Path                              Password  Mode    │
│ Quattro Files   C:\QD2                                No      R     │
│ Word Processing C:\WP                                 No      RW    │
│                                                                     │
│                                                                     │
│                                                                     │
│                                                                     │
│                                                                     │
├─────────────────────────────────────────────────────────────────────┤
│ MENU INSTRUCTIONS                                                   │
│    Select a Volume using the space bar, up arrow, down arrow or first │
│       letter of the Volume.                                         │
│    <ENTER>- List Clients using this Volume.  <DELETE>- UnPublish a Volume. │
│    <F10>- Change the password.               <F2>- Change the Alias. │
│    <ESCAPE>- Return to the previous window.  <F6>- Change the mode. │
└─────────────────────────────────────────────────────────────────────┘
```

Fig. 6-6. Viewing published volumes.

Mounting a Server Volume via TOPSMENU

The mounting of volumes on a server is done through the Client Utilities option of the opening menu. The submenu for Client Utilities is displayed in Fig. 6-7.

The resources that can be mounted are disk volumes or printers. Naturally the mounting can only be done if the above resources have been published. Therefore, the commands File Servers and Printer Servers are meant to show the user a list of all current servers (in the local zone) on the network, with Current Servers meaning any computer that currently has something published.

The File Servers Command

For example, after choosing File Servers, a list of servers appears on the left-hand side of the screen. When the appropriate server is selected from that list, a new list, which is the list of published volumes available on that server, appears on the right. The name for the volume that appears is the alias that was used when the volume was published, so the name of the volume might have spaces or other unusual characters. Refer to the section on publishing if you need a refresher on what alias means. Often this alias is the same name as the actual subdirectory of the server, but not always, as you can see from Fig. 6-8.

To the PC TOPS client, a mounted volume appears as another drive. Although it isn't physically attached to the computer, MS-DOS must have a way to refer to it. This it does with a letter between A and J. You can see the box the menu displays to explain this in Fig. 6-9.

You, the person doing the mounting, are the one who decides what letter identity this new drive will assume. Odds are that the computer you are working at

```
┌─────────────────────────────────────────────────────────────────────┐
│ Fred's XT              TOPS : Client Utilities   Client Utilities   │
├─────────────────────────────────────────────────────────────────────┤
│  Client Utilities Menu                                              │
│    See all the File Servers on the           File Servers           │
│    net, all the Volumes available on a Server,  Volumes Mounted     │
│    all the Volumes Mounted from a Server,    Printer Servers        │
│    and you can Mount an available Volume.    Mounted Printers       │
│                                                                     │
│                                                                     │
└─────────────────────────────────────────────────────────────────────┘


┌─────────────────────────────────────────────────────────────────────┐
│ MENU INSTRUCTIONS                                                   │
│   Select a Command using the space bar, up arrow, down arrow or first│
│     letter of the Command.                                          │
│   <ENTER>- Invoke a selected command.                               │
│                                                                     │
│   <ESCAPE>- Return to the previous window.    <CNTRL-Q>- Exit to DOS.│
│                                                                     │
└─────────────────────────────────────────────────────────────────────┘
```

Fig. 6-7. Client Utilities menu.

already has a drive A, possibly a drive B, and perhaps even a drive C, so those are not usually available choices. Assuming that this client computer does not already have a drive D, the letter D is one logical choice for the first volume you mount. In fact, as you can see from Fig. 6-10, the menu assumes this by default if you press only the Enter key in response to the prompt box. However, you could mount any letter up to J by typing the letter.

The final choice is to select the access mode. Not surprisingly, you can only mount a volume as Read and Write if it was published that way. However, you can mount as Read Only a volume that was published as Read and Write. After choosing the desired option, you can mount other volumes or drop quickly out of the menu to the DOS prompt with the key sequence Ctrl-Q.

When you complete the mount procedure, you have in effect a new disk drive that is identified by the letter you mounted it as. In other words, if you mounted a remote volume as drive D, when you return to DOS, the remote TOPS drive D reacts like any other local drive. For example, to view the files on that drive, give the command DIR D:. You can store files to that drive from within your application programs, or if you have a multi-user application on that server volume, you can run the program from there.

THE REMEMBER OPTION

The TOPSMENU is fairly successful at making some pretty difficult networking tasks very easy to do. The publishing and mounting of disk volumes and printers

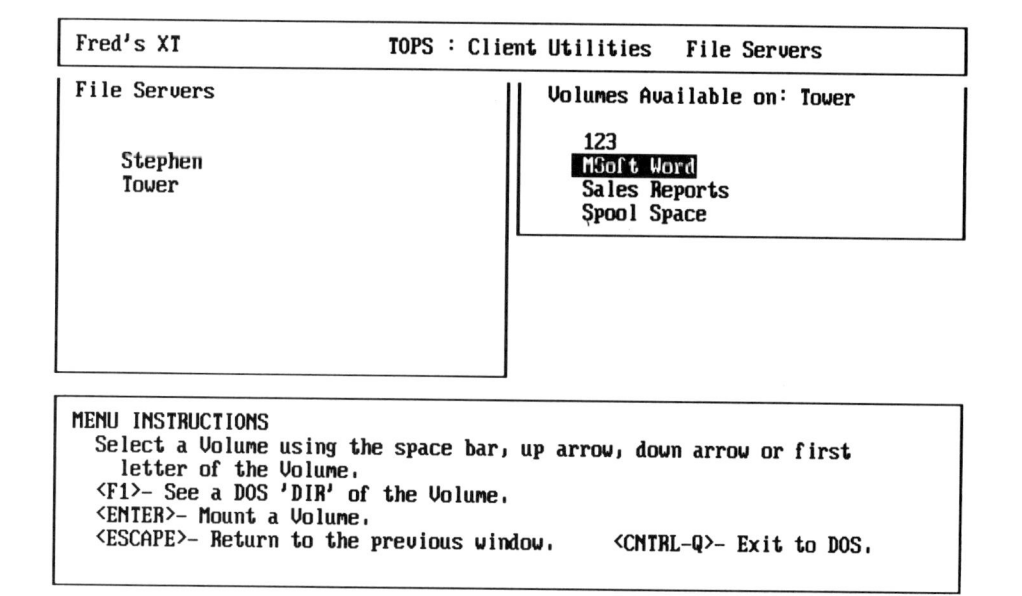

Fig. 6-8. Selecting a published volume.

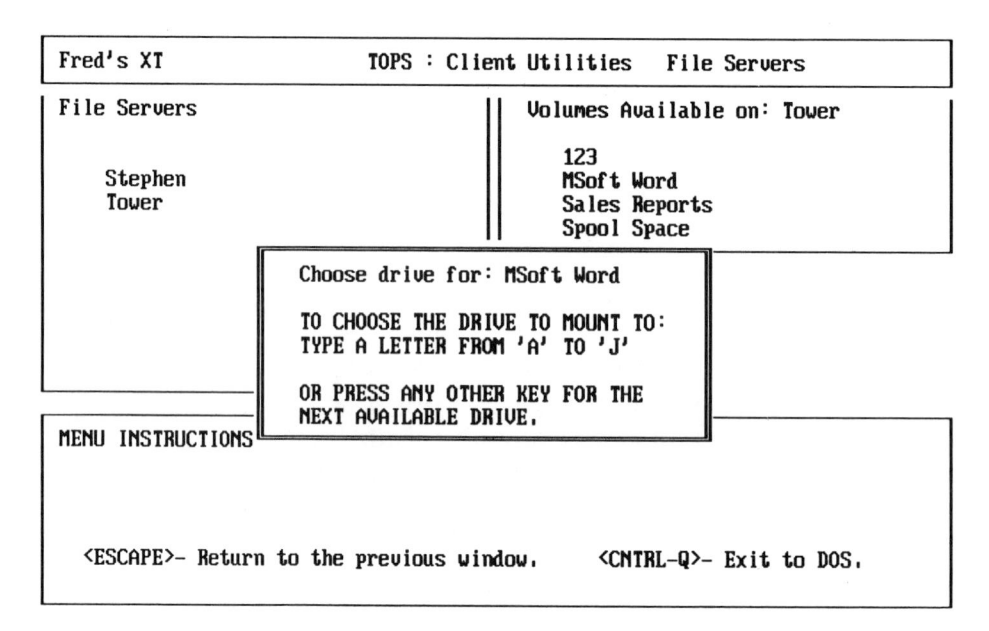

```
┌──────────────────────────────────────────────────────────────────┐
│  Fred's XT              TOPS : Client Utilities    File Servers  │
│  File Servers                 │ Volumes Available on: Tower      │
│                               │    123                           │
│     Stephen                   │    MSoft Word                    │
│     Tower                     │    Sales Reports                 │
│                               │    Spool Space                   │
│              ┌────────────────────────────────────┐              │
│              │ Choose drive for: MSoft Word       │              │
│              │                                    │              │
│              │ TO CHOOSE THE DRIVE TO MOUNT TO:   │              │
│              │ TYPE A LETTER FROM 'A' TO 'J'      │              │
│              │                                    │              │
│              │ OR PRESS ANY OTHER KEY FOR THE     │              │
│   MENU INSTR │ NEXT AVAILABLE DRIVE.              │              │
│              └────────────────────────────────────┘              │
│                                                                  │
│                                                                  │
│      <ESCAPE>- Return to the previous window.                    │
│                                     <CNTRL-Q>- Exit to DOS.      │
└──────────────────────────────────────────────────────────────────┘
```

Fig. 6-9. Drive selection.

is accomplished by making selections from the lists that appear on the screen. Yet if you had to publish and mount the same things over and over again daily, it would probably become an annoying chore. In a lot of real world applications, the server publishes the same volumes and printers every day. The Remember option is a way to take the repetition out of the task.

After the server goes through the steps of publishing, the Remember option writes the information about what is published to a type of file called a batch file. A batch file is a collection of commands or instructions that might otherwise be issued one after another at the DOS prompt. This particular batch file, created by the Remember option, has the name TOPSTART.BAT. The TOPSTART.BAT file is created in the root directory. The next time you use the LOADTOPS command to get TOPS running, your publishing and mounting happens automatically because the TOPSTART.BAT file is executed as a part of LOADTOPS. In fact, the LOADTOPS command runs a batch file called LOADTOPS.BAT which has TOPSTART as its last line of instructions.

One word of caution about using the Remember option. It works great for publishing, but not always so great for mounting. Mounting depends on the server having published what your machine is trying to mount. If the server is not published when you run LOADTOPS on one of its clients, then the mount fails. When the desired volume has been published, you can repeat the mount operation by running TOPSTART by itself instead of through LOADTOPS.

If you are curious to see what is in the TOPSTART.BAT file, you can list its contents by giving the command

TYPE C:\TOPSTART.BAT

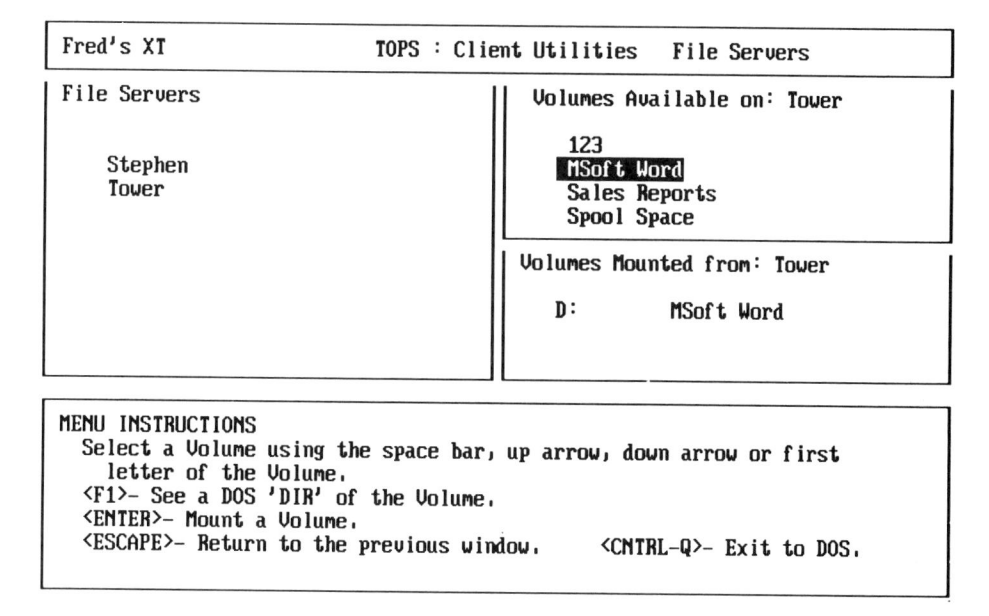

```
┌─────────────────────────────────────────────────────────────────┐
│  Fred's XT                    TOPS : Client Utilities  File Servers │
├───────────────────────────────┬─────────────────────────────────┤
│  File Servers                 │ Volumes Available on: Tower     │
│                               │      123                        │
│     Stephen                   │      ▌MSoft Word▐               │
│     Tower                     │      Sales Reports              │
│                               │      Spool Space                │
│                               ├─────────────────────────────────┤
│                               │ Volumes Mounted from: Tower     │
│                               │      D:         MSoft Word      │
│                               │                                 │
├───────────────────────────────┴─────────────────────────────────┤
│  MENU INSTRUCTIONS                                              │
│    Select a Volume using the space bar, up arrow, down arrow or first │
│      letter of the Volume.                                      │
│    <F1>- See a DOS 'DIR' of the Volume.                         │
│    <ENTER>- Mount a Volume.                                     │
│    <ESCAPE>- Return to the previous window.    <CNTRL-Q>- Exit to DOS. │
│                                                                 │
└─────────────────────────────────────────────────────────────────┘
```

Fig. 6-10. Default drive mounted.

at the DOS prompt and then pressing Enter. What you see is an example of the TOPS command language which has been referred to several times in the preceding sections. Chapter 9 talks at length about this command language and the various ways that it can be used.

One final note for those with a bent to tinker with DOS. The LOAD-TOPS.BAT file is written to assume TOPSTART.BAT will stay in the root directory. If you move it somewhere else, you will have to change the references in LOADTOPS.BAT.

CONCLUSION

The TOPSMENU program is a simple but effective front-end to the TOPS commands. Novice users can navigate the menu, and more experienced users can quickly issue commands through the first letter method. However, sometimes the menu can be cumbersome, and you would like to issue commands direct from DOS. Also, in some situations, you would like to incorporate TOPS instructions into batch files. Control of DOS through direct commands and batch files is covered in Chapter 9. The next chapter addresses the control of printing through TOPS, including the printer options in the Client and Server Utilities menus.

7
General Printing with TOPS

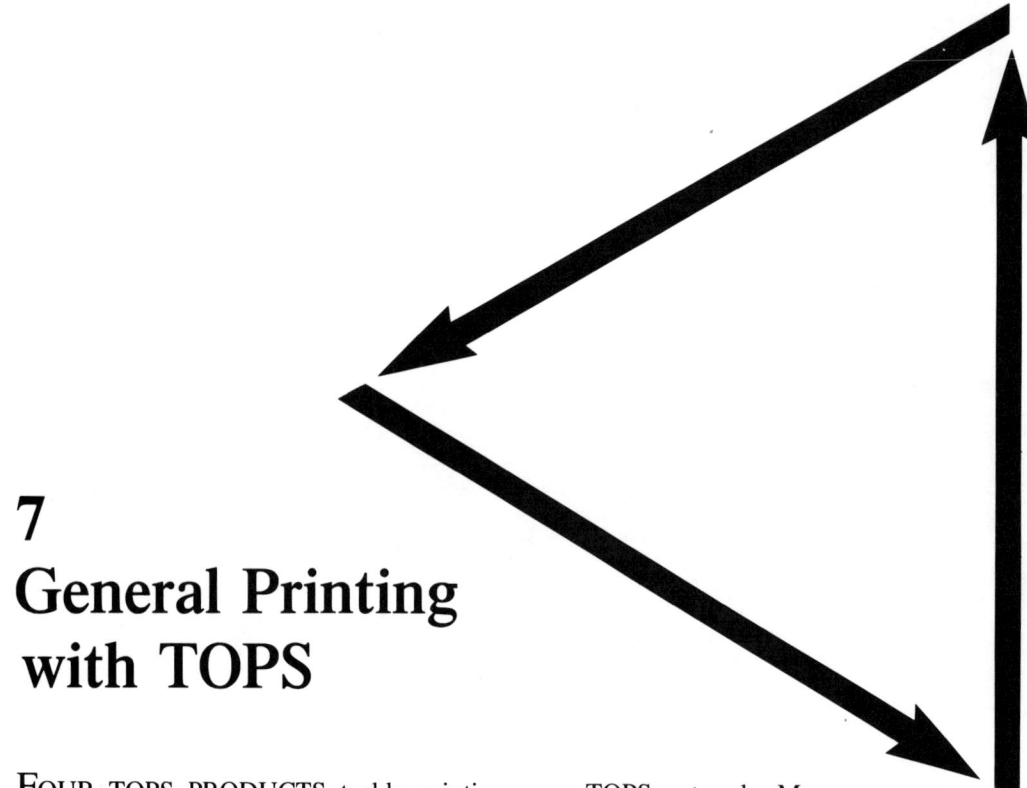

FOUR TOPS PRODUCTS tackle printing on a TOPS network. Mac users get TOPS Spool included with TOPS/Macintosh. With TOPS Spool you have extensive control of printer operations on the network. Buyers of TOPS/DOS get TOPSPRTR to allow remote printing and the TPRINT utility which allows some access to network printers from the DOS prompt. An additional TOPS product for DOS users is TOPS NetPrint which provides network printing directly from an application. This chapter examines network printing in general and the TOPS Spool product in particular. Users of both DOS and Mac systems should familiarize themselves with this material.

THE POSTSCRIPT FACTOR

When discussing printing in the IBM/Macintosh environment that is the specialty of TOPS, special attention must be given to PostScript, the page description language from Adobe Systems. We describe the role of PostScript to prepare you for some of the terminology and techniques that we review in this chapter and the next.

The purpose of a page description language such as PostScript is to tell the printer where to place the ink on the page to match the document you are printing, including characters, their shape, size, and style, as well as images and shading. PostScript is one of several different page description languages in use on printers commonly used by personal computers. Although PostScript is complex and requires considerable amounts of memory to operate, it offers significant advantages in the area of typestyles and image manipulation. Output to a PostScript printer can be scaled up or down from the original and still retain clarity and proportion.

When Apple adopted PostScript to control the LaserWriter from the Macintosh, a new standard for print quality and typestyle flexibility was established. The ability to mix a variety of fonts and graphic images on a page opened up the field of desktop publishing to personal computer users. Because typesetting systems were readily adapted to use PostScript, the ability of software to generate PostScript output became increasingly important. Layout and design could be performed on a Macintosh. Output of respectable quality could be obtained direct from a LaserWriter, or typeset quality could be achieved by transfer to a typesetting device. Users of IBM PCs soon wanted access to the same levels of print quality.

Because the developers at TOPS had come up with a way for PCs to access files on the Mac, it was natural that the TOPS developers also work on products to enable PCs to access LaserWriters. Such products need to address two tasks: the network connection, and the PostScript connection. The *network connection* is the task of transmitting print data over the network wiring, from the PC to the printer. The *PostScript connection* is the task of getting the print output from a PC into the PostScript language. This is not an easy task, but one that has been getting easier as more and more software for the IBM world has added PostScript drivers.

For example, the most widely used word processor on PCs is WordPerfect. With the release of version 5.0 users of WordPerfect users can print directly to a LaserWriter. They can select the LaserWriter from a list of supported printers. The LaserWriter's fonts can be picked from a font list, and no special formatting is required. This makes the PC-to-PostScript connection a lot easier than it used to be. In this case, the TOPS network provides a connection to the LaserWriter, and TOPS software can manage the print process for you. If you are using a program that does not support the LaserWriter but you still want to use a LaserWriter as a printer, then you need to convert the output from the program into a format that PostScript can understand. In this case, TOPS software can perform conversions into PostScript and allow printing to a LaserWriter by a program that is not really PostScript-compatible.

Note that when we refer to the LaserWriter, we really mean to include a large number of different printers with PostScript-like capability that are considered "LaserWriter-compatible," such as the Jasmine DirectPrint or the Qume CrystalPrint Publisher. Also note that PostScript is a page description language used to describe pages to printers; it is not a system of codes used to communicate between computers and printers. The most widely used system of codes is ASCII, and ASCII is used by both Macs and PCs to pass information to printers whether or not the printer is PostScript compatible. To put it another way, PostScript commands are stored and sent in ASCII code.

ABOUT NETWORK PRINTING

If you are somewhat confused at this point by the terms "remote printing" and "network printing," we sympathize. The distinction is confusing, and we will now clarify matters before proceeding. If you look at Fig. 7-1 you will see a diagram of what we are about to put into words.

Some Definitions

A *network printer* is one that has a network port, an AppleTalk connection, which is cabled to the network. A *remote printer* is just an ordinary printer attached to a computer, usually through a parallel or serial port. A network printer is accessible to everyone on the network; it does not need to be published. A remote printer is only available to other network users if it has been published; otherwise it is just used by the computer to which it is attached. A printer that is simply used by the computer to which it is attached is a *local printer*. In general, Macs normally only use network printers, while PCs use remote or local printers and can be allowed to access network printers.

The Remote Printer Scenario

The way that printers on a network are classified and the different ways in which they are used can be clarified by means of the following scenario: you are Fred, you have a PC XT that you use for writing reports. You are connected to a TOPS network which you use primarily to retrieve data about company sales. You frequently print out drafts of your reports so that you can do some old-fashioned editing with a pencil. To print these drafts, and other material such as directory listings and the occasional screen dump, you use a trusty Epson dot matrix printer. This is known as a local printer; it is attached directly to your XT's parallel port. In technical terms, this port is known as LPT1. If you have more than one parallel

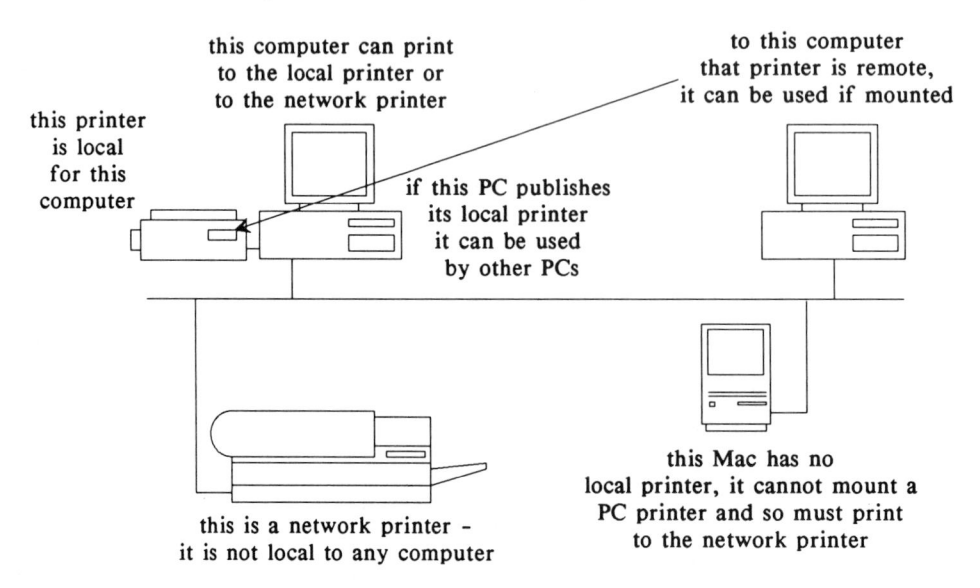

Fig. 7-1. Remote, local, and network printing.

port the second one is known as LPT2, the third is LPT3, and DOS does not provide for more than three of these ports.

In even more technical terms, LPT1 is also known as PRN, the device to which DOS sends print output by default. For example, if you issue the command DIR/W > PRN at the DOS prompt, then DOS sends the wide listing of the current directory's contents to the printer that is attached to LPT1.

To get back your/Fred's situation: the carefully edited final report does not look as good when printed to the dot matrix printer as it does when output on the Hewlett Packard LaserJet II printer in the sales office. This LaserJet is attached to the LPT1 port of the big 80386 machine that is known on the network as Tower. If Fred can persuade the people in sales to publish the LaserJet on the network, then Fred can mount the LaserJet and send documents there to be printed. The steps to publishing the LaserJet on the Tower are as follows:

Load TOPS.
Load TOPSPRTR.
Publish LPT1 as Tower LJet II.

The steps to mounting the LaserJet on Fred's XT are as follows:

Load TOPS.
Load TOPSPRTR.
Mount Tower LJet II as LPT2.

Having mounted the LaserJet, Fred needs to take several additional steps:

Redirect documents from LPT1 to LPT2.
Format documents for the LaserJet as opposed to the Epson.

The exact steps to accomplish these last two tasks depend upon the software that Fred is using. For example, suppose Fred is using WordPerfect 5.0. All Fred has to do is define an "HP LaserJet Series II" with a Port setting of LPT2 and select that printer when printing a final report. Otherwise, the regular Epson printer is selected. This printer has its port defined as LPT1 (for more on the exact WordPerfect commands see your Word Perfect manual.

The Advantages of Remote Printing

You can see that Fred now has two printers he can use. Output directed to LPT1: still goes to the Epson. Output directed to LPT2 is intercepted by TOPS. After all, Fred's XT hasn't got a "real" port called LPT2. TOPS directs the output down the network wire and into the computer called Tower. From there, the output is sent through the parallel cable of the Tower system to the LaserJet. Obviously, this process takes a little time, and the results of the process will appear in another room. However, Fred gets the benefit of better-looking reports, and the total time to print is probably less than on the slower dot matrix next to his XT.

A further advantage of printing to the remote machine is that TOPS "spools" the print task, storing it on disk prior to feeding it into the printer. This means that

Fred's computer unloads the printing work much more quickly than when printing locally.

Fred's company gains as well, because the cost of providing Fred with a LaserJet of his own has been avoided. Indeed, several users can have the benefit of a single LaserJet via TOPS, further reducing the cost per user. TOPS compares quite favorably in price to some of the printer-sharing systems currently on the market and offers full network facilities as well.

The Disadvantages of Remote Printing

Some people are just not comfortable with the idea of telling their PC to print, and then not seeing the results start to emerge from the printer at their desk. Using a remote printer does require a certain amount of faith in your hardware/software. Obviously, you will need to test the arrangement before relying upon it for real work. One situation in which printer sharing raises fewer concerns is in close-knit workgroups where several stations are organized around a shared printer. With the printer and its output in reach, users feel more comfortable, even if they occasionally have to wait for someone else's work to finish first.

Apart from the psychological drawbacks, remote printing does come with several practical limits. If more than one user is printing to the same remote printer, then one print job has to come before the others, leading to a wait for work to be printed that does not occur when you use a local printer. In situations where an expensive printer is being shared by many users, you might want to consider a policy limiting the type of printing that is done at the remote printer. For example, "final drafts only" with rough drafts done on inexpensive local printers. A decent dot matrix printer for a PC only costs a couple of hundred dollars and can placate users frustrated by printing delays. Of course, there are situations where sharing cannot be avoided, for example with special-purpose printers. If all invoices must be printed on the same heavy duty printer and several users are preparing invoices, then waiting for print job completion will be necessary from time to time. TOPS can certainly handle a line, or list of documents to be printed, known as a print *queue* (from the long pony tail worn by Chinese nobility).

In order for TOPS to handle work being sent to a remote printer and hold items in a print queue, it has to take up disk space for temporary storage of files. This space can be on a drive at the computer that is sending the print job, or on any published volume on the network, but it is space that might be in short supply. In situations where a large capacity PC with a printer is acting as file and printer server to many client PCs, you might want to invest in additional disk capacity on the server in order to cope with heavy print spooling. Alternatively, you can have clients mount a directory of the server's hard drive for print spooling, thus avoiding the need to add storage on the client.

Earlier we mentioned that some people dislike having to get their printed output from another room. A further human factor in printer sharing is the control or administration issue. Sharing resources such as a printer inevitably involves compromise. Clear rules for sharing, arrived at by consensus can alleviate part of the problem, but there are always going to be individuals who will get annoyed at such aspects of printer sharing as having to wait for output. Furthermore, there are very real questions when it comes to loading paper (who is responsible?) and using custom forms (can all print jobs be handled on standard paper?). These practical problems need careful thought for printer sharing to be successful.

Bear in mind also that printing to a remote printer requires that the server (the system publishing the printer) loads TOPSPRTR, which consumes an additional 36K of server RAM. This might cut down on the range of applications that the server can handle in the remaining RAM and could require that the server become essentially a dedicated system.

The Network Printer Scenario

A network printer is one that is wired directly into the network. There is no computer controlling access to a network printer; it is there as a separate network device for anyone to use. Nobody publishes a network printer, and you do not have to mount one to use it. So how do you use a network printer? There are three methods:

On a PC use TPRINT to send a file to a network printer from DOS.

On a PC use NetPrint to direct application output to a network printer.

On a Macintosh, print with TOPS Spool installed.

Consider the situation that Fred faces when he hires Kathy to assist in the preparation of reports. Fred's reports, which concern market conditions in a specialized field of industrial goods, were originally intended for internal company use only. However, now that their appearance has been improved by laser printing, Fred's reports can be sold, in slightly modified form, to other companies in the industry, thus providing additional revenue.

Enter Kathy, who has experience in graphic arts and publishing. Kathy is accustomed to preparing documents on a Macintosh and brings her own machine into the office. She convinces Fred that a LaserWriter is necessary to prepare drafts of PostScript documents before they are sent to be typeset. Because TOPS is available, Fred can still type up reports on his XT, share his text files with Kathy, who then incorporates them in the published versions she is preparing on the Macintosh.

When Kathy wants to print a draft of a publication for proofreading and review, she simply selects Print from the File menu of her page layout program on the Macintosh. TOPS Spool takes the document and immediately stores it on disk, allowing Kathy to return to her work on the Mac quicker than if she had to wait for the document to finish printing. TOPS Spool then sends the document to the LaserWriter.

Fred's use of the LaserJet attached to the Tower in the sales office has started a trend. More people are looking to use the same printer, resulting in delays. While

Fred still has the option to print to the LaserJet as long as it is published on the network, he decides to avail himself of the LaserWriter that Kathy uses, because she does not use it all the time.

Fred is using an application that is compatible with the LaserWriter and so has the potential to print directly to the LaserWriter. However, by itself, TOPS/DOS does not allow direct printing from application-to-network printer. Fred cannot mount the LaserWriter. He can either print to disk those documents he wants output on the LaserWriter, and then use the TPRINT utility to send them to be printed, or he can install NetPrint, a separate program that uses the TOPS connection to manage printing from PCs to LaserWriters.

Given these scenarios and some idea of how TOPS printing fits into the typical office, we look at the various parts of the TOPS printing picture, beginning with TOPS Spool on the Mac which takes up the rest of this chapter. The approaches available to DOS users are detailed in the next chapter.

TOPS SPOOL

When we talk about spools, we are not referring to sewing baskets. In the context of printing with computers, *spooling* is simply a technique for storing information to be printed until such time as it is possible or desirable to print it. A spooler is "taking up the slack" as it were and handling printed output while other work is in progress. An operation that takes place while you carry on computing is called a *background task*. Software that records output for a printer and then prints it without interfering with the primary use of a computer is thus called a *background print spooler*.

About Spooling on the Mac

The Macintosh operating system is particularly well suited to performing such background task as print spooling because Desk Accessories are available within any application. TOPS Spool is a background print spooler program with a Macintosh Desk Accessory to run it. The Desk Accessory enables you to turn the spooler on and off and to remove print jobs from the list of documents to be printed (the print queue). You can also use the TOPS Spool DA to change the order in which documents will be printed or save them for printing at a later time.

You need to be aware that whether or not you are doing anything else with the network, TOPS Spool will circumvent the usual Macintosh laser printing process. You can turn off TOPS Spool to use the normal printing channels, but when TOPS Spool is turned on, it redirects the output generated by your application to a temporary disk file instead of sending it directly to the laser printer. This process never takes any more time from your work than is required to actually generate the output data (also called a PostScript file) for the printer and write it onto your disk.

Once this has happened, you can continue in your application, or you can quit and launch another application. At any time, you can spool additional documents to be printed. For example, you can spool your FileMaker report and quit FileMaker. Then you can open a WordPerfect document and spool it without having to wait for the FileMaker report to finish printing. TOPS Spool prints while you work and is unaffected as you move from application to application.

If you are doing a lot of printing or are sharing the printer with others on the network, it is likely that some documents will have to wait their turn before being printed. When the spooler has a job in its queue, it knows to check every few seconds to see whether the printer is available. When the printer is free, the spooler sends the print file from your disk to the laser printer, as shown in Fig. 7-2.

TOPS Spool works from within any standard Macintosh application whenever you use the Print option from the File menu. TOPS Spool also works when you initiate printing from the Desktop by selecting a document then picking File Print. Because the spooling feature records onto disk output that is intended for the printer, TOPS Spool can recover any spooled print jobs that had not been printed prior to a power outage or system crash. This can be of great help in protecting your work against loss.

We recommend that you use the LaserWriter drives and Laser Prep version 5.2, but TOPS Spool is compatible with most LaserWriter drivers since 3.1 (with the exception of 5.1). You will want to coordinate version numbers across the entire network: each station should have versions of the LaserWriter drives and Laser Prep files. Each station that uses TOPS Spool needs 65K of memory and 40K of disk space to run and store the software. Each station also needs at least 75K of disk space for temporary storage of spooled documents. This space can be a published volume on the network or disk space on the local station.

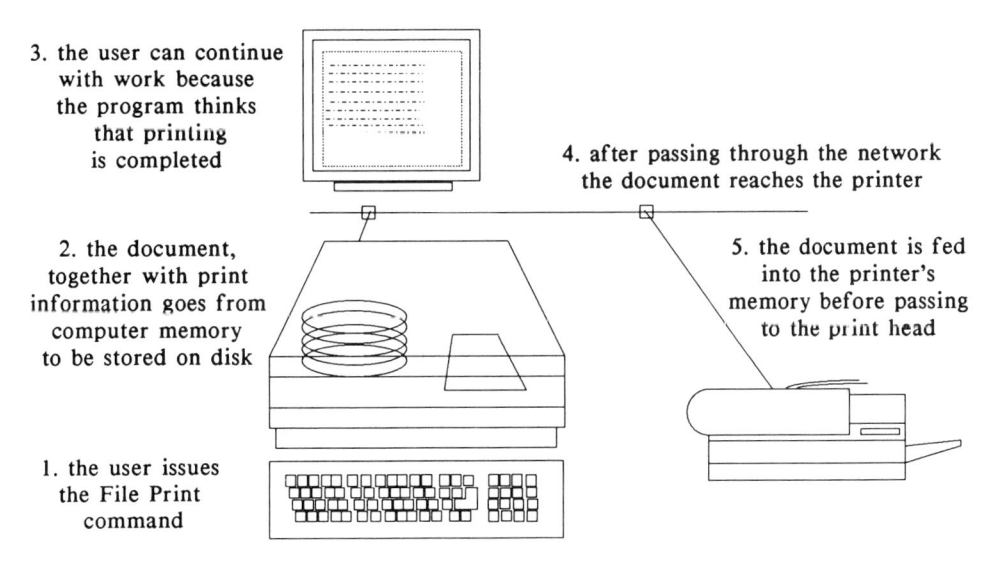

Fig. 7-2. Spooling documents.

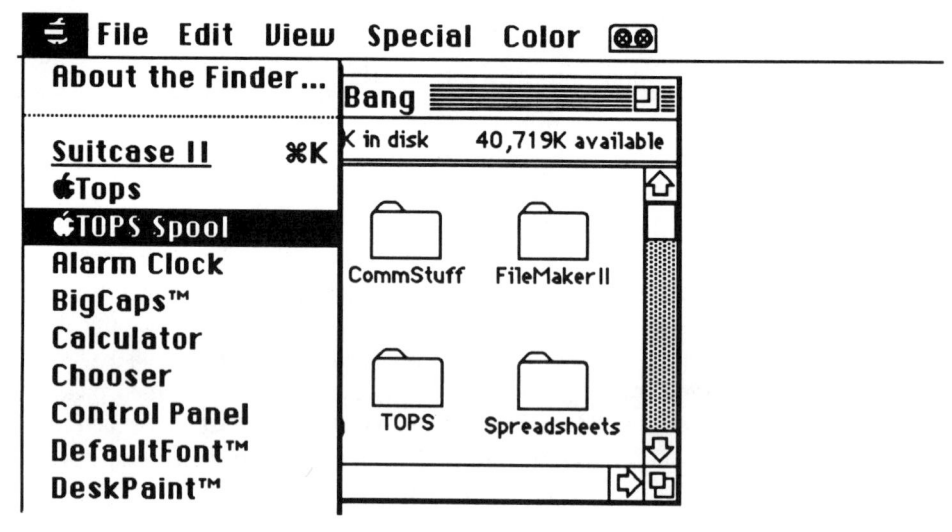

Fig. 7-3. The TOPS Spool DA.

Testing TOPS Spool

After you have installed TOPS Spool as described in Chapter 4, you can quickly test the installation and your connection with a printer. Make sure you are at the Macintosh desktop with no applications active, then follow these directions:

1. Pick TOPS Spool from the Desk Accessory menu (underneath the Apple). If TOPS Spool does not appear on the DA menu, as shown in Fig. 7-3, then

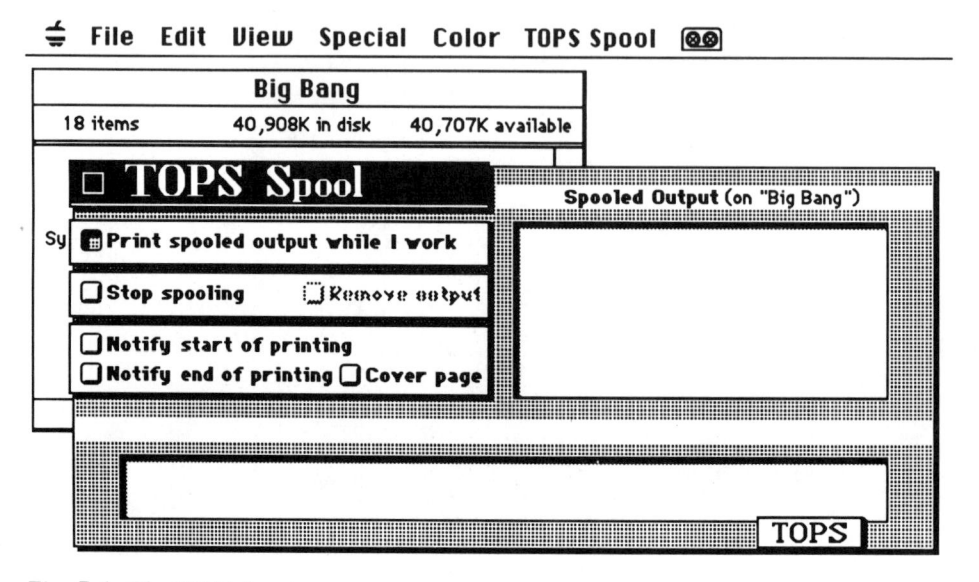

Fig. 7-4. The TOPS Spool menu.

you need to check your installation (consult the manual and Appendix A of this book for help).

2. When you pick TOPS Spool from the DA menu, you will see the menu shown in Fig. 7-4. Also note that there is an added menu item at the right end of the menu bar. This item, TOPS Spool, is covered in a moment. Note that the TOPS Spool DA uses a system of buttons. Clicking on these buttons turns them On and Off, with shading indicating On (this is supposed to show that the buttons are pushed in, while white buttons are popped up). Thus Print spooled output while I work is pushed in/On in Fig. 7-4.

3. Pop up, or turn to white, the one button that is gray in Fig. 7-4, the Print spooled output while I work button. By turning off this feature, you will be able to initiate a couple of print jobs and have TOPS Spool hold the jobs on disk. Click in the close box in the top left corner of the menu to close TOPS Spool DA.

4. Now open the Chooser from the DA menu and do the following:
   a. Check that AppleTalk is active.
   b. Select the LaserWriter you want to print to.
   c. Make sure that background printing is Off.
   The menu should appear something like Fig. 7-5.

5. From the File menu pick Print Directory (shown as Print Catalog on some earlier versions of the System). Then click OK on the print dialog box that appears. A message will appear similar to the one in Fig. 7-6.

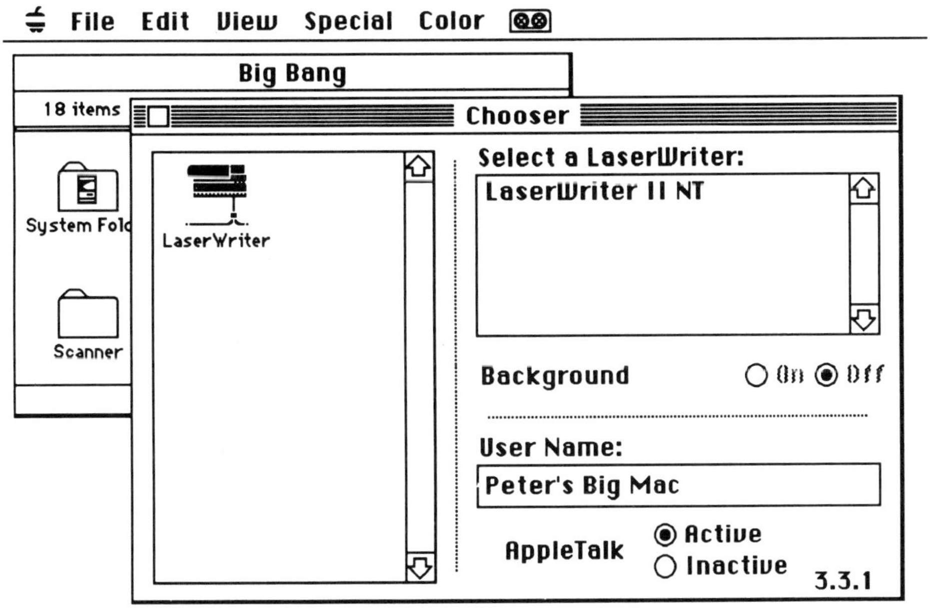

Fig. 7-5. The Chooser menu.

120 Chapter 7

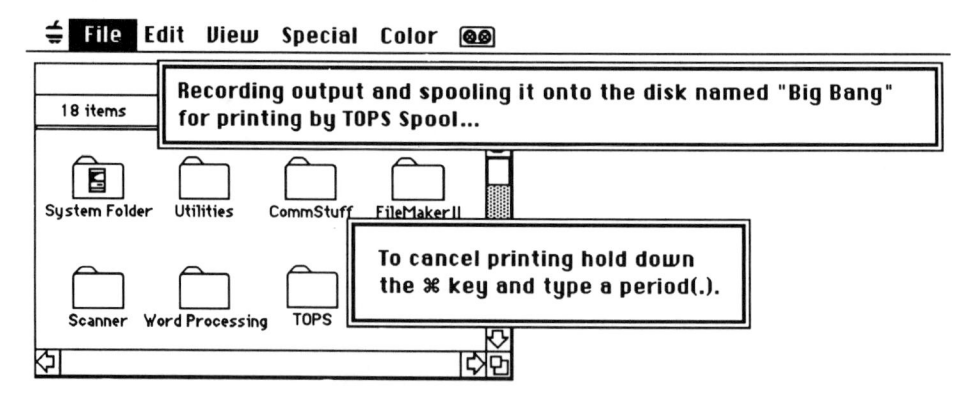

Fig. 7-6. Spooling message.

This lets you know that TOPS is handling the print operation. However, the printer will not receive the directory listing output yet because you told TOPS Spool not to print while you worked. Instead, you will see a blinking icon of a LaserWriter appear over the Apple icon in the top left of the screen, as seen in Fig. 7-7.

6. With the icon still flashing open one of the folders on your disk and again pick Print Directory. Click OK at the print dialog box to confirm printing. Another spooling message will appear.
7. Now pick TOPS Spool from the DA menu and note the items in the print queue, looking something like Fig. 7-8.

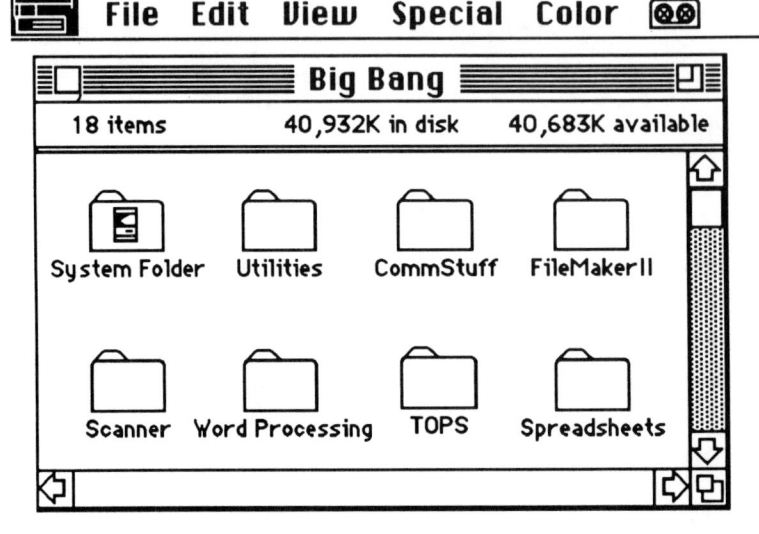

Fig. 7-7. LaserWriter icon.

General Printing with TOPS 121

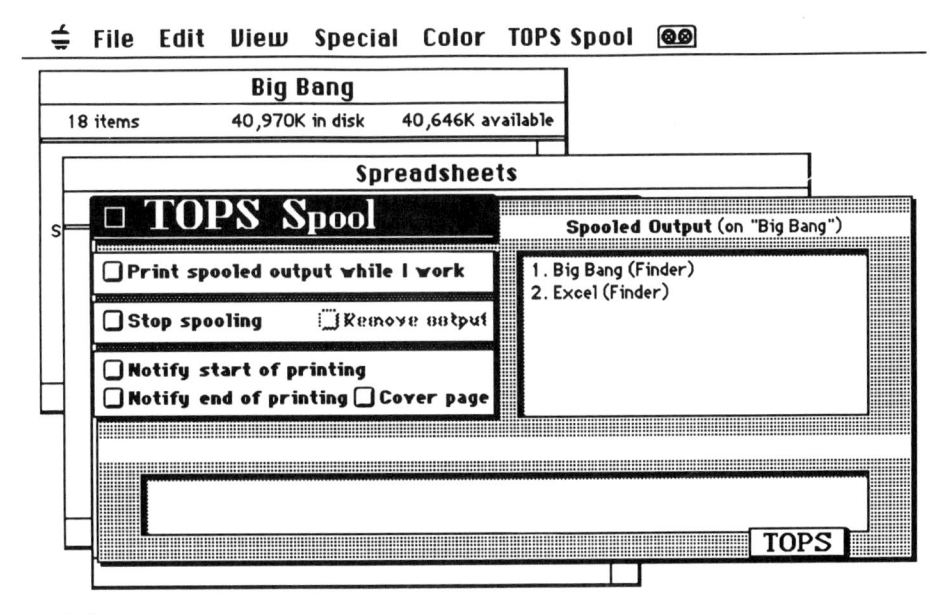

Fig. 7-8. Print queue.

Now click On the Print spooled output while I work button. This will send the two print jobs to the printer, and you will see the menu update their progress.

You might get the message, The LaserWriter needs to be initialized, in which case you will need to pull down the TOPS Spool menu from the right-hand side of the top menu line of the screen and pick Prep Laser, as seen in Fig. 7-9.

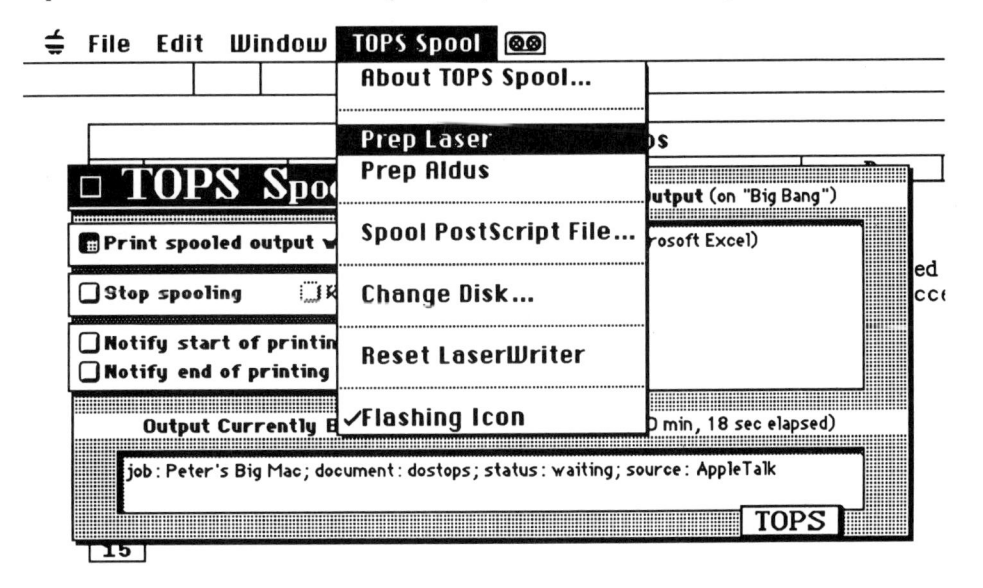

Fig. 7-9. Prep Laser.

This step is necessary when you are the first person to use the LaserWriter to which the print job is being sent.

If you followed the above steps but did not get any printed results, there are several areas you might check as you diagnose the problem. Some of them are fairly obvious but easily overlooked: is the printer turned on? supplied with paper? properly connected? Further steps in problem-solving are described later in this chapter.

What the Spool Information Means

Print information such as that shown in the TOPS Spool DA screen in Fig. 7-8 is very useful when printing is getting hectic. However, you will probably not need to look at this menu if everything is going well. In fact, if you leave the Print spooled output while I work button turned On, TOPS Spool is almost invisible while you print from your applications.

The percent transmitted number shown in the Spool window is the amount of a particular job that has been sent to the laser printer, not the amount that has been printed. The time that is shown is the combination of how long the document has been printing and the time that TOPS Spool spent waiting for the printer to be ready. The bottom portion of the screen tells you who is currently using the laser printer and what job they are printing. The job name is the name entered in the Chooser Desk Accessory. The document name is the name of the file being printed, and the status tells you what the laser printer is doing, for example Idle, Busy, Waiting, or errors such as Out of paper.

The TOPS Spool Menu

In Fig. 7-9, you can see the menu that appears under TOPS Spool in the menu bar. The items on this menu are:

About TOPS Spool   shows the version number for TOPS Spool.

Prep Laser   initializes the laser printer: use this if your file is the first to be printed after the laser printer is turned on (a message like the one in Fig. 7-10 appears if this is necessary).

Prep Aldus   initializes the laser printer when using PageMaker (TOPS Spool tells you if this is necessary).

Spool PostScript File   allows you to spool either a text file or a PostScript file that has been previously saved to disk.

Change Disk   selects the disk on which your spooled output will be saved, used to spool onto a network volume, as described later.

Reset LaserWriter   lets you restart the LaserWriter remotely, sometimes necessary if the LaserWriter has been initialized with a different version of the Laser Prep file (A better solution is to standardize versions; do not use this command if someone else is in the process of printing).

General Printing with TOPS 123

```
  File   Edit   Search   Format   Font   Special   Windows
```
```
                                    Doc 1: Grocery List
                                 Doc 2: Sales Letter1
                              Doc 3: Sales Report1
```

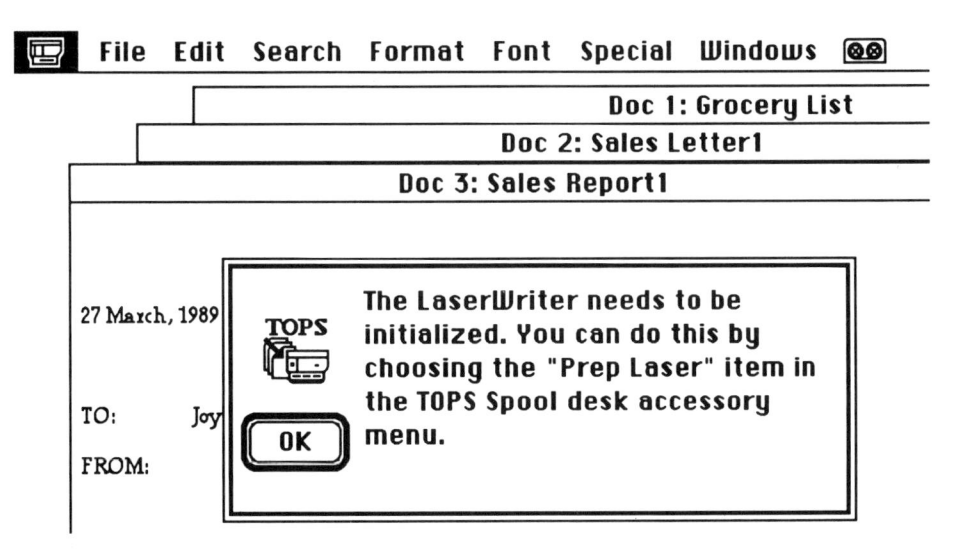

27 March, 1989

TOPS

The LaserWriter needs to be initialized. You can do this by choosing the "Prep Laser" item in the TOPS Spool desk accessory menu.

[OK]

TO: Joy

FROM:

Fig. 7-10. The Prep Laser message.

Flashing Icon allows you to control the flashing LaserWriter icon that normally appears over the Apple when TOPS Spool is spooling; when Flashing Icon is checked, the icon will display during printing.

Spooling to Mounted Volumes

On a floppy-only Macintosh, you might be short of disk space. TOPS Spool needs from 75K to 120K of free disk space for spooling operations. You can mount a volume published by another computer on the network and use space on that disk for spooling. To do this, use the Change Disk command on the TOPS Spool menu, as seen in Fig. 7-11.

Do this *after* you have used TOPS to mount the volume. Note that TOPS Spool always begins spooling to the System folder of the startup disk. This means that on a Macintosh that regularly needs to spool to a remote disk, you need to use the Change Disk command every time you start the computer. Also bear in mind that spooling to a mounted volume increases network traffic. TOPS Spool must send messages and files back and forth between computers as well as to the printer. You will find that printing using spooling to a remote disk is slower than using a local disk.

Changing Print Job Order with TOPS Spool

You can easily change the order of print jobs when you have two or more jobs in the queue at any one time. Suppose you have sent Grocery List to print followed by Sales Letter 1 followed by Sales Report 1. You realize that the Federal Express agent will arrive any minute to pick up the Sales Report. You pick TOPS Spool from the DA menu. The scene will look something like Fig. 7-12.

124 Chapter 7

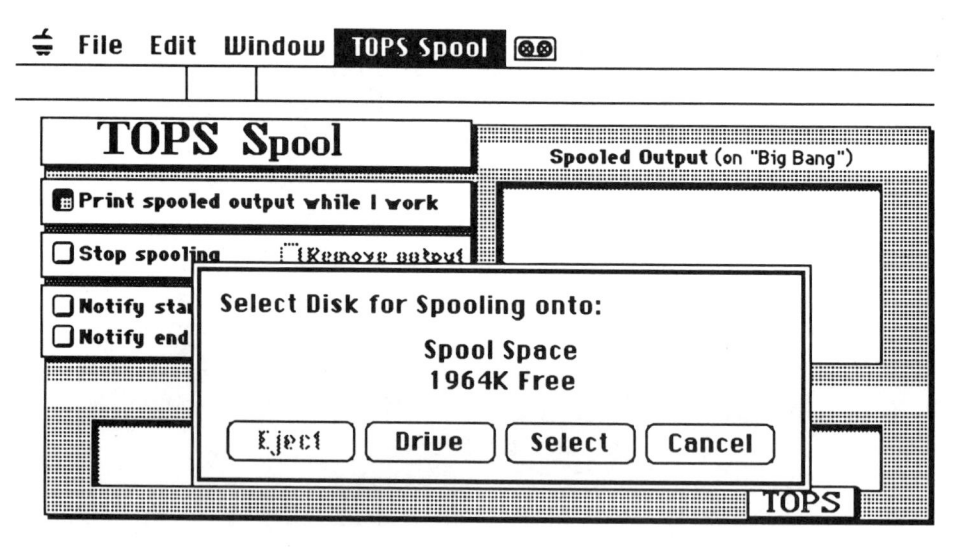

Fig. 7-11. Changing drives for TOPS Spool.

In the window titled Spooled Output, click on the item that is numbered 3 and drag it to the top of the list. There will be a dotted outline around the item as it is dragged as shown in Fig. 7-13.

Because the output being displaced is currently printing, you will be asked if you want to cancel the printing or cancel the change in the order, as seen in Fig. 7-14.

You decide that the report is more important than your grocery list and cancel the current printing. The report is printed next, just as the Federal Express agent arrives. Now the order of the spooled outputs in the queue has been changed.

Fig. 7-12. Three items in queue.

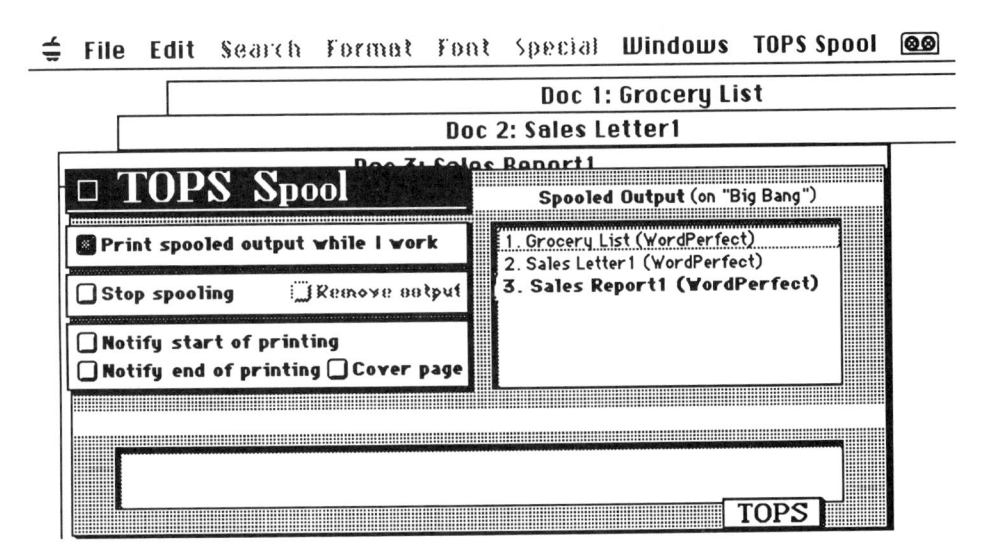

Fig. 7-13. Changing print order.

Turning Off TOPS Spool

Sometimes it might not be convenient to print documents, for example, when the printer is being serviced. However, you might still want to line up print jobs ready to go when the printer is fixed. If you click Off the Print spooled output while I work button, then all documents that you print are held on disk until you click the button back on. You can use this feature for such situations as holding up printing until you go to lunch.

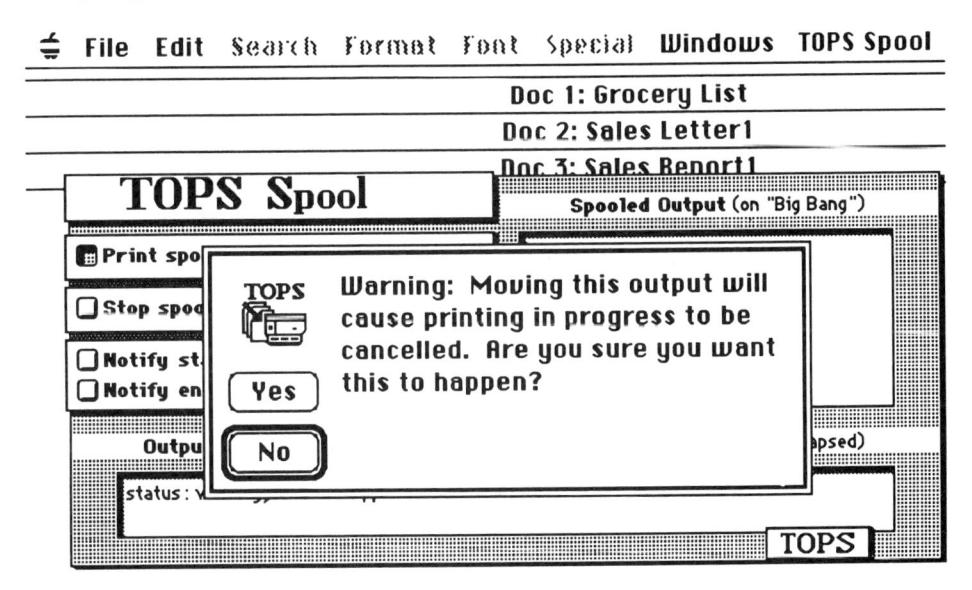

Fig. 7-14. Cancelling current print job.

Sometimes you might want to print in the old-fashioned way, before you installed TOPS Spool. You can print without TOPS Spool by clicking Off the Print spooled output while I work button and clicking On the Stop spooling button. Your printing operations will function just as they did before you installed TOPS Spool.

Other TOPS Spool Techniques

When several users are sharing a printer, the print output tray can quickly fill up with documents from several different users. TOPS Spool gives you the option of sending a cover page with each print job. When you click On the Cover page button you get a sheet of paper printed after every print job that carries the name of the user, the name of the document being printed, along with the day, date, and time at which the document started printing. The information is centered and appears as follows:

Fred
Sales Report
Saturday, April 1, 1990, 1:45 PM

Some programs, such as MacWrite, which do not use the normal print channels in the Macintosh operating system, are not able to give the name of the document to TOPS Spool and so this area on the cover page is blank.

The ability to print a cover page means that whoever passes out documents from the network printer does not have to guess who gets what.

Another pair of features that can assist network administration tasks are Notify start of printing and Notify end of printing. When selected, these options give on-screen message boxes like the one seen in Fig. 7-15.

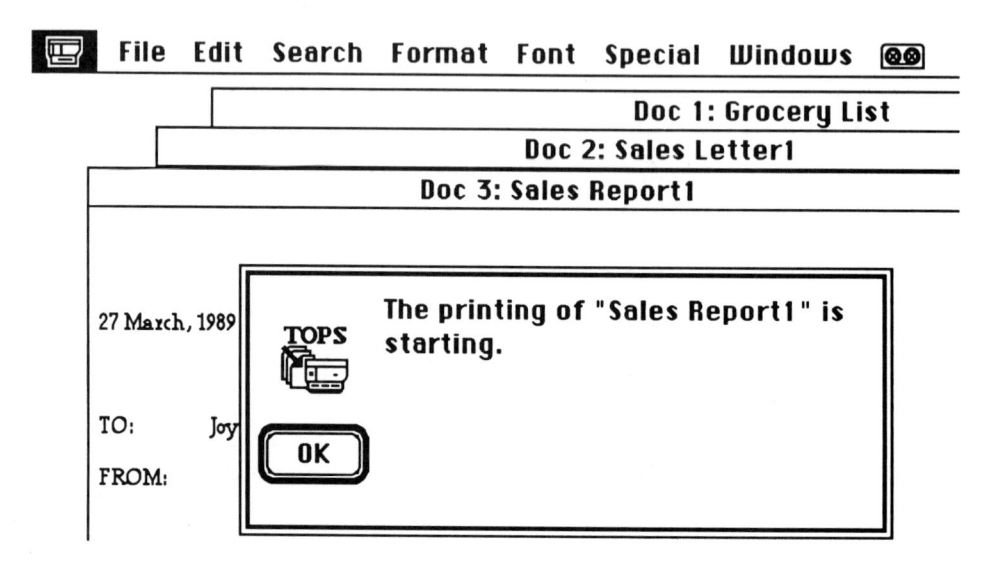

Fig. 7-15. Start printing message.

You can press Enter or click OK when these messages appear, or they will go away by themselves after about ten seconds. The idea is to inform you of the progress of print tasks, particularly when sharing a printer. For the user who has the luxury of unshared access to a printer, these options are not needed.

TOPS Spool Difficulties

If you followed the steps in the manual for installing and using TOPS Spool but encounter problems in getting printed results, there are several areas you might check to diagnose the problem. The first step is to pick TOPS from the DA menu and pick Prep Laser from the TOPS Spool menu item. The Ready light on the LaserWriter should flash on and off several times. If it does not, then you are not communicating with the printer. You will need to check network connectors to make sure the printer is actually connected.

Another area to check is the Chooser. Check that AppleTalk is active, make sure that you have selected the LaserWriter you want to print to, and make sure that background printing is turned off. Beyond this you should check for the following problems.

Installation problems. TOPS Spool cannot be installed if all of your Desk Accessory slots are full. If you have problems completing the installation, try removing one or two DAs with Font DA/Mover and then reattempting the TOPS Spool installation. Remember to use the Special Restart command before trying to use a newly installed TOPS Spool. Make sure that Spool and Spool Installer are in the System folder before running Spool Installer. Do not try to install TOPS Spool with Suitcase 1.0 installed.

Nothing prints. Either the TOPS Spool option to Stop spooling has been turned on, or you might have lost the drive that was being used for spooling (either by ejection or dismounting). Try using a local drive for spooling by using the Change Disk option on the TOPS Spool menu. Other possibilities include corrupted System files. Try copying the documents LaserWriter and Laser Prep from a recent copy of the System Tools disk into your System folder and then reinstalling TOPS Spool.

Can't find TOPS Spool DA. If you know TOPS Spool was installed properly, make sure that you have not launched the current application from a volume on the network that has a System folder without TOPS Spool installed. Close the application and launch from the local drive.

CONCLUSION

By now you should have a pretty good handle on the terms and conditions of network printing. If you are a Macintosh user, you know what you need in order to print across the network. If you use a PC, you will be aware that there are several paths you can take to network printing. The details of these are discussed in the next chapter.

8
The DOS Side of Sharing Printers

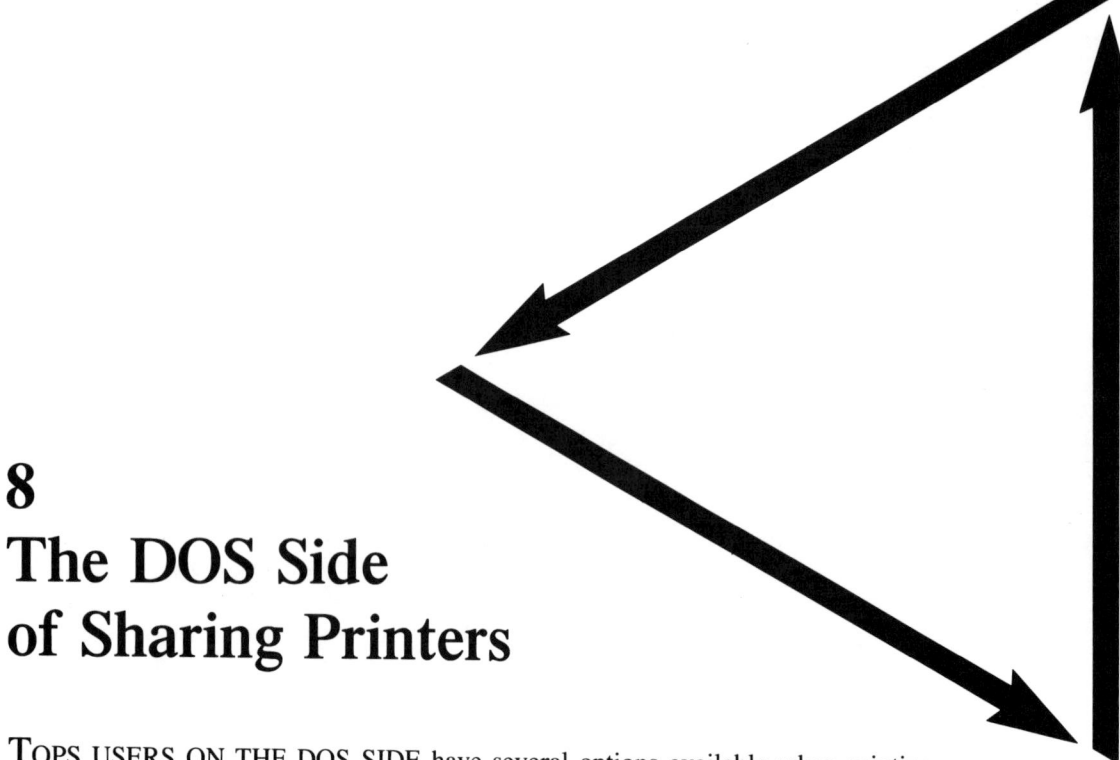

TOPS USERS ON THE DOS SIDE have several options available when printing on a network. TPRINT is a utility that allows some access to network printers from the DOS prompt, and TOPS NetPrint provides network printing directly from an application. NetPrint generates PostScript output and so can be used as a PC-to-LaserWriter connection as well as part of a TOPS network. These options are discussed in this chapter, beginning with a look at the printers you might encounter on a TOPS network and how they are classified.

POSSIBLE PRINTERS

An environment with a mixture of Macintosh and MS-DOS computers can have several kinds of printers. Some may be for Macintosh use only, some for PC use only, and some can be shared by both. The following sections explains some of these options.

Macintosh Printers

The printers that the Macintosh typically uses are either dot matrix ImageWriters or a laser printing LaserWriters. There might be other brands in use with Macs in your office, but these are usually compatible with either ImageWriters or LaserWriters. ImageWriters are usually attached locally to a single Macintosh. An option card can be purchased for the ImageWriter, however, that allows it to become a station on the network, and that way all the Macintoshes on the network can share it. The Laserwriter on the other hand, comes with this network capability built in. Printers such as the Apple LaserWriter and compatibles that have a network connection can also be used by the MS-DOS computers on a TOPS network.

The PCs print to these network printers in two ways. One way is through the TOPS software called NetPrint (explained later in the chapter). NetPrint is a memory resident print redirector. If memory limitations do not allow NetPrint's use, a nonresident utility called TPRINT.EXE can send print files from the DOS line. Thus both Macs and MS-DOS computers can share the kinds of printers that support network connections.

Parallel Printers

Another type of printer used in the MS-DOS world is the parallel or serial printer. This would include models such as the Epson FX and LQs, Hewlett Packard LaserJets, IBM models, and many others. These printers usually do not have the option of being put directly on the network. Instead, they must be attached locally to a single PC. They can be shared using TOPS, but only if the PC to which the printer is directly attached publishes the printer so that others can mount it. Note that Macintoshes cannot mount PC printers, nor can PC users mount Macintosh printers. The publishing and mounting of printers is a DOS-only feature. Macintoshes only share printers attached directly to the network.

While it is possible to connect an Apple LaserWriter serially to a PC and then to publish it, in practice this makes little sense, because the serial connection would limit the printer speed to 9600 baud, compared to a network speed of 230,000 baud for an AppleTalk network and 770,000 baud for FlashTalk. Another negative about the serial connection is that it would prevent the Macintoshes from sharing it. Using the network connection (labeled AppleTalk on the Apple LaserWriter) is the most efficient way to do it.

PUBLISHING AND MOUNTING PRINTERS

To become a printer server with TOPS means that you make a printer that is locally attached to your PC available to the network. When a client mounts a remote printer, it can be used just as if it were actually attached locally. This is because TOPS redirects print commands over the network to the printer server whenever the user of the client computer gives a print command from within an application program (or from DOS).

Printer Publishing

The printer publishing concept is the same as that for publishing disk volumes. So when entering TOPS menu, the user would choose Server Utilities. The TOPSPRTR software program must be run in order to publish a printer. When this software is not running, the printer publishing choices do not appear in the Server Utilities menu, as seen on the left of Fig. 8-1. When TOPSPRTR is running, the menu screen will appear as it does on the right-hand side of Fig. 8-1.

Chapter 8

```
┌─────────────────────────────────────────────────────────────┐
│ Tower              TOPS : Server Utilities  Server Utilities│
├─────────────────────────────────────────────────────────────┤
│ Server Utilities Menu                                       │
│   Publish a Volume to allow network access.  Publish a Volume│
│   You will be prompted for the full          Volumes Published│
│   pathname.  You must choose an              File Clients   │
│   alias, mode and password.                  Hide Name      │
│                                                             │
└─────────────────────────────────────────────────────────────┘


┌─────────────────────────────────────────────────────────────┐
│ MENU INSTRUCTIONS                                           │
│   Select a Command using the space bar, up arrow, down arrow or first│
│     letter of the Command.                                  │
│   <ENTER>- Invoke a selected command.                       │
│                                                             │
│   <ESCAPE>- Return to the previous window.   <CNTRL-Q>- Exit to DOS.│
└─────────────────────────────────────────────────────────────┘
```

```
┌─────────────────────────────────────────────────────────────┐
│ Tower              TOPS : Server Utilities  Server Utilities│
├─────────────────────────────────────────────────────────────┤
│ Server Utilities Menu                                       │
│   Publish a Volume to allow network access.  Publish a Volume│
│   You will be prompted for the full          Volumes Published│
│   pathname.  You must choose an              File Clients   │
│   alias, mode and password.                  Hide Name      │
│                                              Publish a Printer│
│                                              List Published Printer│
│                                              My Printer Clients│
└─────────────────────────────────────────────────────────────┘


┌─────────────────────────────────────────────────────────────┐
│ MENU INSTRUCTIONS                                           │
│   Select a Command using the space bar, up arrow, down arrow or first│
│     letter of the Command.                                  │
│   <ENTER>- Invoke a selected command.                       │
│                                                             │
│   <ESCAPE>- Return to the previous window.   <CNTRL-Q>- Exit to DOS.│
└─────────────────────────────────────────────────────────────┘
```

Fig. 8-1. The two versions of Server Utilities.

While MS-DOS generally allows for three parallel printers to be hooked up to any one PC, you are limited to publishing only one of these printers with TOPS. As mentioned earlier, the ports that the printers are attached to are called LPT1, LPT2, and LPT3. When the command is given to publish a printer, you will be required to say which LPT the printer being published is attached to, as in Fig. 8-2.

If you only have one printer on the computer, it is probably a safe bet to assume that it is attached to LPT1. If you have two printers, and you are not sure which is attached to LPT1 and which to LPT2, you can find out by tapping the Print Screen key (usually abbreviated PrtSc). The printer that responds is LPT1.

As with disk volumes, printers must be given aliases as they are published. It is not very descriptive if the network sees a published printer simply as LPT1. If however, the printer was published as HP Laserjet, or Tower LJet II, as in Fig. 8-3, there is little question as to what the device is.

The final task of printer publishing is to specify a spool directory, the disk space where print jobs are spooled. A spooled print job is one that is temporarily stored while waiting for the printer. This spooling is necessary because if a printer has more than one user it is quite likely that at some point the printer will be busy with one user's job when a second user tries to print. To alleviate the traffic jams, the printer server is going to spool (temporarily store) the job, so that the user doesn't need to sit and wait until the printer is actually free.

In spooling, TOPS actually creates a file that exists only for the duration of the job, and the spool directory is where the file is stored. When the print job finishes, the file is automatically deleted. This could be any existing subdirectory, or a special directory created specifically for spooled files. The directory must already exist

```
┌─────────────────────────────────────────────────────────────────────────┐
│ Tower                          TOPS : Server Utilities    Publish a Printer │
├─────────────────────────────────────────────────────────────────────────┤
│ Publish a Printer                                                       │
│                                                                         │
│     Printer:                                                            │
│                                                                         │
│                    ┌──────────────────────────────────────┐             │
│                    │ Choose printer port to Publish:      │             │
│                    │                                      │             │
│                    │     LPT1 (PRN)                       │             │
│                    │     LPT2                             │             │
│                    │     LPT3                             │             │
│                    └──────────────────────────────────────┘             │
├─────────────────────────────────────────────────────────────────────────┤
│ MENU INSTRUCTIONS                                                       │
│   Select a Printer using the space bar, up arrow, down arrow or first   │
│     letter of the Printer.                                              │
│                                                                         │
│   <ENTER>- Choose a Printer Port.                                       │
│   <ESCAPE>- Return to the previous window.    <CNTRL-Q>- Exit to DOS.   │
└─────────────────────────────────────────────────────────────────────────┘
```

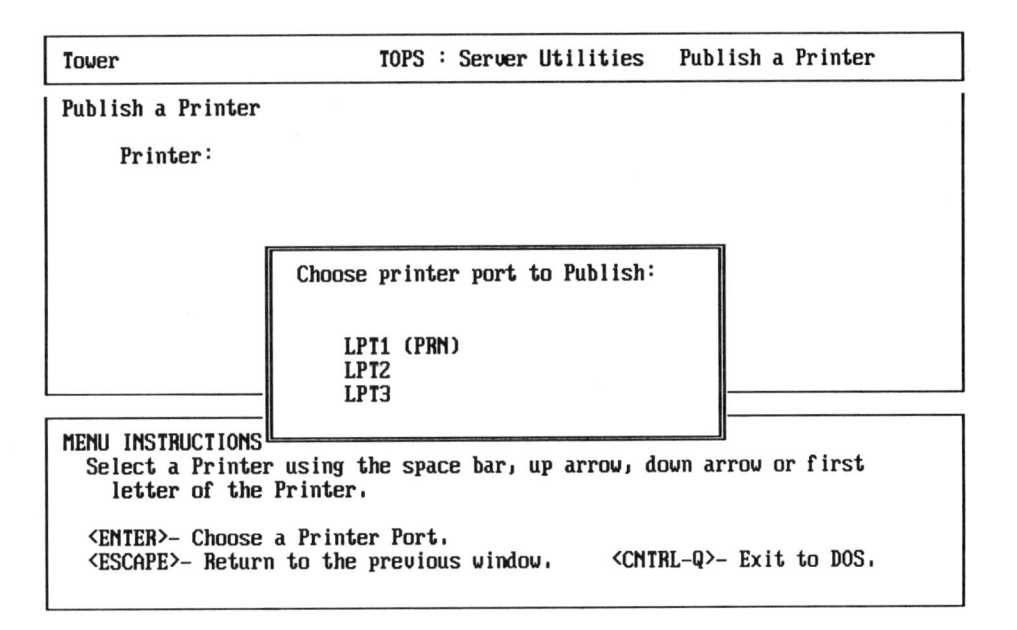

Fig. 8-2. Publishing a printer.

```
┌─────────────────────────────────────────────────────────────────────────┐
│ Tower                          TOPS : Server Utilities   Publish a Printer │
├─────────────────────────────────────────────────────────────────────────┤
│ Publish a Printer                                                       │
│                                                                         │
│     Printer:      LPT1 (PRN)                                            │
│     Alias:        Tower LJet II                                         │
│                                                                         │
│                                                                         │
│                                                                         │
│                                                                         │
│                                                                         │
├─────────────────────────────────────────────────────────────────────────┤
│ MENU INSTRUCTIONS                                                       │
│   Type each item as requested and press <ENTER>:                        │
│     1-16 character alias by which you want this Printer known on the network. │
│     0-31 character password with which you wish to secure access.       │
│     Full Pathname to the spool directory you must designate.            │
│   <ESCAPE>- Start over.                       <CNTRL-Q>- Exit to DOS.   │
└─────────────────────────────────────────────────────────────────────────┘
```

Fig. 8-3. Naming the printer.

if you are naming it as the spool directory. If it doesn't, TOPS returns the error message Directory is not a valid path.

When many jobs stack up waiting for the printer, a line (called a *queue*) forms and the jobs are finished on a first-come/first-serve basis. The queue can be managed through the use of the TOPS command language. The details are discussed in the later section of this chapter entitled "Managing the Print Queue."

Publishing Serial Printers

Serial printers can be published as well as parallel printers. However, if the printer is serial, then the printer is no doubt hooked to a COM port rather than an LPT port. Although TOPSPRTR does not allow you to specify a COM port for the printer you publish, MS-DOS allows you to substitute the name of an LPT port in place of a COM port by using the MODE command.

If you are already using the serial printer locally, you will probably recognize the MODE command in the form:

    MODE COM1:96,8,1,N

This command initializes or prepares the first COM port to communicate at 9600 baud, with a word length of 8, 1 stop bit, and no parity. These numbers are parameters that DOS needs to know in order to successfully use the COM port. Check your system or printer manual for the correct baud rate, word length, stop bits, and parity when setting up a serial printer.

To publish a serial printer, you use an additional MODE command before starting the TOPS menu. Give the following command at the DOS prompt:

MODE LPT #: = COM#

A typical command might be:

MODE LPT2: = COM1

The result is that what DOS formerly referred to as COM1 is now referred to as LPT2. So having renamed your COM1 port to LPT2 port, you can publish the serial printer as LPT2.

Mounting Printers from the TOPS Menu

Mounting a printer is a client function. Begin by selecting Client Utilities on the opening TOPS menu screen. Choose Printer Servers on the submenu to see the list of stations with published printers.

When you select one of these printers to mount, you need to specify what LPT port you are mounting it as. The LPT port that you mount as does not have to be the same as the LPT port the server published. If you don't have a local printer of your own, the best mounting choice is probably LPT1. But if you already have a printer of your own attached to LPT1, then you would choose LPT2, as seen in Fig. 8-4.

Note that if you are going to print screens to a mounted printer, it works only if you mount the printer as LPT1. This restriction is part of DOS and not something that TOPS can change.

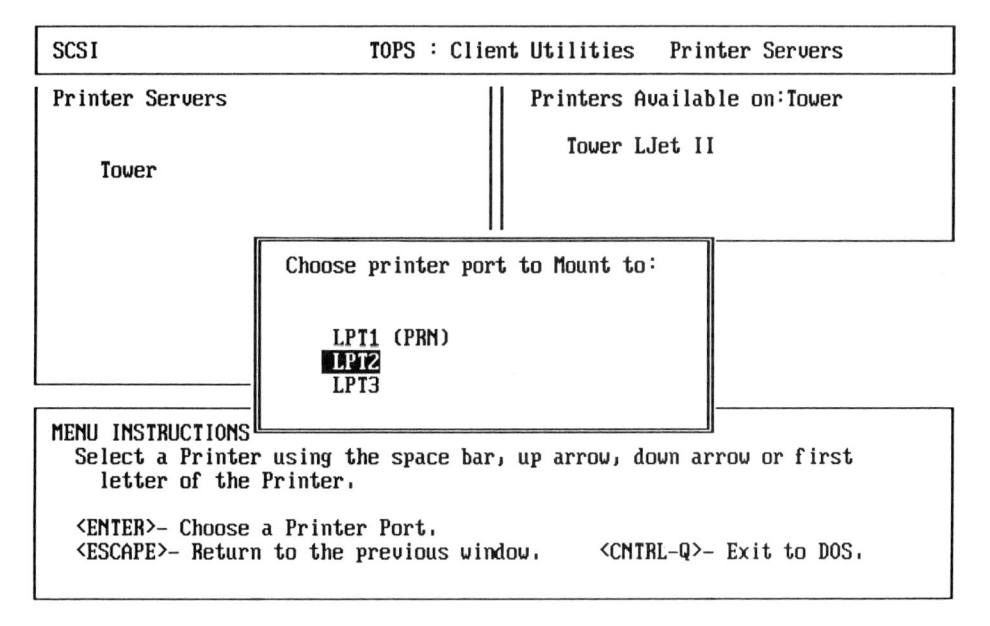

```
┌─────────────────────────────────────────────────────────────────┐
│ SCSI                      TOPS : Client Utilities   Printer Servers │
│ Printer Servers                  Printers Available on:Tower      │
│                                       Tower LJet II               │
│     Tower                                                         │
│                                                                   │
│              ┌──────────────────────────────────┐                 │
│              │ Choose printer port to Mount to: │                 │
│              │                                  │                 │
│              │          LPT1 (PRN)              │                 │
│              │          ▌LPT2▐                  │                 │
│              │          LPT3                    │                 │
│              └──────────────────────────────────┘                 │
│ MENU INSTRUCTIONS                                                 │
│   Select a Printer using the space bar, up arrow, down arrow or first │
│     letter of the Printer.                                        │
│                                                                   │
│   <ENTER>- Choose a Printer Port.                                 │
│   <ESCAPE>- Return to the previous window.    <CNTRL-Q>- Exit to DOS. │
└─────────────────────────────────────────────────────────────────┘
```

Fig. 8-4. Mounting a printer.

Upon mounting a printer, TOPS redirects all print requests sent to the port specified in the mount, over the network to the server. In other words, if you mounted a printer as LPT2, then whenever you direct printing to LPT2 (whether through an application or from the DOS line), TOPS will steer the print job to the server.

Using Mounted Printers

Printing from within applications is the easiest technique for printing to a mounted printer. All you have to do is set up your application program for the correct printer port and type of printer. Then you can print in the normal way from within your application. The print job is sent to the computer with the remote printer where it waits in a queue until the printer is free. There might be a slight delay before actual printing begins because TOPS waits for approximately 30 seconds before printing.

To use the remote printer, you probably will want to configure the application program that will print to that printer. This means changing the default settings, the configuration file, or some similar procedure which varies from program to program. The exact commands differ between applications. Essentially you need to tell the application to use the appropriate LPT port, as well as the correct printer type. For example, if you mount an HP Laserjet as LPT1, then configure your application programs to use an HP Laserjet on LPT1. If you mount the printer as LPT2, then naturally you would do the same for LPT2. If you will vary your jobs, printing some to a locally attached printer at LPT1 and others to a remote printer mounted as LPT2, then you will have to change your application programs back and forth appropriately.

Printing Screens on a Remote Printer

TOPS does not interfere with your ability to do a screen dump to a printer. You can do a print screen on a remote printer using the normal PrtSc key on your PC's keyboard and the screen will normally print on the printer to which you have redirected your LPT1: port. The exceptions to this statement come from the limitations of DOS and not TOPS. As you might know, DOS does not support screen dumps from some graphics cards, and from some software such as Windows, screen dumps are somewhat difficult to get. This situation is not affected one way or the other by TOPS.

USING TPRINT

An alternative to printing from within an application is to first store the file to be printed and then send it to the printer from outside the application. TOPS/DOS allows you to do this with a TOPS utility called TPRINT.EXE. This program, which is supplied with TOPS/DOS, differs from the NetPrint program described later, in the following respects:

1. TPRINT, like NetPrint, also directs output out of the network interface card, but TPRINT is not RAM-resident. It will not remain in memory. It also will not spool print jobs.
2. TPRINT does not work from within the application program you are using. To use TPRINT, you must either exit the application or use a DOS shell from within the application if it has such a shell feature.
3. TPRINT allows you to send either PostScript print files or ASCII (text) print files from the DOS line. These are usually created from within your application by telling the application to print to a file. Note that ASCII file printing is not supported on some network laser printer models.

Because TPRINT is intended as a replacement for the PRINT command supplied with DOS, you might want to replace your PRINT.COM file with the TPRINT.EXE supplied with TOPS. This will prevent you from accidentally using the DOS PRINT program when you intended to use TPRINT. Instead of removing PRINT.COM, which you might need again at some point, you can rename it DOS-PRINT.COM. Note that some applications call the PRINT command when executing, in which case you might have to keep it around or alter the program to work with TPRINT.

Using TPRINT To Print to a Network Printer

The use of TPRINT is relatively straightforward. Basically, what you need to specify is the path and name of the file. Suppose you want to send a PostScript print file called CHARTDAT.EPS from the \DATA subdirectory of the QUATTRO directory, to a LaserWriter. The command can be given as:

TPRINT /X C:\QUATTRO\DATA\CHARTDAT.EPS

TPRINT finds the first available LaserWriter in the local zone of the network, feeds it the CHARTDAT.EPS file, and assumes that the file is PostScript. The /X signifies that you are printing to a network printer.

Several optional "switches" can be applied to the TPRINT command to indicate, for example, whether the file to be printed is a PostScript or plain text file. The full syntax of TPRINT for network printing is listed in Table 8-1.

The /D instruction can be used with LaserWriter models prior to the Series II. The D stands for Diablo emulation mode, a print mode on the earlier LaserWriters that can be set by software. This mode is used to print non-PostScript information, for example, if you need to print a file that is not PostScript but is plain text.

Note that many of the options in Table 8-1 can be skipped. For example, the device name can be left out if the network only has one network printer, or you are not picky about which network printer the output prints from.

The TPRINT process can be further enhanced by creating a configuration file for TPRINT. This file, called TPRINT.DAT, would be an ASCII file containing the device name and the desired options. All you would need to type then would be

Table 8-1. Syntax of the TPRINT command.

/X	Print to a network printer, as opposed to the local printer.
device name/N	The name of the device to which you want to print. Names with spaces in must be enclosed by quotes, including the /N, as in "Fred's Laser/N" with no space between name and /N.
device type/Y	The type of device you want to print to (TPRINT will assume it is a LaserWriter if you do not specify type.
zone/Z	Location of the printer if it is not in the local zone, only required when printing to a device outside the current zone.
/D	Invokes Diablo 630 emulation on a PostScript printer such as Apple LaserWriter.
filename	The name of the file to be printed, including path if not in current directory. Multiple files can be sent if separated by a comma and a space, as in
	TPRINT /X "Fred's Laser/N" C: \WP\LET1.TXT, C: \WS\MY.DOC
/S	Shows status of a printer on the network (omit filename when using /S). For example:
	TPRINT "Fred's Laser/N" "Sales Office/Z" /S
	will return the following if the printer is busy:
	Fred's Laser:LaserWriter@Sales Office reports: status: busy

Use TPRINT without the device name to list names of printers on the network:

- ☐ To list all devices in the current zone of a specific type use TPRINT with the device type argument.
- ☐ To list all devices in the current zone regardless of type use TPRINT followed by an equals sign.
- ☐ To list all devices in a specific zone use TPRINT with a zone argument, as in TPRINT "Sales Office/Z" = to list all printers in the Sales Office zone.

TPRINT and the filename (see the section later in this chapter for more on how to set up a TPRINT.DAT file).

Using TPRINT To Print to a Published Remote Printer

You can use the TPRINT command to send output from one PC to a printer that is attached to another PC. This is referred to as printing to a remote printer. Of course, you must mount the remote printer first, using either TOPSMENU or a TOPS command from the DOS command line. In this role TPRINT is simply an alternative to printing from within an application.

The TPRINT syntax for printing to a remote published printer is

TPRINT /R LPT#: d:\path\filename1, d:\path\filename2

where /R specifies that the printer is remote, and LPT# is the port you mounted the printer as. For example, the following command sends two letters to be printed on a remote printer mounted to LPT3:

TPRINT /R LPT3: D:\WP\SALES1.LET, D:\WP\QUERY.LET

If you do not include an LPT#, TPRINT uses the printer you have assigned to LPT1. Three options can be used instead of a filename. /Q displays the queue on the remote device; /S displays the status of the printer; /T deletes all of *your* print jobs from the remote printer queue. To delete a specific file from the print queue you issue a print command with the filename followed by /C. These commands are described in more detail in the next section.

Managing the Print Queue with TPRINT

TPRINT can be used to list or delete documents that are in the print queue of published printers. The queue, as you recall, will reside on the server. As a client, you can list or delete only your documents from the queue. The server, on the other hand, can delete any document from the queue.

To list the queue, and see the names of the documents, the command is:

TPRINT /R LPT#: /Q

In Fig. 8-5, you can see an example of how the queue list would look. In this example, C:\MARTY was the spool directory specified upon publishing.

To delete a specific document from the queue, the command would be:

TPRINT /R LPT#: /C d:\path\filename

To delete all of your documents from the queue the command is:

TPRINT /R LPT#: /T

```
C:\123R3>tprint /r lpt2: /q
Network print utility for TOPS/DOS version 2
Copyright (C) Sun Microsystems, Inc. 1988. All rights reserved.
TPRINT.EXE     Version 2.10  10/17/88

Type TPRINT /? for help.

No Background Print Queue installed.

Queue entries for printer 'Tower LJet II' on 'Tower':

        Jobid    Client                      Jobsize    Status
        -----    ------                      -------    -------
            1    SCSI                           1872    Printing

C:\123R3>
```

Fig. 8-5. Print queue displayed.

Looking at Network Printers with TPRINT

You can check the availability of network printers by using some of TPRINT's options. For example, to display a list of all of the LaserWriters in the zone called Sales, you would enter:

TPRINT Sales/Z /N

To see if there are any ImageWriters in the local zone, you would enter:

TPRINT ImageWriter/Y

To see all printers of all types in the local zone enter:

TPRINT /Y

To check the status of printers (busy or idle), use the /S option. Thus, to check the status of the LaserWriter called Bill's Laser in the local zone use:

TPRINT "Bill's Laser/N" /S

You will get back a message on screen as to the current status. In Fig. 8-6 you can see an example of these commands and the response from TPRINT.

Your Local Printer and TPRINT

The simplest way to print to your local printer is to specify its port in your applications. However, you can use TPRINT to do local printing but you must first

```
Network print utility for TOPS/DOS version 2
Copyright (C) Sun Microsystems, Inc. 1988. All rights reserved.
TPRINT.EXE      Version 2.10  10/17/88

Type TPRINT /? for help.

There is a (2F) background print queue installed.

--------------------------------------------------------
Looking for all net devices of type "LaserWriter"...
These are the types of devices in the local zone.

LaserWriter
FileMaker 4.0
Top2Server
Top2Station
Top2Serial

Hit any key to continue...

--------------------------------------------------------

The Background Print Queue is Empty

♦ Sat  6-16-1990 C:\>
```

Fig. 8-6. Status reports.

load INITPRIN.EXE. This program, included on your TOPS disk, allows you to queue up files to be printed locally while you are working on other tasks. It should be loaded after you load TOPS, but before you run TPRINT.EXE. However, if you have already published a printer and have the TOPSPRTR module loaded, you do not need to load INITPRIN to take advantage of this feature.

To load INITPRIN program for printing to a local printer on LPT1, just type INITPRIN LPT1: at the DOS prompt and press Enter (change the LPT number if your circumstances are different). The program will verify that there is an active device LPT1. If a printer is on-line, INITPRIN displays the following message on the screen:

Name of Print device: LPT1.

Unless you specify otherwise, INITPRIN assumes you want to print to the LPT1 port.

Once INITPRIN has been loaded successfully, you can use TPRINT to queue up a file or list of files for printing and for managing the queue. The commands are the same as for remote printing with TPRINT, except that /P is used instead of /R. For example, the command

TPRINT /P C:\WP\DOCS\REPORT.STC

sends the document REPORT.STC to the local printer. The command

TPRINT /P /Q

displays a list if all the print jobs in the local print queue.

Saving Your TPRINT Settings

If you find that you are making extensive use of TPRINT you can establish predefined settings for it. This avoids the need to remember all the rules and syntax each time you want to print a file. By creating a file on your disk called TPRINT.DAT and putting TPRINT commands in it, you instruct TPRINT to use those settings. Each time TPRINT runs, it looks for this file; if it does not find it, the default settings are used. As with the TOPSKRNL.DAT, you must edit your TPRINT.DAT file using EDLIN or a word processor, text editor, or utility that creates true ASCII files (for example the Sidekick Notepad, PC-Write, WordStar in nondocument mode or WordPerfect with DOS Text Save).

Suppose that you normally use TPRINT to send files to the LaserWriter called Pete's Laser in a zone of the network called The O Zone. A typical command might be:

TPRINT /X "Pete's Laser" "The O Zone/Z" CHARTFUN.EPS

A TPRINT.DAT file for your use might contain the following:

/X "Pete's Laser" "The O Zone/Z"

Then you can enter:

```
TPRINT CHARTFUN.EPS
```

TPRINT will send a file named CHARTFUN.EPS to a network LaserWriter called Pete's Laser in The O Zone. You can see how a TPRINT.DAT file can cut down on the typing it takes to use TPRINT.

Note that the file TPRINT.DAT must be located in the subdirectory from which you print. Therefore, if you commonly print from multiple subdirectories, each subdirectory should have its own TPRINT.DAT file. The plus side of this requirement is that each TPRINT.DAT file can have different settings.

PRINTING WITH TOPS NETPRINT

When a printer has an AppleTalk or FlashTalk connection, it can be hooked directly onto the network and shared by any TOPS station, whether an IBM PC or Macintosh. NetPrint, which is another RAM-resident TOPS program, is the tool for allowing PCs to print to a network printer. NetPrint can be loaded along with TOPS, or by itself. TOPS is not required to be running for NetPrint to work, although the interface card drivers (PSTACK with either ALAP or ELAP) are necessary.

NetPrint works by emulating one of the computer's LPT ports and performs the following services, depending on how you configure it:

1. NetPrint works in the background to spool and redirect output from an application which is set for PostScript printing to an LPT port, out the network interface card to a PostScript, networked LaserWriter. It can also redirect output to a non-PostScript printer on the network.

2. NetPrint translates generic output from applications that have no PostScript driver into PostScript before redirecting to the PostScript printer. This requires loading of an additional translating program.

Getting Started with NetPrint

Like other TOPS software, NetPrint comes with a program Setup that takes care of basic software installation. Follow the instructions in the manual, and Setup will copy the necessary files to your hard drive. You can install NetPrint in the same directory as TOPS/DOS. You can install onto floppy disks as well, just by copying all of the files to either a boot disk or a plain formatted disk. The total size of the minimum NetPrint files needed to run the program is 39K. This requirement is in addition to the 45K required by ALAP and PSTACK which must be run before NetPrint can be used. This means you will have a hard time getting NetPrint on the same boot disk as TOPS/DOS if you have 360K floppies. However, if you have 720K or larger disks, you can probably combine NetPrint with TOPS/DOS on a boot disk, depending on what features you want to use. The minimum files required to run NetPrint are:

ALAP.EXE (AppleTalk driver program)
PSTACK.EXE (AppleTalk driver program)
PAPOVL.EXE (print overlay for AppleTalk)
KEYINT.EXE (serial number control)
NETPRINT.EXE (the NetPrint program)
NETPRINT.DAT (the NetPrint configuration file)

Remember, you do not have to run all of TOPS/DOS before loading NetPrint if you only want to use NetPrint. For example, suppose you have turned on your PC and have not yet loaded TOPS. You would enter the following commands at the DOS prompt to run just NetPrint:

ALAP   then Enter   (initializes AppleTalk)
PSTACK   then Enter   (controls AppleTalk command stack)
NETPRINT   then Enter   (loads the NetPrint program)

The program NETPRINT.EXE calls the programs KEYINT.EXE and PAPOVL.EXE automatically. In Table 8-2, you can see a list of the NetPrint files and their uses.

Table 8-2. NetPrint files and their uses.

Filename	Purpose
NETPRINT.EXE	Main program.
NETPRINT.DAT	Configuration information file.
PRINT.EXE	Substitute for DOS file PRINT.COM.
KEYINT.EXE	Must remain in the NetPrint directory.
CONFIGUR.EXE	Configuration program.
TWINDOVL.EXE	Manages the menus.
PAPOVL.EXE	Must remain in the NetPrint directory.
FXPS.EXE	Epson to PostScript conversion.
FXPS.DAT	Configuration information file for the Epson to PostScript conversion.
PROPS.EXE	Proprinter to PostScript conversion.
PROPS.DAT	Configuration information file for the Proprinter to PostScript conversion.
PCSCREEN.FS	Fast PC screen font file.
PCSCREEN.SL	Slow PC screen font file.
EPSON.BAT	Sample batch file to run NetPrint with Epson to PostScript conversion.
PROPRINT.BAT	Sample batch file to run NetPrint with Proprinter to PostScript conversion.
REPORTQ.EXE	Reports on status of print queue.
BATS <DIR>	A subdirectory of sample batch files for popular word processors.

Note that some versions of NetPrint are not aware that TOPS/DOS no longer needs the ATALK.SYS driver in the CONFIG.SYS file. If you are using TOPS/DOS 2.1 check whether NetPrint's Setup program has placed the line

   DEVICE=ATALK.SYS

in the file CONFIG.SYS. If the line is there, you can remove it. See Chapter 9 for more on editing SYS and BAT files.

Like TOPS/DOS and TOPS/Macintosh, TOPS NetPrint is serialized. This means that you need to buy a copy for each station on the network. If you load two PCs from the same copy of NetPrint and they both attempt to run NetPrint, the second station will not load due to serial number conflict.

Using PRINT.EXE versus PRINT.COM

To provide command line access to the print queue that it creates, NetPrint comes with a utility called PRINT.EXE. This is intended as a substitute for PRINT.COM that comes with DOS. The TOPS program PRINT.EXE does all that PRINT.COM does and more, so in order to avoid confusion, you can disable PRINT.COM by either moving it off your system disk or renaming it. On a hard disk system, you will probably find PRINT.COM in the DOS directory. You could use the command

   RENAME PRINT.COM DOSPRINT.COM

to change the name of the program to DOSPRINT.COM. That way the program is available if you have to use it, but calls for a program called PRINT go to the PRINT.EXE file in the TOPS directory.

Configuring Your NetPrint Setup

Once you have the NetPrint files copied to your system, you will probably want to configure the program for your specific needs. The default configuration is shown in Table 8-3 which shows you what parameters can be altered. Use the program referred to as CONFIGURE (actually CONFIGUR.EXE) to alter the way TOPS NetPrint is set up on your PC. This program is a series of menus from which you pick the necessary options. The main areas are seen on the left of the Main Menu, shown in Fig. 8-7.

The options you pick are stored in a file called NETPRINT.DAT, a standard version of which is provided with the program. The most common use for TOPS NetPrint is sending the output from a word processing program to a LaserWriter on the network. Because most word processors support PostScript printers, this is the default configuration. In this configuration, TOPS NetPrint is used only for redirecting and print queueing.

The menu system follows the TOPS menu style with instructions and suggested keystrokes in the lower part of the screen. In many menus, you can see a list of possible answers by pressing the Right arrow key and then using the Spacebar to browse through a list of possibilities. When you leave the menu system, you can choose to save the changes to a configuration file (NETPRINT.DAT). If you already have NetPrint loaded, you have to decide whether to write the changes into the currently loaded version or not. If you choose not to save the settings in a file or write them to a current session, then you loose the changes and NetPrint continues

Table 8-3. NetPrint's default configuration with parameters.

Number of copies:	Can be from 1 to 63, with default of 1.
Queue size:	Maximum number of separate print jobs allowed in a queue, can be from 1 to 32, default of 12.
Wait time:	Number of seconds to wait before sending document to printer, can be from 0 to 1000 seconds, default of 20.
Store temp files:	Name of directory in which to store the temporary files generated by NetPrint (cannot exceed 50 characters for combined drive and path name.
Manual feed:	Either YES or NO, with NO as default. Use YES to generate a pause for inserting paper by hand. Setting has no effect if not using PostScript emulation.
Auto Form feed:	For the ImageWriter this sets top of form on next page after one page is complete. Normally set to YES.
NetPrint Port:	The printer port that NetPrint intercepts, typically LPT2 if you have a local printer on LPT1. Use LPT1 if you have no local printer, or if you want to print screens.
Default device:	Choices are LASERWRITER, IMAGEWRITER, LOCAL PRINTER, and NET DEVICE, with default being LaserWriter.
Device names:	Name of the device, default being = which is the first available LaserWriter. When using CONFIGURE program you can press Right arrow to see list of names. Press Spacebar to go through list, press Enter to select highlighted name.
Zones for devices:	Appears only if there is more than one zone. Press Right arrow to see list, press Spacebar to go through list, press Enter to select highlighted name.
Auto Translate:	For translating screen dumps set to YES
PCScreen font:	Set to YES to use the special screen font, which must be downloaded with the command PRINT PCSCREEN.FS/X
Conversion:	Convert printer output to PostScript. Set to NONE by default, which works with programs that can drive PostScript printers. The DIABLO option is rarely used. Set to POSTSCRIPT to translate from one of the emulated printers, Epson FX or Proprinter.

```
┌─────────────────────────────────────────────────────────────────┐
│     xt              NET PRINT CONFIGURATION         Main Menu   │
├─────────────────────────────────────────────────────────────────┤
│                                                                 │
│                                          ▌Setup▐                │
│       Set up NetPrint's communications module                   │
│       defaults; where to store files, which port   Device       │
│       to intercept, queue size, copies to print    Translate    │
│       and the like.                                Special      │
│                                                    Exit with Changes │
│                                                    Quit, no Changes  │
│                                                                 │
│                                                                 │
├─────────────────────────────────────────────────────────────────┤
│   MENU INSTRUCTIONS                                             │
│     Select an item using the first letter of the command,       │
│     the space bar or the up or down arrow.                      │
│                                                                 │
│     <ENTER>- Invoke the selected command.                       │
│                                                                 │
└─────────────────────────────────────────────────────────────────┘
```

Fig. 8-7. Main menu.

to work with the defaults. This allows you to explore the configuration process without upsetting anything.

When you run CONFIGUR from the DOS prompt in the disk/directory where you have stored NetPrint, the program (which is actually called CONFIGUR.EXE and can be run by typing CONFIGUR) reads the file NETPRINT.DAT. If you have not yet used the program, you are asked to provide a user name; this is used to identify your work in the print queue and appears in the top left of the CONFIGURE menu screens. If you have run the program before, you have the choice between modifying the current settings in the NETPRINT.DAT file or altering the settings for just the current session, without overwriting NETPRINT.DAT, as shown in Fig. 8-8.

In Fig. 8-9, you can see the Setup menu. This is where the most commonly used settings are stored.

The Number of copies is normally set to 1. The Queue size, measured in documents sent to print from the current station, can be reduced to save on memory space but less than six is probably too restrictive.

Depending on the speed of the PostScript driver that the application programs use, NetPrint's Wait time might need to be increased. The wait time is a setting that tells NetPrint to pause before assuming the end of a document and sending the job to the printer. TOPS NetPrint waits at the end of each print job for an amount of time you specify in the CONFIGURE program. This wait time is necessary because DOS does not place an end-of-file character at the end of print files. Therefore, there is no signal that the end of the file has been sent to TOPS NetPrint. The TOPS NetPrint wait setting assures that the complete data file has been sent.

```
                    NET PRINT CONFIGURATION

TOPS NetPrint for the PC, Copyright
(C) Sun Microsystems, Inc.
1986, 1987. All Rights Reserved.



        NetPrint is loaded and a configuration file exists.
        Type C to use defaults from the configuration file.
        Type B to use defaults from the background software.



MENU INSTRUCTIONS
    Type a single letter to answer the question.
```

Fig. 8-8. The current session question.

The default setting is 20 seconds. This means that TOPS NetPrint will wait 20 seconds before processing the file (translating it to PostScript when necessary and sending it to the LaserWriter). You should experiment with your particular situation to find the ideal time. Some applications might need several minutes of wait time for calculations made in the middle of printing jobs. However, if you have just

```
   xt                   NET PRINT CONFIGURATION          Setup
                           SETUP SETTINGS
        Number of copies (1 - 63):     ►1
        Queue size (1 - 32):           ►12
        Wait time (0 - 1000 seconds):  ►20
        Store temp files in Directory: ►c:\TOPS\
        Manual feed:                   ►NO       YES
        Auto Form feed for ImageWriter: ►NO      YES
        NetPrint Port:                 ►LPT1     LPT2     LPT3



   MENU INSTRUCTIONS
        <↓> or <SPACE>- Go to the next item.  <↑>- Previous item.
        <←> or <→> or <ENTER>- Change the setting of the current item.
        <F2>- Return this item to its default setting.
        <F10>- Exit using current settings.
        <HOME>- Return this screen to default settings.
        <ESCAPE>- Return to the previous window.  <CNTRL-Q>- Exit, make no changes.
```

Fig. 8-9. The setup settings.

printed a file from within an application, and you know that the application has finished sending it to TOPS NetPrint, you can speed up the operation by pressing PrtSc. This forces TOPS NetPrint to process the file before the wait time is completed. If the wait time is insufficient, it might prematurely assume the end of a document, a condition which results in incomplete printouts. In that case, increase the wait time.

The best place to store the temporary files used by NetPrint is probably the TOPS subdirectory, which is the default setting. You can use a remote volume that has been published by another user and then mounted by the current station, but this does increase network traffic considerably and can result in long wait periods for printing to complete.

The Manual feed and Auto Form feed settings refer to control of paper in the printer. If you are driving a PostScript printer with a PostScript-compatible program, the program controls paper feeding. If you are using an emulation mode to print then you might need to tell the printer to pause for paper insertion (Manual feed = YES). If you are printing to an ImageWriter, you will probably want to set Auto Form to Yes so that a new sheet of paper is automatically fed in at the end of each print job.

The NetPrint Port should be configured for LPT1, LPT2, or LPT3. Typically, LPT1 is fine if you have no other printer, but if you have a local printer, use LPT2 or LPT3. The PostScript conversion should be set to None if you are using application programs that have PostScript drivers, such as WordPerfect 5.0, or if the printer is non-PostScript. If the printer is non-PostScript, set the application for the proper printer driver on the proper printer port and NetPrint will do the rest.

Configuring NetPrint Devices

Normally, you do not need to change the device settings of NetPrint. The default setting is to print to the first LaserWriter on the network, a setting that is shown in Fig. 8-10.

Note that you can choose to print to a local printer, ImageWriter, or other network device. If you want to print to a specific printer that is named on the network, you must enter the name in the appropriate field, otherwise the = sign is used, which means print to the first device of the desired type. You can press Right arrow to see a list of named devices that are currently active on the network (printers must be turned on to be seen). For example, to print to a LaserWriter called xx you would first select LaserWriter as the Default device, then press Down arrow to move to the field called LaserWriter Name. Press Right arrow and a list of names appears, press the Spacebar to go through the list to highlight the name you want and then press Enter to select it. This saves problems with misspelled names.

For networks with more than one zone a further three options appear: Zone for LaserWriter, Zone for ImageWriter, Zone for Net Device. These are marked with an asterisk (*) if the devices are in the local zone. Otherwise the zone name must be

```
┌─────────────────────────────────────────────────────────────────────────┐
│  xt                         NET PRINT CONFIGURATION           Device    │
├─────────────────────────────────────────────────────────────────────────┤
│                          DEVICE SETTINGS                                │
│                                                                         │
│   Default device:              ▶LASERWRITER  IMAGEWRITER  LOCAL PRINTER │
│                                 NET DEVICE                              │
│   LaserWriter Name:            ▶LaserWriter II NT                       │
│   ImageWriter Name:            ▶=                                       │
│   Net Device Type:             ▶LaserWriter                             │
│   Net Device Name:             ▶=                                       │
│                                                                         │
│                                                                         │
│                                                                         │
│                                                                         │
├─────────────────────────────────────────────────────────────────────────┤
│   MENU INSTRUCTIONS                                                     │
│       <↓> or <SPACE>- Go to the next item.  <↑>- Previous item.         │
│       <←> or <→> or <ENTER>- Change the setting of the current item.    │
│       <F2>- Return this item to its default setting.                    │
│       <F10>- Exit using current settings.                               │
│       <HOME>- Return this screen to default settings.                   │
│       <ESCAPE>- Return to the previous window.  <CNTRL-Q>- Exit, make no changes. │
└─────────────────────────────────────────────────────────────────────────┘
```

Fig. 8-10. The device settings.

entered. Again, you can use the Right arrow for a list and the Spacebar to browse through it.

Configuring NetPrint Translation

If your application programs do not have any kind of PostScript drivers, then you can configure the application for an IBM Proprinter and configure NetPrint to do PostScript conversion. This is done at the Translation Setting menu, set up as seen in Fig. 8-11.

The Auto Translate Screen Dumps option is set to Yes as is the PCScreen font downloaded setting. The conversion setting is Postscript. Note that to do this conversion, you must load an additional background program called PROPS.EXE, which does the conversion to PostScript. To use the PCScreen font, you need to copy the file PCSCREEN.FS to the printer after NetPrint has been loaded. The following steps are thus required to run NetPrint with PostScript conversion and the PCScreen font:

```
ALAP
PSTACK
NETPRINT
PROPS
PRINT PCSCREEN.FS/X
```

Issue these commands one after another at the DOS prompt, or incorporate them into a batch file. Note that PROPS.EXE performs the conversion to PostScript from

```
┌─────────────────────────────────────────────────────────────────────────┐
│   xt                   NET PRINT CONFIGURATION            Translate     │
├─────────────────────────────────────────────────────────────────────────┤
│                          TRANSLATION SETTINGS                           │
│                                                                         │
│   Auto Translate Screen Dumps:      ►NO          YES                    │
│   PCScreen font downloaded:         ►NO          YES                    │
│   Conversion:                       ►NONE        DIABLO      POSTSCRIPT │
│                                                                         │
│                                                                         │
│                                                                         │
│                                                                         │
│                                                                         │
├─────────────────────────────────────────────────────────────────────────┤
│   MENU INSTRUCTIONS                                                     │
│       <↓> or <SPACE>- Go to the next item.  <↑>- Previous item.         │
│       <←> or <→> or <ENTER>- Change the setting of the current item.    │
│       <F2>- Return this item to its default setting.                    │
│       <F10>- Exit using current settings.                               │
│       <HOME>- Return this screen to default settings.                   │
│       <ESCAPE>- Return to the previous window.  <CNTRL-Q>- Exit, make no changes. │
└─────────────────────────────────────────────────────────────────────────┘
```

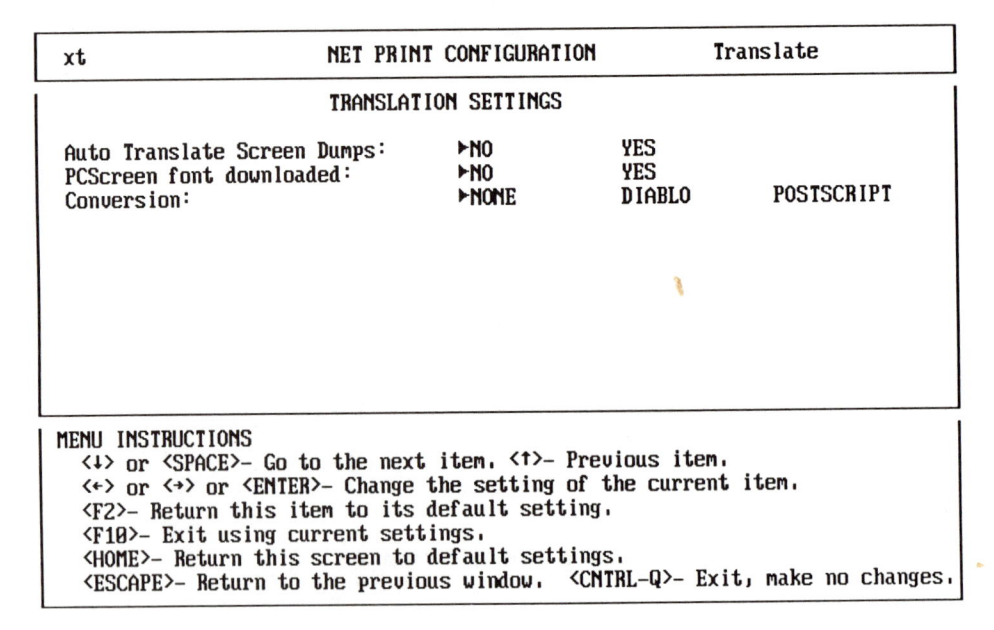

Fig. 8-11. Translation settings.

IBM Proprinter, a model that most applications support. If an application does not support the Proprinter, then substitute the program FXPS which emulates the Epson model FX-80. You also have a choice when it comes to the PCScreen fonts. The file PSCREEN.FS is a fast font, said to look rougher than the slow font PCSCREEN.SL. We suggest you use the FS version unless you find the output to be too coarse.

If you do not need PostScript conversion, for example, if you are using Word-Perfect and have selected the Apple LaserWriter printer, the settings in Fig. 8-11 would be NO, NO, and NONE. You cannot have NetPrint do screen dumps on the LaserWriter while it is not set up for PostScript conversions for application output. However, you can use such screen print utilities as Inset to print screens to the LaserWriter.

When you pick POSTSCRIPT as the conversion setting, then you will need to review the secondary menu seen in Fig. 8-12 that provides details of the translation process.

The default settings that are shown will probably fit most needs. A single plain font in 12 point size is used. The font is a Courier style that is similar to the PC screen display font. The ability to use additional fonts, described later in this chapter, is activated by selecting YES for the Multiple fonts settings. Note that there are serious limitations to the font selection process and the conversion system in general.

Some user environments require a mixture of configurations for printing to application programs that have PostScript drivers and some that do not. In this situation, NetPrint must be reconfigured as you switch from application to applica-

```
┌─────────────────────────────────────────────────────────────────────┐
│    xt              NET PRINT CONFIGURATION         Translate        │
│                    TRANSLATION SETTINGS                             │
│  Auto Translate Screen Dumps:      NO        ▶YES                   │
│  PCScreen font downloaded:         ▶NO       YES                    │
│  Conversion:                       NONE      DIABLO    ▶POSTSCRIPT  │
│  Multiple Fonts Enabled:           ▶NO       YES                    │
│  Using default font:               ▶Times                           │
│  Default font size:                ▶12                              │
│  Italics:                          ▶NO       YES                    │
│  Bold:                             ▶NO       YES                    │
│  LaserWriter paper tray size:      ▶LETTER   LEGAL                  │
│  Legal size is not available for Epson translator.                  │
│   Translator must be loaded; uses an additional 32K RAM             │
├─────────────────────────────────────────────────────────────────────┤
│ MENU INSTRUCTIONS                                                   │
│    <↓> or <SPACE>- Go to the next item. <↑>- Previous item.         │
│    <←> or <→> or <ENTER>- Change the setting of the current item.   │
│    <F2>- Return this item to its default setting.                   │
│    <F10>- Exit using current settings.                              │
│    <HOME>- Return this screen to default settings.                  │
│    <ESCAPE>- Return to the previous window.  <CNTRL-Q>- Exit, make no changes. │
└─────────────────────────────────────────────────────────────────────┘
```

Fig. 8-12. The PostScript translation settings.

tion. This task can be simplified by writing batch files that load the applications and, at the same time, reconfigure NetPrint. This is possible because the NetPrint configure program allows for making changes with commands from the DOS line, as described later in this chapter.

Running NetPrint

Not much work is really involved in actually running NetPrint because it does most of its work in the background. The main trick is to load it correctly and simplify the loading procedure through the use of batch files. The specific procedure for loading NetPrint depends on whether you are going to use PostScript conversion. In Table 8-4, you can see the two most common procedures compared, assuming that you are going to print to a LaserWriter on the network. When the NetPrint loading process is complete, you can print from you applications to the LaserWriter.

If you have an application like WordPerfect 5.0 that supports the LaserWriter, then you will not be using PostScript conversion. Select the LaserWriter as your printer and print normally. When you use the application's print command, you will notice disk activity as the print job is spooled and hear a beep as the print job is sent to the printer. In this case, NetPrint is working as a print spooler similar to TOPS Spool. While the DOS environment does not have a Desk Accessory facility like the Macintosh, most DOS applications allow you to access the command line, from which you can issue PRINT commands to manage the print queue.

If you have an application that does not support PostScript, you need to load NetPrint's conversion software and to configure the application to print as though

Table 8-4. Two NetPrint loading procedures.

Assuming that you are going to print to a LaserWriter on the network, the following commands would be used to load NetPrint:

1. For applications that do not support PostScript, where you want NetPrint to do translation, emulating an Epson printer and using the PCScreen font, assuming that you have configured NetPrint for these settings, stored in NETPRINT.DAT

ALAP	Load the AppleTalk driver
PSTACK	and other required files
KEYINT	for the network connection
PAPOVL	used by NetPrint.
NETPRINT	Load NetPrint.
FXPS	Load Epson FX emulator.
PRINT PSCREEN.FS/X	Download font to printer.

2. For applications that do support PostScript, where you just want NetPrint to do spooling and printing. The CONFIGUR line changes both the NETPRINT.DAT file, and the currently loaded NetPrint settings.

ALAP	Load the AppleTalk driver
PSTACK	and other required files
KEYINT	for the network connection
PAPOVL	used by NetPrint.
NETPRINT	Load NetPrint.
CONFIGUR /W− /T45	Turn off PostScript translation, increase wait time to 45 seconds.

you were using either an FX-80 or an IBM Proprinter, depending on whether you use FXPS.EXE or PROPS.EXE. When you issue the application's print command, you will notice disk activity as the conversion is performed and the print job is spooled to disk. There may be a period of time during the conversion process when the keyboard does not respond. A beep signals when the translation begins and another beep when translation is completed. For very long files, you might want to take a break until the translation process is completed.

Managing the NetPrint Queue

The queue that NetPrint creates is a local queue on the machine running NetPrint. Each machine running its own copy of NetPrint has its own queue. There is no network queue, as there is with published printers. The local queues on all the machines running NetPrint compete for the networked printer on a first-come/first-served basis.

The local queue can be managed with a command called PRINT, which is given from the DOS line. Various options used with PRINT specify what the action is. To list the print queue, the command is just PRINT, as seen in Fig. 8-13.

```
• Sat  6-16-1990 C:\TOPS>print
PRINT - NetPrint access utility for TOPS/DOS version 2
Copyright (C) Sun Microsystems, inc. 1987. All rights reserved.
PRINT         Version 2.00    12/06/87
Net Print version 2.00 is resident.  PostScript Translator not installed.

The Print Queue:

#1: C:\TOPS\qq.eps  is currently printing.

Default Device (LaserWriter II NT :LaserWriter@*) reports:
status: busy; source: AppleTalk.

• Sat  6-16-1990 C:\TOPS>
```

Fig. 8-13. Example of the print queue.

To delete a specific document the command is:

PRINT d:\path\filename/C

To delete all the jobs, the command would be PRINT/T. The PRINT command can even be used to unload NetPrint from memory, with the syntax PRINT/U.

Running CONFIGURE without Menus

You can run the CONFIGURE program from the DOS command line using arguments and thus avoiding the menus. If you give any arguments to CONFIGURE, it takes the actions you specify and returns immediately. This allows you to incorporate the CONFIGURE command into batch files. The two kinds of arguments to CONFIGURE are:

Slash arguments—begin with the / character.

Equals arguments—an argument name followed by an equals sign followed by a setting.

The general syntax for the CONFIGURE command with arguments is:

CONFIGURE [NETPRINT.DAT] slash-arguments LPT# equals-arguments

If you include the NETPRINT.DAT file, CONFIGURE will get the default settings out of that file and make the changes to that file and to the background as well. The arguments you can use with CONFIGURE are given in Table 8-5.

A typical example of placing the CONFIGURE command into a batch file arises when you are using two applications, one of which supports PostScript while the other does not. You can see such a batch file annotated in Table 8-6.

TOPS NetPrint Emulation Tips

If your application does not support a PostScript printer and you are emulating an IBM ProPrinter or Epson FX-80, TOPS NetPrint looks at the setting in the CON-

FIGURE program for the font to be used in the printing process. There are two possible default fonts. If you, or any user on the network, has downloaded the TOPS NetPrint PCScreen font, this is the default font. If the PCScreen font has not been downloaded, the font defaults to Courier.

Both PCScreen and Courier are monospaced fonts, so they resemble closely the spacing on your PC's screen. The PCScreen font can print all the characters that appear on your PC's screen while the Courier font can only print the regular letters, numbers, and punctuation, not the graphics characters. Any of the LaserWriter's fonts can be used by TOPS NetPrint. When you are using an application that has a

Table 8-5. The CONFIGURE command arguments.

General syntax is to enter configuration filename, followed by / options, the printer port to be used, then = options, as in:

CONFIGURE MYPRINT.DAT /options LPT1 = options

In the following list, a plus (+) in an argument means either type + to turn a feature on, or − to turn a feature off. The letter x indicates a number. The slash arguments are:

/M+	Set manual feed mode.
/Nx	Set x number of copies.
/O	Print to "Other Device".
/L	Print to a LaserWriter.
/I	Print to an ImageWriter.
/A	Print to local printer.
/D+	Set the LaserWriter to Diablo 630 emulation.
/W+	Set PostScript translation.
/S+	Save PostScript files.
/C+	Save character screen.
/Tx	Set wait time.

The equals arguments are:

T=size	Size of the paper tray, either "letter" or "legal".
L=name	LaserWriter's name.
I=name	ImageWriter's name.
O=name	Other device's name.
Z=name	Zone's name.
F=fssbi	Set default font. See later in chapter for information on the use of "fssbi" codes.
Dxm=set	Sets dip switch "xm" on or off. The set argument be "ON" or "OFF".

If the names you are using in the equals commands contain spaces or special characters, the entire argument must be in quotes. For example, if the LaserWriter's name is "Steve's LW", your command might look like:

CONFIGURE /L LPT1 "L= Steve's LW"

LaserWriter driver, you use the appropriate application commands to select fonts. If you are driving a LaserWriter through emulation mode, you have to use a special technique in order to activate and print alternate fonts by inserting formatting codes into the text of the document to signal TOPS NetPrint to use the appropriate font.

Adding the appropriate sequences of characters to your word processing file tells NetPrint that the following text should be in a different font or font size. All the

Table 8-6. An annotated CONFIGURE batch file.

The following batch file will run NetPrint for an old-fashioned word processor then load WordPerfect, and finally restore settings. The old word processor does not support PostScript and has to print to LPT1. These settings are stored in NETPRINT.DAT. At the end of the batch file, these settings are restored.

@ECHO OFF
    Turns off screen response to batch file commands.
CLS
    Clears the screen.
CD\TOPS
    Changes to TOPS subdirectory.
NETPRINT
    Loads Netprint, which reads settings from NETPRINT.DAT.
CD\HACK
    Changes directory.
HACK
    Runs HackWriter, an old word processing program that does not have PostScript support.
ECHO Run WordPerfect now? Press Ctrl-C to say No, otherwise . . .
    Gives user opportunity to stop batch file by typing Ctrl-C otherwise they press any key to continue.
PAUSE
    Gives "Press any key to continue . . ." message
CONFIGURE NETPRINT.DAT /L /W− LPT2: "L=Fred's LW"
    Changes settings in NETPRINT.DAT and in the background, to specify printing to a LaserWriter in the current zone called Fred's LW, requesting that all printing to LPT2 be intercepted and that translation be turned off.
CD\WP\DOCS
    Moves to WordPerfect data directory.
\WP\WP
    Runs WordPerfect from WP directory.
CONFIGURE NETPRINT.DAT /L /W+ LPT1: "L=Fred's LW"
    Changes settings in NETPRINT.DAT and in the background, to specify printing to a LaserWriter in the current zone called Fred's LW, requesting that all printing to LPT1 be intercepted and that translation be turned on.

text that follows the formatting code is in the new font until another recognized sequence of characters is inserted into your text. You can add codes to the text to invoke different fonts and font sizes using two methods:

Long method enters codes that fully specify the font and size to use.

Short method defines abbreviated codes and use those abbreviations.

Examples of the codes can be seen in Table 8-7. However, before you get too excited by this feature, you must consider the limitations involved. Programs that do not have PostScript drivers usually cannot respond to the effects of different fonts or sizes you specify. This means that line lengths, margins, tabs, and other formatting might print out quite unlike what you expect. Furthermore, NetPrint does not right-justify text and so the "typeset" look that you might have in mind might not be obtainable. Because many programs on PCs use fixed character fonts, they do not have the ability to represent proportional fonts on the screen, thus your printed page will not look like the screen representation of it. Nobody, including TOPS, is claiming that NetPrint offers desktop publishing for systems that do not support PostScript.

Using TOPS NetPrint from the DOS Command Line

The TOPS NetPrint PRINT.EXE command uses the same syntax as the DOS 3.0 PRINT.COM program does, but TOPS NetPrint extends the DOS PRINT.COM program to take advantage of features which are available in a network environment, such as the presence of multiple printers. TOPS NetPrint also extends the

---

Table 8-7. Format code examples.

Syntax of the format code is:

\\\f ss bi\\\

where \ is the escape character selected in CONFIGURE, f is the font name, ss is font point size (previous size assumed if this is omitted), b is bold, and i is italic.

Font name codes:

a	Avant Garde	b	Bookman	c	Courier	h	Helvetica
n	New Century	p	Palatino	i	PCScreen	s	Symbol
t	Times	z	Zapf Chancery				

For example,

\\\p 14 b\\\

causes text which follows to print in Palatino 14 point bold.

Use \\\1p 14 b\\\ at beginning of document to define font code and then use \1 to invoke font.

---

commands to take advantage of specific features of NetPrint, such as multiple copies, manual versus auto feed, PostScript conversion, and so on. If you use TOPS/DOS and are familiar with the TPRINT command, you will find it very easy to learn the PRINT command. These two commands are very similar.

The PRINT options should be listed at the end of the filename. They are evaluated right to left. There should be no spaces between the end of the filename and the options selected with that filename. Invalid options result in an error. A sample PRINT command line might look like this:

PRINT filename/C

Notice that there is no space between the filename and the optional instruction. The full syntax of the command is listed in Table 8-8.

NetPrint Problems

A common error when using NetPrint is to forget to install the AppleTalk driver. This results in an error message when NetPrint tries to load. Simply run ALAP and PSTACK, then run NetPrint again. A less common error is a problem

Table 8-8. Syntax of the PRINT command.

/C	Clears all errors (as in DOS PRINT).
/P	Sets print mode (as in DOS PRINT).
/T	Sets terminate mode (as in DOS PRINT).
/Q	Provides queue information on a redirected port.
/U	Unloads TOPS NetPrint and/or emulation module.
/R	Sends file to the redirected printer port.
/S	Gives status of redirected or named printer.

Device commands:

/L	Send print file over TOPS to LaserWriter.
/I	Send print file to an ImageWriter with tabs of eight spaces.
/A	Send print file to local printer.
/O	Send output to other network device.

Actual printer commands:

/Nx	Print x number of copies (x can be from 1 to 63).
/M	Set printer to manual feed

Translation commands:

/W	Translate to PostScript. Will override a default of "no translation."
/X	Do not translate to PostScript (use when files are already in PostScript format such as EPS). Will override a default of "do translation."
/D	Activate LaserWriter's Diablo 630 mode.

loading PAPOVL.EXE and KEYINT. Normally these programs are loaded by NetPrint but we have found that sometimes they are not found, particularly if you load NetPrint from a directory other than the one in which they are stored. For example, if you have PAPOVL.EXE and KEYINT.EXE in the TOPS directory and the PATH on your system includes the TOPS directory, then you should be able to load NetPrint from any other directory, just as you can load TOPS/DOS. However, if you get the message PAP installation error!, you might want to try loading all files as separate command line items, as in:

    ALAP
    PSTACK
    PAPOVL
    KEYINT
    NETPRINT

This seems to get around the problem of TOPS finding the program files. This approach avoids the limitations of the other method of loading NetPrint, changing to the NetPrint directory and then running NETPRINT.

When you load NetPrint, it looks for the NETPRINT.DAT file. If you do not have such a file in the current directory, then the program defaults, listed earlier in Table 8-3, are used. Conceivably you could load NetPrint from different directories for different applications, using different NETPRINT.DAT files in each directory. This would give you a means of switching configurations, as long as you unloaded NetPrint between applications (using the PRINT /U command).

NetPrint and the JKL Files

Sometimes when you load NetPrint, you might get a message about *.JKL files. This is not an error message and NetPrint proceeds with loading, but it is a warning that you have unnecessary files still in place. The JKL files are created by NetPrint when it is spooling. The files store information on disk until it is sent to the printer. If you have a system crash or other calamity, before the documents represented by the files have been printed, then they remain on the disk. This allows you to recover the data, simply by printing the files with the PRINT command. The JKL files are if several types:

    PSCRNxx.JKL   Print Screen file
    CHARSxx.JKL   Character stream file
    PTRxxFIL.JKL   PostScript file

In each case, *xx* stands for a pair of letters, as in PSCRNAA.JKL, PSCRNBA.JKL and so on. These files are stored in the spool directory specified in your configuration, typically C:\TOPS. Normally NetPrint deletes these JKL files when printing is successfully completed. However, you can actually tell NetPrint to keep these files all the time. Just use the Special Settings menu of the CONFIGURE program, seen in Fig. 8-14.

Be aware that keeping these files consumes disk space at a considerable rate. To remove these files use the DOS command

DEL *.JKL

in the spool directory.

NetPrint and Dip Switches

You might sometimes have a problem with the printed results of NetPrint when using emulation (either Proprinter or FX-80). One area that can be particularly difficult is reconciling dip switch settings. Dip switches are the small On/Off or Close/Open switches inside printers and other devices. By altering dip switch settings in a printer, you can affect the way it operates. This means that it is difficult for a program like NetPrint to reliably emulate all FX-80s or all Proprinters because you might want to use printer features that involve switch settings different from the factory defaults. In order to address this problem, NetPrint's CONFIGURE program has a special menu, seen in Fig. 8-14.

The Proprinter has just one bank or row of dip switches, while the FX-80 has two. You can either consult you printer manual or the NetPrint manual for the meaning of the different dip switch settings. What NetPrint is allowing you to do is customize the printer that is being emulated into PostScript output on the LaserWriter. Turning on the switches on the menu selects the desired special features, and NetPrint will attempt to translate those through to PostScript. As you might imagine, this is pushing the limits of the emulation process, and results are not always

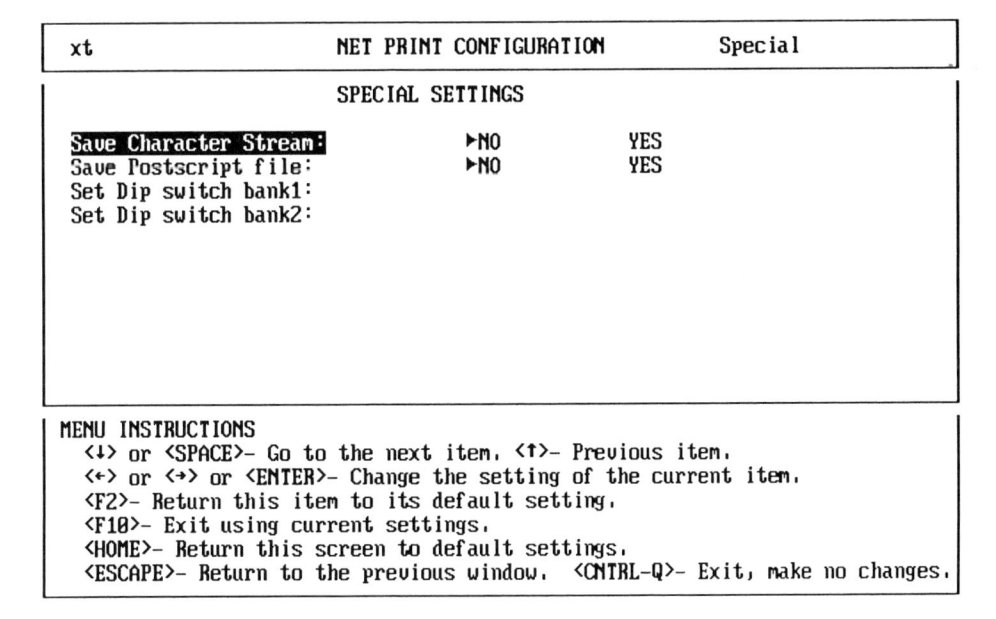

```
┌──────────────────────────────────────────────────────────────────────┐
│ xt                       NET PRINT CONFIGURATION         Special     │
│                           SPECIAL SETTINGS                           │
│    Save Character Stream:      ▶NO          YES                      │
│    Save Postscript file:       ▶NO          YES                      │
│    Set Dip switch bank1:                                             │
│    Set Dip switch bank2:                                             │
│                                                                      │
│                                                                      │
│                                                                      │
│                                                                      │
│ ┌──────────────────────────────────────────────────────────────────┐ │
│ │ MENU INSTRUCTIONS                                                │ │
│ │    <↓> or <SPACE>- Go to the next item. <↑>- Previous item.      │ │
│ │    <←> or <→> or <ENTER>- Change the setting of the current item.│ │
│ │    <F2>- Return this item to its default setting.                │ │
│ │    <F10>- Exit using current settings.                           │ │
│ │    <HOME>- Return this screen to default settings.               │ │
│ │    <ESCAPE>- Return to the previous window.  <CNTRL-Q>- Exit, make no changes. │ │
│ └──────────────────────────────────────────────────────────────────┘ │
└──────────────────────────────────────────────────────────────────────┘
```

Fig. 8-14. Special settings.

reliable. Because NetPrint assumes the emulation you want to do involves the default switch settings, you are best advised not to alter the Special Settings unless you are very well acquainted with the printer in question.

Notes on Printing Screens

We mentioned earlier that TOPS NetPrint supports the use of the PrtSc key to print the screen contents (create screen dumps) on a LaserWriter. With the TOPS NetPrint port set to LPT1, this allows users to immediately send a file to the printer from within their word processing program.

Note that under NetPrint pressing PrtSc has a slightly different meaning; it translates and queues any pending captured character streams, including print tasks spooled under NetPrint. If there are no character stream files, no print jobs pending, then the contents of the screen are sent to the printer without waiting for the delay. If a file is pending and you want to print the contents of your screen immediately, you must press the PrtSc key twice.

If you use the PCScreen fonts, your screen will print as expected. If you do not, some screen characters (especially the nonalphabetic characters) might not print correctly. Another approach for screen capture is to use a program like Inset that performs enhanced screen print duties and that can print to a LaserWriter. However, the memory overhead required to run Inset and NetPrint *and* an application may be prohibitive. See Chapter 14 for more on memory constraints and ways to get around them.

CONCLUSION

Given the variety of techniques that the TOPS software makes available, it is likely that most printing needs will be well served. In the case of DOS systems, you might need to issue some lengthy instructions to print with TOPS, but many of these can be incorporated into batch files for ease of use. In the next chapter, we discuss batch files in greater detail, showing you how to combine TOPS commands for automated network and printer control.

9
Commanding TOPS/DOS and the Utilities

IF YOU ARE A REASONABLY ACCOMPLISHED MS-DOS USER, sometimes you might prefer to issue commands directly to TOPS, bypassing the TOPS menu. Both TOPS/DOS and TOPS NetPrint provide an extensive set of commands that can control network operations without using menus. In addition, a number of utility programs provided with TOPS/DOS can assist you in the smooth and efficient running of PCs on a TOPS network. For the most part, the TOPS/DOS commands form a consistent and easy to use command language. Indeed, even if you are not very experienced with DOS, a couple of activities, such as shutting down the published volumes before you power down a server, are more easily done by typing commands than by selecting from the menus.

This chapter discusses the TOPS commands and utilities and their uses. The commands are roughly grouped into those for the server, those for the client, those for file maintenance (which can be either a server or client task), and those for the TOPS/DOS utilities. In addition, one of the most powerful features of this command language is the ability to incorporate it into batch files. Batch files can significantly automate network startup, so some practical examples of how to write such batch files are included in this chapter. The chapter concludes with some batch files strategies for overall DOS system management.

ABOUT DOS COMMANDS

When you issue a command at the DOS prompt, DOS reads or interprets what you have typed. The program COMMAND.COM that is on all system disks is actually called the *command line interpreter* because it interprets instructions entered on the DOS command line. For example, in Fig. 9-1, you can see a DOS session in which the user typed DIR /W then pressed Enter.

A list of the files in the current directory is displayed. DOS interprets the characters DIR as a command. The /W is a *switch* or option that modifies the command, in this case to mean wide directory. The command DIR /P means directory with a *pause* between screens of file listings. You can further supplement the DIR command with *filters* and *pipes* as in

DIR | SORT | MORE

which filters the file listing sorted into alphabetical order and displays one screen at a time with the More prompt, as seen in Fig. 9-2.

The way that TOPS commands are issued follows a similar pattern. Just as COMMAND.COM does the interpretation for DOS, the program TOPS.EXE does the interpretation of commands for TOPS. However, before exploring TOPS.EXE in detail, we need to cover a few more aspects of DOS itself.

The PATH Factor

In Fig. 9-3, you can see that the DIR/W command was followed by typing WP and pressing Enter, which produced an error.

Because the DIR command is one of those retained in memory by DOS at all times, a so-called *internal* command, DOS was able to execute the command. The command WP was not so successful because WP refers to the program WP.EXE that is not in the current directory of the disk. What happens when you type a bunch of letters, like WP or QUATTRO, and press Enter, is that DOS tries to interpret them

```
♦ Sat   6-16-1990 C:\DOS>DIR /W

 Volume in drive C is TOWER 386
 Directory of  C:\DOS

 .                  ..                 BAT              4201      CPI       5202      CPI
 ADDEVICE BAT       APPEND   EXE       ASSIGN   COM     ATTRIB    EXE       BACKUP    COM
 C        SYS       CHKDSK   COM       COMMAND  COM     COMP      COM       COPYQM    COM
 COUNTRY  SYS       DDIR     COM       DEBUG    COM     DISKCOMP  COM       DISKCOPY  COM
 DISPLAY  SYS       DOSPRINT COM       EDLIN    COM     EGA       CPI       EXE2BIN   EXE
 FASTOPEN EXE       FC       EXE       FDISK    COM     FIND      EXE       FORMAT    COM
 GRAFTABL COM       GRAPHICS COM       GWBASIC  EXE     HARDPREP  EXE       HARDRIVE  SYS
 INITPART MAC       INITPREP MAC       JOIN     EXE     KEYB      COM       KEYBOARD  SYS
 LABEL    COM       LCD      CPI       LINK     EXE     LL        EXE       MIPS      COM
 MKCONFIG EXE       MODE     COM       MORE     COM     NLSFUNC   EXE       PARK      COM
 PRINTER  SYS       RAMDRIVE SYS       RECOVER  COM     REPLACE   EXE       RESTORE   COM
 SELECT   COM       SHARE    EXE       SORT     EXE     SUBST     EXE       SYS       COM
 T        BAT       TOUCH    EXE       TREE     COM     XCOPY     EXE       DESKTOP
 QCOPY    EXE
            66 File(s)   1632256 bytes free

♦ Sat   6-16-1990 C:\DOS>
```

Fig. 9-1. Issuing DOS commands

as instructions. To do this DOS first looks to its internal commands. If it does not find an internal command spelled like the characters you entered, DOS looks for an executable program file by that name on the disk.

If DOS cannot find a program in the current directory that matches the characters you have entered, DOS looks to any path that has been set. A path is an instruction issued to DOS to tell it which disks or directories from which you will be calling programs. For example, the statement

PATH=C:\;C:\DOS;C:\QUATTRO

issued at the DOS prompt tells DOS to look in the root directory (C:\) followed by the DOS directory (C:\DOS) followed by the directory in which you have stored Quattro (C:\QUATTRO). Suppose you have a path setting like the one above, and you issue the command CHKDSK from any directory on your system. The program file CHKDSK.COM is usually stored in the directory called C:\DOS, which has been included in the path, so DOS will find the CHKDSK.COM program and execute it. (Although CHKDSK is a DOS command, it is not an internal command that

```
      Sat   6-16-1990 C:\DOS>DIR | SORT | MORE


              67 File(s)    1589248 bytes free
        Directory of  C:\DOS
        Volume in drive C is TOWER 386
        .            <DIR>         7-27-88    5:12p
        ..           <DIR>         7-27-88    5:12p
        4201         CPI     17089 2-02-88   12:00a
        5202         CPI       459 2-02-88   12:00a
        ADDEVICE     BAT       309 9-15-86   12:00p
        APPEND       EXE      5794 2-02-88   12:00a
        ASSIGN       COM      1530 2-02-88   12:00a
        ATTRIB       EXE     10656 2-02-88   12:00a
        BACKUP       COM     30280 2-09-88   12:00a
        BAT          <DIR>         8-13-88    4:10p
        C            SYS        37 9-15-86   12:00p
        CHKDSK       COM      9819 2-02-88   12:00a
        COMMAND      COM     25308 2-02-88   12:00a
        COMP         COM      4183 2-02-88   12:00a
        COPYQM       COM     13336 1-11-89   11:41a
        COUNTRY      SYS     11254 2-02-88   12:00a
        DDIR         COM       796 1-04-80   12:14a
        DEBUG        COM     15866 2-09-88   12:00a
        DESKTOP                  0 4-26-90    2:27p
        -- More --
```

Fig. 9-2. DOS command with filter and pipe

is always available, it is an external command that has to be read from disk when it is executed.)

You can see the current path setting of your system by simply typing PATH at the DOS prompt and pressing Enter. You cannot edit the PATH setting, you have to issue a new path statement to replace one setting with another. For example, typing PATH=C:\WP and pressing Enter changes the path from whatever it was to just the directory WP.

The AUTOEXEC.BAT Factor

When you install TOPS, it modifies or creates an AUTOEXEC.BAT file that contains the PATH command and the name of the directory in which you installed TOPS. If you already have a PATH statement in your AUTOEXEC.BAT file, then the TOPS directory is added to the statement, as in:

PATH=C:\;C:\DOS;C:\QUATTRO;C:\TOPS

The AUTOEXEC.BAT file is a list of commands that DOS carries out whenever a system is started or restarted. A typical AUTOEXEC.BAT might contain the following:

O'CLOCK
PATH=C:\;C:\DOS;C:\QUATTRO;C:\TOPS
PROMPT $D PG

The first of these commands sets the time and date, using the program O'CLOCK which comes with some system clock boards. The second line sets the PATH, while the third sets the prompt, the characters that appear when DOS is loaded.

Many newer systems do not need AUTOEXEC.BAT command(s) to set the date and time, but just about every system benefits from a PATH command and a PROMPT statement. This is because default prompt is simply the letter of the current drive, as in C>. However, you can change this to show such information as the

```
C:\>CD \DOS

C:\DOS>WP
Bad command or file name

C:\DOS>CD \

C:\>WP
Bad command or file name

C:\>
```

Fig. 9-3. Failed command

date ($D) followed by the path ($P) followed by the greater than sign ($G) which looks like this in the screen:

   Tue 4-1-1990 C:\>—

The advantage of a prompt like this is that when you move to a different directory you can see from the prompt what the current directory is:

   Tue 4-1-1990 C:\TOPS>—

Every time you turn off your computer, it forgets such things as the PATH setting and the prompt you want to use, reverting to a simple C>. You can include a PROMPT setting command in your AUTOEXEC.BAT to get the prompt you want every time the system is turned on.

Regular BATs

The AUTOEXEC.BAT is a special type of file known as a batch file, because it contains a collection of items to be processed, a *batch*. All batch files have the extension BAT. This is one of the special group of DOS extensions that is recognized by COMMAND.COM as programs. The other two common program file extensions are COM and EXE. An example of a batch file besides AUTOEXEC.BAT is the file that loads TOPS/DOS, the full name of which is LOADTOPS.BAT. To execute a batch file, you simply type the first part of the name at the DOS prompt and press Enter, as in:

   C:\>LOADTOPS   Enter

The DOS command interpreter looks for a program file called by the name you have entered. If there was a program called LOADTOPS.EXE or LOADTOPS.COM, then DOS would run those. If those files do not exist, then DOS looks for a BAT file called LOADTOPS, and executes the instructions in it.

While AUTOEXEC.BAT is a special file that DOS looks for every time the system is started or restarted, regular batch files can have any valid eight-character filename. Short names are sometimes convenient, like LT.BAT. You could rename LOADTOPS.BAT as LT.BAT and save some typing when you load TOPS.

One feature of batch files that can pose problems is the question of *nesting* or including a batch file within another batch file. For example, suppose you have a batch file called DW.BAT that clears the screen and displays a wide directory, using these commands:

   ECHO OFF
   CLS
   DIR/W

Now you make a batch file called DWP.BAT that prints the wide directory:

```
ECHO OFF
CLS
DIR/W > PRN
```

Suppose that you want to view the directory before printing, so you change DWP.BAT to run DW.BAT first, as in the following:

```
DW
DIR/W > PRN
```

This will not work because DOS is controlled by the last batch file that it is told to run. When you run the last version of DWP.BAT, it runs DW.BAT, which controls DOS and ends without returning control to DWP.BAT. To get around this problem, later versions of DOS, including 3.3, allow you to use the CALL command within batch files. Thus, a version of DWP.BAT that uses this:

```
CALL DW
DIR/W > PRN
```

would run DW.BAT and then return control to DWP.BAT and carry out the second line of the file. An alternative to CALL is the use of COMMAND /C, as in:

```
COMMAND /C DW
DIR/W > PRN
```

The only problem with these approaches is the lack of compatibility with earlier versions of DOS that do not support CALL or COMMAND /C.

We return to batch files later in this chapter and introduce some of the special commands that you can use to make your batch files more sophisticated.

Now that we have looked at some of the basic elements of batch files and the control of DOS commands, we look more closely at controlling TOPS from the DOS prompt.

THE TOPS COMMAND FORMAT

We have seen that the part of DOS that finds commands and executes them is called the command interpreter. Just as MS-DOS needs a command interpreter, which in DOS's case is called COMMAND.COM, so does TOPS. With TOPS, this command interpreter is called TOPS.EXE, which is in your TOPS subdirectory if you have installed on a hard disk. (If you are using floppy disks the location of TOPS.EXE depends on the size of disk you are using; it is located on disk two of the original 360K program disks.)

TOPS Commands in General

All of the TOPS commands are preceded with the name of the interpreter. For these commands to work no matter what the current directory, make sure the path to TOPS.EXE is included in your DOS search path. A list of the various commands and how they can be abbreviated is given in Table 9-1.

Table 9-1. TOPS/DOS commands with abbreviations, parameters and explanation. Note that items in the square brackets [] are optional command parameters.

Command	Abbr.	Description
TOPS HELP	HE	to get help with TOPS commands, use alone or with /A for help with all commands, or with name of command.
TOPS STATION	ST	[/PR] [name or OFF or ON] to name station.
TOPS ZONE	ZO	[/T or /N] [zone or * or ?] to set zone.
TOPS DIR	DI	[/PR] [/Z zone] [server] to list servers, volumes, and printers.
TOPS MOUNT	MO	d: TO server volume [/Z zone] [/R or /RW] [/P [password]] to mount volumes.
TOPS MOUNT	MO	1pt#: TO server printer [/Z zone] [/P [password]] to mount printers.
TOPS UNMOUNT	UM	[d: or 1pt#: or /A] to unmount volumes or printers.
TOPS PUBLISH	PU	d:path AS volume [/R or /RW][/P [password]] [/X] to publish volumes.
TOPS PUBLISH	PU	1pt#: AS printer USING d:path [/E] [/P [password]] to publish printers.
TOPS UNPUBLISH	UP	[volume or printer or /A] to unpublish volumes or printers.
TOPS REMEMBER	RM	[filespec] to store sequence of operations.
TOPS CSTAT	CS	[d: or 1pt#:] to view client status.
TOPS PSTAT	PS	[/C [name]] [/D] [/F] [/F [/V volume]] [/PR [printer]] to view published status.
TOPS LOGOUT	LO	[/PR] name or /A to logout a crashed client.
TOPS SHUTDOWN	SH	To logout, unmount, unpublish and shut down your station, prior to unloading TOPS.
TOPS UNLOAD	UL	PRTR or KRNL(CLNT) or TALK(TALC) or TNETBIOS or ATALK or /A to unload TOPS from memory.
TOPS PAUSE	PA	[/PR or /Q] suspend TOPS background activity.
TOPS RESUME	RE	[/PR or /Q] resume TOPS background activity.
TOPS ERR	ER	Report network errors.
TOPS VER	VE	Display current TOPS version.

Switches:

/R = Read	/RW = Read & Write	/P = Password
/A = All	/Z = Zone	/C = Client
/D = Directories	/V = Volumes	/F = Files
/PR = Printer	/X = No XSYNC	/PS = Print Setup
/S = Status	/Q = Queue	/E = Erase

Remember that the following are **not** TOPS interpreted commands:

TOPSMENU	Loads menu-driven TOPS command program.
TOPSPRTR	Loads background TOPS Printer Server.
TNETBIOS	Loads TOPS/DOS NETBIOS module.

You might find yourself using some of these commands frequently, and some of them not at all. Whatever the case, they all follow the same basic command format, so if you learn how to do one, its fairly simple to do another. If you ever forget the command structure, you can get an on-screen reminder by using the command TOPS HELP, whose output you see in Fig. 9-4.

A more detailed help screen for any particular command can be summoned by being more explicit in the help request. To display a detailed screen for the publish command, for instance, give the command TOPS HELP PUBLISH. TOPS responds to that with the screen you see in Fig. 9-5.

A couple of rules involved with this command syntax are very important and are listed here. These rules apply to all of the commands and should always be kept in mind:

```
                              TOPS COMMANDS
================================================================================
TOPSMENU           loads menu-driven TOPS command program
TOPSPRTR           loads background TOPS Printer Server
TNETBIOS           loads TOPS/DOS NETBIOS module
TOPS   HELP        [command | /A]
TOPS   STATION     [/PR] [name | OFF | ON]
TOPS   ZONE        [/T | /N] [zone | * | ?]
TOPS   DIR         [/PR] [/Z zone] [server]
TOPS   MOUNT       d:    TO    server  volume   [/Z zone]  [/R | /RW] [/P [password]]
TOPS   MOUNT       lpt#: TO   server   printer  [/Z zone]  [/P [password]]
TOPS   UNMOUNT     [d: | lpt#: | /A]
TOPS   PUBLISH     d:path AS  volume   [/R | /RW] [/P [password]]  [/X]
TOPS   PUBLISH     lpt#: AS  printer  USING d:path  [/E]  [/P [password]]
TOPS   UNPUBLISH [volume | printer | /A]
--------------------------------------------------------------------------------
  /R = Read     /RW = Read & Write  /P = Password  /A = All      /Z  = Zone
  /C = Client   /D  = Directories   /V = Volumes   /F = Files    /PR = Printer
  /X = NoXsync  /PS = Print Setup   /S = Status    /Q = Queue    /E  = Erase
================================================================================
Hit any key to continue, or type <ESCAPE> to quit...

                          TOPS COMMANDS (cont'd)
================================================================================
TOPS   REMEMBER    [filespec]
TOPS   CSTAT       [d: | lpt#:]
TOPS   PSTAT       [/C [name]]   [/D]    [/F]    [/V [volume]]  [/PR [printer]]
TOPS   LOGOUT      [/PR] name | /A
TOPS   SHUTDOWN
TOPS   UNLOAD      PRTR | KRNL(CLNT) | TALK(TALC) | TNETBIOS | ATALK | /A
TOPS   PAUSE       [/PR | /Q]
TOPS   RESUME      [/PR | /Q]
TOPS   ERR
TOPS   VER
--------------------------------------------------------------------------------
  /R = Read     /RW = Read & Write  /P = Password  /A = All      /Z  = Zone
  /C = Client   /D  = Directories   /V = Volumes   /F = Files    /PR = Printer
  /X = NoXsync  /PS = Print Setup   /S = Status    /Q = Queue    /E  = Erase
              [] = Optional Command Parameter          '|' = OR
================================================================================

Sat   6-16-1990 C:\TOPS>
```

Fig. 9-4. TOPS HELP

Commanding TOPS/DOS and the Utilities **167**

1. A specification such as d:\path means that you must supply the proper drive letter and path name.
2. Names that include spaces must be enclosed in quotation marks. For example if your volume alias is Word Processing, you must express that in the command language as "Word Processing".
3. Items enclosed in [] brackets indicate optional arguments

```
TOPS HELP for PUBLISH
===============================================================================
TOPS  PUBLISH    d:path  AS  volume  [/R | /RW]  [/P [password]]  [/X]
-------------------------------------------------------------------------------
Argument            Meaning
-------------------------------------------------------------------------------
 PUBLISH            Makes a Volume of files and directories available to Clients
                    on the Network.
 d:path             Full drive and directory specification of the directory to be
                    published.  All subdirectories of the published directory are
                    made available to the network.
 volume             Network visible name (Volume Alias) of the public directory.
 /R                 Publish the Volume with Read Only access allowed.
 /RW                Publish the Volume with Read and Write access allowed.
 /P password        Assigns the argument "password" to the Volume to verify
                    whether Clients requesting access rights to that Volume have
                    permission to do so.  If the "/P" is specified with
                    no password following, you will be prompted for the password.
 /X                 This option prevents running the XSYNC utiltity to update the
                    directory to be published.  This option should only be used if
                    there has been NO file activity in the directory while TOPS
                    was not installed or the directory was not published.
===============================================================================
Hit any key to continue, or type <ESCAPE> to quit...

===============================================================================
TOPS  PUBLISH    lpt#: AS  printer  USING  d:path  [/E]  [/P [password]]
-------------------------------------------------------------------------------
Argument            Meaning
-------------------------------------------------------------------------------
 PUBLISH            Makes a locally attached Printer available to TOPS Clients
                    on the Network.
 lpt#:              Indicates the LPT port which is being made public.  The "#"
                    should be replaced by the LPT number (1 - 3).
                    PRN: can be used instead of LPT1:.
 printer            Network visible name (Printer Alias) of the printer you're
                    publishing.
 d:path             Full drive and directory specification of a directory to
                    contain the spool files for this Printer.
 /P password        Assigns the argument "password" to the Printer to verify
                    whether Clients requesting access rights to that Printer have
                    permission to do so.  If the "/P" is specified with
                    no password following, you will be prompted for the Printer
                    password without it being displayed on the console.
 /E                 Cleans out the spool directory.  All files with the extension
                    "TPQ" in that directory will be erased.
===============================================================================

Sat  6-16-1990 C:\TOPS>
```

Fig. 9-5. Help with PUBLISH

Furthermore, the use of uppercase and lowercase is generally immaterial when issuing commands at the DOS prompt. The only time that it is significant is when spelling passwords (which are case-sensitive). You might, for aesthetic reasons, want to pay attention to case when giving names to volumes and printers. Using Fred's XT looks nicer to many people than FRED'S XT but TOPS recognizes both as meaning the same thing.

Server Commands

As you recall from Chapter 6, the basic server commands are the publishing of volumes and printers. Also, before powering down a computer that has become a server, you should make certain that the server has no active clients. All of these tasks can be done through the TOPS command language.

As you can see from the TOPS help screen in Fig. 9-4, all the commands begin with the word TOPS, followed by the particular action you wish to initiate. Depending on what you are doing, other *parameters* (sometimes called arguments or instructions) follow.

To publish a disk volume for example, the command specification must include the path of the directory being published, the directory's network volume name (alias), the write permissions (read only or read/write), and the password (if used). The command syntax is thus:

TOPS PUBLISH d:\path AS volume [/R or /RW] [/P [password]] [/X]

Suppose that you want to publish the directory C:\123\SALARIES so that someone else can access it. You want to guard the information with a password, the three characters: POE. You want the further protection of read-only status. You decide to use the name Salary for the published volume. The command would be:

TOPS PUBLISH C:\123\SALARIES AS Salary /R /P POE

If the files in the SALARIES subdirectory do not change much, for example, if they are mainly for reference purposes, you might decide to use the /X option with the PUBLISH command. This prevents TOPS from updating the directory information for the published directory. Because TOPS will have retained this information since the last time the directory was published, you can speed up the publishing process with this option. However, it should only be used if you understand the way TOPS maintains directory information. For more on this subject, see the section later in this chapter on the XSYNC command.

To publish a printer, you must specify the printer port, the printer network alias, the spool directory, and, once again, a password if you want to use one. The syntax of printer publishing is:

TOPS PUBLISH LPT# AS printer USING d:\path [/P password] [/E]

Let us consider a real world example. If a user named Rich were publishing an HP Laserjet connected to LPT1 of his PC, and if he had created a directory called

SPOOL on his C drive to store his clients' spooled files, Rich would publish his printer with the following command:

 TOPS PUBLISH LPT1 AS "Rich's Laserjet" USING C:\SPOOL /E

Note the quotes around the alias because the alias name had a space in it. Note also that Rich did not include a password (it was optional), although he did include the /E, which instructed TOPS to delete any old spool files that for whatever reason might not have printed the last time he published the printer.

 When a server wants to cease being a server, before powering down that server should unpublish all published volumes. While there is a command that individually unpublishes volumes, it is often easier to shutdown all published volumes in one step. The command for this is quite intuitive and is given as:

 TOPS SHUTDOWN

If the server has active clients at the time the shutdown is attempted, TOPS does not allow this action and returns the message Can't SHUTDOWN with active Clients. In that event, the proper etiquette is to identify the clients and ask them to unmount so that the server can shut down properly. It is easy to identify the servers with the command called PSTAT (short for published status):

 TOPS PSTAT

The PSTAT command returns a list of all the active clients. PSTAT also has options to list what clients are mounted on which directories, and whether or not those clients have open files. For a more complete listing of the PSTAT options, enter the command TOPS HELP PSTAT. You can see the response in Fig. 9-6.

```
TOPS HELP for PSTAT
===========================================================================
TOPS   PSTAT      [/C [name]]   [/D]   [/F]   [/V [volume]]  [/PR [printer]]
---------------------------------------------------------------------------
Argument          Meaning
---------------------------------------------------------------------------
  PSTAT           PSTAT stands for Publisher STATus, and displays information
                  about Volumes and Printers that you've published for use by
                  other stations on the network.  Depending on the arguments,
                  information about which Volumes and Printers have been made
                  public, who is using them, and the active directories and
                  files will be displayed.
  /V              Displays which Volumes have been published.
  /V volume       Displays the current status of the specified Volume.
  /PR             Displays which Printers have been published.
  /PR printer     Displays the current status of the specified Printer.
  /C              Displays a list of Clients currently accessing your Volumes.
  /C client       Displays the current status of the specified client.
  /D              Displays a list of active (open) directories.
  /F              Displays a list of active (open) files.
===========================================================================

Sat   6-16-1990 C:\TOPS>
```

Fig. 9-6. The PSTAT command

If it is not possible to have the client unmount the server, as with a crashed client, there is a brute force method for logging out clients. It's done with the command

TOPS LOGOUT client

where client is the network name of the client you want to get rid of. Alternatively, you can logout all the clients by using:

TOPS LOGOUT /A

The LOGOUT command could cause clients to lose data if they are actively using the server's volume! LOGOUT should only be used in cases where the clients were brought down without unmounting, or you have no way of asking them to unmount. Do not logout a client if that client has open files! Close the open files by first saving or quitting. The only exception to this rule would be in the case of a crashed client, in which case the LOGOUT command is the only way to do it.

After all the clients are disengaged, the shutdown command will work successfully. In addition to shutting down, if the server wants to unload TOPS from its memory, perhaps so that it can run a memory intensive application program in stand-alone mode, it can be accomplished with the command:

TOPS UNLOAD /A

Note the space between UNLOAD and /A. The command will not work without it. Also note that what you are doing here is removing a memory-resident program. This has serious implications for the operation of your system.

Unloading Problems

The fact that TOPS/DOS is a *memory-resident program*, one that remains loaded while other programs come and go, can impose restrictions when you want to unload TOPS. The main point to make here is that care is required when using memory-resident programs, otherwise known as *TSR*s for Terminate and Stay Resident. If you have loaded another memory-resident program *after* TOPS/DOS, then you should unload that program first, before unloading TOPS. For example, to shoot some of the screens in this book, we used a TSR program called INSET. We loaded INSET after TOPS. This meant that we could not unload TOPS without first unloading INSET. The reason for this lies in the memory structure of DOS systems. Basically, DOS stacks up programs in memory. If you remove a program from within the stack, the system tends to topple over or crash. Programs need to go in and out in order: "Last In, First Out."

Fortunately, TOPS is aware of this problem. Issuing the UNLOAD command when another program has been loaded after TOPS and remains in memory results in an error message, and the UNLOAD command is not executed. The message reads:

Unable to UNLOAD TOPS KRNL because interrupt 17H has been changed by another loaded, memory-resident program. Unload that program and try TOPS UNLOAD KRNL again.

The solution is simple enough: unload the TSR, then unload TOPS. Unfortunately, some TSR programs are not "well-behaved" and do not unload cleanly. In such cases, you might need to reboot your system to unload TOPS. In a few cases, TOPS might not catch the fact that it was not the last TSR to be loaded. Unloading in such cases can result in a completion of the UNLOAD command but a "flaky" condition in your system. You should be able to spot this condition fairly easily and identify the TSR that is causing the problem. The answer to the problem is to reboot to unload TOPS, rather than use the UNLOAD command.

Client Commands

One of the primary needs of a client who would use the TOPS command language would probably be the mounting of volumes. If you want to do mounting through a batch file or from the DOS line so as to skip the use of the TOPS menu, it can be done with the command TOPS MOUNT.

The mount specification must include the name of the server that is being mounted, the volume (alias) name, the write access, the name of the zone (if not the local one) and the password if required. The MOUNT command's syntax is

TOPS MOUNT d: TO server volume [/RW] [/P password]

where d: represents the drive the mounted volume will be referred to as. The argument server is the name of the server that has published the volume, and volume means the volume's name on the server. For example, suppose the Fred's XT has published a volume called Salary, with a password of POE. You want to mount this volume on your system as drive G, but you want it to be read-only. The command would be:

TOPS MOUNT G: TO "Fred's XT" Salary /R /P POE

Remember that names with spaces in them must be enclosed in quotation marks. To mount printers the command is:

TOPS MOUNT LPT# TO SERVER PRINTER [/P password]

Other commands can help to support the use of the mount command. TOPS DIR for example, displays a list of servers and can be extremely useful for checking correct names and the spelling of servers and their resources. You can use the switch /PR to see a list of printers. Thus the command TOPS DIR lists the file servers whereas TOPS DIR /PR lists the printer servers.

A client has the responsibility to unmount volumes before powering down. TOPS UNMOUNT disengages individual volumes. The syntax structure is the same as TOPS MOUNT. TOPS SHUTDOWN is the quicker method as it dismounts everything at once.

TOPS UTILITIES

While TOPS/DOS works quietly in the background to do such clever things as list Macintosh folders as directories, it is making use of certain features of DOS to maintain the data it needs to carry out these tasks. TOPS/DOS creates a number of *hidden* files on DOS disks to track published volumes and foreign files. In general, the management of these special files is done automatically by TOPS with no need for user intervention. However, as you become more experienced with TOPS, and as you encounter problems that need troubleshooting, you will need to know how to handle these special files.

The TOPS/DOS utilities are not *internal* commands, but programs that must be read from disk every time that they are run. This means that you do not have access to these utilities outside of the directory they are stored in unless that directory is included in the PATH command. Fortunately, the normal installation of TOPS/DOS places the utility programs in the TOPS directory which is then added to the PATH statement in the AUTOEXEC.BAT. If you get the message Bad command or file name when you run a TOPS utility, check the location of the utility and the current PATH setting. Also, check the way you have spelled the command and its options.

Hidden Files

If you are not familiar with it, the term "hidden files" may bring to mind scary new vistas of DOS file management. In fact, several hidden files are already on your hard disk. You cannot see these with the DOS DIR command, but you can use a utility program like FA.EXE, a part of the Norton Utilities, to list such files. For example, in Fig. 9-7, you can see a DOS session in which the user attempted to remove a directory called KEY, which appeared empty when the DIR command was used.

The user then applied the FA command, and the hidden file was revealed.

Because not everyone has Norton Utilities and the regular DOS commands are not up to handling hidden files, TOPS/DOS includes utilities to assist you. These

```
Sat   6-16-1990 C:\KEY>CD\

Sat   6-16-1990 C:\>RD \KEY
Invalid path, not directory,
or directory not empty

Sat   6-16-1990 C:\>C:\NU\FA \KEY\*.*
FA-File Attributes, Advanced Edition, (C) Copr 1987, 1988, Peter Norton

C:\KEY
    xdirstat.tps  Archive              Hidden

  no files changed

Sat   6-16-1990 C:\>
```

Fig. 9-7. The FA listing of XDIRSTAT.TPS

utilities, XSYNC, XDIR, XDEL, TDIR and TDEL, aid in the maintenance and viewing of something called the TOPS Extended Directory files.

Using XSYNC

Whenever you publish a volume from a PC, TOPS creates a file on that volume called the TOPS Extended Directory. This is a DOS file that has the name XDIRSTAT.TPS. In this file, TOPS keeps a list, a special directory of the files in the published volume. To a large extent, this list duplicates the DOS directory, but if the volume contains Macintosh or Unix files, XDIRSTAT.TPS maintains information about Macintosh icon types and the longer names of Macintosh or Unix files. In the case of Macintosh files, XDIRSTAT.TPS links the data and resource forks of Mac files copied into a DOS volume. The TOPS Extended Directory works to assist the normal DOS directory and is an essential part of the TOPS system.

You can view the contents of the XDIRSTAT.TPS file with the XDIR command described later in this chapter. Note that the XDIRSTAT.TPS file is not automatically erased when a volume is unpublished. This is to allow TOPS to reuse the information and so save time in subsequent operations. Also note that the XDIRSTAT.TPS is not visible within a normal DOS directory because it is hidden, using the special DOS hidden attribute.

You might have noticed a certain amount of disk activity when you publish a volume on your PC. In some cases, this can take several seconds because TOPS is checking each directory and subdirectory in that volume. Volumes that have been published before already have Extended Directories, XDIRSTAT.TPS files, in them. If such a file does not already exist, it is created. When an XDIRSTAT.TPS file already exists, TOPS updates it to reflect changes that have been made since the volume was last published. During the time that volume is published, TOPS automatically keeps the XDIRSTAT.TPS file up-to-date.

The role of the XSYNC utility is to update the Extended Directory file to account for changes that occurred while the volume was not published. TOPS uses XSYNC automatically whenever you use TOPS to publish volumes. However, because updating the Extended Directory can take time, you might not want to run XSYNC every time you publish a volume. You can turn XSYNC off so that it does not run automatically. This leaves you with the option to run XSYNC only when you need to.

There are two situations in particular where you might want to consider disabling XSYNC. First of all, if a volume is published whenever you start your computer, TOPS is updating the XDIRSTAT.TPS file automatically all the time and XSYNC need not be run each time the volume is published. This is the case if you are publishing a volume with your AUTOEXEC.BAT file and never have occasion to unpublish it. The ongoing maintenance of XSYNC obviates the need for XSYNCing.

Secondly, if you are publishing a large set of directories, such as a whole hard drive, you know that TOPS take quite a time to complete the publishing operation.

However, if you know you have only changed files in one or two subdirectories since the last time the drive was published, you can manually run XSYNC on those particular subdirectories before you publish the entire drive.

So, how do you prevent XSYNC from running automatically? Well, if you are publishing using TOPSMENU, you can hold down the Alt key and press X at any time while you are in the Publish a Volume submenu of the Server Utilities menu. To let you know the change has taken place and is in effect, TOPS gives you the message NO XSYNC in the top right corner of the menu window. To enable XSYNC, press Alt–X again. The NO XSYNC message will disappear. Remember that unless the NO XSYNC message is displayed, TOPSMENU will run XSYNC as it publishes a volume.

If you are doing your publishing from the DOS prompt as described earlier in this chapter, use the /X option of the PUBLISH command. If you want to manually run XSYNC, for example to prepare a volume for publishing, use the command at the DOS command line, with the following syntax:

XSYNC [?] [/S] [/Y] [/D] [d: [path]]

The command's switches are described in Table 9-2.

Using XDIR

The XDIR utility can be used for two different purposes, either to view the contents of the Extended Directory file described in the previous section or to view the contents of a remote published volume. In the first instance, XDIR lists all DOS and Unix files plus the data and resource forks of Macintosh files, as seen in Fig. 9-8.

The Macintosh resource forks are actually DOS hidden files. When displaying a Macintosh file, XDIR lists both the real name of the Macintosh file and the name

Table 9-2. The XSYNC switches.

?	Display HELP information about the command on screen.
/S	Update the XDIRSTAT.TPS file in the specified directory and all nested subdirectories.
/Y	Override the Y/N confirmation you are usually required to enter before XSYNC updates a directory.
/D	Delete Macintosh Desktop file in the specified directory. (Any published PC volume that has been mounted on a Macintosh and appears on the desktop will have a Desktop file written to it. If the Desktop file becomes corrupted, or you need to remove the directory, this option will delete it.)

Use d:\path to specify the drive and path on which to run XSYNC. If no path is specified, XSYNC starts in the current drive and directory.

```
XDIR:  Displaying information for directory: C:\MARTY

XDIR counts:  entries:    13  (ndirs:    0, ndata:    7, nrsrc:    6)
XDIR info:    BirthDate:  6-16-90    8:53a
              ModDate:    6-16-90    9:18a

NetName         Type      RealName
-----------     ----      --------
QNORTH1 WQ1     Data
VENDOR  WP      Data
Desktop         Data
R-DESKT0        Rsrc      Desktop
CASHBUD0        Data      CASHBUDGET
R-CASHB0        Rsrc      CASHBUDGET
R-OPTIQ0WP      Rsrc      OPTIQ.WP
INDEPTH0        Data      InDepth Report
R-INDEP0        Rsrc      InDepth Report
LETTERT0        Data      Letter to Editor
R-LETTE1        Rsrc      Letter to Editor
Novella         Data
R-NOVEL0        Rsrc      Novella

♦ Sat  6-16-1990 C:\MARTY>
```

Fig. 9-8. The XDIR command

given to it by TOPS. The TOPS resource fork names begin with the letters R-.

When viewing the contents of a remote published volume, XDIR displays the Macintosh or Unix real name as well as a network name created by TOPS, as you can see from Fig. 9-9.

The TOPS/Macintosh InterBase program and the TOPS/Sun Name Binding Protocol Daemon convert the native name into a TOPS network name that can be used by DOS. The syntax for the XDIR command is:

XDIR [?] [/A] [d: [path]]

```
♦ Sat  6-16-1990 C:\MARTY>XDIR J:

XDIR - Extended Directory Viewing Utility for TOPS/DOS Version 2
Copyright (C) Sun Microsystems, Inc.  1987, 1988.  All rights reserved.
XDIR            Version 2.10      10/17/88

XDIR:  Displaying information for directory: J:\

NetName         Type      RealName
-----------     ----      --------
CASHBUDG        MacF      CASHBUDGET
INDEPTH_        MacF      InDepth Report
LETTER_T        MacF      Letter to Editor
OPTIQ.WP        MacF      OPTIQ.WP

♦ Sat  6-16-1990 C:\MARTY>
```

Fig. 9-9. Network name displayed.

where ? is used to display HELP information and /A means display all the information in the XDIRSTAT.TPS file. If you do not include /A, you see only the DOS-usable name, the real name, and the file type for each entry. You can see the effect of the /A option in Fig. 9-10.

Note that the drive and path on which to run XDIR must be stated or else XDIR looks in the current drive and directory.

Using XDEL

This utility deletes all the TOPS-created hidden files in a directory, such as the resource forks of Macintosh files, the Desktop file, and the XDIRSTAT.TPS file. These files are normally removed in order to delete a directory. Be careful, however, because the deletion of a Macintosh resource fork renders a Macintosh application file and some data files unusable. The syntax of the XDEL command is:

XDEL [?] [/S] [/Y] [/N] [d:[path]]

where ? is used to display HELP information and /S means run XDEL recursively, that is, in the specified directory and all branching subdirectories. You can see the XDEL command at work in Fig. 9-11 where it was used to remove a hidden file from the KEY directory seen earlier.

The /Y option is used to override the confirmation required before XDEL updates a directory. Enter /N if you want to be prompted before the deletion of each file. The drive and path on which to run XDEL must be stated or else XDEL starts in the current drive and directory.

```
XDIR - Extended Directory Viewing Utility for TOPS/DOS Version 2
Copyright (C) Sun Microsystems, Inc. 1987, 1988. All rights reserved.
XDIR            Version 2.10    10/17/88

XDIR: Displaying information for directory: J:\

NetName: CASHBUDG           Type: 6      RealName: CASHBUDGET
    Fileno:    1920   Flags:    0        FndrInfo: XLBNXCEL
    BirthDate: 2-01-88  6:32p            ModDate:  6-19-89    9:15a
    Size:         5934                   AuxSize:       0
NetName: INDEPTH_            Type: 6      RealName: InDepth Report
    Fileno:    1925   Flags:    0        FndrInfo: WORDMACA
    BirthDate: 6-19-89  9:13a            ModDate:  6-19-89    9:13a
    Size:         3060                   AuxSize:     730
NetName: LETTER_T            Type: 6      RealName: Letter to Editor
    Fileno:    1923   Flags:    0        FndrInfo: WORDMACA
    BirthDate: 6-19-89  9:13a            ModDate:  6-19-89    9:13a
    Size:         3060                   AuxSize:     730
NetName: OPTIQ.WP            Type: 6      RealName: OPTIQ.WP
    Fileno:    191d   Flags:    0        FndrInfo: TEXTTOPC
    BirthDate: 6-11-90 11:20p            ModDate:  6-11-90   11:20p
    Size:        25357                   AuxSize:       0

• Sat  6-16-1990 C:\MARTY>
```

Fig. 9-10. The XDIR /A option

```
• Sat  6-16-1990 C:\>XDEL \KEY

XDEL - System File Deletion Utility for TOPS/DOS Version 2
Copyright (C) Sun Microsystems, Inc.  1987, 1988. All rights reserved.
XDEL            Version 2.10    10/17/88


WARNING - Please read this!

XDEL makes assumptions about zero-length files and will delete some of them.
It will also delete any DOS hidden files which are portions of
Macintosh applications (usually they are named with 'R-').
In addition, the TOPS extended directory files (hidden DOS files
with the name XDIRSTAT.TPS) will automatically be deleted.

If there are any files which you want preserved, please use caution.
You may use the TOPS system utilities TDIR and TDEL for more precision,
or the /N option to be prompted for each USER file being deleted.

XDEL:  Deleting TOPS files for directory:  C:\KEY
       Proceed?  (y/n)
```

Fig. 9-11. The XDEL command

Using TDIR

The TDIR utility displays the contents of a specified directory, which is what XDIR does. However, unlike XDIR, TDIR presents its results in DOS-directory format, but including hidden files. You can see the output of this command in Fig. 9-12.

This command is handy when you want a more familiar look at files. The summary of file types is also useful because it distinguishes between hidden system

```
• Sat  6-16-1990 C:\>DIR \KEY

Volume in drive C is TOWER 386
Directory of  C:\KEY

.              <DIR>      6-16-90   8:39a
..             <DIR>      6-16-90   8:39a
       2 File(s)   1665024 bytes free

• Sat  6-16-1990 C:\>TDIR \KEY

Tops Directory of C:\KEY

.              <DIR>      6-16-90   8:39a
..             <DIR>      6-16-90   8:39a
XDIRSTAT TPS      1404    6-16-90   8:40a     (hidden)
       2 Normal File(s)
       1 Hidden File(s)
          1665024 bytes free

• Sat  6-16-1990 C:\>
```

Fig. 9-12. The TDIR command

files used by DOS and other hidden files. You can use TDIR within a directory or use a path statement to specify the drive/directory you want to examine.

Using TDEL

The TDEL utility deletes hidden files one at a time, accomplishing the same end as XDEL but with greater protection against accidental erasures. The syntax is:

```
TDEL [d:[path]] filename
```

If no path is specified, it looks in the current directory. If you provide a resource fork filename, TDEL deletes just that file. If you specify a data fork filename, then TDEL deletes both the data fork and the associated resource fork. You can see TDEL at work in Fig. 9-13.

Using TCOPY

As we mentioned in Chapter 5, the TCOPY utility allows you to copy files with DOS while preserving the special Macintosh file structure. In normal file reading and writing across the TOPS network, TOPS keeps track of both parts of the Macintosh file fork structure despite the fact that there is no real equivalent in the DOS operating system. If you use the plain DOS COPY or XCOPY commands to copy a file from a mounted Mac drive onto a PC, or to copy a DOS or Mac file from the PC to a Mac volume, then the special file structure required by the Macintosh is corrupted and you will have difficulty using the file.

```
            Volume in drive C is TOWER 386
            Directory of   C:\KEY

            .           <DIR>       6-16-90    8:39a
            ..          <DIR>       6-16-90    8:39a
                 2 File(s)    1665024 bytes free

    + Sat  6-16-1990 C:\>TDIR \KEY

    Tops Directory of C:\KEY

            .           <DIR>       6-16-90    8:39a
            ..          <DIR>       6-16-90    8:39a
            XDIRSTAT TPS    1404    6-16-90    8:40a      (hidden)
                 2 Normal File(s)
                 1 Hidden File(s)
                    1665024 bytes free

    + Sat  6-16-1990 C:\>TDEL \KEY
    File not found

    + Sat  6-16-1990 C:\>TDEL \KEY\XDIRSTAT.TPS

    + Sat  6-16-1990 C:\>
```

Fig. 9-13. The TDEL command

Instead of the DOS commands XCOPY and COPY, use the TCOPY utility. TCOPY has a full range of options to cope with most situations. The syntax of the command is as follows:

TCOPY path\file [path\file] [/P] [/S [/C]] [/W] [/D] [/F] [/U] [/M m/d/y]

If no path specified, then, like COPY, the command assumes current drive and directory is assumed. If no file is specified, then all files are copied. The characters * and ? in file are treated as wildcards unless the /W option is given. Note TCOPY does not allow a file to be copied onto itself.

The /P option prompts before copying each file, allowing you to specify all files and then decide on each one in turn as they are listed by the TCOPY command. Use /S when you want to include files in subdirectories of the current or specified directory. The /S option recursively copies all subdirectories, and if the destination does not have matching subdirectories, then they can be created by TCOPY. You will be prompted before the new directories are made unless the /C option is specified.

Sometimes you will find the characters * and ? in Macintosh filenames. Use the /W option with TCOPY so that characters * and ? are not treated as wildcards. On the other hand, when you want TCOPY to act just like the DOS COPY command, use the /D option. In DOS mode, the TCOPY command will work only with DOS names and data; TOPS extended information is not copied. TOPS does not need to be loaded for TCOPY to work in this mode. The /T option translates Macintosh and Unix text files into DOS format.

The TCOPY command has some options useful when backing up files. Specify the /U option to copy updated or newly created files (those whose ARC flag is not set to Yes). To copy files modified since a particular date use /M followed by the date, as in:

TCOPY *.* J: /M 07/01/90

This instruction copies all files of the current directory that have been modified since July 1, 1990, to drive J.

If you do copy a DOS file from a PC to a Mac using the DOS COPY command, it will lack a resource fork on the Mac. You can create a resource fork for the file by opening it with ResEdit. This sounds complex but is fairly easy to do and is described in Chapter 12.

TOPS BATCH FILES

The TOPS DOS command language becomes an especially powerful tool when placed into a batch file. In fact, TOPS comes with several examples of batch files. This section explains what they do and how you can enhance them or write your own to customize your environment.

As we saw earlier in this chapter, a batch file is essentially a series of different commands combined together into one. These commands sequentially execute when the file they are stored in is summoned. Batch files are useful in situations where the same commands are often repeated, such as when a server always publishes the same volumes and/or printer.

Making Batch Files

All batch files are distinguished by the extension BAT that is added to the end of the filename. The contents of a batch file are nothing more than typed characters. These are the same characters you might type if you were separately executing the commands that the batch file stores. In other words, if you can type, you can write a batch file. You need only start up your favorite word processor, create a file (including the BAT extension), and line by line type out the series of commands that you want executed.

There is one twist to this procedure. You must store the file in text only format. This format also goes by the names DOS Text (WordPerfect), Unformatted (Micro-Soft Word), Non-Document (Wordstar), and ASCII (many others). For example, if you write the batch file in WordPerfect, you can use the Ctrl–F5 command to save it. After Ctrl–F5, you press 1 for DOS Text and then press 1 again for Save. Enter the name of the file and press Enter. A simple way to write batch files at the DOS prompt is to use the COPY command.

Another method of making a text file is to copy text from the screen (sometimes referred to as the CONsole by DOS) to a file. To do this you can use the following command syntax at the DOS prompt:

COPY CON FILENAME.EXT

Thus you could create a file called LOAD.BAT by typing

COPY CON LOAD.BAT

and then pressing Enter. DOS responds by giving you a blank line on which to type. Type the first command that you want in your batch file, taking care to type accurately, using the Backspace key to back over any mistakes and retype them. When the line is correct, press Enter and proceed with the next line of the file. You cannot go back and edit a line after you have pressed Enter. If you make a mistake, you must exit the file and re-create it. To exit the file, which automatically saves it, press F6 or Ctrl–Z at the end of the last line. Then you press Enter. The characters ^Z signify the end of the file and DOS writes the text to disk.

Another drawback of the COPY CON method is that DOS does not warn you if a file of the same name already exists. This means that if you issue the command COPY CON LOAD.BAT and already have a file called LOAD.BAT in the current directory, the contents of that existing file are overwritten by the new material. DOS offers the program EDLIN.COM as an alternative to COPY CON. In EDLIN, you have a very basic line editor, meaning that you edit line by line, with each line numbered. The advantage of EDLIN over COPY CON is that you can go back and change specific lines, add lines, and delete lines. Instructions on how to use EDLIN can be found in any DOS manual. If you are doing extensive work with DOS and want to write batch files with something less weighty than a full-blown word processor but more sophisticated than EDLIN, you might want to consider QuickDOS II, a DOS disk manager that comes with a built-in ASCII editor that is very easy to use.

Using Batch Files

When the name of a file is entered at the DOS prompt, and DOS finds that the file's extension is BAT, DOS knows that it should execute the commands inside the file. The file LOADTOPS.BAT, which starts the TOPS/DOS server software, is one example. The commands inside LOADTOPS execute when LOADTOPS is typed at the DOS prompt. LOADCLNT.BAT, which is a way to load a client only version of TOPS/DOS, is another example. In addition, if you have used the REMEMBER option from the TOPS menu, you have created a batch file called TOPSTART.BAT that does publishing and mounting.

Here is a line-by-line interpretation of the LOADTOPS.BAT file in which you can see the use of an **if** statement to give the batch file a decision making capability:

alap

    loads the FlashCard driver.

pstack

    loads the network protocols.

topstalk

    loads the network redirector.

topskrnl

    loads entire network kernel (server and client).

echo off

    DOS command that suppresses screen output.

if not exist \topstart.bat goto nostart

    tells DOS to go to the line called :nostart if there is no file in the root directory called topstart.bat.

echo on

    resumes screen output.

topstart.bat

    executes the topstart.bat file.

:nostart

> this is the line, named in the above goto statement, which ends the execution of the file.

By naming a line in the file with a colon and a word (in this case :nostart) and then using the if not exist statement, the batch file can direct DOS past the line that runs topstart.bat if that file does not exist. The use of goto with a name is very convenient when you want to give your batch files some flexibility.

In the case of LOADTOPS, the goto step was necessary because of a feature of batch files under earlier versions of DOS that we mentioned earlier: if a batch file tells DOS to run another batch file, then the second batch file controls DOS, and DOS will not return to the original file. In programming terms, you cannot *nest* batch files unless you use the CALL command. Under versions of DOS that do not support CALL, a simple call to a batch file is the last line of a batch file that gets executed.

For a further example of batch files you might already have used, here are the contents of a sample TOPSTART.BAT:

```
TOPS /q STATION "Rich's PC"
TOPS /q PUBLISH C:\LOTUS123 as "LOTUS FILES" /RW
TOPS /q PUBLISH C:\WP as "WORDPERFECT FILES" /R
```

In this case, the TOPSTART.BAT file creates the user name, and then publishes two subdirectories. The first subdirectory, called LOTUS123 on the hard disk, is published with the alias of LOTUS FILES, in a read-and-write mode. The second subdirectory, WP, is also published with an alias and in read-only mode.

As we mentioned earlier, one of the most common batch files used in the DOS world is AUTOEXEC.BAT, the special file that is automatically executed when the computer starts up. Many users like to fully automate the network's server by placing the LOADTOPS command into the AUTOEXEC.BAT FILE, so that TOPS automatically starts at the time the computer is booted. Two sample AUTOEXEC.BAT files listed below show how this can be done:

```
PATH=C:\;C:\DOS;C:\TOPS
PROMPT $P$G
LOADTOPS.BAT
```

Note that if a batch file is named within a batch file, it should be preceded by either CALL or COMMAND C as in the example below:

```
PATH=C:\;C:\DOS;C:\TOPS
COMMAND /C LOADTOPS.BAT
PROMPT $P$G
```

If COMMAND /C were not included, the AUTOEXEC.BAT would have terminated at LOADTOPS. The only time this isn't necessary is when the second batch file is the last line. In the first example, because LOADTOPS was the last line anyway, COMMAND /C was purposely left out.

Client computers can also use the AUTOEXEC.BAT file to their benefit. The primary difference between the server's and the client's AUTOEXEC is that the client would call LOADCLNT.BAT rather than LOADTOPS.BAT. The client might also choose to load NetPrint:

```
PATH=C:\;C:\DOS;C:\TOPS
COMMAND /C LOADCLNT.BAT
PROMPT $P$G
NETPRINT
```

Another application for batch files might be valuable if NetPrint were used in an environment where only some of the application programs had PostScript printer drivers. In the case when loaded applications do not have PostScript support, a PostScript translating program would need to be loaded, and NetPrint's configuration would have to be changed. This could be handled by writing a batch file for loading the application, that also loads the PostScript translator and reconfigures NetPrint accordingly. Then when the application was closed, the batch file could also set things back the way they were before. Following is an example called DB.BAT that shows how this could be done for use with an application like dBASE III.

PROPS.EXE	Loads the PostScript translator.
CONFIGUR /W+	Reconfigures NetPrint to use the translator.
DBASE	Loads the application program.
CONFIGUR /W−	When application is closed, the batch file continues to execute and this line resets NetPrint.
ECHO Y | PRINT/U	Unloads PostScript translator (the Y is important because you must confirm unloading of PROPS.EXE by typing Y).

The above example assumes that NetPrint was already loaded when this batch file is run. If that is not the case, add the NetPrint command to the beginning.

Finally, a batch file can be useful if the client normally mounts the same volumes on the server. This is one case, however, where it might not be advisable to include the mount commands in the AUTOEXEC.BAT file of the client, or in a TOPSTART.BAT file. The reason for this caution is that the mount commands will not properly execute unless the server is already published. If the client powers up before the server, then the client's mounts will fail and not be repeated unless the machine is rebooted. Consequently, mounting might be best left in the user's control.

A simple step to help the user in this case is to use the Remember option on the TOPS Menu to create the TOPSTART.BAT FILE and then rename the file to something else such as MOUNTUP.BAT. When the client needed to log on to the network drives, they need only type the command MOUNTUP. Below is a listing that shows how a MOUNTUP.BAT might look. This example mounts the volumes published by the server in the earlier example:

TOPS MOUNT d: TO "Rich's PC" "Lotus Files" /RW
TOPS MOUNT e: TO "Rich's PC" "WordPerfect Files" /RW

The above example assumes that the volumes were published in the local zone, without a password, as readable and writable. This file would include another line if a printer were also being mounted.

A SYSTEM OF BATCH FILES

The commands that are placed in the AUTOEXEC.BAT file of a system vary, depending upon how the system is configured. You can see what is in the AUTO-EXEC.BAT file by moving to the root directory and typing TYPE AUTOEXEC.BAT then pressing Enter. As an example of what might be contained in the AUTO-EXEC.BAT, consider the following listing:

```
PROMPT $D $P$G
PATH C:\;C:\DOS;C:\BAT;C:\TOPS
CALL LOADTOPS
MENU
```

The first line tells DOS to show you the date and time in the prompt, so that it appears like this:

Tue 1-30-1990 C:\TOPS>—

The second line sets the appropriate paths so that DOS can always find programs stored in the root directory, the DOS directory, the BAT directory, the TOPS and the DOS directory. The third line calls the LOADTOPS batch file, while the fourth line tells DOS to run a program called MENU, described in a moment.

You could change the last line of the above batch file to an application name if you always wanted to load a particular one every time you started up the system. However, the MENU program gives you a choice of programs to run. The MENU program is actually just another batch file.

You can write batch files to run applications when there are several steps involved. For example, a batch file called X286.BAT might run Excel and could contain the following commands:

ECHO OFF	Turn off screen echo
CD \WINDOWS\FILES	Change to \WINDOWS\FILES subdirectory
C:\WINDOWS\EXCEL	Run Excel
C:	Log onto drive C
CD\	Return to the root directory

This tells DOS to change to the FILES subdirectory of the WINDOWS directory, and then load Excel from the WINDOWS directory.

After the third line of the above batch file has been carried out, control of the computer is passed to Excel. However, the rest of the batch file is held in memory. When the user quits Excel, the fourth line of the batch file picks up control of the system, telling DOS to log onto drive C if the logged drive has changed, and to return to the root directory. Note that the ECHO command turns off the display of DOS commands on the screen so that they do not distract the user.

A DOS Menu System

You can use a system of batch files to take care of loading different application programs and also several versions of the same program, using different parameters. The last line of the sample AUTOEXEC.BAT told DOS to run the batch file called MENU.BAT. This file might contain the following:

```
ECHO OFF
CLS
C:
CD\
TYPE MENU.MSG
```

The MENU.MSG file is another ASCII file that draws a menu. This can be a fancy boxed arrangement, as seen in Fig. 9-14.

The fancy boxes can be drawn quite easily in word processors such as WordPerfect and DisplayWrite 4 that have a cursor draw feature, together with the ability to save files as ASCII text. Alternatively, you can use a simple text list, as seen in Fig. 9-15.

If the MENU.BAT file is stored in any of the directories specified in the PATH statement of the AUTOEXEC.BAT, you can use it at any time. Thus you could modify the X286.BAT file to read:

ECHO OFF	Turn off screen echo
CD \WINDOWS\FILES	Change to WINDOW\FILES subdirectory
C:\WINDOWS\EXCEL	Run Excel
MENU	Run MENU.BAT

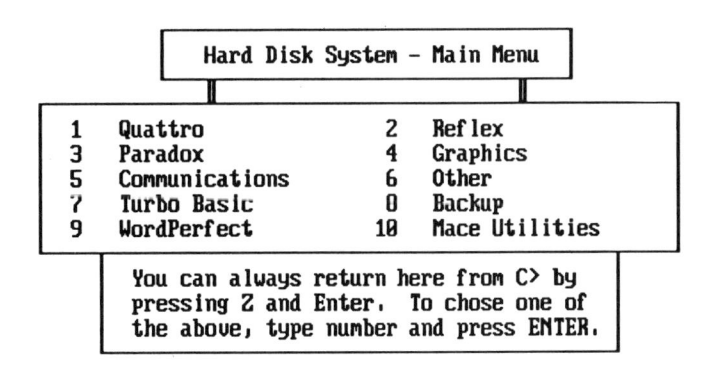

```
┌─────────── Hard Disk System - Main Menu ───────────┐
│                                                     │
│   1   Quattro           2   Reflex                  │
│   3   Paradox           4   Graphics                │
│   5   Communications    6   Other                   │
│   7   Turbo Basic       8   Backup                  │
│   9   WordPerfect      10   Mace Utilities          │
└─────────────────────────────────────────────────────┘
      │ You can always return here from C> by        │
      │ pressing 2 and Enter.  To chose one of       │
      │ the above, type number and press ENTER.      │
      └───────────────────────────────────────────────┘

  ◆ Sat   6-16-1990  C:\>
```

Fig. 9-14. Fancy MENU.MSG

Note how the contents of MENU.BAT now take care of the return to C:\ and display of MENU.MSG.

The next step in refining the system is to change the name of X286.BAT to 2.BAT. This means that when users look at the menu message and decide on the second option, they can type 2 and press Enter, and Excel will be loaded. When they quit Excel, they will return to the menu.

Consider the files listed in Fig. 9-16. These allow you to select and run several different programs, including Excel with several different initially loaded files.

Parameter Passing

In the system described in Fig. 9-16, the names of the files to be loaded are supplied in the batch file, but this might be considered too restrictive. You can have a menu option that allows the user to specify a file by using batch file feature called *parameter passing*. As we saw with TOPS commands, a parameter is a piece of information supplied on the command line when a command is issued. For example, in the command statement WP REPORT.DOC the file REPORT.DOC called is a parameter, as is the spreadsheet SALES.XLS in the statement EXCEL SALES.XLS.

You can build parameters into your batch files. Consider this modified version of the X286.BAT or 2.BAT file:

ECHO OFF	Turn off screen echo
CD \WINDOWS\FILES	Change to \WINDOWS\FILES
C:\WINDOWS\EXCEL %1	Run Excel with parameter 1
MENU	Run MENU.BAT

Here the characters %1 stand for the first parameter supplied with the batch file name. Thus, if you had the above code in a file called 2.BAT you could enter 2 SALES at the DOS prompt, and Excel would be loaded, complete with the worksheet SALES.

You can use the parameter passing technique with TOPS batch files for such variables as station names. For example, here you can see the contents of a file

```
PC Menu System:

1  Load TOPS
2  Load 1-2-3
3  Load WordPerfect
4  Format a floppy disk
5  Run Norton Utilities

Type number and press Enter


C:\>
```

Fig. 9-15. Simple text file MENU.MSG

called START.BAT that is an alternative to TOPSTART. This file uses a parameter instead of a fixed station name to start TOPS:

```
TOPS /q STATION %1
TOPS /q PUBLISH C:\WP\DOCS as DOCS /RW
```

When the user enters START XT then XT is used as the station name. If the user enters START Fred then Fred is used as the station name.

Up to ten parameters (%0 through %9) can be passed in batch files. If you need more, then you should explore the SHIFT command or the use of named parameters with the SET command. These are described in most DOS manuals and discussed extensively in *Advanced MS-DOS Batch File Programming*, (Windcrest book No. 3197) by Dan Gookin.

A Rebooting System

You might need to alter the configuration of your system to accommodate TOPS together with programs that are memory hungry. While TOPS and most other memory-resident programs can be unloaded from memory, no commands alter the information loaded from your CONFIG.SYS file. This is the file that tells DOS about such parameters as files and buffers, as well as device drivers you want loaded, such as RAM disks, Bernoulli drives, and so on. (In fact, earlier versions of TOPS/DOS used a device driver called ATALK.SYS instead of ALAP and PSTACK. This meant that the whole of TOPS could not be unloaded from the command line like it can with version 2.1.)

Some device drivers occupy a lot of memory, and so might need to be unloaded before TOPS and a memory-intensive application can be run. To unload a

```
AUTOEXEC.BAT   (place in root directory)
PROMPT $P$G
PATH=C:\;C:\DOS;C:\BAT;C:\WINDOWS
MENU
```

```
MENU.BAT   (in \BAT)
ECHO OFF
CLS
C:
CD\
TYPE MENU.MSG
```

```
Main Menu
1 Excel with SALES.XLS
2 Excel with SHEET1
3 WordPerfect
Type number, then press Enter
C:\>
```

```
MENU.MSG   (in root)
Main Menu
1 Excel with SALES.XLS
2 Excel with SHEET1
3 WordPerfect
Type number, then press Enter
```

```
1.BAT   (in \BAT)
ECHO OFF
CD \WINDOWS\FILES
C:\WINDOWS\EXCEL SALES
MENU
```

```
2.BAT   (in \BAT)
ECHO OFF
CD \WINDOWS\FILES
C:\WINDOWS\EXCEL
MENU
```

```
3.BAT   (in \BAT)
ECHO OFF
CD \WP\FILES
C:\WP\WP
MENU
```

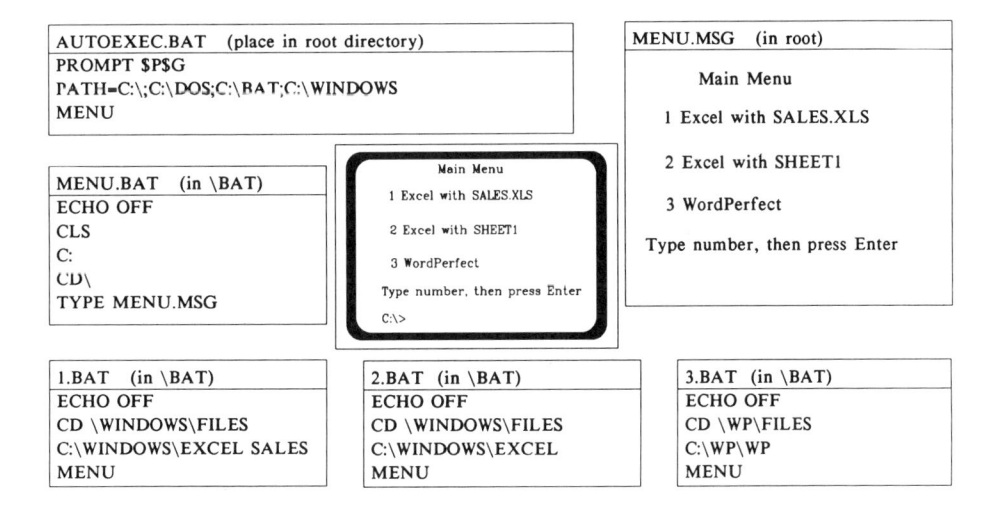

Fig. 9-16. DOS menu system.

device driver requires altering the CONFIG.SYS and rebooting the system. To perform this from a batch file requires a simple little utility called REBOOT.COM. This enables you to set up a batch file that reboots the system for you, after changing the current CONFIG.SYS file. A set of files to perform this operation are described in Chapter 14 in the section on RAM Cram.

CONCLUSION

Through its extensive support of the DOS command line, TOPS/DOS can be highly automated and worked into the overall control system of a PC. As you become increasingly proficient in batch file writing, you will find many ways to simplify operations for yourself and others using BATs.

10
Word Processing and Translating

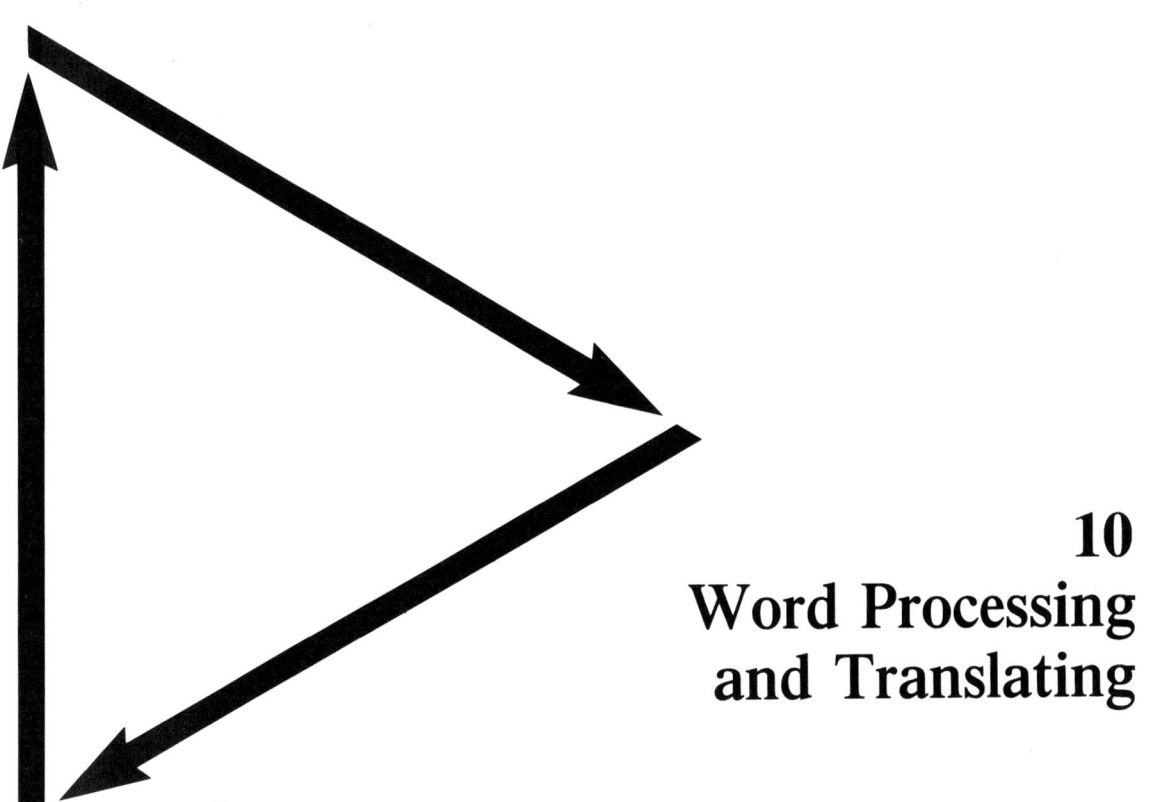

SO FAR IN THIS BOOK, we have looked at the nuts and bolts of networking PCs and Macs with TOPS, from the cabling to the menus and commands. This is the first of three chapters that attempt to put this technical information into a practical and functional perspective, looking at TOPS networking. We look at TOPS from the point of view of typical users, faced with typical problems, in the solution of which TOPS can play a significant part. This chapter and the next two assume that you didn't buy TOPS just to see if it works, but that you had a real need for some aspect of what the product can do. We also assume that you will not mind bearing with us while we review some of the basic issues that are behind many of the problems that TOPS can help solve.

WHY THINGS ARE AS THEY ARE

The growth of the microcomputer to the level of a universal phenomenon, to the one on-every-desk status of the telephone, is well under way. The advantages of linking these powerful information processors is increasingly apparent. Even small companies can save large amounts of time and effort by avoiding the need to re-process information from one medium to another. The sales figures for last quarter that appear in one person's presentation to investors might be needed the next day in someone else's presentation to vendors, or someone else's work on the next quarter's budget. A big step to greater efficiency was taken by putting the information on computer in the first place, the presentation looks better, the numbers were revised faster. But if everyone who needs the numbers has to reenter them the gains from computerization are eroded. By sharing the data electronically, one input operation serves numerous output functions.

Diversity

Given the enormous potential benefits of electronic sharing, what are the obstacles? There must be obstacles, otherwise everyone would already be connected. In the opening chapters, we briefly addressed the issues of cost in relation to networking. Certainly there is expense involved in networking, but then again the move from calculators and typewriters to microcomputers was expensive. So cost is only an obstacle as long as it exceeds perceived return on investment. We have seen that TOPS is a relatively inexpensive addition to a computer system. There are issues of security and privacy, but these are being addressed by such features as the password protection and selective access offered by TOPS. So what obstacles to electronic sharing of text and data remain?

The answer seems to be diversity. That is the number of different arrangements used to store information, store it in such a way that it is not directly accessible to others. The cost of networking and the administrative effort required to coordinate installation and use of a network is not justifiable if the users simply cannot read each other's data. For example, suppose that the sales figures are gathered by a custom dBASE application that collates data from retail invoices. The dBASE files reside on a PC that is on the network. The person who is creating the presentation to the board is also on the network and so has an electronic path to the files. However, if the presentation is being prepared with a program that cannot read dBASE files, the network is not really a big help.

So a major obstacle to the productive sharing of text and data across a network is the diversity of file formats being employed by the applications that are currently in use. Individuals buying microcomputers for their own use have been relatively free to choose whichever application they like the best. Many have enjoyed exercising this freedom because it was a pleasant change from the strict rules that governed the world of the mainframe. The early model of the personal computer user is one who inputs the data and outputs the data. The format that the data is stored in makes little difference to this microcosm until the wider community of users is considered. Then it makes sense for a PC user to buy a program that stores in the XYZ format if that user wants to store some data files on a disk and pass them on to another XYZ user.

But storing files on a floppy is not an investment like buying a network connection. Once you have decided that a network is worth installing, you need to consider who can share what with whom, and possibly draw up rules about which formats must be used. This is one of the areas where the human factor of networking comes on strong. Once you start dictating parameters about application selection, then you are running contrary to some of the freedom of choice that is so valued by personal computer users. There are several approaches to this problem.

The Glorious Unified Company-Wide Standard

One approach to the diversity of file formats is summed up as "make everyone use the same program." This approach promises great benefits. Training and support costs will be reduced because there is only one program to support. Upgrading, a major headache now that every quarter there is a major new version of at least one major software program, that will be simplified. Document sharing will be free from the hassles of document conversion.

The negative aspects of this approach are considerable and really hinge on one factor—it is unrealistic. For a start, you need a piece of software to standardize on. Many corporations have found that it is hard to find one piece of personal computing software that "does everything" and does it well. Programs that attempt to integrate word processing, spreadsheet, database, and graphics have generally failed when compared with what can be accomplished by specialized stand-alone applications. Furthermore, unless you can find an application that runs the same across several hardware platforms, including IBM and Macintosh, then you will effectively be taking the "all one machine or else" approach that has proved very unpopular.

The "one for all" approach might stand a chance if today's business world were less volatile, and the work force less mobile. At least one company has worked hard to establish a company-wide personal computing standard, only to be merged with another company that is on another standard. Even if the corporate leadership does not change, the personnel using the computers most certainly will. These days many new employees come complete with computing skills and computer philosophies, and it is too much to expect that they will all think the same way. Besides, even if you can establish a company standard and make it stick, there is always the outside world to think about. You can hardly impose your standard on your business partners and customers, and these days a lot of information passes between partners over electronic links. The bottom line is that diversity is a fact of life. To run an effective personal computer network, you need to be able to understand what is feasible when it comes to file sharing and file conversion.

WORD PROCESSING AT WORK

The one thing that users of personal computers do with their computers, more than anything else, is word processing. The ability to empower even the clumsiest typist to create great looking documents is still a major selling point for microcomputers. In companies, such as law firms, that rely on the properly printed word, the benefits of word processing on a personal computer include the ability to store on disk documents that used to take up whole filing cabinets, and reuse those documents through simple file retrieval rather than retyping.

Word Processing on TOPS

Where does TOPS fit in the word processing task of the typical office? One common answer seems to be "where word processing turns into desktop publishing." One of the great legends of the computer industry is how the Macintosh rode into corporate offices of the back of desktop publishing (DTP). Although there are now some excellent products for desktop publishing on the IBM, the fact is that the Macintosh has established itself as the tool of choice for many graphic artists involved in publications, from *USA Today* to the lowliest newsletter. A typical arrangement is to have basic word processing done on an IBM and then transfer the file to a Mac for incorporation in a DTP document.

Before looking at some of the problems and solutions involved in this IBM-to-Mac transfer, we want to look at the several good reasons for thinking that this arrangement will continue to be popular. At the risk of annoying some devout Mac fans, we suggest that, for straight word processing there are few benefits to be gained from moving from an IBM to a Mac. Many people who know how to do word processing learned on IBMs and are very comfortable with the old monochrome, mono-spacing, IBM monitor. They have a hard time adjusting to mouse oriented editing and do not need the fonts, styles, and graphics of the Mac. For example, most of this book was typed on an IBM XT clone using WordPerfect 5.0. For editing the text was printed out double-spaced in Courier 10 pitch, a non-proportional font that is easy to edit. The only styles that were used were the occasional bold face and underline.

Some material was prepared on a Mac II using MacWrite II and WordPerfect for the Mac. The files were then accessed across TOPS. We found that you can navigate a document and perform search and replace operations just as fast on the XT as you can on a Macintosh II. Because the book was written in chapters, the 360 K capacity of an old 5.25 inch floppy disk was not a problem. The only place that we missed extra speed was in spell checking, and so TOPS was sometimes used to read files from the XT to an 80386 machine where the spelling checker worked much faster. The street price of an IBM XT clone equipped with a 20 MB hard disk is around $800. You cannot buy the most basic Macintosh for that price. This price differential will ensure that PCs will be doing word processing for some time to come. While you might argue that WordPerfect is not an easy program to learn, if it is the only program a user learns, the time it takes is not that great. Where the Macintosh excels in the area of layout, graphics, and the ease with which new users can learn a variety of programs. If you spend enough on extra equipment the Macintosh can now handle entire book production projects including all of the page formatting, typesetting, and illustration.

Another area in which TOPS keeps cropping up as part of a word processing solution is in offices where the Mac has gained a stronghold and is being used heavily for word processing. More and more we are finding that whole sections of a company have "gone over to the Mac" but still need a way of sending word processing documents to those sections still "on IBM." So, given that Macs and IBMs will need to share word processing documents for some time to come, let us look at how this sharing is accomplished.

Reading Versus Translating

One of the easiest scenarios to deal with in IBM/Mac word processing is where both sides are using the same word processor. This means that you can read the files from other user's directly into your program without using a translation program. You might have to take a few extra steps, but essentially the procedure is automatic. For example, if the IBM folks are using WordPerfect 4.2 and the Mac people are using WordPerfect Macintosh, then file sharing is relatively painless. Users on the IBM side need do nothing special. Users on the Mac side can open WordPerfect-PC files simply by pointing at them

When a Macintosh volume has been mounted by the PC, the WordPerfect-PC Retrieve (F10) command can be used to specify Macintosh WordPerfect files. The List Files command (F5) can also be used to read a directory of the Macintosh drive and select files for editing. Users on the Mac side can open WordPerfect-PC files simply by pointing at them in the File Open dialog box.

Users of WordPerfect-Mac will see a special dialog box when attempting to open a file that was created by WordPerfect 4.2. This box asks you to confirm that the file being opened is in WordPerfect 4.2 format, rather than plain text, as you can see from Fig. 10-1.

You need to make sure that the 4.2 format button is checked and then click OK to bring in the WordPerfect-PC file. All formats and text attributes such as boldface and underline will be carried over from the PC to the Mac. Note that special versions of WordPerfect 4.2 can run under other operating systems besides DOS, such

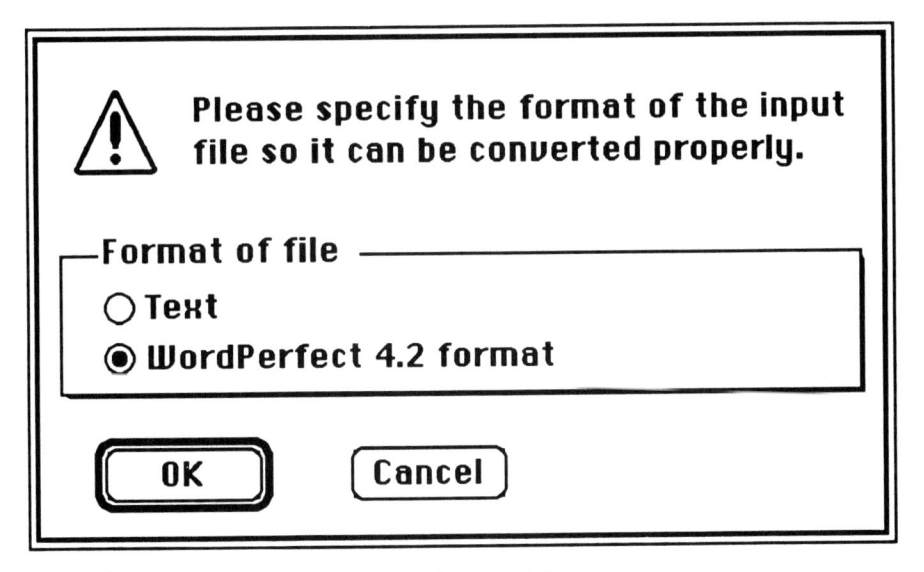

Fig. 10-1. Confirming Conversion of WordPerfect 4.2.

as Unix. If you have Macintoshes networked to Unix systems you can read WordPerfect files from Unix machines.

Of course, many PC users are now working with WordPerfect 5.0 and so to share files with users of the first version of WordPerfect-Mac they must use 5.0's Text In/Out command to save into 4.2 format. Unfortunately this strips the document of some features such as graphics which are not supported by 4.2.

Font selection is also lost when saving from 5.0 to 4.2 if the PC document is not formatted for an Apple printer. However, if you format your document in 5.0 for the Apple LaserWriter and then save it as a 4.2 document, WordPerfect on the Mac will recognize the font and pitch selection.

WordPerfect 5.0 on the PC automatically reads in 4.2 documents and so you should not have problems reading documents created by Macintosh WordPerfect if you save the file in the correct format. The Save As command on the File menu in WordPerfect-Mac has several options, as you can see from Fig. 10-2.

These options are also available when you have read an IBM WordPerfect document into WordPerfect-Mac and want to resave the file. You can store as either Mac or IBM. The Other option provides access to different formats which WordPerfect may support in the future.

When you use Microsoft Word 5.0 on the PC together with Word 4.0 on the Macintosh, you will find that document sharing is very easy. Word-Mac 4.0 will read Word-PC 5.0 files directly from a published volume that has been mounted on the Mac with TOPS. This works whether you use the normal Word-PC 5.0 format or the Rich Text Format option in the Transfer Save menu. Word-PC 5.0 can read documents created by Word-Mac 4.0 if they are saved in the correct format. In Fig.

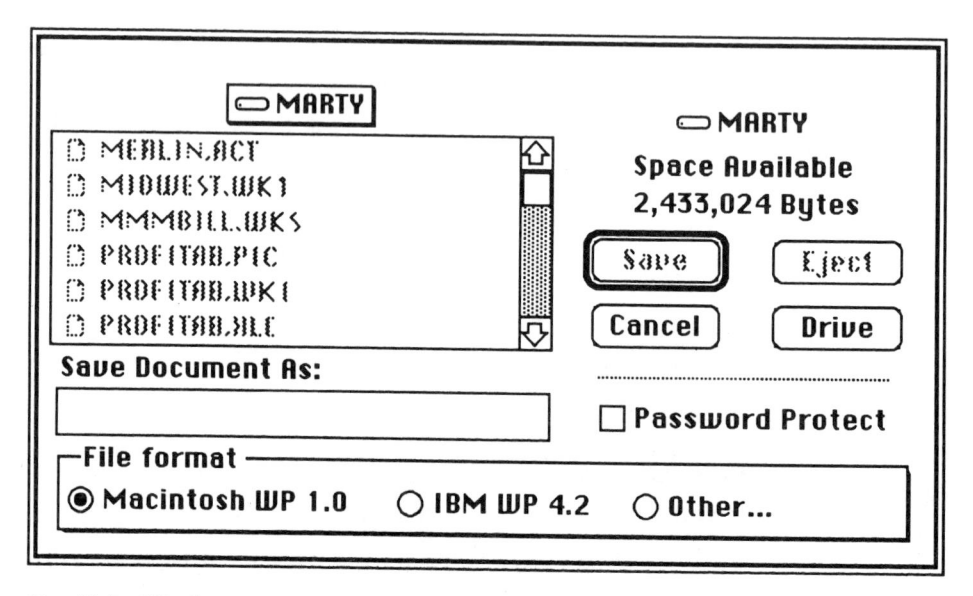

Fig. 10-2. File Save As in WordPerfect-Mac.

10-3, you can see the Format option on Word's File Save As menu lists the MS-DOS version of the program.

THE TRANSLATION ALTERNATIVES

When the time comes to look outside of your applications for file translation you have a variety of options. One option comes with TOPS/Macintosh. This is the program called TOPS Translators, described in detail in the next section. Another option comes free with the Macintosh System software. This is the Apple File Translation facility. Beyond this, commercially available programs offer file translation. Some of these are mentioned later on in this chapter. However, we want to concentrate on those that are free, and freely available.

The cost of TOPS Translators is not a measure of its worth. We have found this program to be reliable and produce impressive results where other software has stumbled.

USING TOPS TRANSLATORS

As you can tell from either the preceding discussion or your own experiences, the need to translate data from Macs to IBMs and back, from one word processing format to another, is common. For this reason TOPS includes a translation utility with TOPS/Macintosh network software called TOPS Translators. The technology used in this program is actually licensed from a company called DataViz, Inc., and they license similar technology to other companies, including Apple. DataViz translators are incorporated into several other conversion products such as MacLink Plus, and the company is continually expanding the list of formats that it covers.

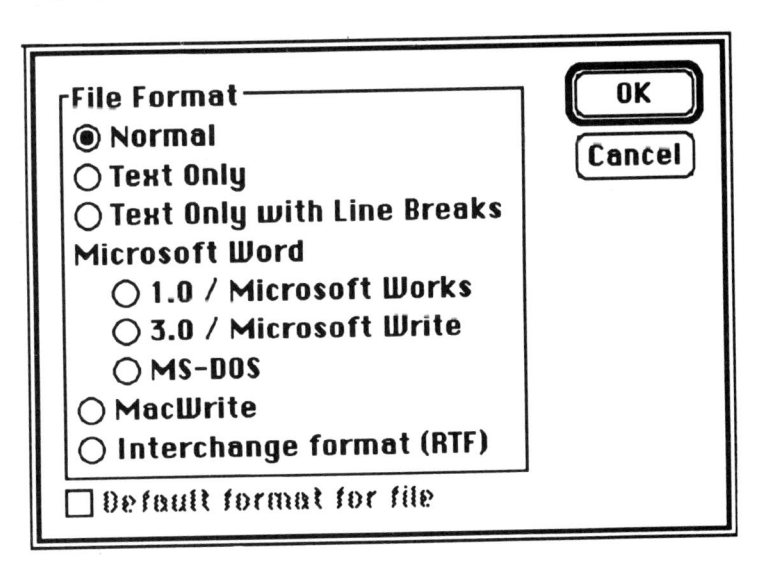

Fig. 10-3. File Save As in Word-Mac.

Starting TOPS Translators

When you first load the application, you will see a screen with two windows. The window on the right is "Foreign" formats, meaning those used by IBM applications. On the left is the Macintosh Formats window, as seen in Fig. 10-4.

The big arrow marked Direction indicates that the current translation direction is toward Macintosh Formats, away from "Foreign" Formats. The Direction arrow controls the translation process. Click on the arrow and it changes to the other direction, Mac to IBM. You can also change the direction of the translation with the radio buttons on either end of the arrow. The two other buttons on the TOPS Translators screen are Set Translators and Select Files. You use Set Translators to specify the formats involved in the conversion process and you use Select Files to specify which files will be converted. Note that the menu for TOPS Translators consists of three items: File, Preferences, and Log. The Edit menu is not available while using TOPS Translators and the Log menu is not available until you have performed a file conversion.

You might also note from Fig. 10-4 that the screen is called Untitled. This refers to the settings or choices you have yet to make about the direction and type of translation that will take place. When you have made these choices, you will be able to name the settings for later use and the name will appear instead of Untitled. You can store settings either before or after you have performed a file conversion.

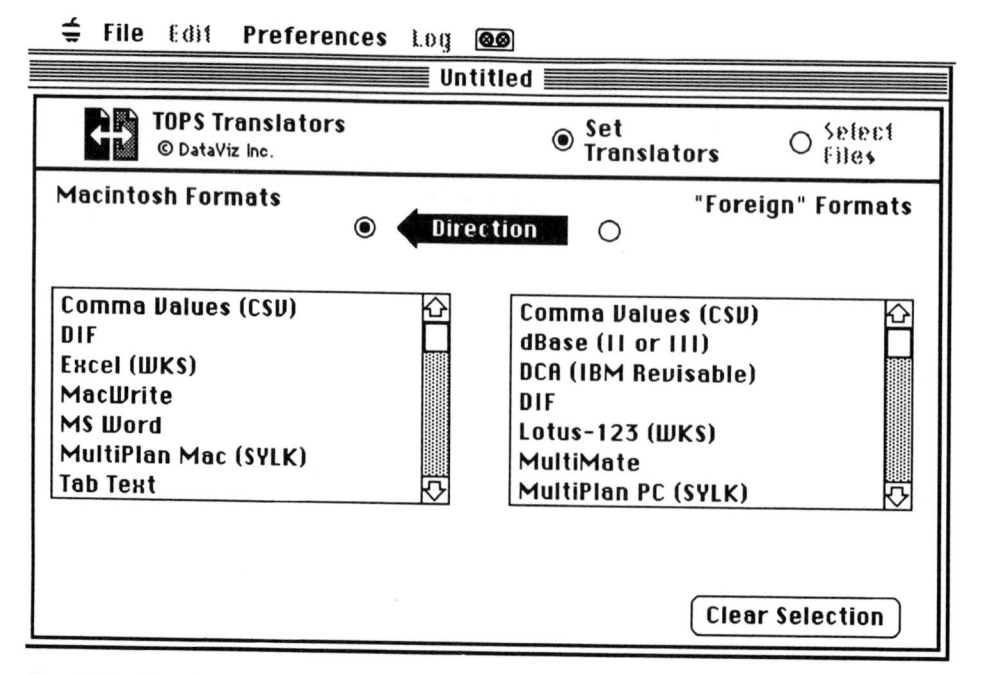

Fig. 10-4. Opening screen: TOPS Translators.

The Transaction Process

The first step in the translation process is to Set Translators. This means two things—telling TOPS Translators the direction of the translation (either from a Macintosh format to a "foreign" format, or to a Macintosh format from a "foreign" format), and then specifying the exact formats involved in the translation, for example, from WordPerfect PC to MacWrite. After setting the translators, you will select the actual files involved, indicating the name and location of the file you are translating from, as well as the name and location of the file you are translating to. When the parameters of the operation have been set up, you tell TOPS Translators to proceed with the conversion. The whole process is fairly straightforward thanks to the Macintosh interface. You can conveniently process several files at once and keep a log of transaction activity for the record.

A Translation Example

Suppose you have a standard contract document that was created on a PC with WordPerfect and you would like to translate it on a Mac with MacWrite. We will follow the steps involved in making this translation. Before launching TOPS Translators, you might want to think about where the source file is, the one you will be translating from, and where you would like the target or destination file to be stored. Suppose the source file, the WordPerfect document, is in a directory called MARTY on the hard disk of your PC. You should publish this directory so that it is available when you begin the transaction. You can mount the published volume either before or during your use of Translators.

When you click on TOPS Translators to launch the program, the first screen you see is the Set Translators menu, seen earlier in Fig. 10-4. The first thing to do is find the foreign format from which you will be translating. Use the scroll bar to browse down the right-hand window until WordPerfect (PC) appears. Click on this format to select it, as seen in Fig. 10-5.

Note that as soon as you select the foreign format, the left-hand window shows you what Macintosh formats are available for this transaction. Until you pick one of the Macintosh formats, the Select Files choice remains grayed. In Fig. 10-6, you can see that the MacWrite format has been picked and the Select Files choice is available.

If you find that you have made a mistake or that you have selected the wrong format, you can click on the Clear Selection button in the lower right of the TOPS Translators screen.

Now that the specific formats and the direction of the translation have been chosen, pick Select Files. This reads a list of files into each of the two windows. As you can see from Fig. 10-7, the formats that you have chosen are shown above the appropriate window.

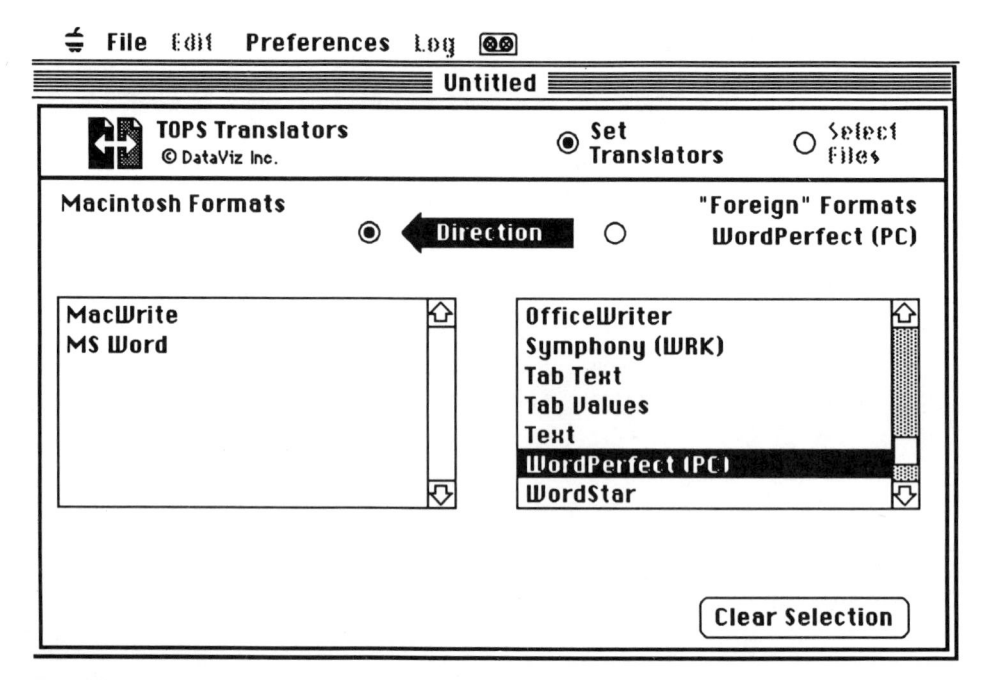

Fig. 10-5. Selecting the Foreign Format.

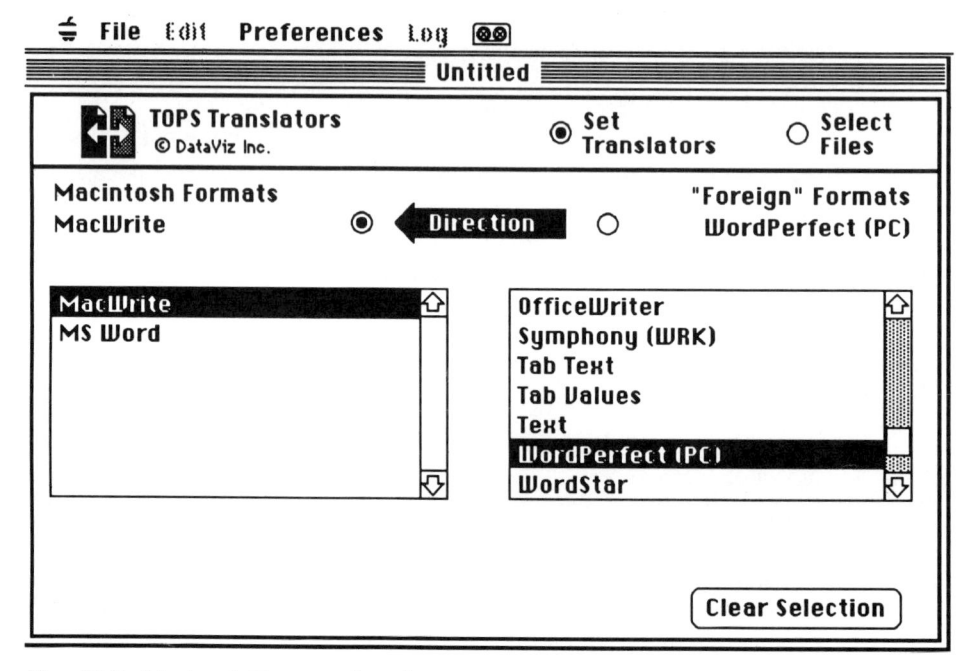

Fig. 10-6. Macintosh Format selected.

Word Processing and Translating **199**

The Macintosh side (left) lists files and folders on the desktop of the Macintosh drive that launched TOPS Translators. Note that TOPS Translators goes to the top of the HFS and does not default to the folder in which the TOPS Translators software is stored. At first, the foreign window lists the same files as the Macintosh window and you must change to the drive that contains the PC files. This was done already in Fig. 10-7.

If you have not already mounted the PC drive that you want to translate from, you can use the TOPS DA to mount it now. You can click on the Drive button to change the drive that is being displayed in either window. Use the Open, Drive, and Eject buttons to select the volume for the source file. If the file is in a folder, you can double-click on the folder name in the list or select the folder by clicking once open it by clicking Open. When you have found the file you want to convert, click on its name to select it. In Fig. 10-8, you can see that MERLIN.ACT was selected and that selecting a file activates the Convert button in the bottom middle of the screen, as you can see in Fig. 10-8.

The next step is to check the location for the destination file. By default, TOPS Translators will place it on the desktop of the Macintosh drive shown on the left. If you want the file to be placed in a particular folder you should open that folder now. If at this point you should decide that you do not want to proceed, you can simply return from the Select Files screen to the Set Translators screen by clicking Set Translators in the upper right-hand corner of the screen.

When you have selected the destination for the converted file, you can click on Convert to begin the processing of the file. You might be wondering what name the

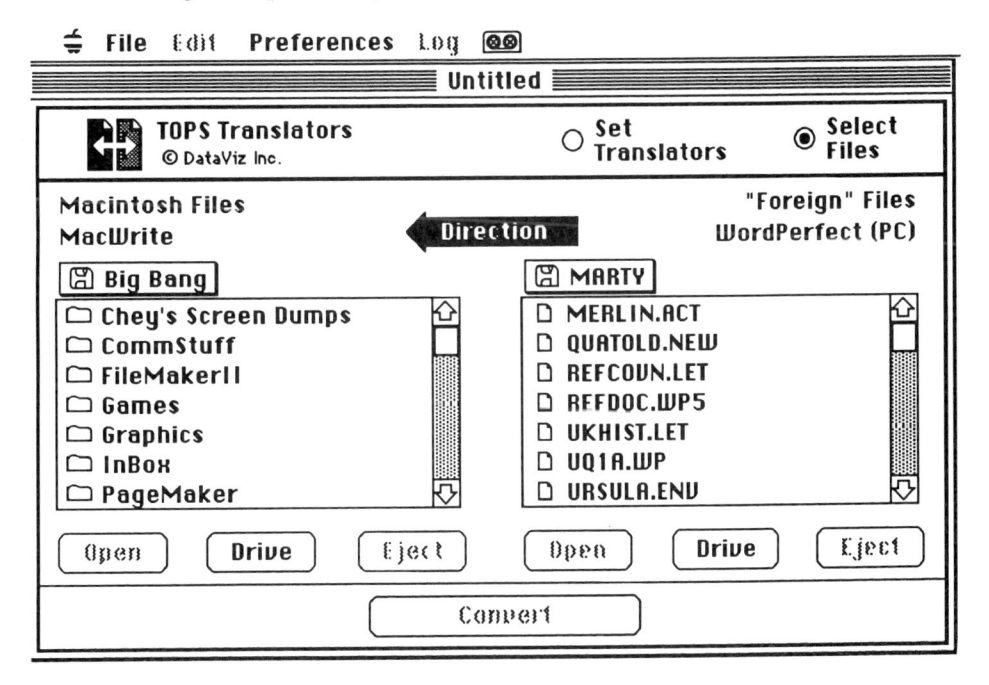

Fig. 10-7. Select Files window.

new file will have on the Mac. TOPS Translators automatically creates a name out of the PC filename, placing a suffix on the end that indicates the new format. However, TOPS Translators prompts you to confirm the name and gives you a chance to cancel the operation with the screen seen in Fig. 10-9.

You can edit the name, confirm with OK, or abort by clicking Cancel. Note that this screen repeats the name of the disk that will receive the newly created document.

When you click OK, the screen changes to give you a report on the progress of the conversion, showing a percentage of complete figure. Do not be alarmed if this figure is negative or in the thousands. Such wild numbers occasionally appear but do not seem to be related to any real problems in the conversion process. When the completion is completed, the progress screen will look like Fig. 10-10.

Note that TOPS Translators will not immediately proceed with translation if you have picked a name for the destination file that duplicates an existing file on the destination volume. Instead you are presented with a warning and must either allow the existing file to be overwritten or change the destination filename.

When the conversion is completed you should look for the message 0 Warnings, 0 Errors seen in Fig. 10-10. This is a good sign! If there are errors, a warning will appear in place of this message. To look at specifics of the error you can use the Show Log button. If there are no errors you can simply click on the Done button.

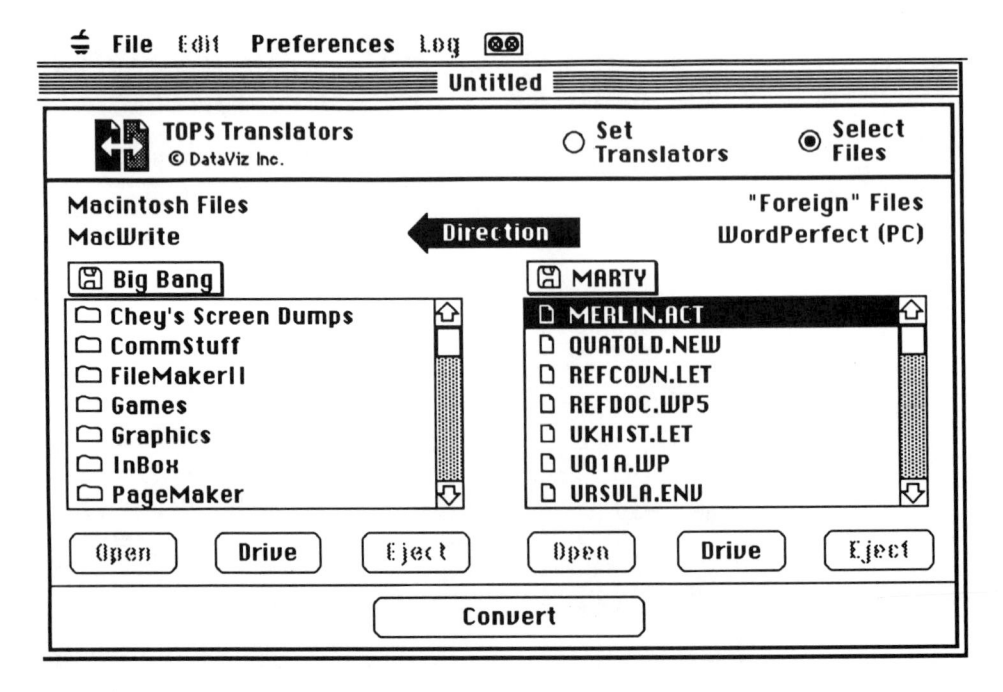

Fig. 10-8. The source file selected.

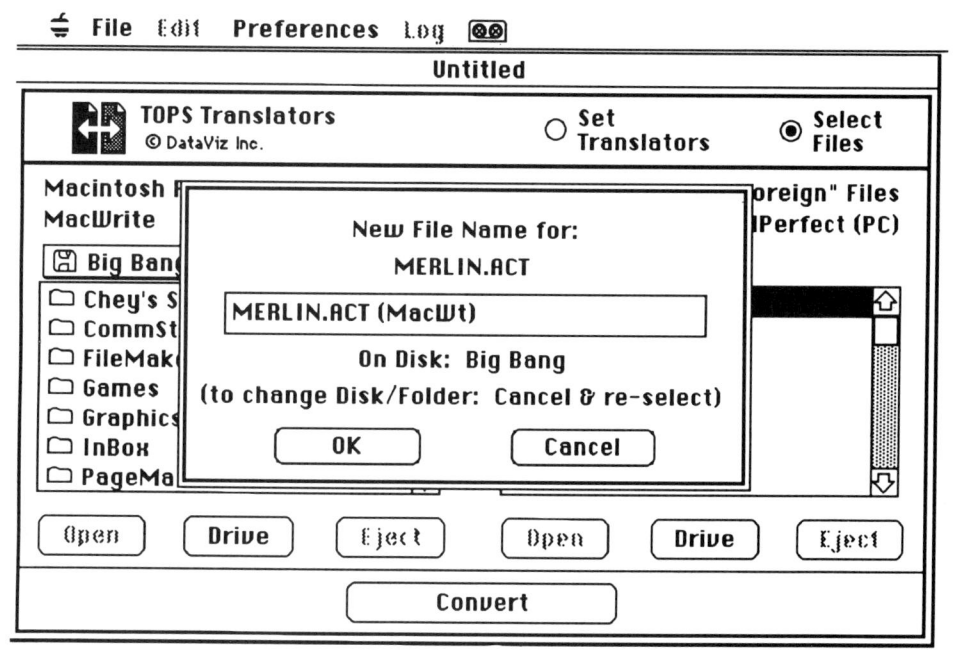

Fig. 10-9. The name confirm screen.

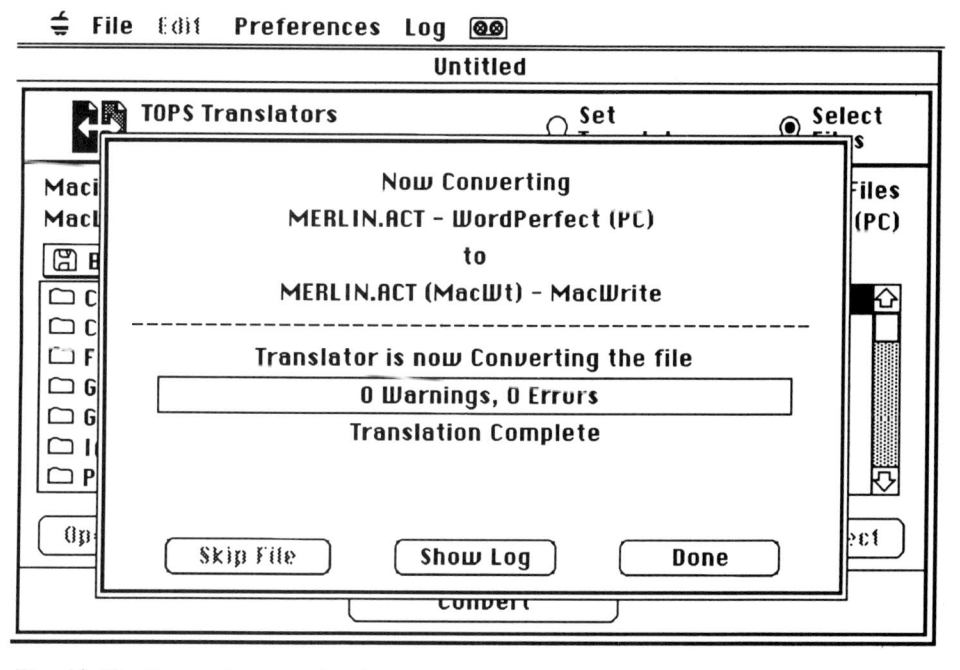

Fig. 10-10. Conversion completed.

The Transaction Log

The Show Log button on the progress screen in Fig. 10-10 is a means of accessing the record that TOPS Translators keeps of your conversion activity. Also, a Log menu item becomes available after a conversion has been performed. In the case of the occasional single file conversion activity this is not particularly useful unless you have a lot of errors. Where the Log comes in very handy is when you have a large number of files to convert and need help in keeping track of which files you have worked on. In Fig. 10-11, you can see a log of the example we have just demonstrated.

This is a very thorough account of what has just transpired. You can put the log away by clicking on Hide Log. While viewing the log, you can pick the Log menu to print the log, save it, or clear it. During a session with TOPS Translators after some conversion has taken place, you can pull down the Log menu and select Show Log. You can see the Log menu in Fig. 10-12.

The Print Log option is useful if you want to review your work with TOPS Translators or need to track activity for office records. When you pick Save Log As, you can use a typical Macintosh Save As menu to assign a name to the log and store it on disk.

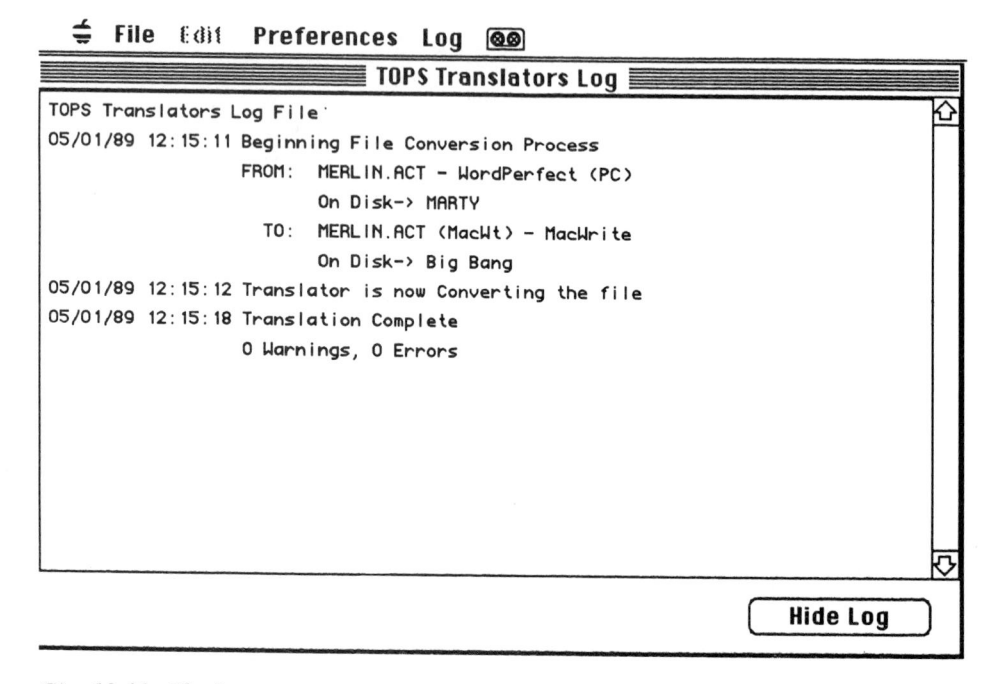

```
File  Edit  Preferences  Log

================= TOPS Translators Log =================
TOPS Translators Log File
05/01/89 12:15:11 Beginning File Conversion Process
                FROM:   MERLIN.ACT - WordPerfect (PC)
                        On Disk-> MARTY
                  TO:   MERLIN.ACT (MacWt) - MacWrite
                        On Disk-> Big Bang
05/01/89 12:15:12 Translator is now Converting the file
05/01/89 12:15:18 Translation Complete
                        0 Warnings, 0 Errors




                                              [ Hide Log ]
```

Fig. 10-11. The Log.

Multiple File Translation

You can select more than one file for transfer and translation by TOPS Translators. To do this, use the normal Macintosh mouse procedures: hold down the Shift key while dragging the mouse to select a range of files for translation. Hold down Shift while clicking the mouse on individual files will select, or deselect, one file at a time from the list. The multiple files you pick must be in the same folder or subdirectory and destined for the same folder or subdirectory. All selected files will go through the same conversion.

When you tell TOPS Translators to convert a group of files, you get a series of the "name that file" dialog boxes that TOPS Translators provides for you to check the name of the file you want to create. When the transaction proceeds, you can use the Skip File button to skip over a file in the group that is being processed. After translating multiple files, the Show Log command will show all of the status or error messages which appeared during translation. When the translation is finished, the message Translation Complete appears, the Done button replaces the Cancel button, and you are back at the Select Files screen. To translate additional files you can use the Select Files commands. If you want to change file formats, click Set Translators. This replaces the Select Files screen with the Set Translators screen. You can click Clear Selection to make all the formats available.

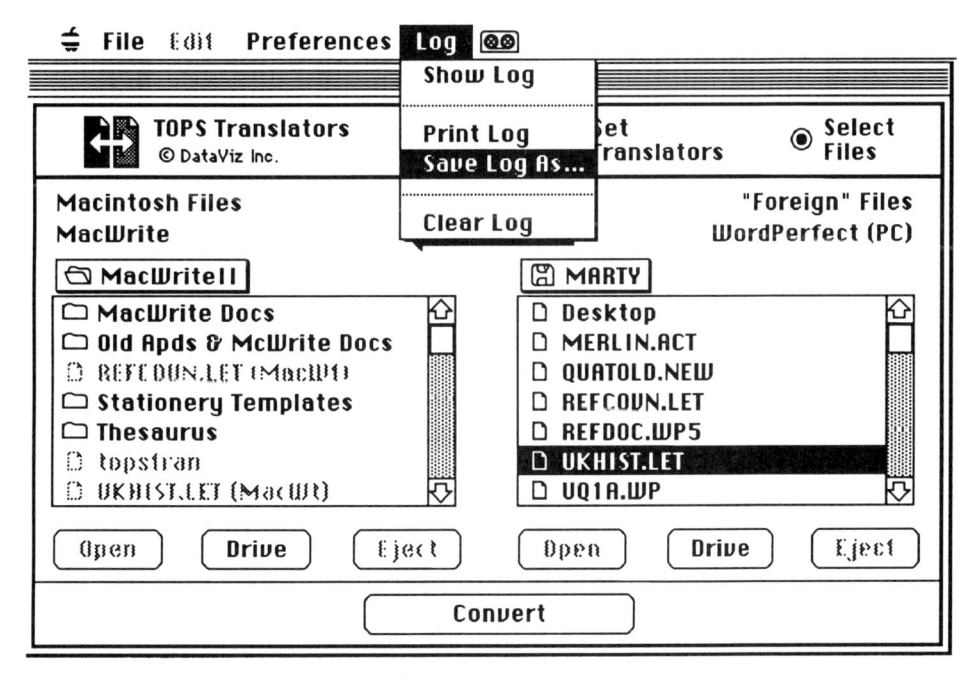

Fig. 10-12. The Log menu.

When you have finished working with TOPS Translators, select Quit in the File menu. You will be prompted to save the last set of translation choices to a special file that can be used to start TOPS Translators with the same selections. You can either create this settings file or choose Cancel to quit. The next section discusses the use of stored settings.

TOPS Translators Settings

As you can see from Fig. 10-13, the File menu under TOPS Translators contains commands for settings documents and for quitting TOPS Translators.

TOPS Translators lets you save your translation settings in a special TOPS Translators settings document so that you do not have to choose the settings each time you run the program. If you save your settings, you can simply double-click the icon for that document instead of the TOPS Translators icon. When you open a settings document, the Select Files screen appears immediately. The Macintosh and "Foreign" formats and the translation direction are already picked for you.

To create a settings document, first establish your choices. For example, if you found that you were often called upon to translate WordPerfect documents from the PC to MacWrite, you could set up the conversion as seen in Fig. 10-6 and then pick Save Settings As from the File menu. You could call the settings file something like WP-PC 2 McW. You can see such a file in Fig. 10-14.

Next time you need to convert a WordPerfect document from a PC to MacWrite, you can double click on the appropriate settings file and you will go straight

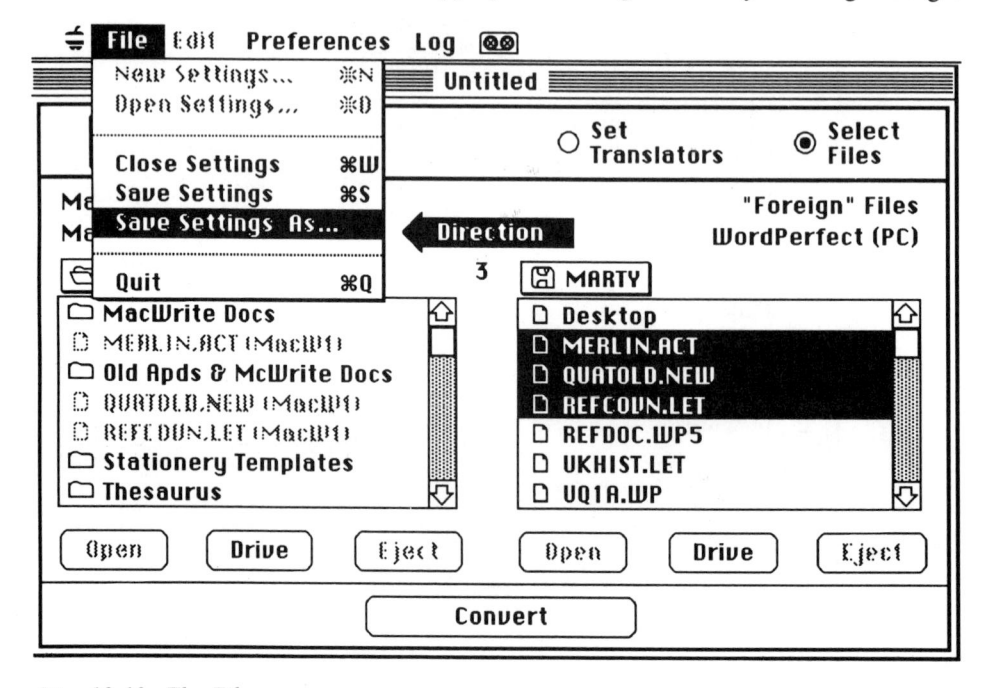

Fig. 10-13. The File menu.

Word Processing and Translating **205**

to the Select Files screen. Note that you cannot store your volume preferences in a settings file.

When you launch TOPS Translators with a settings file or save previously untitled settings, the name of the file is shown at the top of the window, replacing the name Untitled seen in previous figures. When you are using named settings you can close one settings file and then use the New Settings command from the file menu to create a fresh settings document. The Open Settings command opens a settings document stored on disk and immediately puts into effect the settings that it contains. The Close Settings option closes the current settings document. You will be given the option to save the current settings if you have not already done so. In typical Macintosh style, the Save Settings option stores the current settings into the currently named settings document or gives you a chance to assign a name to untitled settings. The Save Settings As option stores the current settings, giving you the option to specify the name and location for the file. The Quit option closes the settings document and quits TOPS Translators, giving you the chance to save the settings if you have not already done so.

The Special Preferences

The Preferences menu that appears when you are using TOPS Translators contains three options. The Special option allows you to change the default settings for displaying files, formats and translation status messages, using the dialog box you see in Fig. 10-15.

The meaning of these options and their uses follows.

Show All Applications. This option is used to override the default setting of the Set Translators screen which is to display only Macintosh formats in the left

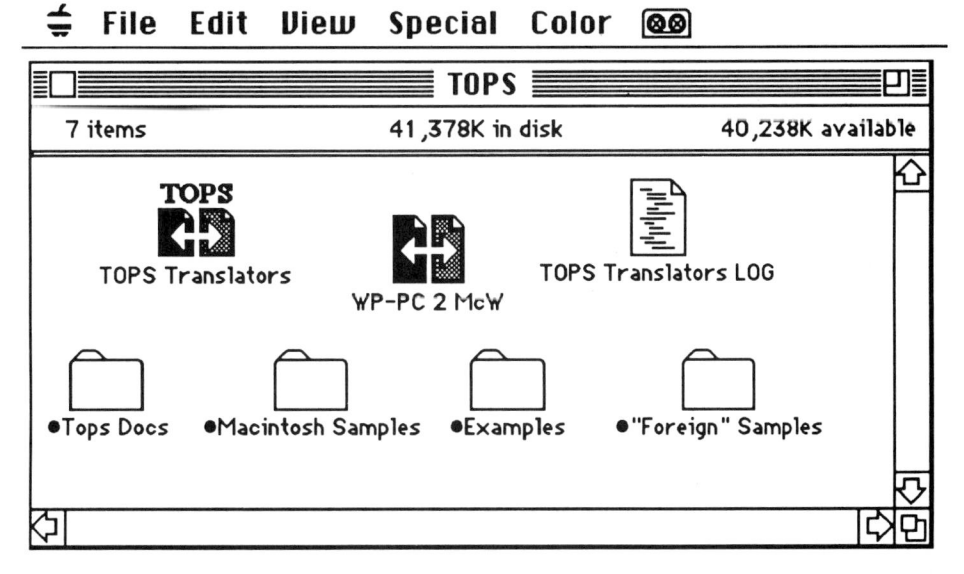

Fig. 10-14. Settings file.

window and DOS formats in the right window. Check the buttons on this line to display both Macintosh and DOS formats in the left or right window. This option may be useful if you have a mixture of files in your volumes.

Show All Files. TOPS Translators normally displays only files that are in the formats you selected in the Set Translators screen. Thus when MacWrite is specified as the format on the left of the Set Translators screen, only MacWrite documents appear in the Macintosh window of the Select Files screen. To display all files in the left or right window, check the appropriate buttons on this line. You might need to select this option if a DOS file you need does not appear in the "Foreign" files box, or a Mac file you expect to see does not appear in the Macintosh list.

Normally TOPS Translators attempts to uses the three letter extension of DOS filenames to identify their format. For instance, dBASE III automatically assigns the extension DBF to database files that it creates. When you choose the dBASE format in the "Foreign" formats box only filenames that end in DBF appear in the "Foreign" files window. If the extension has been changed for some reason, you will not be able to see the file under the default settings in TOPS Translators. This rule does not apply to DOS files created by applications that are not specific about extensions, such as WordPerfect. Also note that some PC programs such as 1-2-3 permit different extensions for different versions. TOPS Translators shows both WKS or WK1 when 1-2-3 is the chosen format.

An analogous problem can arise on the Mac side, for example when program versions change. Mac files typically use the resource fork to identify the program

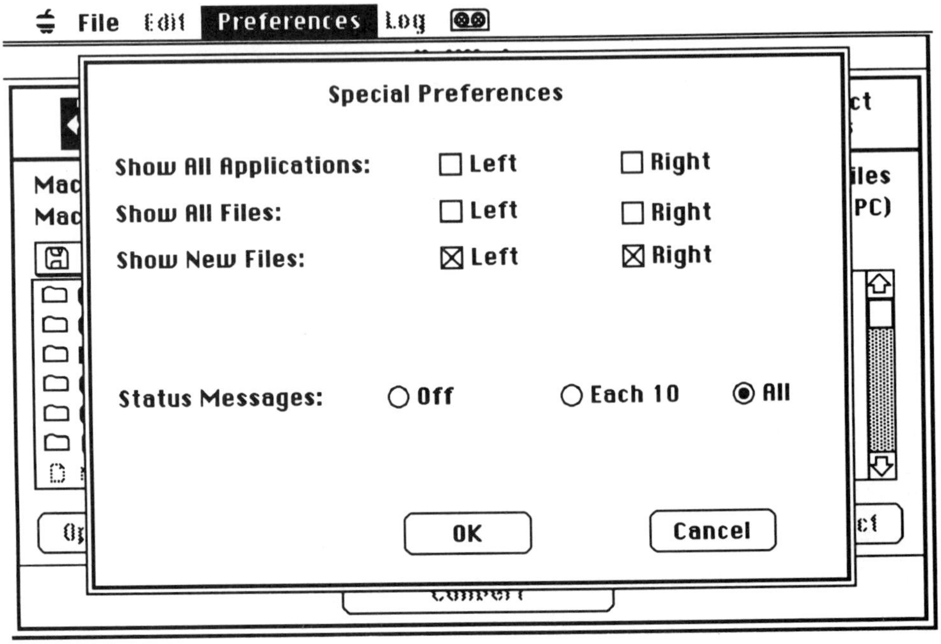

Fig. 10-15. Special Preferences.

that created the file. This information is visible on screen when you list files with the By Name option. As part of a version change in a program the programmers might alter the file type so that, for example, a MacWrite II document is not included in a list of MacWrite documents. In this case, the discrepancy has a positive effect, because MacWrite II files are not converted correctly by older versions of TOPS Translators, resulting in the error message seen in Fig. 10-16.

This type of problem is understandable; after all, translation technology is constantly attempting to keep up with new versions of software. You should try to get the latest version of TOPS Translators from your dealer.

There are times when a Macintosh file will loose track of the identity of the program that created it. This means that, for example, a WordPerfect-Mac document can be left off the TOPS Translators list of WordPerfect-Mac files, even when the file is still there. By using the Show All Files option, you can ensure that the file is shown. In fact, we have used this feature to resurrect damaged WordPerfect files, converting them into MacWrite then reading them back into WordPerfect-Mac, which can read MacWrite files.

Show New Files. TOPS Translators normally obtains new directory information for the target disk and refreshes the display in the target file window after it creates a file. This means that new files can be seen right away. If you uncheck this button for one of the windows, the directory is not retrieved after each translation and new files are not shown in that file window until some other operation causes the directory to be retrieved.

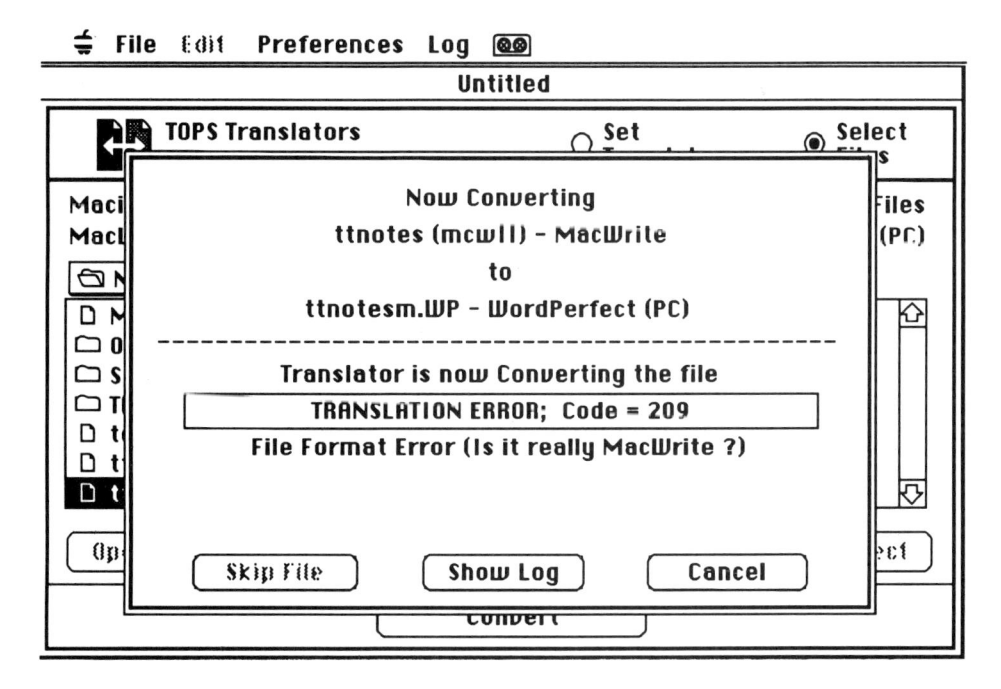

Fig. 10-16. File type error.

Status Messages. This option determines how frequently status messages are displayed during translations. For instance, when converting paragraphs of a word processing document, status messages can be turned off or they can be displayed for each paragraph or for every ten paragraphs.

NOTE: the Localize option that appears on the Preferences menu sets the Foreign Character Set for various European languages. See the "Update and Release Notes" for more information. If you are using the U.S. version of TOPS Translators, this option is gray.

File Control Preferences

The option called File Control on the Preferences menu controls the way that file names are assigned to converted files and how to TOPS Translators handles conflicting file names and translation errors. You can see the dialog box in Fig. 10-17.

The File Control option is particularly useful when doing multiple transfers and translations. The choices follow.

For New File Names. The choices here are clearly spelled out. You can do all the file name assignments yourself, or you can let TOPS Translators assign the file names for you.

In Case of File Name Conflicts. If you let TOPS Translators assign file names, you can choose to resolve the conflicts yourself. For example, when a file of the same name already exists, you will be informed and given an edit box in which

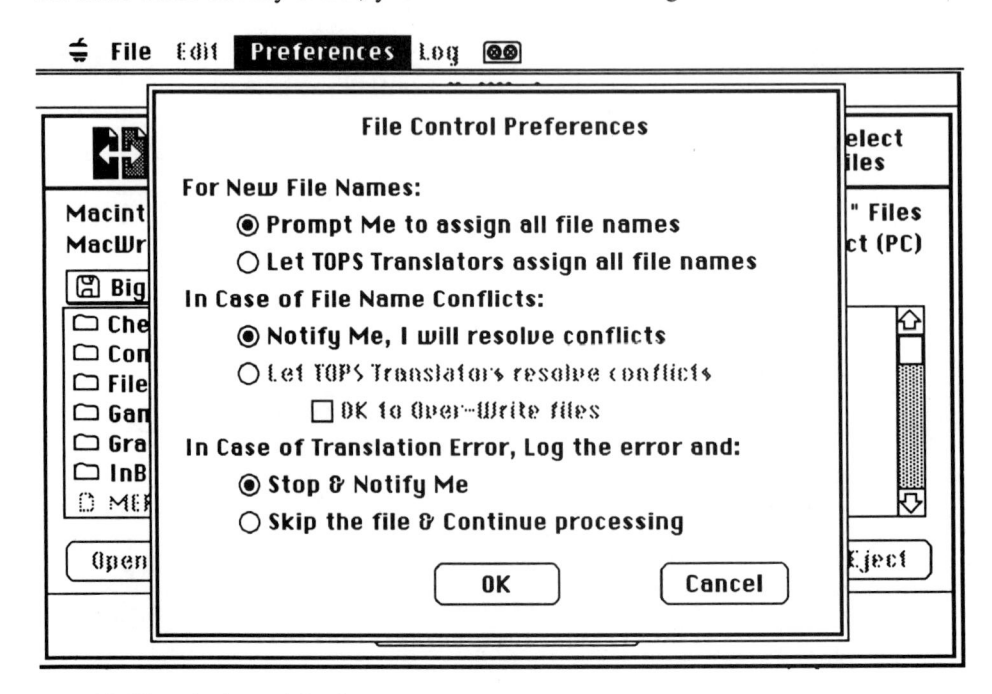

Fig. 10-17. File Control Preferences.

to type an alternative name. The other option is to let TOPS Translators resolve conflicts for you. The program does this by adjusting the file name or, if you check the OK to Over-Write files box, by overwriting the output file.

Translation Error. If you are trying to run a conversion on the wrong file type, you can choose to have TOPS Translators stop immediately and notify you, or to simply skip the file with the error and continue processing all other files in the list. In either case, the error is reported in the Log.

The Available Formats

The structure of the TOPS Translators software involves separate programming for each direction of the conversion process, a reader, and a writer. Normally one translator reads the format that a given Macintosh or MS-DOS application uses and another translator writes that format. Thus, you have a reader for MultiMate files and a writer for MacWrite files. TOPS Translators contains readers and writers for many popular word processing formats. Among these are MacWrite, Microsoft Word, WordPerfect, MultiMate, WordStar, DCA, and plain text formats. In addition, many other applications can open files in these formats. For example, files in MacWrite format can be opened by Write Now, Microsoft Word-Mac and Page-Maker-Mac.

On the PC, many word processors have utilities or alternate formats to read or write WordStar, MultiMate, DCA, or text files in addition to their own proprietary formats. By using one of the formats supported as an intermediate file format, documents can be converted to and from many of the most popular IBM PC word processors. The word processing translators identify and translate the following formatting: rulers, margins, paragraphs, indentation, tabs, tabular tables, bold, underline, italics, print styles, superscripts, and subscripts. In general, the translators ignore page breaks and footnotes. We review specifics of each translation, beginning with Multimate. Note that much of what is said about the translating Multimate files applies to the other PC word processing formats.

Translating Multimate

The Multimate translators in TOPS Translators allow you to convert both the text and the formatting of a PC Multimate file into a functional MacWrite or Micro-Soft Word document on the Mac including all text, paragraphs, margins, and print styles. The most basic elements of a document are its paragraphs. TOPS Translators makes every attempt to convert paragraphs so that they appear the same on the Mac as they did in Multimate. Some differences do occur during translation, however.

Margins. You might notice that these differ somewhat from the original when they have been converted because Multimate's margins are set in characters, while MacWrite and MS Word margins are set in inches. You also might notice that more characters and words are included in each line on the Mac than on the PC. This is again because of the basic differences between the way page layout is handled by the two operating systems. The Macintosh supports proportional print fonts, where each character takes an amount of space that is proportional to its shape. For example, "MMM" takes up more space in a Macintosh document than "iii". Multimate on the PC, however, prefers to deal in fixed-length print fonts, where each character requires an equal amount of space, regardless of its size.

Print Control Codes. As with most word-processors, Multimate users are able to specify how a particular piece of text within a document should appear when printed. These settings are represented and displayed within Multimate file by special print control codes. TOPS Translators converts these codes to formats on the Macintosh as shown in Table 10-1.

Columns. When columns of text or numbers are set in a Multimate document using tabs, TOPS Translators is able to duplicate and align them in MacWrite or MS Word. Even when a single column is created in Multimate using just spaces, TOPS Translators is able to correctly re-create it on the Mac. However, when multiple columns are created in Multimate, with spaces versus tabs between them, then TOPS Translators is not able to fully translate the effect. Instead, because of the Mac's handling of proportional characters, the second column is not aligned. If Multimate users stick to using tabs between columns, this nonalignment can be avoided.

Hyphens. Typically, two types of hyphens can occur within a word processing document: "hard" and "soft." The former always appear within certain words, such as "good-bye" and "close-up." Soft hyphens, however, occur only when a multisyllable word must be broken between two lines. In Multimate, soft hyphens may be

Table 10-1. TOPS Translators converts these Multimate codes to formats on the Macintosh as shown.

Multimate Function	Multimate Code	Formats TOPS Translators Converts To
Bold	Alt–Z	as bold
Underline	Alt–_	as underline
Superscript	Alt–Q	as superscript
Subscript	Alt–W	as subscript
Shadow	Alt–X	as shadow
Bold/Underline	Alt–Z_	as bold/underline
Alternate Pitch	Alt–C	*Pitch Translated to*
		1 24 point
		2 18 point
		3 14 point
		4 12 point
		5 12 point
		6 9 point
		7 9 point
		8 9 point
		9 9 point

inserted using the Shift–F7 combination. The requested soft hyphen then appears on the screen as a special character. On the Mac, however, the need for these soft hyphens frequently disappears due to the shifting of lines within paragraphs. When this occurs, TOPS Translators removes them for you during translation.

Page Breaks. Because Macintosh word processors can fit more words within each line and paragraph, a page of Multimate text often requires fewer lines when translated to the Mac. As a result, TOPS Translators does not attempt to translate page breaks between the two products.

Centering. In Multimate, MacWrite, and MS Word, a control code represents the centering of a line within a document. TOPS Translators correctly translates this code between the products.

Translating IBM DisplayWrite

This section deals with a format that is sometimes called *DCA* or *IBM Revisable Form Text*. Documents stored in Revisable Form Text (RFT) files are binary files in the DCA (Document Content Architecture) format. This format can be created and read with utilities provided with many products such as Microsoft Word for the Macintosh and WordPerfect. However, the main source of RFT files is probably IBM's DisplayWrite series of word processors from the now defunct DisplayWriter, a dedicated word processing computer, to DisplayWrite 5/2, an advanced word processing program running under OS/2. Probably the most common incarnation of DisplayWrite is DisplayWrite 4. The RFT format is not the normal or default storage format of DisplayWrite 4 files, but users of DisplayWrite 4 can access a built-in ability to convert documents into two special formats, Revisable-Form Text (RFT) and Final-Form Text (FFT). These formats can be read by other word processing programs that have conversion abilities. Some programs can also produce text in these formats so that DisplayWrite 4 can read their documents.

Final-Form Text. Called FFT for short, Final-Form Text is a special format used by several different IBM word processing products. Creating an FFT version of a DisplayWrite 4 document allows you to print the document with systems or application programs other than DisplayWrite 4 that support FFT documents. An FFT document contains special print formatting codes that enable the other programs to do this. You can convert DisplayWrite 4 documents to FFT documents plus convert FFT documents generated by another system or application program to DisplayWrite 4 documents. You convert documents to and from FFT with the Document Conversion option in the Utilities menu. Also, you can specify FFT documents in the Print Document menu to print them without actually converting them. Once the DisplayWrite 4 document is converted to an FFT document, it can be viewed or printed with systems or application programs that support the FFT format (for example, IBM DisplayWrite/36). When the FFT document is converted to a DisplayWrite 4 document, you can revise or print it using DisplayWrite 4. After conversion, both the original document and the converted document remain on your disk. If you no longer need the original document, you can delete it using Erase in the Utilities menu. By reading an FFT document into DisplayWrite 4, you can then save it as

RFT, making it available to users of the Macintosh through the TOPS Translators program.

Revisable-Form Text. Called RFT for short, this format is IBM document storage format that allows exchange of documents between DisplayWrite 4 and a wide range of other systems and application programs. A DisplayWrite 4 document converted to RFT can be used with IBM DisplayWrite/36, IBM DisplayWrite/370, IBM DisplayWrite 3, and IBM DisplayWrite Assistant. Within DisplayWrite 4, you can also use RFT documents originally created by DisplayWrite /36, DisplayWrite /370, DisplayWrite 3, and DisplayWrite Assistant. The RFT format makes DisplayWrite 4 documents available to Macintosh users through the TOPS Translators program.

For DisplayWrite 4 users, a semi-automatic system for converting RFT documents is generated by another system or application program to DisplayWrite 4 documents and documents created by DisplayWrite 4 to RFT documents. You can convert RFT documents to DisplayWrite 4 documents the same way you convert DisplayWrite 3 documents, simply by specifying the RFT document name in the Revise Document menu. You can also convert documents to and from RFT through the Utilities menu. The Get File command used with an RFT document converts it to DisplayWrite 4 and inserts it into a DisplayWrite 4 document. This is a useful way to handle copying one or more pages of a RFT document while you are editing a DisplayWrite 4 document.

If you are going to be doing a lot of document exchange using the RFT format in DisplayWrite 4, you will probably want to go to the Revisable Form Text Defaults menu in Profiles and set the Provide RFT options in the End/Save menu to Yes. This gives you the added options for the F2 key, as seen in Fig. 10-18.

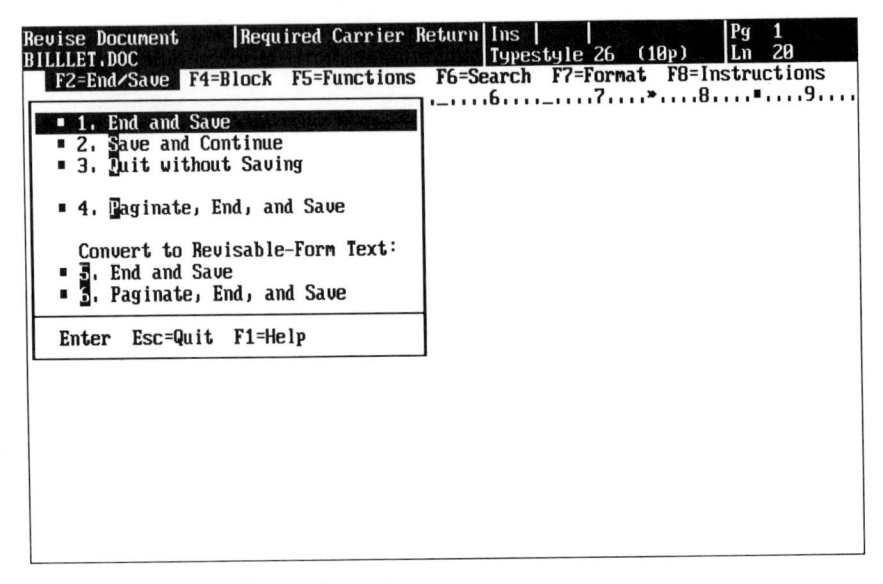

Fig. 10-18. DisplayWrite 4 file saving.

This way you can convert a DisplayWrite 4 document to RFT after creating or revising the document by selecting one of the Convert to Revisable Form Text menu items in the End/Save menu. Note that when you revise a RFT document, DisplayWrite 4 automatically provides the RFT menu items in the End/Save menu, regardless of your Profile setting.

TOPS Translators and DisplayWrite. TOPS Translators allows you to convert both the text and the format of a DisplayWrite (DCA) file into a functional MacWrite or MS Word document on the Mac so that you can start with a DisplayWrite document on a PC and transfer and translate it to the Macintosh using TOPS Translators. As with Multimate documents, some differences do occur during translation. Margins might differ somewhat in the converted document because DisplayWrite margins are set in characters, while Macintosh products set margins in inches. Because the Macintosh supports proportional print fonts, but DisplayWrite documents generally do not, there might be differences in line endings and word wrapping between the two documents.

Print Control Codes. As with most word-processors, DisplayWrite users are able to use special print control codes to specify how a particular piece of text within a document should appear when printed. TOPS Translators converts all of the following codes to a MacWrite or MS Word document: bold, underline, superscript, subscript, bold and underline (text marking).

Columns. When columns are set with tabs, TOPS Translators is able to duplicate and align them when translating to the Macintosh. When multiple columns are created in DisplayWrite using spaces (as opposed to tabs), then TOPS Translators is not able to translate the effect fully. The result is that, because of the Mac's handling of proportional characters, the second column is not aligned. The use of tabs for column alignment in DisplayWrite will avoid this problem.

Hyphens. In DisplayWrite, soft hyphens might be inserted by moving the cursor to a line, pressing function key F5 and then pressing Return. The requested soft hyphen then appears on the screen as a special character. On the Macintosh, however, the need for these soft hyphens frequently disappears due to the shifting of lines within paragraphs. When this occurs, TOPS Translators removes them for you during translation.

Page Breaks. TOPS Translators only translates required page breaks in DisplayWrite documents. Normal page ends are simply ignored during the translation to allow for the fact that Macintosh documents typically get more text onto a page.

Translating WordStar

Care needs to be exercised when translating WordStar files. WordStar supports many features included in word processing software, but does so rather differently. For example, the Tab key in most word processing software places a tab control code in the document. Normally this code can be identified by a translator and properly expressed in the new file so that tab alignment is preserved. In WordStar, however, the tab key does not put tab indicators in the document. Instead, WordStar counts character positions and adds spaces to determine where to place a tabbed character. Because character widths are not constant in most Macintosh fonts, using spaces instead of tabs does not preserve column alignment. To preserve alignment, TOPS Translators uses the fixed-width Monaco font for all documents translated from the WordStar format.

As with most word-processors, WordStar users are able to specify how a particular piece of text within a document should appear when printed. These settings are represented and displayed within a WordStar file by special print control codes. TOPS Translators converts these codes to the Mac as follows:

>Bold is translated.
>Doublestrike is converted to bold.
>Strikeout is translated for MS Word.
>Strikeout is converted to outline for MacWrite.
>Superscripts are translated.
>Subscripts are translated.
>Underline is translated.
>Alternate is converted to 9 point type size.
>Bold/underline is translated.

Columns. With TOPS Translators's other translators, columns in a document that are set with tabs can be fully translated and aligned. Unfortunately, WordStar does not allow its users to mark columns in any special way. Even when originally established with tabs, WordStar internally represents the distance between columns as just spaces. So, TOPS Translators converts WordStar files to the mono-spaced Monaco font on the Mac. You are of course free to change the file to one or more of the Macintosh fonts as you prefer, but you will need to do some work to get columns to line up.

Hyphens. In WordStar, soft hyphens are prompted for and inserted automatically when reblocking a paragraph. They then appear on the screen highlighted. On the Macintosh, however, the need for these soft hyphens frequently disappears due to the shifting of lines within paragraphs. So, TOPS Translators removes them for you during translation.

Page Breaks. Because Macintosh word processors can fit more words within each line and paragraph, a page of WordStar text often requires fewer lines when translated to the Mac. As a result, TOPS Translators does not attempt to translate page breaks between the two products. Instead, the dot commands for forced (.pa) and conditional (.cp) paragraphs are moved with the file's text so that you can easily review their placement and decide if they are still appropriate.

OTHER TRANSLATION SOURCES

In addition to TOPS Translators, your Macintosh probably has several other facilities for file translation. We examine them here as supplements or alternatives to the TOPS Translators program.

Apple File Exchange

Apple includes Apple File Exchange (AFE) with System 6.0 software. The real purpose of including AFE with the System software is to show that Apple is serious about coexisting with other computer systems, particularly IBM. AFE is both a working program, and a set of guidelines for programmers working on coexistence issues. The Apple File Exchange Folder on your system probably looks something like Fig. 10-19.

You might not have a document called Exchange Settings because this is created by AFE when you use it, much the same way as a TOPS Translators settings document. The DCA-RFT/MacWrite document is a set of translators used for DCA to MacWrite conversions. These translators are included by Apple as an example of what can be done with AFE. You can get other translators that work with AFE. In fact, the main source of such translators is DataViz, the maker of TOPS Translators.

When you launch the AFE program, you see a screen like the one in Fig. 10-20, which bears a striking resemblance to the TOPS Translators screen.

The menu above the parallel file lists contains an item called Mac to Mac. There are other menu items if you have a drive that is capable of reading foreign files. For example, you can use AFE to read MS-DOS files and ProDos files, *if* you have the right hardware, such as the Apple SuperDrive. You might wonder why Apple is not recognizing the mounted TOPS drive in Fig. 10-20 as foreign drives. This is because TOPS makes them look like Mac drives to the Mac.

When you pull down the Mac to Mac menu, you see a list somewhat like the one in Fig. 10-21, which shows the translations available at this point.

If you have other translators on your system, you can add them to the menu by using the Other Translators option. In fact, you may need to use this option to add the DCA/MacWrite translators if they are not already there. You do this with the menu seen in Fig. 10-22.

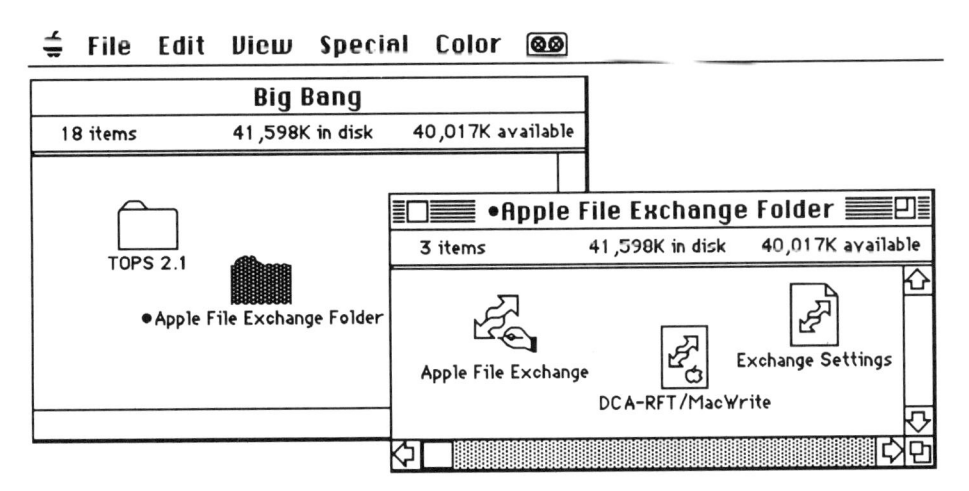

Fig. 10-19. The AFE folder.

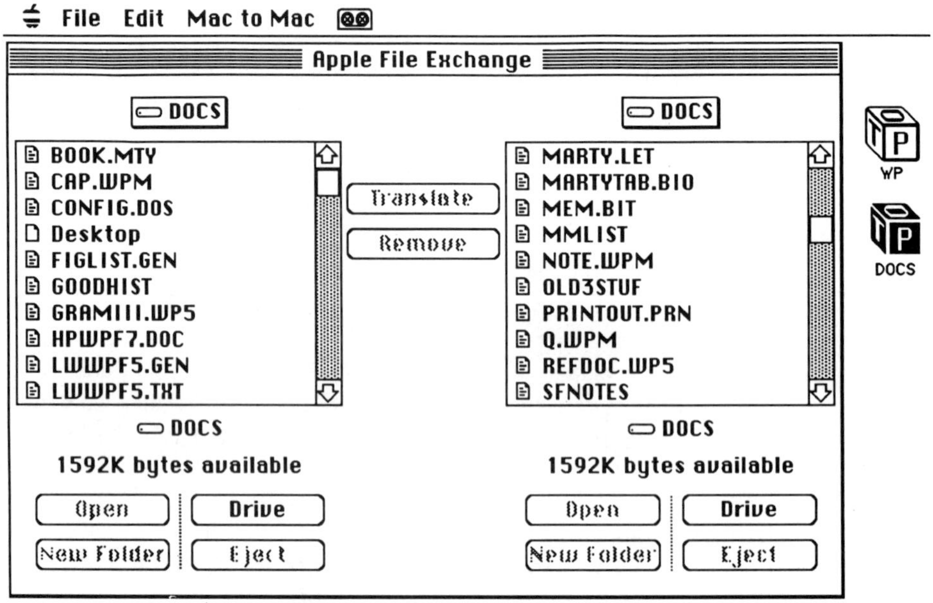

Fig. 10-20. The AFE opening screen.

From the Mac to Mac menu you pick the translation you want. We selected MacWrite to DCA. You are then returned to the file lists where you can pick the source file that you want from the side that is on the feather end of the Translate arrow, as seen in Fig. 10-23.

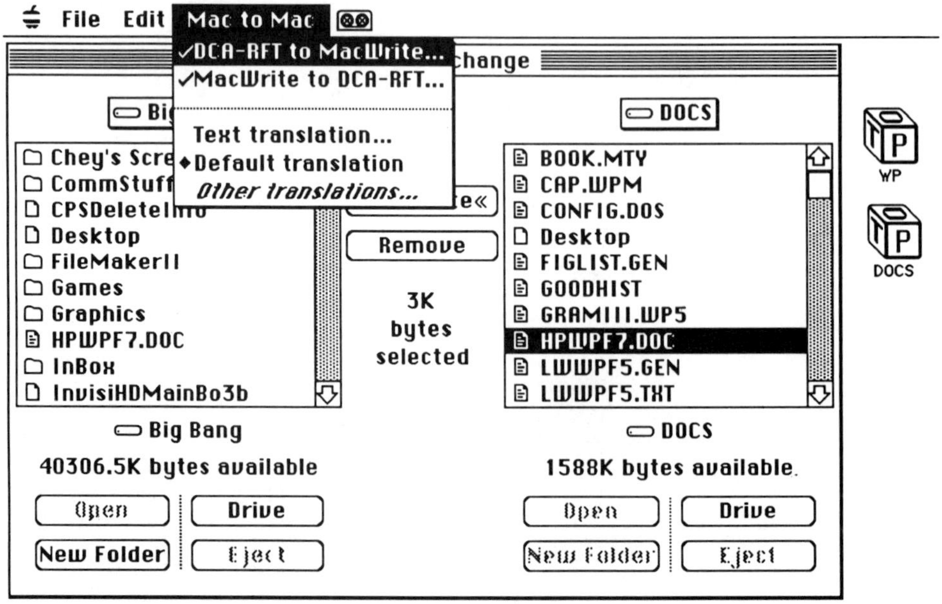

Fig. 10-21. The Mac to Mac menu.

Word Processing and Translating **217**

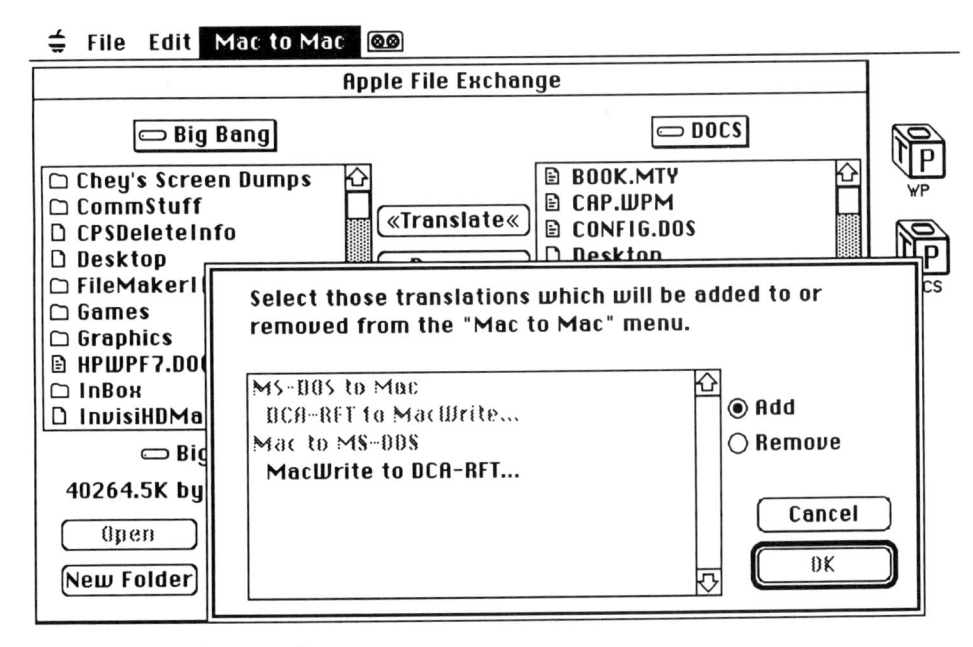

Fig. 10-22. Adding translators.

You have Drive and Folder buttons on either side to navigate your disks. Like TOPS Translators, AFE catches duplicate names and gives you a chance to adjust them. Messages and activity are also logged and stored if you request. After translating, you can store the settings you used.

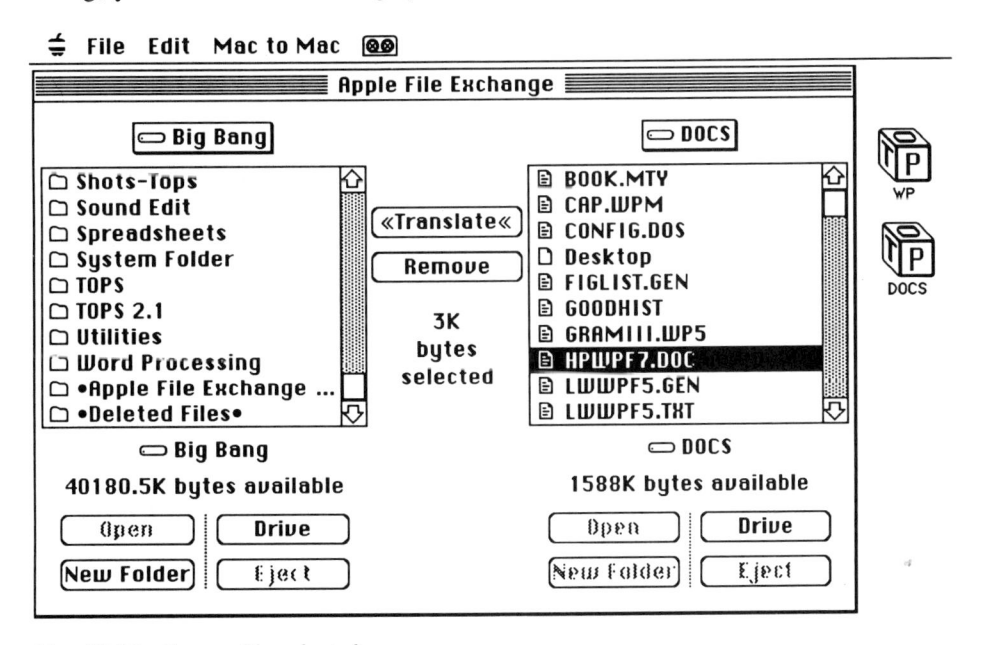

Fig. 10-23. Source file selected.

218   *Chapter 10*

While much of AFE is like TOPS Translators, a facility in AFE is a little different. The Text Translation option seen earlier on the Mac to Mac menu offers a series of options for translating ASCII or text files, as seen in Fig. 10-24.

You can either use a straight copy, which will transfer a file from one place to another, according to the drives you select back at the file lists. The other options show the flexibility of the program across the various Apple formats. If you choose MS-DOS to Mac you can adjust numerous parameters, as seen in Fig. 10-25.

These options address some of the more annoying aspects of text translation such as foreign characters and tabs and spaces.

The Text Translation aspect of AFE may be of interest if you have been using the TOPS Copy command to make a Macintosh text file out of PC documents. As you may recall, the Copy option on the TOPS menu allows you to swiftly transfer a file from one volume to another without having to mount the volume. The Copy option is available when you have selected a file rather than a folder on one side of the TOPS menu, and opened folder rather than just a drive on the other side. When you click on and pull down the Copy option, you get the screen seen in Fig. 10-26.

The Copy All Data option makes a straight copy, whereas the Copy Text Only option filters the file into text. You can use the Help feature of the TOPS menu to get information about the file, and the first screen, with date and size, is shown in Fig. 10-27.

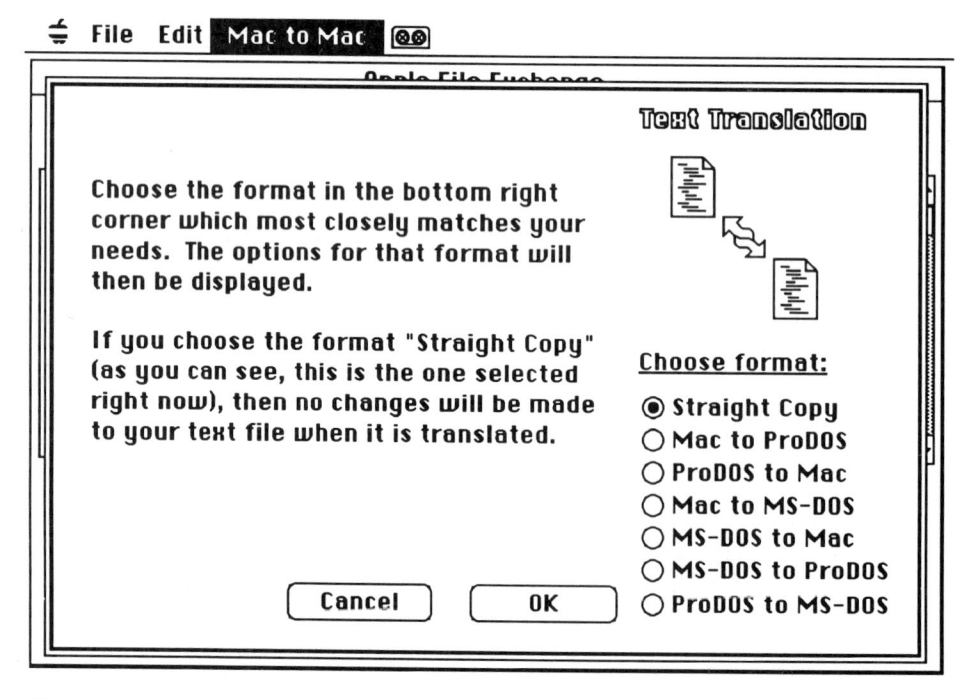

Fig. 10-24. Text Translation.

```
≜  File  Edit  Mac to Mac  ⊙⊙
```

```
For converting MS-DOS text files to Mac:        Text Translation
Carriage Return, Line Feed (CR/LF):
   ☒ Replace CR/LF with just CR.         ⇔
Special characters (å, ü, £, etc.): ⇔
   ⦿ Change to closest single character.
   ○ Change to multiple characters.
   ○ Neither.                                    Choose format:
Tab Character:
   ○ Replace tabs with spaces.                   ○ Straight Copy
        Tab stop every [8]   spaces.             ○ Mac to ProDOS
                                                 ○ ProDOS to Mac
   ○ Replace sequence of [2]  or more            ○ Mac to MS-DOS
        spaces with a tab.                       ⦿ MS-DOS to Mac
                                                 ○ MS-DOS to ProDOS
   ⦿ Neither.    [ Cancel ]    [  OK  ]          ○ ProDOS to MS-DOS
```

Fig. 10-25. The MS-DOS to Mac options.

The second screen of the Help facility shows the filtered view, in this case a bit of a mess because this file is a 1-2-3 worksheet and will not do well as a text file on the Mac. You can see the filter effect in Fig. 10-28.

If you get a readable view in this screen, then your file might do well when transferred to the Mac as a text only document.

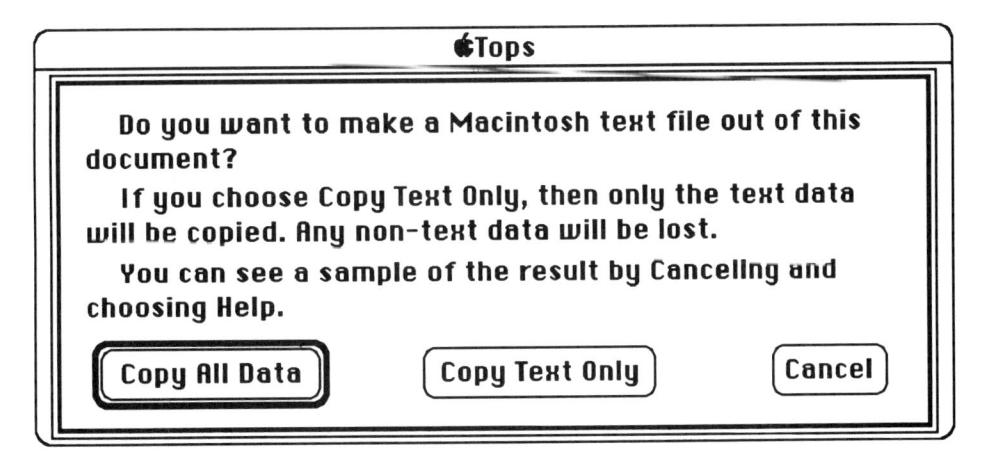

```
                        ◆Tops
   Do you want to make a Macintosh text file out of this
   document?
       If you choose Copy Text Only, then only the text data
   will be copied. Any non-text data will be lost.
       You can see a sample of the result by Cancelling and
   choosing Help.

   [ Copy All Data ]      [ Copy Text Only ]      [ Cancel ]
```

Fig. 10-26. The Copy options.

220   Chapter 10

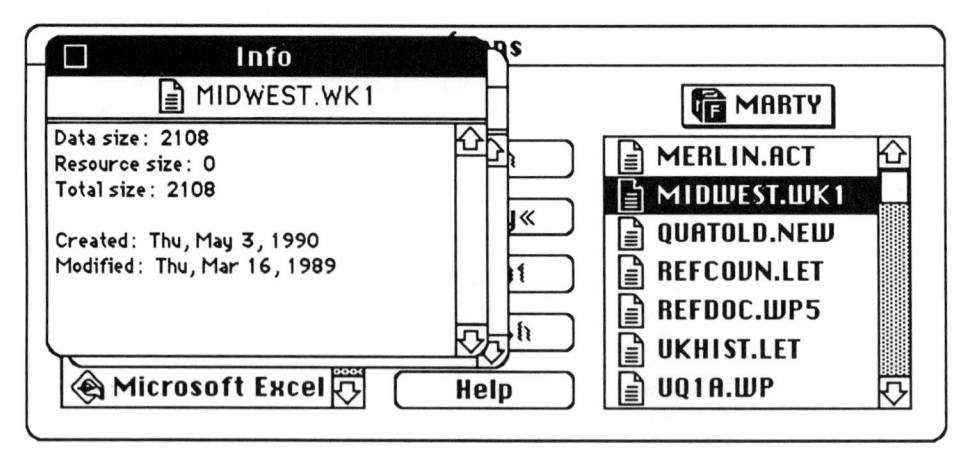

Fig. 10-27. About the file.

To sum up the AFE facility on the Macintosh, it does not add a great deal to the facilities already included in TOPS, but future enhancements by Apple and others may make available a wider range of translators that meet your specific needs.

Other Formats

Many other file formats available on both the IBM PC and the Macintosh are not directly addressed by AFE or TOPS Translators. Fortunately, many MS-DOS and Macintosh programs can use intermediate file formats. In some cases, files can be converted without the aid of TOPS Translators. For instance, Microsoft Word on the Macintosh can read Word files from the PC. WordPerfect on the Macintosh can read files formatted by WordPerfect on the IBM PC.

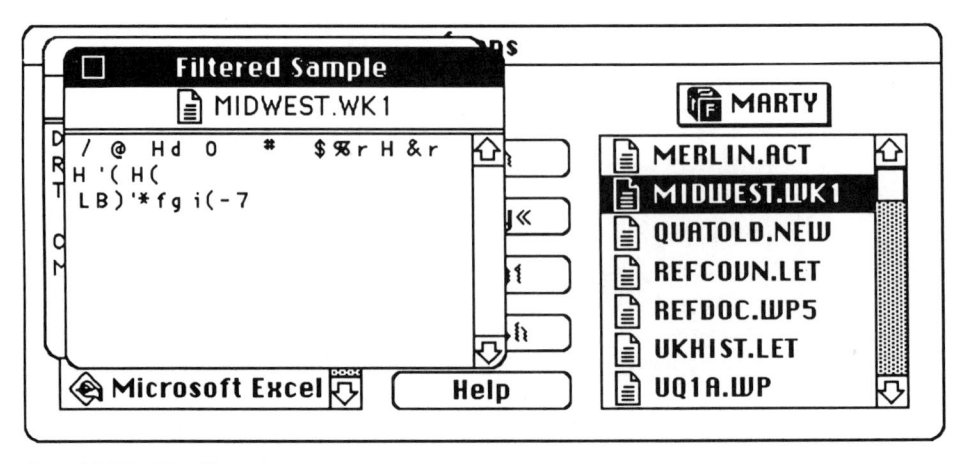

Fig. 10-28. The filtered view.

However, once again the question of program versions needs to be considered as each new release of a major program seems to cause some discrepancy in file formats. For example, during 1988-89 most users of WordPerfect on the IBM were converting from 4.2 to 5.0. The new version offers faster operation plus richer formatting features such as a variety of fonts and styles like italic, as well as the ability to include graphics in documents. Meanwhile, version 1.0 of WordPerfect 1.0 on the Mac was unable to read 5.0 files. The transfer between WordPerfect versions thus has to take place at the older, 4.2 level. When you use WordPerfect 5.0 on the PC, you use Ctrl-F5 to save a document in the 4.2 format, selecting item 4, Save WP 4.2 and then assigning a document name.

Intra cultural Transfers

So far we have concentrated conversions that cross the barriers of competing machine cultures: IBM and Mac. However, you might be networking all IBM or all Mac systems, but this does not necessarily remove the need to perform document conversions. So a word about conversions on the same system are in order.

WordPerfect's CONVERT

In Fig. 10-29, you can see the screen that appears when you start up the program called CONVERT which comes with WordPerfect on the IBM.

Actually, to get to this point, you need to specify the file that you want to convert from and the file you want to convert to. You can do this on the DOS command line by typing the filenames and path, as in:

CONVERT C: \MARTY\LETTER.DOC A: \LETCONV. DOC

If you just enter CONVERT, the program prompts for the names. The source filename must be a valid file in the directory you specify, but CONVERT does not check what kind of file it is. By default, the output goes into the directory you loaded CONVERT from, unless you specify a path with the target filename. You

```
1 WordPerfect to another format
2 Revisable-Form-Text (IBM DCA Format) to WordPerfect
3 Navy DIF Standard to WordPerfect
4 WordStar 3.3 to WordPerfect
5 MultiMate Advantage II to WordPerfect
6 Seven-Bit Transfer Format to WordPerfect
7 WordPerfect 4.2 to WordPerfect 5.0
8 Mail Merge to WordPerfect Secondary Merge
9 WordPerfect Secondary Merge to Spreadsheet DIF
A Spreadsheet DIF to WordPerfect Secondary Merge

Enter number of Conversion desired
```

Fig. 10-29. Formats that CONVERT can handle.

then pick a file translation you want to perform. Note that some of these formats are not simply WordPerfect documents. You type 1 to select an output format. The list seen in Fig. 10-30 appears.

When you pick the format you want, the conversion takes place and the program quits. If you have specified duplicate filenames you are warned by CONVERT even before you get to pick the format.

You can perform multiple conversions by grouping files with similar names using DOS wildcards. For example a group of files called CHAPTER01.WS, CHAPTER02.WS and so on could be converted from WordStar to WordPerfect by entering:

CONVERT C: \WS\CHAPTER??.WS C: \WP\CHAPTER??.WP

This would take you to the format choices. You can actually pick the format choice on the command line as well, by using the number. Thus entering

CONVERT C: \WS\CHAPTER??.WS C: \WP\CHAPTER??.WP

would allow CONVERT to do the conversion with no further input. Obviously, you could include CONVERT in batch files to automate file conversion activity.

Microsoft's Rich Text Format

Just when you thought you had all of the acronyms down pat, along comes RTF, the *Rich Text Format* from Microsoft, not to be confused with the RFT from IBM. What Microsoft hopes to accomplish with RTF is a means of transferring text together with a high level of intelligence about the format of the text, including pitch, font, style, and so on. You might have read earlier that WordPerfect documents converted from 5.0 to 4.2 on the PC lose all font and some style information. The RFT is designed to overcome such limitations. You can see this format implemented in WriteNow 2.0, a very nice word processor from T/Maker. In Fig. 10-31, you can see the Save As menu in WriteNow.

The file type list includes WriteNow plus the others you see in the figure. The last on the list is the RTF format. We saved a document with several fonts using the RTF format and were able to open it on the Mac under Microsoft Word 4.0 and

```
1 Revisable-Form-Text (IBM DCA Format)
2 Final-Form-Text (IBM DCA Format)
3 Navy DIF Standard
4 WordStar 3.3
5 MultiMate Advantage II
6 Seven-Bit Transfer Format
7 ASCII text file

Enter number of output file format desired
```

Fig. 10-30. Formats that CONVERT can write to.

have all of these elements preserved. Microsoft Word interprets the information in the file and displays it as formatted text although the actual contents of the file are a readable longhand set of parameters.

When saving with Save As using Word 4.0 on the Mac, you have a variety of formats from which to choose. Just click on the File Formats option, and you will see a list like the one in Fig. 10-32.

A number of Microsoft program formats are supported. Note the RTF format at the bottom of the list. Look for more applications to support this format in the future.

A TRANSLATION APPLICATION

One area of growing interest to people who work with a lot of text is the increasing sophistication of *optional character recognition* or OCR. When it works properly, an OCR device can take printed text and turn it into a computer document, avoiding the need to retype. A typical OCR system for a microcomputer consists of hardware—an image scanner—and OCR software (for example, a Hewlett-Packard ScanJet and OmniPage from Caere). This technology offers a way to get text into your computer when the electronic connection just cannot be made.

The Need to Scan

Consider this situation: a potential customer draws up detailed specifications for a project that you are going to bid on. The specs are mailed to you, twenty pages of nicely typed text that you need to share with coworkers. Typically, you photo-

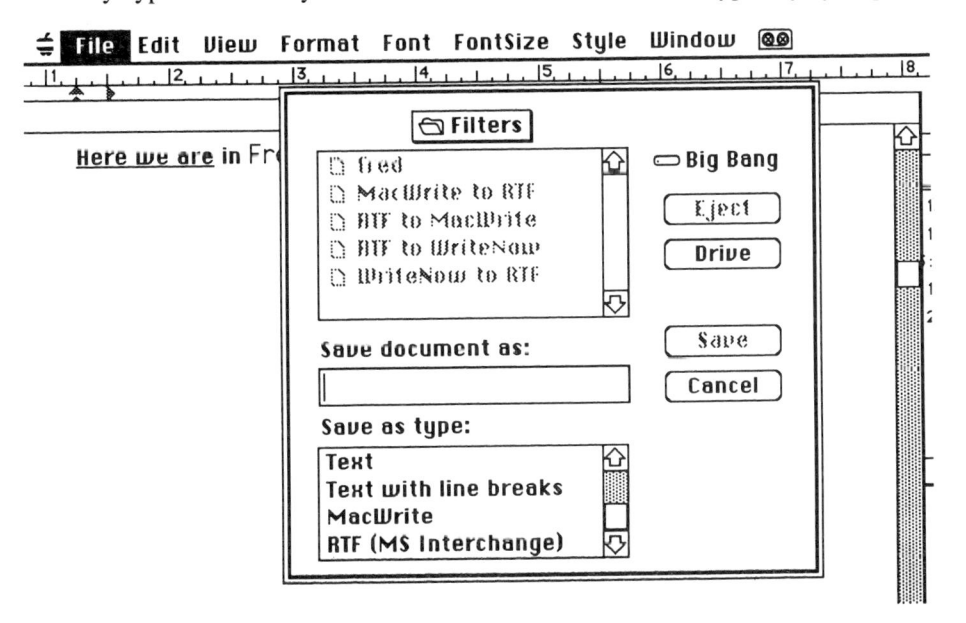

Fig. 10-31. Saving with WriteNow.

copy the document and distribute it. Then several people realize that a lot of text of this document will need to be regurgitated as part of the bid document that you submit. You can hardly ask the customer to submit the document on disk, and even then it might not be a format your software can read. Without a scanner, this means that you will have to type in the text you want to use. With a scanner, you can input the text in a matter of minutes per page. If you have a network, you can then share the document with coworkers. In fact, you can avoid the need for photocopying by publishing the scanned document.

This is only one area where scanning can increase productivity. Consider the law office that is converting from typewriters to word processors. Hundreds of pages of boiler plate text, standard contracts, and the like, need to be made available on the word processing system. As fast as legal secretaries can type, few can keep up with a scanner. Typing speed is often low on the priority list for academics, but the need to access large amounts of text via computer is great. Scanning of documents can save hours of typing when preparing class materials, papers, and reports. You can even use an OCR system as a disaster recovery mechanism. Suppose you have been writing an article and saving it to floppy disk. You print out a copy to edit, take out the disk, turn off the computer, and promptly spill coffee on this disk. The disk cannot be read, even with Mace Utilities or PC Tools. However, you can scan the draft you have back into the computer!

An additional benefit from buying a scanner for text recognition is the ability to scan in images, photographs, art work, and diagrams that might be needed in your line of work. We will talk more about using scanned images in Chapter 12.

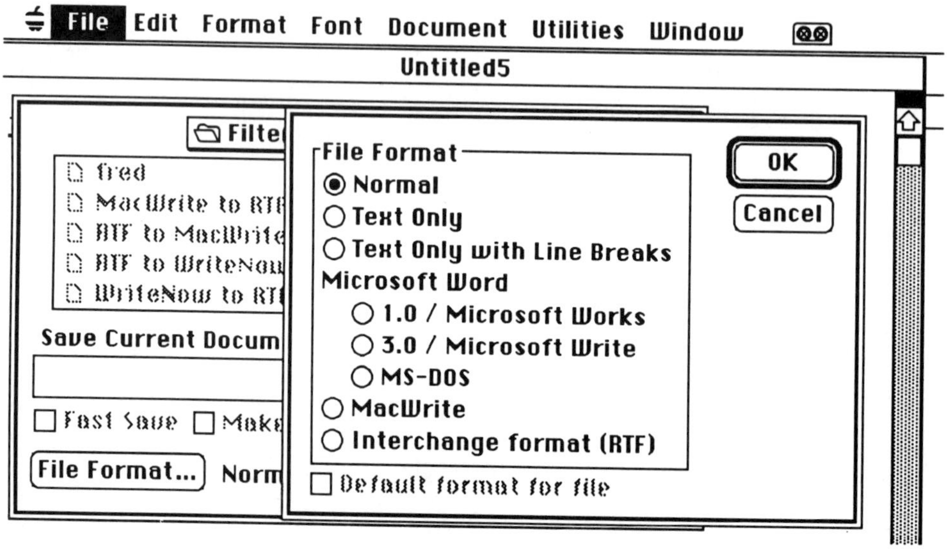

Fig. 10-32. File Formats in Word 4.0.

Scanning and Networks

Why are scanners and OCR systems relevant to networks? Because they are an excellent example of fairly expensive technology that might be hard to justify on a "one per person" basis because few jobs require constant access to a scanner. However, if half a dozen people will have access to the scanner, then it is much easier to justify the expense. Most scanning devices must be attached to a server. Scanners cannot perform as an intelligent network device like the LaserWriter. But a network still means that there is multiple access to the equipment. The role of TOPS is of considerable relevance here because there are different scanning and OCR options in the IBM and Mac worlds. The wealth of graphics programs on the Macintosh means that you might be better off scanning images into a Macintosh, and the graphics orientation of Mac hardware also helps when it comes to text recognition.

A good example of this is the OmniPage package from Caere. This optical character recognition system does an excellent job on everything from newsprint to books to typed memos. You can scan a document into a text file or into a formatted word processing file where such features as boldface are often read correctly from the source document. The program knows about multiple columns and can read a magazine article column-by-column. You can even read tables of numbers into a spreadsheet format. However, OmniPage for an IBM costs a lot more than OmniPage for the Mac. The Mac package really needs a Mac II with at least 4 megabytes of Ram, but the IBM version also requires heavy duty hardware, a top-end machine that is 80386-based. The difference in cost comes from the fact that the IBM package includes a circuit board containing a coprocessor. The Mac package is software only, software that utilizes the advanced graphics capability of the Mac. By attaching a scanner to a Mac II on a TOPS network, you can use OmniPage to read in text files and then share them with anyone else on the network.

A Scanner Test

To test this arrangement, we connected a Hewlett-Packard ScanJet to our Mac II and scanned the document you see in Fig. 10-33.

The ScanJet is modestly priced and certainly not top of the line as scanners go. In fact, HP offers a ScanJet Plus that provides better graphics capability (256 scales of gray, as opposed to 16 on the ScanJet). But for text scanning, you do not need great graphics performance. Another advantage of the ScanJet is the fact that it is a generic scanner, neither IBM or Mac oriented. You buy an interface kit to connect to the machine of your choice, giving you the option to "go either way." You also need to buy a set of cables to make the hookup. The connection to the Mac is made via the external SCSI port. HP includes software to test the connection and some nice image scanning and editing software. These operate as DAs on the Mac so you

226   *Chapter 10*

```
     OmniPage is an excellent tool for many different
professionals.  The ability to read columns like this is very
impressive:

     Name              Manufacturer

     Word              Microsoft
     WriteNow          T/Maker
     MacWrite II       Claris
     WordPerfect       WordPerfect

The way that it (almost always) reads !@#&*! like this is also
amazing.  So far this has been Courier 10 pitch, but if we
switch, to:
any form of TIMES font, the program keeps on reading properly.
```

Fig. 10-33. Sample document.

can scan an image, edit it, and the paste it into a document, without leaving the document.

When you have hooked up your scanner and copied the OmniPage software unto your Mac, you can begin. You place the document on the scanner *bed*, a flat piece of glass like a photocopier. Then you choose your settings, from a screen like the one seen in Fig. 10-34.

You can choose two formats of ASCII file, + MacWrite (pre-MacWrite II) and Excel. The Excel file is a text file, but can be opened directly by Excel. The options on the right are best explained from the bottom up. The column settings refer to how you want OmniPage to treat columns of information. Choosing Single column means that everything on the same line is read as a line, whereas Multiple column

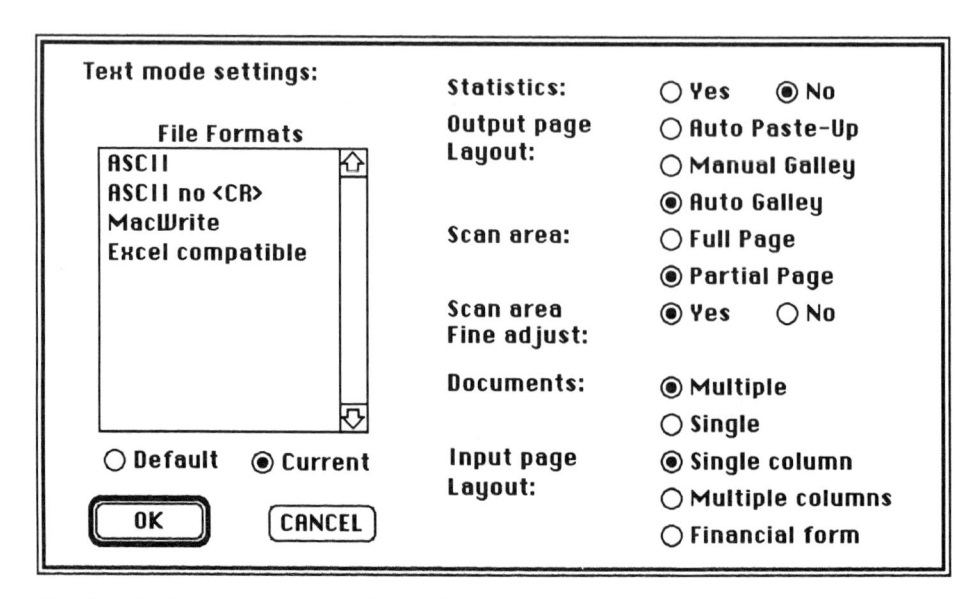

Fig. 10-34. Setting up a scan with OmniPage.

means that OmniPage will read down one column then go back to the top of the second, and so on, as is often the case with newspaper articles. The Financial form option works with the Excel format to separate the columns ready to be read into a spreadsheet.

When you scan documents that are longer than one page, you can pick Multiple documents to keep on scanning the whole document into one file. When you want to scan only part of the page, you can select Partial Page with Fine adjustment to get a precise look at what will be scanned. If there are several different areas of text on a page, you can manually adjust the order in which the sections are read into the file using the Output options. Otherwise, OmniPage will make a best guess for you.

When the settings are established you pick OK to proceed. The scanner head moves across the document in about ten seconds. Right after this a small view of the document page appears, as seen in Fig. 10-35.

This is just a graphic image at this point. If you need to select a part of the page you do so now. You can zoom in on the page to fine-tune the area that is being scanned. Otherwise, if you have picked the Full Page option, OmniPage goes right to the task of reading the image, giving results after a few seconds, as seen in Fig. 10-36, where the progress meter is seen.

The document that was scanned here was the example shown earlier. To scan a second page, you would click Scan More.

Once scanning is complete you can view the document and edit it if it is in ASCII format. You can see from Fig. 10-37 that the text is letter perfect.

While the change in font is not translated into the file, the font change did not upset the recognition which was 100%. Even the set of punctuation marks was deciphered. The columns were also preserved.

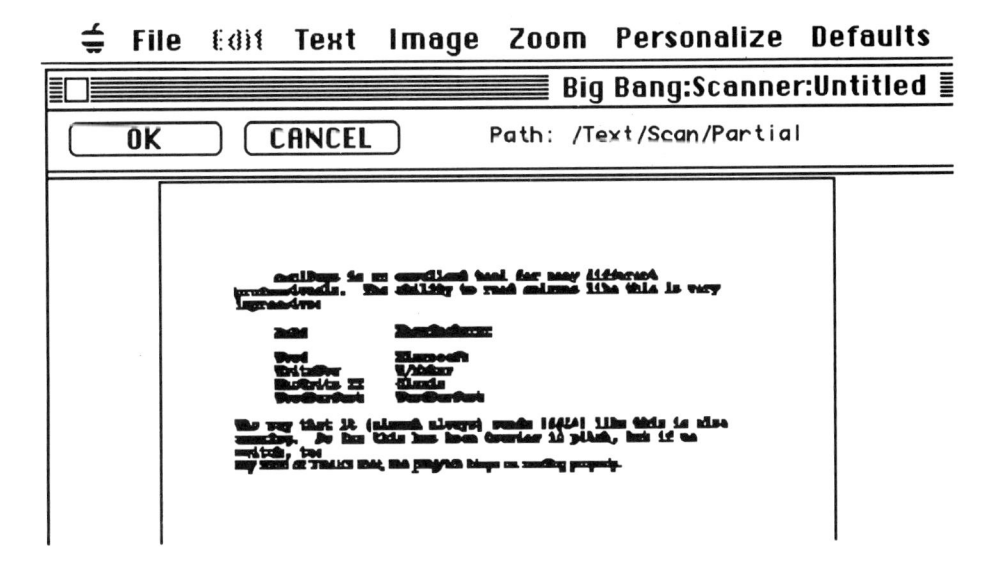

Fig. 10-35. Initial view.

Fig. 10-36. Scanning progress.

We then opened the document into MacWrite II and got the results seen in Fig. 10-38.

Here you can see that the underlying layout was preserved. The margin settings were altered slightly but a ruler was created for the columns. Just for the heck of it, we transferred the document from MacWrite format to WordPerfect 4.2 format using TOPS Translators. The results were then readable on the PC, complete with underlining and the original margins!

A WORD PROCESSING STRATEGY

Companies in which employees use a variety of word processors will have to develop some type of strategy for dealing with the sharing of documents. This may

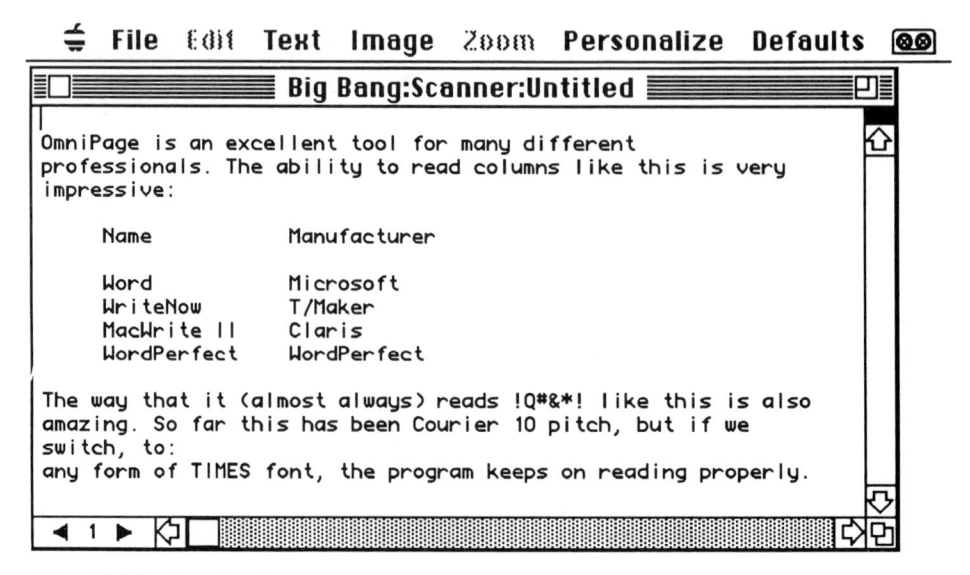

Fig. 10-37. Completed scan.

mean selection of the lowest common denominator for file format, one that can be read and created by the largest number of programs. At this time, the IBM format called DCA or RFT is probably the most widely read file format that retains document formatting information.

However, unless the entire organization is standardized on one program, there will need to be rules for use of various document formats, characters, and features that do not work well in translation. For example, most translators fall down on foreign characters such as ñ, ¥, and £. These may come through translation as gaps or simple dashes, rather than the correct character. Some users will not need such esoteric features and so there can be a hierarchy of formats from the simplest ones used by those least fussy about the appearance of their text, or by those who pass on text to others, up to those used for final document review and printing.

Among widely available formats, DCA format does a pretty good job of catching most document features, including foreign characters. Many companies put up with the limitation of DisplayWrite 3 in order to take advantage of the DCA format stored by Displaywrite 3 when the RFT extension was used. However, even in the DCA world things are not always compatible. For example, the DCA files created by DisplayWrite 4 are not read correctly by several programs like WordPerfect on the PC that are supposed to read DCA. This can be traced to subtle changes in the DCA format implemented by IBM. You will find that TOPS Translators has a hard time with RFT files created by DisplayWrite 4. While DisplayWrite 4 has no problem reading Displaywrite 3 files and other RFT files generated by translators and converters, the flow would seem to be one way at this time.

Ironically, it is Microsoft's RTF, Rich Text Format, that offers the most complete storage of text features, down to font names, sizes, and styles. However, until

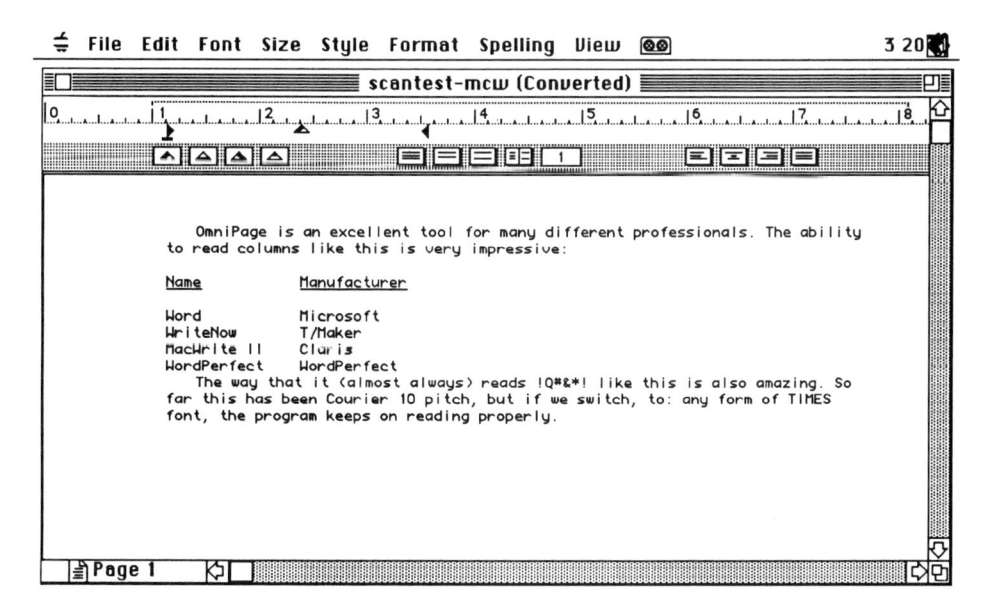

Fig. 10-38. Results in MacWrite II.

it is adopted more widely you will need to look among Microsoft products, such as Word 5.0 on the PC and 4.0 on the Mac, for this format. We did find that Write Now 2.0 uses RTF, so the trend may be for wider use of this format. Until the day when all systems use a universal format for words and the way they are to be printed, you will need to coordinate activities on a network when exchange of text is required to increase productivity.

CONCLUSION

While the proliferation of formats and the inconsistencies of program versions can be frustrating at times, the TOPS network at least simplifies the underlying task of file exchange and sharing. The TOPS Translators do a good job of converting text and bridging those gaps that remain between built-in conversion routines that are seen in an increasing number of word processors. As software makers, like computer support staffs, realize that no single format is going to "take over" in the foreseeable future, then the path toward openness will grow wider, with more and more programs offering innate conversion features. While the word processor that reads and writes the most formats is not bound to be the one that sells the best, it is likely to do very well in the pluralistic environment of today's networked office. In the next chapter, we look at working with spreadsheets and databases across the network.

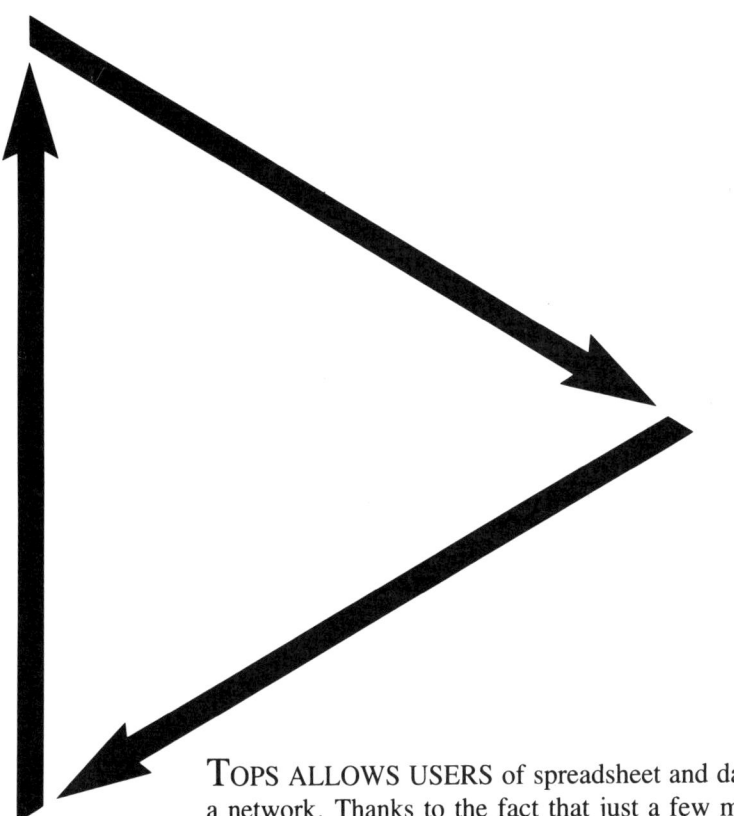

11
Spreadsheets and Databases

TOPS ALLOWS USERS of spreadsheet and database software to share files across a network. Thanks to the fact that just a few major programs dominate the spreadsheet and database markets, there are several standard formats for such data. This means that exchanging data between programs and systems is fairly easy, but there are some limitations. Because spreadsheets can perform a vital role in the running of today's businesses and people tend to rely on the answers they provide, it is important to be clear on what works and what does not when moving data between different spreadsheet programs and between spreadsheets and databases.

A LEGAL DISCLAIMER

While discussing the use of word processing software over TOPS in the preceding chapter, we did not spend much time talking about a question that applies with equal force in the spreadsheet and database arena: can several users each load the same program across TOPS by accessing it from a server? The answer is a highly qualified "Yes" accompanied by both practical and legal disclaimers. The practical limits are first of all machine-dependent. No Mac is going to run an application written for PCs and vice versa, although Macs can load Mac-specific applications that are stored on a PC that is acting as a server. When several PCs use the same application, users will need to account for differences in hardware such as display systems. An example of how that is handled is discussed later under running Excel on a network.

A further practical restriction is performance. Now that TOPS is Ethernet-compatible, it is feasible to load a run applications from a server, if the network is operating at Ethernet speed. At FlashTalk speed, the loading time for applications is very slow. The program performance depends upon the amount of disk access involved. For example, WordPerfect on the PC works reasonably well when loaded by an XT from an 80386 server over FlashTalk, but applications such as dBASE and Excel become very slow.

Beyond the practical limits, which might erode as new network hardware improves performance, the legal limits remain: you must buy as many copies of a program as you use. This is what most software makers say in their licensing agreements. Although some companies, such as WordPerfect offer special packages for network access that can work out to be less than buying several individual packages, the basic rule of thumb is that if you have three people using a package at once, then you must buy three packages. For example, the documentation for the program called FileMaker states: "Your FileMaker licensing agreement allows two or more people to use FileMaker simultaneously in a network environment only if you own the same number of copies of FileMaker as the number of people using FileMaker on the network."

While future trends might look more kindly upon networks and at least alleviate the need to warehouse multiple packages just to prove that you have them, for the present, those who want to live within the law must live with the terms of the software license agreement. This tends to become more problematic in larger corporate networks, rather than the sort of ad hoc workgroups that TOPS so often works for. However, nothing in this book should be construed as suggesting that you use your network to avoid buying the legal minimum of software for your operation, whether you load it from a server or from each machine.

A SPREADSHEET EXAMPLE: EXCEL

The spreadsheet program with the largest installed base in the IBM world is still 1-2-3. However, in recent years, the 1-2-3 standard has been improved and challenged by other products, notably Quattro from Borland International and Excel from Microsoft. Excel is of particular interest when discussing IBM/Mac connectivity because, like Microsoft Word, it is a program with both IBM and Mac versions. In our discussions, we refer to "Excel-PC" when making a point about Excel on the IBM and we use "Excel-Mac" when talking about the Macintosh version. If we simply use "Excel," we are saying something that applies to both editions of the program. We use the word "edition" to refer to differences between programs based on different operating systems, as opposed to "versions" which are upgrades of the same product.

To achieve a Mac-like appearance and functionality on the IBM, Excel uses Microsoft Windows, a multi-tasking operating environment that fits between DOS and application software to give a similar look and feel to programs. You can see this environment in Fig. 11-1 where Excel can be seen running.

Note the File and Edit menu items, common features of Windows-based applications and Macintosh software. Because the two programs run in much the same

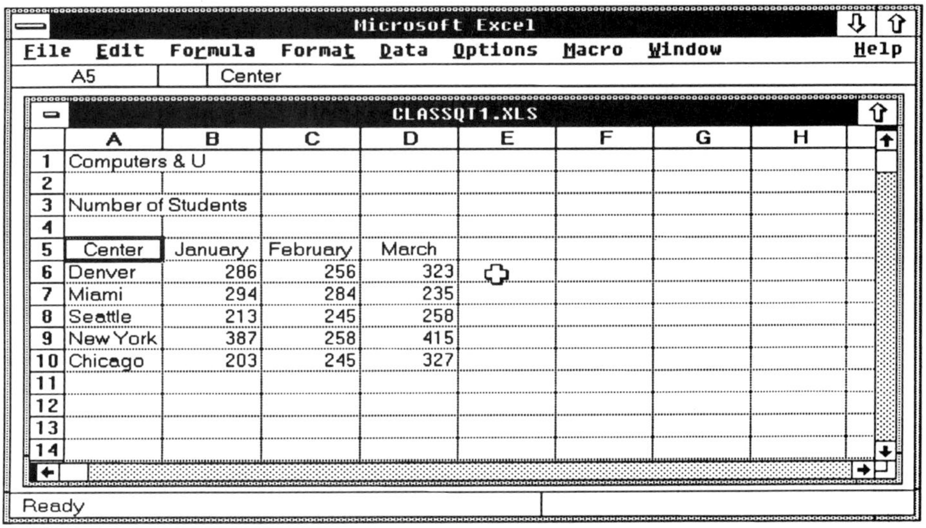

Fig. 11-1. Excel on the PC.

way, companies that have both IBMs and Macs can cut down on training costs for spreadsheet users if they use Excel. You can see the similarities when you compare Fig. 11-1 with Fig. 11-2, which shows Excel on the Macintosh.

We expect that Excel-PC will continue to increase its share of the IBM spreadsheet market because of the advanced features it provides and the availability of a

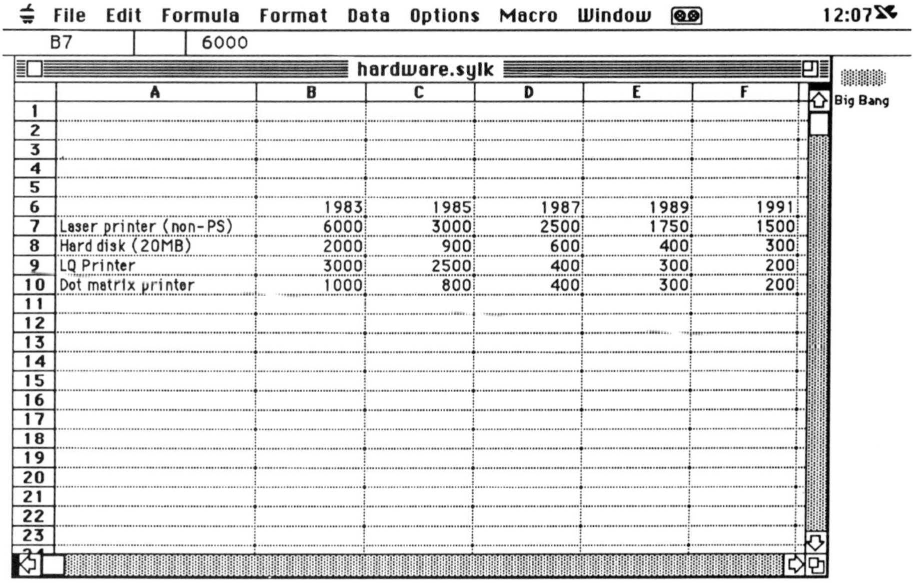

Fig. 11-2. Excel on the Mac.

companion product on the Mac. Unfortunately, there are some differences between the two editions of Excel. For example, Excel 2.1 on the PC has text formatting but version 1.5 for the Mac does not. You can supply text to an Excel 2.1 chart with a link text from a worksheet. What tends to happen is that Microsoft upgrades one edition and then the other, so that Excel 2.2 for the Mac will do some things that Excel 2.1 for the PC will not.

The IBM/Mac Excel Connection

When you share files between Mac and IBM editions of Excel, all numbers, text, cell formats, and most values are shared, as are cell protection, calculation, and display settings. Macro sheets can be exchanged, but charts cannot. However, the big gap is the requirement that the files must be stored in the SYLK format, Microsoft's generic *symbolic link* format, not the regular Excel format.

To begin the process of sharing data with Excel-PC, the Mac user must use Save As and pick the SYLK file format when storing the file that will be shared. A suitable name for the file should be chosen to assist the PC user in finding the file. Because Mac files do not automatically have extensions, nothing will indicate that the file is a SYLK file unless an extension, such as .SLK is created as part of the name. You can see this in Fig. 11-3.

Using a name that conforms to DOS rules is also a good idea. When the file is read by a PC, Excel's File Open command can be used to read in the SYLK file automatically.

When transferring Excel-PC files to a Mac, you will want to follow the Save As procedure and store in the SYLK format. You might find minor differences between versions of Excel like cell shading which some earlier versions of Excel-Mac do not support. The one area of difference between Mac and PC versions of Excel that can have a significant effect on calculations is the treatment of dates. The date problem does not appear when you bring Excel-Mac worksheets to the PC, but going the other way with date information can be a mess.

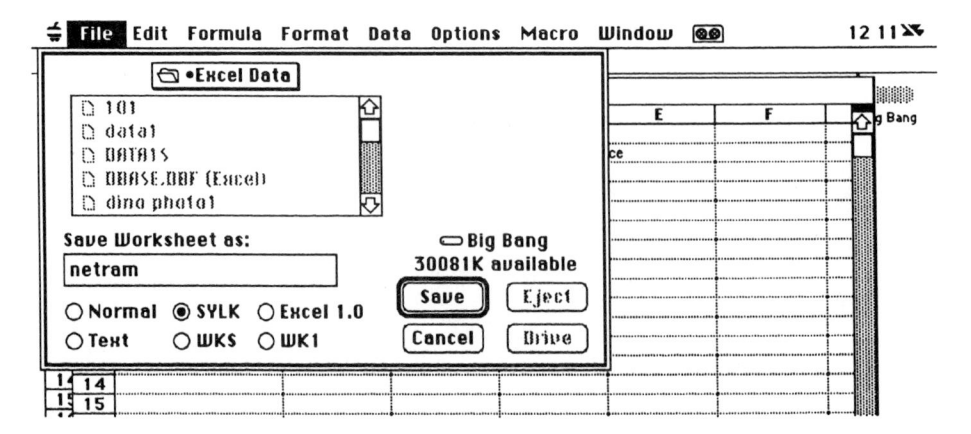

Fig. 11-3. Saving as SYLK in Excel-Mac.

The problem with dates arises because Excel-Mac uses a base date of January 2, 1904, instead of the January 1, 1900, date used in Excel-PC and 1-2-3. When Excel-PC reads Excel-Mac worksheets, it takes care of the difference automatically. But in order for dates in a Excel-PC worksheet to be read correctly by Excel-Mac, you need to *begin* the PC worksheet with the Sheet Options setting 1904 Date System checked under the Options Calculation menu, seen in Fig. 11-4.

This requirement is something of a pain because you might have existing worksheets that you want to export that did not use this setting. Microsoft might endow future versions of Excel-Mac with the ability to make the translation automatically. In the meantime, you can get around the problem by copying an existing worksheet into a new sheet in which the 1904 date setting has been made.

Excel and dBASE

Excel can use data from files generated by dBASE or a compatible program. Suppose you need some market research data for a project and you can acquire the data on disk. You want to analyze the data using Excel, but the data is only available in dBASE format. This presents no problem if you are using Excel-PC because in most cases Excel-PC can accurately read dBASE files with the File Open command. You only need to specify the filename in the Open dialog box, as seen in Fig. 11-5, and Excel-PC will read it into worksheet format.

If you are using Excel-Mac, then you need to use TOPS Translators to convert the file from dBASE to Excel-WKS format before Excel-Mac can read the file.

Notice that when Excel opens a file, the top left corner of the Excel window tells you how much of the file has been read from disk, from 0 to 100 percent. This

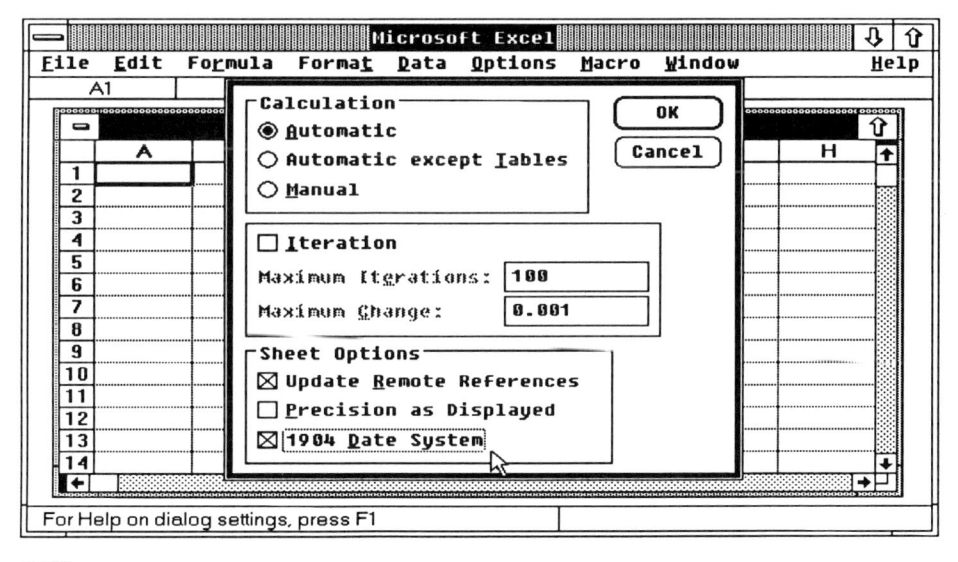

Fig. 11-4. Taking care of dates in Excel-PC.

area of the screen also tells you the type of file being retrieved, normally Excel. When you retrieve a dBASE file with Excel-PC, the message reads DBF to let you know the type of file. If you try to open a dBASE file with Excel-Mac, this message says Text and the file is not read properly. While PC users might think that the type of file was obvious from the extension on the filename, Excel's file type message provides an extra precaution against mixing of file types. For example, nothing will stop you from creating a file in text format that has an Excel filename extension. To avoid possible loss of data, always check the file type message when retrieving a file to make sure that the type is correct.

When you open a dBASE file with Excel-PC, the program creates a worksheet with the dBASE field names in the first row, as you can see from Fig. 11-6.

The width of the columns is determined by the length settings of the dBASE fields. Note that Excel has read the DATE field entries as dates. Otherwise, there is no formatting of numbers carried over from the dBASE file (the numbers in the LOAN field were comma formatted in dBASE).

In Fig. 11-6, you can also see that the name Database has already been assigned to the field names and records so that you can immediately begin to use the data as a database in Excel. This is done automatically by Excel-PC. The range name Database is particularly important when you save a worksheet that was opened from a dBASE file. If you have made changes to the data and want to save the file in dBASE format, you need to bear in mind that Excel-PC will only save the part of the worksheet that is defined by the name Database. This is because dBASE files only contain field names and records, they do not contain rows of titles and formulas such as you can add with Excel.

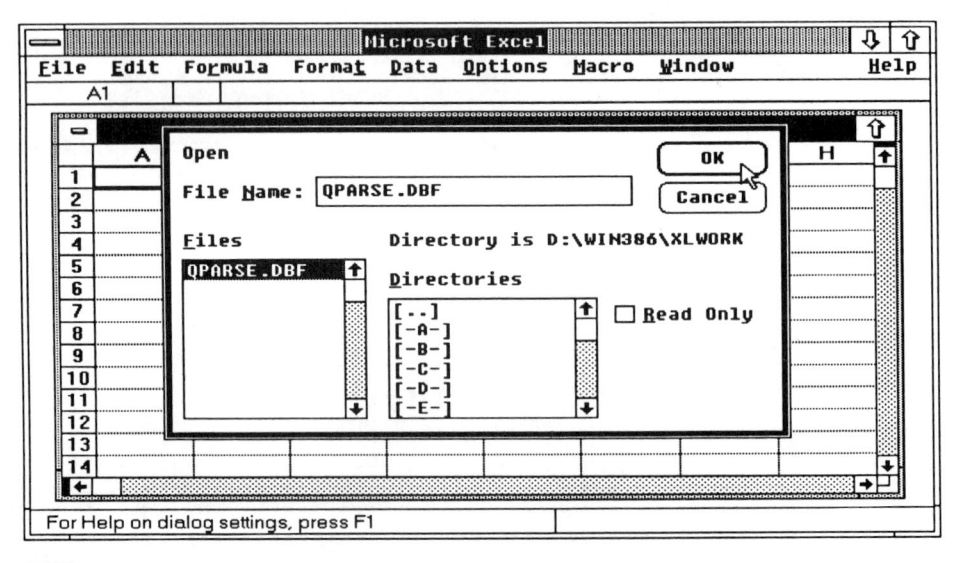

Fig. 11-5. Opening a dBASE file with Excel-PC.

When you go to save a worksheet that was opened from a dBASE file, you will be shown the Save As options, discussed in a moment, and one of the DBF options will be selected. Excel's default course of action when saving a foreign format file is to save the file in its original format. You must change the File Format selection to Normal to save the file as an Excel worksheet.

Exports from Excel

Suppose you have assembled important market research data in an Excel worksheet. You need to pass on this information to someone using a program other than Excel. One of the easiest ways to export files from Excel is to load the worksheet in question and use the Save As command from the File menu. When using Excel-PC, you will notice that the Save Worksheet As dialog box has an Options button. This leads you to the dialog box you see in Fig. 11-7, with its smorgasbord of nine file formats.

The available file formats, together with their use are listed in Table 11-1. Suppose your market research data is in a worksheet called MRD1.XLS and you want to share on the network with an associate who uses 1-2-3, Release 2. At the Save Worksheet As dialog box, check the WK1 option button. This causes Excel-PC to change the filename extension to WK1. Thus MRD1.XLS will be saved as MRD1.WK1. When you pick OK to confirm the save operation, the file will be translated to the correct file format for 1-2-3, Release 2 (use the WKS option to store files in the 1-2-3, Release 1A, format). You can publish the file on the network where it can be read by your associate who uses 1-2-3. (You might also want to pass

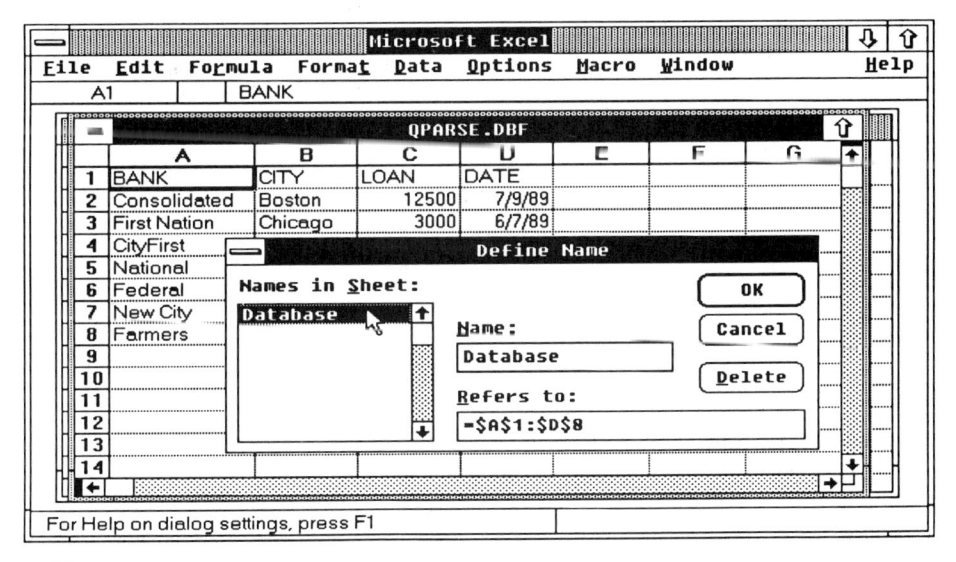

Fig. 11-6. A dBASE file with names defined.

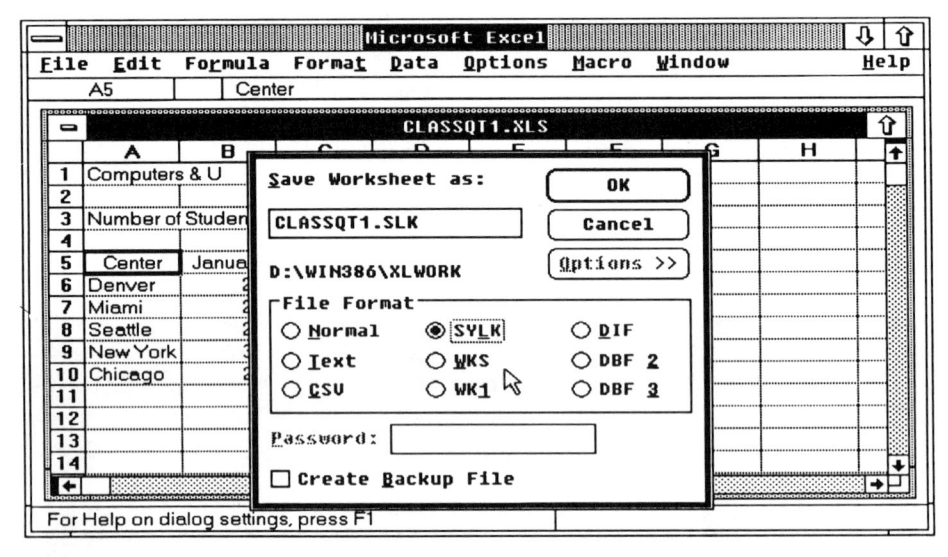

Fig. 11-7. The Save Worksheet As dialog box.

along some notes about how Excel deals with data that has no direct equivalent in 1-2-3, an aspect of file translation that is discussed later in this chapter.)

Note that when you use Excel-PC to save a file with the WK1 extension, the filename in the title of the worksheet window is also changed to reflect the new format. Thus, in the example, the default name for the next File Save operation will

Table 11-1. Excel file export formats.

Type/Extension	Used for
XLS	Normal format
SYLK (SLK)	Transfer of data to another spreadsheet program such as Multiplan or Excel-Macintosh 1.5.
Text (TXT)	Transfer data to or from a word processor.
WKS	Transfer of data to Lotus 1-2-3 Release 1A or Symphony.
WK1	Transfer of data to Lotus 1-2-3 Release 2 or 3.
CSV	Transfer of data with comma separated values to or from a word processor.
DBF2 (DBF)	Transfer of database range to dBASE II.
DBF3 (DBF)	Transfer of database range to dBASE III.
DIF	Save values, not formulas, for programs that do not support other formats.

be MRD1.WK1. To help you keep track of worksheets in non-normal formats, Excel treats every File Save command as a File Save As command when the active worksheet was last saved in a foreign format. This prevents you from carelessly opening an Excel worksheet, making changes to it, saving it as a 1-2-3 worksheet, and then closing the file without saving the changes in the Excel format. This is particularly important when you are using Excel-specific formulas that cannot be saved in files that use the 1-2-3 format.

Although Excel-PC automatically changes the filename extension to match the File Format option you have selected, Excel does not check extensions you enter against the file format. For example, if you use File Save As options when the current worksheet is SALES1.WK1 and you edit the worksheet name to read SALES1.XLS but do not change the File Format option from WK1 to Normal, Excel-PC will store your worksheet in 1-2-3 format but with an Excel-sounding name. Given that 1-2-3 files lack some important features of Excel files, this type of error can cause serious corruption of worksheets and should be avoided.

The Macintosh version of Excel does not have an Option button in the File Save As dialog box but you can pick between a number of options, seen earlier in Fig. 11-3. You should use a filename that indicates the format of the file.

Reading 1-2-3 Files into Excel

Because Excel is often used in offices that have prior experience with 1-2-3, there is often a need to translate old 1-2-3 files into Excel worksheets. The basic procedure with Excel-PC is simply to use the File Open command and list WK? files, picking the file you want to translate from the file list. With Excel-Mac you will also use the File Open command. For example, if you have published your PC directory containing 1-2-3 worksheets, a Mac user can mount that volume and read the worksheets directly.

1-2-3 Conversion Factors

In most situations 1-2-3, data is read by both editions of Excel exactly as it was stored by 1-2-3, including numeric formats, label alignment, formulas, and range names. If there are graph settings in the 1-2-3 file, these will be ignored by Excel-Mac but Excel-PC gives you the opportunity to Create Lotus 1-2-3 graphs? Answering Yes will cause Excel-PC to create a new chart for each graph defined in the 1-2-3 worksheet, each one linked to the worksheet that you are opening. An answer of No tells Excel-PC to ignore the graph settings in the 1-2-3 file and they are lost. (Even if you have defined graphs in 1-2-3, you might want to create your Excel charts from scratch.)

Because 1-2-3 does not display gridlines, all 1-2-3 worksheets will appear in Excel without gridlines, although you can add these later with the Options Display command and the Gridlines check box. Formats for 1-2-3 values read into an Excel worksheet are converted according to the settings shown in Table 11-2. Where a standard Excel format equivalent for a 1-2-3 format does not exist, then a custom format is created, as in the case of a 1-2-3 format with four decimal places. Date formats from 1-2-3 are read correctly by Excel, as well as date values. The two exceptions are dates beyond the year 2078, which Excel cannot handle, and dates transferred to the Macintosh, discussed earlier.

Databases defined in 1-2-3 files are fully converted by Excel, the only exception being the output range in 1-2-3. Because Excel uses no permanent definition of the output area used by the Data Extract command, the 1-2-3 output range definition is not retained. Data tables created in the 1-2-3 worksheet appear as tables of values when translated into an Excel worksheet because the Excel Data Table system uses array formulas that have no equivalent in Excel. You will need to redefine the data tables in Excel.

Odd Names

You will find that Excel recognizes 1-2-3 range names and retains them. Cell coordinates of range names are made absolute in keeping with normal Excel range name practice. In addition to range names you defined in the 1-2-3 worksheet, Excel records such settings as the print range. The print range appears in the Excel version of the worksheet as Print_Area. You may want to make a point of using the Define Names command after importing 1-2-3 worksheets, just to check that all essential names have been carried over, and also to get rid of any unnecessary names that might linger from 1-2-3. For example, 1-2-3 records the last area used for a Data Fill

Table 11-2. Formats for 1-2-3 values.

1-2-3 Format	Excel Format
Fixed, 0 decimals	0
Fixed, 2 decimals	0.00
Scientific, 0 decimals	0E+00
Scientific, 2 decimals	0.00E+00
Currency, 0 decimals	$#,##0 ; ($#,##0)
Currency, 2 decimals	$#,##0.00 ; ($#,##0.00)
Percent, 0 decimals	0%
Percent, 2 decimals	0.00%
Comma, 0 decimals	#,##0); (#,##0)
Comma, 2 decimals	#,##00.00 ; (#,##0.00)
General	General
+/−	General
D1 (dd-mmm-yy)	d-mmm-yy
D2 (dd-mmm)	d-mmm
D3 (mmm-yy)	mmm-yy
Text	General
Hidden	;; (numbers) or ;;; (text)

command and Excel retains that as the name _Fill. Data table settings are recorded as _Table1_In1 and so on.

Translating Formulas from 1-2-3 to Excel

Excel has more functions than 1-2-3 and generally more formula options, such as arrays. However, some subtle differences when translating 1-2-3 formulas into Excel are listed here.

Range Operators. While Excel uses colons as the range operator, as in =SUM(B2:B20), 1-2-3 uses double periods, as in @SUM(B2..B20). Excel automatically translates these. The use of commas for multiple arguments, as in =SUM(B2:B20,C2:C20), is identical in both programs.

Mathematical Operators. The precedence of operators is slightly different between 1-2-3 and Excel, although this should not affect too many formulas. While 1-2-3 does exponentiation before anything else, Excel places negation over exponentiation, so that =−4^4 returns positive 16 in Excel whereas 1-2-3 would make −16 out of this. This only affects your worksheets if you use both negation and exponentiation. The use of parentheses can overcome this difference.

Calculation Order. In 1-2-3, you can perform row-wise and column-wise calculation, a feature that allowed 1-2-3 to use older spreadsheets that were designed before natural calculation was available. Because Excel only does natural calculation you will not want to transfer 1-2-3 worksheets based on row- or column-order calculation until you have altered them to work with natural calculation.

Offset Numbering. One of the most confusing of 1-2-3's features is the *offset column* or *row*. This is the position number of a specific column or row in a table, with the first offset being 0. For example, in a vertical lookup table, offset column 1 is the second column in the table, the first one after the lookup values. Excel simply numbers columns and rows beginning with 1. In converting 1-2-3 formulas, Excel adds 1 to the offset number in lookup functions and in statistical functions. In the case of the CHOOSE function, Excel subtracts 1 from the offset number. However, you might want to check complex VLOOKUP, HLOOKUP, and CHOOSE formulas (use the Formula Find command to do this).

The MOD Function. Excel's handling of the MOD function also differs from 1-2-3. For example the formula =MOD(−3.5556,3) returns the answer 2.4444 in Excel, but the same formula in 1-2-3 returns −0.5556. If you are importing a 1-2-3 worksheet that contains MOD formulas that might be handling negative values, you will want to use Excel's Formula Find command to check out the results and possibly modify the formulas.

Financial Negatives. Because Excel considers payment and principal arguments in financial functions to be negative, it changes the sign of such arguments when converting 1-2-3 financial functions. In any IRR function statements imported from 1-2-3, the guess and values arguments are transposed by Excel to meet Excel's argument order.

Statistical Functions. As you know, Excel ignores labels in ranges used in statistical functions, such as AVERAGE. However, 1-2-3 gives labels in such ranges a value of zero. This means that you need to watch such functions and the results they give. The use of labels in a range being averaged can throw off the @AVG function in 1-2-3 because the label is counted as an entry. You might have gone to some lengths to work around this limitation in 1-2-3 but will not need to in Excel.

Error Messages. The 1-2-3 error message NA is translated as #N/A!. The ERR message is translated as #VALUE! (There are only two error messages in 1-2-3 and so there is no distinction within 1-2-3's ERR messages as to the cause of the error).

Translating 1-2-3 Macros

When you import a 1-2-3 worksheet that contains macros, Excel reads the macros as simple text entries and records the range names assigned to the macros. No effort is made to do anything with the macros. However, if you have invested time and energy in developing your 1-2-3 macros, you might get excited when you learn that Excel-PC provides a program called the Macro Translation Assistant. Unfortunately, while this program does attempt to convert both Multiplan and 1-2-3 macros into Excel macros, the success rate varies widely, depending upon the type of macros involved. This really cannot be blamed on the Macro Translator because the entire approach to macros is different in Excel, and many 1-2-3 macros do not need to be translated anyway. For example, macros to center numbers are not needed, as Excel does this with formatting.

To attempt to convert your 1-2-3 macros to Excel-PC, you first open the worksheet containing the macros, then use the Run command to load what is billed as the Macro Translator (Alt-Space, U, Alt-M, Enter). The Macro Translation Assistant menu appears, with only one item, Translate. When you pick this, the choice is between 1-2-3 and Multiplan. When you pick 1-2-3, a list of currently opened worksheets appears and you select the one containing the macros that you want to translate. You do not have to open a macro sheet prior to this because Excel-PC will place the macros in a fresh sheet automatically.

When Excel-PC knows the worksheet you want to translate from, a list of range names appears. All range names beginning with \ are automatically selected. You can pick and choose range names, including macro code that is not named with \ or deselecting macros that you know are redundant. The Verbose option tells Excel-PC to present messages about translation problems as they occur. When you pick OK, the translation process begins and messages about the status of the task appear. When the process is complete, you are asked if you want to close the Macro Translation Assistant. Pick Yes to get back to the worksheet and check out the results, pick No to go on with further translation.

What Excel-PC has done during translation is open a fresh macro sheet and enter code that emulates the 1-2-3 macro code. The macros are named for their 1-2-3 originators. While the Macro Translation Assistant does succeed at what some would consider to be a very difficult task, it rarely writes clean code. The situation generally escalates with more complex macros and you can even put the translation process into a loop, filling up a macro sheet with code as it tries to handle menu branches and subroutines in 1-2-3 macros. In general, you will find that Excel's features are so rich and its macros so much more sophisticated in their structure, that you will want to rewrite many of your 1-2-3 macros anyway. You can use the Macro Translation Assistant as a starting point in some cases, much like the macro recorder. Users of Excel-Mac who want to use macros from 1-2-3 worksheets can do so if they have access to Excel-PC. By using the Macro Translation Assistant on the PC to create an Excel macro sheet saved in SYLK format that can then be read by Excel-Mac, the 1-2-3 macros can be brought into the Mac version of Excel. However, all of the caveats about macros that are translated from 1-2-3 still apply on the Mac side.

Other Excel/1-2-3 Factors

Despite the limitations mentioned, Excel does a great job of understanding the vast majority of 1-2-3 calculations. However, as with any electronic spreadsheet work, you should not assume that what looks at first glance to be correct is actually so. Check all results from imported models to make sure that nothing has been lost in translation.

EXCEL AND MULTIPLAN

In several areas, Excel accommodates users of Microsoft's other spreadsheet program, Multiplan. Excel can read and write Multiplan-compatible worksheets using the SYLK format. By saving Multiplan files using the Symbolic option, under the Transfer Options command, you can open them with Excel's File Open command. The Symbolic option stores files with the DOS extension SLK in Microsoft's own *symbolic link* format, referred to as the SYLK format. Use *.SLK in the File Name box to list SYLK files in Excel. The SYLK format does not support charts.

When Excel reads a SYLK file created by Multiplan, it correctly understands numeric and text entries, name, formats, formulas, and protection settings. However, because Excel lacks a bar graph format, any Multiplan worksheet cells that have this format are given the general format in Excel. There are one or two other areas of difference between the two programs. Linked spreadsheet formulas from Multiplan are turned into external array formulas in Excel. The Multiplan functions DELTA and ITERCNT have no function equivalents in Excel, but you can use Excel's Maximum Change and Maximum Iterations settings under the Options Calculation command to simulate these Multiplan functions. You will also need to check that the column-wise calculation used in Multiplan has translated correctly into Excel's natural order calculation.

Sending Excel worksheets to Multiplan begins with the Save As option where you pick the SYLK format. You cannot export Excel macro sheets or charts to Multiplan. When you retrieve the Excel file into Multiplan, you will find most numeric formats, as well as column widths and alignment, are preserved. However, custom Excel formats might be lost and there might be formulas that Multiplan does not understand, either because Multiplan lacks all of Excel's functions or because Multiplan does not support array arguments or array formulas. Furthermore, Multiplan only supports 5 arguments per function statement as opposed to Excel's 14. Also, Multiplan is only 4095 rows by 255 columns, as opposed to Excel's 16,394 rows and 256 columns. In cases where Excel formulas cannot be translated by Multiplan, there either will be an error message or the formula will simply be ignored.

LIMITS TO EXCEL FILE EXCHANGE

When exchanging files between programs with differing capabilities, it is not surprising to find that sometimes something is "lost in the translation." The next few sections point out the areas to watch for when moving data between programs and systems.

Exporting from Excel to dBASE

The most important thing to bear in mind about exporting data from an Excel worksheet to the dBASE file format, either through the Excel-PC Save As feature or via the TOPS Translators conversion facility is that you can only export the area of the worksheet named Database. Within this area, any fields that are calculated values will be converted to values when they are stored in the dBASE format. While the dBASE file will adhere to the decimal place settings of the numeric formats in the Excel worksheet, you cannot export format characters such as comma separators, dollar signs, or custom formats.

There are significant differences between the file format used by dBASE II and that adhered to by dBASE III and later versions. For this reason, Excel-PC and TOPS Translators include separate options for the two formats. If you need to export a worksheet from Excel-PC to dBASE II or a program that reads dBASE II files, then be sure to check the DBF 2 option, rather than DBF 3.

From Excel to 1-2-3

While you can save Excel worksheets as 1-2-3 worksheets, you cannot export Excel macro sheets or charts. Furthermore, because Excel has more features and functions than 1-2-3, there are going to be areas where the Excel worksheet does not translate well. These are listed in Table 11-3. You might want to keep these areas in mind if you are designing Excel sheets that you know will be distributed to 1-2-3 users.

Usually labels, simple formulas, and values from Excel are correctly saved in the 1-2-3 format. When Excel is saving a formula into the 1-2-3 file format and sees that 1-2-3 will not recognize it, the formula is converted to a constant value. The functions that 1-2-3 does not support are listed in Table 11-4. Excel will alert you to conversion errors by displaying an alert box as the file is being saved. You can be alerted to each conversion problem or choose to see only a summary when the conversion is complete. The summary does not tell you where all the errors are, just how many there are.

Standard numeric formats are cleanly converted from Excel to 1-2-3, but custom formats are not. If Excel finds no suitable 1-2-3 equivalent for a numeric format, the number is stored unformatted. Obviously, font and border formats are not retained in the 1-2-3 file, and all values are right-aligned when they are passed to 1-2-3. The various Excel error messages are boiled down to two in 1-2-3. The #NA! error becomes NA, all others, such as #NUM! and #NAME? become ERR in 1-2-3.

UNLISTED PROGRAMS

You or your associates might be working with a spreadsheet program that has not been mentioned yet. For example, when you are working with Excel-PC, some popular programs are not specifically listed in Excel's file formats, such as the databases R:BASE and Paradox, or the spreadsheets VP Planner and Quattro. Can these programs share data with Excel? Yes, if they use one of the listed formats as an intermediate format. For example, the spreadsheet Quattro can save files in both WK1 and DBF format as well as its own format. To transfer data from Quattro to Excel, you save the file WK1 in Quattro, then retrieve into Excel. To pass data back to Quattro, save the Excel worksheet as WK1, which can then be read by Quattro.

Many other programs have this multiple file format capability, thus allowing fairly easy exchange of data. For example, Microrim's R:BASE database program has a utility called Gateway that can read and write many popular formats. Borland's Reflex 2.0 database on the PC can read and write 1-2-3, Paradox, dBASE, and Quattro files. The Macintosh database called FileMaker can write SYLK files that can be read by Excel on both the PC and the Mac.

Table 11-3. *Problem areas in converting Excel worksheets to 1-2-3.*

Array formulas—converted as constants.
External references—converted as constants.
PV, FV, and PMT function statements that use future value and type arguments—turns formula to a constant.
NPV function statement with mulitple cash flow arguments (as opposed to a single range of values)—becomes a constant.
Gridlines, font, and border formats—not translated.
Print settings—not translated.
Data tables—turns results to constants, will need to be redefined.
Multiple windows—lost.
Titles—not retained.
Named values—turned to constants.
Range names not meeting 1-2-3 range name rules—lost.

Table 11-4. Excel functions that 1-2-3 does not support.

AND (Excel's #AND# is an operator, not a function)
AREAS
COLUMN
COUNT (@COUNT is equivalent to COUNTA)
DCOUNT (@DCOUNT is equivalent to DCOUNTA)
DOLLAR
DPRODUCT
DSTDEV (@DSTD is equivalent to DSTDEVP)
DVAR (@DVAR is equivalent to DVARP)
FACT
GROWTH
INT
IPMT
ISBLANK
ISERROR
ISLOGICAL
ISNUMBER (@ISNUMBER is equivalent to ISNONTEXT)
ISREF
LINEST
LOGEST
LOG (@LOG is equivalent to LOG10)
LOOKUP
MATCH
MDETERM
MINVERSE
MIRR
MMULT
NOT
OR (Excel's #OR# is an operator)
PPMT
PRODUCT
ROW
SEARCH
STDEV (@STD is equivalent to STDEVP)
SUBSTITUTE
TEXT
TRANSPOSE
TREND
TYPE
VAR (@VAR is equivalent to VARP)
WEEKDAY

TOPS TRANSLATORS AND SPREADSHEETS

In addition to the file saving alternatives offered by applications themselves, users who are crossing the IBM/Mac boundary can use the TOPS Translators to convert files from and to a variety of formats. The TOPS Translators software, operation of which was described in the last chapter, comes with readers and writers for popular spreadsheet formats. These include WKS (from the original Lotus 1-2-3 and many other products), WRK (from Lotus Symphony), WK1 (from 1-2-3, version 2), and SYLK (from Multiplan, Excel and many other products).

As TOPS Translators sees it, a spreadsheet is a grid of cells that can contain formulas, format specifications, and numeric values or text. The TOPS Translators spreadsheet readers decode this information and organize it in a way that can be used by the TOPS Translators writers to build spreadsheets or other files that can use all or some of the information. TOPS Translators does not attempt to convert macros. But there are many uses that TOPS Translators is good for. For example, you can build a spreadsheet on the Mac that has the same formulas, formats, and values as a Lotus spreadsheet. You can create a file type, such as DIF, that only uses the values, possibly as an intermediate format on the way from a spreadsheet to a database program. You might want to use the results of a Lotus spreadsheet in a desktop publishing project, you could do so by means of Tab Text output. This takes the Lotus values and places them in a tabbed text file in the same format that would be visible on the Lotus screen.

TOPS TRANSLATORS AND DATABASES

Databases are generally record-oriented. They contain text and numeric values, format specifications, structural information that identifies relationships between data items and/or records, and so on. TOPS Translators contains readers for the dBASE format. It also contains many writers that are capable of using the text and numeric values and the format specifications from the database while ignoring the structural information. This makes it possible to use values and formats from dBASE II or III files to build databases in spreadsheets or in other database products which provide their own structure information.

For example, to use dBASE information in an Excel-Mac spreadsheet, select dBASE as the input format and Excel (WKS) as the output format. To use the same information in another database product, select dBASE as the input and CSV, DIF, or SYLK as the output. When using this approach, you will be creating files that look, on the Mac, like blank pages. You cannot open these documents until you have opened the Macintosh application that needs to read them. From within the application you can open the translated file using the appropriate commands.

Comma Separated Values (CSV)

A CSV file contains ASCII text records with all values separated by commas, text values surrounded by double quotes, and a carriage return at the end of each record. One such record is created for each row or record in the original input file. The format of the text or numeric values within each record matches the format specifications from the original input file. This file format is accepted by many newer application packages. It provides an easy way to bring data from an existing spreadsheet or database into a new one.

PC dBASE II or III

The data files created by dBASE-PC are ASCII files in a proprietary format. They contain database structure, text, and numeric values. dBASE II and III have subtle differences it comes to file format, so you should choose the appropriate format for the version you are using. dBASE is more than just the files in which data is stored. For users to print out the data stored in dBASE, report formats have to be designed. The reports occupy files. To automate procedures in dBASE, you write programs of instructions, which are also stored in files. These are not translated by TOPS Translators or spreadsheets like Excel-PC. To read these files and use them, you need dBASE-PC itself or a dBASE- compatible program such as FoxBASE+.

Mac dBASE

The Macintosh version of dBASE creates data files in the DBF format of dBASE II or III that can be used in dBASE Mac or any Macintosh product that accepts the dBASE DBF format. Unfortunately, dBASE Mac cannot use the report and programming files from dBASE on the PC. However, FoxBASE+ Mac can use these files.

FILEMAKER, A MACINTOSH DATABASE

On the Macintosh side of the database software market you will find that a product called FileMaker has established a strong position. This is not a relational database like dBASE Mac or 4th Dimension, but it is more than a flat-file database, offering multiple views of the same data file. While FileMaker is easy to use for simple applications, it can be used to develop sophisticated systems through the use of scripts and layouts. Although FileMaker, the latest version of which is marketed by Claris, and known as FileMaker II, only runs on Macs, it has good file exchange facilities, runs well on a network, and is a good database choice for Mac users on TOPS. As you can see from Fig. 11-8, FileMaker offers good support for graphics in database reports and records.

FileMaker has built-in commands that allow you to exchange data with other programs. Typical applications of this would be to share data with PC users who do not have FileMaker, to export data for graphs to be used in a presentation, or to use FileMaker's finding and sorting capabilities on a mailing list that was initially entered in a word processing document. You can use the Output To command to create a file in a format that can be used by other applications. You also can copy data from another application into a FileMaker file with the Input From command.

The Input From and Output To commands can be used to exchange data with a variety of file formats—text files, BASIC files, and the SYLK files used by Excel. You can also output FileMaker data to a merge file format that allows you to combine FileMaker data with a form letter created in a word processor. The Input From and Output To commands work together, allowing you to share FileMaker data with another application, work on it there, and then pull it back into FileMaker. You can use FileMaker's features on data created by remote systems in other applications, then output the data to a file that can be used by the original application.

Output from FileMaker

When you input data from another application to FileMaker, you can choose whether to add new records or update existing records in the current file. For example, you might use data from Excel to do update records in a FileMaker file once a month. Note that if you are using FileMaker on a floppy disk system and plan to employ the Input From or Output To command, you should keep your System, Finder, and the files you are working with all on disks that are in drives. This will help you avoid excess disk swapping.

When you use the Output To command, FileMaker creates a new file, called the output file, in the file format you choose. The records you are browsing in the current file are copied to the new file in the order you are browsing them, so you

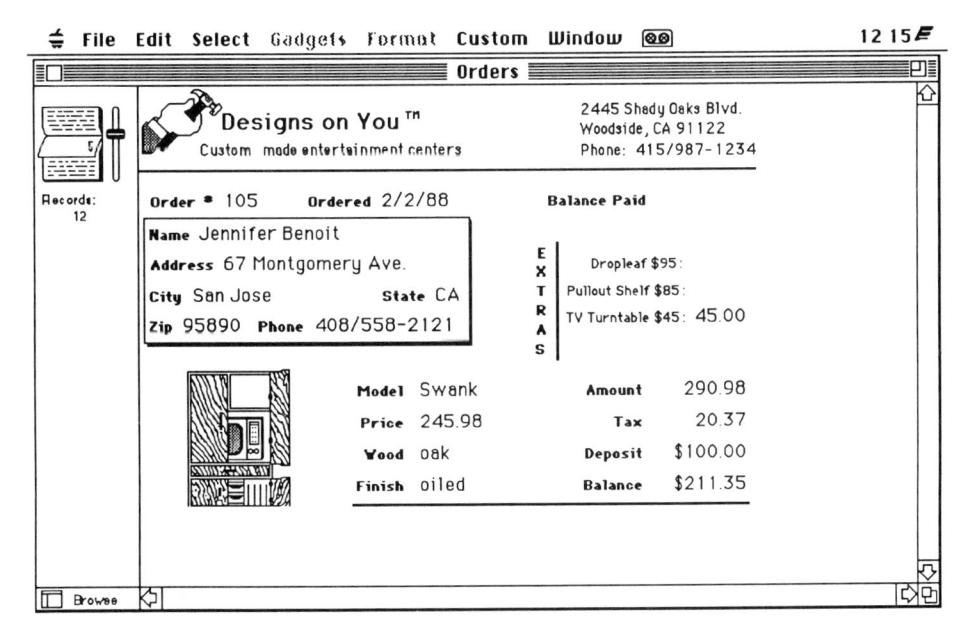

Fig. 11-8. A FileMaker example.

can use the Find, Omit Records, and Sort commands to specify which records you want copied and the order in which they are output. You choose which fields to output from the current file and their order by specifying an output order. You can output values from text, number, date, and calculation fields in the current file to the output file. You can also specify whether number, date, and calculation fields are to be output using number and date formats from the current layout or unformatted.

FileMaker remembers the output order you specify, as well as the file format you choose, so if you create an output file from the same FileMaker file on a regular basis, you do not have to respecify this information. If you need to change the order later, you can add or remove fields in the output order, or erase the order and specify a new one. You can output FileMaker data to the following file formats.

Text file (tabs). The text file format is a common format that can be used by most word processors and many other applications. For example, you can open a text file from within MacWrite or Microsoft Word; it has the same format as a document you save as Text Only. Field values are separated by tabs; records are separated by return characters. If you have return characters in a field value, they are output as ASCII vertical tab characters. If numbers and dates are not formatted or you request that the formatting not to be copied into the output file, the values will be output exactly as you typed them. Otherwise, the same format is used as when you browse or print records in FileMaker using the current layout.

BASIC file (commas). This is the same format as the one listed in TOPS Translators as Comma Separated Values (CSV), one that can be read by BASIC programs. This format is generated from a BASIC program with the PRINT# or PRINT USING# statements. Applications such as dBASE can read files in BASIC format. Field values are separated by commas; records are separated by return characters. If you have return characters in a field value, they are output as spaces. All field values are enclosed in quotation marks, with the exception of unformatted numbers. If your field value contains double quotation marks, FileMaker outputs them as single quotation marks. If a number field includes text or symbols, only the number is output. FileMaker outputs only the first 255 characters of a text field because that is the maximum size that can be read by BASIC.

SYLK file. This is the Microsoft format that stores data in rows and columns. It is used by spreadsheet spplications such as Microsoft Excel. Each field is output as a column, starting with column 1. Each record is one row, starting with row 1. If a number field includes text or symbols, only the number is output. SYLK interprets each cell as a piece of text or a number. FileMaker outputs dates and formatted numbers as text in quotation marks. If a number is unformatted or you choose not to use numeric formatting from the layout, the number is output as a number (no quotation marks). No more than 245 characters can be output for any field.

Merge file. Similar to the text file, this format can be used in creating personalized form letters and other standard documents. For example, Microsoft Word can combine data in a merge file with text in a main document to print form letters or other documents that merge standard text with variable data. The merge file is equivalent to the file Microsoft Word refers to as a *data document*. Field values are separated by commas; records are separated by return characters. The first record is a header record listing the field names. If you have commas in a field value, the entire field is surrounded by quotation marks. If you have quotation marks in a field value, the field is surrounded by quotation marks and the quoted word(s) is surrounded by two sets of quotation marks, for example, "the " "Best" " Model". If you have return characters in a field value, they are output as ASCII vertical tab characters. (This is the same character that is typed with Shift–Return in Microsoft Word.) If numbers and dates are not formatted or you specify that you don't want the formatting to be copied into the output file, the values will be output exactly as you typed them. Otherwise, the same format is used as when you browse or print records in FileMaker using the current layout.

Performing an Output

The full instructions for using the output commands can be found in the FileMaker manual. Essentially the procedure is to select the fields of your FileMaker database that you want copied to the output file. These will be text, number, date, and calculation fields. Picture and summary fields cannot be output. You first open the database that you will be exporting from, use the Find and Omit commands if you want to select certain records to be left out of the transfer to a new file, then sort the records if you want them output in a special order. On the Browse screen, you then choose Output To from the File menu. You will need to give the file a name. Use a name that includes the type of the file you will be creating and try to conform to DOS rules if you are going to share the file with PC users. When you click New, you will be shown a screen similar to the one in Fig. 11-9 where the SYLK format has been chosen.

Select, in order, the fields you want transferred to the new file and click the Move button, seen in Fig. 11-9. You can double-click on a field name in the field list to move it. To move all the fields at once in their original order, click the Move All button.

At this point, FileMaker will ask if you want to include calculation fields. Bear in mind that the values in calculation fields can be output to any file format, but you cannot read these values back into calculation fields in FileMaker. If the application you are exporting to supports calculated fields, you can establish the calculated values there. Just remember that you output calculated data from the current file, then read it back without modification of either the input file or the FileMaker file. You click on Include to keep fields in the Output Order. You click on Exclude to keep calculation fields out of the Output Order. You can remove a field from the Output Order list by clicking the field name in the Output Order list, then clicking Move. To erase the whole Output Order list and start over, click the Move All button.

So far the output file has not been created and no data has been copied. You click the Output button to have FileMaker go ahead and copy the data to the output file. You can click the Exit button to return to the current FileMaker file without creating the output file. You can stop the process of copying data to the output file after you have clicked Output, hold down the Command key, and type a period. After the data is copied into the output file, FileMaker returns to the Browse screen in the current file.

In the Finder, the icon for the new output file looks like a blank page. To open the output file, you must first launch an application that can read the file format you have chosen for the output file (text file, BASIC file, SYLK file, or merge file).

Input to FileMaker

To copy data from another file format into a FileMaker database, use the Input From command. For example, you might want to take advantage of FileMaker's layout capabilities to present data generated by Excel. You might have captured data from an on-line database into a text file and want to prepare it for analysis. The file that you copy the data from is called the *input file*. When you copy data from a file created with another application into a FileMaker file, you specify an input order that tells FileMaker what fields are in the input file, and the order in these fields appear. You also specify the file format of the input file, and chooose whether the data in the input file should be used to add new records to the FileMaker file or to update existing records. FileMaker saves the information you specify, so if you periodically copy the same field values from another file into a FileMaker file, you don't have to respecify the input order or the input file format.

You can copy text, number, and date values into the current FileMaker file from these file formats: text, BASIC (CSV), and SYLK. The input file should contain data in one of the following forms.

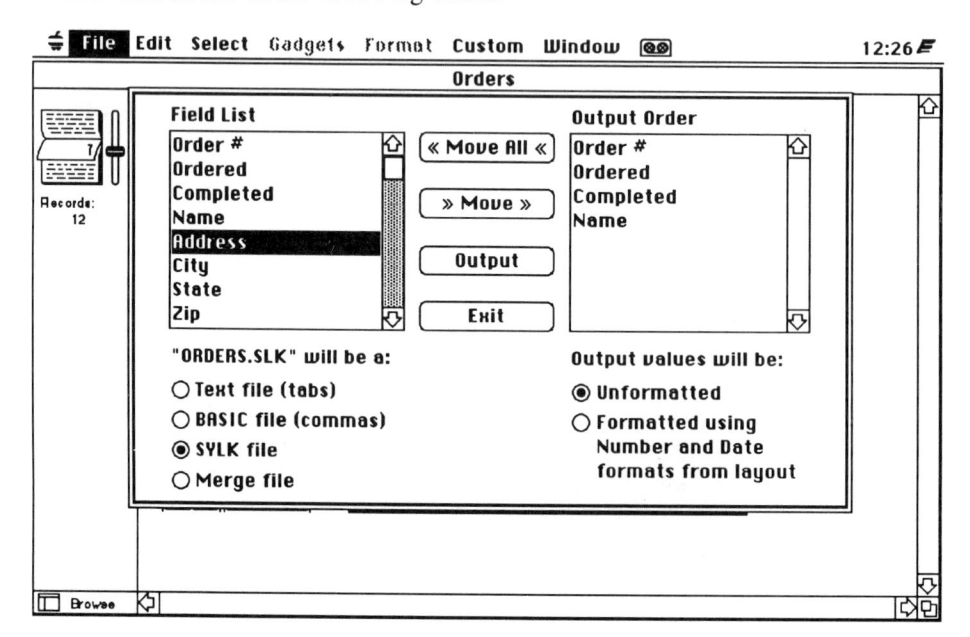

Fig. 11-9. Creating a SYLK file from FileMaker.

Text. Field values are separated by tabs; records are separated by return characters. If you are using the text file to add new records, FileMaker uses the field values in the text file to fill fields in each new record according to the Input Order. If there are fewer field values in the text file than fields in the Input Order, some fields in the new record will be empty. If there are more field values in the text file than fields in the Input Order, some fields in the text file will not be input. Similarly, if you are using the text file to update records, and the number of field values for a record in the input file doesn't match the number of fields in the Input Order, some fields will not be updated, or some field values in the input file will not be used (depending on whether there are too few or too many field values for the record in the input file).

BASIC (CSV). Field values are separated by commas or return characters. If the field value is in quotation marks, the separator is optional. Field values in quotation marks can contain commas and return characters. FileMaker uses the same rules for the format of the input file as BASIC uses for the INPUT# statement, except that FileMaker can exceed BASIC's limit of 255 characters for a field value copied into a text field.

SYLK. Each column contains data for one field; each row contains one record. This is the format used to exchange data between versions of Excel and Multiplan.

If you want to use the incoming data to add new records to an existing database, FileMaker copies values from the input file into new records at the end of the current file, with the new records grouped as the records found. This means that you can immediately browse just the records that were added. You can locate empty fields, invalid dates, or duplicate values that might have been accidentally created by using the Find command. Alternatively, you can go on to browse all the records in the expanded file by using the Find All command.

When you are using the incoming data to update existing records in a FileMaker database, FileMaker replaces field values in the records you are browsing in the current FileMaker file with values from the input file. For this reason, you should make sure that the order of records you are browsing exactly matches the order of information in the incoming file. You will also need to specify that the input order exactly matches the sequence of field values in the input file. The first field value in the input file replaces the contents of the first field in the Input Order in the current file, the second replaces the second, and so on. For safety's sake, make a backup copy of your existing FileMaker database before you begin updating records with data from another file.

To input data from a text, BASIC, or SYLK file to a FileMaker file follow these steps:

1. If you are updating records in the current FileMaker file, first make a backup copy of the current file, then make sure you are browsing only the records to be updated, in the order the information appears in the input file.

2. Open the FileMaker database into which the new information will be going. Then, from the File menu in the Browse screen, choose Input From. Select the

file that is the input file and click the Open button. You will see a screen like the one in Fig. 11-10. Choose whether to add new records or update current records by clicking the appropriate check box.

3. Move field names from the Field List to the Input Order to let FileMaker know which fields will be supplying information from the external file. The order of these must match the existing order of field names in the FileMaker database.

4. When your selections are complete, click the Input button to begin copying data from the input file to the current FileMaker file. If you need to, you can click Exit to return to the current file without copying data from the input file.

Note that inputting from a large file might take some time. When the process is completed the information from the input file is copied into the current file, FileMaker displays the Browse screen. If you have added new records, you will be browsing just the new records. The status area shows the number of records added as the number of records found. If you have updated current records, the status area is the same as before you input data (found, sorted, and the same number of records). Check the file to make sure the updated records are as you want them before discarding the backup copy of the file that you made before updating.

As you can see, the process of moving data in and out of FileMaker is relatively simple, making the program a useful solution for database applications on networked Macintoshes. As you will see in a later section, FileMaker offers useful

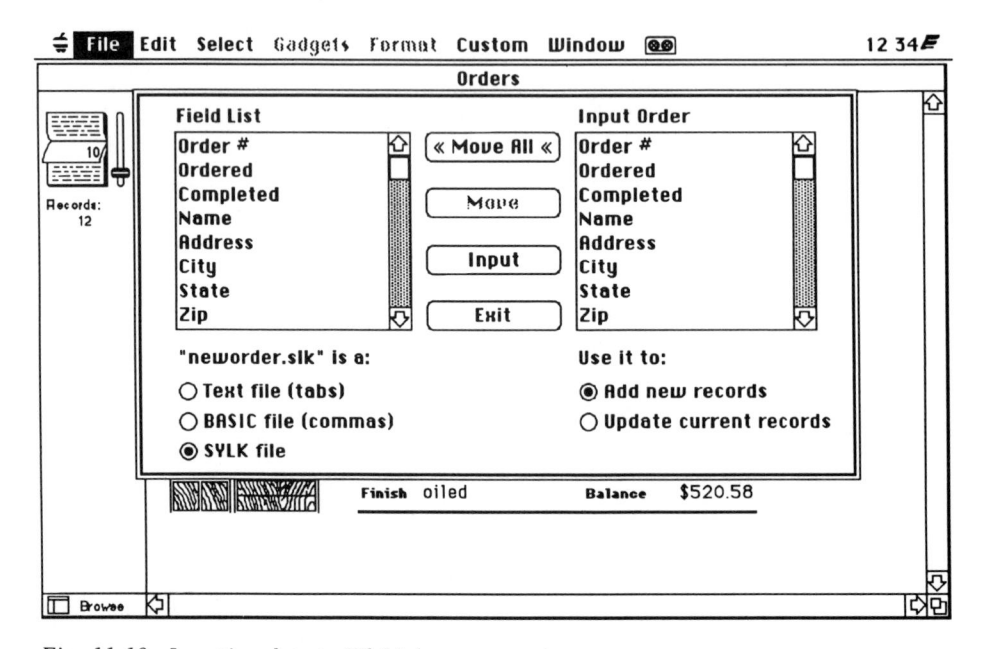

Fig. 11-10. Inputting data to FileMaker.

features that are network specific, allowing the sharing of files across a TOPS network.

RUNNING EXCEL ACROSS TOPS

So far we have talked about file translation and sharing files over TOPS, now we need to talk about how you organize spreadsheet and database applications programs on the network and establish functional connections with TOPS. We will look at Excel first. This gives us a chance to address the question of how to run TOPS and Excel together on an IBM, which is not always easy to do.

Running Excel-Mac

First of all, what about running Excel-Mac from a Macintosh server? So far we have talked as though each computer on the network should load its own copy of Excel, then use TOPS to share file storage areas to permit communal access to important data. In fact, you can have several users load Excel from a Macintosh server, although a faster model such as the IIcx is required for satisfactory performance. The important question is, "What do you gain from running Excel-Mac as a server-based application." Because you have to purchase a required number of copies of Excel anyway, and there is as yet no network edition of Excel, the answer is not a lot. This might change with future releases of the product.

Running Excel-PC

If you have installed and used Excel on the PC, you will know that it is a resources hog requiring a fast processor, a fast hard disk, and a good graphics card to provide acceptable response times. Consequently, you will probably not want to load from a remote system if you are using FlashTalk. If you are running TOPS over Ethernet, then the performance degradation might not be too bad. Some techniques can help you organize network access to Excel-PC.

The basic arrangement is to install Excel on the file server by naming the desired file server drive and directory when running the Setup program. However, this arrangement has some limitations. Unless all stations on the network use the same display and mouse you will need to install separate versions of the program, either in separate network directories, or on the separate stations. A booklet called *Getting the Most From Your Hardware With Microsoft Excel* is now included with the Excel-PC package. This contains valuable hardware- and software-specific installation and operation details. The booklet can be obtained from Microsoft Customer Service.

Just because you are using Excel on a network does not mean that all users must conform in their style of Excel operation. Those aspects of the program, such as screen colors, that are specified by the WIN.INI file that controls Windows, can be individually established. The basic procedure for individualizing your version of

Excel when loading the program from a network server is to make a copy of the WIN.INI file that is on the network server and store the copy locally. Then start Windows/Excel from the local directory containing the copy of WIN.INI. Windows always uses the first WIN.INI it finds and so will read WIN.INI from the current directory before looking to the network file server.

You can proceed to customize settings because the changes will be saved into the copy of WIN.INI that started the program. If you later start Windows/Excel from your system and do not begin from the directory in which WIN.INI is stored, you will still make use of your own WIN.INI if the directory it is stored in precedes the file server drive/directory in your system's PATH statement. Remember that the first WIN.INI found is the one used, so careful attention to your PATH statement will allow you to control which WIN.INI is in effect.

Excel File Sharing

You can share both IBM and Mac Excel data files over the network and establish links between worksheets created by different users. However, you need to consider the question of document access in such an environment. Within Excel, a system exists to control access to worksheets that are being used. If you attempt a normal File Open on an Excel document that is already open you will get a message telling you that you can only open the file as a Read Only document. A read-only document is one that you can view, but not edit, one from which you can copy data and establish links, but not one you can update or change. You can intentionally open files as read-only documents turning on the Read Only option in the File Open dialog box. Opening a file with Read Only checked means that another user cannot alter the document until you close it.

If you are storing Excel documents in an area of the network to which other users have free access, you might want to use password protection on the documents (using the Save As command). Unless you share the password with others, they will not be able to open the document. To allow viewing of the file by others but prevent editing, you can use the Format Cell Protection command and Options Protect Document command, issuing a password to control the protection status.

A TOPS-Excel Scenario

Even if you have your PCs connected via FlashTalk and require each one to have its own copy of Excel, TOPS has some benefits. For example, any laser printer on the network can be used to print Excel documents.

Suppose you have a Macintosh and a PC in your office and both are running Excel. The Macintosh is being used to design and prepare presentations that use Excel data. The PC is used for a lot of data entry into Excel. If both systems are connected with TOPS, the PC with Excel can be used to update files on the Mac, or the Mac could read the needed files directly from the PC. This eliminates the need for other types of file transfers and actually allows live access between systems. While the need to save files in SYLK format cannot be avoided because you will be running Excel-Mac on the Mac and Excel-PC on the PC, the relatively high cost of additional storage space on the Macintosh can be avoided by storing files on the PC. The PC files can be read onto the Macintosh where advanced graphics programs can be used for such applications as publication design.

The following notes will help make the Excel connection on TOPS:

1. *On the Mac*. Nothing special needs to be done. To make Mac Excel worksheets and macro sheets available to PC Excel, just save as SYLK files. Publish the folder in which the files are saved to make them accessible to other network users.

2. *On the PC*. Unless you have a specialized configuration that runs TOPS without using the 640K of normal DOS memory, you will need to run TOPS in a slimmed down configuration in order to run Excel as well. You can run in Client mode to save memory. This allows you to mount Mac folders and other directories from other PCs as drives on your PC. You can read and write with these volumes, but you cannot publish your drives for access by others.

3. *Client Mode*. To operate TOPS in client mode on the PC, use the command LOADCLNT instead of LOADTOPS to load the appropriate files. If you normally use the AUTOEXEC.BAT to load the full version of TOPS, you will need to unload the full version, using the command TOPS UNLOAD/A, and then reload with the client command in order to regain memory space. Alternatively, you can modify your AUTOEXEC.BAT to always load the client version of TOPS.

4. *Slimmer Windows*. If you load TOPS in client mode on your PC, then try to load Excel and get the message Insufficient memory to run Excel, do not despair. There are further steps you can take to gain more memory. One alternative is to use the run-time version of Windows, the one that comes with Excel, rather than the full version (variously known as Windows 2.1, Windows/286, Windows/386). Another tactic is to slim down your CONFIG.SYS and AUTOEXEC.BAT files. A third approach is to use a DOS extender to gain access to more memory.

If you have an 80386 machine you may already have heard the bad news: Windows/386 and TOPS do not get along well. This problem is discussed in more detail in Chapter 14. However, Windows/286 and TOPS work fairly well together on an 80386, and the run-time version of Windows does well on 80386 machines.

If you still have insufficient memory to run Excel after loading TOPS in client mode and using the run-time version of Windows, check what other settings are in your system's CONFIG.SYS. Unnecessary device drivers should be removed. Check that you are not loading unnecessary device drivers for graphics cards and add-on devices. For example, the device driver for a Bernoulli drive typically uses 12K of RAM. While you cannot remove the device driver and still use the Bernoulli drive, you might decide to reconfigure your system to get to TOPS and Excel loaded. You might also find drivers from devices that are now defunct have been left in your CONFIG.SYS. If you check the PATH setting in your AUTO-EXEC.BAT, you might be able to remove excess directories. Too many paths eat up an important area of memory. If all of these tactics fail, see the discussion of RAM-cram, and ways to overcome it in Chapter 14.

While you may find that making changes to accommodate TOPS is irksome at first, the ability of TOPS that lets you read Mac folders as drives with the File Open command is more convenient than many of the other cabling and disk drive systems that offer PC-to-Mac connectivity. Furthermore, hardware and software developments might soon remove the memory constraints that currently hamper the TOPS connection.

Using Excel-PC and NetPrint

A slightly different application of TOPS technology for Excel-PC users is to let you access to the Apple LaserWriter printer. Using the TOPS product called NetPrint you can print direct from Excel-PC to an Apple LaserWriter over a TOPS network. However, you need to coordinate both the NetPrint settings and the Windows/Excel print setup in order for this to work.

When you configure NetPrint, use the CONFIGURE program to specify which port of your computer you want NetPrint to reroute to the LaserWriter. If you use LPT3, you can retain a local printer as LPT1 while anything that you tell your computer to print on LPT3 will be captured and rerouted by NetPrint. You must also specify that you do not want PostScript emulation in NetPrint and you do not need to load the screen font. After you use CONFIGURE, the settings will be stored in a file called NETPRINT.DAT. You can run NetPrint without loading the full TOPS network. The files that need to be run to load NetPrint are as follows.:

```
ALAP
PSTACK
PAPOVL
KEYINT
NETPRINT
```

You can place these commands into a batch file to save typing.

To set up the Excel side of the equation, use the Control Panel to install the Apple LaserWriter, picking LPT3 from the Connections menu. When using the printer-specific Setup command for the LaserWriter, set a job timeout of about 20 seconds. Set the Handshaking to Software. You can set the Header to Download each job, or you can use the technique described for PostScript printers in Chapter 14 to create a header file that is copied to the printer from DOS.

When you select the LaserWriter to print an Excel document, you will notice that NetPrint spools the document to disk before printing it. This means Excel is not held up for long by the printing process, which TOPS carries out in the background. A system of beeps is used to keep you informed of the spooler's progress as it prepares the document to be sent to the printer.

RUNNING OTHER SPREADSHEETS ACROSS TOPS

IBM users on a network can run other spreadsheets besides Excel. Quattro, 1-2-3, VP Planner, and SuperCalc can all be loaded from file servers over TOPS. You probably will not want to do this if your PCs are connected with FlashTalk, but Ethernet connections are fast enough to support remote loading. Although loading across the network takes longer than local loading, most spreadsheet software is memory-resident and so the program will not need to do much reading from disk once it has loaded. This statement needs to be qualified when it comes to some newer versions of the above programs, which have become so large that disk access is required. If you are using Quattro Professional, SuperCalc 5, VP Planner, or 1-2-3 Release 3, you should get the network version of the software if you plan to load over a network. In some cases, you might need to coordinate hardware configuration for users loading the same version of the software or establish local driver sets of each user.

The non-network versions of these packages offer simple first-come file access. The first user to read a file gets read/write access to it, other users can read the original of the file from disk but cannot modify it. Excellent password protection is offered by all four packages and should be used as a major level of security. Users who are storing files in common-access areas should also use cell protection in worksheets to prevent accidental damage to spreadsheet data.

RUNNING FILEMAKER ON TOPS

As we mentioned earlier, FileMaker is a database manager and forms design application that can run over TOPS. Several levels of security are provided for network use. However, with permission, you can access information in a coworker's file at the same time as the coworker is using the file. Sharing FileMaker databases helps users get work done more effectively and efficiently because information management and communication typically involves sharing different pieces of information with different people.

When using FileMaker on TOPS any user can host a file residing on a file server or in a folder mounted using TOPS. While you can use FileMaker on AppleTalk, an AppleTalk user can host only those files residing on their own Macintosh. By taking advantage of FileMaker network commands, you can begin sharing files and working simultaneously with coworkers relatively quickly. By simply toggling FileMaker's Exclusive command in the File menu, multiple users can share the same file. When you issue the Exclusive command, the check mark that is normally next to that button disappears.

From this point on, the first person to open a file is the *host*. Anyone can host a file residing in a folder mounted using TOPS. All subsequent users are *guests*. Guests can access nonexclusive files open on other Macintoshes using the Network button in the Open dialog. Once the file is opened by the guest, the host and the guest can begin sharing the same information residing in the host's file. All the additions, deletions, and modifications made to the file appear in each user's window and are saved to the disk from which the host opened the file.

Information that should not be changed or needs to stay confidential is easily protected with passwords and other features. For example, you can let one user only browse your file, another user only browse and edit your file, and keep access to the entire file to yourself. With multiple users sharing the same information, limiting who can open your files and see your information is a primary concern. For example, if you have a file containing coworkers' salaries, you wouldn't want everyone to have access to the file. By limiting file access to a few individuals, the integrity of the salaries tracked in the file can be maintained.

To make a FileMaker file available to multiple users, you can open a nonexclusive file in a folder published using TOPS. If you are storing the file in a folder published using TOPS, you might want to limit access using the password command in TOPS. Alternatively, you can limit the folder to be write-protected, one writer only, or many writers; however, to host a file, you must have at least write access to the file. With two or more people using the same FileMaker file at the same time, setting limitations on who can mount published folders using TOPS is a start, but you might also want to limit who can open a file from within FileMaker. For example, if you're using TOPS, you can limit who can mount a published folder containing a highly sensitive file. But as soon as one person mounts the folder and opens that file (and the Exclusive command is not checked), a guest can open the highly sensitive file from within FileMaker using the Network button and never encounter the protection set on the published folder. Using a few of FileMaker's features, you can avoid "uninvited" guests by setting limitations on who can open your file, what information they can see, and what they can do once they've opened the file.

FileMaker lets you limit who can open and use your file by letting you create passwords. Passwords are words that you assign and can give users different levels of access to a file. FileMaker lets you limit what information a user can see by letting you create *confidential layouts*. Confidential layouts are layouts that you designate to be available only to users with the correct password. FileMaker lets you limit what users can do in your file by assigning access rights to a password. Access rights are the levels of access you assign to a password that let a user perform actions, such as browsing records in a file.

After you assign passwords to a file, no matter where a user opens the file—from within FileMaker, the Finder, or a folder mounted using TOPS—FileMaker will first ask for a password before opening the file. A *password* is a word (or words) that you type to which you assign a set of access rights to a file (or a word that you type to receive an assigned set of access rights). By creating passwords for a file, you can control who can open the file. By creating a password, making a layout confidential, and not giving a user access to confidential layouts, you can limit what information a user can see. For example, if a file contains a confidential layout and your password does not let you view confidential layouts, all objects on the confidential layout appear in gray, as seen in Fig. 11-11.

By creating a password, you can also control what actions can be performed by assigning various access rights. For example, if a password lets a user only browse records, that user cannot print field definitions or add records to the file. You can mix and match five separate access rights to create different levels of access. For example, you can create one password that lets a user browse and edit records, another password that lets a user browse records and use confidential layouts, and yet another password that lets a user browse and edit records and use confidential layouts and design layouts.

FileMaker also gives you one more level of control: the ability to assign a set of access rights to no password. This means that a user can open a file without typing a password and receive a certain set of access rights to the file. This is useful for making a file available to numerous users while reserving entire access to yourself so that operations such as defining fields can only be performed by you.

You can create any number of passwords with as many levels of access as you want as long as you have access to the entire file. You can also change and delete passwords. When creating passwords, you must create at least one password that lets you access the entire file. If you are creating passwords while others are using the file, the current users will not be affected by it. However, FileMaker will ask any subsequent users for a password.

When designing a layout displaying sensitive information that you do not want other users to view, you can designate that layout to be confidential. By limiting the fields containing sensitive information to layouts that are confidential, you are assured that users can't view that information without the correct access rights. For example, if you place a field called Wages on a confidential layout and on a layout that is not confidential, the Wages field would be gray on the confidential layout (if a user didn't have the correct access rights) but it would be fully visible on the other layout. To maintain the confidentiality of the Wages field, you would place the Wages field only on confidential layouts.

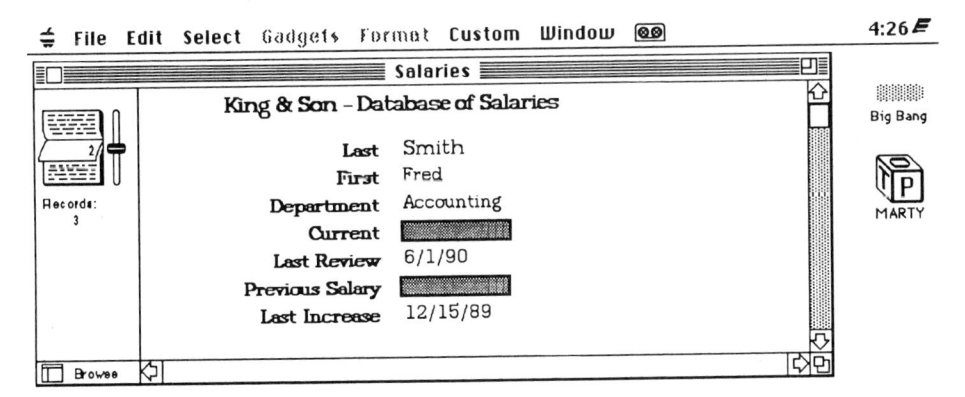

Fig. 11-11. Protected information in FileMaker.

Tips on TOPS and FileMaker

When opening a FileMaker database as a host, it is important to keep in mind the responsibilities associated with opening the file first. The host must open any lookup files associated with the hosted file to ensure that the lookup files will open for any guests. When running FileMaker with MultiFinder, the host must also use only applications that support background processing and only use such applications for short periods of time.

A few operations are best performed as a single user. These include using the Replace, View as List, Delete Multiple, Sort, Relookup, and Print commands in a file containing a large number of records. When you open a file as the host, you get the previous host's sorting order, find requests, page setup, and all changes made to the file by both the previous host and guests. (A guest is the second or subsequent user to open the file.)

You can use the Network button on the Open dialog to open a nonexclusive file as a guest from within FileMaker. TOPS users can also open a file as a guest as you normally would from the Finder as a single user by double-clicking on the file icon, or selecting a file on your disk, a file server, or a folder mounted using TOPS, and then using the Finder's or FileMaker's Open command. When opening a file as a guest, you should keep in mind the responsibilities associated with being a guest. Most importantly, you are using the file through the generosity of the host. This means that if the host asks you, the guest, to close a file, you should comply with the request. You should also be sure to close any files that you are not using. This will ensure better performance for all users.

The Question of Communication

FileMaker is a good example of an application that has good file sharing features built into it. However, you can see that even a relatively simple program like this presents a new level of complexity when working with others. The network dimension to software opens up not just technical issues such as allowing access, but also personal issues such as informing others of what you are doing and deciding who gets to see what. The benefits of electronic communication are impressive. Great amounts of laborious repetition become redundant. The "price" is greater communication between coworkers than when we were all sealed within our booths. However, we should be happy to pay this price as it might well bring us to a clearer picture of what work really needs to be done and how best the doing of it can be organized. By forcing the company or the work group to speak up on issues of access, need-to-know, and work flow, better ways of doing the work might be discovered.

RUNNING OTHER DATABASES ACROSS TOPS

In addition to FileMaker, several other databases on the Mac support TOPS. MultiUser Omnis Plus is a relational database that supports up to 64 users accessing the same database over TOPS. The program features file and record locking, meaning that when one person is updating a record others are prevented from accessing that record. This makes for more reliable multiuser updating of shared databases. Similar features designed to protect the integrity of shared data are provided by the Helix database from Odesta, one of the first relational databases for the Mac.

Of the databases that run on both Mac and IBM, a leading contender is FoxBASE+. This program reads and writes database files between systems and can also swap report and program files between the IBM and the Mac. FoxBASE+ reads and writes dBASE files and is usually referred to as a dBASE-compatible program. However, FoxBASE+ is a strong performer in its own right.

A more recent entrant into the Mac database field is a company that has been in the minicomputer database market for some time—Oracle. They have a product for the Mac that offers a HyperCard interface to database operations. All Oracle products, whether for the IBM or the Mac, feature compatible support for a database system called SQL (often pronounced "sequel"). Essentially SQL is a set of standardized commands or *verbs* that carry out database actions. These are now supported by a wide range of products on larger computers. Smaller computers have been developing SQL capability so as to talk more freely with larger systems. Oracle has used this feature to pull together its whole product line and make all versions compatible from micros to mainframes.

CONCLUSION

By using TOPS as the basic means of interconnection between systems, users of spreadsheet and database software can share information with relative ease. In some cases, the data that is being exchanged needs to be translated first, but the translation options are extensive, and some of them can be automated. Until such time as a universal data format emerges, we need to cope with some minor inconsistencies. At least TOPS gives us transparent access to the basic data resources. In the next chapter, we look at using TOPS when you are working with graphics and desktop publishing.

12
Graphics and Desktop Publishing

IN THIS CHAPTER, we look at some of the applications for TOPS as an IBM/Mac connection in the area of graphics and desktop publishing. The question of exchanging graphics files between systems is examined and we look at how you can incorporate data from multiple sources into documents created with desktop publishing software.

A GRAPHICAL WORLD

In the last decade or so, there has been a tremendous growth in the amount of information that is transmitted *graphically*, that is, by means of pictures and images rather than words. The rise of nonprint visual media such as television and video has played an important role in this trend, as have many other elements, such as the rapid increase in the amount of information that we need to absorb, and the growing velocity of social intercourse that brings people together with common interests but no common language. Look around any modern airport in the world and you will see the almost universal replacement of written instructions with graphic images. These days just about anyone can understand directions from the symbols in Fig. 12-1.

An emphasis on graphics has been part and parcel of the microcomputer revolution. Since the earliest days of the industry, it seems that the standard publicity photo of any new computer had to feature some sort of chart or graphic on the screen. Just as word processors made possible crisp, error-free, multipliable, easily revised documents, so graphics software promised automated image making, with infinitely reproducible, scalable, revisable charts and pictures. In some ways, the promise of graphics software has taken longer to fulfill. Graphics make heavier demands on hardware than text. For many word-related applications it is possible to reduce text to a limited set of standard characters. This is how dedicated word processors, CP/M computers, the first IBM PC systems dealt with most applications. Really flexible graphics are not possible until you can compose them out of a vast number of separate dots. This ability has been grafted on to the original architecture of the IBM PC, with qualified success, but it was designed into the Macintosh from the very beginning.

There were several reasons for putting graphics ability into the guts of the Macintosh. PC users were getting frustrated with the limitations of graphics applications available on the IBM, indicating a strong demand for a machine that could "do graphics." Furthermore, there was growing frustration with the interfaces offered by programs on the PC. As the microcomputer spread beyond the core of dedicated hackers and "early adopters," people complained that programs were hard to learn. The keys you were supposed to press to accomplish a particular task were not obvious, and learning the keys for one program did nothing but confuse you when you went on to another. To a large extent this problem persists in the PC world. To save a file with WordPerfect you press F10 or F7. To save a file with 1-2-3 you press / then F for File, and S for Save. In WordPerfect you type the file name at the bottom of the screen; in 1-2-3 you type it at the top of the screen. In neither program is a menu of commands displayed until you ask for it. When it came time to organize

Fig. 12-1. Universal symbols.

files, early versions of DOS forced you to type cryptic commands and decipher equally cryptic responses. There was no "big picture" of the resources or information at your disposal.

Designers of the Macintosh saw graphics as a solution to these inconsistencies and limitations. A common core of commands would be implemented in every application and, wherever possible, images would be used instead of words. The files, programs, storage space, and other resources of the Macintosh would be visually represented. In a phrase, the Mac would have a "graphic interface." The computer resources to do this would also serve to make possible much more sophisticated graphics work than had so far been possible on a microcomputer. This was underscored by the first suite of programs for the Mac: MacPaint, MacDraw, and MacWrite. From these beginnings the Macintosh has gone on to dominate the "creative applications" side of microcomputing.

Meanwhile, in the DOS world, the rising demand for better graphics and more effective interfaces led to some interesting developments. Cheap clones of the Hercules Graphics Card brought respectable graphics to millions of PC that would otherwise be merely "character-based." From the early Color Graphics Adapter (CGA) standards advanced past the Enhanced Graphics Adapter (EGA) to the Video Graphics Adapter (VGA), with its increased resolution and potential use a wide range of colors. The relatively low cost of powerful PCs based on 80286 and 80386 chips meant that Microsoft could begin to deliver on the promise of Windows, a graphical interface for DOS that was first introduced in 1983.

The effect of these trends on Mac/IBM connectivity has been significant. Consider the case of Aldus PageMaker, an early leader in the field of desktop publishing. The Windows environment allowed Aldus to successfully launch a PC version of what was first released as a Macintosh product. The two editions of the same program run in very much the same way, at least as far as the user is concerned. PageMaker documents created on the Mac can be read directly by the PC, and vice versa. By using Windows, Microsoft has been able to do the same with Excel, in which the latest Macintosh version reads all documents created by the PC version.

By 1989 the "graphics gap" between IBM and Mac had narrowed considerably. Impressive products such as Adobe Illustrator were running on both platforms. The fact that the Mac took an early lead still means that in most cases the flow of graphics is from the PC to the Mac. But as you explore the field of file formats used in graphics work, the shifts in relative positioning between the two worlds, IBM and Mac, will play an important role.

TYPES OF GRAPHICS

In Chapter 10 we saw that word processing programs generate many formats for storing text. The same is true for graphic images produced by computers. In some ways, the situation with graphics is somewhat better than it is for word processing. There are some standards emerging for files that store graphic images. Nevertheless, there is still a wide variety of image storage formats which can be confusing. We will attempt to classify the types of graphics you will encounter on Macs and PCs and then talk about how to share them.

In the DOS environment, some programs use the three letter file extension to indicate a file format. For example, .WK1 indicates a 1-2-3 worksheet and a file ending in .PCX is a PC Paintbrush picture. File format designations on the Macintosh are handled somewhat differently. As you probably know by now, Macintosh files have two parts, called file forks: the data fork and the resource fork. The data fork contains the meat of the file's content, the resource fork contains information about the format of the file and the program that created it. This is what enables you to see the origin of files when you use the By Names option on the desktop. Four-letter codes are used for the file type in each resource fork. These distinguish the formats of Macintosh files like the filename extensions of DOS files. In some situations, it might be necessary to manipulate either the DOS filename extension or the Macintosh file type in order to share graphics files. A section later in this chapter discusses working with Macintosh resource forks.

Charts

The most common form of graphics used by businesses is probably the chart. You might define a chart as a visual representation of numerical data, such as the one seen in Fig. 12-2.

The chart communicates the meaning of the data much faster than a reading of the numbers. When conveying information to the public, to clients, to employees, or to members of the board, a chart can avoid boring the audience with numbers. It

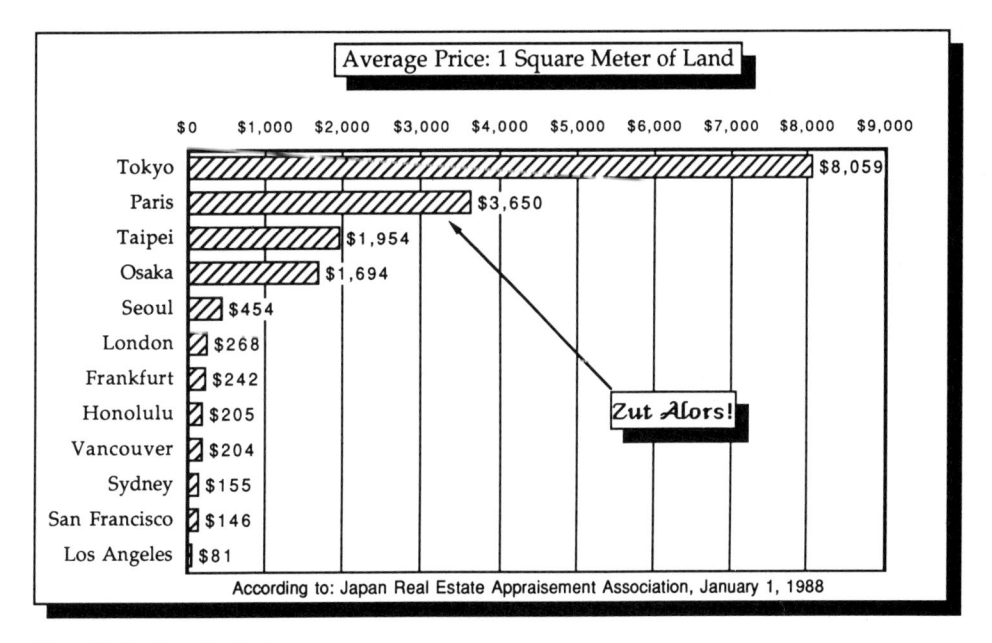

Fig. 12-2. A typical chart.

is generally accepted that the presenter equipped with charts projects a more polished image.

Charts are produced by several types of program. Many spreadsheet programs can produce charts from numbers stored in a spreadsheet, as you can see from Fig. 12-2 where an Excel-Mac graph is displayed. The graph is linked to a spreadsheet data so that a change in data immediately updates the graph. Excel graphs are stored in their own files, separate from the spreadsheet. On the IBM, the extension XLC is given to Excel charts.

Spreadsheet programs can display the graph on-screen and produce printed output. The chart in Fig. 12-3 was printed from Quattro Professional, a spreadsheet program running on the IBM, that display graphs within spreadsheets.

Quattro Professional generates on-screen and printed graphs directly from spreadsheets and normally does not store them in separate files. The first spreadsheet on the IBM to really popularize graphics was 1-2-3. All versions of 1-2-3, up to and including Release 2.01, generate on-screen graphs directly from data in a spreadsheet, but they cannot print graphs from within the spreadsheet portion of the program. Instead, graphs that are to be printed are stored in special files with the extension PIC. These files contain complete instructions about how the graph is to be printed. A similar format was used by Lotus Symphony, and this has given rise to the Lotus PIC format for charts. A number of graphics programs can read Lotus PIC files and then embellish them. In fact, Lotus sells a graphics package called

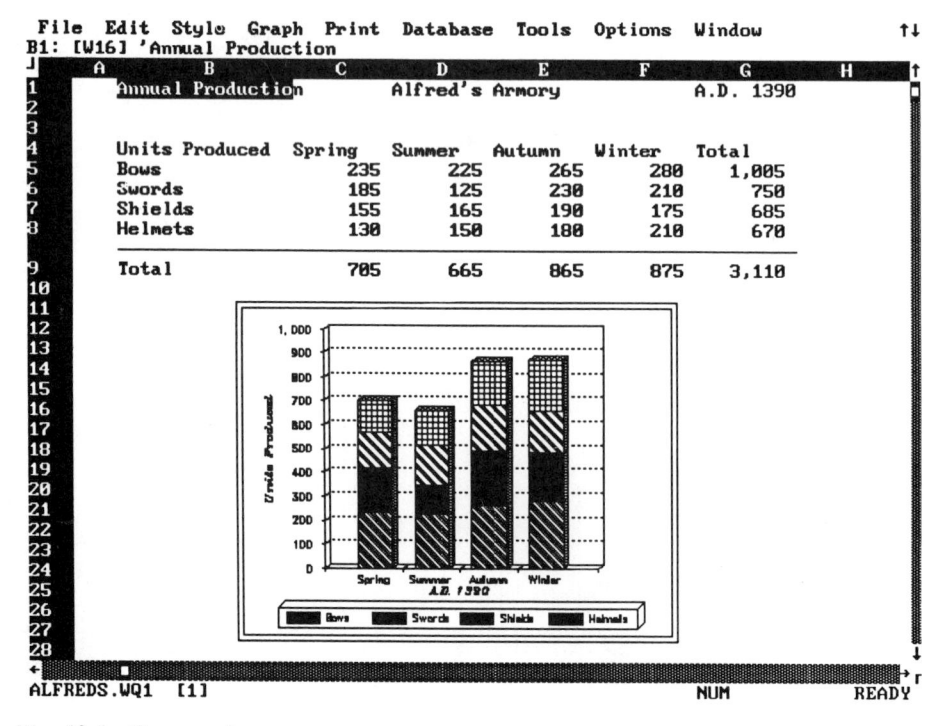

Fig. 12-3. Quattro chart.

Freelance, which can dramatically improve on the rather basic charts produced by 1-2-3. With Release 3 of 1-2-3, you can create CGM files, described later in this chapter.

An alternative to spreadsheets when it comes to making charts are programs like Freelance and ChartMaster which were written just to make charts. Generally referred to as *stand-alone* applications, these charting programs were originally designed to be fed data from the keyboard and generate their output from scratch. Many of them can now read data from standard file formats such as dBASE DBF files and 1-2-3 worksheets.

Among charting programs, there are relatively few standards when it comes to storing charts in files. The Lotus PIC format is somewhat limited in what it can store because 1-2-3's graphing options are relatively limited. Excel charts are much richer but few programs can read them. This is changing as new versions of software become available. While Excel-Mac 1.5 cannot read Excel-PC 2.1 charts, and vice versa, Excel-Mac 2.2 can. Furthermore, the ability of many graphing programs to generate charts from standard data formats opens up considerable possibilities when it comes time to make pictures out of your numbers.

Painted Pictures

In the realm of graphics files, probably nothing is further from charts than paint-type files containing the types of image that painting programs like PC Paint and MacPaint create. Charts are mathematically-based images of numbers embellished with text, and as such they can be stored in a format that describes the numbers, the layout, and the text. Painted pictures, like the one in Fig. 12-4, are

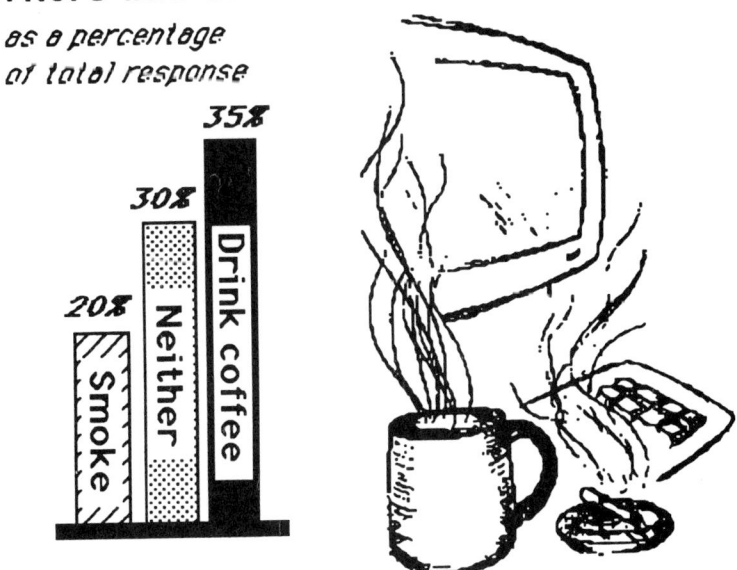

Fig. 12-4. A bit-map picture.

essentially rectangular arrays of dots, known as bit-maps, in which dots known as pixels are either on or off.

While the overall impression of a painted image can be far from a "bunch of dots," that is really all the image is. You can see this basic construction when you zoom in closer, as in Fig. 12-5.

This collection of dots is relatively simple for a computer to describe. Thus the file formats in which paint-type images are stored are fairly easy for programs to work with.

Paint programs are available on both the PC and the IBM. Popular programs on the PC include PC Paint, PC Paintbrush, and Windows Paint. On the Macintosh is MacPaint, Canvas, and a host of others. The formats that have developed in this area follow.

MacPaint. The file format developed for the very first paint-type program on the Mac is still very popular. Most paint-type programs on the Mac can read MacPaint files and store into this format. This format appears as PNTG in the File Type field of the resource fork. See the section on resource forks later in this chapter for more information on this subject.

SuperPaint. One of the most popular paint programs on the Macintosh, SuperPaint can store images into MacPaint or PICT format but also uses a special format that appears as SPTG in the File Type field of the resource fork. Popularity of this program was boosted considerably when Microsoft included free copies of Version 1.1 with packages of Word 4.0.

Fig. 12-5. A magnified bit-map.

PCX. A variety of paint-type programs on the IBM store files in this format, including: PC Paintbrush, Publisher's Paintbrush, and PC Paintbrush Plus. The extension .PCX is used for files in this format.

PIC. One of the first programs to make extensive use of a mouse on the IBM was PC Paint from Mouse Systems. The format used by this program, as well as PC Paint Plus and compatible applications, is called PIC although it is quite different from the Lotus PIC format. The Paintbrush PIC format is also different from the PIC format used by Windows Draw, one of the first drawing-type applications to run under Microsoft Windows. The extension .PIC is thus a tricky one when you have a lot of IBM graphics files to deal with. You will need to keep track of which application produced files with ambiguous extensions, possibly by using part of the filename for this purpose (for example, SUNSETPP.PIC, SUNSETLO.PIC, and SUNSETWD.PIC for files created by PC Paint, Lotus, and Windows Draw respectively).

MSP. When Microsoft introduced Windows as an operating environment for the IBM, the intent was to show how the PC could match the abilities of the Macintosh. Thus they included a simple word processor, Windows Write, and a simple paint program, Windows Paint, along with the Windows operating software. The format used for images created by Windows Paint is MSP.

PIX. When you want to capture, edit, and print graphic images from the screen of your PC, you can use a program called INSET. The format used by INSET uses the extension .PIX. The company that makes INSET also sells a graphics utility for the PC called HIJAAK. This program can convert over a dozen different formats into the PIX format. HIJAAK can also output files to over a dozen foreign formats. A later section of this chapter will deal with HIJAAK in more detail.

TIFF. One of the first graphics formats to be developed by cooperative efforts is the Tag Image File Format, known as TIFF for short. Files of this type on the Macintosh bear the letters TIFF in the Field Type field of the resource fork. On the PC such files are designated by the filename extension. TIF Software vendors Microsoft and Aldus got together with makers of scanner such as Hewlett-Packard to develop the TIFF format for storing files produced by from scanned images. The format is also used by some paint-type software programs such as DeskPaint and Canvas, and there are a number of utility programs, described later, that can convert graphic files both to and from TIFF format. Hewlett-Packard publishes a software program called Graphics Gallery that can produce charts and drawings in the TIFF format. There are several variations on the TIFF format. When you store images from a scanning device, you can use TIFF for both halftones and for gray-scales, described in the next section. There are also uncompressed and compressed TIFF formats, the latter being a means of saving disk space.

Scanned and Gray-Scale Images

The image in Fig. 12-6 was created by scanning a pencil drawing into the Macintosh and then editing it with Hewlett-Packard's Desk-Paint.

The edited graphic can then be stored in a number of different formats. While some scanned images can be stored as paint-type graphics, scanning deserves special attention.

You can group scanned images into three categories: line art, halftone, and gray-scale. An image that is simply composed of black and white lines, such as the sketch in Fig. 12-6, or the graphic in Fig. 12-7, is considered to be line art.

Such images do not have large areas of shading or gray in them and so they translate well into bit-mapped graphics. Images of this kind can be produced by most scanners.

A halftone image is one that has areas of gray in it, sometimes called *continuous tone variations*, rather than just black or white lines. A typical example is a black-and-white newspaper photograph. When an image is scanned as a halftone, the gray areas are converted to a series of black and white dots to approximate varying gray areas. You can see a closeup of a photograph scanned as a halftone in Fig. 12-8.

This process of converting tones to black and white dots is sometimes called *screening*. A screened image can be edited as a bit-map by a paint type program, although the image is much denser than a piece of line art.

Like a halftone image, a gray-scale image is produced from a photograph or other continuous tone original. However, instead of screening the areas of shading, a gray-scale image treats each part of the image as one of a number of levels of gray. Some scanners can support 256 levels of gray while others support 64 or 16.

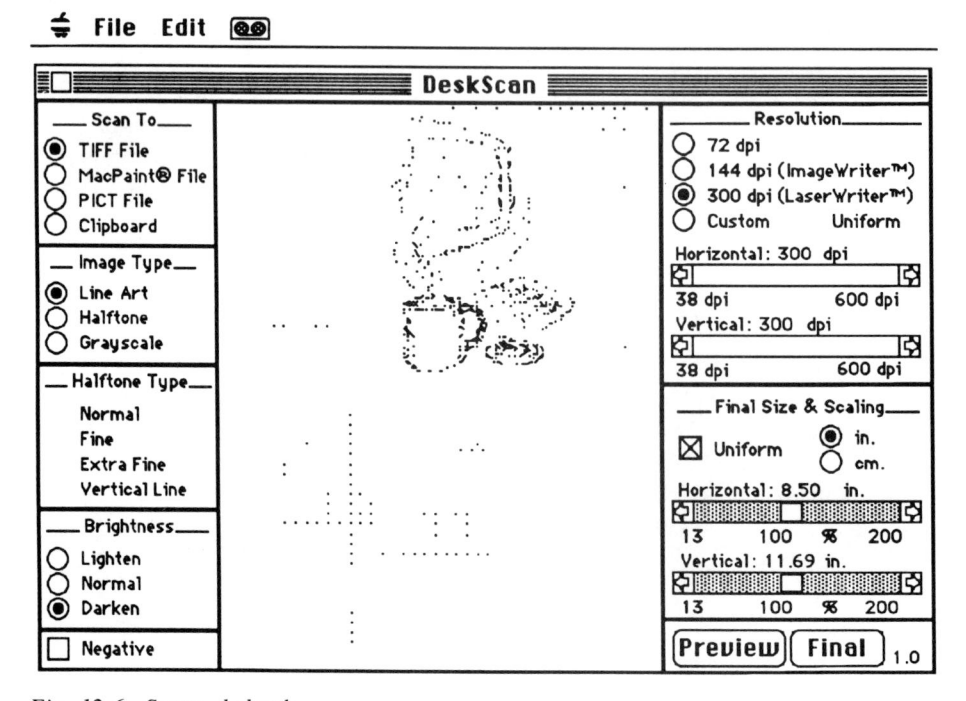

Fig. 12-6. Scanned sketch.

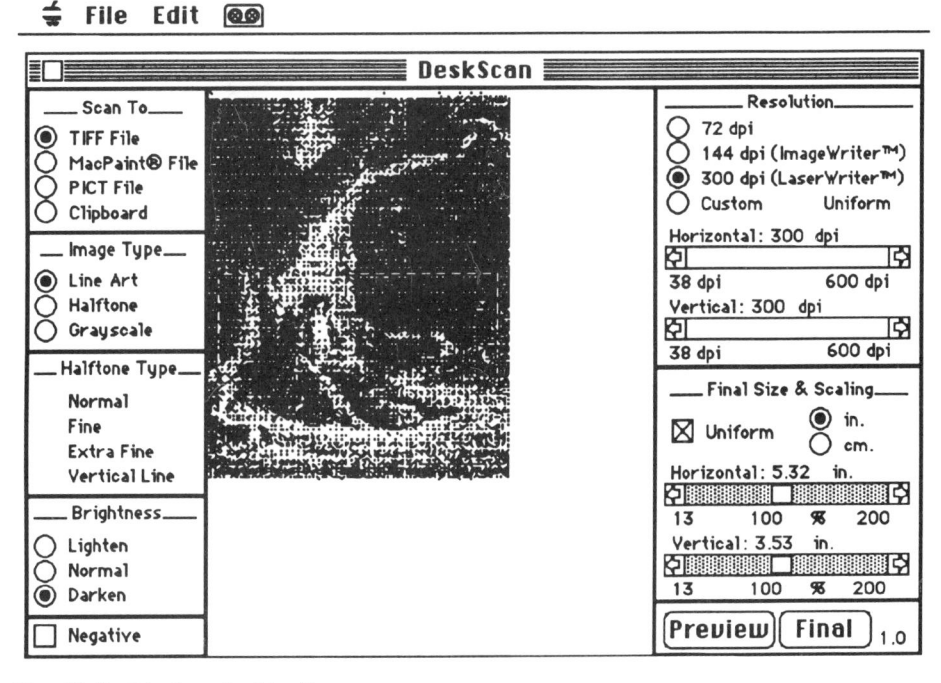

Fig. 12-7. Black and white line art.

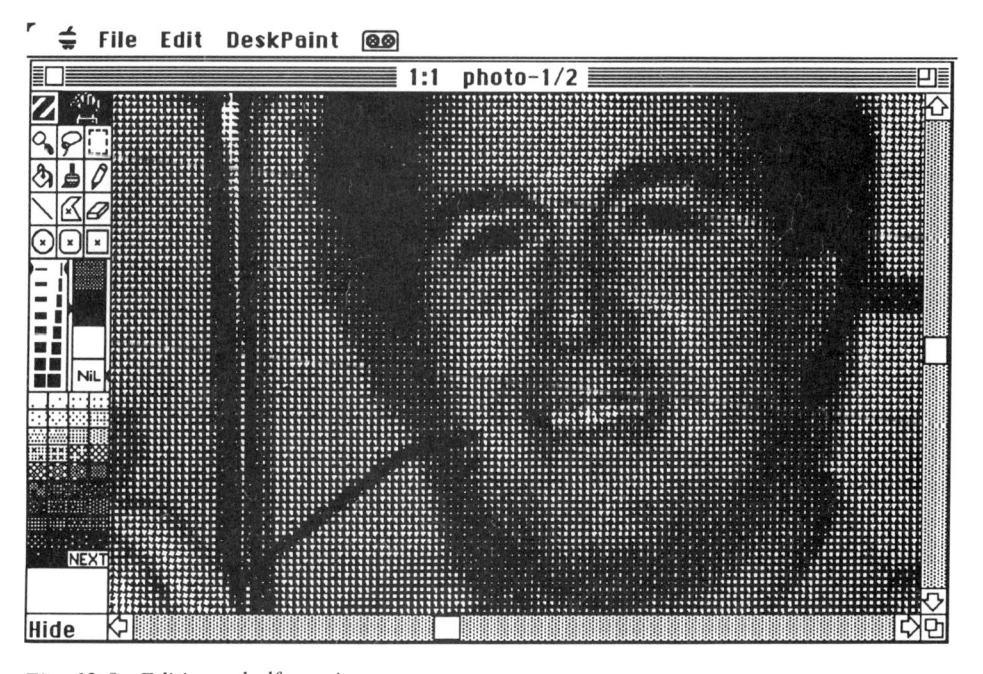

Fig. 12-8. Editing a halftone image.

Even with 16 levels of gray, a photograph is more realistically reproduced by gray-scaling than halftoning. As you might expect, this higher level of appearance consumes more resources: the files created by gray-scaling are larger and the time it takes to display and print gray-scale files is much longer. Because laser printers use a series of dots to print a gray-scale image, the image is actually screened before it is printed by the program that prints it and the printer. You can see the photograph from Fig. 12-8 scanned as a gray-scale image in Fig. 12-9.

This image is being placed in a document composed in PageMaker. Capturing a gray-scale image on-screen with a screen print program is difficult because the screen is captured as a bit-map. However, in Fig. 12-10 you can see an actual LaserWriter print of the photograph in Fig. 12-9.

This image was scanned with a Hewlett-Packard ScanJet using 16 levels of gray. Because of the way that gray-scaling handles the screening of an image, you do not need to scan gray-scale images at high resolutions. The image in Fig. 12-10 was scanned at 75 dpi rather than 300. This produces good results on a laser printer. A resolution of 150 dpi produces good results when printing on a typesetting device such as a Linotronic 100. You might want to use a higher resolution if you plan to enlarge the image significantly.

While gray-scale images consume a lot of space, they offer advantages over halftones. Gray-scales are easier to resize without loss of detail. They are easier to work with in desktop publishing applications such as PageMaker. However, halftones are easier to edit and combine with other art work. Saving halftones in a TIFF file format preserves a great deal of detail, and programs like DeskPaint can edit such TIFF files. When the TIFF format is used to store gray-scale images, editing requires a specialized program such as Darkroom Studio.

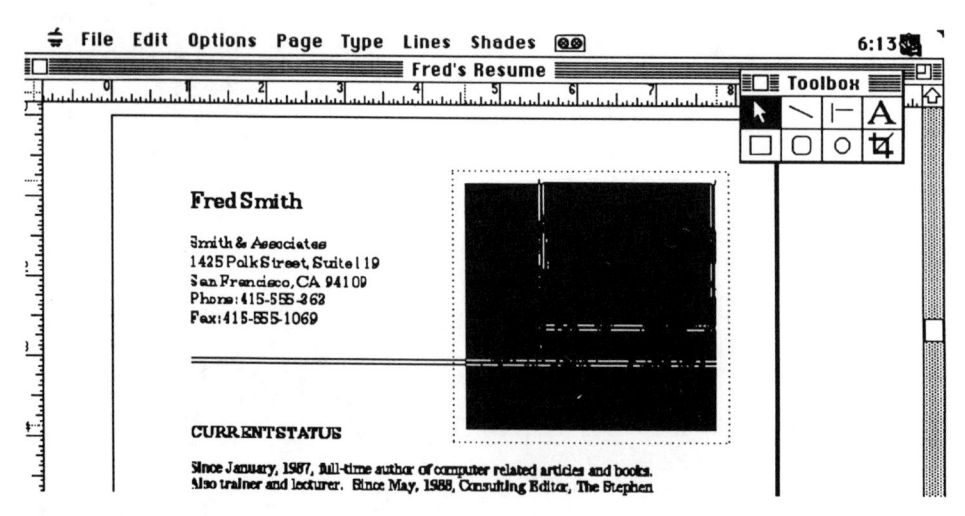

Fig. 12-9. Placing a gray-scale image.

Drawings versus Paintings

The images in Fig. 12-11, along with many of the diagrams in this book, were actually created on an IBM rather than a Macintosh. They were created with Windows Draw Plus, an application that runs under Windows on the IBM.

Although it might not be apparent to the viewer, from the computer's point of view there is a big difference between paint-type images that are composed of pixels or bits and draw-type images that are composed of geometric shapes that can be defined mathematically. The computers in Fig. 12-11 are made up of rectangles, lines, arcs, and other objects. These objects can be overlapped or layered to produce the desired effect. A collection of objects can be combined or grouped to make one compound object which can then be copied, rotated, and otherwise mainpulated as a single entity.

One of the major advantages of draw-type images is that they are much easier altered without distortion. For example, the two computers in Fig. 12-11 are the same drawing scaled differently. The mathematical nature of draw-type images means that they are scaled correctly when their size is changed, whereas increasing or decreasing the size of a bit-map image can produce grainy or blotchy results, as you can see from Fig. 12-12.

What causes this distortion? Paint programs are based on the WYSIWYG principle: What You See Is What You Get. In other words, what is displayed by the

Fred Smith

Smith & Associates
1425 Polk Street, Suite 119
San Francisco, CA 94109
Phone: 415-555-363
Fax: 415-555-1069

CURRENT STATUS

Since January, 1987, full-time author of computer related articles and books. Also trainer

Fig. 12-10. Printed gray-scale image.

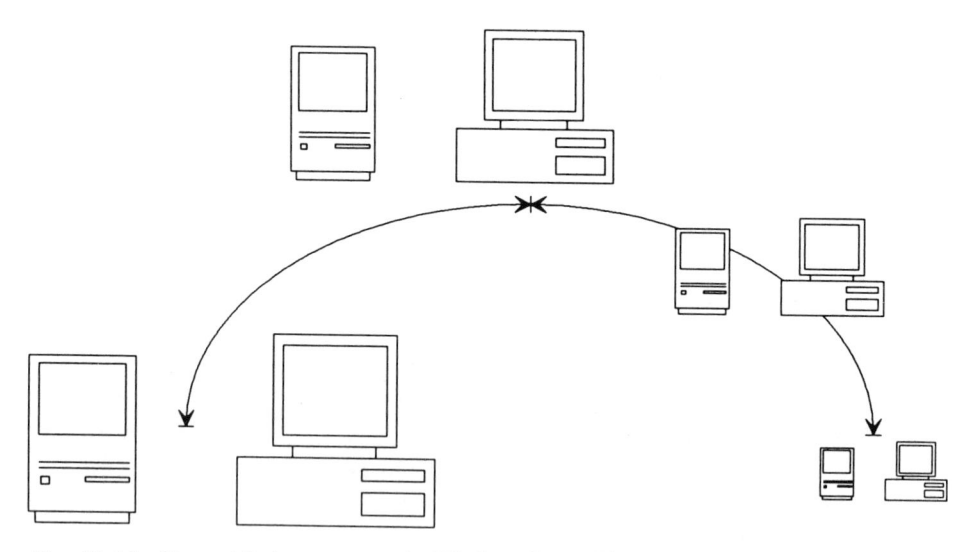

Fig. 12-11. Big and little computers in Windows Draw Plus.

paint program is exactly what is printed out. In a typical paint program, each little square of the screen or pixel is reproduced as dots in the printed image. When you use a paint program to draw a circle, the computer will display it as a pattern of square pixels. The circle might look smooth but a close look will show the jagged edges of a series of squares approximating a curve. When you stretch or enlarge the painted circle the computer looks at the pattern of dots and estimates where to add or subtract dots to accomplish the change. This can lead to distortion, accentuating the jagged edges.

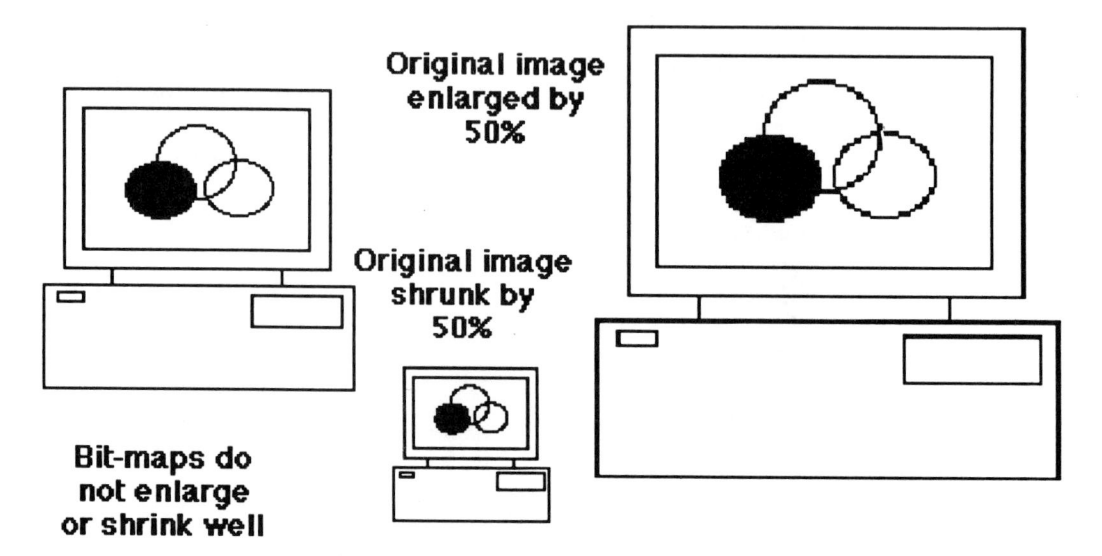

Fig. 12-12. Bit map altered.

When you print out a bit-mapped image, each dot on the screen is read and printed accordingly, distortions and all. The standard Mac screen is composed of 72 dots per inch (72 dpi). If you create a paint image at the Mac screen resolution, then the printer, regardless of its potential printing resolution will print at this 72 dpi jaggies and all. However, printers like the ImageWriter LQ and the LaserWriter can print at higher resolutions (216 dpi and 300 dpi, respectively). This means they have the potential to do better than WYSIWYG. Paint programs are now taking advantage of this greater resolution. For example, you can scan an image at 300 dpi and edit it, as seen earlier in Fig. 12-4 and Fig. 12-5. The image in Fig. 12-5 is magnified considerably, and this is how programs handle the disparity between displayed and printed resolution. The full-size screen image is actually composed of dots that are smaller in size and greater in number than the screen can handle. When you use the program's Zoom command, you can edit these dots and then zoom out to view the effect. Because the printer can handle the higher density of dots, the printed image is actually clearer than the screen image.

While draw-type programs offer some distinct advantages, they are not as adept as paint programs when it comes to producing freeform images. Furthermore, draw-type images are more complex, requiring fairly sophisticated file formats. Not only must information about shapes be stored, but also about fonts used for text. In a paint-type program, text becomes one more collection of dots whereas draw-type programs use fonts that can increase or decrease in size. This means that draw-type files are more difficult to translate from one format to another.

The Draw Formats

Numerous formats are currently in use for draw-type images. Some of the most common are described here.

MacDraw PICT. As the first drawing-type program on the Macintosh, MacDraw established a file format for object-oriented images that is still widely used today. Just about every draw-type program on the Macintosh can save images in this format. You will find the letters PICT in the File Type of the resource fork of such files. Programs like Cricket Draw, Easy 3D, and SuperPaint can create PICT files. Some Macintosh graphics programs, such as SuperPaint and Canvas, can work with both bit-maps and objects. You can thus read a bit-map into Canvas and save it as a PICT file. This makes image easier to scale and resize without distortion.

Scrapbook. On the Macintosh, you have a program called Scrapbook that is part of the system. You can paste images into the Scrapbook from the Clipboard. For example, when you are using Excel, you can copy a chart to the Clipboard and then paste it into the Scrapbook. The Scrapbook stores images in the PICT format so you can paste directly from the Scrapbook into draw-type programs on the Mac.

Glue. An innovative way of creating images in the PICT format on the Macintosh is to use the program called Glue. This actually installs as a printer driver that you can select in the Chooser instead of your ImageWriter or LaserWriter. While the Glue printer driver is selected, you can print from just about any graphics program and what you have printed will be captured as a PICT file. This allows otherwise incompatible output to be shared using the PICT format.

Micrografx PIC and DRW. One of the first companies to back Microsoft Windows as a graphics environment on PC was Micrografx. The products Micrografx products called Windows Draw and In*A*Vision both produce draw-type images. These are stored in files that have a PIC extension, although the format has nothing to do with the Lotus PIC format. More recent Micrografx products, Designer and Draw Plus, use the extension DRW. Some other Windows-based programs, such as PageMaker, recognize these extensions. You can place a drawing created by Windows Draw directly into PageMaker.

Windows GDI Metafiles WMF. Another format supported by Windows applications, such as Pro3D, this format uses the extension .WMF.

Zenographics IMA. Another variation of the Windows metafile format is created by some Zenographics applications such as Mirage. These files have the extension IMA.

Computer Graphics Metafile CGM. A general-purpose draw-type file format that is supported by Harvard Graphics and Lotus Freelance. The extension CGM is used for these files. Lotus 1-2-3 Release 3 can store charts as CGM files.

Videoshow PIC. There is a file format for presentation graphics called North American Presentation Level Protocol Standard (NAPLPS). Several programs, including Microsoft Chart, Lotus Freelance Plus, and Videoshow from General Parametric allow storage in this format.

Autodesk PLT. The most popular program in the field of Computer-Aided Design (CAD) is AutoCAD from Autodesk. This software is capable of creating very complex images and storing them in a number of formats. One format that can be read by other programs, such as PageMaker, uses the extension PLT. Files of this type are created by outputting to the ADI plotter driver and capturing the output in a file. AutoCAD automatically assigns the PLT extension to such files.

Lotus PIC. As we mentioned in the section about charts, several Lotus applications such as 1-2-3 can create simple business graphics. Because these consist mainly of straight lines, polygons, and text, they can be considered drawings. The PIC extension is used for these files which can be read by a wide range of programs.

HP-GL. One of the most popular pieces of equipment for printing out drawings and charts is a plotter, and the most widely used plotters are those made by Hewlett-Packard. To allow programs to tell the plotter pens where to put ink on paper, Hewlett-Packard developed HP-GL, the Hewlett-Packard Graphics Language. Just about every graphics program on the PC can print to an HP plotter using HP-GL. Consequently, one method of exchanging graphics on the PC has been to capture or "print to disk" output intended for an HP plotter. Many graphics programs can now read files in this format as well as create them. You can place HP-GL images in PageMaker documents. There is really no required standard extension for this format although .PLT (for plotter) is required by PageMaker for HP-GL files to be recognized as such.

Encapsulated PostScript Files

One file format belongs under drawings, but is worthy of a separate section, and that is EPS, short for Encapsulated PostScript. As you know by now, PostScript is a language used to describe to printers where to put ink on paper. Due to the fact that PostScript is very sophisticated, it can describe very complex images. The resolution of these images can exceed most display screens and laser printers. For example, the image in Fig. 12-13 is printed at 300 dpi and will not even appear on a 72 dpi screen shot of the program in which it was created.

Even at 300 dpi, the delicate shading of the image is not captured effectively. High-level illustration programs such as Aldus FreeHand and Adobe Illustrator use PostScript to produce images for publication on typesetting equipment.

Technically, just about any graphics image can be described by PostScript. These days, a growing number of programs on both the PC and the Macintosh support a file format based on PostScript. A file in EPS format consists of lines of PostScript programming code together with comments. This information is stored as ASCII text so you can easily read it. If you have ever looked at a program written in Pascal, you will have an idea of what an EPS file looks like. In Fig. 12-14, you can see some of the text of the PostScript file that produced the image in Fig. 12-13.

This format is very effective in some situations. For example, the spreadsheet program Quattro, running on the IBM, can store business graphs in EPS format. The file can then be sent directly to a LaserWriter printer or other PostScript compatible device for printing. This can be done with the TPRINT utility described in Chapter 8. High-level Macintosh and PC graphics programs can store files in EPS format, making it easy to exchange files between them. For example, Adobe Illustrator uses EPS to allow sharing of files between Mac and PC versions.

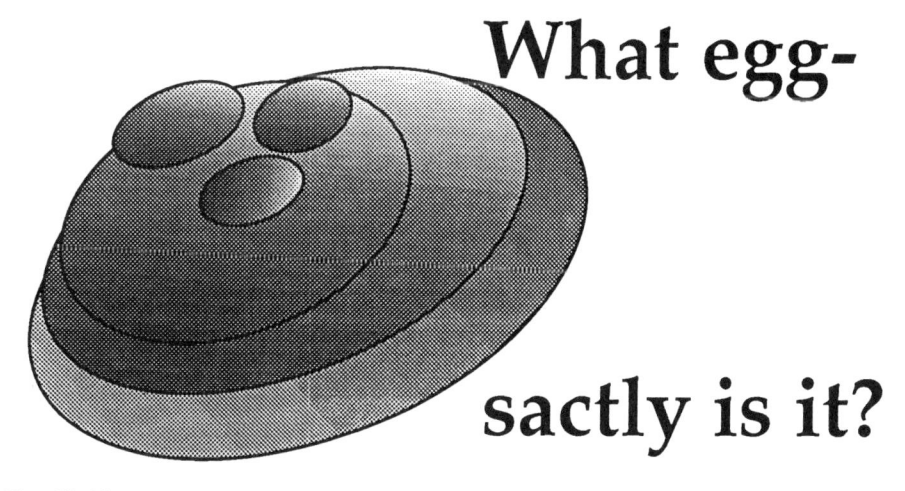

Fig. 12-13. A PostScript image.

SHARING GRAPHICS

The above account of graphics types and file formats should help you navigate the muddled waters of graphics file sharing. Fortunately, there is a strong tendency for software makers to endow their graphics applications with more and more read/write capabilities, thus allowing a lot of direct reading of another program's files and a lot of saving to someone else's format. In cases like this, sharing over a network can be as simple as storing the images to be shared in a published volume where others can read them.

Simple Sharing

We know of one office that has to prepare a lot of brochures and leaflets for promotional campaigns. These documents are created by a number of different individuals. They use their TOPS network to connect a lot of Macs and a few PCs. One Macintosh with a large hard disk drive is used as an electronic clip art file. This Mac has a scanner attached that is regularly used to input images that are stored in a volume published as Art Work. You can see this arrangement diagrammed in Fig. 12-15.

Any user on the network can then use the images to embellish their documents. The users around the network can mount the volume Art Work on their system and then have free access to the files. Alternatively, users who do not want to mount a volume can use the TOPS Copy command to copy files that they need onto their local drives.

```
%!PS-Adobe-2.0 EPSF-1.2                    /bdefbind defbdf
%%Creator : FreeHand                       /xdfexch defbdf
%%Title : eggs                             /ndf1 index wherepop pop popdup xcheckbindif
%%CreationDate : 6/26/89 6:06 PM           defifelsebdf
%%BoundingBox : 48 529 459 756             /min2 copy gtexchif popbdf
%%DocumentProcSets : FreeHand_header 2 0   /max2 copy ltexchif popbdf
%%DocumentSuppliedProcSets :               /graystep .01 def
FreeHand_header 2 0                        /bottom -0 def
%%DocumentFonts : Symbol                   /delta -0 def
%%+Palatino-Bold                           /frac -0 def
%%DocumentNeededFonts : Symbol             /left -0 def
%%+Palatino-Bold                           /numsteps -0 def
%%ColorUsage : Color                       /numsteps1 -0 def
%%CMYKProcessColor : 0 0 0 0.1 (10% gray)  /radius -0 def
%%+ 0 0 0 0.2 (20% gray)                   /right -0 def
%%+ 0 0 0 0.4 (40% gray)                   /top -0 def
%%+ 0 0 0 0.6 (60% gray)                   /x -0 def
%%+ 0 0 0 0.8 (80% gray)                   /y -0 def
%%EndComments                              /df currentflat def
%%BeginProcSet : FreeHand_header 2 0       /tempstr 1 string def
/FreeHandDict 200 dict def                 /clipflatness 3 def
FreeHandDict begin                         /inverted?
/currentpacking wherepop true setpackingif 0 currenttransfer exec .5 ge def
/bdfbind defbind def                       /concatprocs
```

Fig. 12-14. Inside an EPS file.

Complications

When sharing graphics on a TOPS network that is Mac-only, the problems can be minimized if some simple rules are established and the occasional utility program is invoked. The same can be said for IBM-only networks. Complications begin to encroach upon the free flow of images when you have too wide a range of applications or no control over the source of your graphics. Within a work group or department, you might want to try for some level of consensus about which formats will be used.

At the most basic level, MacPaint will work on the Mac side and you can even exchange files between Macs and PCs at this level if you use some type of converter or translator, as described in the next section. While MacPaint files do not preserve all of the details you might want, the format can be read by just about any graphics-related application.

If you need to preserve a greater level of detail, then the TIFF format can be used. This stores bit-maps at a higher level of resolution. A number of PC applications can create and read TIFF format files.

If you are working with object-oriented images, such as those produced with draw-type programs, then you might want to use the PICT format. As we mentioned earlier, applications like Canvas on the Macintosh can work with both bit-mapped and drawn images. This allows you to read in bit-maps and then save them as part of a PICT file, making the bit-map easier to scale without distortion.

At the top end of the graphic file format scale is the EPS format. You might want to standardize on this if you are using illustration-type programs such as Aldus FreeHand and Adobe Illustrator.

Whether your efforts to standardize on a graphics file format succeed or not, you will probably have occasion to convert images from one format to another. Even if everyone on the network is happily using the same format and publishing

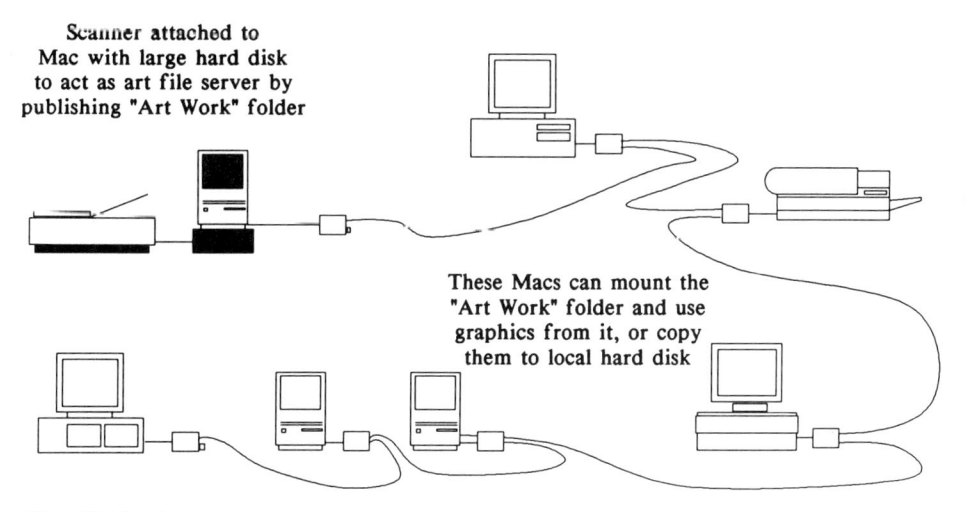

Fig. 12-15. An art network.

their art in volumes on TOPS, there is likely to be a need for someone to read a file in a foreign format. Then translators and converters come in to bridge the gap between formats.

CONVERTERS AND TRANSLATORS

A number of products allow you to convert an image from one format to another. Indeed, newer versions of TOPS Translators include translators for some graphics formats. The following products are mentioned to help you find the path you need between the formats you are using.

TOPS Translators

DataViz, the company behind TOPS Translators, has added several graphics formats to the translators now available. You will find Lotus PIC, TIFF, and PCX formats on the PC side, with PICT and MacPaint on the Mac side. These translators work the same way as the word processing ones described in Chapter 10.

Metafile

Zenographics makes a program called Metafile that handles conversions between the following formats on the PC: AutoCAD DXF files, HP-GL, NAPLPS, and Lotus PIC. The program also comes with a utility called CGMWIN that allows you to transfer files into the Windows Clipboard format. The Windows Clipboard works within Windows-based applications to allow cutting and pasting of data between applications, just like the Clipboard on the Mac.

The Graphics Link

Conversion between several formats is possible with The Graphics Link by PC Quik Art. Supported formats include MacPaint, PC Paint, PCX, Windows Paint (MSP), and TIFF.

Using HIJAAK on the PC

Continuing on the IBM side, a program called HIJAAK can help you deal with the plethora of formats from paintings to fax files. In Table 12-1, you can see a list of all of the formats supported by the latest version of HIJAAK that we used. You can see that MacPaint and TIFF formats are available when you want to transfer files to the Mac. In Fig. 12-16, you can see HIJAAK at work converting a file called TEST.MAC to PC Paintbrush from MacPaint format.

The extension MAC was used to identify the file's source. The source file is stored in a directory that is published on the network, allowing the file to be accessed by a Macintosh and a PC.

Table 12-1. HIJAAK formats.

Amiga ILBM	FAX Teli	Microsoft Paint (Ver 1)
Compuserve GIF	GEM IMG	Microsoft Paint (Ver 2)
FAX Complete PC	Halo CUT	NewsMaster
FAX Generic	HP LaserJet PCL	PC Paintbrush
FAX INTEL (B/W PCX)	HP Plotter PGL	PrintMaster
FAX JetFAX	Inset PIX	Text
FAX JT	Lotus PIC	TIFF (Compressed)
FAX OAZ	Macintosh MacPaint	TIFF (Uncompressed)
FAX Ricoh	MacPaint (No header)	WordPerfect WPG

A very simple interface is used in HIJAAK to allow selection of files and formats. In some cases, you can adjust fonts, resolution, and inversion of the image. You can turn color off if you want to. As an alternative to the menu, you can operate HIJAAK with a command language, similar to the arrangement in TOPS/DOS. This enables you to develop batch files for frequent translation tasks.

In Fig. 12-17, you can see a conversion going the other way. The source file is a PC Paintbrush file. The converted file will be moved to the Mac using the TOPS Copy command.

You have to give the destination file a DOS compatible filename even though it will be used by a Mac. You will also need to alter the resource fork of the file before it can be used on the Mac. Resource forks are discussed in the next section.

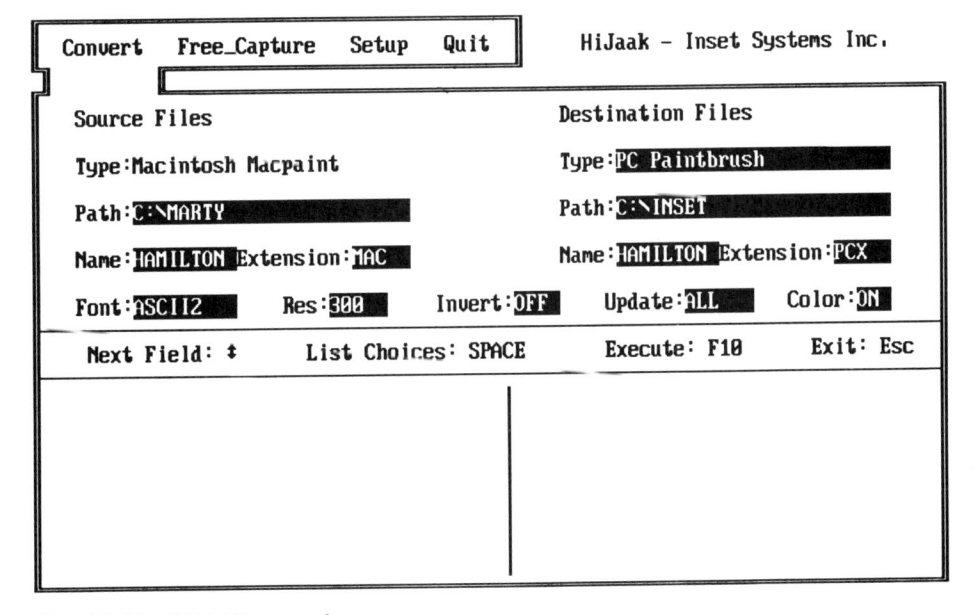

Fig. 12-16. HIJAAK at work.

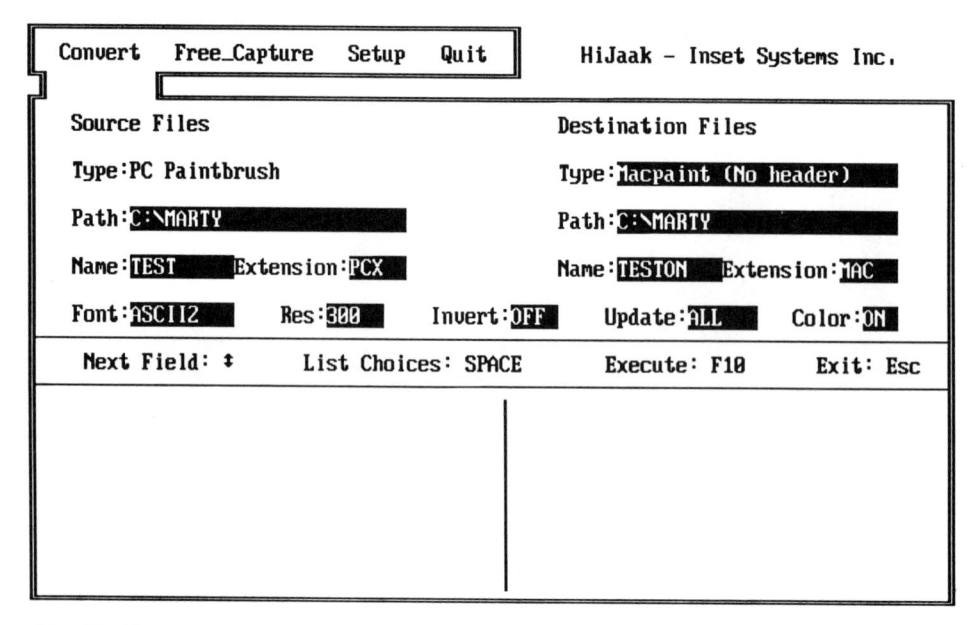

```
Convert   Free_Capture   Setup   Quit          HiJaak - Inset Systems Inc.

Source Files                                Destination Files
Type: PC Paintbrush                         Type: Macpaint (No header)
Path: C:\MARTY                              Path: C:\MARTY
Name: TEST      Extension: PCX              Name: TESTON    Extension: MAC
Font: ASCII2    Res: 300    Invert: OFF     Update: ALL     Color: ON

    Next Field: ↕      List Choices: SPACE      Execute: F10      Exit: Esc
```

Fig. 12-17. HIJAAK creating a Mac file.

The Question of File Forks

Several programs on the PC can now convert images to formats that can be read on the Mac, such as MacPaint and TIFF. However, one problem that can plague attempts to move such files to the Mac from an IBM is the lack of file forks for DOS files. Macintosh files have two parts called file forks: the data fork and the resource fork. The data fork contains the meat of the file's content, the resource fork contains information about the format of the file and the program that created it. This is what enables you to see the origin of files when you use the By Names option on the desktop, as seen in Fig. 12-18.

Files created by MS-DOS have no equivalent of the resource fork. This can lead to problems when trying to read the files on a Mac. If you use a utility program like Mac Tools, you can view information that is in a Macintosh files's resource fork. For example, a MacPaint file examined by Mac Tools appears in Fig. 12-19.

You can see that one category of information is the Finder File Type. In this case it is painting, indicated by the code PNTG. This is what causes the file to appear as a painting icon on the desktop. The information listed in Fig. 12-19 in the field called Finder Creator is MPNT, short for MacPaint. This is how the File Open command can be selective about which files it lists.

Within DOS itself there is no way to create resource fork for a file. However, when TOPS publishes DOS files on the network it creates resource forks for them. A document read from a DOS disk published by TOPS will have the PC icon on it, and will show TOPC in the File Creator field. In Fig. 12-20, you can see a PC document in Mac Tools.

Graphics and Desktop Publishing 285

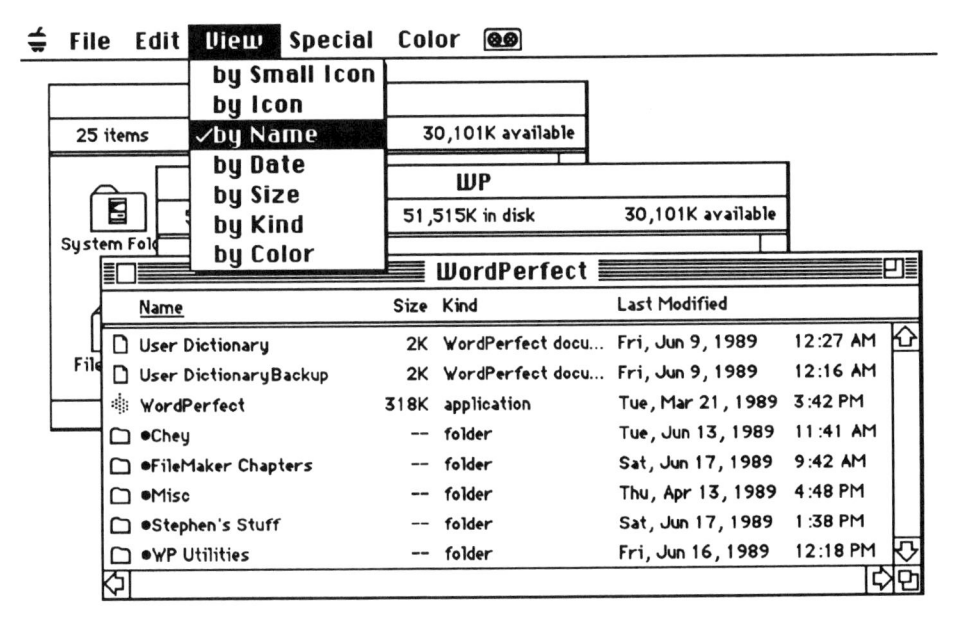

```
 File   Edit   View   Special   Color
              by Small Icon
              by Icon
 25 items   ✓by Name        30,101K available
              by Date
              by Size            WP
              by Kind      51,515K in disk      30,101K available
 System Fol   by Color
                          WordPerfect
  Name                    Size    Kind            Last Modified
  User Dictionary          2K    WordPerfect docu...  Fri, Jun 9, 1989   12:27 AM
  User DictionaryBackup    2K    WordPerfect docu...  Fri, Jun 9, 1989   12:16 AM
  WordPerfect            318K    application          Tue, Mar 21, 1989   3:42 PM
  ●Chey                    --    folder               Tue, Jun 13, 1989  11:41 AM
  ●FileMaker Chapters      --    folder               Sat, Jun 17, 1989   9:42 AM
  ●Misc                    --    folder               Thu, Apr 13, 1989   4:48 PM
  ●Stephen's Stuff         --    folder               Sat, Jun 17, 1989   1:38 PM
  ●WP Utilities            --    folder               Fri, Jun 16, 1989  12:18 PM
```

Fig. 12-18. Viewing files and folders by names.

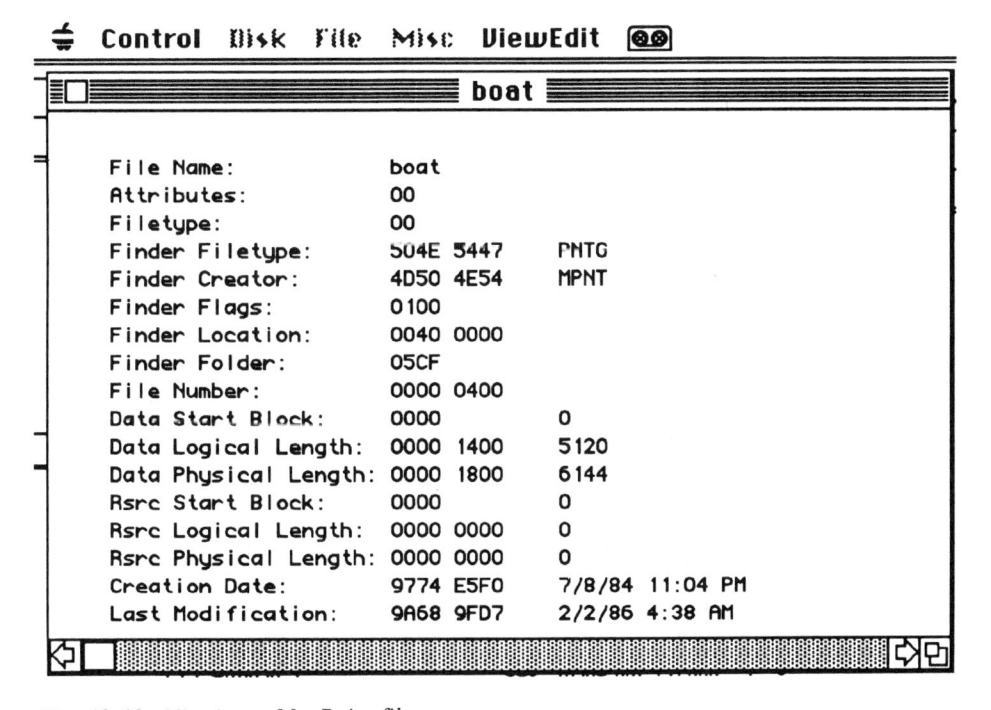

```
 Control  Disk  File  Misc  ViewEdit
                            boat

  File Name:             boat
  Attributes:            00
  Filetype:              00
  Finder Filetype:       504E 5447     PNTG
  Finder Creator:        4D50 4E54     MPNT
  Finder Flags:          0100
  Finder Location:       0040 0000
  Finder Folder:         05CF
  File Number:           0000 0400
  Data Start Block:      0000          0
  Data Logical Length:   0000 1400     5120
  Data Physical Length:  0000 1800     6144
  Rsrc Start Block:      0000          0
  Rsrc Logical Length:   0000 0000     0
  Rsrc Physical Length:  0000 0000     0
  Creation Date:         9774 E5F0     7/8/84  11:04 PM
  Last Modification:     9A68 9FD7     2/2/86   4:38 AM
```

Fig. 12-19. Viewing a MacPaint file.

All files published from the PC on TOPS show TEXT as the File Type. When you use the File Open command in many Mac programs, the file list that appears is actually a filtered list, containing only those files that were created by the program or can be read by it. Use File Open in MacPaint and you only see files that have MPNT as the File Type. The Mac operating system allows filtering of files based on the resource fork. If you are trying to open a MacPaint file that came from a PC, it will not have the correct information in the resource fork and thus not appear in the list. This means that after you translate a file from PC Paintbrush to MacPaint format, using a program like HIJAAK, you still have to alter the resource fork for it to appear in the File Open list of MacPaint or other paint program.

Some Mac programs, notably those like Microsoft Word that have PC cousins, take care of this problem automatically, listing files from a PC and recognizing them as such. In other cases, you will need to step in to edit manually the resource fork for a PC file if you want to use it on the Mac. Indeed, in some cases you might have to create a resource fork. If you use the DOS command to copy a file from a PC to a Mac drive that was mounted by the PC, the DOS file will have no resource fork at all. You can avoid this problem by using the TOPS Copy command. However, in case you need to create a resource fork for a DOS file that was moved to a Mac, we will show you how and also look at how to edit resource forks.

Creating a Resource Fork

One of the easiest ways to create resource fork for a file stored on a Macintosh is to use ResEdit. This is a utility program from Apple that is available from Macin-

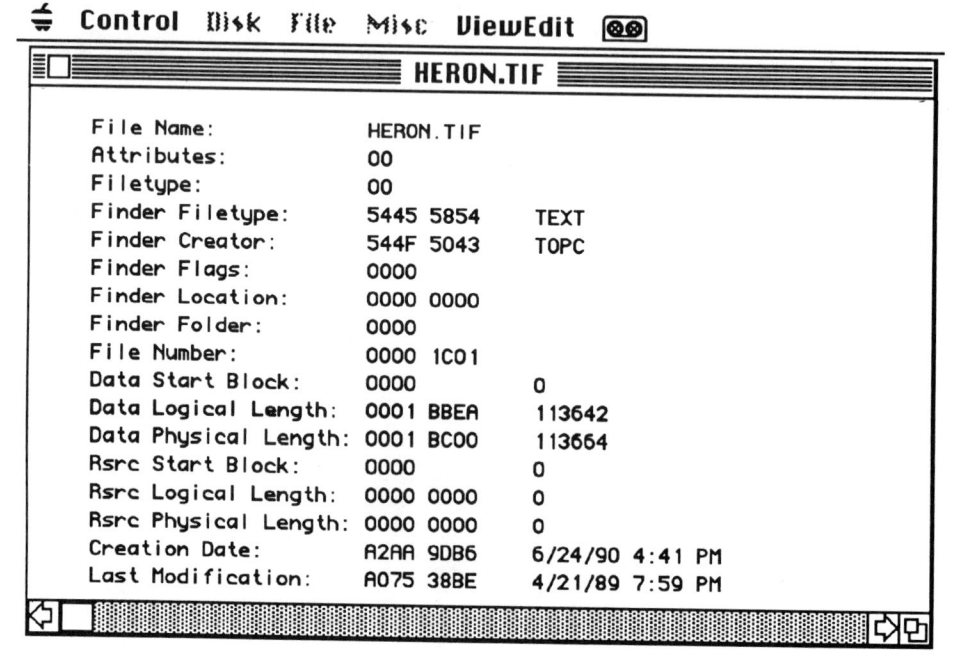

Fig. 12-20. A PC document.

tosh dealers and from bulletin boards such as CompuServe (on CompuServe type GO MAUG to reach the Macintosh area). You can do a lot of interesting things with ResEdit, including edit your system's icons. You can actually do damage to your system files with ResEdit so you should exercise care when using it. However, using ResEdit to create a resource fork for a DOS file is not dangerous. In fact, all you do is start ResEdit and then select the file for which you want to create the resource fork.

When you start ResEdit, one or more small windows will appear, listing files currently available on disk. In Fig. 12-21, you can see that ResEdit has been started and two disks, Big Bang and Marty, are listed.

The next step is to highlight the file you want to work on and pick Open from the File menu (you can also double click on the filename). In Fig. 12-22, you can see what happened when we tried to open the file called TESTON.MAC, a picture that was drawn in PC Paintbrush and then converted to MacPaint format with HI-JAAK.

We were asked if we wanted to add a resource fork. You can click OK to go ahead and do this, *if* you have the file on a Macintosh drive. Because DOS has no direct equivalent of the resource fork, you cannot create a resource fork for a file that is stored on a DOS disk (you will get an error message if you try). You might wonder about this; after all, you know that TOPS allows you to store Mac files on PC disks. Indeed, TOPS preserves the two forks of a Mac file when it resides on a PC disk, but it can only do this after both forks have been created. In order to use ResEdit in our example, we first copied the file to a Mac disk. We did this with the DOS COPY command, which does not know about resource forks.

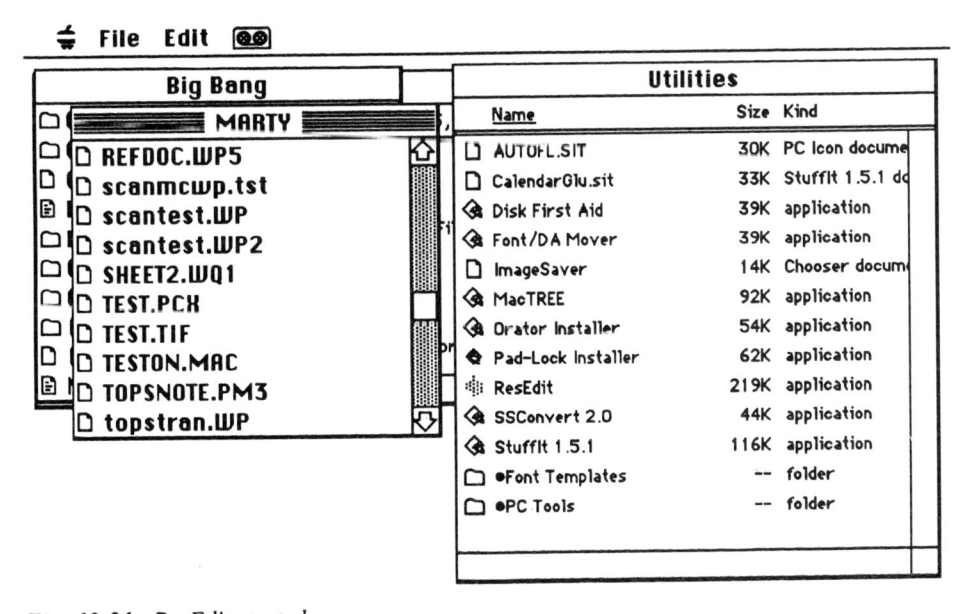

Fig. 12-21. ResEdit started.

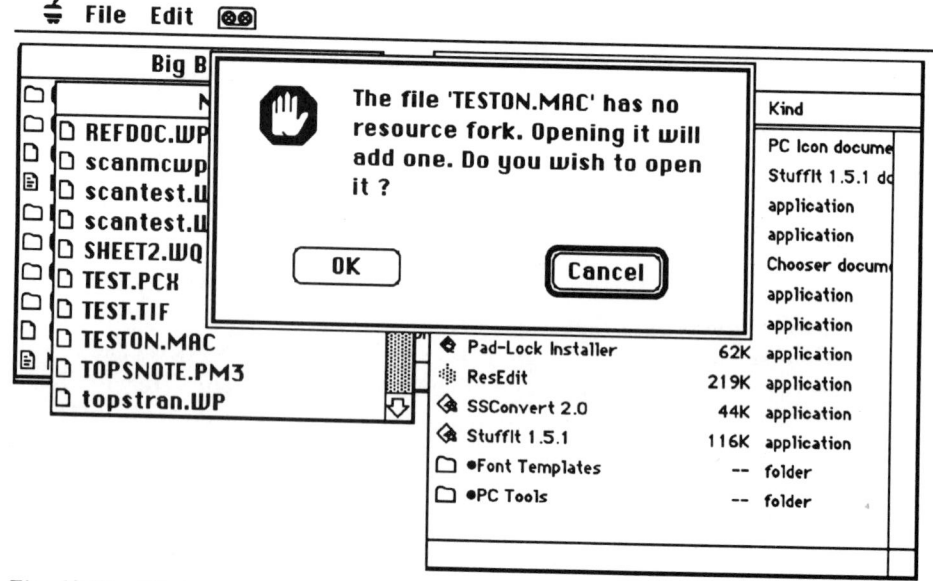

Fig. 12-22. Missing resource fork.

Remember that when you need to go the other way, from Mac to PC, the TOPS Copy command preserves the resource fork of your Mac files, whereas DOS COPY does not. Furthermore, using the TOPS Copy command to move the file to a Mac would automatically create a resource fork. In Fig. 12-23, you can see the TOPS Copy command being used to move the file to the Mac.

After copying the PC document to the Mac with DOS COPY, we used ResEdit and clicked OK in response to the "add" prompt. As you can see from Fig. 12-24, the results do not look very impressive, but they do not need to.

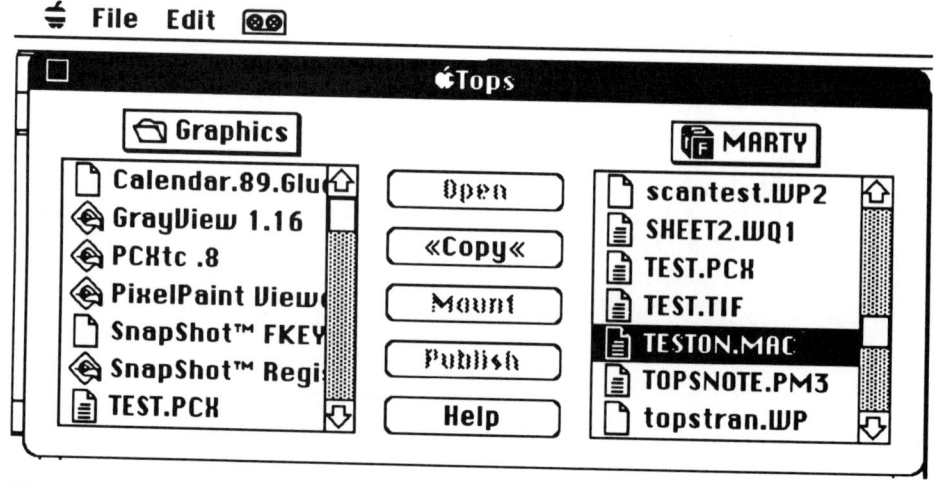

Fig. 12-23. TOPS Copy command.

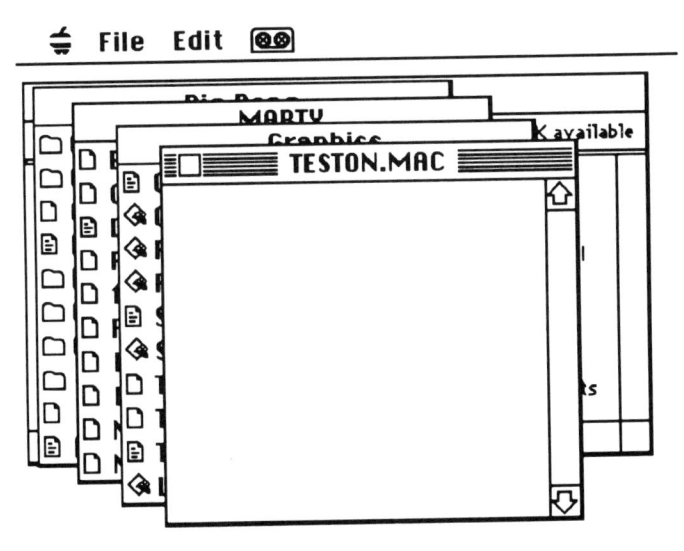

Fig. 12-24. Document opened with ResEdit.

Just double click the close box, or use the File Close command and the task of adding a resource fork is completed. You do not even need to use a Save command. You can tell the difference in Fig. 12-25 where the before and after views show the blank document filled in.

Editing Resource Forks

When you use TOPS to publish a PC drive or copy files from a PC to a Mac, the DOS files will be given a resource fork, but, as we discussed earlier, it might

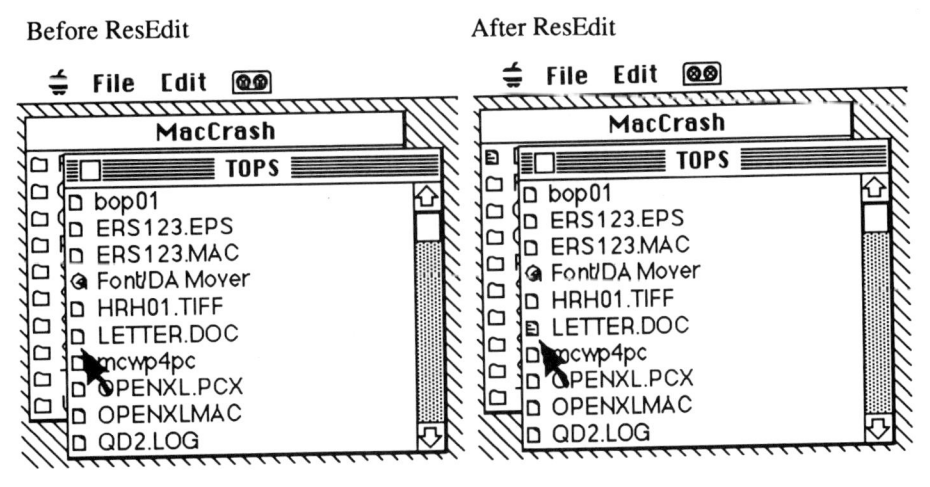

Note the change to document icon in ResEdit file list.

Fig. 12-25. Before and after ResEdit.

not contain the right information for the application you want to use. If you have had to create a resource, it will not have the correct information either. To edit the resource fork, you can either use ResEdit or a commercial file management program like Mac Tools. In Fig. 12-26, you can see the Mac Tools InfoEdit command which presents the File Type and File Creator of a file in an easy-to-edit format.

You can see that the file currently has TEXT as the Type and TOPC as the Creator. In Fig. 12-27, you can see these values changed so that MacPaint is the Creator and the Type is painting, represented by the values MPNT and PNTG respectively.

Now this file will appear in the File Open list when you use MacPaint or another program that can read MacPaint files. The file can be retrieved just as though it were a natural Macintosh file.

Going the Rounds

Although TOPS cannot automatically assign correct resource forks to DOS files, the way that it tracks such subtleties of file sharing as resource forks makes it particularly suited to the exchange of graphic files. We decided to test this with a set of images that begin on the Mac and end up on the PC. This demonstrates some of the techniques you have available when you are connected with TOPS.

We began with a scanned image. In Fig. 12-28, you can see a piece of currency being scanned by a Hewlett-Packard ScanJet using DeskScan software. The

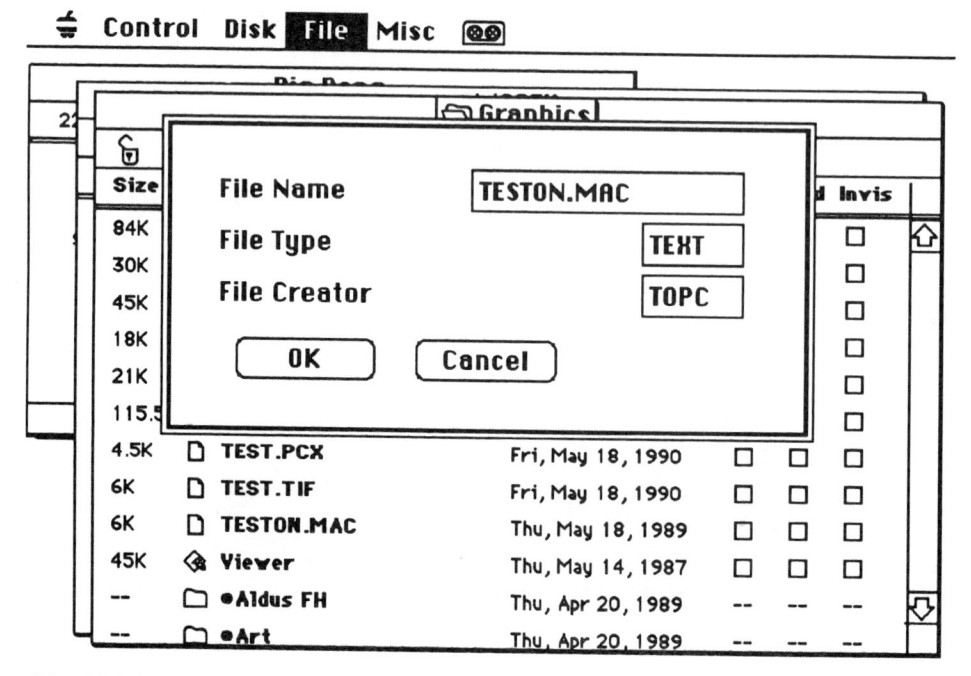

Fig. 12-26. Editing the resource fork.

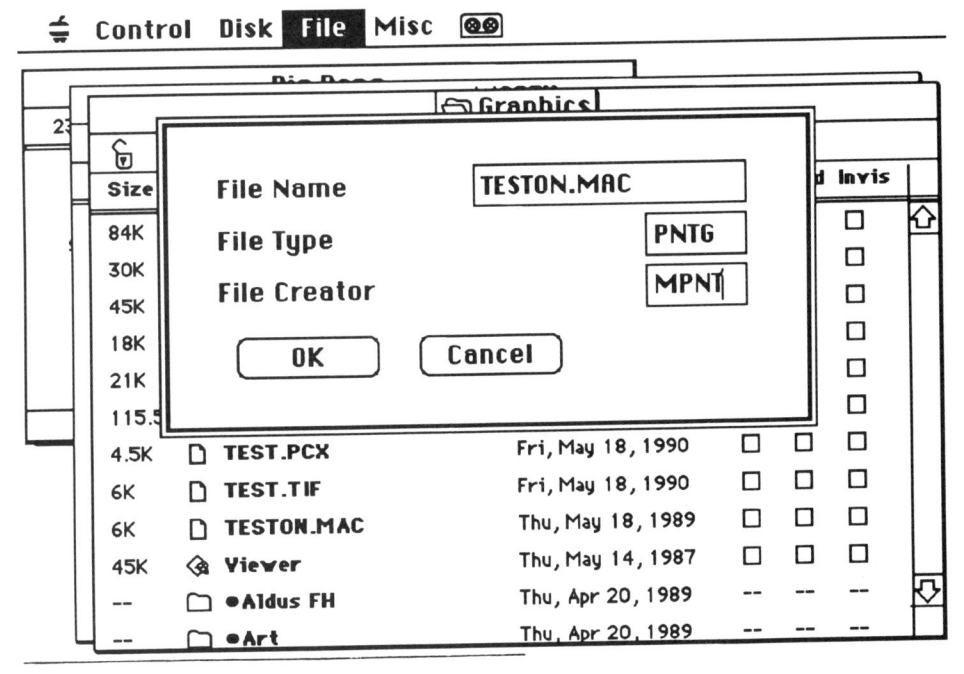

Fig. 12-27. Edited resource fork.

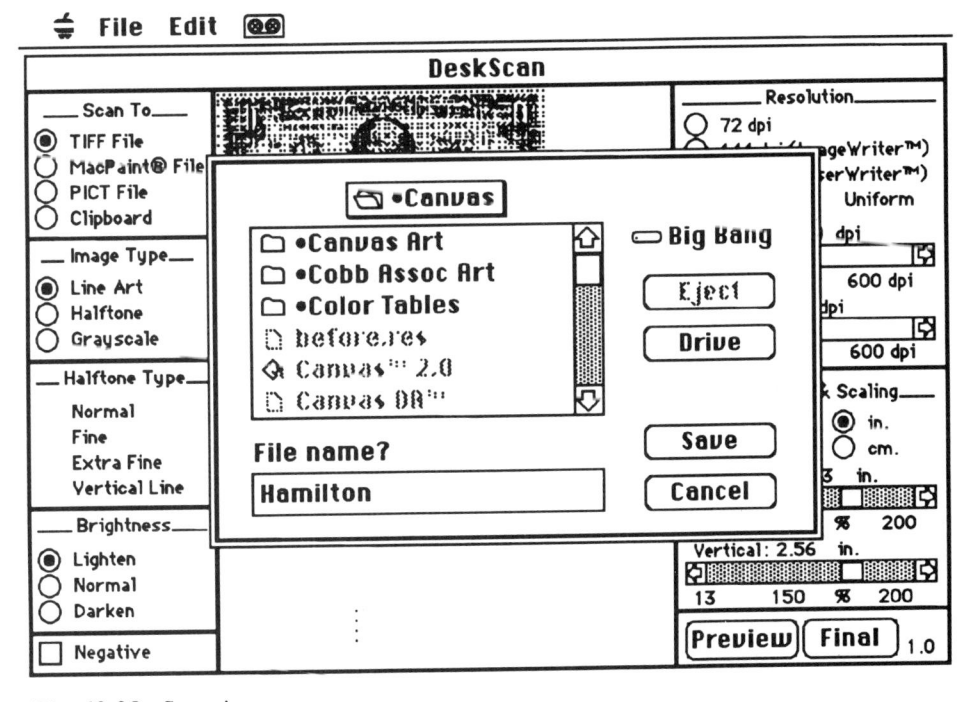

Fig. 12-28. Scanning.

292   Chapter 12

file is about to be saved and you can see that the TIFF format was chosen from the options on the left.

The other options in DeskScan are MacPaint, PICT, or direct to the Clipboard. You can also see that the image was scanned as line art rather than as a halftone or gray scale. This is because the image is essentially a drawing and a line art scan will pick up more detail.

As we discussed in Chapter 8, scanning can be done on either the Mac or the PC. The ability to share files makes it possible to move images in either direction after they have been scanned into the host system. In this case, we began with an HP scanner hooked up to a Macintosh. You can see the scanned image being edited in Fig. 12-29.

Only part of the ten dollar bill was scanned and it is enlarged as it was scanned. The program doing the editing is DeskPaint which comes with the HP scanner. After the image was cleaned up, it was resaved in TIFF format and opened by Canvas. (See Fig. 12-30.)

Here some further editing was done. You can see a smile being broadened in Fig. 12-31 using an 8:1 enlargement of the image.

Canvas allows you to mix both bit-maps and objects. Several rectangles were added to the image, as well as some text, to produce an advertisement. You can see

Fig. 12-29. Editing scanned image.

the resulting image in Fig. 12-32 where the scale is back to 1:1.

Like most graphics programs on the Mac, Canvas supports several formats when performing a File Save As. You can see from the dialog box in Fig. 12-33 that PICT, TIFF, and MacPaint are supported, as well as Stationery Pad and the native Canvas format.

Once you have scanned an image, you can use it in many different applications. For example, to create a more sophisticated image for your advertisement, you might want to use a program like Aldus FreeHand that has access to a lot of PostScript features. In Fig. 12-34, you can see the scanned image in a FreeHand document.

You might not notice much improvement here, but that is because the full effect of PostScript does not appear in a screen picture like the one in Fig. 12-34. After all, the screen is printed at fairly low resolution. Indeed, only a typeset rendering of the image would bring out the delicate shading possible with PostScript routines.

When you have created a PostScript image, you need to save it as PostScript. You can see FreeHand's EPS file export option in Fig. 12-35.

The file can be exported to a PC or saved in a format for the Macintosh. The Macintosh format adds special QuickDraw routines to the file to allow the Mac

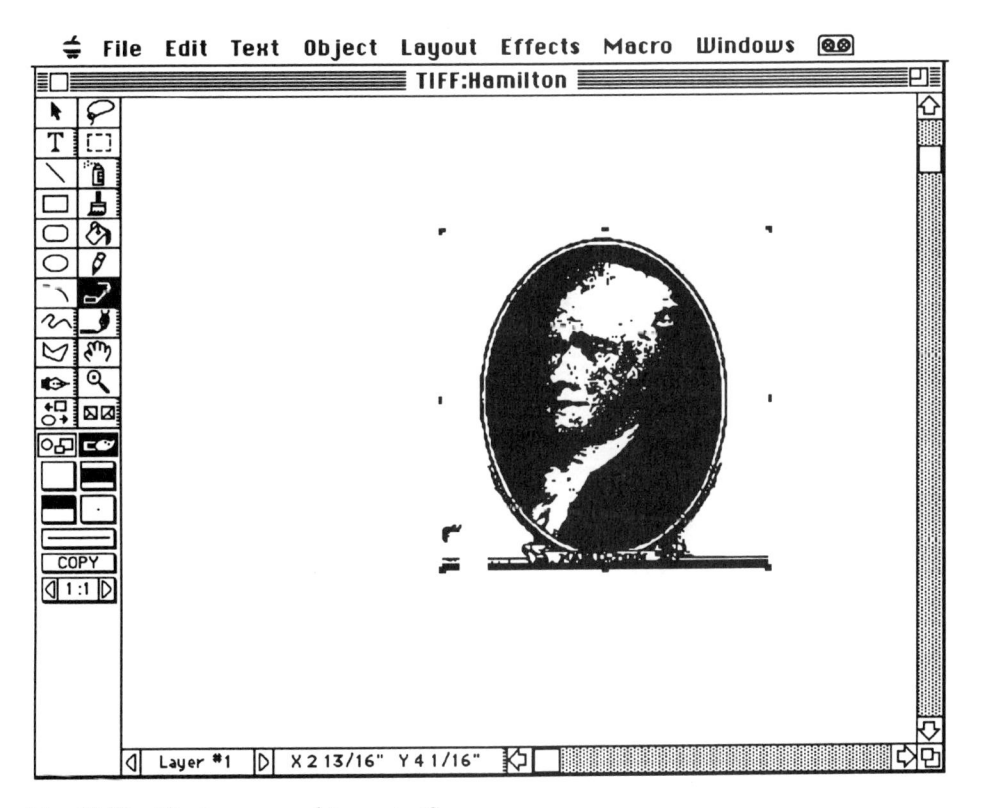

Fig. 12-30. Placing scanned image in Canvas.

monitor to display it. QuickDraw is the system used by the Macintosh to display images on the screen. The display of the PC version will depend on what software uses it.

FreeHand can also save images as TIFF files, using the dialog box seen in Fig. 12-36.

You need to know which variations of TIFF your applications support before choosing from a selection like this. If in doubt, use Uncompressed.

As the last step in the circuit, we used the TOPS Copy command to copy the Canvas image, saved in TIFF format, over to a PC. We used a paint-type program on the PC called Paint-It to open the TIFF file. You can see the result in Fig. 12-37.

This is a fairly faithful rendering of the Canvas image. The heavier text is due to the fact that we used bold on the Canvas image after the earlier view of it. Instead of using the TOPS Copy command, we could have published the Canvas folder containing the file and then mounted it on the PC to read the file. Remember that TOPS Copy allows you to avoid mounting volumes. If you had to make this sort of exchange on a regular basis, then one folder could be designated as a repository of art and published for other users to mount or copy from, as needed.

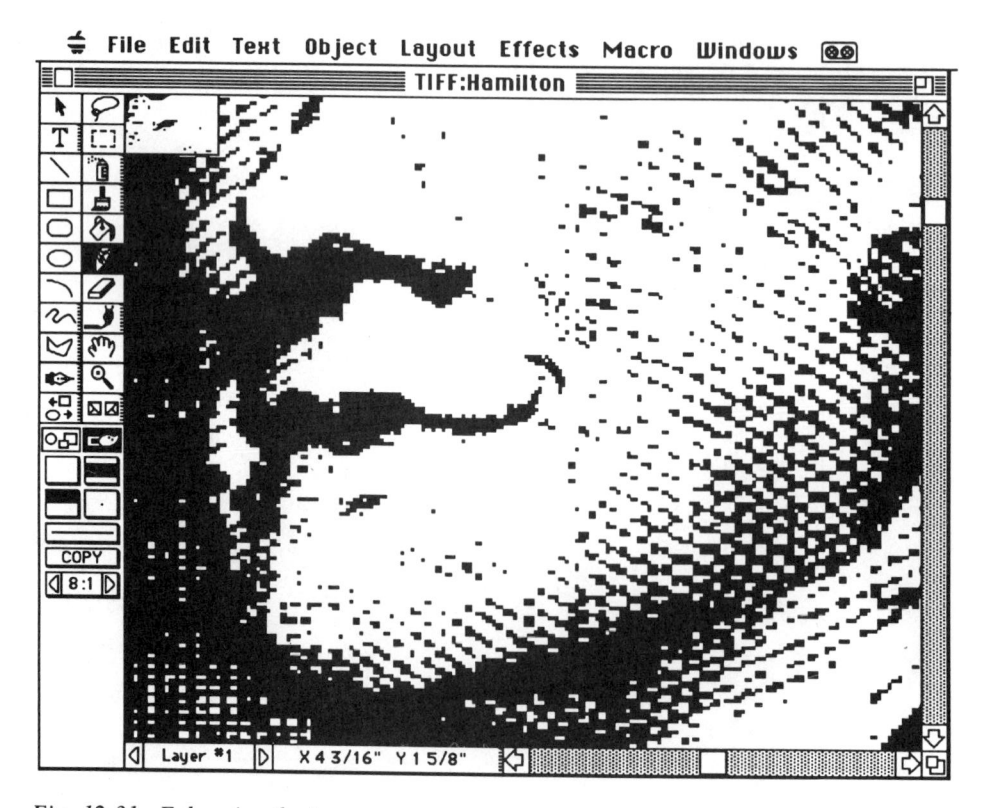

Fig. 12-31. Enhancing the image.

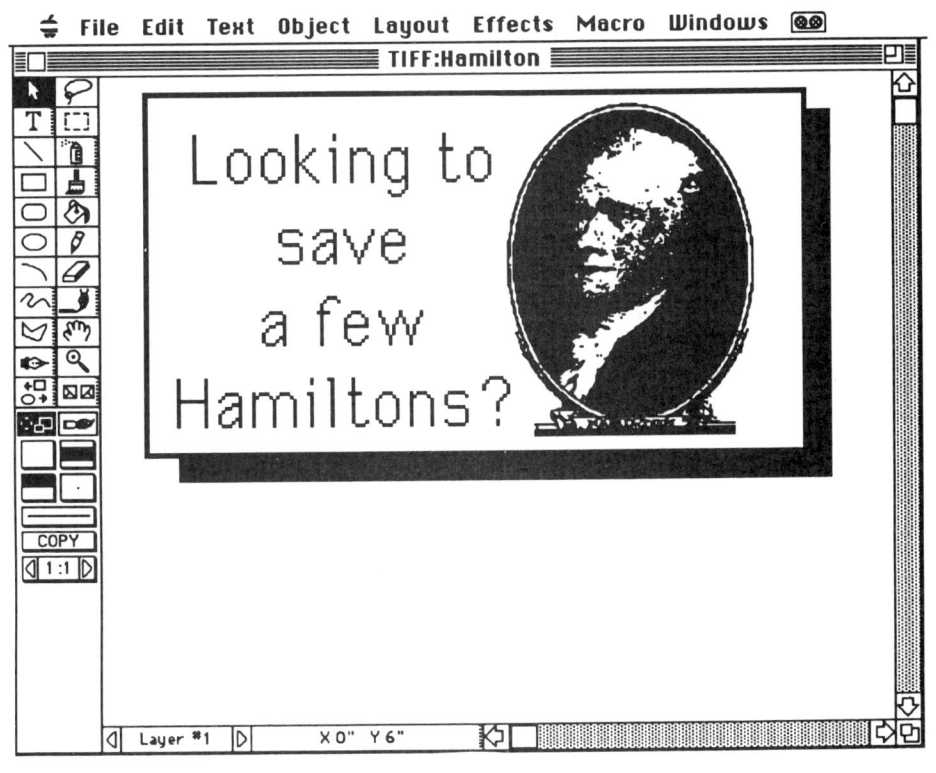

Fig. 12-32. The finished graphic in Canvas.

Fig. 12-33. File Save alternatives in Canvas.

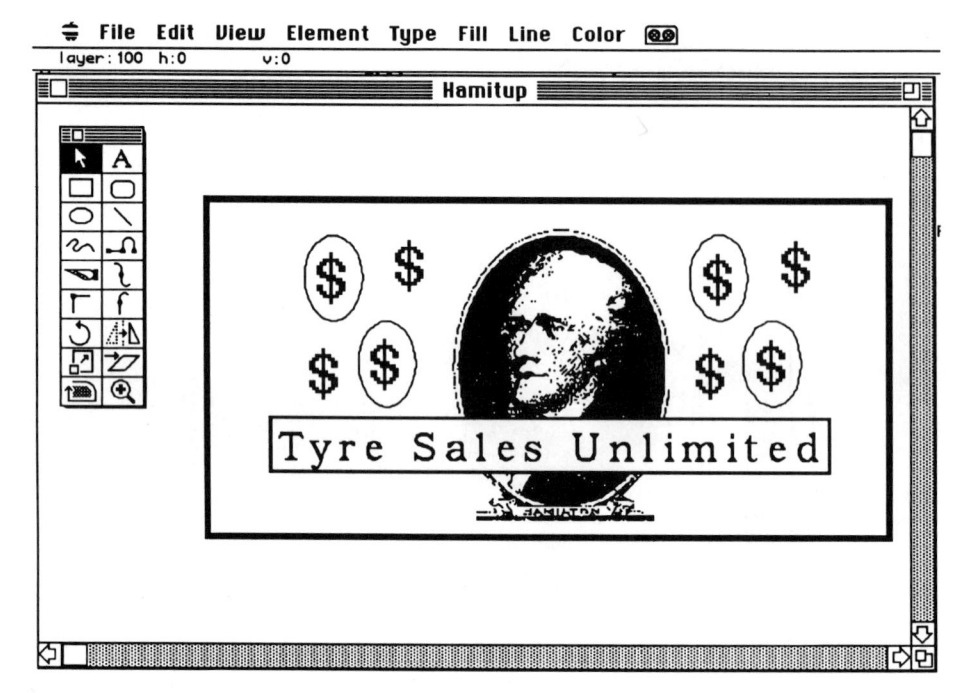

Fig. 12-34. Alternative version in FreeHand.

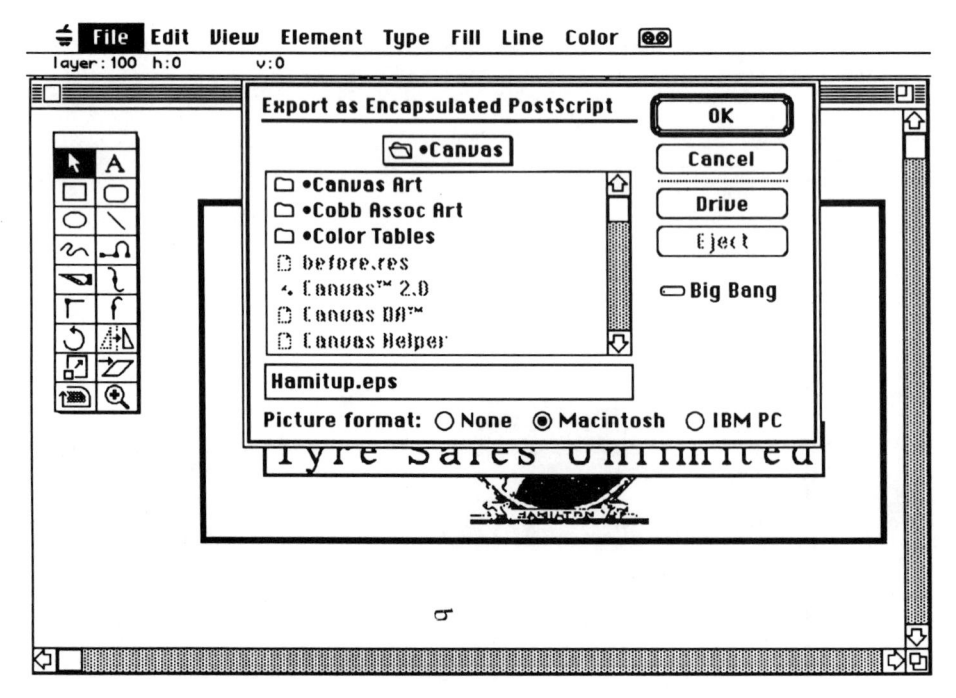

Fig. 12-35. Saving as an EPS file.

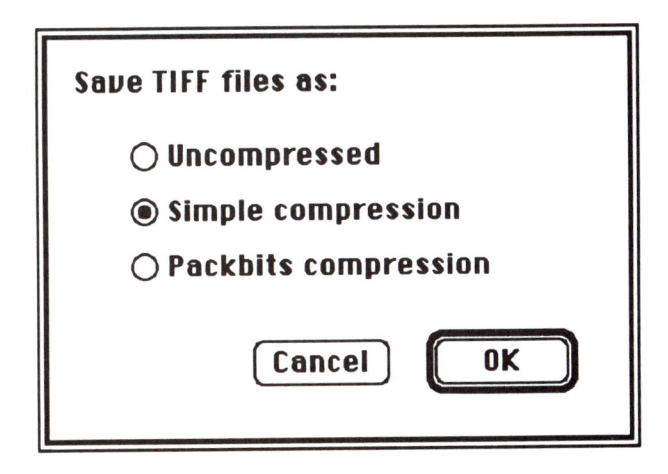

Fig. 12-36. Saving as a TIFF file.

BRINGING IT ALL TOGETHER: DESKTOP PUBLISHING

Desktop publishing is one application that requires users to pull together material available from a wide variety of world sources. For such projects as newsletters, reports, and brochures, you need text, graphics, and even data from spreadsheets and databases. TOPS is an ideal solution in the DTP field as it allows all types of files to be shared. Of the leading DTP programs, PageMaker is the only one to offer almost identical versions on both the PC and the Mac. This makes it an ideal candi-

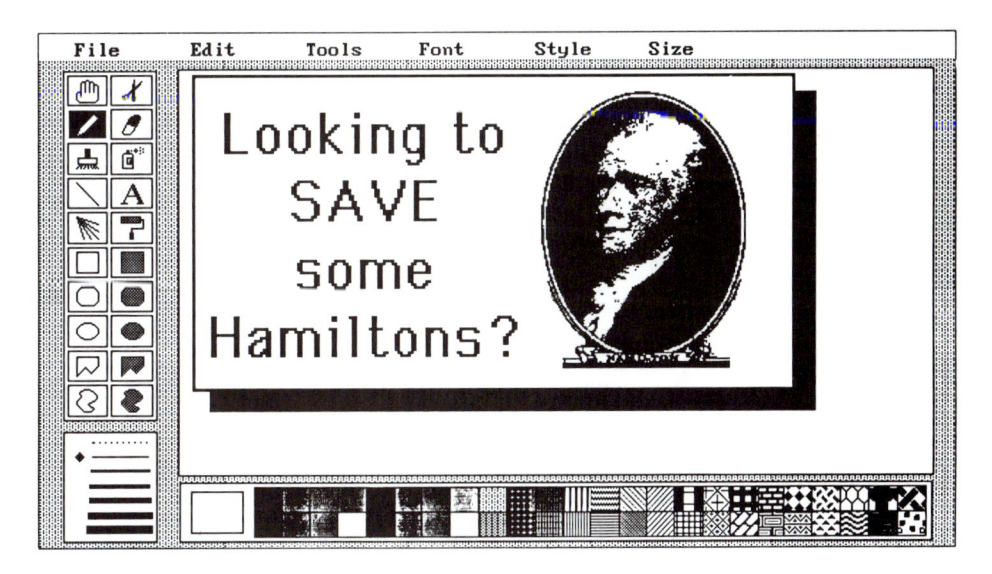

Fig. 12-37. The PC version.

date to handle the demands of interoperating system environments. Furthermore, PageMaker can read a wide variety of file formats, reducing the need for file conversions.

In Fig. 12-38, you can see how PageMaker appears when it is running on a Mac.

Here you can see a PostScript graphic about to be placed. PageMaker reads a wide range of Mac graphics, as you can tell from the list in Table 12-2.

PageMaker running under Windows on the PC looks remarkably similar, as you can see from Fig. 12-39.

Here a piece of text from WordPerfect is about to be placed in a document. PageMaker reads a wide range of text formats, as you can see from Table 12-3. With this ability to read foreign file formats, an ability that expands with each new release of the program, you can pull information from a wide variety of sources into your PageMaker documents.

When you are using PageMaker to assemble documents from files spread out over a TOPS network, you will find the ability to directly place files of differing formats a great advantage. Users who are supplying you with material for the PageMaker document can publish it in volumes that you can mount. However, if a lot of users are supplying information to you, you might want to publish a volume for submissions, which is then mounted by each submitter. This reduces the amount of

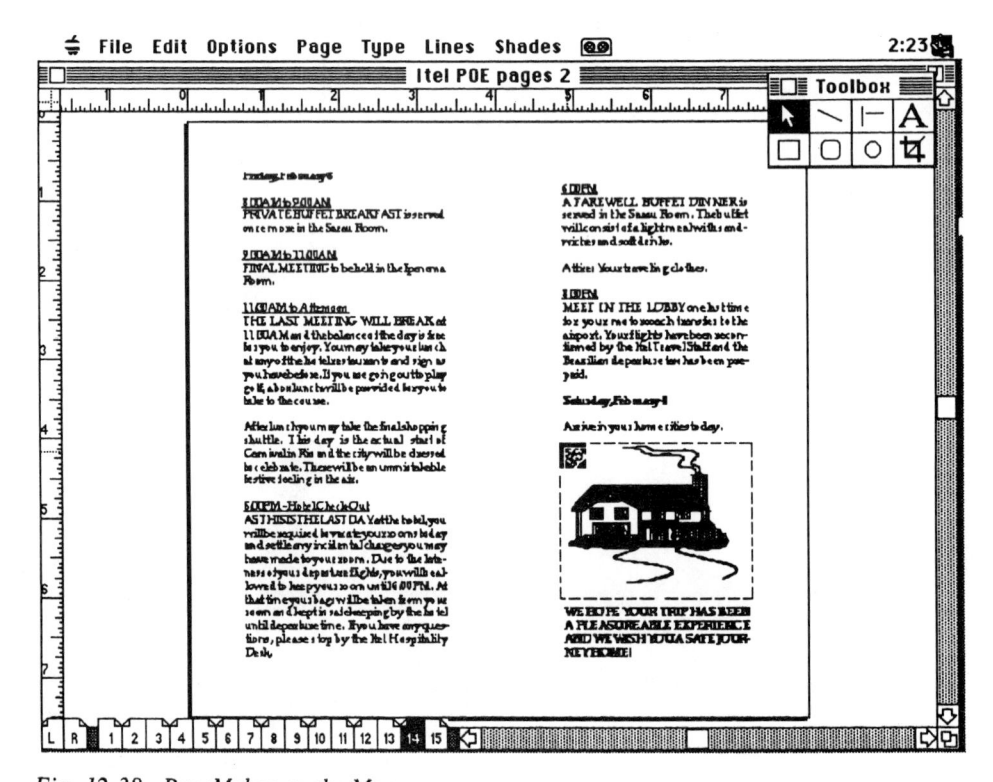

Fig. 12-38. PageMaker on the Mac.

network overhead on the system that is assembling the document. If each submitter has only one or two documents to supply, they can use the TOPS Copy command to copy them to your published volume without having to mount your volume.

Note that when you want to read Mac files into PageMaker on the PC, you need to name the files with the appropriate conventions. While Mac users might bridle at having to be bound by DOS naming conventions, it is a small price to pay for the flexibility that Pagemaker offers.

CONCLUSION

TOPS is an excellent tool when you need to bring together resources that are scattered among many users. When the resources relate to graphics the diversity of file formats can be confusing. However, the examples in this chapter should give you a clearer picture of the types of graphics and their relative merits. The tools to convert images from one format to another are rapidly being developed. While a single format for all images is probably a false shibboleth, the day when most images can be converted to a shareable format is fast approaching. As the quantity

Table 12-2.

Graphics files read by PageMaker (Mac)	Graphics files read by PageMaker (PC)
Adobe Illustrator	Adobe Illustrator
Aldus FreeHand	Aldus FreeHand
Cricket Draw	AutoCad
Cricket Graph	EPS format
Easy 3D	HP Graphics Gallery
FullPaint	HP-GL format
Glue	Lotus 1-2-3
MacDraft	MacPaint
MacDraw	Mirage
MacPaint	PC Paintbrush
MGMStation	PC Paint Plus
PICT format	PC Paintbrush Plus
PictureBase	PC Paint
Scrapbook	Publisher's Paintbrush
SuperPaint	TIFF format
TIFF format	Videoshow
	Windows Draw
	Windows Paint
	Windows Designer

NOTE: Because new formats are constantly being added by Aldus and third-party vendors, we do not claim that this list is exhaustive.

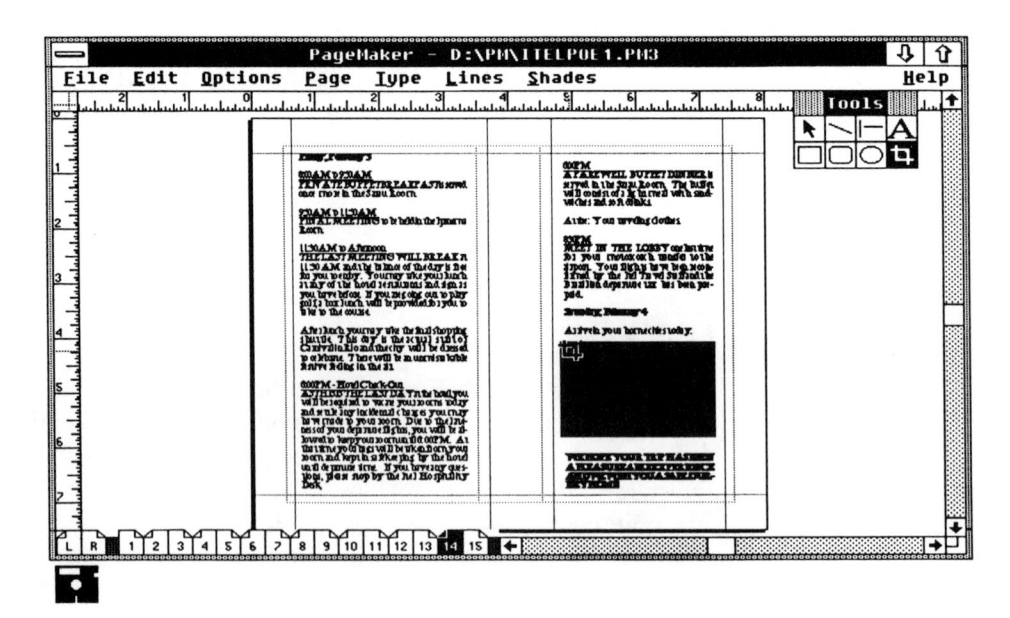

Fig. 12-39. PageMaker on the PC.

Table 12-3. Text files read by PageMaker.

PageMaker Mac reads	PageMaker PC reads
DCA files (PC and Mac)	HP Executive MemoMaker
MacWrite	HP AdvanceWrite
Microsoft Word (PC and Mac)	IBM DisplayWrite 3 and 4 (DCA)
Microsoft Works (PC and Mac)	Lotus Manuscript (DCA)
WordStar PC	Microsoft Word PC
WriteNow	Multimate
XyWrite PC	Samna Word
	Volkswriter (DCA)
	Windows Write
	WordPerfect
	WordStar
	WordStar 2000 (DCA)
	XyWrite

NOTE: Files are read in native format unless otherwise noted. Because new formats are constantly being added by Aldus and third-party vendors, we do not claim that this list is exhaustive.

and quality of images stored on microcomputers increases, we will have more and better graphics resources to share across our networks.

In the list of file formats that HIJAAK can understand, you might have noticed FAX, one of the hottest new forms of communication. In the next chapter, we look at communications between users on TOPS and between TOPS users and other networks.

13
Mail and Communications

THIS CHAPTER DISCUSSES some of the communications possibilities opened up by the TOPS network. With TOPS you cannot only share files with other users, but send messages between workstations on the network. For users spread throughout a building, this can be a valuable communications tool. Using special equipment, you can connect your local network with a network in a remote office, sharing files and sending messages over great distances. Networking dissimilar computers such as the Macintosh and PC is an impressive technical feat. But by no means is it the limit of TOPS capabilities. TOPS products are also available that allow the same Macs and PCs to network to much more powerful desktop workstations from Sun Microsystems and Hewlett Packard. This chapter also deals in more detail with some of the issues of wiring and network connection that have been raised elsewhere.

ELECTRONIC MESSAGES

Communication is at the heart of most human enterprise. This communication takes three main forms: documents, face-to-face conversation, and talking on the telephone. All three modes of communication have their advantages and disadvantages. Technological solutions to problems in all three areas have resulted in a communications revolution in recent years.

Electronic mail is just one of a whole raft of new terms that have been coined, like voice mail, FAX, desktop publishing, and even desktop communications. Computers have been a major part of these new technologies.

The Need for Electronic Mail

These days many offices have sophisticated phone systems with features like call waiting and call forwarding. Many offices also have word processing facilities that use computers to put out professional-looking memos and reports. Why then is there a need for electronic mail? The answer lies in a lot of small but cumulatively significant problems that plague us when we try to "reach out and touch someone" or to "put it in writing." Often when we call someone we simply don't connect. The parties we are trying to reach are too often not at their desk, or on another line. They might be in another time zone, or in an occupation that keeps them away from a phone. This gives rise to telephone tag, missed messages, and crossed wires. One reason for the rapid rise of the electronic facsimile machine or FAX is the ability to get a message through, whether or not the recipient is available for a conversation. However, the pieces of paper that FAX generates have many of the disadvantages of the other pieces of paper that clutter our desks and demand to be filed or tossed, or otherwise addressed.

As computers approach the status of a universal desktop accessory, next to the phone and the calculator, they become a third avenue of communication. The idea behind electronic mail is to use computers to offer an alternative to other forms of communications, an alternative that solves some of the problems of both the telephone call and the printed word. There are two forms of electronic mail. The first uses a remote computer as a repository for messages which can be accessed by anyone anywhere in the world who has a computer equipped with a modem. The second uses a local area network to permit communication within a smaller group of people. You can see both types diagrammed in Fig. 13-1.

Both types of electronic mail share some significant advantages. Being electronic the mail can be read, stored, organized, and replied to, without generating

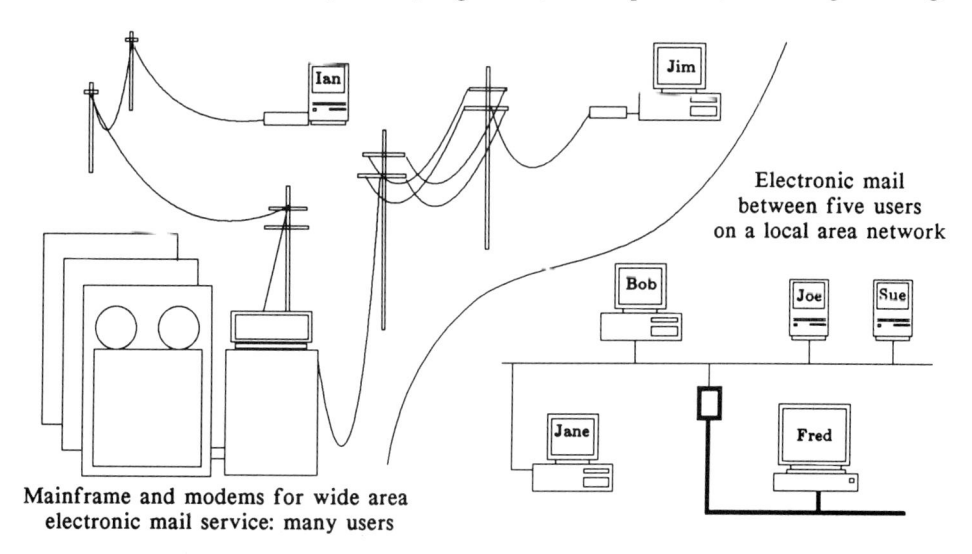

Fig. 13-1. Types of electronic mail.

any paper. Messages sent electronically do not fall on the floor, get accidentally lost, or otherwise disappear. They wait to be read, and, in some cases, can automatically generate a notice of receipt. Electronic mail is faster than any other medium. Unlike phone calls or documents consigned to the mail, electronic communications always get to their destination on the first try, regardless of weather, carrier competence, or recipient reluctance. Furthermore, much electronic communication can be done outside of regular business hours, and some of it can be automated by the computer.

Typical of *wide area electronic mail*, such services as MCI Mail and CompuServe act like electronic post offices with thousands of mail boxes that are in fact nothing more than well-organized file storage space on a large computer system. To communicate via MCI Mail, you must have signed up and received an electronic address. A communications program on your computer dials up the MCI Mail computer, and you can check your electronic mail box. You can then send messages to anyone else who has given you their MCI Mail address. You can type the message while you are *on*-line using a simple text editor that is part of the MCI Mail computer system. Alternatively you can *upload* a message, that is, transmit a document that you typed and stored in a file before you dialed up the mail service. You can read your mail on-screen, or capture it in a file, *downloading* it to your own computer so that you can edit and print it locally. Using an electronic mailing list you can *broadcast* the same message to several different people on the service.

A different kind of electronic mail is possible when all of the computers within an office are wired together as a network. With the right software each computer can send and receive messages to one or more of the others. When you send electronic mail to another user on the network they are alerted, either by a sound or an on-screen message. The sender knows that the message arrived, and the recipient cannot ignore it. A typical example of *local area electronic mail* is InBox, a product that runs on TOPS and works as a desktop communications software tool. With InBox you can send messages, memos, and even data files, from one workstation to another on a TOPS network.

ELECTRONIC MAIL WITH TOPS INBOX

To provide TOPS users with an electronic mail service, SUN MicroSystems, makers of TOPS, acquired InBox from Think Technologies. InBox started out as a Macintosh product and was highly rated as a mail system for AppleTalk networks. A PC version followed, and now you can send messages between Macs and PCs using any TOPS-based network. InBox works as a pop-up program. On the Mac, it is installed as a Desk Accessory. On a PC, InBox can either be run in the background as a terminate and stay-resident program, or it can be run in the foreground.

The InBox Message Center

Setting up InBox on your network is a straightforward task once you have a general understanding of the way that the program works. On each computer that will be using InBox a *personal connection* is installed. This identifies the user and runs the local part of the InBox program for that user. One computer on the network will be designated the message center. This computer does not have to be dedicated to message center operation, which will take place in the background like other network operations. There can even be several message centers on a single network, each with a different name. A computer that is designated as a message center will store messages for all users of that center. For example, in Fig. 13-2, you can see a typical network arrangement with two message centers.

Each InBox user will have a mail box installed in the message center. The procedure for installing InBox is to first set up the message center, then add users to the system. Each user has software installed for his/her machine. Each time a user is added, the message center is updated to include that user.

If you are running TOPS in server mode, where one computer system is providing the bulk of the resources for the network, then this server is the logical place to install the message center. You will need a certain amount of free disk space available to the InBox message center. Although the message center software itself does not take up a lot of room, message traffic can eat up space. See the InBox manuals for instructions on how to estimate storage space needed. If you are running an all Mac network then the message center should be placed on a Mac, preferably one with a large hard disk. Current versions of InBox require a Mac be used for a message center when both Macs and PCs are using InBox. The message center machine must remain on at all times if users of the network are to have round-the-clock access to their messages.

Each user of InBox is assigned a mailbox in a message center. This is used to store messages that have been sent to that user. Once the user reads the message, it can be left in the mailbox, forwarded to another user's mailbox, deleted, or transferred to a disk file on the user's own system. If a message has a data file attached

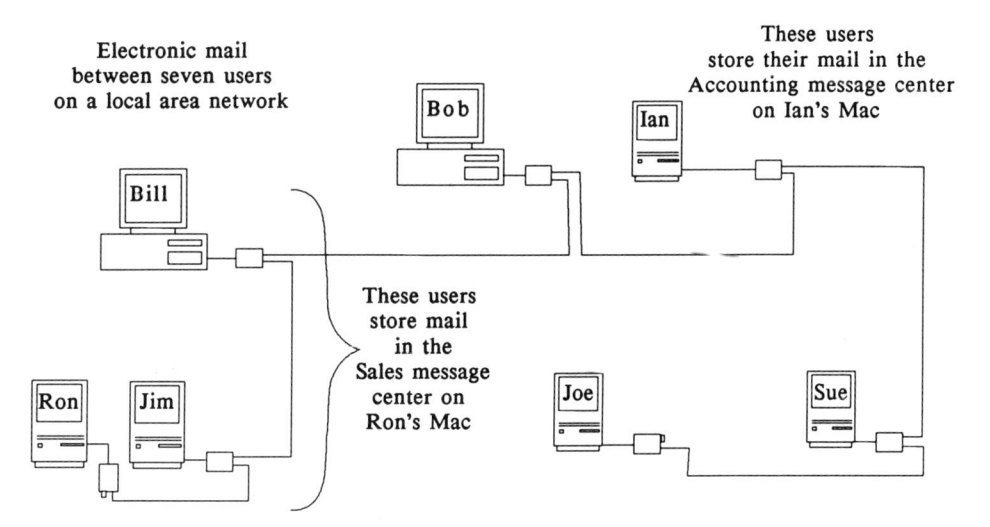

Fig. 13-2. InBox network.

to it, that data file is also stored at the message center until the user has a chance to transfer it to local storage.

Another task performed by the message center is to notify users when they have new messages. This is done by flashing a message on the user's screen, or by sounding a tone. The message center also controls access to mailboxes to prevent unauthorized use or tampering.

A Typical InBox Communication

To give you a feel for what InBox does, look at a typical series of events involved in the use of InBox. We first look at events from the perspective of a Macintosh user. On a Macintosh, you can have InBox load automatically as a DA, or you can choose to start InBox from the desktop using the InBox Startup, seen on the desk in Fig. 13-3.

Here you can see that InBox has been started and the InBox controller has been popped up. The message InBox appears underneath the Apple logo in the top left of the screen to let you know that the program is active. If the program is not active, the message center cannot inform you that you have mail waiting. However, mail can be sent to your mailbox at any time, regardless of whether your system is on or InBox is loaded.

The InBox controller on the Mac features six icons that stand for InBox, Addresses, Phone messages, Memos, Enclosures, and Sending messages. The InBox option lists current messages so that you can read them. The Addr. option displays an address list for the network, allowing you to pick the person or persons to whom

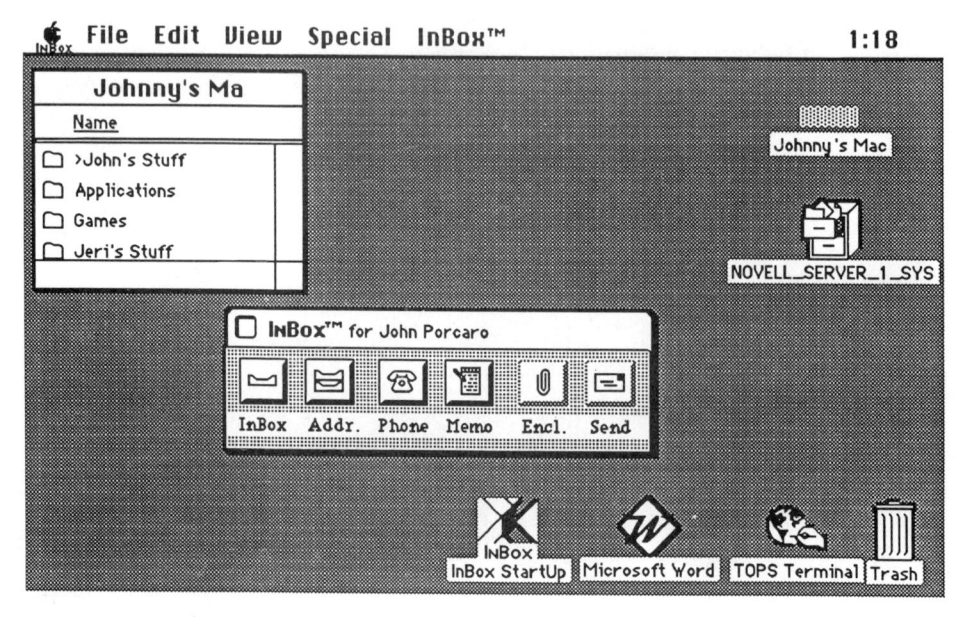

Fig. 13-3. Starting InBox.

you want to send messages. The Phone and Memo options are used to write messages, either in a telephone message or memo format. The Encl. option allows you to attach a disk file to a message so that it can be transferred across the network to the recipient. The Send option is used to transmit messages after they have been written. There is also an InBox menu on the Macintosh menu bar. This provides access to other program features that we discuss later.

Note that the user's name appears at the top of the menu. Unlike some software, electronic mail depends heavily on identification of the user. You do not want your copy of InBox used on someone else's machine as this could give them access to your messages. InBox has several levels of security to prevent unauthorized access and these are discussed later.

InBox makes it relatively painless to write and distribute messages such as memos that otherwise require a lot of repetitive typing and formatting. In Fig. 13-4, you can see that John has selected the Memo icon in order to open up a memo document.

This document is automatically dated and time stamped. The user's name is automatically entered. Writing in the memo area is very simple. The Re: area is usually filled in with a subject for the memo and then you can move down to the body of the memo. Text in the memo will word-wrap when it reaches the right-hand margin and the usual Macintosh editing keys are available. If you are verbose enough to fill the first page, a second is made available. You can see a completed

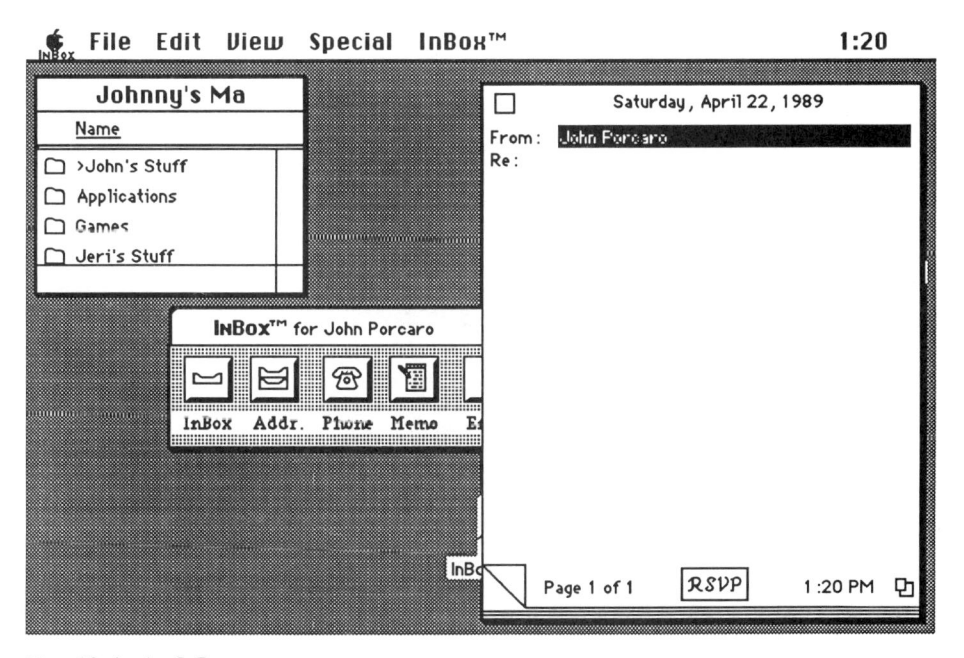

Fig. 13-4. An InBox memo.

memo in Fig. 13-5. Although the memo is headed with the sender's name and the Message Center will inform the recipient of the source of the memo, it is considered good electronic mail protocol to also type your name as sender, as shown.

After completing the memo, the writer clicks on the InBox controller to bring it to the foreground as in Fig. 13-6.

When you are ready to send a memo, you can click on Addr. to pop up a list of users who have mailboxes on the system. This list, seen in Fig. 13-7, is created by InBox from the Message Center information about who is set up on the system.

You can perform several operations with the address list in addition to addressing your mail. You can click the printer icon at the bottom of the list to print out names. You can store the list on disk or discard names that you do not want on your list.

The slider control on the side of the list can be used to browse through it. When you find the name of the party to which you want to address the memo, you click the box beside their name and a check mark appears, as seen in Fig. 13-7. You can pick more than one person to receive the memo, just by clicking on all the names you want. Reclicking a checked name un-checks it. Your own mailbox will appear on the address list in bold type. You can send mail to yourself, as described later.

Note the grayed name at the top of the list in Fig. 13-7. This is a routing list, a collection of names that have been put together by the user. By using a routing list you can send mail to several people at once without having to select names individually. There might also be names marked on the list with a triangle in the margin.

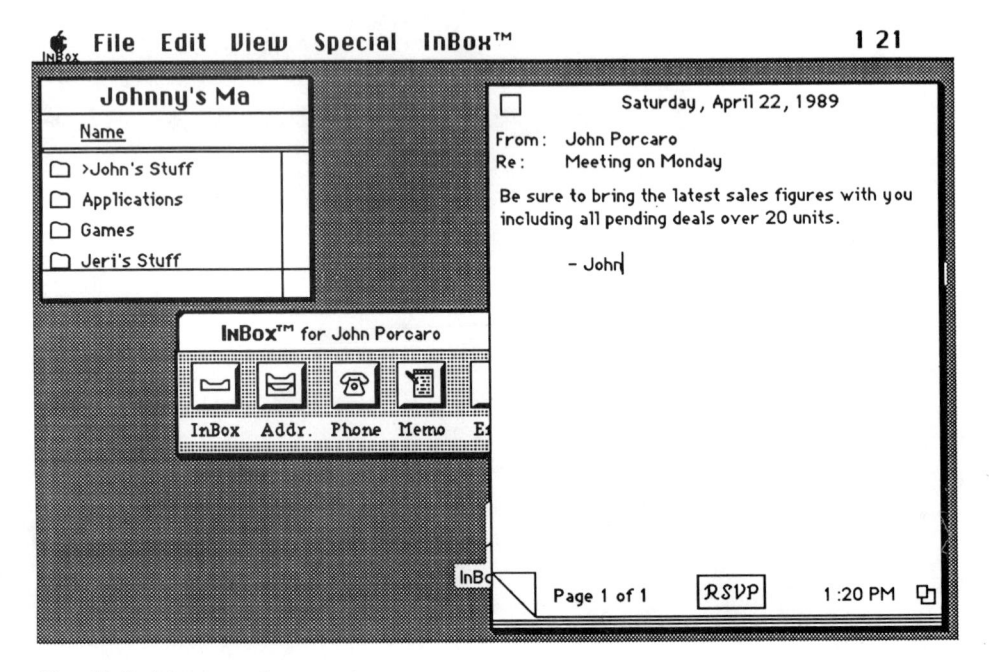

Fig. 13-5. Memo ready to send.

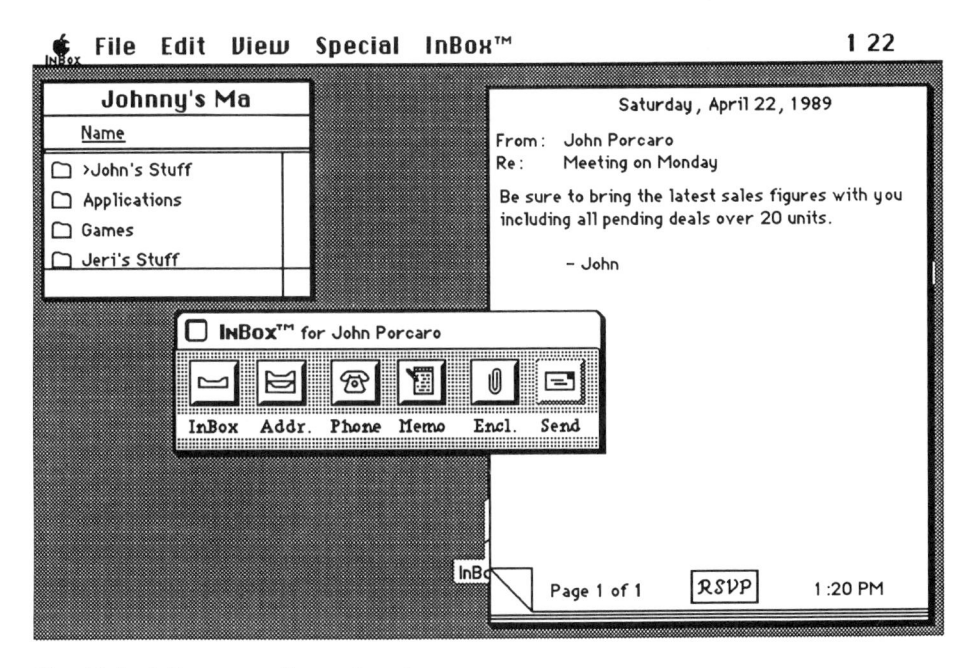

Fig. 13-6. InBox controller activated.

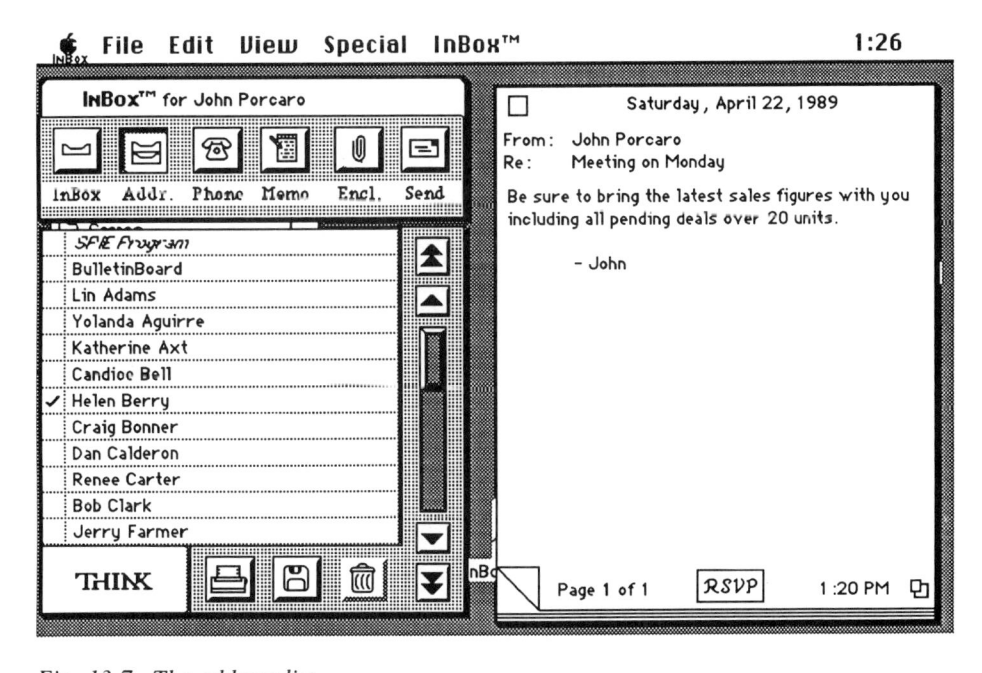

Fig. 13-7. The address list.

These will be the names of other message centers on the network. Click on one of these to get to a list of users in that area.

Having selected the person or persons to whom you want the memo sent, you click on the Send icon. This transmits the message and marks the memo as sent, as seen in Fig. 13-8.

As you can see, the procedure is very simple and much less hassle than getting out a piece of paper. With so much information added automatically, you have very little typing to do besides the meat of your message. When the memo has been sent, you can click on the close box in the top left corner of the memo to put it away. You can carry on with your work confident that everyone you selected from the address list will have received the message. If they are at their computer they will have been alerted to the fact that a message has arrived. If they turn on their system and have unread mail, they are alerted by InBox when it starts up.

On the Receiving End

The recipient of John's memo is a PC user on the TOPS network. As soon as John sent the message, a special beep sounded on Helen's PC to let her know she had mail. Although she was in the middle of a 1-2-3 session, she simply pressed the InBox hot key and the Inbox PC controller popped up, as seen in Fig. 13-9.

The InBox controller on the PC has a similar set of options to those on the Macintosh, with Addr., Phone, Memo, Send, and so on. InBox PC automatically displays a list of messages in the lower half of the InBox screen. You can see the

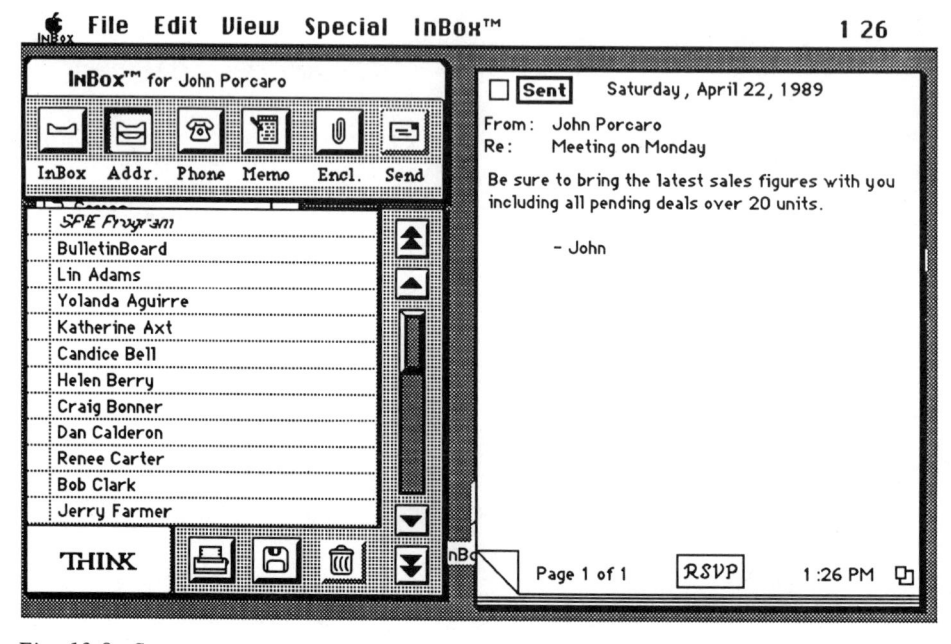

Fig. 13-8. Sent memo.

one from John at the bottom of the list. By pressing the F10 key, Helen can pop up a list of InBox commands, such as Print, Save, Delete, RSVP, Reply, and so on. All on these commands can be issued by pressing Alt and a key letter.

The small diamond next to some messages on the list, including the one from John, is part of a system of icons used on both PC and Mac versions of InBox to distinguish different types of messages. As you might guess, a diamond indicates that the message has not been read yet. A wavy equal sign is placed next to messages that a user sends to himself or herself, a clever application of InBox that is discussed later. Two further symbols are used to manage a sophisticated RSVP system. As you probably know, RSVP stands for "Respondez S'il Vous Plait" which is French for "please reply." When you send a message with InBox, you can request a reply and stamp the message RSVP. InBox will then notify you, the sender, of the exact time and date that the message was read by the recipient. InBox does this by sending you a message, in the name of the person who was asked to RSVP. The message is marked with a § symbol. This feature provides a level of confidence in the system. Instead of sending a message and not knowing if it got to the recipients, you will know for certain that they have read it. The recipient knows that a message is marked RSVP because it will appear on his or her list with ≈ symbol. You might have noticed the initials RSVP on the bottom of the memo in Fig. 13-8. If John had clicked this box, it would have activated the InBox RSVP feature. Note that the RSVP feature does not make someone reply (only good working relationships can ensure that), but it does provide a confirmation that what you have said has been read.

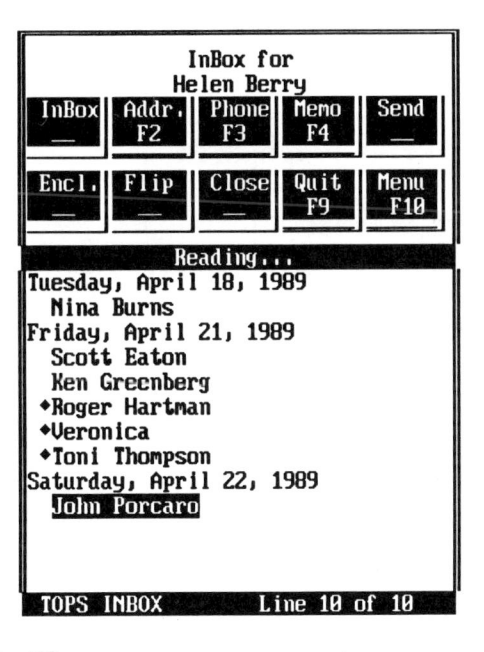

Fig. 13-9. InBox on the PC.

By highlighting a message and pressing Enter, Helen can display the contents of any message. At this point the message from John is highlighted so pressing Enter reveals the contents, as seen in Fig. 13-10.

Here is the exact text of John's message, complete with date and time of sending and a notation that this is incoming mail. If John's message was a lengthy one then Helen could press Escape to make the message side of the display active, as seen in Fig. 13-11, and then use the arrow and cursor movement keys to scroll through it.

One nice feature of InBox is that all messages can be replied to very painlessly. This is very handy for those situations when the bulk of your reply is much the same as the message to which you are replying. Another example is when a message is coming down or up the chain of command. Requests and questions can be passed from one person to another simply by issuing the reply command (Alt-R on the PC) and editing the incoming message. InBox opens up space ahead of the original text into which you can type your reply. When the reply is complete, the outgoing message can be automatically sent to the sender of the original, or re-addressed to someone else.

Making Enclosures

Suppose that Helen sends a message to her assistant requesting the sales figures that John is looking for. In the days before computers, the assistant might have to

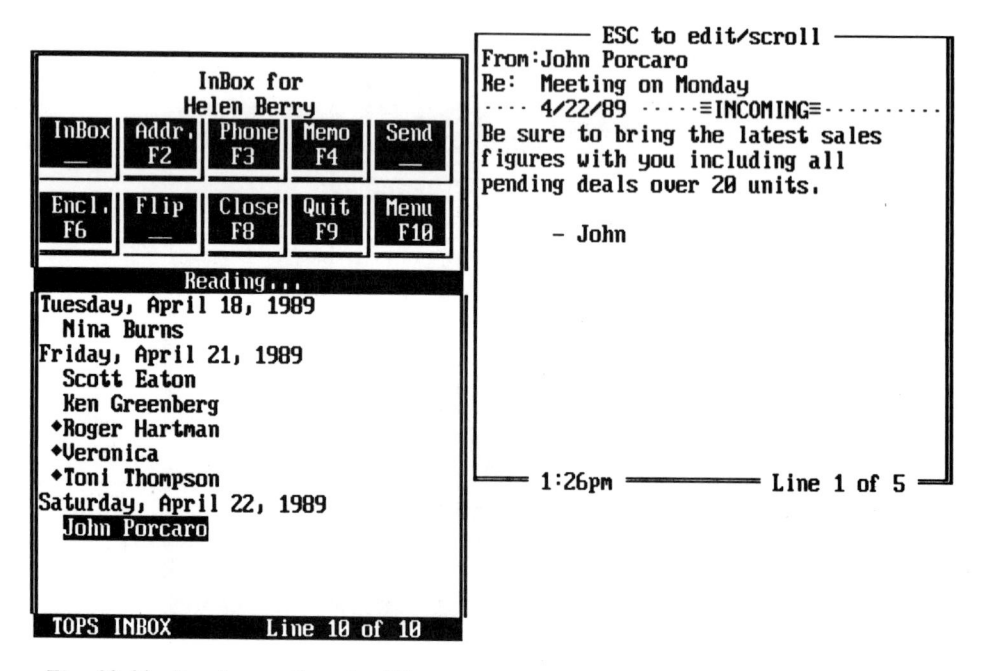

Fig. 13-10. Reading mail on the PC.

type these up from reports and route them through office mail to Helen, or even walk them over. In the computer age, the scenario is often that the numbers are stored in an electronic spreadsheet. In itself, this does not mean efficiency has been maximized. In many offices, the assistant loads the spreadsheet program, prints out the numbers, then carries them to the boss. The boss might want to dress the numbers up a little so asks for the disk file with the spreadsheet on it, loads it, massages it, then prints it out. In the TOPS networked office the scenario is much smarter. Helen's assistant gets the request for numbers as an electronic message. She edits the message into a reply, attaches the 1-2-3 spreadsheet file and dispatches it via InBox. Helen sees the reply, reads it, and receives the file onto her disk. Helen loads the spreadsheet and completes the report. She might even send the report as a spreadsheet to John. Even though John is using a Macintosh, because of TOPS he can store the 1-2-3 file on his system and use Excel to display and print it.

You can see the Inbox Encl. command at work in Fig. 13-12 where John has written a memo to Toni to which he wants to attach a document. When you issue the Encl. command, you use a standard Mac file list to get to the file you want and then click Encl. to attach it to the message. The result is a paperclip in the top right of the message, as seen in Fig. 13-12.

This particular document is a magazine article scanned by OmniPage and then edited by Microsoft Word. When the message is sent, the file is copied to the message center. Because large documents can take a while to send, InBox gives you a status report as the file is being set, as seen in Fig. 13-13.

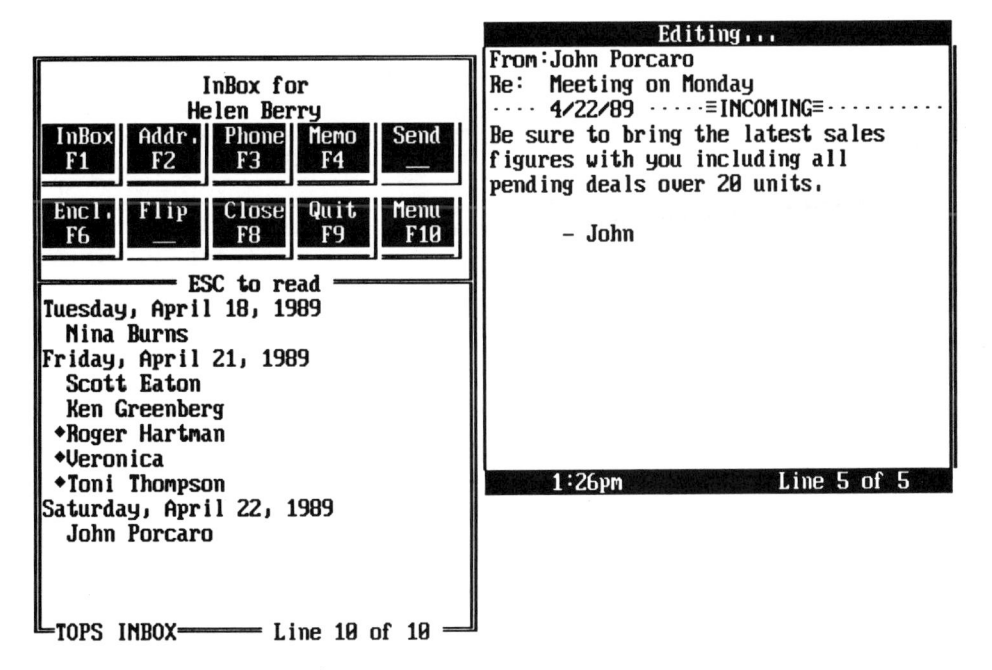

Fig. 13-11. Editing the mail.

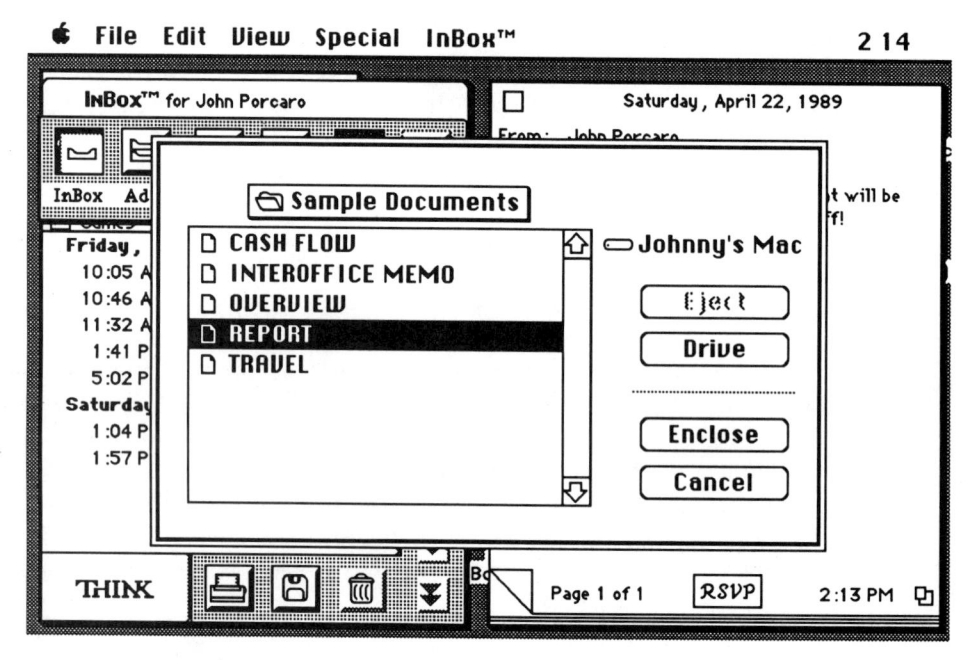

Fig. 13-12. An enclosure.

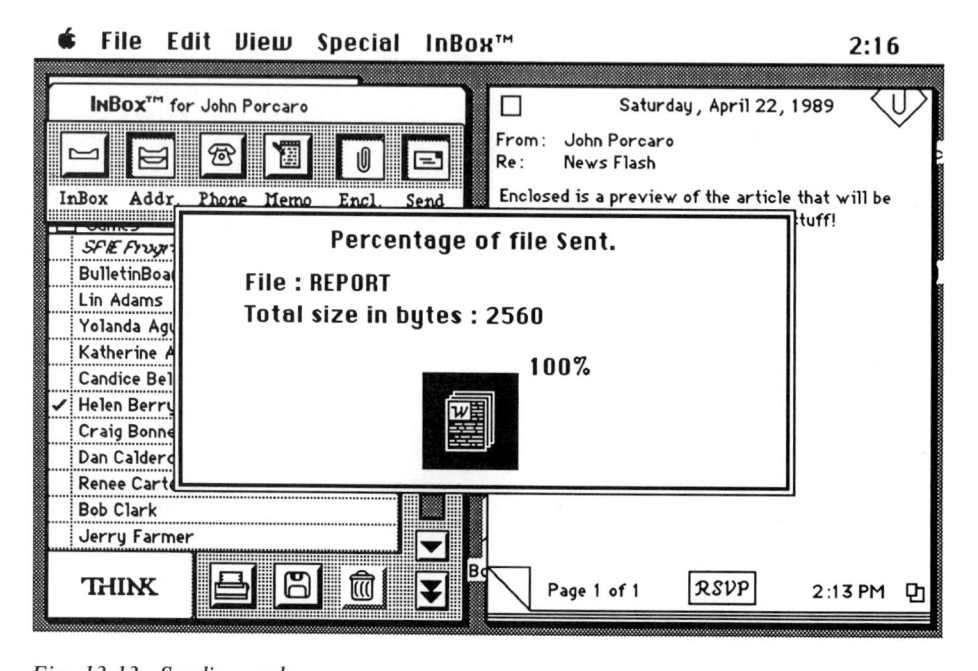

Fig. 13-13. Sending enclosure.

When Helen reads this message with InBox on her PC, it will include the notation =ENCL= to let her know that a file is attached. She can then read this file with her software, or print it out.

More InBox Abilities

In addition to the functions carried out in the above examples, typical communication between coworkers, along with file transfer, there are several other uses to which InBox can be put.

One of them is a specialized message taking task that appears on the InBox controller: Phone. This feature is designed to assist users in taking down, storing, and forwarding phone messages. These are the flimsy little slips of paper that seem to mount up whenever you are away from your desk, the ones that often seem to disappear under desks, papers, and behind filing cabinets, resulting in that embarrassing question from clients and colleagues: "Didn't you get my message?" By using InBox for phone messages, you can ensure that they do not get lost. You can even use InBox to keep a record of telephone contacts with clients. In Fig. 13-14, you can see the telephone message pad that InBox displays when you select Phone from the InBox controller.

Note that there is no name filled in on this message sheet, even though it is on John's Macintosh. The reason is that John answers a phone that is used by several people. In fact, a typical application of InBox is for a receptionist to use InBox on his or her Macintosh when taking calls for employees who are not available. Instead

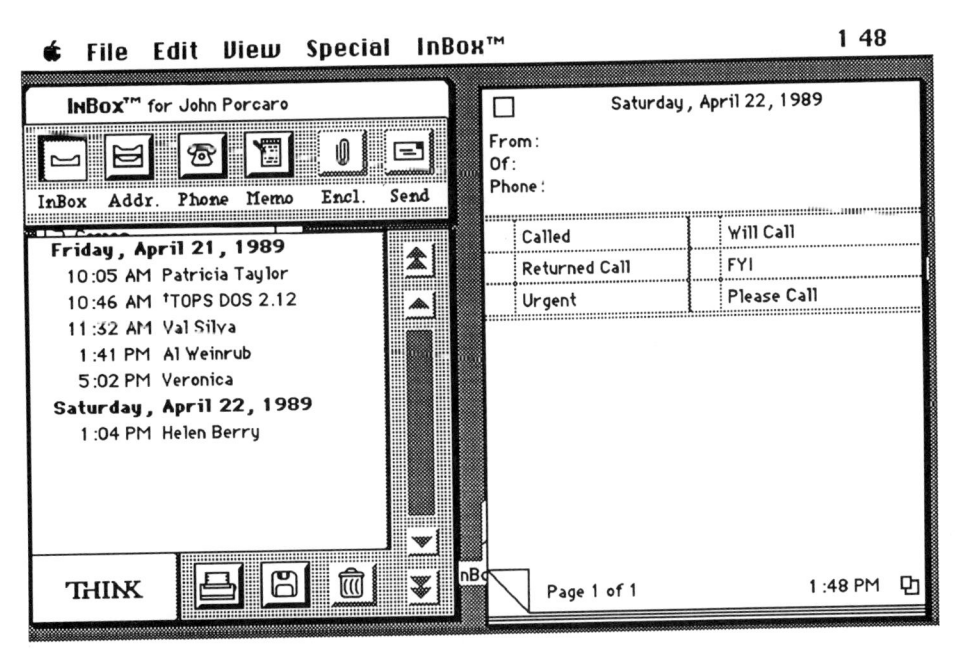

Fig. 13-14. The Phone message.

of having to run all over the office sticking notes on people's desks, the receptionist can simply post the message on InBox, knowing that it will not be lost.

In Fig. 13-15, you can see the InBox Macintosh menu that allows access to some other InBox features.

This is where Mac users issue the commands to reply and forward mail and adjust settings such as showing the times as well as dates of messages.

On the PC side are similar options. Some options are adjusted through the installation process. In Fig. 13-16, you can see the installation menu for InBox PC where the user can select such features as audible alerts for messages, plus visual on-screen alerts, and repeated alerts that sound at intervals until the incoming message is read. Note the Password section in Fig. 13-16, as well as in Fig. 13-17. InBox provides secure access to mailboxes and to the administration of the message center, right from installation.

When the message center is first installed, the administrator assigns a password to the center. Only people who know this password can make changes to the message center. Whenever a new user is added to the system, the user enters a name and chooses his or her password. The name and password must be entered every time that the user accesses InBox. This means that, if you protect your password, only you can read your mail. However, because entering a password is a chore, InBox can be told to remember your name and password so that your access is automatic. This is the way most people work if they can control who uses their computer. In other situations or at times where security is important, the Remember feature can be turned off and InBox will require entry of the password.

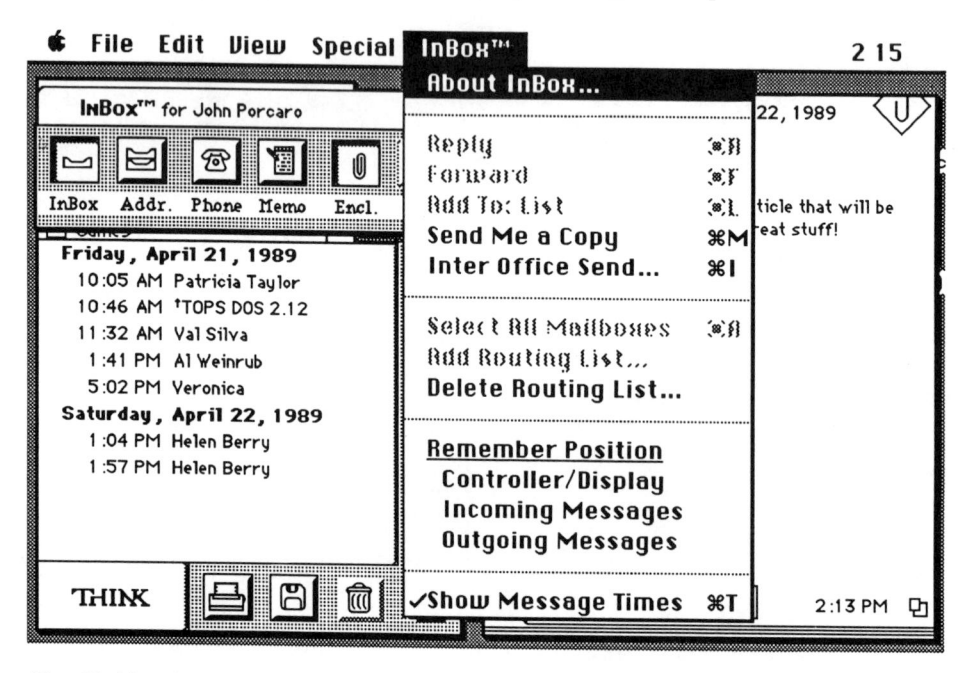

Fig. 13-15. The InBox menu.

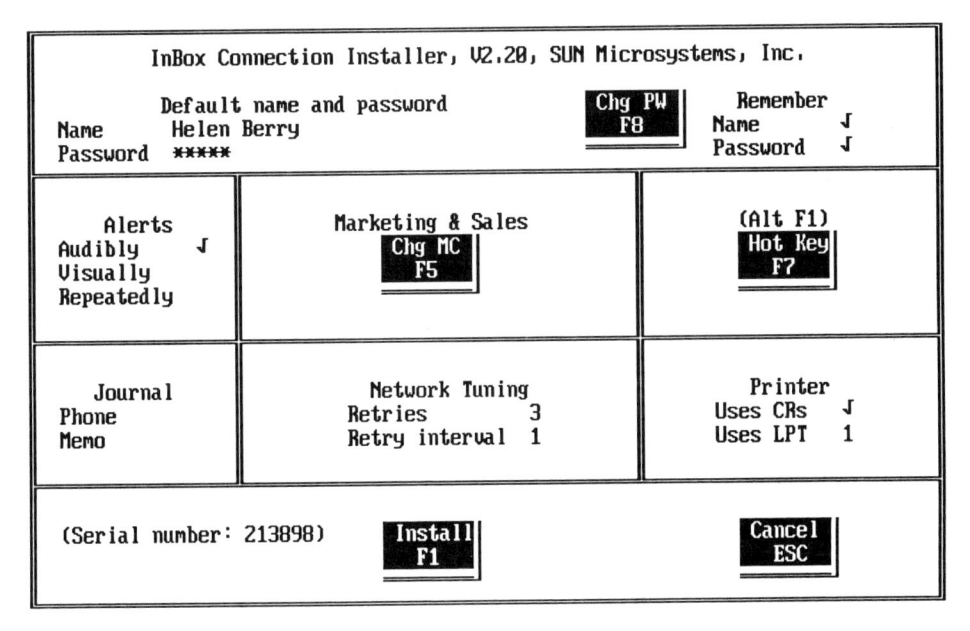

Fig. 13-16. The InBox PC installation screen.

Fig. 13-17. Initial password setting or Mac.

All of the creative uses of electronic mail are beyond the scope of this book, however, several have been listed here to whet your appetite.

Broadcast news. The InBox administrator can send messages to all users in one simple step. This allows prompt notification of changes in the system and housekeeping chores. For example, if the message center needs to be shut down for repairs, everyone can be warned beforehand.

Send to lists. By selecting more than one name on an address list, you can send a message to more than one person. If you like, you can have InBox remember this list as a *routing list* that can be added to the address list. Next time the same group of people need to get one of your messages, you can click once on the routing list. You can also copy names into a memo from a list of selected recipients. For memos that need to show a "To:" list at the top you select the names on the address list and then copy the names into the top of the Memo.

Cut and paste. Lists of recipients are not the only thing you can cut and paste with InBox. Just about any text from anywhere can be clipped from an application into an InBox memo. This saves a lot of retyping. You can also cut text from an InBox message and paste it into an application.

Electronic Mail Security Issues

As the infamous Gumbel-Scott incident of 1989 made painfully clear, electronic mail is not without its shortcomings, the primary one of which is security. (You will recall Bryant Gumbal made several less-than-favorable comments about NBC Today Show costar Willard Scott in a memo sent to NBC management by electronic mail; said comments were revealed when someone gained access to the computer files.)

When entrusting personal comments to an office mail system, electronic or otherwise, caution is the watchword. If you think that what you are writing could end up being read by an unintended audience, exercise discretion in what you say. Beyond that, make sure that you use the security measures built into the system. In the case of InBox, the security system will serve to prevent anyone without your password prying into your messages. If the person to whom you send your messages also uses a password, then what you have consigned to InBox will remain secure.

For super-secure communications, you can make your important remarks in a word processing or spreadsheet file that is password protected. All major applications now let you assign password to files. If you attach the password protected file to your InBox communication, only a recipient who knows the password will be able to read the file. For more on network security and passwords, see Chapter 14.

ANOTHER LOOK AT CABLE CONNECTIONS

Having looked at some of the benefits provided by electronic mail running on a TOPS network, we turn back to some of the issues related to cabling TOPS constraints. We then look at some of the more exotic communication possibilities that TOPS provides.

A Brief Review

Recall the two types of cabling that can be used in an AppleTalk network are LocalTalk cabling and phone cabling. The LocalTalk cabling consists of a LocalTalk connector that attaches directly to the AppleTalk port, and LocalTalk cables. The LocalTalk connector has either a DIN-8 or DB-9 connector to attach to the machine, and then has two DB-8 connectors to which the cables attach. LocalTalk is self-terminating. The other type of cabling is phone cabling. For this, you use standard phone cable to carry the signals. To attach the phone cable to the machine, you need a connector such as a TOPS TeleConnector or Farallon's PhoneNet connector. These connectors have either a Din-8 or a DB-9 connector to attach them to the machine, and two RJ-11 connectors to which the phone cables attach. Phone cabling is not self-terminating and needs terminating resistors to be placed in the appropriate places in the network. The position of the terminating resistors is determined by the topology, which brings us to the question of buses and repeaters.

Buses and Repeaters

An electronic bus is a row of connected computers with termination at the ends (if required). A network can be solely an electronic bus, or it can be made of multiple electronic buses. A repeater is a dumb network device. All it does is pass along signals—no interpretation of, or change to, the information in the signal is made. Signals are merely strengthened. The repeater is seen as two devices on the network, but is not assigned node numbers. In terms of network definition, a repeater does not define a network, all it does is separate two electronic buses. Termination at a repeater is just the same as if the cable ended there. If the repeater connects two electronic buses, then you would terminate at the end of each bus. Two of these ends would be at the repeater. In terms of topology, a network needs to be designed so that any node can reach any other node on that network by going through no more than two repeaters. In large networks that require more than two repeaters, the "trunk with drops" topology can be used to make it so that no node is more than two repeaters away from any other node.

Repeaters have a low signal strength threshold of approximately 2 volts. Any signal that reaches the repeater below this strength will be interpreted as *noise*. This is regarded as garbage and is not passed along by the repeater. This low signal threshold is true of the FlashTalk board as well as AppleTalk interfaces. This means that networks that appeared to be working before the repeater was installed, might stop working when the repeater (or FlashCard) is added. In this case, the network was borderline to begin with. In Fig. 13-18, you can see two electronic buses connected by a repeater.

Note that even though there are two buses, there is only one network. Because there is only one network, the node numbers for all the devices are unique (the numbers in the diagram represent node numbers). Note that the repeater, while it represents two devices on the network, does not have any node numbers.

Defining a Bridge

The bridge provides for "smart" signal passing. The bridge interprets the signal it receives, and only passes it on if the signal is intended for a node on the other side

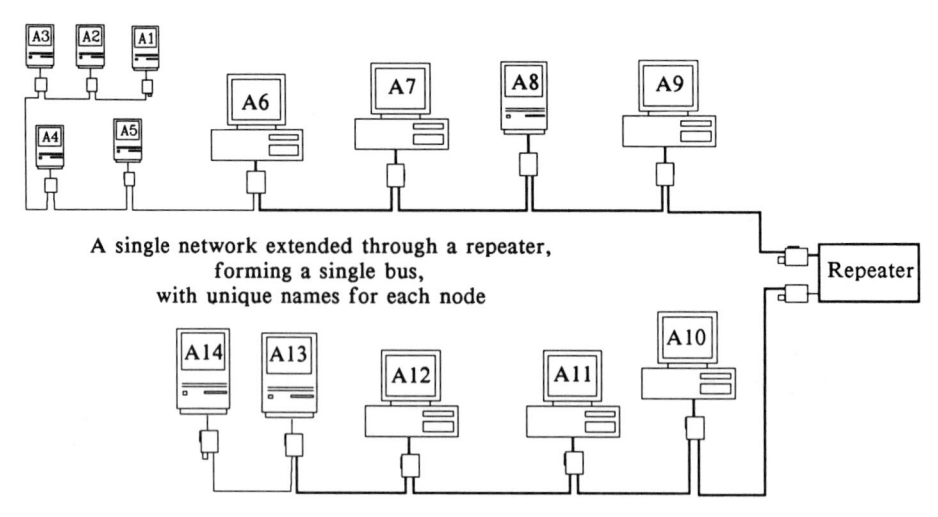

Fig. 13-18. Two buses connected by repeater.

of the bridge. In terms of defining networks, each side of a bridge is its own network. The bridge is seen as one device on each network and is given a different node number by each network. Any communication between nodes in the same network is not passed through the bridge, therefore keeping the lines clear of unnecessary signals. This is not true of a repeater which passes on all signals. Termination with a bridge is the same as termination with a repeater. The numbers in the Fig. 13-19 represent node numbers given by the network.

Node numbers in network A do not have to be unique from node numbers in network B because network A and network B have different network numbers. A nodes address is a combination of network number and node number, so nodes with

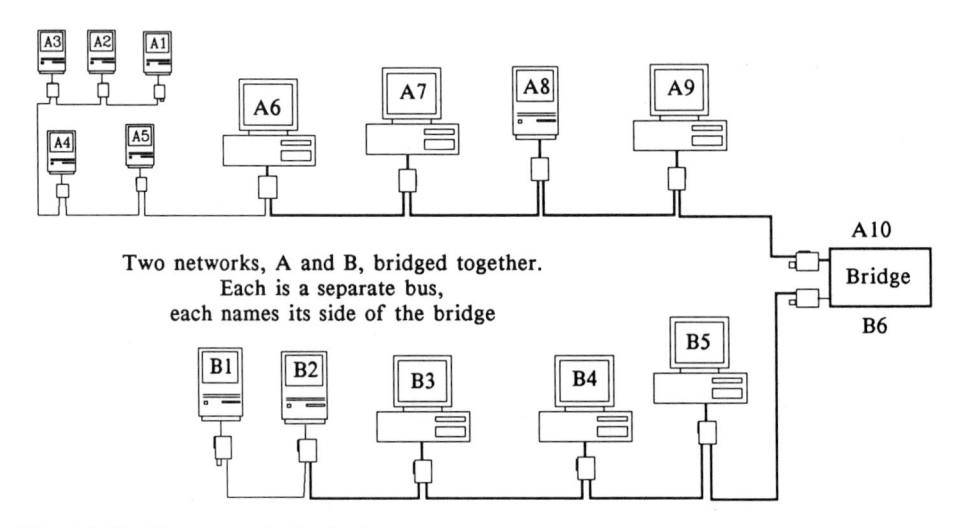

Fig. 13-19. Two networks bridged together.

different network numbers do not have to have unique node numbers in order to have unique addresses. Each side of the bridge is given a node number by the network on that side, so network A gave the bridge a node number of 10, and network B gave the bridge a node number of 6. In this diagram, each network is also one electronic bus.

Defining a Gateway

A *gateway*, such as a Kinetics FastPath, connects two different types of network cabling. The most common gateway that we deal with is a gateway between AppleTalk and Ethernet. A gateway is the same as a bridge in terms of termination and defining networks. The gateway is a smart device that interprets the incoming signal and either adds or removes information to allow that signal to travel on the other type of network wiring. A Kinetics FastPath is used specifically to go between AppleTalk and Ethernet. For communication from AppleTalk to Ethernet, the Appletalk signal is wrapped in an Ethernet header and footer and sent over the Ethernet. The protocol of sending AppleTalk signals over Ethernet cabling is referred to as EtherTalk.

More about Bus Topology

A bus topology is the most simple and most straightforward AppleTalk topology to support. In a bus, the machines are connected or daisy-chained to each other with the cable going from one machine to the next and so on. Termination is put at each end of the bus.

More about Trunk with Drops

In this topology, there is a main bus with no machines on it that is terminated at both ends. This is the *trunk*. The *drops* are lengths of cable that are spliced onto the trunk. Drops are not terminated because there is termination on the trunk. Machines or network hardware are added to the end of each drop. One rule of this topology is that the length of the drop must be relatively short compared to the length of the trunk. Machines or network hardware can be put at the end of a drop. If a machine is to be put at the end of a drop, then only one machine can be put there. If a repeater, bridge, or gateway is put at the end of a drop, then this creates a separate electronic bus, and allows many machines to be added at that drop. If a piece of network hardware is put at the end of a drop, then the separate electronic bus created by that piece of network hardware is terminated as if it were a stand-alone bus, but there is no termination on the drop side of the piece of network hardware. In Fig. 13-20, you can see that the repeater is not terminated on the drop side, but the electronic bus attached to the repeater is terminated at both ends just as if it were independent.

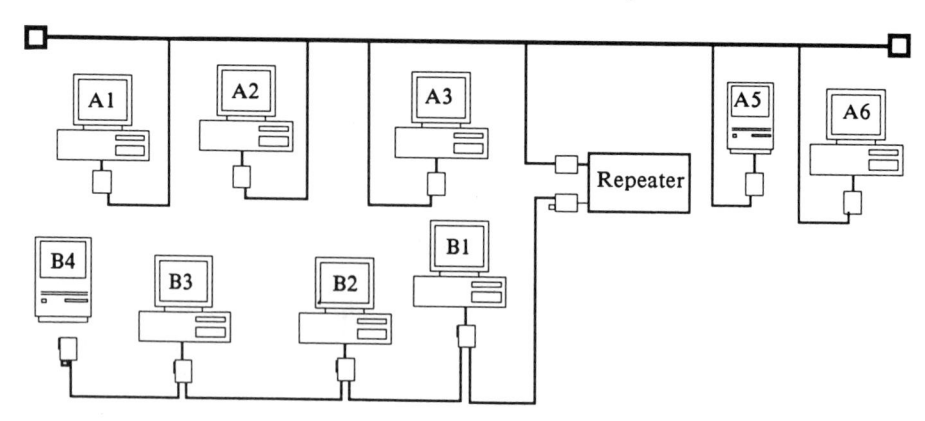

Fig. 13-20. A single trunk with drops network.

Passive Star

The *passive star* topology usually occurs when a network is formed using already existing phone wire. A phone system is wired so that every phone line is connected from the office it is in directly to the phone box (punch-down block). Theoretically, all the phone lines meet at a central point. If this were true, then this topology would work correctly. The problem is that the phone lines do not meet at a single point, they attach to the punch-down block which is in essence a short trunk. Because the punch-down block is a trunk, this topology is effectively a trunk with drops. One rule for a trunk with drops is that the length of the drops must be short in comparison to the length of the trunk. In a passive star, the length of the drops is very long in comparison to the length of the trunk. This is where the problems arise, and this is why a passive star is not a supported AppleTalk topology. If the passive star topology is used, the suggested way to terminate is by placing termination at the ends of the four longest (distance) arms of the star. Machines can be daisy-chained onto the end of an arm of the passive star. However, this increases the length of the arm (or drop), and with that increase comes an increased chance of problems. The distance of an arm of the star is measured from the punch-down block to the last machine on the arm.

Active Star

Wiring for an *active star* is the same as for a passive star (usually using existing phone wire) except that you attach a star controller to the punch-down block. A star controller is essentially a 12-port repeater. Termination is internal to the star controller, so the lines only need to be terminated at the ends of the arms of the star. Every star arm needs termination at its last node. The star arms can support daisy-chained machines, repeaters, or bridges/gateways to other networks.

Network Limits

There are no exact limits on a TOPS network, only advised limits. Some networks can run well when going way beyond the advised limits, but if a network is not working and the cabling length or number of nodes is extended beyond the limit, then the first thing to do is bring these inside the limits. Use the limits in Table 13-1 as a guide.

Wiring Basics

Having considered some of the more exotic wiring alternatives, we should perhaps return to the basic wiring system that is included with FlashBoxes, TeleConnectors, and compatible units. This is ordinary phone wire and modular plugs. We look at several aspects of using this cabling medium. Suppose you want to connect two Mac SEs and a LaserWriter in a workgroup situation like the one shown in Fig. 13-21.

As you can see, the units are fairly close together. You put TeleConnectors on all three devices. Each TeleConnector comes with a 6-foot cable. You will use two of the three cables to complete the network, making sure that there are resistor plugs in all of the empty TeleConnector sockets, as shown in Fig. 13-22.

The resistor plugs close up openings in the cable system, helping to strengthen the network signal by preventing interference. Each TeleConnector comes with a resistor plug.

If the piece of flat wire that comes with each FlashBox and TeleConnector is not long enough for your needs, you can buy additional wire at most hardware

---

Table 13-1. Network Limits.

LocalTalk

Cable length limit per electronic bus—1000

Node limit per bus—32

Phone Cables

Cable length limit per bus
    22 gauge flat—500 to 1000
    26 gauge—1000 to 3000

Node limit per bus—32

Total number of nodes on one network—254
    0 cannot be a node number.
    PCs, Macs, LaserWriters, and net devices are all nodes.
    Repeaters, bridges, and gateways all count as two nodes.

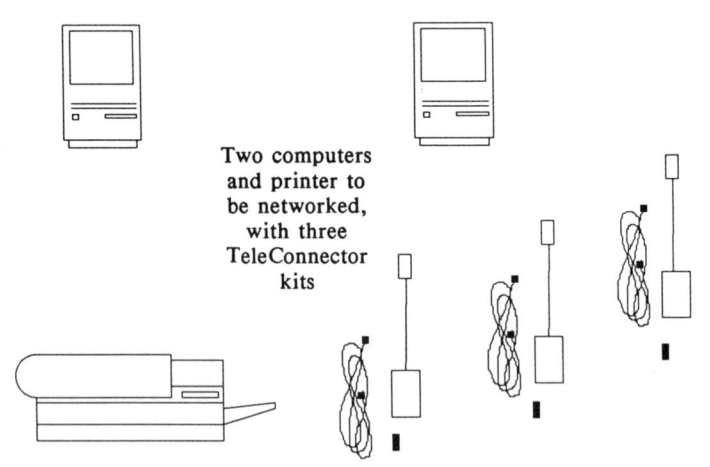

Fig. 13-21. Small network.

stores and Radio Shacks. Look in the telephone section. The wire is the same as you would use to connect a phone unit to the wall and it comes with modular plugs installed at each end. (Note that this is not quite the same as the cord units used to connect handsets to phones, because they use slightly smaller plugs.)

One advantage of this cabling medium is the ability to join two lengths together with a junction box. These only cost a few dollars and can save you buying more cable than you need. Suppose that you want to connect a PC to the network seen in Fig. 13-20. You want to put the new machine on the end of the network, but this is at a desk that is about 9 feet away. You install a FlashCard in the PC and attach the TeleConnector to the FlashCard. You plug a resistor into one socket of the TeleConnector box, and into the other socket you plug the standard length of wire. However, this will not reach to the last TeleConnector on the existing network. So, you

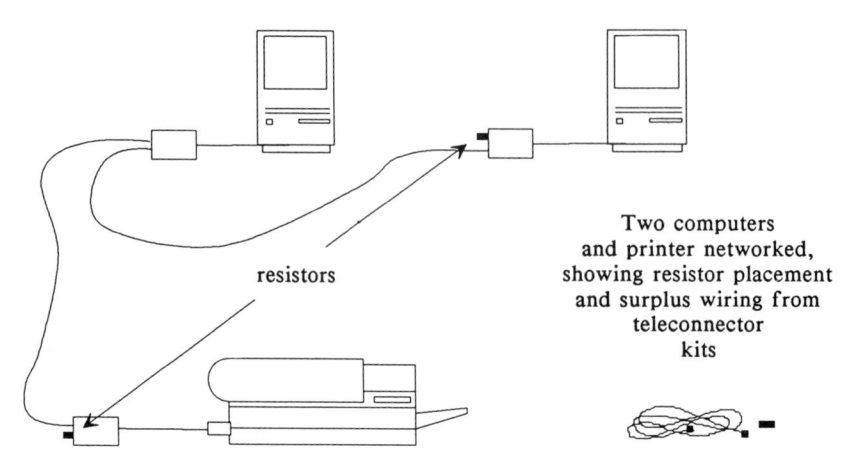

Fig. 13-22. Resistor placement.

run the leftover standard cable from the last TeleConnector of the network and join the two lengths with a junction box, as seen in Fig. 13-23.

Even when the distances are greater, say 20 to 30 feet, you can use junction boxes to connect lengths of cable. For example, many stores have 18-foot cables. Together with the standard 6-foot cable and a junction box, this gives you 24 feet.

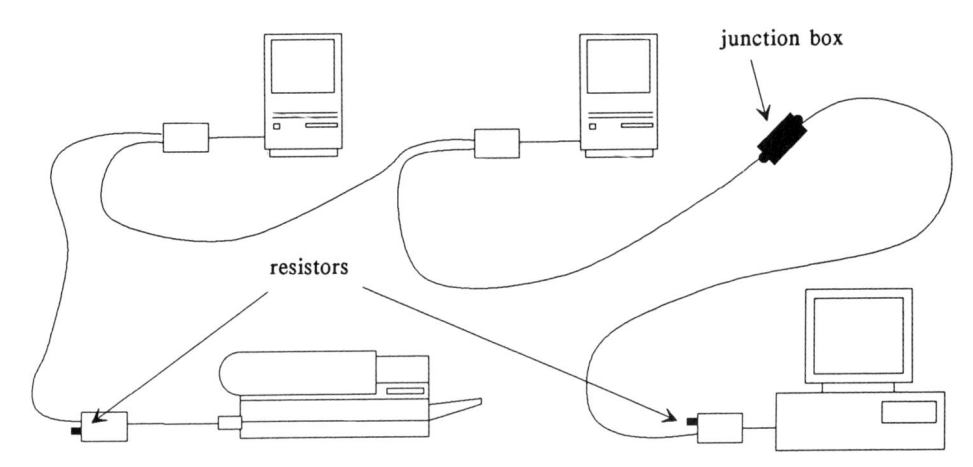

Fig. 13-23. Using a junction box.

A Simple Daisy Chain

The arrangement of equipment used in Fig. 13-24 is referred to as a *daisy chain*, the simplest topology you can use with a TOPS network.

A daisy chain is essentially a network where each device is hooked to two other devices, except at the two ends. The key to the success of a daisy chain is termina-

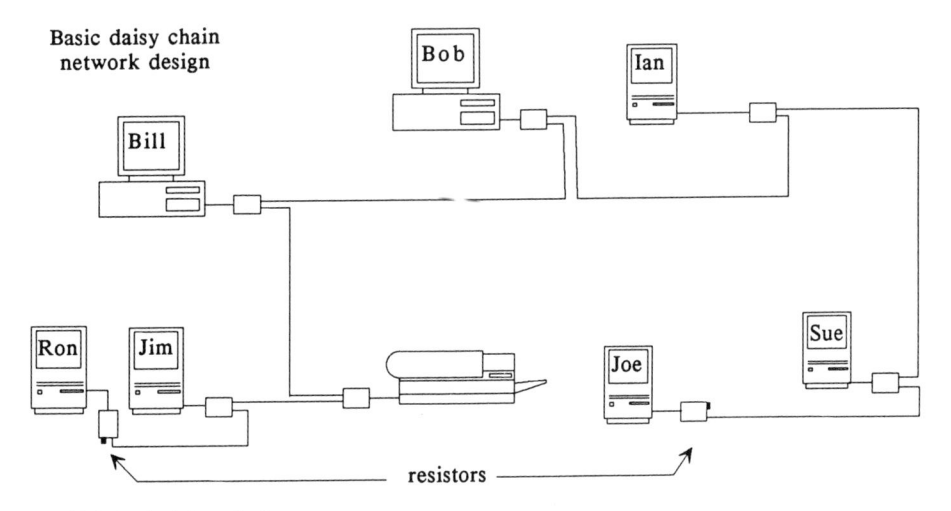

Fig. 13-24. A daisy chain.

tion. Each TOPS connector has two sockets. When you are connecting within the chain each socket holds a wire to the adjacent device in the network. At the two ends, there is only one adjacent device, leaving one socket potentially empty. However, this socket must be terminated to help close off the wiring to outside interference. A terminator is included with each TeleConnector package.

To see how this system works in practice, suppose you need to network the following equipment within a small office: a PC-XT, a PC-AT, a Macintosh Plus, a Mac II, and a LaserWriter. You install the FlashCards in the PC-XT and PC-AT. To each device you attach either TeleConnectors (the PCs and the LaserWriter) or FlashBoxes (the Macs). Then you unwind the lengths of flat telco wire that came with the TeleConnectors/FlashBoxes. Into one of the two sockets in the TeleConnector attached to the PC-XT you plug one end of the wire. You plug the other end into the TeleConnector attached to the PC-AT. The TeleConnector has two sockets. Into the empty one you plug a second piece of telco wire. You can see this stage illustrated in Fig. 13-25.

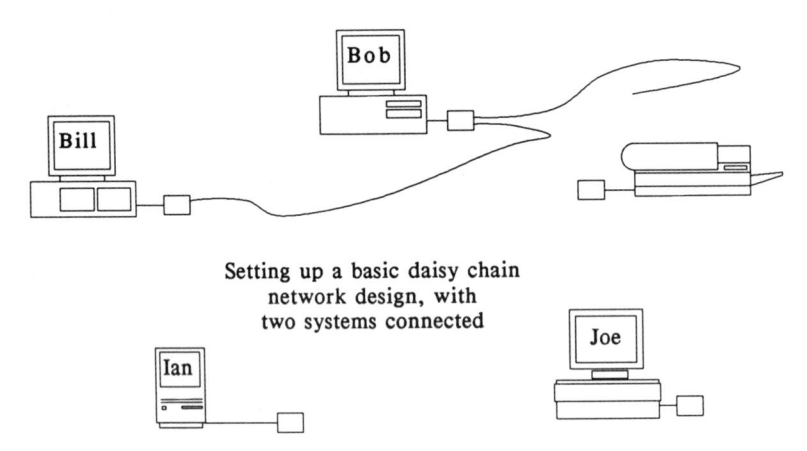

Fig. 13-25. Incomplete daisy chain network.

This wire goes to one of the sockets in the TeleConnector on the LaserWriter. Into the socket next to that is inserted a wire that leads to the FlashBox connected to the Mac II. The FlashBox, like the TeleConnector has two sockets. A fourth piece of wire leads from this FlashBox to the next. All of the devices are now connected, *but* the terminating resistors have not been inserted. They are placed into the two empty sockets, at each end of the daisy chain, as seen in Fig. 13-26.

You are now ready to proceed with software installation and use of the network.

If you want to add a device to the network, you can do so on the end or in the middle. To add a device to the end, simply remove the terminating resistor, plug in the cable to the new device, and make sure that the connector for the new device has its resistor installed. To add a device to the middle of a network, you determine between which two devices you want to insert the new one. You then disconnect

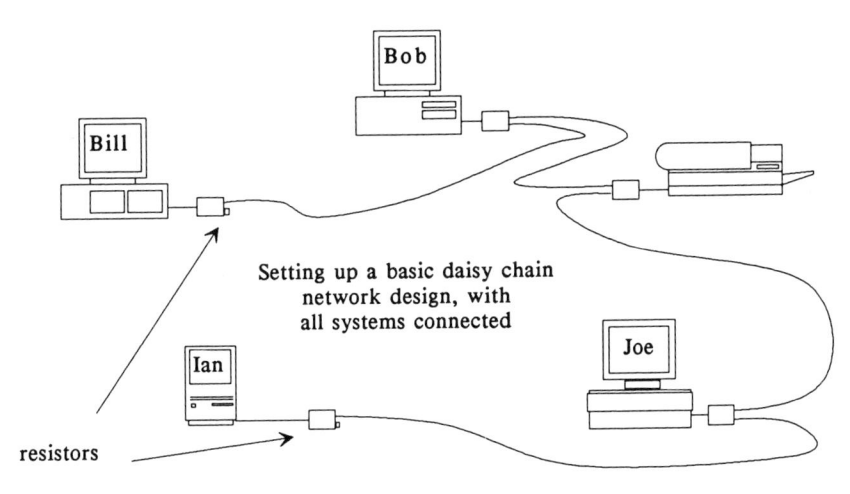

Fig. 13-26. Completed daisy chain.

one end of the cable that connects these two devices, plug it into the new connector, and run a new cable from the new connector to the other existing device, as seen in Fig. 13-27.

If you know that your network will be expanding, you can wire in additional connectors that are not yet attached to devices. This does not interfere with the network operation. However, you should never connect one end of the network chain to the other, as seen in Fig. 13-28. This will seriously interrupt network traffic.

One other note of caution is in order regrading daisy chain networks. You should not connect a daisy chain to a trunk. This will result in serious performance degradation.

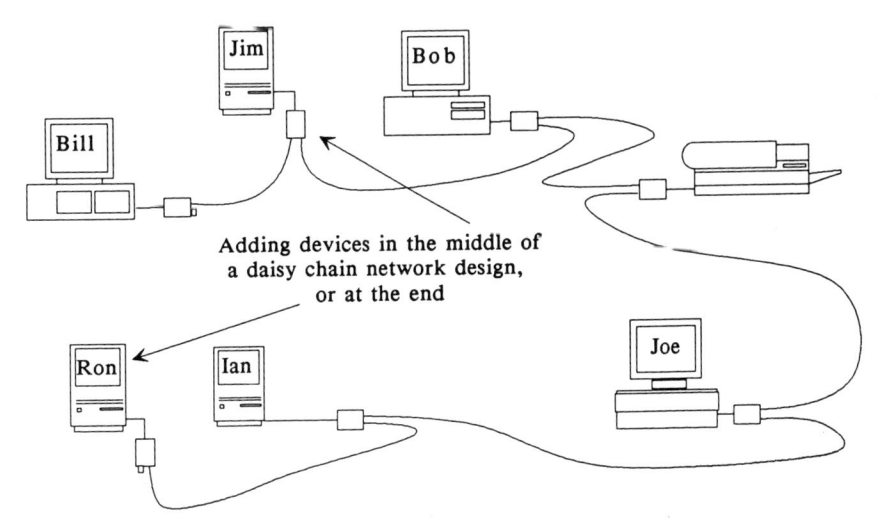

Fig. 13-27. Adding devices.

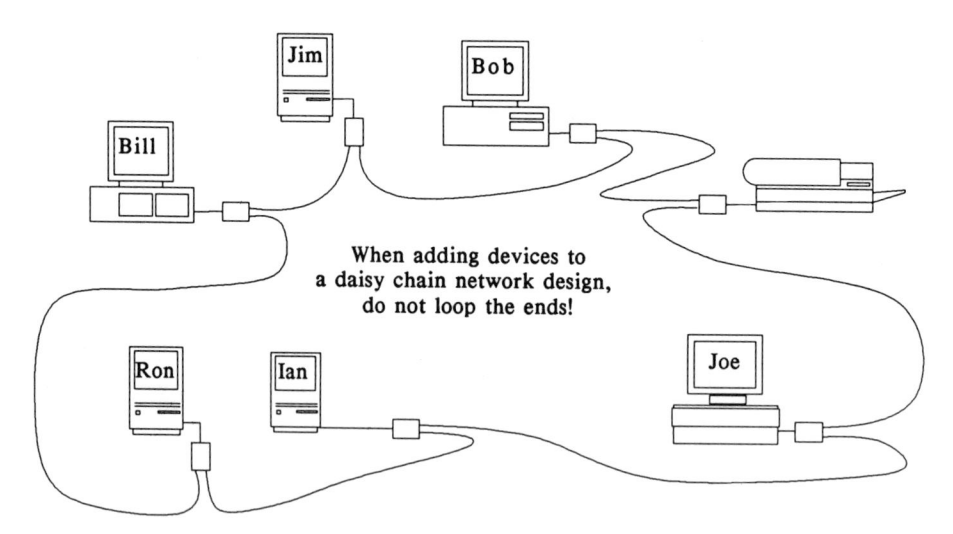

Fig. 13-28. Adding and looping.

Other Approaches

The flat modular phone wiring we are discussing here is sometimes called *flat telco* wire. The same task is performed by a slightly different wire, *round telco*, or direct-connect phone wire. This is the wire that is used in the walls of homes and offices to join outlets together. The thickness of wire is measured in gauges, with lower numbers meaning larger wire. Round telco is usually 22 gauge, which is thicker than flat telco, which is normally 26 gauge. The length to which you can stretch a TOPS network without repeaters will depend upon which of these two wires you are using. With 22 gauge you can go almost twice as far as with 26 gauge before suffering signal loss.

You might have noticed that the flat type of cable we have been discussing actually has several wires within it, usually 4 or 6. TOPS only needs to use 2 of these wires. When used for telephones, only 2 wires are used. This gives you the potential to connect TOPS through the same set of wiring that is already installed for the phones.

There are forms of flat cable that use either foil or just two wires. Do not use either of these forms as they will not work according to the required TOPS specification.

NETWORK TROUBLESHOOTING

Cabling problems are often hard to identify and track down. They are usually inconsistent, and this is actually a good way to identify whether a problem is due to cabling or not. Inconsistencies, especially when they occur in nodes at the ends of buses, almost always point to cabling problems. If a machine is having inconsistent problems when it is at one position on the network, and no problems if it is moved to another position on the network, then you can usually suspect cabling as the cause.

If you suspect cabling problems, the best way to prove this quickly is to create a mini-network of the machines that are having the problem. If two machines on the network cannot see each other, place the machines side-by-side, connect them with a short piece of cable, and terminate at both machines. If the problem goes away, then it was most likely caused by cabling. In TOPS specifically, if a client is often getting the message Trying to connect to (server name) Keep Trying / Give Up, then it might well have a cabling problem.

CONNECTING TO MINICOMPUTERS AND SUPER-MICROS

You can connect powerful minicomputers and so-called super-microcomputers to a TOPS network with special hardware and software. The software side of the connection is achieved by installing TOPS server software on the minicomputer side, for example on a Sun workstation. A special piece of software from TOPS is installed and run on the workstation. This allows the workstation, which is running an operating system such as UNIX, to act like any other TOPS network server. Just as with Mac or PC versions of TOPS, the workstation running TOPS publishes directories for others on the network to use.

For example, if you have a Mac connected to a network on which a Sun workstation is publishing volumes, you can pull down the TOPS window and the Sun server will appear as any other, with the exception of the icon. The icon shows the specific machine type of the server. But just as when the Mac accessed a server that was a PC, that fact the Sun server is non-Macintosh doesn't matter, it is transparent to the user. Similarly, when a PC accesses a workstation server, the published volume is mounted as a drive letter.

Benefits of Minicomputer Connections

In addition to gaining direct access to the files and storage of workstation, this larger connectivity provided by TOPS can produce some other less obvious gains. Through an operating system extension on Sun and other workstations called NFS, the Macs and PCs can network to the machines from over 150 other vendors, including the likes of Cray Supercomputers. In other words, through TOPS and Sun NFS, everything from a Macintosh to a Cray Supercomputer can communicate in a single network. This is not simply a colorful exaggeration. All that is required to make such a connection work is one workstation that is a TOPS server at the same time it is an NFS client to an NFS server. The workstation in the middle acts as a gateway between TOPS and NFS. True, not every business has the need, let alone the resources, to invest in a Cray. The point is that TOPS offers an upward connectivity path to a whole world of other computing platforms.

The use of a more robust server machine such as Sun workstations can provide many times more power in a server than is available in a nondedicated or even dedicated Macintosh or PC server. Often it gives you access to a many times larger storage device as well. The operating systems used by Suns are multi-tasking by design. These machines are natural nondedicated servers. It is quite normal for these servers to handle many different server requests and computing tasks simultaneously.

Another consideration is the level of security that is built into operating systems such as Unix. In the MS-DOS computing world one has to invest in something such as Advanced Novell Netware to come close to the rich features of Unix.

Connection to Larger Sites

One way of making the wiring connection between Macs or PCs, and systems like Sun, is by connecting all the machines with Ethernet. In this case the PCs and Macintoshes would have Ethernet interfaces and plug directly into Ethernet cabling. The other option is to put the Macs and PCs on twisted pair, and bridge the twisted pair to Ethernet. One such bridge is the Kinetics FastPath. The back of the FastPath has fittings for both Ethernet and twisted pair connectors, and so bridges the two wiring systems by attaching between them, as in the diagram in Fig. 13-29.

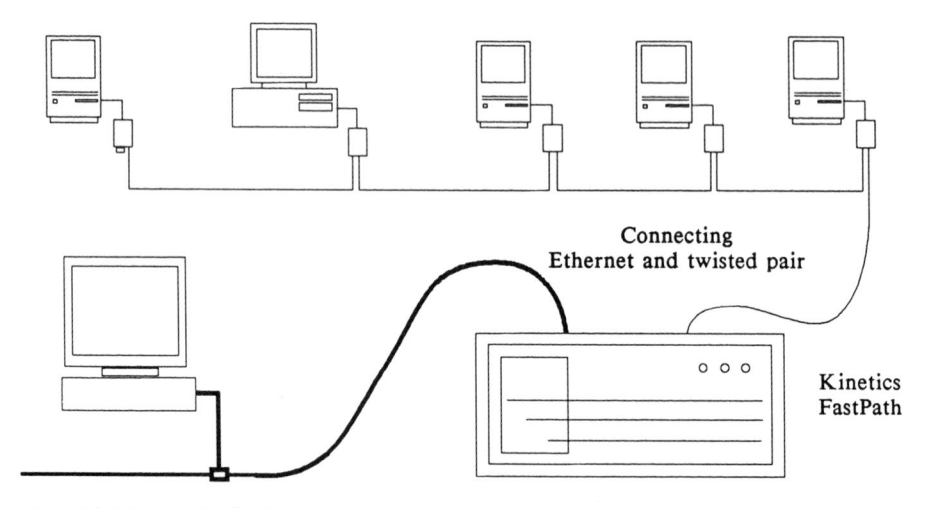

Fig. 13-29. FastPath diagram.

The FastPath can double as an AppleTalk bridge in that the Ethernet and twisted pair sides can be assigned different zone names. As you will recall, *zones* are parts of a TOPS network that are separated, but which you can access. When you use the TOPS menus, users in other zones are listed separately from those in your own zone. You can mount volumes published in other zones and use printers in other zones.

Using the FastPath is more cost effective than an all-Ethernet solution if there are many Macs and PCs on TOPS. Ethernet cards are expensive per node, whereas the FastPath's cost can be spread out among many users. The only downside is a loss of performance for those machines running on twisted pair because of its limited bandwidth.

In addition to bridging two different cabling mediums, the FastPath does a conversion of communication protocols. This is necessary because internode communication is done with Ethernet protocols on the Ethernet side, and AppleTalk on the twisted pair side. An Intel microprocessor in the FastPath runs the conversion software that repackages data as it passes through, from the protocol of its origin, to a form that's acceptable to the protocol of its destination. So for example, as a data packet enters the FastPath from the AppleTalk side, the software in the FastPath encapsulates the packet by placing an Ethernet header at the front and trailer at the back before sending it onto the Ethernet.

Kinetics is the Apple connectivity division of a networking company called Excelan. The strength of the Apple LAN market is reflected in the growing range of products available from Kinetics which has become a leading developer of open-system connectivity products that allow Apple Macintosh computers to participate transparently in multi-vendor networks. With Kinetic networking products, Macintosh users can employ standard network protocols to access systems and services in Macintosh, UNIX, and DOS environments. Some of the current offerings from Kinetics follow.

EtherPort SE. The EtherPort SE is an internal Ethernet option card for the Macintosh SE. The EtherPort SE will allow true AppleTalk software to use high-speed, high-bandwidth Ethernet transparent to the applications. The EtherPort SE provides thin Ethernet (lOBASE2) and standard Ethernet transceiver (lOBASE5) connections on the same card.

EtherPort SEL. The EtherPort SEL is the same as the EtherPort SE, but it also provides direct connection of a Macintosh SE to unshielded twisted pair Ethernet and standard Ethernet.

EtherPort II. The EtherPort II is a controller card for the Macintosh II's NuBus. This will work with both thin and standard Ethernet. The EtherPort II will allow a Macintosh II the ability to participate in an Ethernet network and communicate with other Macintosh computers and network peripherals, as well as dissimilar host computers with Ethernet capability.

EtherPort IIL. The EtherPort IIL is the same as the EtherPort II, but it also provides direct connection of a Macintosh II to unshielded twisted pair Ethernet and standard Ethernet.

EtherPort SE/30. The EtherPort SE/30 is an internal card that will provide connection of a Macintosh SE/30 to either standard or thin Ethernet. Standard AppleTalk-based software packages for file and disk service, multi-user database systems, and electronic mail can run unmodified. In addition, the EtherPort SE/30 supports TCP/IP, DECnet, and OSI protocols.

EtherPort SE/30L. The EtherPort SE/30L is the same as the EtherPort SE/30, but it also provides direct connection of a Macintosh SE/30 to unshielded twisted pair Ethernet and standard Ethernet.

FastPath. As we have mentioned, FastPath is a LocalTalk-Ethernet gateway. This will give LocalTalk networks the ability to connect to standard Ethernet networks such as the UNIX and PC networks. The FastPath supports multiple network protocols simultaneously including AppleTalk and TCP/IP. This can use standard or thin Ethernet. LAN Ranger network management software comes standard with every FastPath.

EtherSC3. EtherSC3 is a general-purpose external Ethernet connection for the Macintosh Plus, SE, or II using the SCSI interface. The Macintoshes can talk to each other using standard AppleTalk software, or to Ethernet-based Unix systems using software based on AppleTalk or other protocols. The EtherSC3 comes with built-in transceiver and BNC connector to thin and standard Ethernet transceiver.

LAN WorkPlace HostAccess. The HostAccess software provides direct access (utilities, terminal emulation, file transfer, and other applications) for the Macintosh user to multiple hosts on an Ethernet network. The HostAccess connects a wide variety of systems supporting TCP/IP.

TOPS Server Software

As mentioned before, TOPS server software for Unix or VMS allows the server to appear to Macs and PCs like any other TOPS server. This is accomplished by adding an extension to the operating system of the Unix server that allows the server to speak the AppleTalk protocol, as well as recognize and send AppleTalk data packets. In Unix, this is done by adding code to the Unix Kernel.

The result is a fairly efficient mechanism for giving clients access to Input/Output on the host. Remember that minicomputers are designed to handle more than one user at once, and more than one task. Their hardware and operating system software are optimized for multi-user, multi-tasking operations. The fact that they are required to do TOPS work in the background is no different from typical multi-user, multi-tasking operations. The overhead involved in handling TOPS server activities is a process that manages the user requests. The load created by client processing is about the same as any user logging onto the system through conventional means.

TOPS client software running on the Mac or PC will fully respect account security of the host. Users must sign on with appropriate account names and passwords. Once logged onto the host, the security of files stored there is treated the same as it is for any other of the host's users.

One noteworthy fact for the administrator who is integrating Macs and PCs into the Unix environments, is the Mac file system's requirement to store the files in two parts, and the Mac Finder's need to have a Desktop file. As happens when the Mac mounts any volume for the first time, the Mac Finder must be able to write a Desktop file to that volume. As for the resource forks, TOPS software manages them by storing them in a .rsrc directory located in the path of the published host directory. TOPS creates a table that keeps track of the Macintosh HFS relationships.

File Conversion

Minicomputer version of TOPS, such as Sun/TOPS, do not have full featured document translators like the Macintosh version comes with, but it does have utilities to convert text (ASCII) files. Unix text, Mac text, and DOS text are all basically the same, but they do differ in how they end their lines. The utilities of Sun/TOPS convert the end-of-line characters from one format to the other. The three utilities are aptly named tomac, tounix, and topc, and are as easy to use as typing tomac -c [path]filename to convert a file from Unix or DOS text to Mac text and vice versa.

Printing on SUN/TOPS

TOPS for the Sun also contains print software that allows you to print from a Sun workstation to a PostScript LaserWriter that is attached on the AppleTalk side of a Kinetics FastPath. Once the TOPS/Sun print utility has been installed, you can print from the workstation using standard document processing commands. It works because TOPS for the Sun creates a new filter for the lpr process that converts the Unix file to PostScript, and supports printing to the AppleTalk addressed printers. The product can also be used in conjunction with other Sun printing products such as Transcript.

REMOTE ACCESS

A *modem* is a device that enables computers to communicate. Short for *modulator-demodulator*, a modem takes data and turns it into a signal that can be sent over wires and telephone lines. A typical use of a modem is to connect your personal computer with bulletin boards and on-line databases. In computer terms, a *bulletin board* is a hardware/software combination that allows the posting of messages and exchange of information via computer. A typical arrangement is a personal computer with a large hard disk and a modem, as seen in Fig. 13-30.

Users of the bulletin board dial its phone number with their computer/modem. The bulletin board system, called the *host* in this situation, answers the phone and a connection is established. The user may be asked to sign in, or log in, possibly by entering a name and/or password which the bulletin board software checks again its records. When log-in is complete, the user can access the messages, read them, and reply. Files stored on the bulletin board system can be copied to the system that is calling in, a process called *downloading*. The caller can add to the information stored on the bulletin board by copying files to the host, a process known as *uploading*. This is a great piece of technology for spreading certain kinds of information. Indeed, TOPS operates a bulletin board service to provide answers to questions and

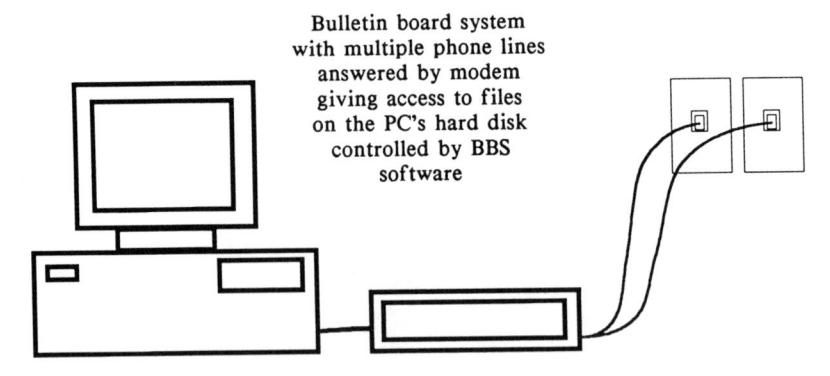

Fig. 13-30. Bulletin board system.

make useful software available to users. The TOPS Bulletin Board Service (BBS) is at 415-769-8774. The service operates at 300, 1200 and 2400 baud. Set your communications software to 8 data bits, 1 stop bit, no parity.

A larger incarnation of the bulletin board is the on-line database, operated on large computers with thousands of users. A popular on-line database is CompuServe which contains news and information about a wide range of subjects, particularly computers. This information is stored on large computers that have modems attached to them. TOPS provides technical information in the Apple Vendors Forum on CompuServe, use GO APPVENA to reach it.

Modems are of significance to networks for several reasons. They allow computers that are remote from the network to access it, either to perform simple file retrieval and storage, or to participate in a full range of network activities. Modems also allow a complete bridge between two networks that are too far apart for network wiring. Using the telephone line as an extension of the network wiring modems can connect two networks into one. Furthermore, a modem can be shared between users on a network, providing each user with a way to contact remote bulletin boards without having to fit each computer with a modem.

BRIDGING TOPS NETWORKS TO REMOTE SITES

In the chapter on cabling, references were made to the ability to link two remote TOPS (AppleTalk) networks together with network bridges. In this way, two physically separate networks at two physically different sites, can act as one large network. Users can mount servers, send mail, and send print jobs to machines at the remote site just as easily as with machines at the local site. This bridging is possible through the products of several different companies. Most of these solutions come from Macintosh-oriented companies and so are Macintosh-oriented solutions. There are, however, companion products that allow PCs to also work in these environments. What follows is a brief overview of how these bridging products work.

The Basics of Bridging

Two things must happen for effective bridging of remote networks. First, a connection must be established between the sites. Many of the following solutions establish these connections through some kind of hardware device that includes or works with a modem, and most likely sends data over a public telephone line. A private or leased line could also be used, but in general private lines are much more expensive and aren't necessary. Quite often the hardware that is used is an intelligent bridge. Among the makers of these products are Shiva, Hayes, and Solano. You can refer to Appendix B for more information on these third-party networking products and their suppliers. Intelligent bridges are supplied with software that stores the network configuration and dials the phone number of a bridge at the other site. This information is downloaded into and stored within the bridge device.

Liaison, a product from Infosphere, is a software-only bridge. It uses the storage and memory of a Macintosh to allow the machine itself to act as a bridge. Liaison allows any Macintosh II with a modem to work as a bridge to a similarly equipped Macintosh II at the remote site.

The second thing that needs to be accomplished in a bridging connection is an adaptation of the network signals that normally run on LocalTalk or twisted pair wiring to a signal that will work with a modem. This task is usually accomplished with software. Something called an *asynchronous driver* comes with the bridging companies product that allows AppleTalk connections to be maintained through the modem and over the telephone wire. *Asynchronous* is a term for the type of communication that low-cost computer modems typically use.

The diagram in Fig. 13-31 depicts how a remote link would be set up with the Hayes InterBridge.

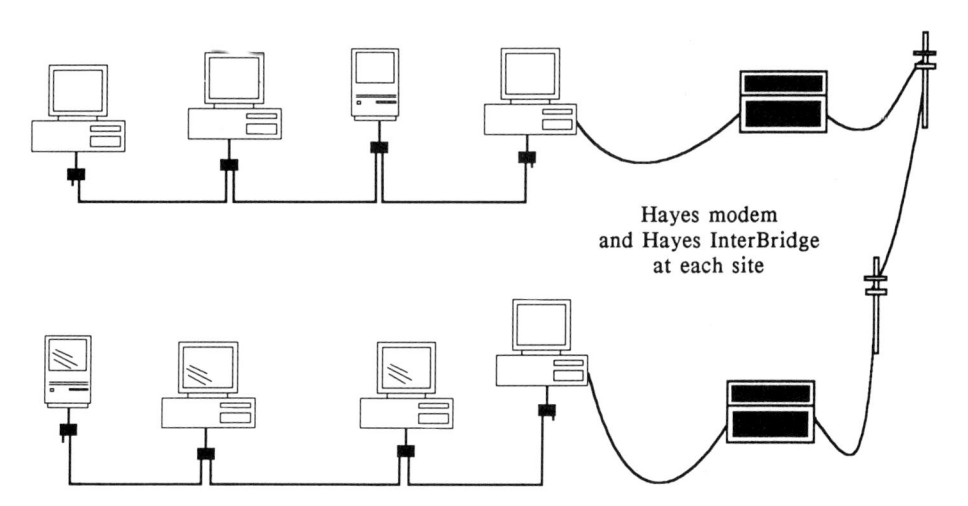

Fig. 13-31. A Hayes Interbridge connection.

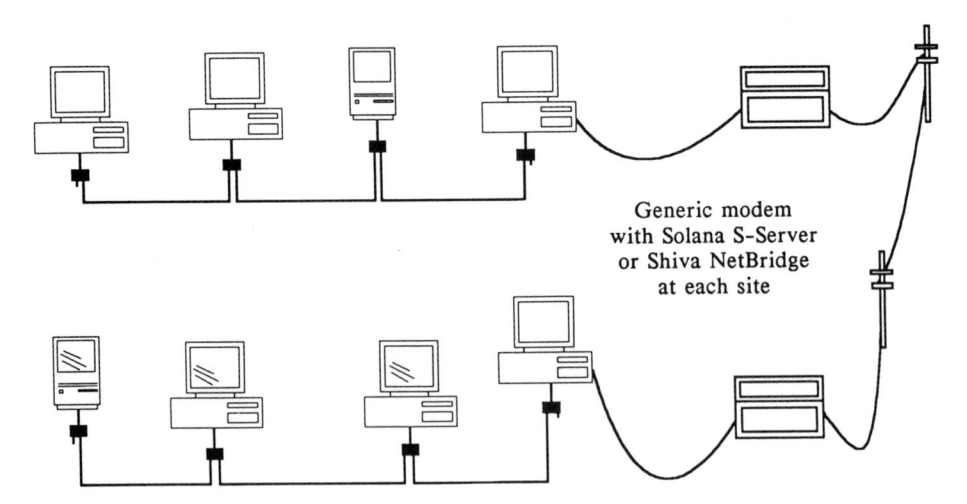

Fig. 13-32. Alternative bridge.

The InterBridge connection only works with a Hayes modem and is able to communicate only with another InterBridge. One must be placed at either site, along with a modem. Slightly different versions of the InterBridge connection are provided by products from Shiva Solano. In Fig. 13-32, you can see a connection where a generic modem is being used with either Shiva's NetBridge, or Solana's S-Server.

A software solution that does away with the need for a separate bridge device is Liaison. The only hardware needed for remote access is a modem. Liaison lets you designate which peripherals on the network can be access from remote locations. One system on the network acts as a Liaison server. A copy of Liaison must be on both connecting systems.

A slightly different type of remote access to your network is provided by Timbuktu Remote. Using a Mac and a modem at a remote location you can call up a modem-equipped Mac back at the office and, using the Timbuktu Remote software, take over control of the office Mac. You can issue commands and run applications from a distance, just as though you were at the keyboard of the office system. This makes possible remote support of users, monitoring of activity, and intervention to solve problems. Timbuktu Remote also permits the exchange of files and messages between the two machines. Of course, both must be equipped with the Timbuktu Remote software.

A different version of distant access is provided by Telefinder. With Telefinder, you cannot take over a remote Mac, but you get low-level access, which means file transfer between systems and message exchange. Another package that offers low-level remote access between Macs is Okyto, from the makers of the popular communications program, Red Ryder. A unique feature of Okyto is the ability to *multiplex*, that is, perform several different communication activities at once. For example, you can exchange messages saying that you want to transfer a file between your remote Mac and the one in the office, begin the transfer, and then continue exchanging messages while the file transfer takes place in the background.

Tips for Remote Bridging

Telephone linked networks are very cost effective within local calling areas. But unfortunately, as the distance between networks extends into long-distance calling zones, it becomes fairly expensive to maintain a constantly open connection between sites. Over long distance lines, it might make more sense to compromise with a half-bridged network from one remote location to another.

A *half-bridged network* means that only one of the linked sites has an intelligent bridge, the other site would probably have only dial-up software. The big difference between a half bridge and a full bridge, is that with a half bridge, the communication to the remote network is one way only, and occurs only with the specific machine that dialed up the other network. The remote computer that calls into another network can see into the network, but the network cannot see out to the other site. With half-bridged networks, the remote site can call in, complete the business on hand, and then hang up. The line does not have to be constantly kept open as with a full bridge.

Half bridges give up some features that full bridges permit, such as complete bidirectional networking of all nodes, but half bridges still have many useful applications. A half bridge is ideal, for example, for the traveling salesperson who gets to a hotel room after the home office has closed and wants to read and send some E-mail messages back to the office on his or her laptop computer from the hotel room. With dial-up software and a modem in the laptop, the salesperson can call the office bridge and read and send messages anytime day or night. They could even send print jobs to the company's Laserwriter.

The same companies that make the full bridges usually sell products to permit half-bridging. Shiva for one, has remote dial-up software for both the Macintosh and PC.

NETWORK MODEMS, FAXES, AND SO FORTH

Specialized communications equipment is one more area where the cost-sharing aspect of network can be explored. These days a reliable auto-dial/auto-answer 1200 baud modem can be purchased for under $200. You can achieve twice the speed with a 2400 baud unit for less than $400. However, if you have five users on a network who all want to use a modem at one time or another to contact a remote database, then you could be faced with $2,000 to equip each one with a good modem. If you raise the speed limit to 9600 baud, the stakes are even higher. At close to a $1,000 per unit, these high-speed modems are attractive in that they substantially reduce connect time. But it will take $5,000 to equip each of five users with their own modem. A better approach might be a network modem, one that serves multiple users connected on a network. Although expensive, this type of modem means that you can take advantage of connections at less total cost. See Appendix B for vendors of network modems.

The rapidly emerging technology of facsimile machines is giving rise to another genre of equipment that can be cost-effectively shared among a group of networked PC users. FAX cards for Macs and PCs are gaining ground as alternatives to stand-alone FAX machines. These cards can manage FAX operations in the background while you are performing other work. They allow you to compose FAX messages from documents on your computer and then send them out. Incoming messages can be read, stored, and printed from the computer keyboard. Look for network-compatible computer FAX systems to emerge, allowing several users to access FAX transmissions through one unit.

14
Tips and Tricks and Other Connections

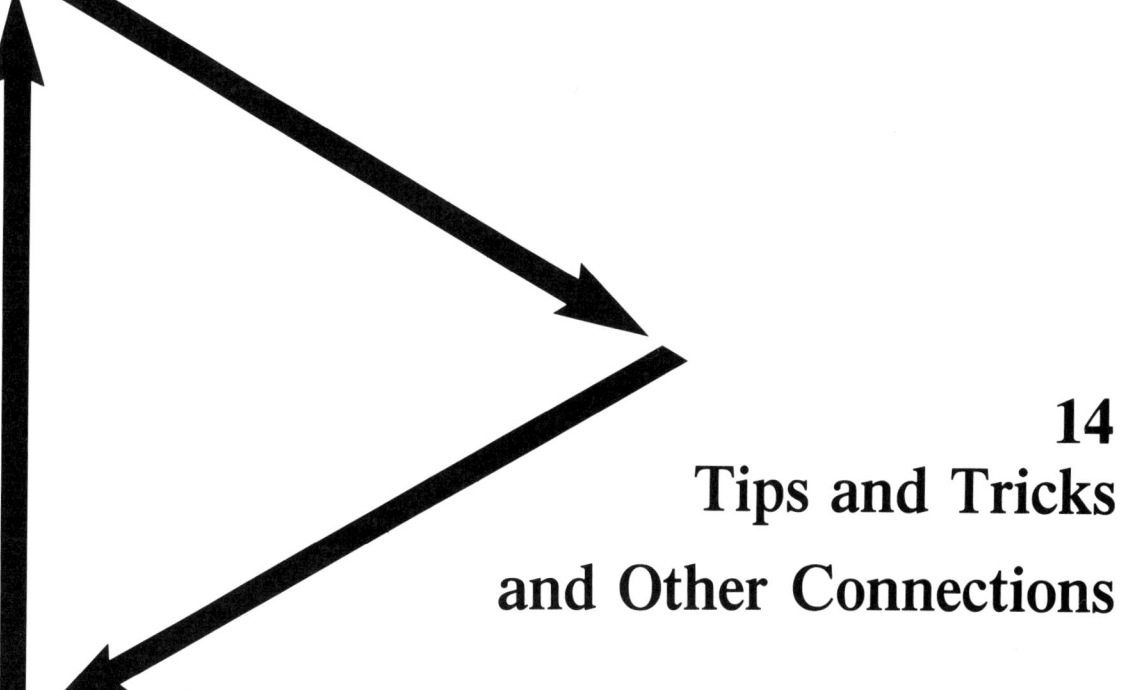

THIS CHAPTER COVERS A VARIETY OF SUBJECTS including techniques for installing network gateways and using TOPS with specialized software such as DESQview and Windows. We also look closely at the need for circumventing the memory constraints of DOS and at memory management techniques that might be helpful.

TIPS FOR TOPS GATEWAYS

This section contains suggestions to help you set up a PC as a TOPS gateway. TOPS networks can be linked to other PC LANs, thereby giving Macs or PCs on the TOPS network the ability to share files with the LAN server. The link-up is obtained by installing TOPS in one of the PC LAN stations, thereby making that station a gateway between the two networks. Note that TOPS cannot be installed on a PC LAN dedicated server. Also note that because the gateway machine is running both the PC LAN software as well as TOPS, there is normally not enough RAM to also run most standard application programs. For this reason the gateway machine is, in most cases, a dedicated gateway.

A General Guide

The installation of TOPS on the gateway PC depends on the particularities of the PC LAN hardware and software, but is relatively straightforward. Once installed, TOPS can then be used to publish the LAN virtual drives, making files on the LAN server available to stations on the TOPS network. The general procedure is as follows:

1. Before loading your LAN software, but with your LAN interface card installed, install TOPS on your gateway station. Any hardware conflicts between the TOPS FlashCard (or other AppleTalk interface card) and the PC LAN network interface card must be resolved. This can require, for example, changing the TOPS FlashCard's board interrupt and/or DMA channel. Refer to the TOPS FlashCard manual or Appendix D of this book for more on how to make these modifications.

2. Some PC LAN operating systems conflict with the TOPS FlashCard's network access interrupt, thereby requiring you to change the interrupt from its default value of 5C to, say, 5D. The setting should be changed on most bridge nodes.

3. With all these conflicts eliminated, the PC LAN software and TOPS software can both be run simultaneously. After rebooting, the normal loading sequence is to first load the PC LAN software shell, then link the PC to the server, as normal, by designating virtual drives. Once the LAN software is loaded, then load the TOPS software (using LOADTOPS).

4. You can automate the startup process for your gateway by putting loading commands in your AUTOEXEC.BAT file, making sure that you load the other LAN software before the TOPS software. Remember that if the LOADTOPS command is executed within the AUTOEXEC.BAT file, it must be preceded by COMMAND/C (DOS 3.1 and 3.2) or by CALL (DOS 3.3) if it is not the last line in the batch file.

5. If you have problems identifying volumes through the TOPS MENU or from the DOS command line, try using the XSYNC command on the volume from the DOS command line, then publish the volume without the XSYNC option.

6. Note that when you link the PC to the LAN server through virtual drive designations, TOPS must be told to regard these virtual drives as physical drives. Before loading your TOPS software, you should modify the drive map line of the TOPSKRNL.DAT file so that your LAN virtual drives are shown as hard drives or, in some cases, floppies. If they are not listed in the drive map, virtual drives will not be available for publishing. You can then load your TOPS networking software and still have access to your LAN virtual drives.

Using the Gateway

Once you have completed the setup as described, publish the LAN virtual drives. They can then be mounted on other stations on the TOPS network, thereby enabling Macintoshes or PCs on the TOPS network to access the LAN server via the gateway. Normally, when publishing directories or drives to a TOPS network, any changes to those directories are automatically seen on your TOPS client stations. However, in the case of a LAN gateway, if your TOPS network contains Macintosh or other non-PC machines, then it is necessary to update the TOPS directory of LAN files periodically. This requires a utility called XDAEMON which can be obtained from the TOPS Bulletin Board or from TOPS Customer Service.

TOPS and PC LAN Compatibility

A number of PC LAN software products and network interface cards are available on the market. Those which have been tested in a gateway configuration with TOPS are listed in Table 14-1. The Tops FlashCard configurations required to eliminate hardware conflicts with LAN interface cards that have been encountered by TOPS are given in Table 14-2. Review some of the more common gateway configurations in the following sections.

Using TOPS with 3Com

The suggested procedure for setting up a TOPS-3Com gateway is to get the computer working on the 3Com network then add the FlashCard and make sure that TOPS and the other network both work together. Note that these instructions can work as a basis for establishing other popular gateways. The equipment required for a TOPS-3Com gateway is as follows:

- IBM PC/XT/AT or compatible (640K RAM recommended)
- 3Com EtherLink Card
- TOPS FlashCard
- TOPS TeleConnector (DB-9)
- PC/MS-DOS Version 3.1 or higher

Table 14-1. Gateway configurations.

Software	Hardware
3COM 3+	3COM EtherLink
Grapevine	Grapevine
Nestar SR-6	Nestar NIC
Novell	3COM EtherLink
Novell	IBM Token Ring PC Adapter
Novell	Standard Microsystems ARCnet
PC-NFS	3COM EtherLink
Starlan	Starlan
Ungermann-Bass	Ungermann-Bass NIUpc

- 3COM 3+ Share Client Version 1.2.1 or later
- TOPS/DOS Version 2.01 or later

The first stage in setting up your TOPS-3Com gateway is to install the 3Com and FlashTalk cards in the gateway computer, then get TOPS up and running. Begin by installing the TOPS FlashCard and FlashCard driver. To eliminate hardware con-

Table 14-2. TOPS settings for gateways.

3COM Etherlink*:
    Set DMA=3 for ATs
    Set DMA=none for PC/XT
        (It is also possible to change DMA channels on the 3Com card instead)

IBM Token Ring*:
    Set Board Interrupt=3

Standard Microsystems ARCnet*:
    Set Board Interrupt=3

Ungermann-Bass*:
    Set Board Interrupt=3
    Set DMA=3 for ATs
    Set DMA =none for PC/XT

Nestar Network Interface Card*:
    Set Board Interrupt=3
    Set DMA=3 for ATs
    Set DMA=none for PC/XT

AT&T Starlan*:
    Set Board Interrupt=3
    Set DMA=3 for ATs
    Set DMA=none for PC/XTIBM PC-Net

Novell S-Net:
    Set Board Interrupt=3

Gateway G-Net:
    Set Gateway to IRQ=4

Local Net D-Link:
    Set Board Interrupt=3
    Set DMA=3 for ATs
    Set DMA=none for PC/XT

Corvus Omninet Card:
    Set Board Interrupt=3
    or change IRQ on Corvus

flicts with the 3Com card, configure the TOPS FlashCard and driver so that the board uses address 310. The board interrupt should be IRQ 3. Set DMA to 3 for an AT. Set DMA to none for a PC/XT. To eliminate software conflicts with the 3Com software, configure the software interrupt as INT=60 although any value between 5D and 6F should be OK.

These configurations require some changes in the FlashCard as described in Appendix D. Use the following parameters with the ALAP command when using LOADTOPS:

ALAP /boardint=3 /address=310 /dma=none /int=60

This should eliminate any hardware conflicts between the FlashCard and the 3Com board. If you have other boards in the gateway it may be necessary to make other modifications. Remember to make sure that the Files=20 and Buffers=20 settings are included in your CONFIG.SYS. Now reboot the gateway computer and load the TOPS software. Make sure that you can communicate with other stations on the TOPS network.

Next you should reboot the gateway computer and load the 3Com client software. Log in to the 3Com server and connect with the server using the link command.

The next step is to configure your TOPS software for use as a gateway by modifying the TOPSKRNL.DAT file. Under the Station Name, assign your gateway computer a unique name. Under Drive Map, modify the last line to indicate all virtual drives linked to the 3Com server. For example, suppose drives D, E, and F are used to link up to the 3Com server. Change the drive map to indicate the virtual drives D, E and F as hard drives. The drive map should read FFHHHHUUUU. If you are mapping to drives beyond J, you must change the "last drive" parameter and the drive map accordingly. See Chapter 4 for more explanation of the drive map in TOPSKRNL.DAT.

Now load your TOPS software and publish your 3Com drives to the TOPS network. Any TOPS network stations that mount these volumes will have access to the 3Com server. Before publishing drives, make sure that the proper permission for read/write exists on the 3Com server.

If your TOPS network contains Macintosh or other non-PC machines, you also need to load XDAEMON. This is a utility that allows all TOPS network stations to see changes made on the 3Com server by periodically updating the TOPS directory of files. Check the XDAEMON documentation for details.

If your gateway works properly, you can automate the startup process by putting 3Com and TOPS loading commands in your AUTOEXEC.BAT file, making sure that you load the 3Com software before the TOPS software. If you encounter problems publishing volumes through the TOPS MENU or from the DOS command line try using the XSYNC command on the volume from the DOS command line, then publish the volume without the XSYNC option.

A TOPS/NOVELL Gateway with 3Com EtherLink Card

This gateway is installed using the same basic procedure as the TOPS-3Com, using the following equipment:

- IBM PC/XT/AT or compatible (640K RAM recommended)
- 3Com EtherLink Card
- TOPS FlashCard
- TOPS Teleconnector (DB-9)
- PC/MS-DOS Version 3.1 or higher
- Novell Advanced Netware 286 version 2.0A or later
- TOPS/DOS Version 2.01 or later

Use the same board and ALAP settings as above. When you have made sure that TOPS works after installing both the EtherLink card and the FlashCard reboot the gateway computer. Load the Novell Netware shell. Log in to the Novell server. Link up to the Server using the MAP command.

Next, configure your TOPS software for use as a gateway by modifying the TOPSKRNL.DAT file. Following the instructions in the previous section, modify the drive MAP to indicate all virtual drives linked to the Novell server. Now you can load TOPS and publish your Novell drives to the TOPS network. Be sure that before publishing drives, the proper permission for read/write exists on the Novell server. If your TOPS network contains Macintosh or other non-PC machines, you also need to load XDAEMON, the utility that allows all TOPS network stations to see changes made on the Novell server by periodically updating the TOPS directory of files. If you automate the startup process by putting Novell and TOPS loading commands into your AUTOEXEC.BAT file, be sure to load the Novell software before the TOPS software. Also, be sure you do not use Novell search drives on the gateway. If encounter problems publishing volumes through the TOPS MENU or from the DOS command line, XSYNC the volume from the DOS command line then publish the volume without the XSYNC option.

A TOPS/NOVELL Gateway with ARCnet Cards

This gateway works with the following equipment:

- IBM PC/XT/AT or compatible (640K RAM recommended)
- Standard Microsystems Corp. ARCnet pc-210 card
- TOPS FlashCard
- TOPS TeleConnector (DB-9)
- PC/MS-DOS Version 3.1 or higher
- Novell Advanced Netware Version 2.0a
- TOPS/DOS Version 2.01

The steps are the same as those in the preceding section, including the ALAP settings which should prevent conflict with the ARCnet card. Remember to make the necessary changes to the FlashCard board as well as using the proper software settings.

A TOPS/Novell Gateway with IBM Token Ring PC Adapter

This gateway works using the following equipment

- PC/XT/AT or compatible computer (640K RAM recommended)
- IBM Token Ring PC Adapter
- TOPS FlashCard
- TOPS TeleConnector (DB-9)
- PC/MS-DOS Version 3.1 or higher
- IBM Token Ring driver
- TOPS/DOS Version 2.01 or later

The Token Ring driver can be any of the following:

- TOKREUI or TOKREUI & NETBEUI
- DXMAOMOD.SYS & DXMCOMOD.SYS
- Novell 286 Version 2.0A (ANET3 shell generated for Token Ring, configuration #1 of 4, primary adapter for GENOS/GENSH).

To eliminate hardware conflicts with the Token Ring card, configure the TOPS FlashCard and ALAP as follows:

```
ALAP /boardint=3 /address=310 /int=5D
```

If you still need help setting up a gateway, or with other aspects of connecting with TOPS, you can contact TOPS Technical Support at 415-769-8711 or the TOPS Bulletin Board Service (BBS) at 415-769-8774. The service operates at 300, 1200, and 2400 baud. Set your communications software to 8 data bits, 1 stop bit, no parity. TOPS technical questions can also be answered over AppleLink (D0098) or in the TOPS user conferences on the BIX and CompuServe networks.

A TOPS/PC-NFS Gateway

This gateway connects a TOPS network to a PC LAN that uses the NFS protocol. NFS stands for Network File System, designed and promoted by Sun Microsystems as a means of providing transparent access to remote file systems so that data on any computer can appear like local data to any other computer. NFS is part of ONC, Open Network Computing. This is a product family promoted by Sun and endorsed by many other vendors with the goal of connectivity in mind. The idea is that by following some common guidelines for software architecture across operating system boundaries, more computers will be able to talk to each and share data, with less inconvenience to the user. To this end, Sun has freely shared the NFS protocols with other vendors.

You can set up a PC-NFS gateway to Sun computer systems with the following:

- an AT compatible 80286 or 80386 system
- a 3Com EtherLink Card as PC-NFS card
- TOPS FlashCard
- TOPS Teleconnector (DB-9)
- PC/MS-DOS Version 3.1 or latter
- PC-NFS Version 2.81
- TOPS/DOS Version 2.0 or latter

With the PC-NFS card installed in the gateway computer, install the TOPS FlashCard and FlashCard driver. Configure the TOPS FlashCard and driver as to eliminate hardware/software conflicts with the PC-NFS card (Board address of 310, Board Interrupt = 3, DMA = 3 on an 80286, possibly DMA = none on an 80386, Access Interrupt = 60). These changes should eliminate conflicts between the FlashCard and the 3Com card.

After rebooting the gateway computer, load the TOPS networking software, and verify a connection with other stations on the TOPS network. Reboot again and load the PC-NFS software. Run the NFSCONF program. Link up to the Sun drives using the menu system. Now configure your TOPS software for use as a gateway by modifying the TOPSKRNL.DAT file as in previous examples, giving it a unique name and modifying the drive map to indicate all virtual drives linked to the PC-NFS server. Now load your TOPS software and publish your PC-NFS drives to the TOPS network. Any TOPS network stations that mount these volumes will have access to the Sun server. Before publishing PC-NFS drives, you should check that the proper read/write permissions exist on the Sun server. Use chmod 777. As with other gateway situations, if your TOPS network contains Macintosh or other non-PC machines, you also need to load XDAEMON.

Note that you can also create a TOPS to Sun gateway using the TOPS/Sun product running on your Sun. This provides a smooth connection to Sun systems which can then act as a gateway to many diverse systems that use NFS.

Using TOPS with Unix

If you work in a mixed Macintosh and Unix environment, you might have noticed some differences in the way the two systems structure files. The Unix file structure is very similar to the DOS file structure, and also very different from the Macintosh. TOPS/Sun also implements a procedure for storing both forks of a Macintosh file on the Unix server. Each Unix directory used by TOPS contains a subdirectory named .rsrc. When a Macintosh file is stored on a Sun workstation by a Macintosh TOPS user, the data fork is placed in the main directory and a file corresponding to the resource fork is placed in the .rsrc subdirectory.

To see how this works in practice, consider a Macintosh user on the network who creates a folder, or Unix directory, on the Unix volume. The volume is called marty and stores Macintosh files. When you are on a Unix workstation and use Unix commands to view the contents of the directory, you can see the files containing the Macintosh data forks in marty:

```
manager% ls -a  marty
   .rsrc   doc    notes
   account  help
```

The files containing the resource forks appear in marty/.rsrc, as in:

```
manager% ls -a marty/.rsrc
.     account   help
..    doc       notes
```

Then to copy, move, or delete Macintosh files stored on a Unix computer, first publish them, mount the folders on your Macintosh, and then use Finder to drag or delete the files. If you are on a Unix computer and want to copy, move, or delete a Macintosh file, you must remember to perform the operation on both the resource and data forks. To copy the file called sales to the directory /usr/local/marty, enter the commands:

```
manager% cp sales /usr/local/marty
manager% cp .rsrc/sales/usr/local/marty/.rsrc
```

To move the file doc into the directory /usr/local/marty, enter the command:

```
manager% mv doc /usr/local/marty
manager% mv .rsrc/doc /usr/local/marty/.rsrc
```

Finally, to delete the file called notes in marty, enter:

```
manager% rm notes manager% rm .rsrc/notes
```

If you copy a Macintosh application to a PC or Unix server, any Macintosh on the network can access the application if the PC or Unix volume is published. Once the Macintosh user mounts the volume containing the application, he or she can work on existing documents or even create new ones—and store them back on the PC or Unix hard disk or any other available disk on the network.

Storing your Macintosh applications on a PC or Unix hard disk turns the PC or Unix computer into a file server for the Macintosh. If your Macintosh doesn't have a hard disk, this method can be more convenient than using a floppy. It provides you with a lot more storage, and it is also somewhat faster.

Even if your Macintosh has its own hard disk, copying your applications and files onto another computer can be a useful backup system, however bear in mind the "for archival purposes only" rule and abide by the software license agreement when using an application on the network.

As you might know, the Macintosh has two file system models. The older flat file system called MFS has no hierarchy (folders are an illusion maintained by the system software), and the newer Hierarchical File System (called HFS) has files that are contained in folders nested within a hierarchy of folders. TOPS supports both MFS and HFS. Because the Macintosh HFS file system is different from the Unix file system, there are issues you should be aware of that affect the TOPS interaction between Macintoshes running HFS and Unix-based computers.

HFS is fully supported by TOPS/Sun version 2.1, and is transparent to users of the TOPS network. When a Macintosh TOPS client wishes to access a file stored on the Unix server, a *daemon* (Unix program running in the background) on the server is consulted to determine the Unix directory name corresponding to the Macintosh directory number. This daemon, **rpc.hfsd,** maintains the directory number and pathname database.

The Macintosh directory number and Unix pathname database is initialized by invoking the utility program *hfs build*. This program is run automatically at startup time and whenever a new directory is published. No intervention is necessary either by the System Administrator or the clients of the Unix server.

Current versions of the Macintosh Finder (6.1 and earlier) maintain a file called the Desktop that contains information about Macintosh folders and files. The Desktop file is used to hold information relating to the size, shape, and position of windows, the type of file display (large icon, small icon, by name, etc.), and file notes. When you make a change to one of these things, the Finder records that change by writing it in the Desktop file. A new Desktop file is also written to a published volume when you mount that volume on a Macintosh client.

Whenever a volume is accessed with the Macintosh Finder, the Finder looks for a Desktop file. If it does not find one, it attempts to create one. When a volume is published initially, it must be published either One writer only or Many writers for the Macintosh Finder to accept and create an icon for it. Once a Desktop file has been created for a particular volume, the volume can be published read-only. The Finder will then be able to use the mounted TOPS volume.

The present version of the Macintosh Finder was not designed for multi-user access. This can cause some confusion when more than one client tries to access the same volume, because only one Finder at a time can write to the Desktop file. When two clients have mounted a volume, the first user's Finder gets write access to the Desktop File. The second user has read-only access, but his or her Macintosh gives no indication that this is the case. Consequently, the second user has the illusion of writing to the Desktop, but in fact, no changes (changing comments in the Get Info box of a file or rearranging a window, for example) are recorded. This confusion can be avoided by publishing a volume One writer only over TOPS. Then users will see a padlock icon in the upper left corner of the Desktop if someone else is writing to the folder.

SOME SPECIAL SITUATIONS

The next few sections cover a variety of technical areas in which you might need assistance when running your TOPS network. They include problems running TOPSMENU, compatibility with AppleTalk networks, and setting up NetPrint with Microsoft Word on the PC.

Problems with TWINDOW

You might have noticed the program TWINDOVL.EXE on your TOPS/DOS disks and in the TOPS directory. This is an overlay program that provides a windowing environment for TOPSMENU and for TOPS NetPrint's installation and configuration programs. As a TOPS user, you do not run TWINDOW directly. It is automatically called by the aforementioned programs when they are invoked. On some PCs, you might get a message No available interrupts for TWINDOVL.EXE when running TOPSMENU. This means that the BIOS in your machine does not clear the interrupt vectors upon booting, and the program that called it, that is TOPSMENU, aborts.

There are several possible solutions to this problem. The most immediate is to avoid using TOPSMENU or CONFIGURE by issuing commands from the DOS command line. For example, use the command language

TOPS /Q MOUNT J: TO Fred Excel /RW

to mount the volume that Fred published as Excel on your system as drive J with read/write privileges, rather than use TOPSMENU.EXE. As you recall from Chapter 9, command line requests to TOPS are processed by TOPS.EXE.

A more lasting approach might be to get your computer's manufacturer to provide you with a ROM BIOS that initializes the *interrupt vector table* in a more conventional manner. What is meant by vector interrupt table is described in the next section, which will help the technically adept to effect a "hack" or fix for this problem using the DOS utility called DEBUG.

By way of background, we should say that TWINDOVL requires an available interrupt vector in the range 60–67 hex. TWINDOVL defines an available interrupt vector as one that contains either hex zeroes (00 00 00 00) or a pointer to the assembler instruction IRET (dummy interrupt return). It requires this in an attempt to be programmatically "polite." If it simply installed itself at interrupt 60 (or some other interrupt vector), regardless of whether or not some other interrupt handler were already installed at that location, nasty things could happen. So, TWINDOVL scans the interrupt table from 60–67, looking for an unused interrupt or dummy return. It is the job of a computer's ROM BIOS to initialize the interrupt vector table at boot time. The ROM BIOS in certain machines puts neither zeroes nor pointers to dummy returns in any of the interrupt vectors in the range 60–67, thus causing the above error to occur.

With the DOS DEBUG utility you can patch an interrupt vector in the range 60–67 with zeroes, so that it is available for use by TWINDOVL. The procedure is as follows:

1. Determine which interrupt vector you wish to patch. It is necessary to select an interrupt that isn't being used. In this example, we patch interrupt 60.

2. Determine the beginning and ending address of the interrupt vector to be patched. The beginning address of interrupt 60 is 0:180, and the ending address is 0:183 (each interrupt is four bytes long).

3. Using the DOS COPY CON command, EDLIN, or some other text editor, create a text file with the following lines:

    f 0:180 183 0
    q

    Note that in line one, 0:180 183 is the beginning and ending address of interrupt 60. If you were patching interrupt 61, the line would read:

    f 0:184 187 0

4. Give the file a name. In this example, we name it ZEROMEM.

5. In your AUTOEXEC.BAT file, place the command

    DEBUG<ZEROMEM

    where ZEROMEM is the name of the text file you created. Note that the < sign tells DOS to take input from the file that follows the <.

From now on, every time you boot your computer, an interrupt vector will be made available to TWINDOVL.

Compatibility between AppleShare and TOPS

With newer versions of the AppleShare network, chooser volumes mounted on an AppleShare client by AppleShare can be published via TOPS on the same Mac to the TOPS network. This means that if you are connected to an AppleShare server and mount the volume Fred from the server, you can then publish Fred to the TOPS network. The AppleShare volume Fred is then available for access from any TOPS station on the network, including MS-DOS machines. This way TOPS allows MS-DOS connectivity to the AppleShare server. Any AppleShare volumes that are mounted on a client Mac and then published via TOPS will appear in the available volumes list of a PC TOPS window. The volume can then be mounted by the PC and accessed like any other TOPS volume.

However, AppleShare users should be aware of several issues. TOPS does not recognize the folder access rights of AppleShare. Publishing an AppleShare volume via TOPS gives the same access privileges to every TOPS station that can access the volume. If an AppleShare user published a private volume or folder via TOPS, the volume or folder would be globally available to every TOPS station. When an AppleShare volume is accessed through any TOPS station, it appears to the AppleShare server that the AppleShare client who originally mounted the volume is accessing the server. Thus the access rights of the original client are extended to all TOPS stations and bypass the privilege scheme on the AppleShare server.

In a mixed AppleShare/TOPS environment, volume and folders can be safely accessed through AppleShare or TOPS but not both at the same time. An AppleShare volume or folder that has been first mounted by an AppleShare client and then published via TOPS should not then be mounted through both AppleShare and TOPS simultaneously on another AppleShare client Mac.

AppleShare shows all folders on the mounted volume, whether or not the client has access rights to the folders. If an AppleShare volume has first been mounted by an AppleShare client, published via TOPS on the client Mac, then viewed through the TOPS window on any TOPS station, all the folders in the volume are listed. If the volume is mounted via TOPS and private folders are opened with the Finder, the folder's window is empty. Attempting to mount a private folder via TOPS causes an error message.

TOPS should not be installed on the AppleShare server Macintosh. The reason for this is that AppleShare keeps a copy of the server directory that would not be properly updated if a server volume is modified by clients using TOPS stations. The TOPS installation on the AppleShare server Macintosh might work if all volumes were published from the server Mac as read-only volumes, though there is probably no reason to configure a network as such.

Microsoft Word and NetPrint

Unless otherwise stated, the following comments apply to versions 2.x, 3.x, 4.x, and 5.0 of Microsoft Word. For Word to print properly to an Apple LaserWriter over NetPrint, you must first modify both its landscape and portrait mode initialization files. An initialization file is a PostScript dictionary defining terms used by Microsoft Word's PostScript driver. This file must be appended to the print file, or sent to the LaserWriter beforehand, for the LaserWriter to properly interpret Microsoft Word's PostScript output.

If you have Word 3.x, the portrait and landscape initialization files are named APPLASER.INI and APPLAND.INI. If you have Word 4.0 or 5.0, the files are named POSTSCRP.INI and POSTSCRL.INI. If you have Word 2.x, the portrait initialization file is named MSSETUP.PS (there is no landscape mode initialization file). The exact same modifications must be made to both the portrait and landscape initialization files. However, we only show the portrait mode modifications in the steps below.

Word 2.x. Copy MSSETUP.PS to MSSETUP.OLD. Using Word, make four editing changes in MSSETUP.PS. Two lines at the beginning of the file must be commented out and made inactive. Do this by adding percent signs to the beginning of the line. The two lines originally look like:

```
userdict /msdict known {stop} if
serverdict begin 0 exitserver
```

The modified lines look like:

    %userdict /msdict known {stop} if
    %serverdict begin 0 exitserver

Search the file for the words currentfile closefile. Use the SEARCH feature of Word to locate them. These two words will appear between two brackets flanked by /PSe and def, such as:

    /PSe {...currentfile closefile...} def

You should delete these two words or overwrite them with spaces. The modified line would look like:

    /PSe {... ...} def

At the end of the file, six lines need to be deleted:

    save
    /Times-Roman findfont 30 scalefont setfont
    100 500 moveto
    (Ready for Microsoft Word output) show
    showpage
    restore

The last character in the file is a Ctrl–D (hex 04), a diamond shape. Delete this character. Note that you will see a second diamond shape that cannot be deleted. This one will not interfere with NetPrint.

Now save the file without formatting. This initialization file is now network compatible. Repeat the above steps for the landscape mode installation file. You are now ready to configure NetPrint. Run the NetPrint CONFIGUR program and go into the Translate menu. Set the Conversion option to NONE. Alternatively you can run the WORDPS.BAT batch file located on your NetPrint disk. Then exit to the Main menu and select the Setup menu. Set the NetPrint Port option to the port you will be printing from within Word.

Now run Word and you should now be able to print as you normally would. All output will be redirected to your PostScript printer. Be sure to select the PostScript driver in the Word Printer Options menu and the same printer port that you selected in NetPrint.

Word 3.x First copy APPLASER.INI to APPLASER.OLD. Using Word, make three editing changes in APPLASER.INI. Two lines at the beginning of the file must be commented out and made inactive. Do this by adding percent signs to the beginning of the line. The two lines originally look like:

    userdict /msdict known {stop} if
    serverdict begin 0 exitserver

The modified lines look like:

```
%userdict /msdict known {stop} if
%serverdict begin 0 exitserver
```

Search the file for the words currentfile closefile. Use the SEARCH feature of Word to locate them. These two words will appear between two brackets flanked by /PSe and def, such as:

```
/PSe {...currentfile closefile...} def
```

You should delete these two words or overwrite them with spaces. The modified line would look like:

```
/PSe {... ...} def
```

The last character in the file is a Ctrl–D (hex 04), a diamond shape. Delete this character. Note that you will see a second diamond shape that cannot be deleted. This one will not interfere with NetPrint.

Now save the file without formatting. This initialization file is now network compatible. Repeat the steps above for the landscape mode installation file, and you are ready to configure NetPrint. Run the NetPrint CONFIGUR program and go into the Translate menu. Set the Conversion option to NONE. (You can, instead, run the WORDPS.BAT batch file.) Then exit to the Main menu and select the Setup menu. Set the NetPrint Port option to the port you will be printing from within Word.

You will now be able to print with Word as you normally would. All output will be redirected to your PostScript printer. Be sure to select the PostScript driver in the Word Printer Options menu and the same printer port that you selected in NetPrint.

Word 4.0. First copy POSTSCRP.INI to POSTSCRP.OLD and then, using Word, make three editing changes in POSTSCRP.INI. Two lines at the beginning of the file must be commented out and made inactive. Do this by adding percent signs to the beginning of the line. The two lines originally look like:

```
userdict /msdict known {stop} if
serverdict begin 0 exitserver
```

The modified lines look like:

```
%userdict /msdict known {stop} if
%serverdict begin 0 exitserver
```

Now search the file for the words currentfile closefile. Use the SEARCH feature of Word to locate them. These two words will appear between two brackets flanked by /PSe and def, such as:

```
/PSe {...currentfile closefile...} def
```

You should delete these two words or overwrite them with spaces. The modified line would look like:

```
/PSe {... ...} def
```

The last character in the file is a Ctrl–D (hex 04), a diamond shape. Delete this character. You will see a second diamond shape that cannot be deleted. This one will not interfere with NetPrint. Now save the file without formatting. This initialization file is now network compatible, and you can repeat the steps for the landscape mode installation file.

Now run the NetPrint CONFIGUR program and go into the Translate menu. Set the Conversion option to NONE. (You can, instead, run the WORDPS.BAT batch file.) Then exit to the Main menu and select the Setup menu. Set the NetPrint Port option to the port you will be printing from within Word. You will now be able to print as you normally would. All output will be redirected to your PostScript printer. Be sure to select the PostScript driver in the Word Printer Options menu and the same printer port that you selected in NetPrint.

Word 5.0. After you have copied POSTSCRP.INI to POSTSCRP.OLD, use Word to make three editing changes in POSTSCRP.INI. Four lines at the beginning of the file must be commented out and made inactive. Do this by adding percent signs to the beginning of the line. The four lines originally look like:

```
userdict /msinifile known
{msinifile (POSTSCRP) eq {stop} if} if
serverdict begin 0 exitserver
userdict /msorigstate known {msorigstate restore} if
```

The modified lines look like:

```
%Userdict /msinifile known
%{msinifile (POSTSCRP) eq {stop} if} if
%serverdict begin 0 exitserver
%userdict /msorigstate known {msorigstate restore} if
```

Now search the file for the words currentfile closefile. Use the SEARCH feature of Word to locate them. You should delete these two words or overwrite them with spaces. The last character in the file is a Ctrl–D (hex 04), a diamond shape. Delete this character. The second diamond shape cannot be deleted, but this one will not interfere with NetPrint. Now save the file without formatting. This initialization file is now network compatible. Repeat the steps for the landscape mode installation file.

Run the NetPrint CONFIGUR program and go into the Translate menu. Set the Conversion option to NONE. (You can, instead, run the WORDPS.BAT batch file.) Then exit to the Main menu and select the Setup menu. Set the NetPrint Port option to the port you will be printing from within Word. You will now be able to print as you normally would. All output will be redirected to your PostScript printer. Be sure to select the PostScript driver in the Word Printer options menu and the same printer port that you selected in NetPrint.

NetPrint 2.0 and Windows/286 (Version 2.11)

To marry these two products requires a certain amount of matchmaking skill. We suggest the following approach:

1. Install NetPrint.
2. Run the NetPrint Configure program, choosing Translate from the Main menu. From the Translate menu move the cursor to Conversion and change its value to NONE. Press Escape until you are back at the Main menu, then choose Setup. From the Setup Menu move the cursor to Wait Time. Change the Wait Time to 40 seconds. Then move your cursor to NetPrint Port and select the port that you will print from within Windows. Press F10 to exit and save your changes. Load NetPrint.
3. Install Windows. Select the Apple LaserWriter (or other PostScript device) as your printer and choose LPT1, LPT2 or LPT3 as your printer port (make sure the port is the same as the one you selected for the NetPrint port in Step 1).
4. You must also disable the Windows Spooler by editing the section of the WIN.INI file titled [Windows] and change the line Spooler=yes to Spooler=no.
5. If you selected LPT2 or LPT3 as your printer port when you installed Windows, you will have to edit the WIN.INI file. When printing to LPT2 or LPT3, Windows writes directly to the hardware, bypassing DOS. NetPrint expects the application to call DOS for print services. By adding a port called LPTx.TXT= (where x is the number of the parallel port), we force Windows to send output to a file called LPTx.TXT. Any file with the prefix LPTx will be treated by DOS as output to the parallel port. This method forces Windows to go through DOS instead of directly to the hardware. To add this port option, edit the part of the WIN.INI file titled [PORTS]. Add a line that says LPTx.TXT= (where x is the number of the port). NOTE: If you don't follow this procedure, you won't get any output at all from Windows and NetPrint.
6. Load Windows and go into the Control Panel by double clicking on the file CONTROL.EXE. Drop down the menu Setup and select Connections. A dialog box with two windows will open up. On the left you will have a list of printers and on the right a list of ports. Click on the PostScript printer you have installed. Then click on the LPTx.TXT= option on the right side and click OK. Exit the Control Panel.

You are now ready to print. Start by creating and printing a small document from Write. If you are successful, then print a long document. If you are having problems, verify each of the steps above and make sure you have reviewed all of the items in the General Considerations section following. While these steps might seem somewhat elaborate, remember that steps 5 and 6 normally only apply if you use a port other than LPT1.

Windows 2.03 and 286 with PageMaker and AppleTalk

To set up this configuration, first load the file TOPSPAP.EXE by entering the command TOPSPAP on the DOS command line while in TOPS subdirectory. Now install Windows and select the Apple LaserWriter printer. Select any port. Because Windows does not offer an AppleTalk port option during installation, you will add the AppleTalk port manually after the installation of Windows has been completed. After installing Windows, install PageMaker. Because Windows is already installed, PageMaker will not give the user the opportunity to install a printer or port.

Once PageMaker has been installed manually, copy the file APPLETLK.DLL into the Windows subdirectory. This file, which can be found on the drivers disk that comes with PageMaker, contains the code that adds the AppleTalk port logic to windows. The DLL stands for *Dynamic Link Library*. Next you must tell Windows that the APPLETLK.DLL file is available by adding a line to the WIN.INI file. Go in to Windows and double click on WIN.INI. Windows will bring the file up in the editor called Notepad. Locate the line that reads [PORTS]. Underneath that line, on a line by itself, add the line:

Appletalk = Next

Now locate the line that says Spooler = and make sure the word NO follows. Now use the File menu to save the WIN.INI file. Exit Windows and then reload it so that the changed WIN.INI will be in effect.

Use the Windows Control Panel to install a PostScript printer such as the Apple LaserWriter. To do this, you double click on the file CONTROL.EXE. Then select the Installation menu and Add a new printer. The Control Panel will prompt you to insert the disk with the printer driver in drive A. You should insert the driver's disk that comes with PageMaker so that the PostScript driver installed is the correct one (it should be dated 5/18/88 as TOPS has not tested any other version of the driver).

Once you have added the PostScript printer, you should drop down the Setup menu in the Control Panel and choose the Connections option. A dialog box with two windows will open up. On the left is a list of printers and on the right a list of ports. Click on the PostScript printer you have just installed, then click on the Appletalk port on the right side. Click OK and exit the Control Panel. Next, call up PageMaker. Drop down the File menu and select Printer setup. Click on the Postscript printer on Appletalk selection. If you want to locate a PostScript printer in a another zone have them click on Setup and then Appletalk, and select the correct zone. Click on OK until you are back in the PageMaker main screen.

You are now ready to use this setup. Create a new PageMaker document with just a few words in it and try printing. If you are successful, try printing one of the example files (preferably a long one with graphics in it). If you don't get any output, go through all the items in the General Considerations section of this document. Then repeat (or verify) all of the above steps.

PageMaker with Run-Time Windows and AppleTalk

To install PageMaker using the Windows run-time edition and the AppleTalk option, you first install PageMaker. During the installation process, select a PostScript printer on the AppleTalk printer port (as opposed to LPT1, COM1, and so on. The PostScript printer driver is named PSCRIPT.DRV. The AppleTalk port software interface file is named APPLETLK.DLL. After the installation process, both of these files should be in the PageMaker directory. If you cannot find them in the PageMaker directory, you can copy them from the PageMaker DRIVERS disk. If you have to copy the files over, make sure you go into the PageMaker Control Panel. Go into PageMaker and drop down the menu from the bar in the upper right corner. Select Setup, then Connections to select the PostScript printer on AppleTalk port. If the Appletalk port option does not appear in the Control Panel, you need to edit the WIN.INI file and add it. For instructions on how to do this, see the previous section.

Once you are sure PageMaker is installed correctly, add /INT=60 to the ALAP line in your AUTOEXEC.BAT, as in: ALAP /INT=60. Reboot the computer, load TOPSPAP.EXE from the TOPS subdirectory. Load PageMaker. Go into the Control Panel to make sure the printer selected is a PostScript device on the AppleTalk port. Also, make sure that the spooler is turned off by dropping down the menu from the bar in the upper right-hand corner and selecting spooler. If spooler=YES in WIN.INI, follow the instructions above to change it to NO.

You are now ready to try printing. Start by create and print a small document from Write. If you are successful, print a long document. If you are having problems verify each of the steps above and make sure you have reviewed all of the items in the General Considerations section.

Printing with Windows and TOPS: General Considerations

To troubleshoot printing problems with Windows and TOPS, you should strip your system down to the basics and then build up, determining at which point the problem arises. This approach is the standard diagnostic technique for PCs. First, make sure that the CONFIG.SYS file contains only the very basics:

```
FILES=20
BUFFERS=20
```

You will also have DEVICE=ATALK.SYS if you are using TOPS 2.0, but we suggest using 2.1 and eliminating this driver from CONFIG.SYS. The values for FILES and BUFFERS can be higher, but should not be lower.

Also, rename your AUTOEXEC.BAT file so that it is disabled. The troubleshooting process is much easier if you eliminate all possibilities of interference with something in this file. Make sure you can print from DOS first. Use TPRINT or PRINT to send an ASCII file. Find out whether the user has ever had NETPRINT or the APPLETLK.DLL option working. Sometimes questioning along these lines can uncover new information about the problem.

RAM-CRAM: THE PC MEMORY PROBLEM

As you might already have discovered, everything is not rosy on the DOS side of the network world. Loading TOPS followed by your favorite application can result in an message saying Insufficient memory. Even after you have loaded an application, you might find your workspace is severely limited. Using your favorite spreadsheet after you have loaded TOPS can mean that worksheets that once loaded completely might no longer fit. In this section, we explore the problems encountered by DOS network users that have been termed *RAM-cram*. This is the need to put into random access memory (RAM) more programs than will fit comfortably (cram). We discuss the structure and use of memory in DOS systems and then present some solutions to the problem. We would like to point out that this is not simply a TOPS problem. All DOS networks take up memory, as can be seen from the chart in Fig. 14-1.

This is based on typical configurations. We show the amount used for DOS as 70K although DOS 3.3 itself only takes up 53K. The other 17K is room required by typical CONFIG.SYS settings.

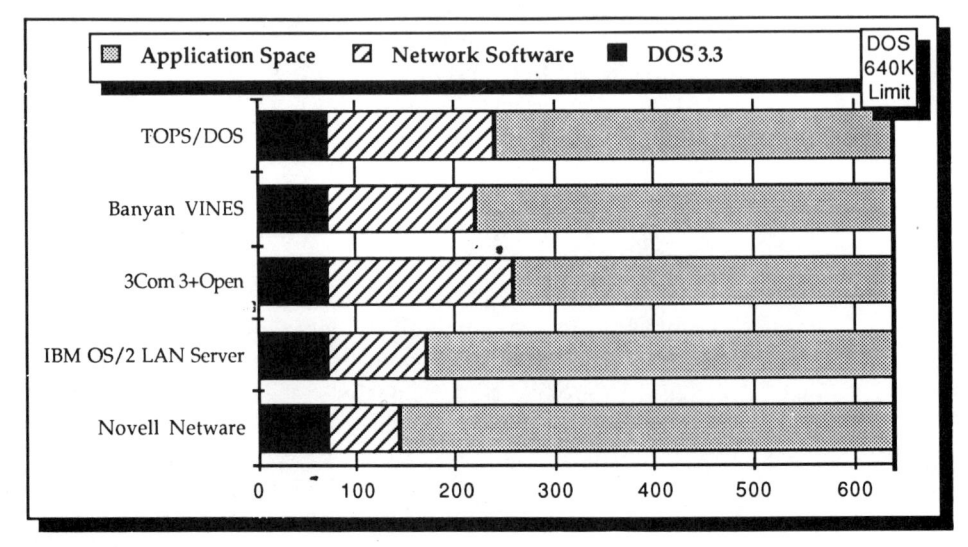

Fig. 14-1. RAM used by networks.

Types of Memory

So that we are all clear on the terminology used in the following sections, we briefly review the memory aspect of personal computers built in the tradition of the IBM PC. The two types of memory in a PC are Read-Only Memory (ROM) and Random Access Memory (RAM). ROM holds instructions, permanently burned into the chips, that your computer uses immediately after the power is turned on, before even a disk is read. RAM is where all of the instructions, the programs that the computer is to execute are held prior to being carried out. RAM is also where data is held before it is sorted onto disk. When you turn off the power to your computer, you wipe out the contents of RAM.

Consider how memory works in a typical session with a typical piece of application software such as WordPerfect. (For the sake of clarity and brevity this tale is simplified somewhat, but it is basically a true story.) First, you turn on the computer. Almost immediately, instructions are read from ROM. This includes the testing of memory that gives the numeric display in the top left of the screen, as well as the BIOS instructions (Basic Input Output System) that lay the ground rules for the exchange of information between different parts of the system such as keyboard, display, disks, and so on.

The ROM instructions tell the computer to look to the drive(s) to find software on disk. When the computer finds a disk with DOS on it, DOS is read into memory. DOS actually consists of several parts, the two most important being the hidden system files and the command processor, COMMAND.COM. After COMMAND.COM is loaded, DOS looks for two special files that tell it about the computer, CONFIG.SYS and AUTOEXEC.BAT. The CONFIG.SYS file is a list of settings for DOS to use, plus instructions about any special equipment that is part of the hardware configuration. The AUTOEXEC.BAT file is a list of instructions about what DOS should do first, like set the date and time and display a menu of programs.

As manager of the flow and storage of information, DOS then allows you to issue an instruction that loads a program, such as WordPerfect. WordPerfect is read from disk into RAM. DOS remains in RAM as well. You type some text from the keyboard and this is held in RAM. You issue the save instruction and a copy of the text in RAM is stored on disk, but remains on screen as well for further editing. When you are done editing you resave the document, replacing the old version on disk with the new one, and then exit WordPerfect, which removes both text and the program from RAM.

How Much Is Enough?

The preceding story is simple enough, if you have enough RAM to hold both DOS and WordPerfect. How much is enough, and how much have you got? Like file storage space on disk, RAM is measured in bytes and kilobytes. If you type CHKDSK at the DOS prompt and press Enter you will see a report on memory, such as 655360 bytes total memory, 554688 bytes free. This indicates the total amount of memory recognized by DOS, plus what's used.

When the IBM PC was first introduced, it came with 65,536 bytes or 64 kilobytes of RAM. This was considered a lot of RAM at the time. Competing systems such as the Apple II had 48K of RAM in standard configuration, and only the hottest CP/M machines had 64K. WordStar, one of the most prevalent applications of the day, was only 32K in size, so 64K was more than enough. Because the "power users" back then had 64K CP/M machines, the designers of DOS figured that ten times that much would be sufficient "user RAM" for DOS and any future applications, hence the figure of 640K which is the maximum amount of user RAM that DOS can recognize.

This sounded like a reasonable limit at the time. However, users kept demanding more features from software, and each new wave of programs required more RAM. These days the most widely used word processing program on PCs is WordPerfect, which takes up about 320K. New functions have been added to DOS, which used to occupy less than 30K but now requires some 80K. In addition to DOS and regular application programs, a new breed of software, called TSRs or *terminate-and-stay-resident* programs, gained popularity and consumed RAM. A TSR program, such as the original Borland SideKick, is loaded into memory after DOS but before application software and stays there as you unload one application and then load another. This way a TSR program can offer the same features, such as a notepad or clipboard, within whatever application you are using. The TOPS software is a type of TSR program in that it is loaded before applications and continues working while you work within applications.

There is also pressure on memory limits from the thirst for more exotic hardware. The designers of the original PC and DOS could not anticipate every type of storage system, communications equipment, and hardware interface that was to be developed for PCs. Equipment like removable hard disks, FAX boards, and MIDI interfaces simply did not exist then. However, DOS was designed so that someone who designed a new piece of equipment could also write a piece of software that told the PC how to relate to that equipment. This specialized software is called a device driver, and many products for the PC come with a device driver. In fact, early versions of TOPS/PC used a device driver to integrate the FlashCard into the PC (this is now done with the ALAP program). The problem with device drivers is that they are loaded into memory when the computer starts up, right after COMMAND.COM. You cannot use such equipment as Bernoulli boxes without these drivers occupying space in memory. This is how the 640K limit of DOS came to be such a squeeze: bigger and better applications and versions of DOS, plus TSR software, and specialized equipment. Then along came networking to really top things off!

Memory Architecture

You might wonder why DOS has not been altered to recognize more than 640K. The answer lies in the original design of the PC and what many users have seen as the necessity to keep each new wave of PC designs compatible with the last. Understanding the problem begins with understanding addresses. In order for a computer to keep track of the data it handles, it needs to know where it is. The location of each byte that is going to be processed needs to be defined. This is done by assigning a unique address to every byte. You can think of a delivery person attempting to make deliveries. If every customer has a unique address, the job of locating them is made much easier. In a computer, each piece of data that is processed has to pass through memory. Every address in memory has to be coded in binary code. If you have eight digits or bytes to work with, you can come up with 256 unique addresses. With 16 bits you can create 65,536 combinations or unique addresses. The 8088 chip used in the first PCs had the capacity to use 20 bits for addressing. This was a function of the physical design of the chip. This results in a maximum potential number of addresses of 1,048,576. This is exactly 1 megabyte worth of addresses or addressable memory. The 8088 chip can be said to have a *1 megabyte address space*.

However, not all of this space can be used by programs that you load from disk. Some of the area needs to be reserved for information passing through memory from and to displays. There needs to be room to address the basic input/output system (BIOS) that controls how the pieces of hardware communicate with each other. To allow for these factors IBM engineers pre-allocated 640K for programs, 384K for system overhead. Remember that this 640K is the limit of user RAM. In addition to this user RAM, there is the memory area occupied by ROM. The total amount of ROM and RAM that a PC can work with is limited by the type of chip or the central processing unit that is running the system. The CPU chip must move data and program code in and out of memory. The Intel 8088 and 8086 chips that powered the first PC can address up to 1024 kilobytes or 1 Megabyte of memory. This space or area is made up of the 640K of RAM, plus 128K of memory reserved for use by video boards, plus 256K of space reserved for the system ROM (640K + 128K + 256K = 1024K or 1MB).

So, beyond the 640K of user RAM, the rest of the PC's 1MB total address space is reserved for system operations, a 384K range of memory locations where the CPU finds data or instructions for its own use. As you can see from Fig. 14-2, the space from 640K to 768K is for video buffers, the data used to draw and redraw the screen display.

Optional or installable ROM modules, such as those used by hard disk controllers and enhanced graphics boards, fit between 768K and 896K. The computer's own built-in ROM, that starts the computer running, is addressed from 896K to 1,024K. Note that we are talking address space here, not actual memory chips. What we are saying is that the 8088/8086 processors can see a total memory space no bigger than 1024K, of which no more than 640K can be RAM. Even if you have more than 640K worth of RAM chips, DOS will not recognize it.

However, the address area above 640K is rarely full. An 80-column, 25-line text display uses 4K of video memory. The Monochrome Display Adapter occupies just the area from 704K to 708K. Only the most colorful EGA and VGA modes fill

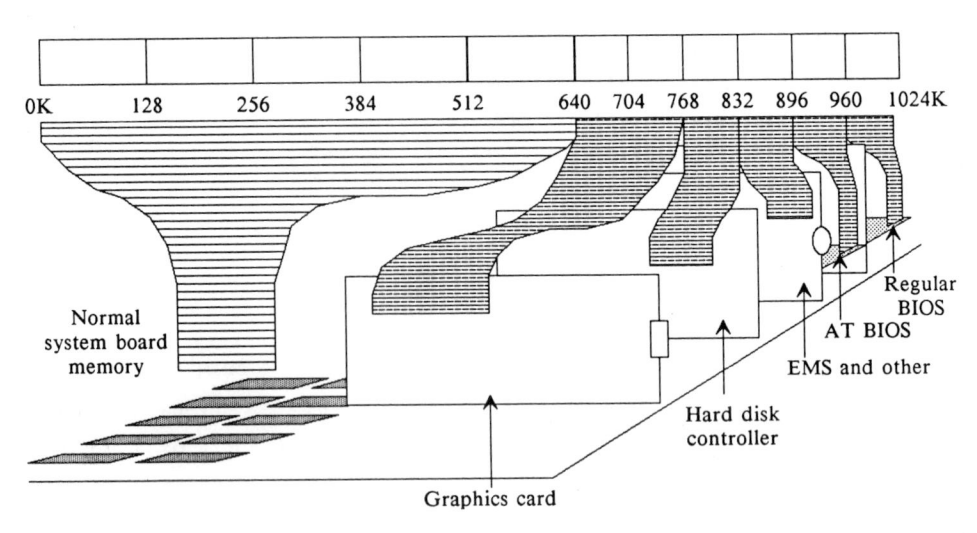

Fig. 14-2. Memory map.

or exceed the 128K assigned to video. Only IBM's PS/2 models, not PCs or ATs, use all the address space above 896K for system ROM. Having vacant space in high memory can come in handy. Having a 64K gap amidst the video buffers and BIOS routines makes possible EMS expanded memory, described in a moment. You can see a list of memory usage in Table 14-3.

Table 14-3. Memory usage.

Decimal	Segment	Contents
0K	0	Standard
64K	1000	Memory
128K	2000	includes
192K	3000	DOS
256K	4000	terminate and
320K	5000	stay resident
384K	6000	programs
448K	7000	and regular
512K	8000	software
576K	9000	applications
640K	A000	EGA displays
704K	B000	Video displays (including EGA)
768K	C000	Hard disk ROM, EGA, bootable Bernoulli boxes
832K	D000	ARCnet cards, EMS, accelerator boards, token ring
896K	E000	AT reserved ROM space
960K to 1 MB	F000	ROM Bios

Although the 8088 CPU stops at 1MB of RAM, the 80286 found in the PC AT can address 16MB, and the 80386 CPU can address as much as four gigabytes (4096MB). Compared with the mess of addresses below it, RAM above the 1MB boundary is fairly simple. It is known as extended memory, straightforward additional space for 286 or 386 systems running OS/2, Xenix, or some 386-specific software. Unfortunately, a 286 or 386 using DOS runs in something called *real mode*. This was designed into the chip for backward compatibility with earlier computers. The 8088 based PCs were around so long that hardware designers built their peripherals to take advantage of the addresses above 640K. Altering the limit would affect your ability to use many popular hard disk controllers, video boards, and so on.

The real mode of 80286 and 80386 chips has the same 1MB address limit as the 8088. There is an alternative mode that can be addressed by operating systems other than DOS. This is called the *protected mode*, and it can use large extended memory spaces. Very few DOS programs, a few utilities or disk caches, actually do anything with extended memory. For example, many PC ATs come with 384K of actual RAM memory installed beyond 640K but DOS cannot use it. An AT with 1MB of built-in RAM gives the same CHKDSK report of available memory as one with 640K. Some 1MB systems use the extra memory as *shadow RAM*, loading a copy (or shadow) of sluggish video and BIOS ROM code into RAM for quicker performance. Shadow RAM makes screen displays more responsive, especially for EGA, but won't stop programs from displaying Out of memory messages.

There is a way to use a little more RAM than 640K. A trick called XMS (*eXtended Memory Specification*) was developed by AST, Intel, Microsoft, and Lotus. XMS allows DOS to use 64K of extended memory for a DOS-recognizable system total of 704K. Microsoft Windows/286 is the first program to recognize the bonus, gaining 43K of usable space from it. XMS support is sure to show up in more programs, but for the most part, extended memory is a dead end for DOS.

EMS Architecture

Compared with the simple linear addressing of extended RAM, expanded memory relies on a technical trick known as *paging* or *bank-switching*. This trick takes a window within the region visible to the processor (the 8088's 1MB address space) and swaps different areas, or *pages*, of expanded memory in and out of that space as needed. What happens is that an unused 64K section of the memory between 640K and 1,024K is used as the address for a larger area, sort of like a mail drop that is one stop on the postal route but which has boxes for lots of customers. The CPU is fooled, busily operating within this virtual space on data whose real or physical address can be many megabytes away.

Simple bank-switching is nothing new, but EMS is a sophisticated scheme. It involves hardware and software working together with the extra RAM and memory-mapping hardware on an EMS board, combined with a software driver added to your CONFIG.SYS file. This driver, the *expanded memory manager* (EMM), lets

DOS and your applications recognize the paged memory. Given at least 64K of contiguous, vacant address space above 784K (one of the unused gaps), EMS creates a page frame holding at least four 16K pages. The memory manager can map any 16K segment, anywhere within expanded RAM, into any of these pages, fielding CPU requests while preventing collisions among multiple programs and data areas.

The original *Expanded Memory Specification*, EMS 3.2, supported 8MB of expanded memory, mostly as workspace for spreadsheets and other data files. AST and other firms modified that standard to create the *Enhanced Expanded Memory Specification* (EEMS), which can swap more pages, including some below the 640K line as well as in the page frame above it. This helps environments such as DESQview shuffle programs in and out of conventional memory. Now EMS 4.0 has surpassed the EEMS standard. With EMS 4.0, you get support for up to 32MB at 8MB per expansion slot. This is swapped into pages almost anywhere below 1MB, and it has many more functions and routines for executing program code as well as handling data.

DEALING WITH RAM-CRAM: OUTSIDE TOPS

Now that we have reviewed why memory is organized the way it is in a PC, we can look at some techniques for getting around the limits imposed by this state of affairs. Typically your problem will arise when trying to load an application program after you have just installed and loaded TOPS. You want to run TOPS in the background, maintaining the network connection, while you work on your application. Another scenario is that you have loaded TOPS and your application, but are running out of memory to handle the data files you normally work with. There are some steps you can take to manage TOPS itself, but first we look at ways of getting more out of your memory.

Slimming Your CONFIG.SYS

Computer systems that have been around for a while can accumulate a lot of unnecessary additions. You might have noticed this in the disk file department, dozens of files that have been on a hard disk for ages, but nobody is sure why. A similar thing can happen to your CONFIG.SYS. Some applications add information to CONFIG.SYS when they are installed. Some hardware requires that lines be added to CONFIG.SYS. If the application or hardware falls into disuse, it can be removed, but the additions to CONFIG.SYS might remain. A good example is the ATALK.SYS driver supplied with FlashCards. This is no longer necessary because TOPS uses a memory-resident program instead of installed driver. Devices loaded in CONFIG.SYS can take up precious memory, so remove ones you no longer need. Make sure you know why what is in your CONFIG.SYS is there.

Mapping out Your Memory

A valuable tool for checking out what you have in memory and where it is located is a utility program called a *memory mapper*. Several of these are available from bulletin boards such as IBMNET on CompuServe. In Fig. 14-3, you can see the type of information displayed by one of these programs, PMAP.

This is a screen report of the current configuration of an 80386 computer after TOPS has been loaded. While this is not as graphic as you might like your maps, the documentation that comes with PMAP explains what sections of the report mean.

Some of these programs are free once you have downloaded them, others are shareware that you pay for after you decide to use them. If you are doing extensive work with memory, for example configuring several different machines, then a program of this kind is very helpful.

Hardware Solutions

If you are using a PC XT or other 8088/8086-based PC, you have limited hardware options when it comes to extra memory. You can add EMS memory for use by programs like 1-2-3, but you cannot access that memory for use with TOPS. However, a company called RYBS Electronics offers a product called HIcard that uses something called *Advanced Memory Specification* to help out PC XT users. The HIcard is a board that is installed into your PC and is fitted with up to 512K of memory. This can be used to bring 512K machines up to 640K, but it also provides memory beyond that. Using AMS software, this memory can be incorporated into the system to be put to use. The SYSMAP software that comes with HIcard maps out the memory usage in your PC before and after the card is installed. You are

```
Sat  6-23-1990 C:\>PMAP
pmap 1.32 Copyright (C) 1986-1988 by The Cove Software Group/C.J.Dunford

Addr Program   Parent    Parameters        Han Blks   Size    Vectors
---- -------   ------    ----------        --- ----   ----    -------
0FC6 command   command                      0   2      3536   22 23 24 2E F1
10B8 inset     command                      0   2    120256   09 10 17 20 21 61
                                                              E7 EC ED EF FB
Total conventional free memory                  3    401328
Largest conventional free block                      401216
Extended memory installed                             73728
Next program will load at 2E16

Expanded memory summary:

     Block      Size     Name
     -----      ----     ----
       0      524288
     Free    2146304
     Total   2670592
     Page frame segment: 9000h
```

Fig. 14-3. PMAP display.

shown how much "HIDOS" memory you have available and how much regular RAM will be freed up if you load such things as mouse drivers and network drivers into this HIDOS area. Gains of 100K to 200K in regular RAM required by applications are possible. Note that HIDOS is the term that RYBS uses for memory beyond 640K, memory that can be addressed by using those addresses not need by BIOS, display adapters, and other equipment.

The software used by HIcard is very reliable, taking care of potential conflicts between calls on memory and making operation of the HIDOS transparent to the user. All that you have to do to utilize the extra RAM space is load into those programs that are best suited to that region, such as the TOPS software. To load TOPS into high memory, you could add extra commands to the LOADTOPS.BAT file. You need to use the LOADHIGH command to run programs in high memory. Depending upon how much memory you have installed, you could use:

    LOADHIGH ALAP
    LOADHIGH PSTACK
    LOADHIGH TOPSTALK
    LOADHIGH TOPSKRNL

This would place the main sections of TOPS software into the high memory area, freeing up over 100K in regular memory, often enough to make the difference when trying to load large applications.

Another hardware solution is available for users of AT and PS/2 systems that are based on the 80286 chip. The ALL CHARGECARD is a device that adds powerful memory management capabilities to 80286 machines. Using the chips on the ALL CHARGECARD, you can choose to reorganize your memory usage in several different ways, including access to high memory areas such as those accessed by the HIcard. The ALL CHARGECARD does contain memory itself, but allows you to reorganize all types of memory in your system: motherboard RAM, EMS, and extended memory. This can permit you to run TOPS together with applications that would otherwise not be able to fit in memory.

Software Solutions

Because 80386 systems have the capacity to address larger memory areas and have better memory management functions built into their hardware, you can use software solutions to achieve results on an 80386 that require hardware solutions on earlier systems. Two examples of this are HI386 from RYBS, the makers of HIcard, and 386^{MAX} from Qualitas. In Fig. 14-4, you can see the way 386^{MAX} looks at your memory. You can treat extended memory as expanded, access high DOS memory, and perform other tricks.

To use 386^{MAX} with TOPS you use a similar type of LOADHIGH program to place TOPS into the high memory area away from regular RAM. Using programs of this nature does require that you coordinate several aspects of your computer system: video display, hard disk controllers, and network interface card. A lot of optional commands with 386ᴹᴬˣ allow you to alter the way it runs in order to avoid conflict with other programs. In some situations, problems with high memory will require extensive analysis to resolve conflicts. For example, some VGA cards such as FastWrite VGA from Video7 use up an area of memory often used by memory swapping routines. If you load the VGA BIOS into RAM as described in the VGA utilities manual, you get around this conflict, but you will need to coordinate memory addresses with your memory expansion software. Some cards such as the FastWrite also take up a DMA channel, requiring that you give up the DMA access on your FlashCard. This is done by using ATALK/DMA-none in your LOADTOPS.BAT However, this sacrifices the higher speed of FlashTalk.

TOPS and the Quarterdeck Expanded Memory Manager

DESQview is a multi-tasking windows environment for DOS-based machines, made by Quarterdeck Office Systems. The current version is 2.2 plus. You can run DESQview on just about any machine running DOS 2.0 or higher, on an 8088, 8086, 80286, or 80386 microprocessor. On 386-based machines, DESQview is most commonly used in conjunction with Quarterdeck's 386 Expanded Memory Manager, QEMM-386, to form a combination generally referred to as DESQview386. You can run DESQview on a 386 without QEMM-386, but you lose significant memory-management capability, ending up with an environment virtually identical to DESQview on a 286, only faster. The current version of QEMM-386 is 4.2 plus. Note that DESQview and QEMM-386 are separate products which must be purchased separately, that can be used together or independent of one another. For the reason stated above, it is rare to find someone running

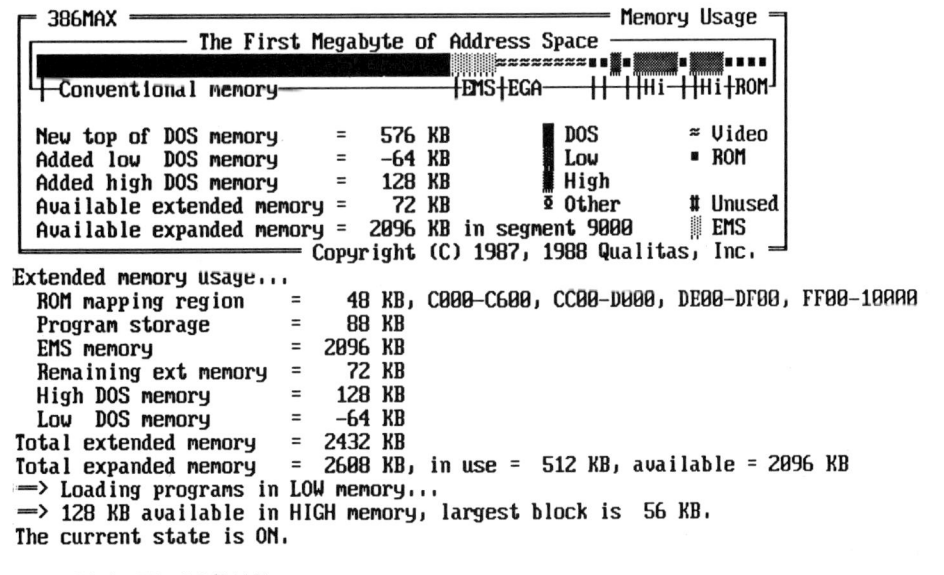

```
┌─ 386MAX ═══════════════════════════════════════════ Memory Usage ═┐
│            The First Megabyte of Address Space                    │
│████████████████████████████████▓▓▓▓▓▓▓▓▓▒▒▒▒▒▒▒░░░░░              │
│└─Conventional memory─────────┘└EMS┤EGA├──┤├─Hi─┤├Hi┤ROM┘           │
│                                                                    │
│   New top of DOS memory      =    576 KB     █ DOS    ≈ Video     │
│   Added low  DOS memory      =    -64 KB     █ Low    ■ ROM       │
│   Added high DOS memory      =    128 KB     █ High               │
│   Available extended memory  =     72 KB     ▒ Other   # Unused   │
│   Available expanded memory  =   2096 KB in segment 9000  ▓ EMS   │
│                   Copyright (C) 1987, 1988 Qualitas, Inc.         │
Extended memory usage...
   ROM mapping region      =     48 KB, C000-C600, CC00-D000, DE00-DF00, FF00-10000
   Program storage         =     88 KB
   EMS memory              =   2096 KB
   Remaining ext memory    =     72 KB
   High DOS memory         =    128 KB
   Low  DOS memory         =    -64 KB
Total extended memory      =   2432 KB
Total expanded memory      =   2608 KB, in use =  512 KB, available = 2096 KB
 ═> Loading programs in LOW memory...
 ═> 128 KB available in HIGH memory, largest block is  56 KB.
The current state is ON.
```

Fig. 14-4. The 386MAX map.

DESQview on a 386 without QEMM-386. However, for reasons that will become clear, many people who do not own DESQview buy and use QEMM-386 as their 386 Expanded Memory Manager of choice.

We can suggest QEMM-386 as a solution to TOPS/DOS users on 386 machines who are having trouble running their applications in conventional RAM. QEMM-386 has two major functions. Firstly, like 386^{MAX}, it can transform extended memory into expanded memory (LIM EMS 4.0 and EEMS 3.2), which can then be accessed by programs designed to take advantage of expanded memory, as well as by DESQview, which can use it to create "virtual" DOS environments for simultaneous operation of multiple programs. Secondly, it can map RAM into the unused addresses between 640K and 1MB and allow a user to load TSR modules (such as TOPS modules), into it, thus making more conventional RAM available to applications.

These two functions are optional, and can be managed separately from one another, but the first will have a significant impact on the second, for the following reason. How much HIDOS RAM is available is a function of the particular machine architecture and attached peripherals (display adapter, etc.) and of whether or not you invoke Expanded Memory Emulation. Managing Expanded Memory requires a 64K page frame in HIDOS RAM. DESQview can perform many of its expanded memory operations without a page frame, but most applications that use expanded memory require the page frame to access it. This function therefore reduces the amount of HIDOS RAM available to TSRs by 64K. Obviously, from the point of view of someone who merely wishes to get TOPS "out of the way," it would be best to disable Expanded Memory Emulation. But the price you pay is effectively to render useless all that expensive Extended Memory with which your 386 is loaded.

This presents an interesting dilemma for someone running TOPS and QEMM-386 without DESQview. Do they disable Expanded Memory Emulation, get as much as possible of TOPS into HIGH DOS RAM, and have the maximum amount of conventional RAM (but no Expanded RAM) available for their applications? Or, conversely, do they enable Expanded Memory Emulation, which forces them to put more of TOPS into conventional RAM, but makes Expanded RAM available to their applications? If you are running DESQview386, you get less benefit out of disabling Expanded Memory Emulation, because DESQview can use half of the page frame area anyway to clear its code out of conventional memory, and because certain DESQview features require a page frame.

QEMM-386 consists of a device driver (QEMM.SYS) and two command-line utilities (QEMM.COM and LOADHI.COM). QEMM.SYS is loaded from CONFIG.SYS with a command of the form:

DEVICE=[d:][path]QEMM.SYS [options]

If QEMM.SYS is installed, DESQview, when launched, will recognize it, and take advantage of the services it provides. QEMM.SYS works by using the "virtual 8086" mode of the 386 microprocessor to provide such services as Expanded Memory Emulation. It has three possible *states* in this regard—AUTO, ON, and OFF. AUTO means that Expanded Memory is available only when a program needs it. ON means it is always available, and OFF means it is not available. The default state (which can be set as an option to QEMM.SYS) is AUTO. The current state can be checked and set using QEMM.COM. The default state for Expanded Memory Emulation is enabled. To disable it, add the option FRAME=NONE to QEMM.SYS. HIDOS RAM mapping is enabled by adding the option RAM to QEMM.SYS. This forces the initial state to ON, and it cannot be overridden.

To load TSRs into HIDOS RAM, use the utility LOADHI.COM with a command of the form:

    LOADHI [d:][path]program

There must be a contiguous section of high memory that is large enough to load the TSR, or LOADHI.COM returns an error and loads the TSR into conventional RAM. You can get a map of the first 1MB of RAM by entering the command QEMM without any parameters. This also returns the current state of QEMM.SYS, and the amount of Expanded Memory, if any.

DESQview386 and TOPS. We recently tested DESQview386 2.2 (as well as QEMM-386 4.2 as a stand-alone memory manager) with TOPS/DOS 2.1 and NetPrint 2.0 on a Compaq386/20 with 2MB RAM, VGA, and Compaq DOS 3.31. Results were uniformly excellent on both AppleTalk and Ethernet *if* the basic rules of DESQview/QEMM/TOPS compatibility are followed:

1. Do not run DESQview on a TOPS server. There appears to be a basic incompatibility between DESQview and TOPS' server functionality. This applies not only to DESQview386, but also to DESQview on a 386 without QEMM-386, as well as to DESQview on a 286, 8086, or 8088. It is fine to have the full client/server software loaded, but if you have something published and someone tries to access it, you will have problems. Usually, both client and server will eventually hang. Note that we found no problem being a TOPS server when just QEMM-386 was loaded and active, unless DESQview was loaded as well. We did not test being a print server, but we would expect similar results.

2. The LAP driver (ALAP or ELAP) must have DMA set to NONE if QEMM-386 is loaded and active state is ON. This is true in the case of ALAP and ELAP503, although the symptoms using ALAP are much more dramatic. If ALAP is set to use DMA 1 or 3, and QEMM is ON, you will hang up your system when you load TOPS or NetPrint. If QEMM is AUTO, you will probably hang at some point after loading DESQview or otherwise accessing Expanded Memory from an application. The problems seem to take longer to develop when using ELAP503 with a DMA channel, but they were unavoidable. Because the default for ELAP503 is DMA=0, this is not normally a problem. The rule of thumb is, if you are using QEMM-386, disable DMA.

3. With DESQview, configure the LAP driver to use a software access interrupt other than the default. The default software access interrupt used by all the TOPS LAP modules is 5C. We suggest configuring the driver to use some other interrupt, such as 60. This can be most easily accomplished through the CONFIGURE option in the SETUP program.

4. Load TOPS and/or NetPrint *before* loading DESQview.

All of the TOPS and NetPrint functions can be executed from within DESQview *except* for the actual loading of the memory resident modules. When the above four rules were followed, all the TOPS network functions we tried worked flawlessly. We were able to see network servers and printers, print to network devices, mount remote volumes, (and publish and act as a server, if DESQview was not loaded), do bidirectional copying between two machines, and run programs remotely, both from the command line in DOS with QEMM.SYS on, as well as from DOS Windows in DESQview. You can even create a DESQview Program Information File for TOPSMENU and CONFIGUR, and run them in a DESQview Window.

In one interesting experiment, we modified the Program Information File for Microsoft Word 4.0 to run off drive D, then we mounted a Macintosh folder, copied the contents of my Word subdirectory into it, launched Word remotely off the Mac drive, opened a Word document, edited it, saved it, and printed through NetPrint, all from within DESQview with QEMM.SYS active. We were able to perform all these functions both with TOPS and NetPrint loaded in conventional RAM, as well as when various TOPS and NetPrint modules had been loaded into HIGH RAM with LOADHI.COM.

Tests of DESQview were performed with the previous version of DESQview, version 2.01, and its companion QEMM-386, version 4.1, with identical results, with one exception. If you try to load a TSR with LOADHI.COM, and there is insufficient contiguous HIGH RAM available. LOADHI will inform you of the fact, and load the program into conventional RAM. If this occurred with a TOPS module under QEMM-386 4.1, TOPS functions would no longer work. It was necessary to LOADHI only those modules which would fit in HIGH RAM, and do a conventional load on the others. This problem did not occur with QEMM-386 4.2. It is important to keep in mind that different architectures and designs are employed in different 386-based machines. This can sometimes result in different behavior from TOPS with 386 Expanded Memory Managers on different machines. We have seen the exact same programs and configurations work on one 386 machine and fail on another. However, in general, reports from the field have been uniformly positive regarding TOPS and DESQview386 when the previously-mentioned rules are followed.

Software Application Decisions

Problems with PC hardware and software can bring out the philosopher in all of us. When you examine what you want versus what you can achieve, given the limits of RAM, the cost of the solutions, the need to network, and so on, you must begin the painful process of compromise. This might mean that you give up some network functions, perhaps some favorite TSR programs, or you even consider changing your application software. While this might sound like a radical step, situations where software is already in a state of flux can add network considerations to the overall evaluation process. For example, consider the field of PC spreadsheets. Here a battle royal is going on between the new versions of 1-2-3, Quattro Professional, and Excel, plus SuperCalc 5, and VP Planner. All of these programs offer feature lists that extend well beyond the previous standards in electronic spreadsheets, and many users are considering moving to a new application standard. When you factor in the need to work within the memory constraints imposed by networking, the evaluation process can take a new turn.

In the case of spreadsheets, it would seem that Excel has the biggest memory problems. Because Excel needs Windows to run, extra overhead is involved. You can load DOS, TOPS, Windows, and Excel, but just barely. Furthermore, Windows/286 works better with TOPS than Windows/386, and it is the latter that holds a lot of attraction to users because of it's memory management advantages. Unfortunately, these are obtained at some expense. Windows/386 breaks a lot of the rules for DOS programs, writing directly to the hardware rather than through DOS. This makes it hard for TOPS to intercept some operating system calls. While setting DMA to NONE can help, we have found a lack of stability when running TOPS and Windows/386.

The memory management features in 1-2-3 Release 3 enable it to load nicely on top of TOPS and use both extended and expanded memory. For example, after loading DOS 3.3 and TOPS on a 1 megabyte 80386 system, we had 402,688 bytes of conventional memory free. After loading 1-2-3 Release 3, we had a worksheet status report of 230,478 bytes available memory, indicating that 1-2-3 was using the extended memory of our system automatically. We had no trouble running Release 3 of 1-2-3 from one PC on another over TOPS provided there were compatible hardware configurations.

Another program that offers the linked spreadsheet capability of 1-2-3 Release 3 and Excel, together with presentation quality graphics, is Quattro Professional 2.0. This program features an interesting technology called VROOM (*Virtual Real-Time Object-Oriented Memory Manager*) developed by Quattro's publisher, Borland International. This system deals with program code in small chunks, thus allowing as much program code to be loaded from disk as possible, and as little as will fit if memory constraints are tight. Because the software code for Quattro Professional does not have to be fit into memory as an all-or-nothing package, the software will work with a wider range of hardware and software. The tighter your memory situation, the more the program will need to read from disk for certain operations, but you can definitely run Quattro Professional nicely on top of TOPS. We had no problems loading Quattro Professional across TOPS, and Borland's autodetect feature means that the same software could be loaded onto different display systems without any adjustments.

So, as you look at your application software and the recurring need to upgrade and improve, factor in the memory needs of networking, and you might reach better compromises. You can also expect to see more solutions for RAM-cram appearing as an increasingly broad group of users encounters this hurdle.

New Stations: The Macintosh Advantage

Another radical solution to memory constraints in the PC world is to move to a different planet: buy a Mac. This is not meant as an evangelist endorsement of the Mac. There are some aspects of using Macintoshes that are less than perfect, as anyone who has seen the little bomb icon can attest. However, the memory architecture of a Mac is quite different from that of a PC and you do not have the same problems trying to run TOPS plus applications. Sure, you can run out of memory on a Mac, but if you buy more memory, it can be accessed by TOPS—which is not always the case on the PC. There is no practical upper limit when running TOPS and applications on a Mac and so, as your needs expand, your Mac can eat up more memory without hitting that RAM-cram barrier that plagues PCs. If you already have some Macs and you need to expand your network with more stations, buying Macs ensures that you can run on the network and use your applications as well.

DEALING WITH RAM-CRAM: within TOPS

You can make some changes to the way you run TOPS that can get around the RAM limit when running TOPS. These are marginal solutions, incremental steps that can help you squeak by. They are not put forward as answers to the overall problem.

Run As Client Only

If you do not need to publish volumes from your PC, you can run in client mode rather than full client/server mode. You can mount another user's volumes and read/write with them. To run TOPS in client mode, you use LOADCLNT.BAT rather than LOADTOPS.BAT. If you have not yet used LOADCLNT.BAT, make sure that any changes you made to customize LOADTOPS.BAT are also incorporated in LOADCLNT.BAT. Also, if you have loaded the full version of TOPS, you must unload it before using the client mode, otherwise you will not free up any memory.

Reducing TOPSKRNL.DAT

A number of settings in TOPSKRNL.DAT, such as maximum number of files, can be reduced to save a small amount of memory. TOPS uses these settings to set aside space in memory for network activity. Review your TOPSKRNL.DAT and see how the current settings relate to your work pattern. The default settings represent an average user. If you do not have heavy network traffic, try reducing settings and then testing your system. You might be able to get by with lower settings for such items as remote files and remote servers and still enjoy acceptable performance using less memory.

Loading and Unloading TOPS

If you do not need constant access to network functions, you might be able to remove TOPS from memory for some operations where memory is at a premium. Using the batch file techniques described in Chapter 9, you can create a batch file to load a memory intensive program. This batch file would first issue the command

```
TOPS UL /A
```

to remove TOPS from memory. Then the batch file would load the application. A line after the application loading command could reload TOPS by calling the LOADTOPS.BAT or LOADCLNT.BAT files. Bear in mind that TOPS is best loaded and unloaded as the last memory-resident program, so you will need to factor this into your batch file procedures.

TOPS TIPS

The following sections contain miscellaneous tips and suggestions for efficient running of your TOPS network.

TOPS Spool Tricks

When printing from your Mac on TOPS Spool, it is possible to get into what appears to be a dead end. The problem arises when a document that you have sent to the LaserWriter passes over into the land of eternal winking lights, where the Ready light on the LaserWriter keeps flashing but nothing ever comes out. This can happen with complex graphic images or faulty output from an application. So you decide to use TOPS Spool to cancel the printing of this document only to be told that the printer is busy and TOPS Spool is waiting. Sometimes even turning off the printer does not work at this point. The busy message stays on screen and there appears to be no way to get the message off the screen and return to your Macintosh application. However, the regular Mac command for stopping printing, Command plus the period (.) has been known to break out of this situation, even though the message on screen does not mention this Stop print command. So, if you seem unable to break out of a print spool cycle, try pressing Command and a period.

Another TOPS Spool trick can be very helpful when your Mac has misbehaved. You might have found that a good rule of thumb on the Mac is to save a file before you print it. However, there are times when we don't follow our rules, and so you can end up sending an unstored document to print, then having a system crash. This can result in the loss of the document. However, all is not lost when using TOPS Spool. When you send a document to print with TOPS Spool, it stores a copy of the document in a preprint file. When you restart your system after a crash that prevented complete printing of a document, TOPS Spool knows that a document was not printed properly. When you select TOPS Spool from the DA menu, it advises you of unprinted output. You can tell TOPS to go ahead and repeat the print job, thus giving you a hard copy of the unsaved document.

A Problem with XCOPY

We have encountered a minor problem with TOPS when using the very handy DOS command XCOPY. As you might know, the regular COPY command in DOS, used to copy files from one disk/directory to another, reads one file at a time when it copies a group of files. This means a lot of reading/writing activity. The XCOPY command reads a group of files at once, then writes them at once, substantially speeding up the copy process. XCOPY has other advantages as well. For example, it does not poop out when all the files won't fit on the target disk. However, you can encounter problems XCOPYing to a TOPS drive. For example, you have mounted a remote volume as drive J and want to copy several files to it. You use

```
C:\STUFF>XCOPY *.* J:
```

but TOPS replies in typically alarming fashion: Invalid drive specification. However, we have found that you can log on to the TOPS drive, and at what would be the J prompt in this case, use XCOPY, as in:

```
C:\STUFF>J:
J:\>XCOPY C:*.*
```

A similar problem seems to affect some DOS file manager utilities like the very useful QuickDOS II. An indispensable tool for copying, moving, and manipulating files, QuickDOS II unfortunately will not log on to a remote drive that has been mounted.

About Security

These days there is a lot of talk about computer security, particularly about breaches of security in large networks. Much of this talk is not relevant to local area networks.

External attack. Unless your LAN has a modem attached to one of the systems and that modem is programmed to answer the phone, you need have no fear of outside access to your LAN. Indeed, if you have ever attempted to set up a modem so that it will answer the phone, you know that this is not easy to do. Unless a working phone answering system has been set up, the mere presence of a modem will not give an outsider access. Only sophisticated electronic eavesdropping equipment can get data from your LAN if there is no phone access to it. Even then, if you have used password protection on data access with TOPS, plus used the file password protection built in to most applications such as Word, Excel, 1-2-3, and Word-Perfect, then you need have nothing to fear.

Internal attack. The main cause for concern when it comes to the security of data on your LAN is *internal* breaches, attacks from someone who works within the company. Deflection of prying eyes can be approached at four levels. The more levels you use, the more secure your data will be:

1. *Machine access.* Use a third-party software or hardware product to limit use of machines. These products require that a user sign in or use a key before they can use the machine. This prevents casual unauthorized use.

2. *Storage area access, Level 1.* Do not put sensitive files in published folders or directories. Because TOPS allows you to publish less than a whole drive, simply keep sensitive files out of the areas that you publish. *Never* use the Remember feature to automatically publish an entire drive. Not only does this make security more difficult to enforce, but it is a waste of resources. Bear in mind that publishing one part of a disk does not give other users access to the rest of the disk or to the rest of your system.

3. *Storage area access, Level 2.* Use the TOPS Password option to limit access to the areas that you do publish. This option is always presented whenever you publish with TOPS/DOS. On the Mac, you must pull down the Publish button to see the password option, which appears as shown in Fig. 14-5.

    By using a password here only those who know the password will be able to mount the published volume.

4. *File access.* Use the password protection feature of your application to add password protection to sensitive files. It is amazing how many users overlook the excellent protection afforded by many popular applications such as 1-2-3, WordPerfect, and Excel. You have paid for this protection and, if you are serious about securing data, you should use it.

Of course, using passwords is a pain, and so you should decide if the need for security is real. If it is, then you will want to make sure you use proper passwords.

Fig. 14-5. Access control in TOPS/Macintosh.

Password Pointers

Using a password in TOPS or in an application like Excel is of little or no use if you use a useless password. Common examples are "password," "pass," "your first name," "the filename," and so on. Believe it or not, you can buy lists of common passwords, so the serious data thief is likely to guess most words that do not have the following features:

- At least eight characters.
- Mixture of text and numbers.
- Some odd characters, like @ and commas.
- Mixture of upper and lowercase.
- A lack of logic.

While some applications are not sensitive to upper and lowercase distinctions, and others do not permit odd characters, all allow you to use the last feature: a lack of logical connection between the content of the file and the password protecting it. For example, a banker might use the names of birds to protect a series of salary recommendation files. Combined with the other features, something like this would be difficult to guess:

Robin@5769

Because such a name would also be difficult to remember, you must also make proper provision for recording and securing passwords. A sheet of paper locked in a drawer is usually a good technique. You can use a spreadsheet or word processor to list files and their passwords. The more paranoid might want to code the passwords on the printed listing.

Bear in mind that the more security you use, the more cumbersome users will find network operations. For this reason you should seriously address the question of what needs to be secured, and how serious the threats to that security are. For more on this subject, see *Stephen Cobb's Complete Guide To PC and Network Security*, Windcrest (Book No. 3280), 1990.

About Backup

Every computer user should know about backup, the need to make copies of important files in case something happens to one of them. We store so much valuable information on computers these days that the loss of a disk can put a serious dent in our work, not to mention our attitude and the bottom line.

Every user should take responsibility for keeping backups of his or her own work. Participating in a network does not absolve users of this responsibility, particularly when the network is a democratic and independent one like TOPS. If you are running TOPS in a central server configuration where most people store their data on large capacity central disks, then you can provide something like a tape backup unit on the server and perform automated backups each night of the whole set of data, using the software that comes with the tape backup unit. However, if you are using TOPS in the distributed mode, where there is no central storage, then you should make sure everyone on the network knows that they are responsible for their own backup.

A Batch File Reboot System

In some situations, PC users will find that they need several different configurations of their system to accommodate the various devices and memory management systems needed for PC networking. The configuration information contained in CONFIG.SYS cannot be altered once you have booted up your system. The only way to alter the configuration is to change the CONFIG.SYS and then perform a *warm boot*, that is, press Ctrl-Alt-Delete to have your computer restart. Now you can develop a series of CONFIG files that have different names such as WINTOPS.SYS that is designed for running TOPS with Windows, and MAXTOPS.SYS that is designed to run TOPS with a memory management program in place. You can copy one of these to CONFIG.SYS and then reboot to use it.

You might want to incorporate this action into a batch file, offering the user a choice of configurations, selectable from a menu, as with the batch file menu system described in Chapter 9. The problem with this is that there is no DOS command for reboot. However, you can create such a command, a file that performs a reboot. Then you can create a pair of batch files that allow you to choose between two configurations by typing either 1 or 2 and pressing Enter. The file called 1.BAT might prepare the system for Windows and TOPS and could look like this:

```
COPY WINTOPS.SYS CONFIG.SYS
COPY WINTOPSA.BAT AUTOEXEC.BAT
REBOOT
```

Another file called 2.BAT could prepare the system a different way and look like this:

```
COPY MAXTOPS.SYS CONFIG.SYS
COPY MAXTOPS.BAT AUTOEXEC.BAT
REBOOT
```

Note that both files copy special CONFIG and AUTOEXEC.BAT files over the current ones, and then reboot the computer.

You could elaborate on this system by creating a standard AUTOEXEC.BAT and CONFIG.SYS. These could be put in place after every reboot to make sure that when the next user came along a standard setting was in place. To use a standard setting, you would include in every version of AUTOEXEC.BAT a final line that called a batch file named REFIT.BAT. This file would contain the lines:

```
COPY CONFHOLD.SYS CONFIG.SYS
COPY AUTOHOLD.BAT AUTOEXEC.BAT
```

Because these would be executed after the reboot, they would place the standard files (CONFHOLD and AUTOHOLD) in position for the next time the system was turned on.

To create the REBOOT.COM file that makes this system possible, follow these instructions, beginning at the DOS prompt:

1. Type DEBUG and press Enter. You will get a minus sign as you prompt.
2. Type A 100 and press Enter. You will get a series of numbers in response. We got 4197:0100 but you might get different digits for the first four, the rest will be the same.
3. Type MOV AX,40 and press Enter. The number prompt will change to something like 4197:0103. Now type the following, ending each line with Enter:

   MOV DS,AX
   MOV WORD PTR [72],1234
   JMP FFFF:0

   The prompt should now be something like 4197:0110.
4. Press Enter again and the minus sign prompt will return. Type R CX and press Enter. You will get a colon as your next prompt.
5. Type 10 and press Enter. The minus prompt will return. Type N REBOOT.COM and press Enter, followed by W and Enter. You will get a message Writing 0010 bytes. Now type Q and press Enter.

You have now made a program file called REBOOT.COM that will perform the same action as Ctrl-Alt-Delete. Be careful how you use this as it will not ask you if you are sure! However, properly used, it can be a very handy utility. If you use a zero instead of the number 1234, you can make a program that performs a *cold boot*, that is, one which makes your system perform a parity check on memory.

Other Batch File Tricks

A handy way to make batch files more flexible is to have them ask for user input. There are several ways of doing this. One of the simplest forms of input is provided by the batch command PAUSE. When you insert the pause command into a batch file you can give the user a chance to say no. For example, we use the following file called DELBAK.BAT that clears away old BAK files:

```
@ECHO OFF
CLS
ECHO About to delete all BAK files, press Ctrl-C to abort
PAUSE
DEL *.BAK
```

When you type DELBAK and press Enter, the screen gives the following response:

About to delete all BAK files, press Ctrl-C to abort
Strike a key when ready . . .

The last line of the response is generated by the PAUSE command. If the user presses any normal key, then the batch file continues. If the user presses Ctrl–C, then the batch file is stopped, and the screen asks Terminate batch job (Y/N). If the user types N then the batch file continues. If the user types Y, the batch file is ended. You can use this type of pause mechanism in batch files that perform TOPS operations, giving the user a chance to alter the course of the batch file. For example, if you have included LOADTOPS in your AUTOEXEC.BAT you will have TOPS loaded every time your system boots. However, you might want to have the option to prevent that, to run without TOPS on some occasions. By adding the following to the LOADTOPS.BAT file you can give yourself that option:

```
ECHO About to load TOPS network, press Ctrl-C to abort
PAUSE
ALAP
PSTACK, and so on . . .
```

One limitation of the PAUSE command is that if you use Ctrl–C to abort the batch file, the whole batch file terminates. You might want to build a variety of responses into your batch files. You can do this with a public domain DOS utility like ASK.COM or with ASK.EXE that comes with the Norton Utilities. These little programs allow you to solicit a variety of user replies and carry on the batch file according to the response.

FUTURE DEVELOPMENTS

Here we are at the end of what has been a very interesting project. We have enjoyed working with TOPS, and we have enjoyed the prospect that what we have written will help you work with TOPS. While the last chapter has raised some technical questions that might seem a little overwhelming, most aspects of operating TOPS are relatively easy once you are familiar with the basic concepts involved. When it comes to the more exotic connections between different network systems and different levels of computers, the matters necessarily increase in complexity. However, the trend is definitely toward more effective connections between hardware and between programs. Look for new version of applications to offer better file translation between Macs and IBMs, even direct file reading such as you now have in Excel, PageMaker, and a few other programs.

As for TOPS itself, it will continue to grow as a popular means of getting people together on networks. Future developments in PC technology will probably remove the RAM limit and allow all popular applications to run together with TOPS on a broad range of machine types. The InBox electronic mail facility will continue to improve, particularly on the PC side where more sophisticated programming will allow better pop-up menu access. Stay in touch with your TOPS dealer for word on the latest developments and be sure to register all TOPS purchases with Sun Microsystems so that you will receive news of upgrades and new products. Finally, if you have tips, tricks, and comments on TOPS to share, try using the TOPS bulletin board, described in the previous chapter, as well as the TOPS area on CompuServe (use GO APVENA to get to Apple Vendor Forum A where TOPS is in library 5). Of course, your suggestions are also appreciated by the authors of this book. Any suggestions that we use will be acknowledged in the next edition, and you will be eligible for a free copy. Please write us care of Windcrest Books.

Appendix A
TOPS Error Messages

THIS APPENDIX LISTS ERROR MESSAGES you might encounter while using your TOPS software. We begin with messages you might encounter on IBM systems with TOPS/DOS. Then we look at the TOPS/Macintosh and TOPS/Spool messages.

ERRORS WITH TOPS/DOS

This listing is by alphabetical order according to the first word in the message. In some cases, we have given examples of the error. In others, we have suggested why the error occurred and what you might try to solve or prevent it. When we give examples, we generally use the root directory of drive C as the location of files. If you are using a different directory or drive, you will need to make the corresponding changes.

Another volume is already mounted on this drive.

The drive letter you specified during the mount operation has already been used for a remote volume. Choose another drive letter or unmount the other volume.

AppleTalk Driver not installed.

This means that TOPS has not been loaded into memory before you tried to use TPRINT. Enter LOADTOPS command, then TPRINT will work. To use TPRINT without the memory overhead of TOPS, load the LAP driver (ALAP or ELAP) and PSTACK only, before using TPRINT.

Bad Path, cannot find: <name>.

The pathname specifying which directory should be published is not correct. Verify that you typed in the drive specifier and name correctly and that the directory actually exists.

Bad path specifier
As in C:\>TOPS PUBLISH

The pathname specifying which directory should be published is not correct. Verify that you typed in the correct drive specifier and name and that the directory actually exists.

Cannot find directory: <name>.

The directory you are trying to publish or use as a spool directory does not exist.

Cannot find printer: <name>.

The printer name you selected is no longer in the list of available printers. Check the printers available for the given server.

Cannot find server: <name>.

The named server is not found on the network. Try refreshing the servers in the File Servers submenu of TOPSMENU with the Home key, or use TOPS DIR, to verify that the server is still active. Try this twice if you don't see it the first time. If you see the server's name, try the command again (twice if necessary). If it fails, check for a bad network connection.

Cannot find volume: <name>.

The volume name you selected is no longer in the list of available volumes. Check the volumes available window for the given server for a list of available volumes.

Can't do Server Utilities without TOPS Server installed.

You are trying to access server utilities after loading client-only version of the software. Unload TOPS with TOPS UL /A and use the LOADTOPS load command.

Can't UNLOAD TOPSPRTR while printers are published.

You must unpublish printers before unloading them.

Can't UNLOAD TOPSKRNL while Volumes are Published.

You must unpublish all volumes before unloading TOPSKRNL.

Can't UNLOAD TOPSKRNL while Volumes or Printers are mounted.

You must unmount all volumes and printers before unloading TOPSKRNL.

Can't unmount your current drive: <drive>
As in C:\>TOPS UNMOUNT

If you specified a drive, the drive you specified is your current drive and cannot be unmounted until you log on to a different drive. If you used the /A option, the current drive is one of the drives mounted by a remote volume. You must change your current drive. Try unmounting from a local drive.

Client <client> not found.
As in C:\>TOPS LOGOUT

The specified client was not found in your list of active clients. Check TOPS PSTAT /C to verify that they are still using your volumes or printer.

Directory already published
As in C:\>TOPS PUBLISH

A subdirectory or a parent directory of the directory you are trying to publish has already been published. Try the TOPS PSTAT /V command to see which volumes are already published.

Directory: <name> or sub-directory is already published.

A subdirectory or a parent directory of the directory you are trying to publish has already been published. Try the VOLUMES PUBLISHED window to see which volumes are already published.

Drive already assigned to remote volume
As in C:\>TOPS MOUNT

The drive letter you specified in the MOUNT command has already been used for a remote volume. You should choose another drive letter or unmount the other volume.

Drive does not exist or no disk in drive.

The drive specified to publish or mount was not a legal drive specifier. For publish, it could be a non-local drive. For mount, it might be out of the legal range. If it is a legal specifier of a floppy drive, make sure the disk is properly in the drive.

Drive not valid
As in C:\>TOPS UNMOUNT <drive>, C:\>CSTAT <drive>

The drive you specified is not valid. Try the TOPS CSTAT command to verify that the drive you entered is local or mounted to a remote volume.

Error 2000 or 2001, Stack overflow

Check that your DOS version is properly installed on your computer. To do this, type COMMAND and press Enter. Make note of the version of DOS displayed and then type VER and press Enter. Do the two responses mention the same version? If the version numbers are different, then DOS is installed incorrectly and you need to reinstall DOS on your PC.

Error <number> returned trying to XSYNC <path>.
As in C:\>TOPS PUBLISH

TOPS was unable to run the TOPS utility XSYNC on the directory you are trying to publish. This could happen if the path specified is invalid, the utility XSYNC.EXE is not in one of the directories specified by the PATH environment variable, or there is not enough memory to run XSYNC from within TOPS. Try running XSYNC directly from the DOS command line, with the following syntax:

As in C:\>XSYNC /s /y <path>

If the error was due to a shortage of memory, this command should complete successfully. You should then attempt the PUBLISH command with the /X option.

EXEC failure.

You might see this message when attempting to load a remote application. To fix the problem, the path for the TOPSEXEC.COM file (line 6 in the TOPSKRNL.DAT file) must be modified to point to the drive and directory where your TOPSEXEC.COM file is located. Reload TOPS after making this change.

Invalid directory
As in C:\>TOPS PUBLISH

The directory you are trying to publish does not exist.

Invalid mode argument
As in C:\>TOPS PUBLISH, C:\>TOPS MOUNT

The argument which was passed as the mode was not one of the legal options. Check the format of the command using TOPS HELP.

Invalid parameter to PSTAT
As in C:\>TOPS PSTAT

One of the parameters you entered for the PSTAT command was not valid. Check TOPS HELP PSTAT for the syntax of the PSTAT command.

Invalid password
As in C:\>TOPS MOUNT

The password entered on the command line or at the prompt was not correct. Try the command again, and be careful typing the password.

Memory error (not enough)
As in C:\>TOPS DIR

TOPSKRNL couldn't allocate memory for a temporary buffer. Try the command again. If it returns the same error, you might want to increase the buffer size in the TOPSKRNL.DAT file and reload TOPS.

Name conflict C:\>TOPS STATION <name>

The name you have chosen has already been used by someone on the network. You must choose another name.

Name conflict, choose another Server name.

The name you have chosen has already been used by someone on the network. You must choose another name.

Name too long
As in C:\>TOPS STATION, C:\>TOPS PUBLISH

The station name or volume name or printer name you specified is too long. The limit on PC station names is 15 characters. The limit on PC volume or printer names is 16 characters.

Network error
As in C:\>TOPS DIR <server>, C:\>TOPS MOUNT

This is a general network error. If it happens frequently (that is, with many servers), there might be a bad network connection somewhere on the net. Otherwise, the server you are trying to list the volumes or printer from or connect to might be stuck in an error condition.

No available interrupts for TWINDOVL.

TWINDOVL.EXE is the windowing program used by TOPSMENU (and the CONFIGURE program of TOPS NetPrint). See Chapter 14 for problems with this program and ways to get around them.

No more volumes may be published.

You have reached the limit of remote volumes you can publish. Try unpublishing some or increasing the relevant values in the TOPSKRNL.DAT file and reloading TOPS.

No network driver.

You have tried to start TOPS by loading only TOPSTALK, without first loading ALAP (or ELAP) and PSTACK.

Not ready error reading drive X:
Abort, Retry, Fail

This is actually a DOS error that can arise when you are loading TOPS and have specified a drive in your drive map that is removable, such as a Bernoulli Box. Simply type F for Fail and TOPS will continue to load successfully.

No volume specified to UNPUBLISH
As in C:\>TOPS UNPUBLISH

You did not specify which volume is to be unpublished or use the /A option. You must enter the name of the volume you wish to unpublish or use the /A option to unpublish all your volumes.

Null pointer assignment

Check that your DOS version is properly installed on your computer. Enter COMMAND and press Enter. Make note of the version of DOS displayed. Next, type VER and press Enter. Check the version of DOS it displays. If the version numbers are different, then DOS is installed incorrectly and you need to reinstall DOS on your PC.

PAP open failed. Network error. File not sent.

This indicates that your PC is not seeing the network print device due to bad cabling, a poor connection, or an improperly terminated network. It is also possible that the device is not turned on or not set to AppleTalk mode. See the Troubleshooting section for information about how to check LocalTalk connections.

Path: <name> does not refer to a local physical drive.

The drive specifier in the pathname specifying which directory should be published is not a local drive. Verify that you typed in the correct drive specifier.

Printer: <name> is in use, cannot be unpublished.

The printer you wish to unpublish has active clients. You should either ask them to disconnect or use the LOGOUT command in the PRINTER CLIENTS window to close them out from your printer.

Serial number conflict
As in C:\>TOPS STATION <name>

The serial number of the TOPSKRNL you are using is the same as that of someone else on the network. Make sure you are not using someone else's TOPS disk.

Server has active clients
As in \>TOPS STATION <name>

Your server has active clients while you are trying to set a new station name. You must wait until there are no active clients to change your station name.

Server has incompatible version
As in C:\>TOPS DIR <server>, C:\>TOPS MOUNT

The server you wish to access has an incompatible version of TOPS. You should upgrade to the latest version of TOPS on all systems.

Server not found
As in C:\>TOPS DIR <server>, C:\>TOPS MOUNT

The named server is not found on the network. Try refreshing the servers in the File Servers submenu of TOPSMENU with the Home key, or use TOPS DIR, to verify that the server is still active (you might want to try it a second time if you don't see it the first). If you see the server's name, try the command again (twice if necessary). If it fails, check for a bad network connection.

Server too busy to accept connection
As in C:\>TOPS DIR <server>, C:\>TOPS MOUNT

The server whose volumes or printer you were trying to list or whose volumes or printer you were trying to mount is being used by its limit of clients. Try another server.

Station name already initialized
As in C:\>TOPS STATION <name>

Your station name has already been initialized and is ON. If you want to change your station name, turn the name OFF using the TOPS STATION OFF command first.

Station name not initialized
As in C:\>TOPS DIR, C:\>TOPS PUBLISH, C:\>TOPS MOUNT

You are trying to use the network without providing a network name for your station. Use the TOPS STATION command to set your station name.

The DMA buffers cross an absolute 64K boundary. To use DMA, the driver must be relocated.

The location of the network driver in your computer's RAM is such that the buffer for DMA data transfer is falling across an absolute 64K boundary. TOPS will still work, but the driver will not use DMA, and FlashTalk will be disabled. You can relocate the driver by modifying the amount of memory used by any program which is loaded before it. A simple way to do this is to increase the setting of your FILES or BUFFERS statement in CONFIG.SYS.

The driver cannot find the network board. Please check the jumper settings and command line options in the manual. The Lap driver is not installed. The driver will not be installed.

You will see this message if you do not have a TOPS supported network interface card installed in your PC. Or, your network interface board is either not seated properly, seated in a nonfunctioning slot, set at an I/O address different from that specified in the CONFIGURE option of the SETUP program, or is defective.

The Lap driver is not installed. The driver will not be installed.

You need to load ALAP (or ELAP) before PSTACK.

There are incompatible versions of TOPS on this network.

The server you wish to access has an incompatible version of TOPS. You should upgrade to the latest version of TOPS on all systems.

There is another Station already logged in with this Serial Number.

The serial number of the TOPSKRNL you are using is the same as someone else's on the network. Make sure you are not using someone else's TOPS disk.

This operation cannot be completed while a Client is using this volume.

This volume has active clients while you are trying to change the alias, password, or mode. You must wait until there are no active clients to make these changes.

This printer is already assigned to TOPS NetPrint.

Either abandon the printer assignment or request a different printer.

This printer is already published or reassigned.

Either abandon the printer command or request a different printer.

This server is password protected. You must provide the password.

The server you have selected requires a password. Either input the appropriate password or request a different server.

This server is either not there or not servicing requests.

The server whose volumes or printers you were trying to list or whose volume or printer you were trying to mount is overloaded and not currently servicing your requests. Try refreshing the servers on the network window with the Home key to verify that the server is still active (you might want to try it a second time if you don't see it the first) or try again in a few minutes.

This server is overloaded and cannot serve you at this time.

The server whose volumes or printers you were trying to list or whose volume or printer you were trying to mount is being used by its limit of clients. Try another server.

Too many volumes mounted
As in C:\>TOPS MOUNT

You have reached the limit of remote volumes you can mount. Try unmounting some or increasing the relevant values in the TOPSKRNL.DAT file and reloading TOPS.

TOPS: Command (<command>) not found. Type TOPS HELP for a list.
As in C: \>TOPS <command>

The command you entered wasn't recognized as a TOPS command. Make sure there wasn't an error entering the command and try TOPS HELP to get a list of the valid TOPS commands.

TOPS HELP command (<command>) not found.
As in C:\>TOPS HELP <command>

The command you entered wasn't recognized as a TOPS command. Try TOPS HELP to get a list of the valid TOPS commands.

TOPS illegal option (<option>), ignored
As in C:\>TOPS <option> <command>

There was an option entered before a TOPS command was specified. The only option recognized in that way is the /Q option which prevents the copyright message from being displayed.

TOPS memory error type: <number>.

TOPSKRNL couldn't allocate memory for a temporary buffer. Try the command again. If it returns the same error, you might want to increase the buffer size in the TOPSKRNL.DAT file and reload TOPS.

TOPS Network error type: <number>.

This is the dreaded general network error. If it happens frequently, there might be a bad network connection somewhere on the network. Otherwise, the server you are trying to access might be stuck in an error condition. Check the remote system for problems.

TOPS: no arguments specified. Enter TOPS HELP for more information.
As in C: \>TOPS

There were no arguments or commands entered after TOPS on the command line.

TOPS: TOPSKRNL not installed, aborting.
As in C:\>TOPS

You tried using TOPS without having the background software (TOPSKRNL.EXE) installed.

TOPS: You must load TOPSPRTR before you can Publish a Printer.

TOPSPRTR controls all printer functioning. Be sure to load TOPSPRTR before publishing a printer.

TOPSRRNL error detected: insufficient memory TOPSKRNL installation aborted.

You have set the parameters in TOPSKRNL.DAT so high that there is insufficient memory available to load TOPSKRNL. Reduce some of the settings and try again.

TOPSPRTR is not installed

Printing cannot occur unless an installed TOPSPRTR is available. Return to the TOPS installation program and install TOPSPRTR.

Topstalk: Insufficient memory.

The default size of the memory buffer for TOPSTALK and TOPSTALC is set to handle network usage corresponding to the default settings in TOPSKRNL.DAT. If you have increased these settings, and you have published and or mounted extensively, you might get this error. The solution is to increase the TOPSTALK buffer size (not the same as TOPSKRNL buffer size, line 21 of the TOPSKRNL.DAT file). To increase the TOPSTALK buffer size, add a parameter to the TOPSTALK or TOPSTALC command of the form: /M=x000, where x equals the size (in K) to which you wish to set the buffer. Thus, if you were a very heavily-used server, and you wished to increase the buffer size to 20K from its default size of 10K (the maximum is 30K), the command would read: TOPSTALK /M=20000.

Unable to write to remember file.

There has been some error in writing the file TOPSTART.BAT. See if your disk is full on your current drive.

Unable to XSYNC <name>: <number>.

TOPS was unable to run the TOPS utility XSYNC on the directory you are trying to publish. This could happen if the utility XSYNC.EXE is not in one of the directories specified by the PATH environment variable, or there is not enough memory to run XSYNC from within TOPSMENU. Try running XSYNC directly from the DOS command line, with the following syntax:

C:\>XSYNC /s /y <path>

If the error was due to a shortage of memory, this command should complete successfully. You should then attempt to publish the volume without running XSYNC by using the Alt–X option.

Unknown error condition
As in C:\>TOPS

There might be some error conditions that are not documented here or in the TOPS manual. You might want to note the circumstances and the error number and contact TOPS Technical Support about such an error.

Unknown error type <number> on call <number>.

There might be some error conditions that are not caught by TOPSMENU. If you come across one, please note the circumstances, the error type number and the call number and contact TOPS Technical Support.

Unrecognized argument to PUBLISH: <arg>
As in C:\>TOPS PUBLISH

One of the parameters you entered for the PUBLISH command was not valid. Check TOPS HELP PUBLISH for the syntax of that command.

Volume in use
As in C:\>TOPS UNPUBLISH

The volume you wish to unpublish has active clients. You should either ask them to disconnect or use the TOPS LOGOUT command to close them out from your server.

Volume: <name> is in use _ cannot be unpublished.

The volume you wish to unpublish has active clients. You should either ask them to disconnect or use the LOGOUT command in the FILE CLIENTS window to close them out from your server.

Volume not found
As in C:\>TOPS UNPUBLISH

The volume name you entered was not in the list of currently published volumes. Check TOPS PSTAT /V for a list of published volumes.

You cannot reassign your current drive.

You have attempted to mount a volume on the drive that is your current drive. You must change your current drive before you can reassign this drive.

You cannot unmount your current drive.

You have attempted to unmount the drive that is your current drive. You must change your current drive before you can unmount this volume.

You have reached the limit of volumes you can publish or mount.

You have reached the limit of remote volumes you can publish or mount. Try unmounting or unpublishing some volumes or increasing the relevant values in the TOPSKRNL.DAT file and reloading TOPS.

MACINTOSH ERRORS WITH TOPS

The following sections contain error messages you might encounter while using TOPS/Macintosh or TOPS Spool. The listings are grouped by function. After each message, we give an explanation that supplies the error solution.

When Starting TOPS/Macintosh

The following messages might appear on your screen while you are starting up your Macintosh with TOPS installed on your startup disk:

Install TOPS?

This will appear if you are holding down the Option key or the mouse button while you are starting up your Mac, actually a handy way to bypass TOPS if you need to for diagnostic purposes.

TOPS: Cannot Open AppleTalk.

TOPS tries to open AppleTalk as soon as it is installed. If it can't, it presents this message and then uninstalls itself. The most likely cause is that the AppleTalk drivers aren't installed in your system.

When Opening TOPS Desk Accessory

No List Manager (Pick 0).

The Desk Accessory needs this system resource to run. You probably have an old System file.

Please Install TOPS First.

The Desk Accessory cannot run until the TOPS driver has been installed. You must either start up from a disk with TOPS in the System folder, or you must run the Start TOPS program.

Please use 31 or Fewer Characters.

Your network name can have a maximum of 31 characters.

Sorry, That Name is Already in Use. Please Try Another.
Two different users cannot use the same network name.

You'll have to use another one while the other user is logged on the network.

Sorry, Name Registration Error.

For some reason AppleTalk couldn't register your network name. Try again. If it still fails, try simplifying your environment. You might be trying to run other AppleTalk programs at the same time. There may be conflict from other background programs that use a lot of memory. Try eliminating one of these. If all else fails, try another name.

Sorry, your serial # is Already in Use by:

Each station on your network must have a different serial number. You must use a different copy of TOPS with a unique serial number in order to sign on to the network.

Warning: TOPS Has Been Damaged.

If the TOPS driver becomes damaged, it will present this message once as soon as the damage is detected. You should save your work and unmount any remote volumes as soon as possible. Current connections will be maintained as long as possible, but any attempt to use the TOPS Desk Accessory will present one of the two messages below:

Warning: This Copy of TOPS Has Been Damaged! Please Return it From Backup.

If the TOPS driver has been damaged before you start using it, this message appears the first time you try to use your Desk Accessory. To replace the damaged driver, copy the file called TOPS from your Disk I master and replace the working copy of the TOPS file.

Warning: This Copy of TOPS has been damaged! Please Save Your Work and Reboot as Soon as Possible.

If TOPS is already in use when the driver becomes damaged, this message will appear when you try to use your Desk Accessory.

When Using the TOPS Desk Accessory

That Server is Running a Different Version of TOPS.

Your Macintosh is running a different version of TOPS than the server, and they might or might not be compatible. Make sure that all stations are running the same version of TOPS.

That Server is Running an Incompatible Version of TOPS.

Your Macintosh is running a different version of TOPS than the server, and they are definitely not compatible. You will have to upgrade TOPS either on your Macintosh or the server. (You can also see this message if a serial number conflict is detected after sign-on.)

Sorry, That Server is Not Responding.

You will get this message if the server does not respond within a certain amount of time, typically 30 seconds. Either the server has shut down or crashed, or the person using the server is doing something that blocks its network activity, such as running a program that doesn't support Desk Accessories.

Sorry, Can't Open That Volume.

You will get this message if TOPS cannot open a particular volume and a more specific error message is not available. Again, the message is probably due to the server's failure or an activity that blocks network activity.

Sorry, Can't Open That Directory.

You will get this message if TOPS cannot open a particular directory and no more specific error message is available. You might also receive this message when you double click on a file icon. Files cannot be opened from the TOPS Desk Accessory.

Sorry, Can't Read That Directory.

You will get this message if TOPS cannot read a particular directory, and no more specific error message is available.

When Mounting or Unmounting Volumes

That Volume is Write Protected and Has No DeskTop File. You Can Use It From an Application, But the Finder Will Reject It.

Although the Desktop file is usually invisible because the Finder doesn't display its icon, the Finder (version 6.1 and earlier) requires a Desktop file on every volume. If there is no Desktop file, the Finder tries to create one. However, the creation fails if the disk is write protected. The way to access such a volume is to "initialize" it. Publish the volume with the Publish option One writer only or Many writers, then mount it from a remote Macintosh, and let the remote Finder create the Desktop file. Then republish it write-protected. From then on, you should not have problems with the Desktop file. Alternatively, you can enter an application and then mount and unmount the volume without ever returning to the Finder.

Sorry, No More Than 6 Remote Volumes May be Mounted at Once.

When this message appears, you must unmount one of your previously mounted volumes before you can mount another. Although any number of volumes can be published, a station can only mount 6 remote volumes at a time.

Warning: You Have Open Files on That Volume. The Safest Way to Unmount it is to Return to the Finder and Drag its Icon to the Trash.

This message usually appears when you try to unmount a volume from the TOPS Desk Accessory while the Finder is running. The Finder keeps an invisible DeskTop file open on each volume, and it can have information in memory that needs to be written out. If you return to the Finder and drag the icon to the trash, then the Finder itself is responsible for the unmounting, and it will flush the Desk-Top properly. If you are running an application when you get this message, then a document from the remote volume might still be open. If so, you can close it and then unmount from the Desk Accessory without returning to the Finder. But returning to the Finder is always the safest course of action, because that forces the application to properly close its files.

When Publishing Volumes

Sorry, Two Published Volumes May Not Have the Same Name.

You will get this message if you try to publish a volume or a folder with a name that is identical to something you have previously published. Each server's volumes must have distinct names. You should return to the Finder and rename the volume you are trying to publish.

Warning: "   " Has Active Users. If You Continue, They May Lose Their Work.

You will get this message if you try to unpublish, eject, or unmount a volume that someone else is currently using. You should cancel the operation, click Help to get a list of users, and ask them to save their work.

When Copying Files

That Volume is Write-Protected.

You will get this message if you try to copy a file to a write-protected volume. You should have the server republish the volume in a mode that allows writing.

Sorry, There is Not Enough Space on That Volume.

You will get this message if you try to copy a file to a volume that doesn't have enough room. You will have to delete some files on the destination volume or copy to another volume.

Please Use 31 or Fewer Characters.

If the destination volume already has a file with the same name as the one you are trying to copy, you are given a chance to specify a new name. You get this message if you try to specify a name with more than 31 characters. You should edit or retype the name.

Break This Server Connection?

If your Macintosh ever seems to be "stuck" while the network activity light is blinking, then you are connected to a server that has become unable to respond. If the server's case is really critical (someone has tripped over the power cord, for example), your Macintosh will stop trying within 30 seconds. You can tell if you are in the middle of a network operation by looking at the upper left corner of your screen. A tiny "light" will blink on and off while your Macintosh is waiting for the server to respond. Be careful about choosing Give Up unless all your work has been saved. Some programs crash when you break one of their operations.

Sorry, Network Error.

This message is given in the rare case of a network error that isn't covered by any of the other more detailed error messages. It usually pertains to network hardware.

Sorry, Out of Memory.

Try closing some files and/or unmounting some volumes to free up enough memory. If you have an all-Macintosh network, you could also restart and delete the InterBase file.

Sorry, That Operation Failed.

This message is given when the Desk Accessory is unable to read the specific error message it wants from the disk.

Do you want the output currently being printed to be cancelled too?

If you turn off the Print spooled output while I work option while one of your outputs is still being printed, this warning message will appear. You can allow the laser printer to finish by clicking on the NO button.

The installer can't install the driver and/or the Desk Accessory because there aren't enough free slots available.

There are too many Desk Accessories already installed in your System file. Remove an unwanted Desk Accessory with the Font DA/Mover and try installing TOPS Spool again (you might have to remove two). If you are using Suitcase 1.0, you need to move it out of the System folder, restart your Macintosh, and install TOPS Spool. Then move Suitcase back into the System folder and restart your Macintosh again. Suitcase 2.0 is compatible with TOPS Spool as long as there are no more than 14 Desk Accessories installed in the System file.

The installer can't run because of a naming conflict with the TOPS Spool driver and/or Desk Accessory.

This occurs in the unlikely case that you already have a Desk Accessory or driver called TOPS Spool installed in your System file.

The installation failed because of a Resource Manager error (disk full?).

This installation error most likely occurs when your disk or its directory is full. If there is enough free disk space, this error can be caused by an unexpected system error. Restart your Macintosh and try installing TOPS Spool again. If the problem persists, call your dealer or TOPS Technical Support.

The LaserWriter needs to be initialized. You can do this by selecting the "Prep Laser" item in the TOPS Spool menu.

If a spooled document is the first one to print on the laser printer since it was turned on, you must choose the Prep Laser option in the TOPS Spool Desk Accessory in order to initialize the laser printer. This installs the contents of the Laser Prep file in the LaserWriter, which is needed for most LaserWriter printing (the most notable exception being PageMaker printing). The Laser Prep file must be in your System folder. The Print while I work option is automatically turned off until you select Prep Laser, then automatically is turned back on.

The LaserWriter needs to be initialized for PageMaker. You can do this by selecting the "Prep Aldus" item in the TOPS Spool menu.

If a spooled PageMaker document is the first one to print on the laser printer since it was turned on, you must choose the Prep Aldus option in the TOPS Spool Desk Accessory in order to initialize the laser printer for PageMaker. This installs the contents of the Aldus Prep file in the LaserWriter, which is needed for PageMaker printing. The Aldus Prep file must be in your System folder. The Print while I work option is automatically turned off until you select Prep Aldus, then is automatically turned back on.

The printing of FILENAME has been cancelled because AppleTalk is not connected.

In order to print to a laser printer, your Macintosh must be connected to AppleTalk. When you have connected the AppleTalk cables to the printer port of your Macintosh, start up the AppleTalk software with the Control Panel or Chooser Desk Accessory.

The printing of FILENAME has been cancelled because of a communications error.

Because of excessive network traffic, the connection to the LaserWriter has been broken and the printing of the output from FILENAME was cancelled. Printing will start over again with FILENAME as the next spooled output to print.

The printing of FILENAME has been cancelled because the LaserWriter could not be found.

Check to see that an existing LaserWriter is selected in the Chooser. If spooled output is directed towards a LaserWriter that does not exist on the network, it should be removed from the queue and reprinted after selecting a new LaserWriter. There might also be a physical break somewhere on the AppleTalk network, or possibly the laser printer has failed or simply been turned off. Check your connections and/or restart your laser printer.

The printing of FILENAME has been cancelled because of a System Error.

This error message results when any unexpected system error occurs, and typically results from an error in reading the spooled output. If it occurs, go back to your application and spool your output again.

This output will not be spooled because there is insufficient memory to do so.

Too much spooled output has been accumulated. In this case, printing proceeds directly, bypassing the spooler.

Some previously spooled output was found. Do you want to start printing it?

TOPS Spool is designed to survive a system shutdown without losing any spooled output. This statement appears after you restart a Macintosh where previously spooled output remains to be printed. It can also appear after you use the Change Disk...option in the TOPS Spool Desk Accessory menu. If you click the NO button, previously spooled output is not removed; instead, the Print spooled output while I work option is turned off.

Spooling was cancelled because of a System Error.

An unexpected system error occured while spooling the output. In this case, the output is lost and must be spooled again. This typically occurs if your disk becomes full while spooling.

Warning: Moving this output will cause printing in progress to be cancelled. Are you sure you want this to happen?

If you change the order of the outputs in the list of Spooled Output by dragging your first output after it has begun printing, its printing must be cancelled. This warning statement gives you a chance to cancel the change.

Warning: There is spooled output still not printed. Are you sure you want to do this?

This warning statement appears if you attempt to change the disk that TOPS Spool is writing its spooled output on when spooled output remains to be printed. If you click the YES button, the spooled output is not lost, but it will not appear in the list of Spooled Output until you change back to that disk again.

TOPS Spool shows the message "LaserPrint Error: Limitcheck (or Typecheck), Offending Command <<error message>>.

The most likely cause is that another user used a different version of the LaserWriter and LaserWriter Prep files. Check the LaserWriter driver versions by selecting Print...and looking in the upper right-hand corner of the LaserWriter print dialog box. Make sure all the users on the network have the same version of the LaserWriter drivers.

Screen (bitmap) image of Chicago font is being created because it does not reside in the printer.

This message appears when a spooled document contains screen fonts. Screen fonts, such as Chicago, do not have a corresponding LaserWriter font. LaserWriter fonts are stored in a PostScript format, while screen fonts are stored in a bitmap format. When the LaserWriter recognizes a screen font, it prints a bitmap image.

Errors in TOPS Translators

Typically, you will find that errors occurring within TOPS Translators cause a numbered message to be displayed. This number should be used to locate the message in the Appendix of the TOPS Macintosh manual. Remember that TOPS Translators must be run from a hard disk or an unlocked floppy disk. If the TOPS Translators application is launched from a locked floppy disk, you might get errors −1 and −51 during the translations and the translation log will not be created correctly.

Appendix B
TOPS-Related Product Directory

IN THIS APPENDIX, we have attempted to pull together all of the product references scattered throughout the book. We have split the listing into two main parts. We begin with products and what they do, and follow that with the addresses of manufacturers and suppliers. This arrangement avoided the duplication of address information.

With any product list, a couple of caveats are in order. We are not endorsing products by listing them. For performance data on products, we urge you to check for product reviews in the latest magazines, check with other users (for example through a bulletin board like CompuServe). We are not claiming that this list is complete or up-to-the-minute. In this business, few lists can account for every product in a field and few publications come out often enough to include everything that is "now" available.

MACINTOSH CONNECTORS AND CABLING SYSTEMS

TOPS TeleConnectors. Part of the TOPS TeleConnector System. TOPS Tele-Connectors provide the electrical drop from the Mac or PC to the network wiring (twisted pair telephone wire). A network connector is needed to connect every network device (computer or network printer). *Sun MicroSystems, TOPS Division.*

TOPS FlashBox. Hardware and software for the Macintosh that upgrades AppleTalk networks to FlashTalk speed. Works with Apple's LocalTalk as well as TOPS Teleconnectors and Farallon PhoneNET and compatibles. The FlashBox should be used on networks that are all FlashTalk capable (that is all Macs use FlashBox and all PCs use FlashCard). *Sun MicroSystems, TOPS Division.*

LocalTalk. AppleTalk cabling system from Apple Computer Corp. LocalTalk is shielded wiring with DIN-3 connections. A network connector is needed to connect every network device (computer or network printer). *Apple Computer Corporation.*

PhoneNET. AppleTalk cabling system from Farallon Computing. PhoneNET connectors provide the electrical drop from the Mac or PC to the network wiring (twisted pair telephone wire). A network connector is needed to connect every network device (computer or network printer). *Farallon Computing.*

Dupont Fiberoptic. The Dupont System is Fiberoptic cabling and connectors for AppleTalk Networks. They provide the electrical drop from the Mac or PC to the network wiring (fiberoptic). A network connector is needed to connect every network device (computer or network printer). *Dupont Connector Systems.*

MACINTOSH ETHERNET CARDS

EtherLink/SE and EtherLink/NB. Software and Ethernet adapters for the Macintosh SE and the Macintosh II. The EtherLink adapter is installed in an expansion slot on the Mac II or Mac SE. The card works with either thick or thin coaxial Ethernet cabling. *3Com Corporation.*

EtherPort SEL/SE and EtherPort IIL/II. Software and Ethernet adapters for the Macintosh SE and the Macintosh II. The EtherLink adapter is installed in an expansion slot on the Mac II or Mac SE. The card works with either thick or thin coaxial Ethernet cabling. *Kinetics, Inc.*

EtherPort SE/30. The EtherPort SE/30 is an internal card that will provide connection of a Macintosh SE/30 to either standard or thin Ethernet. Standard AppleTalk-based software packages for file and disk service, multi-user database systems, and electronic mail can run unmodified. In addition, the EtherPort SE/30 supports TCP/IP, DECnet, and OSI protocols. *Kinetics, Inc.*

EtherPort SE/30L. The EtherPort SE/30L is the same as the EtherPort SE/30, but it also provides direct connection of a Macintosh SE/30 to unshielded twisted pair Ethernet and standard Ethernet. *Kinetics, Inc.*

EtherSC3. EtherSC3 is a general-purpose external Ethernet connection for the Macintosh Plus, SE, or II using the SCSI interface. *Kinetics, Inc.*

Dove Fastnet. Software and Ethernet adapters for the Macintosh SE and the Macintosh II. The EtherLink adapter is installed in an expansion slot on the Mac II or Mac SE. The card works with either thick or thin coaxial Ethernet cabling. *Dove Computer Corporation.*

PC APPLETALK CARDS

TOPS FlashCard. AppleTalk interface card for IBM PCs and compatibles. It allows PCs to be networked to Macintoshes or other PCs using twisted pair cabling systems. The FlashCard transmission rate is 770 kbps, roughly three times the speed of standard AppleTalk. *Sun MicroSystems, TOPS Division.*

Apple PC Card. Appletalk interface card for IBM PCs and compatibles. *Apple Computer Corporation.*

Hercules Network Plus Card. Appletalk interface card for IBM PCs and compatibles that also includes a Hercules color monitor adapter. *Hercules Computer Technology, Inc.*

Daystar PC and PS/2 Cards. Appletalk interface card for IBM PCs and compatibles and for IBM PS/2 computers. TOPS recommends the Daystar PS/2 card be used on TOPS clients only, and not TOPS servers. *Daystar Digital, Inc.*

TandyLink Card. Appletalk interface card for IBM PCs and compatibles. *Tandy, Inc.*

PC ETHERNET CARDS

EtherLink II (3C503) and EtherLink II/MC (3C523). Software and Ethernet adapters for the IBM PC and PS/2. The EtherLink adapter is installed in a PC expansion slot. The card works with either thick or thin coaxial Ethernet cabling. *3Com Corporation.*

Ethercard Plus and Ethercard Plus/MC. Software and Ethernet adapters for the IBM PC and PS/2. The EtherLink adapter is installed in a PC expansion slot. The card works with either thick or thin coaxial Ethernet cabling. *Western Digital.*

APPLETALK REPEATERS

TOPS Repeater. Electronic signal repeating device that boosts network signals to extend network lengths. The repeater also will allow extend the number of devices (32 by default) that can operate on an electrical network. *Sun MicroSystems, TOPS Division.*

PhoneNET Repeater. Electronic signal repeating device that boosts network signals to extend network lengths. The repeater also will extend the number of devices (32 by default) that can operate on an electrical network. *Farallon Computing.*

PhoneNET Star Controller. An intelligent 12-port repeating device. The Star Controller is a central hub that can be installed in a building telephone closet and can repeat signals down multiple network branches. The Star Controller also includes some diagnostic software that can help track network problems. *Farallon Computing.*

APPLETALK BRIDGING DEVICES

Hayes InterBridge. Expands the connectivity of AppleTalk networks with both local and remote bridging capabilities. Locally, networks can be separated into zones to minimize work group traffic. Two Interbridges linked via modems can bridge two remote sites into a single network. *Hayes Microcomputer Products, Inc.*

Shiva Netmodem, NetSerial, NetBridge and TeleBridge. Shiva makes a product line of AppleTalk devices that enhance or can be shared on AppleTalk networks.

NetModem is a modem with an AppleTalk connection that can be shared by any Macintosh on the network that has the Shiva asynchronous driver in its System folder.

NetSerial is a connector that allows non-AppleTalk serial devices, such as an HP LaserJet to be connected to AppleTalk networks.

The NetBridge is a local bridging device that can separate large networks into smaller work groups and/or zones.

The TeleBridge can link two remote networks into a single network. *Shiva Corporation.*

Solana I-Server, C-Server, and R-Server. The C-Server will allow non-AppleTalk serial devices to be connected to AppleTalk networks.

The I-Server is a local bridging device that can separate large networks into smaller work groups and/or zones.

The R-Server can bridge two remote networks into a single network. *Solana Electronics, Inc.*

Infosphere Liaison. Liaison is a software product that will permit a Macintosh II to act as a remote AppleTalk bridge or as an AppleTalk/Ethernet bridge. To act as a remote bridge the Macintosh II must be equipped with a modem. To act as an AppleTalk/Ethernet bridge the Mac II must be fitted with an Ethernet interface card (see list of cards above). *InfoSphere, Inc.*

Kinetics FastPath. An intelligent AppleTalk to Ethernet bridge. The FastPath will reroute AppleTalk data packets over Ethernet cabling, and vice versa. The FastPath will also act as a TCP/IP gateway for Telenet terminal applications running on a Macintosh. FastPath supports multiple network protocols simultaneously including AppleTalk, TCP/IP and DECnet. This can use standard or thin Ethernet. LAN Ranger network management software comes standard with every FastPath. *Kinetics, Inc.*

APPLETALK NETWORK PRINTERS

In addition to the Apple LaserWriter, there is the AST TurboLaser, GCC Business LaserPrinter, NEC Silent Writer, and the QMS Laser. New PostScript compatible models are appearing quite frequently now. Check with manufacturers as to AppleTalk compatibility.

APPLE MACINTOSH PRINTER DRIVERS

MacPrint. Printer drivers that allow the Apple Macintosh to print to non-Apple printing devices such as the HP LaserJet. *Insight Development Corporation.*

Printworks. Printer drivers that allow the Apple Macintosh to print to non-Apple printing devices such as the NEC Spinwriter. *SoftStyle.*

NETWORK MANAGEMENT SOFTWARE

As networks grow in size, you need assistance in tracking the flow of information, spotting bottlenecks, and diagnosing problems. This is the role of network management software.

LAN Ranger. Network management software that comes standard with every Kinetics FastPath. Runs on Macintoshes with graphical display of network performance. *Kinetics, Inc.*

CheckNET DA and TrafficWatch. These two programs from Farallon Computing help you keep tabs on network activity. The CheckNET DA quickly shows who is using the network at the present time. TrafficWatch does the same thing, but also tracks activity over time to produce statistics on device usage, by whom, and so on. This kind of information helps you optimize performance and add new devices in the right places.

OTHER USEFUL ITEMS

This section holds a miscellany of programs that we have mentioned as being useful when mixing PCs and Macs on a TOPS network.

ResEdit. For those who want to change the Mac trashcan icon to a black hole or garbage heap, plus edit other icons, resources, and file forks. Free from Apple Computer Corporation.

PC Tools Deluxe. Talk about gender confusion, this product comes in PC and Mac versions. The version for the Mac is very useful as it gives you access to resource forks so that you can edit them, overcoming one of the big hurdles in PC-to-Mac file transfer. Also provides file encryption with password protection, a file finder, a diskette recovery, and file undelete system. Plus you get a program for optimizing your hard disk which we have found helps prevent system crashes caused by system folder corruption. *Central Point Software.*

HIJAAK. A program for converting graphic files between many different formats on the PC. Can also create files in MacPaint format form PC files but you must edit the resource fork to read into MacPaint. *INSET Systems.*

PCX to TIFF Converter. A pair of programs to convert graphics from PCX to TIFF and back come with Paint-It, a paint program for the PC that stores in TIFF format and edits Mac TIFF files without conversion. This software comes with the DEXXA Mouse. *DEXXA International.*

Mace Utilities. One of the first commercial programs to offer recovery from disk formatting on PCs. Also has disk optimizing, caching, and other useful features for the PC user.

Norton Utilities. The first commercial software to enable PC users to recover deleted files. Also offers disk optimization routines, batch file programming extensions, and a powerful disk editing features.

QuickDOS II. A personal favorite when it comes to managing files on a PC hard disk. Quick file locate, group, move, copy, and edit facilities with a simple menu system that runs in a variety of colors. This program can be used as a DOS shell for launching programs. *Gazelle Systems.*

NAMES AND ADDRESSES

3Com Corporation
3165 Kifer Rd.
Santa Clara, CA 95052
(408)562-6400

Apple Computer Corporation
20525 Mariani Ave.
Cupertino, CA 95014
(408)996-1010

Daystar Digital, Inc.
5556 Atlanta Highway
Flowery Branch, GA 30542
(404)967-2077

Dove Computer Corporation
1200 North 23rd St.
Wilmington, NC 28405
(919)763-7918

Dupont Connector Systems
515 Fishing Creek Rd.
New Cumberland, PA 17070
(800)237-2374

Farallon Computing
2201 Dwight Way
Berkeley, CA 94704
(415)849-2331

Hayes Microcomputer Products, Inc.
P.O. Box 105203
Atlanta, GA 30348
(404)449-8791

Hercules Computer Technology, Inc.
921 Parker St.
Berkeley, CA 94710
(415)540-6000

InfoSphere, Inc.
4730 SW Macadam Ave.
Portland, OR 97201
(503)226-3620

Insight Development Corporation
1024 Country Club Dr., Suite 140
Moraga, CA 94566
(415)376-9451

Kinetics, Inc.
2540 Camino Diablo
Walnut Creek, CA 94596
(415)947-0998

Papiewski, John
P.O. Box 7444
Elgin, IL 60121

Shiva Corporation
155 Second St.
Cambridge, MA 02141
(617)864-8500

SoftStyle
Pacific Office, Phoenix Technologies Ltd.
7192 Kalanianaole Hwy., Suite 205
Honolulu, Hawaii 96825
(808)396-6368

Solana Electronics, Inc.
7887 Dunbrook Rd., Suite A
San Diego, CA 92126
(619)566-1701

Sun MicroSystems, TOPS Division
950 Marina Village Parkway
Alameda, CA 94501
(415)769-9669

Tandy, Inc.
P.O. Box 1052
Fort Worth, TX 76101
(817)390-3011

Western Digital
2445 McCabe Way
Irvine, CA 92714
(714)474-2003

Appendix C
The Basics of PC and Mac Operation

IN THE COURSE OF PUTTING TOGETHER a mixed IBM/Mac network some people from both sides will get their first taste of life on the other. We want to shed some light on the crosstraining process that such contact sometimes requires. Unfortunately, the process of trying to work with a Mac can make an experienced PC user feel stupid, and having to use a PC can put a dent into the self-esteem of accomplished Mac users. Of course, one of the advantages of TOPS is that it lets you use the machine you like and still communicate with the other side, but we are talking about the times when, for whatever reason, you have to use "one of the other ones."

PHILOSOPHY AND HYPE

One of the principle barriers to seeing clearly across the great IBM/Mac divide is the hype that is put out by both sides. Most people know that the Macintosh was introduced with tremendous fanfare as a radical alternative to the PC. This led many early adopters of the Mac to treat it with an evangelical fervor. Apple encouraged this as a basic business strategy. However, in all the talk about how simple and easy to use the Mac is, two important facts tend to get overlooked. First, as a machine a Mac is no less complex than a PC. The Mac operating system is no easier to understand than DOS. Of course, the Mac evangelists said, the point is that you don't need to understand the Mac's operating system to use it, and the same is not true for the IBM. We would have to say that when a Mac runs properly you don't need to understand the operating system, but when things go wrong, it is every bit as complex as a PC.

The second fact that is overlooked in talk of Mac-easy is that there a lot of people out there who know DOS, people to whom DOS is an open book. These people are a much larger group than the group who can say the Mac operating system is an open book. Because the Mac operating system is trying to do so much for you and for the programs that run under it, it gets to be a very involved system.

The bottom line on operating systems is that computers are complex, but logical. They are sometimes hard to figure out, but everything that they do, they do for a reason. Systems can be learned, and the learning curve rises fast. The more you know about an operating system, the easier it is to guess the next step. Persevere and you will prevail!

MAC TYPES WORKING WITH DOS

Unless you are working with a PC that is running Windows, the PC world will look different from screen one. Some PCs do have a menu system or shell that appears when the machine is booted. This usually gives a list of programs that can be run, and the keys used to run them, but basically a PC just sits and waits for you to tell it what to do. The operating system, DOS, has to be told what to do every step of the way. If you want to run an application and you don't have a shell program installed, you will have to navigate the DOS hierarchical folder system, known as the directory tree, to find the application. You will need to type the exact name of the application to run it. Some applications let you type in the program name plus a document name to load both at once, like double clicking on a document on the desktop, but need to know the program name and there is often no way of telling which application created it.

We have tried to make the sections on TOPS/DOS clear enough so that a Mac user could at least navigate through the steps required to connect the PC to TOPS. However, if you are having problems getting to grips with DOS, we suggest some books at the end of the appendix that might be helpful. Remember, DOS is very literal, and works line-by-line rather than from the big picture. If you need to do much work with the filing system on a PC you might want to check out a program like QuickDOS II that helps you manage files, listing them in sorted order, and presenting the basic filing commands in a menu, as seen in Fig. C-1.

Note the file at the top of this alphabetical list. It is the Desktop file that TOPS creates to help Macintoshes read the file information from the PC disk. Also note

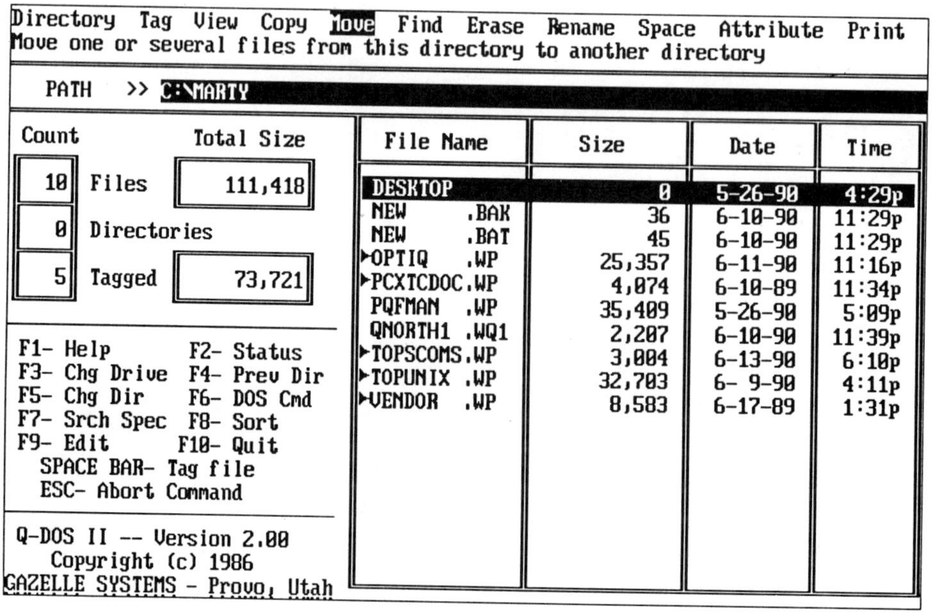

Fig. C-1. The Quick DOS file list.

the files with triangles next to their names, these are tagged files and will be affected by the next command, such as Move, which can move either of them to another directory/folder.

When you have doubts about the origin of a file or its contents, QuickDOS II allows you to view the file contents. You can even edit files, such as batch files, using the QuickDOS editor. Another handy feature of QuickDOS is the ability to show the directory structure as a picture. You can see this in Fig. C-2.

You can select directories from the tree to view their files or add directories.

DOS TYPES WORKING WITH MACS

Fortunately for you, today's Macintoshes come with a very good tutorial in from Apple that will teach you clicking and dragging and other mouse operations, as well as review the menu system. The Apple manuals are pretty good for basic operations, and so we suggest that you start there, irksome as that may be to a DOS power user who knows BATs from bytes. Really, that seems to be the crux of the problem when DOS users work on Macs. Try this exercise: imagine a completely menu-driven PC, for example, one with Windows completely and properly installed. Now imagine that this is the first computer you have ever seen. In essence, this is the Mac. Now, in your imaginary scenario you start picking menu items, appreciating the consistency of menu choices between applications, the touches of humor, and the pretty pictures. But suddenly you realize you have no idea what is happening in the background, behind the desktop. If you know DOS, you will

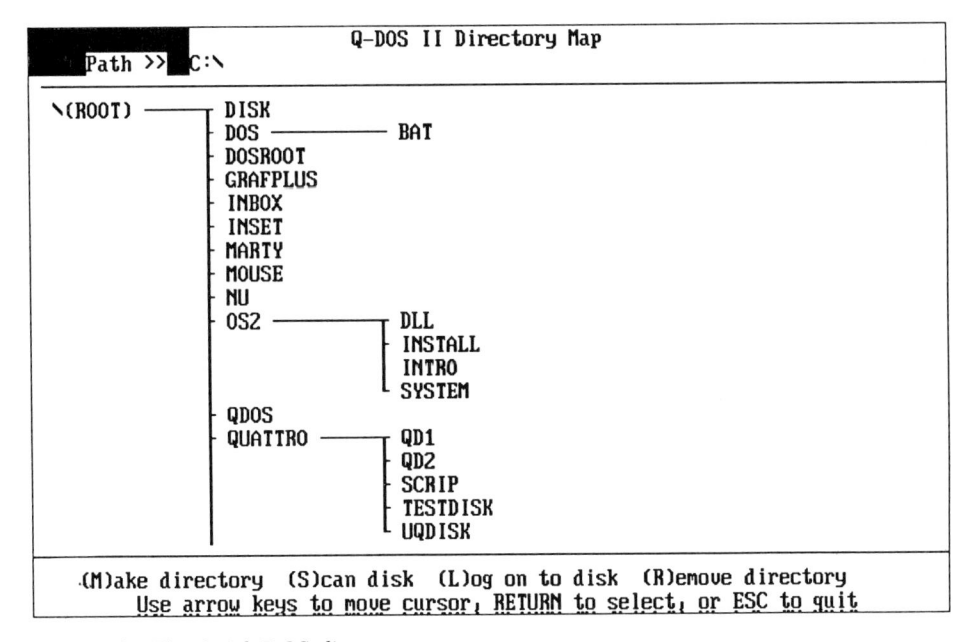

Fig. C-2. The Quick DOS directory map.

probably not feel comfortable lacking this information about what is going on behind this wonderful menu system. If you have a PC you can always bail out to DOS, then DIR, TYPE, and CD your way around. On the Mac, there is no way to dive into the operating system, at least not without a hefty background in programming. You have a choice. You can study up on the Mac to feel comfortable with it. Alternatively, you can live with the uncertainty, just knowing what commands and routines you need to get by.

In Fig. C-3, you can see a typical Macintosh opening screen, a desktop complete with hard disk, floppy disk, and trash can.

The contents of the window called Big Bang are the root directory of the disk with the volume label Big Bang. Each folder, WP, Graphics, and so on, is a directory. The System folder is the equivalent of DOS directory with a big difference. Program files placed in there can be automatically loaded at system startup time. Click the box in the top left corner of the window and the window will disappear into the grey box called Big Bang that represents the disk. Double click on the floppy disk called TOPS demo and a window like Big Bang will open to reveal the contents of the disk. Click on the floppy and drag it to the trash can and it will be ejected. Pressing Command–E from the keyboard will also eject a disk.

If you can't find the Command key, it's the one with the cloverleaf on it. Note that already a familiar lack of consistency and clarity starts to appear: this Mac is not quite as simple as it seems.

You can also click on a floppy disk to make it the current item, shaded black, then pick Eject from the File menu. Three ways to do the same thing. Note that the trash can eject method requires that the can turn black before an item is really "in" it. Drag a file or folder to the trash, and it is deleted. Programs cannot be deleted

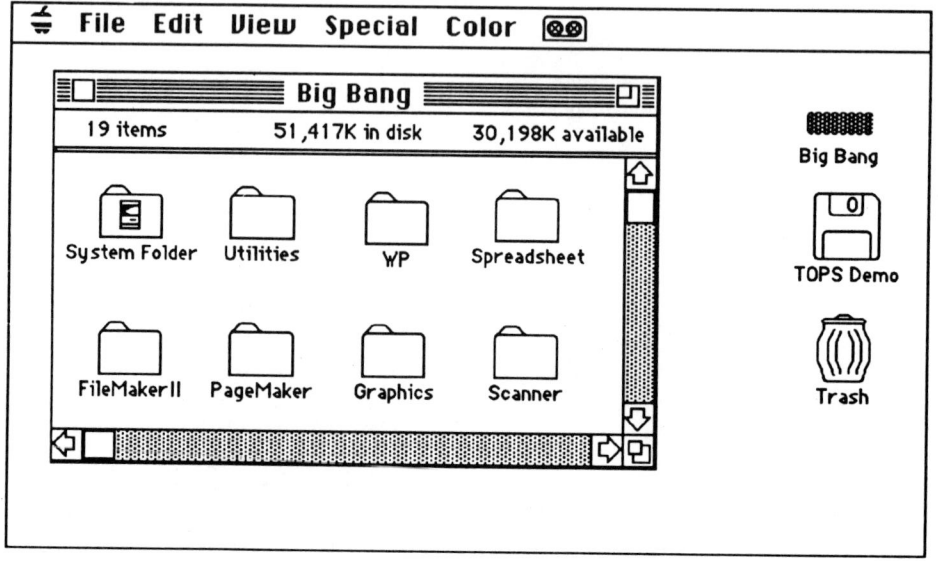

Fig. C-3. Typical Macintosh desktop.

without warning, but files can. Note that the trash can is bulging, indicating that someone just dragged a file there. For some time after a file is placed in the trash it can be removed and thus "unerased." There is a Mac equivalent of Norton Utilities for the Mac called PC Tools Deluxe, Mac Version. And so it goes. You will find that the Mac does yield its secrets, often faster than DOS. Do not feel that you have gone back to square one, but don't expect to be able to create batch files and perform other such DOS tricks on the Mac—at least not right away.

Finally, a word of consolation and warning to those venturing into the Mac world. Expect to see a fair number of messages called "System Error" and accompanied by a small drawing of a cartoon bomb. When you get one of these, your Mac has basically turned itself off, given up the ghost, and said "let's start over." There is one button on this message, Restart. In DOS terms, this is the equivalent of someone pressing Ctrl–Alt–Del for you, without your asking. When you restart, you will have lost everything that was not stored on disk. As an average user, you are likely to get a fair number of system errors. Tell this to a confirmed Mac evangelist, and you will probably hear that you are somehow responsible for this, the mix of programs you have chosen, the way you have organized your files, something you have done is causing this. However, DOS users have come to expect that programs described as "IBM compatible" will run on an IBM compatible machine without causing the system to crash, and without conflicting with other programs you might reasonably expect to use. Indeed, it is doubtful if anyone could sell software for the IBM if they labelled it like some Mac programs: "May cause system errors when used with certain other software."

Take heart, the crash was probably caused by buggy software, and not something you did. The exact mix of programs you were using at the time may just not be possible. On the System Error message you may will see a notation such as ID=10. This is the identification code for the error. Sometimes you can find out what this means, helping you to prevent further occurrences. However, do not look to the Mac manual to tell you what the error code means. Some are assigned by the application you are using. Apparently ID=10 means that the program you were using caused the crash, as opposed to another program or the system software. As we said, an operating system is an operating system, they are all complex, and no amount of graphics can alter that. However, the longer that the Mac is around, the better it will get, and learning it now will prepare you for the future.

Suggested Reading

The Macintosh Bible. Full of tips, tricks, and suggestions, this book will help you see the "big picture" and fill in some of the cracks in the details. While the evangelistic tone is a bit much at times, much can be learned from this innovative title.

Making MS-DOS Work for You. A good basic guide to using the PC operating system, written from a human point of view. (Windcrest, Book No. 1848).

Appendix D
Installing and Configuring FlashCards

THERE ARE TWO SIDES to the process of installation and configuration of Flash-Cards. Hardware must be set or adjusted, and software must be told about the changes.

THE HARDWARE SIDE

For your PC to talk to a network it needs a network interface card. This is a printed circuit board with a bunch of chips soldered onto it and a connector that will protrude from the back of your system unit. There may also be some switches on the card. There are two steps to installing a network card. First, you must place the card in the computer, then you must configure your software to work with the card. We will look at both aspects here, beginning with getting the card into the system. While we will be concentrating on the FlashCard, many of the comments will apply to other network cards as well, such as EtherLink cards.

Setting Up the Card

Before you place your network card into the computer, you need to consider the card's settings. These are switches that determine how the card communicates with your computer. The switches can be small blocks of switches, called *DIP switches*, or *jumper blocks*. The latter are plastic blocks that have a piece of copper inside them. The block is fitted over two pins, making a connection between them, thus turning the switch on. The FlashCard uses jumpers, but other network cards may use DIP switches. You can see the layout of switches in Fig. D-1.

Each piece of equipment in your system has to be able to communicate with the rest of the system, particularly the central processing unit (CPU). To do this, there are several channels that can be used. To avoid conflicts between different devices that might want to use these channels, you set the switches on the card for specific channels. The card comes with default settings that probably work in most cases. However, if you know that there will be a conflict, or discover one, then you can change the switches. Conflicts can be revealed after you install your card and find that either TOPS will not work, or that a device that worked before no longer functions reliably. The following settings can be switched on the FlashCard.

IRQ. To interrupt the CPU and pass along information, your PC has *Interrupt Request lines*, called IRQs. There are typically eight of these, with most of them pre-

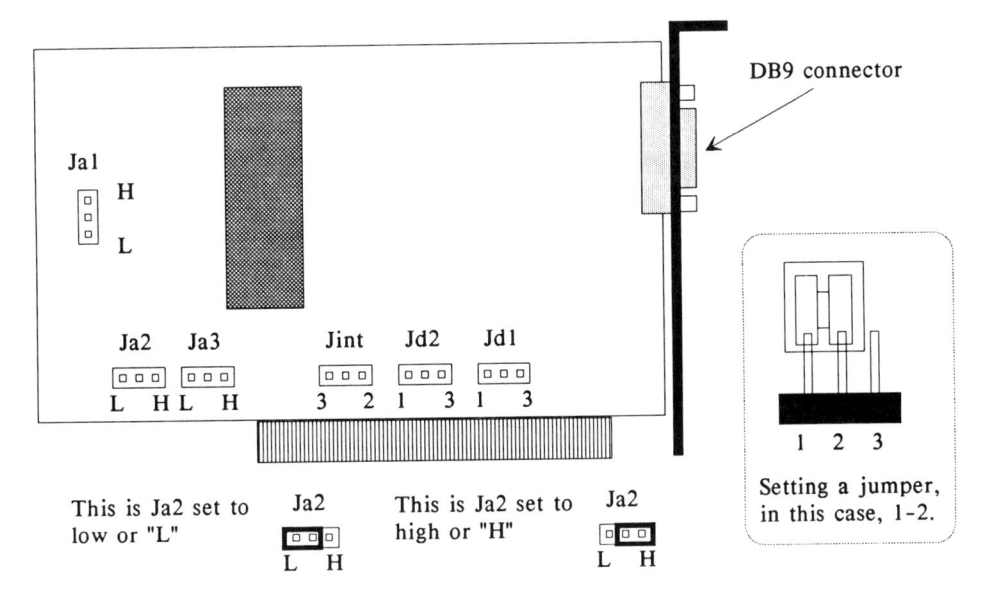

Fig. D-1. Jumper settings on Flash Cards.

assigned. For example IRQ1 is used by the keyboard, IRQ5 is used by the hard disk controller, and IRQ6 by the floppy controller. There are two IRQ lines used for communications, for serial ports if you have them installed. These are the ports used by modems and sometimes by mice. Typically IRQ4 is used by COM1, while a second serial port, COM2 will use IRQ3. The FlashCard can use either IRQ2, the default, or IRQ3, which will conflict with any device that is using COM2, including an internal modem configured as COM2. You can run out of IRQ lines and may have to give up some equipment. For example, the FastWrite VGA card uses IRQ2. This means you have to use IRQ3 for your FlashCard and that squeezes out COM2. On one machine configured like this, we had to give up a mouse that was connected to COM2, because we already had a modem on COM1. We tried replacing the serial mouse with a bus mouse, one that has its own port card and does not use a serial port. However, a bus mouse still needs an IRQ line from somewhere and we were not able to find an unused one. This is one reason that IBM introduced the Micro Channel architecture, as a way to add more access to the computer from peripheral devices. Future cards will use the MCA technology.

DMA. In addition to IRQs, PCs also have *Direct Memory Access* channels (DMAs) that allow direct communication between devices and the CPU. There are three of these, and the FlashCard can use DMA1 or DMA3. By using a DMA channel, the FlashCard can communicate at higher speeds, using FlashTalk. If you have specialized equipment installed on your system, such as a Bernoulli Box, and you encounter problems using the FlashCard, you should check to see what DMA channel the other equipment is using. The controller card for a Bernoulli Box is typically set for DMA3. This will not conflict with the default use of DMA1 on the FlashCard. However, there may be situations where all DMAs are used up. In such cases, you can set the FlashCard to not use a DMA channel, but this prevents you from using FlashTalk's higher speeds.

I/O Address. Each piece of equipment in your system needs an address, an assigned address in your system's memory so that information going to and coming from the equipment can be properly delivered. At times different equipment can try to use the same address. The FlashCard will work at several different addresses so you can change the address to resolve conflicts with other devices.

Adjusting the Switches

Because such a variety of hardware can be used on a PC, sometimes there is a need to resolve conflicts between a network card and other devices. To change the card's settings observe the table at the end of this Appendix) and move the jumpers onto the correct pins. To move the pins, grasp the card firmly after touching the metal chassis of your system or other grounded object. Handle the card—gently, by the edges, but not by the gold-striped connector. You can use a paperclip or small pointed tool to ease the jumper off the pins. Do not apply too much pressure or the jumper will flip off and they are hard to find (and harder to buy if you lose one).

Putting in the Card

The basic procedure for installing a network card is: turn off your computer and unplug it, open the box, find an empty slot, insert card, close box. The box is your system unit. Opening it is usually accomplished by unscrewing one or more retaining screws, then lifting or sliding the case off the chassis. Finding a free slot is not too difficult, just look along the row of cards that are lined up at right angles to the back of the chassis, called the *back-plane*. Use the empty slot closest to the big silver box that is the power supply. If there are no empty slots then you will have to consider compromising on your equipment options.

After locating a free slot, you will probably need to remove the silver-colored plate that is covering it. Remove the retaining screw and take out the plate. Inserting the card is done by holding the card with the port facing the rear of the chassis, and the gold-edged connecting tongue pointing downwards. The tongue is introduced to one of the slots with two rows of gold teeth, lined up, and then pressed into place. Considerable pressure is sometimes required, particularly if the slot has not been used before. The bottom end of the shiny silver retaining bracket needs to be able to slide down into the chassis or it will hold up the seating of the card. After the card is seated, you can use the retaining screw to secure the bracket on the back-plane. Now turn plug in your PC and turn it on. You can turn on your PC without the cover on, **if** you keep fingers and other body parts away from the wiring. The current in the wires are mainly 5 and 12 volt, but do not take chances. Also avoid spilling drinks into the open chassis. Running without the cover for long periods is not recommended as the cover is part of the cooling system. However, running without the cover is helpful if you need to remove different cards to resolve problems.

When the PC is on, make sure that it works the way it did before the card was installed. If something is not working, check the switch settings. The basic diagnostic technique for new cards is to remove all cards except the display and drive controllers, then add the new card. If this arrangement works then add back the other cards one at a time testing each time a card is added. this way you can tell which card is conflicting with the new card.

THE SOFTWARE SIDE

Your PC will not know that you have added a network card with AppleTalk capabilities unless you tell it through some form of program. The software that tells a PC about a hardware device is called a *device driver*.

Driving the Device

There are two methods of driving devices on a PC. You can either load the device driver as part of the basic program configuration read into memory from CONFIG.SYS at startup, or load the driver as a memory-resident program from the DOS command line, either manually, or as part of the AUTOEXEC.BAT. Early versions of TOPS used this approach and supplied a file called ATALK.SYS which was then included in the CONFIG.SYS with the line:

```
DEVICE=ATALK.SYS
```

The advantage of the CONFIG.SYS approach is that it is automatic and happens regardless of what you do with your AUTOEXEC.BAT. The disadvantage of the CONFIG.SYS approach to loading device drivers is that you cannot unload them without altering the CONFIG.SYS and rebooting, a cumbersome and often inconvenient requirement. For this reason TOPS went to a program approach, using the file ALAP.EXE instead of ATALK.SYS. You run ALAP from the DOS command line, usually as a part of a batch file like LOADTOPS.BAT. Because ALAP is run as a program, it can be unloaded, using the TOPS /UL ALAP command. This makes it much more convenient to load and unload TOPS, necessary on some occasions when you want to run memory intensive programs, or test your system.

Because such a variety of hardware can be used on a PC, there is often a need to resolve conflicts with your network card and other devices. If your network card does not work with the default settings on the card, you will need to adjust switches, or jumpers, as described above. On the software side, you add software options or switches to the device driver in order to synchronize it with the network card settings. There is no need to use command line software switches if your card is using the default settings.

When TOPS used the ATALK.SYS device driver, these switches were added to the line in the CONFIG.SYS, as in:

```
DEVICE=ATALK.SYS /BOARDINT=3
```

When you use the ALAP command, you add the switches on the command line, as in:

    ALAP /BOARDINT=3

This setting changes the IRQ line from the default of 2, to the alternative of 3. To change the DMA channel from the default of 1, use either /DMA=3 or /DMA=none. Note that only 80286 and 80386 system can use DMA=3. Alter the address for the board I/O from the default of 398, with /ADDRESS=390 or /ADDRESS=310. To specify a software interrupt other than the default of 5C, use /INT=6F or any other hexadecimal address from 5C to 6F. You can disable FlashTalk, the high speed transmission mode, with the switch /FLASHTALK=0. We do not suggest that you use the /FLASHTALK=0 setting because TOPS automatically disables FlashTalk when either of two machines who are communicating do not have FlashTalk capability, or have their DMA set to none. Remember that the /BOARDINT, /DMA, and /ADDRESS settings must correspond with your FlashCard settings. A typical command line for a system using no DMA and IRQ3 might look like this:

    ALAP /BOARDINT=3 /DMA=none

EtherLink Cards

When installing Ethernet cards for use with TOPS, you might have to make changes to the default configuration as you sometimes do with the FlashCard. When you want to run TOPS on a 3Com Ethernet card instead of ALAP.EXE, you run either ELAP503.EXE or ELAP523.EXE. These load the Ethernet driver for the 3Com InterLink II card and the 3Com InterLink/MC card, respectively. This command is followed by switches similar to those used with ALAP. The possible settings for ELAP503 are as follows:

/BOARDINT	2, 3, 4, or 5 with default of 3.
/DMA	1, 2, 3, or none with default of none.
/ADDRESS	250, 280, 2A0, 2E0, 300, 310, 330, 350 with default of 300.
/INT	5C to 6F with default of 5C.
/XCRTYPE	1=Thin, 2=Standard, referring to cable type. used by Ethernet, with 12 as the default.

For example, an EtherLink II card configured to use IRQ2 and thick/standard cable would use this command:

    ELAP503 /BOARDINT=2 /XCRTYPE=2

The EtherLink/MC card uses ELAP523.EXE and is for the IBM PS/2 systems and other machines with the Micro Channel architecture. This is a method for adding cards to a computer that offers some improvements over previous systems. The Micro Channel is intelligent, reading encoded data from the card and using it to modify operations without the need for user intervention. The result is that the only option you can change through Setup is INT, where the default value is 5C, as on most other cards.

Like the settings for ALAP, the ELAP settings can be configured with the Setup program that comes with TOPS/DOS 2.1. Configuring your driver with this program is described in the next section.

Configuring with Setup

With TOPS/DOS 2.1 you get a program, officially called "Software Installation and Configuration," that helps you configure your network card. We will refer to this program as Setup and you start it with the name SETUP entered at the DOS command line. When you get to the main menu, you will have three choices: Install, used to install the TOPS/DOS programs; Update, used to upgrade from older versions of TOPS to the current one; or Configure, which is what you use to alter the ALAP statement in LOADTOPS.BAT and LOADCLNT.BAT to match your card settings.

When you type C ("to configure driver for network card"), you are prompted to enter the directory you are using for your TOPS software and the drive you are using for booting TOPS. Having entered this information, you proceed to a choice between three different cards: FlashCard, EtherLink II, and EtherLink/MC, as seen in Fig. D-2.

There is a fourth option on the list, None of the above. Selecting this takes you back to DOS after suggesting that you consult the manual for the network card.

When you pick the FlashCard option, you get a list of the configuration factors, with the first one, IRQ, selected. In the lower part of the screen, you can see a reminder that changing the default settings with the software will require a matching

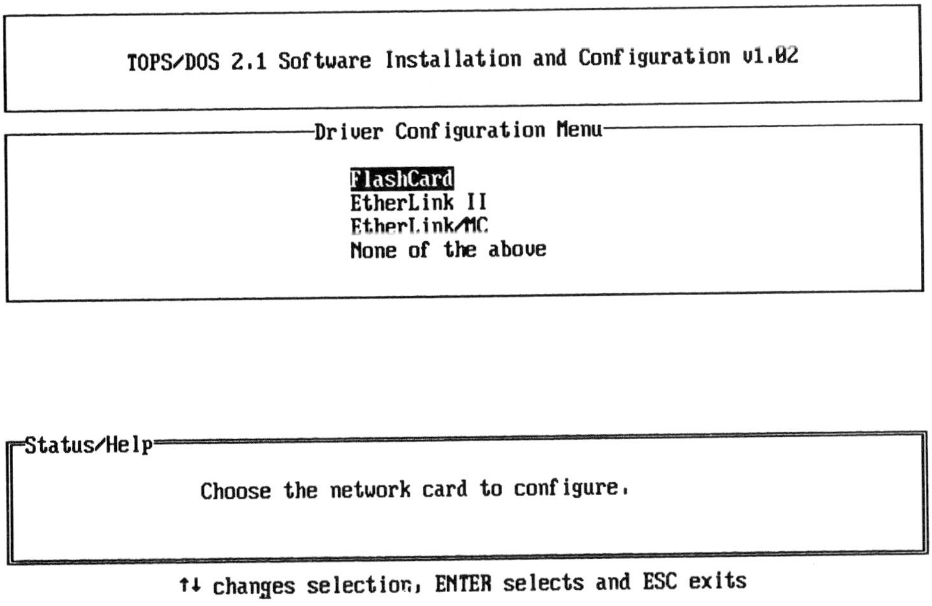

```
┌─────────────────────────────────────────────────────────────────┐
│      TOPS/DOS 2.1 Software Installation and Configuration v1.02 │
└─────────────────────────────────────────────────────────────────┘
┌──────────────────────Driver Configuration Menu──────────────────┐
│                                                                 │
│                    FlashCard                                    │
│                    EtherLink II                                 │
│                    EtherLink/MC                                 │
│                    None of the above                            │
│                                                                 │
└─────────────────────────────────────────────────────────────────┘




┌─Status/Help─────────────────────────────────────────────────────┐
│                                                                 │
│              Choose the network card to configure.              │
│                                                                 │
└─────────────────────────────────────────────────────────────────┘
              ↑↓ changes selection, ENTER selects and ESC exits
```

Fig. D-2. Configuring network card with Setup.

```
┌──────────────────────────────────────────────────────────────┐
│         TOPS/DOS 2.1 Software Installation and Configuration v1.02 │
└──────────────────────────────────────────────────────────────┘
  ┌──────────────────FlashCard Configuration──────────────────┐
  │             Board IRQ Line      2            ┌─┐          │
  │             DMA Channel         1            │2│          │
  │             Board I/O Address   398          │3│          │
  │             Enable FlashTalk    Y            └─┘          │
  │             Software Interrupt  5C                        │
  └───────────────────────────────────────────────────────────┘


  ┌─Status/Help─────────────────────────────────────────────┐
  │  Board IRQ default is 2.  If you do not use the default setting, │
  │  you must change a jumper on the FlashCard.             │
  └─────────────────────────────────────────────────────────┘
   Press ↑↓ to select value, <ENTER> to record value, and <ESC> to return to menu
```

Fig. D-3. Flash configuration.

change to the hardware defaults. Note that this screen reads the current settings from LOADTOPS.BAT if you have such a file installed already. Otherwise the screen shows the defaults. After using the Up or Down arrow to highlight the setting you prefer for IRQ you press Enter. This moves the highlighting to the next setting category, DMA, as seen in Fig. D-4.

You proceed in this fashion through all five categories and are then prompted to save your changes, entering Y for yes or N for reentering data (press Escape to abort the entire configuration operation). When you select Y, you will see the Setup program modifying the LOADTOPS and LOADCLNT batch files. You are then returned to DOS with final message confirming installation.

If you have not already loaded TOPS, you can proceed with the LOADTOPS or LOADCLNT command. If TOPS is already loaded with other settings you can unload it with TOPS /UL /A. If you have mounted drives and published volumes, TOPS /UL A will not work unless you first use the TOPS SHUTDOWN command.

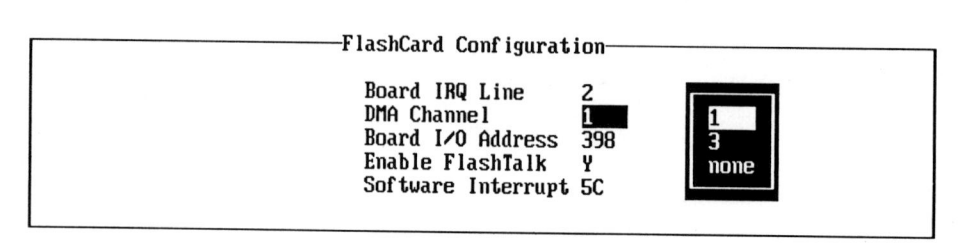

```
  ┌──────────────────FlashCard Configuration──────────────────┐
  │             Board IRQ Line      2            ┌─┐          │
  │             DMA Channel         1            │1│          │
  │             Board I/O Address   398          │3│          │
  │             Enable FlashTalk    Y            │none│       │
  │             Software Interrupt  5C           └─┘          │
  └───────────────────────────────────────────────────────────┘
```

Fig. D-4.

Other Software Changes

Depending upon your system and the software you are using, you might need to make some other software changes to accommodate the network card. For example, when running Windows/386 you can encounter serious conflicts with TOPS. This is because Windows/386 likes to use direct hardware requests for some operations that normally go through DOS. You should modify the Windows/386 configuration file, WIN.INI, to include the line

virtualhdirq = 0

in the section titled [win386]. This should help to resolve hardware interrupt request conflicts with TOPS.

Note that when you use the Setup program to configure your ALAP statement, both LOADTOPS.BAT and LOADTOPS.CLNT are altered. However, there is nothing to stop you from editing either one of these files to make the settings different. For example, you might have an entirely different configuration when you run in client mode and so want different settings in LOADCLNT.BAT. Refer to Chapter 9 for more on batch files and editing them.

Glossary

access To *access* a computer, printer, or modem means to communicate with that hardware and its associated software. To *access* an application means to run that application. To *access* a file means to read, write to, or read and write to it.

alias A name (16 characters maximum) given to a volume or printer when it is published. This is the volume or printer name as seen by other stations on the network.

AppleTalk A set of network communication protocols for LocalTalk cabling systems. The driver that controls how the network devices address, send, receive, and read the information transmitted over the network.

application file or application program A file containing an executable program. The program will perform a particular task, such as word processing, database management, networking, etc.

ASCII The American Standard Code for Information Interchange, ASCII is a standard way of representing text in microcomputer operating systems.

AUTOEXEC.BAT A DOS batch file that executes automatically on system start-up.

background tasks Functions performed by the computer while allowing the computer to be used for other activities. Background functions are not apparent to the user. For example, while printing a document in the background, the computer can still accept and process data intended for another document.

back up To copy the contents of a disk, directory, or file to another hard or floppy disk. (A backup file or disk is the copy used to protect the original.)

batch file A text file containing DOS commands intended for execution in a batch. Entering the batch file name at the DOS prompt executes the commands in the order in which they appear in the file.

bridge A hardware device that connects two similar networks (zones). Bridges extend networks to expand the resource pool and control network traffic by forwarding only transmissions intended for a different zone.

BIOS Basic Input/Output System, the basic routines used to manage communication between hardware and software. Normally stored in ROM.

client A station (PC or Macintosh) that uses the resources made available by servers on the network.

data file A computer file containing information or data that can be read or processed by an application. This could be a word processing document, spreadsheet or database file, or simple text. Most data files have information formatted in a way that can be processed only by the particular application that created it. Text files have no formatting.

data fork One of the two parts of a Macintosh file, the data fork stores the data or text. See also *resource fork*.

Desktop file A file used to store the Macintosh working environment, such as window size, shape and position, file display type (large icon, small icon, etc.), and file notes.

device Any piece of hardware that you can attach to a network; for example, computers, printers, file servers, bridges, gateways, modems.

directory A self-contained group of files stored on a disk. Directories can be created within other directories, forming a hierarchy of directory and subdirectory levels (root directory, second-level directory, etc.). Also used to refer to a listing of files within a directory.

disk A device used to store information processed by your computer. Hard disks and floppy diskettes are common storage devices.

DOS The operating system (Disk Operating System) used by IBM PC and compatible computers.

driver The portion of network software responsible for getting communication out onto the network and for ensuring that it gets to its destination station without error. Different interface cards require different drivers.

DMA channel Direct Memory Access, a channel of communication between hardware and software. There are only a few of these channels built into the IBM architecture and so some devices are not able to use them. Conflicts can occur unless your hardware has DMA settings correctly made.

Ethernet A physical network cabling system (usually consisting of shielded wire) that links computers and peripheral devices on a network. Capable of transmitting data at up to 10 megabits per second.

EtherTalk A network driver that supports AppleTalk protocols over an Ethernet cabling system using an Ethernet interface card.

file locking A system used by network (multi-user) applications to prevent data files from being written to by more than one user at any one time.

filename conventions The rules for constructing file names. These differ from one operating system to another. DOS filenames can be up to 8 characters with an optional 3-character extension. Macintosh filenames can be up to 31 characters long.

file server A station on a network that makes files available to other stations on the network.

Finder The application that maintains the Macintosh desktop. It keeps track of documents and applications and transfers information to and from disks.

FlashTalk A LocalTalk network driver developed by TOPS. It is similar to AppleTalk, but transmits data at up to three times the AppleTalk rate.

gateway A device used to connect two dissimilar networks. Maintains both a hardware connection and a software interface between the two systems of network protocols. An example is a LocalTalk/Ethernet gateway.

hexadecimal A base 16 numbering system. The 16 digits count from 0 to 9, then A to F.

Hierarchical file system (HFS) A filing system used by the Macintosh operating system in which files are organized according to a hierarchy of folders within folders.

interrupt The temporary suspension of a program by a computer to perform other tasks. Usually, it is in response to a signal from a peripheral device or other external source. In the IBM, there are a limited number of IRQ lines, channels to the computer from devices such as modems, mouse, and other hardware. Correct setting of IRQ lines to avoid conflicts is important.

Internet A network that spans local area networks by linking them together, often over long distances.

local Files, software, or hardware stored in or connected to a computer. See also *remote*.

Local Area Network (LAN) A network localized in a single workplace or institution. Compare to a wide area network, which spans long distances and usually links local area networks.

LocalTalk A physical networking system made by Apple that links computers and peripheral devices together to permit communication and data transmission. Also refers to any LocalTalk compatible cabling system.

memory (disk, RAM, ROM) The data storage area of a computer system, usually composed of three types. Generally, we refer to disks as storage and to RAM and ROM as memory. However, you will read references to disks as memory.

- *Disk memory* is the main data storage area of a computer. Application and data files are stored even with the computer turned off.
- *RAM (random-access memory)* is memory used to hold application programs when they are being executed. Turning off the computer clears the memory.
- *ROM (read-only memory)* is memory on which data is permanently stored, or burned in. You cannot write to ROM.

mount To connect to a server so that a remote published volume or printer can be used as if it were local.

multi-user applications An application designed to be run by more than one user at a time.

network Devices (computer stations, printers, peripherals) connected by cabling or phone to permit information exchange. To share or send information to machines on a network, the information must be transmitted according to certain rules or protocols. See also *Local Area Network*.

network interface card A computer card that forms the physical connection between a microcomputer and a network cabling system.

network name The name which a computer, printer, or volume displays to the network.

node An AppleTalk term referring to a station on the network.

password A unique character string that the user must enter to access certain files, folders, or volumes. Passwords provide network security.

partition A portion of a memory device, such as a hard disk, that is accessed as if it were a separate device.

path The route through a hierarchical file system, from one directory down through the hierarchy, to a file.

port The device or connector on a computer where peripheral devices are attached. For example, a printer port.

PostScript A page-description language used by certain types of printers to compose documents a whole page at a time and print them.

printer redirection A process by which print files are intercepted and sent to a remote or network printer rather than a local printer port.

printer server A station on a network that makes its local printer available to other stations on the network.

protocol A set of rules that govern the transmission of information across a network. Many kinds of rules at different levels govern data communication, just as in spoken communication.

publish To make a resource such as files or printers available to other stations on a network. See *File Servers* and *Printer Servers*.

Queue The line of print jobs waiting to be printed on a printer.

RAM Random-Access Memory is memory used to hold application programs while they are being executed. Turning off the computer clears the memory. DOS machines have a maximum of 640K of conventional RAM memory.

read-only access An access mode that allows a user to read, but not change, a file's contents.

read-write access (R/W) An access mode that allows a user to read and/or change (write) a file's contents.

record locking A system used by some network application programs to allow several users on a network to access the same data file, but does not permit more than one user to make changes to a particular record in that file at any one time.

remote Files, hardware, or software stored in or directly connected to a station on a network other than your own. See also *Local*.

resource fork One of two parts of a Macintosh file, the resource fork contains information about the icons, graphical interface, menus, and other information about the nature of the file. DOS cannot read or display the information in a resource fork. See also *datafork*.

ROM Read-Only Memory is computer memory that contains permanently stored information vital to computer operation. It is not lost when the computer is turned off or the power is interrupted in any way.

root directory The top level directory of a DOS hierarchical file system. Server A station that makes its resources, such as files, printers, and other peripherals, available to other stations on a network.

single-user application Applications designed to be run by one user at a time.

spooler An application that lets printing take place in the background, that is, without interfering with your computing tasks. Print jobs are placed in a queue and printed as the printer becomes available. Local spoolers put your local print jobs in a local queue. Network spoolers put print jobs from all stations in a central queue.

station Each computer on the network is a station. Each station receives a name from its user when the user signs onto the network. PC station names can be up to 15 characters long. (Macintosh station names can be up to 31 characters long.)

syntax The grammar of a command. The command format that lets the computer application understand what you want it to execute, including particular options you want invoked.

text file A file containing text only (no formatting information). Several conventions exist. ASCII is most common for microcomputers. See also *data file*.

UNIX A widely used, multi-user, multi-tasking operating system originally developed by Bell Laboratories and used on Sun Workstations.

unmount To break the connection to a remote volume, or printer.

unpublish To make unavailable any resource a server has made available to the network by publishing.

volume A directory or subdirectory that has been published (made available) to the network. (When a directory is published, all subdirectories and files in that directory are also published.)

write to Transfer information from the computer's RAM memory to a disk drive. When you write a file to a disk, you store the information on the disk.

zone A logical grouping of network(s) within a larger group of interconnected networks joined together through bridges. Zones are used to subdivide a very large network so as to control traffic and make networking within a work group easier.

Index

A

access control, 260-261, 375
active star topology, 322
advanced memory specification, 365
Advanced MS-DOS Batch File Programming, 187
ALAP, 21, 78, 98
alternative bridge, 336
Apple File Exchange
  adding translators to, 217
  Copy options, 219
  file information option, 220
  folder in, 215
  Mac to Mac menu for, 216
  MS-DOS to Mac options, 219
  source file selection, 217
  translator, TOPS-type and, 215-220
AppleShare, 10, 14
  TOPS compatibility with, 350
AppleTalk, 13, 14, 27, 38, 39, 45, 46, 48, 49, 50, 54, 59, 318, 401, 402
  PageMaker and, 357
  PC cards, 400
  Windows 2.03 and, 356
  Windows/286 and, 35
AppleTalk Network System, 12, 13, 14
  memory, 360-363
  open systems interconnect (OSI), 14
ARCnet, 13, 14, 344
arguments, CONFIGURE, 151, 152
Ashton-Tate, 35
asynchronous driver, 335
ATALK, 98
AUTOEXEC, 97-98

B

background tasks, 116
backup copies, 376
bank-switching, 363
batch files, 163-164, 179-188
  creation of, 180
  DOS menu system for, 185
  parameter passing, 186
  tips for use of, 378-379
baud rate, 14
boot disk, 11
bridges (see also bridging), 3, 45, 47, 48, 49, 83, 319-320
bridging, 334-337
  alternative bridge, 336

AppleTalk devices, 401
  asynchronous driver for, 335
  Hayes Interbridge connection, 334, 335
  tips for, 337
broadcasting, 304
bulletin board, 330, 333
bus topology, 42, 43, 44, 45, 321
buses, 319

C

cables, 40-45, 318, 328
  product directory for, 399
Canvas, 293, 295
CD-ROM, 9
central processing unit (CPU), 12
charts, 267-269
client/server networks, 12
clients, 10, 11, 12, 30, 31
coaxial cable, 40, 48
cold boot, 378
color graphics adapter (CGA), 266
comma separated values (CSV), Excel and, 248
command format, TOPS, 164-171
  client commands, 171
  command parameters, 168
  general rules, 164
  listing of, 165
  server commands, 168-170
  unloading problems, 170
command line interpreter, 159
communications (see also electronic mail) 302-338
  active star topology, 322
  bridge definition, 319-320
  buses, 319,321
  connections for, 318-328
  daisy chain topology, 325-328
  EtherPort, 331
  FAX, 337
  file conversion, 333
  gateway definition, 320
  minicomputer and super-micro connections, 329
  modems, 337
  network limits in, 323
  passive star topology, 322
  remote access, 333-334
  Sun/TOPS, printing on, 333

  TOPS server software for, 332
  troubleshooting networks, 328-329
  trunks and drops, 321
  wiring basics, 323
Compaq, 26
Complete Guide to PC and LAN Security, 33
Complete Guide to PC and Network Security, 376
CompuServe, 14
computer-aided design (CAD), 18
Computer Graphics Metafile CGM, 278
CONFIG.SYS, 21, 97-98
configurations (see topologies)
CONFIGURE command, 151, 152, 153
connection, 37-51
  active star topology, 322
  bridges, 47, 319-320
  buses, 44, 45, 319, 321
  cable standards, 40
  cabling, 40-45
  coaxial cable, 40, 48
  communications, 318-328
  daisy chain topology, 325-328
  DIN-8, 43
  Ethernet and twisted pair combination, 49-50
  EtherPort, 331
  fiberoptic cables, 40
  FlashTalk, twisted pair cabling and, 42
  gateways, 320
  Hayes Interbridge, 334, 335
  IBM PC, 39-40
  larger site, 330
  Mac connectors, 37-39
  minicomputer and super-micro, 329
  network limits, 323
  passive star topology, 322
  product directory for, 399
  repeaters, use of, 44, 46, 319
  RJ-11 plugs, 43
  star topology, 50-51
  telco wire, 328
  topologies, 42-43
  TOPS/Macintosh, 54
  trunks and drops, 321
  twisted pair cabling, 40
  wiring basics, 323
continuous tone variations, 272

424 Index

copy command, TOPS/Macintosh, 88-90
Corvus, 7

D

daisy chain topology, 325-328
data fork, 35, 36
data storage, personal computers, 10, 11
Datapoint, 13
dBASE, 21, 35
    Excel and, 235-237
    exporting from Excel to, 244
    Mac, Excel and, 248
    PC II or III, Excel and, 248
dedicated server, 77
    clients and, 78
default, 18
Desk-Paint, 271
desktop communications, 302
Desktop file, 87
desktop publishing, 192, 297-302
    PageMaker for, 298-300
DESQview, 367-370
device, network, 18, 19
Digital Equipment Corp, 13
DIN-8 connectors, 43
DIP switches, 157-158, 410
direct memory access (DMA) channels, FlashCard and, 411
disk format, personal computer, 7
diskless workstations, 11-12
DisplayWrite, translator, TOPS-type and, 211-213
distributed network architecture, 12
distributed service, 25
DOS commands, 24, 159-164
    AUTOEXEC.BAT factor, 162
    batch files and, 163-164
    command line interpreter and, 159
    PATH factor, 160
downloading, 304, 333
drops, 321
DRW, 278
DuPont Connector Systems, 14
dynamic link library, 356

E

EBM, 9
electronic mail (see also communications), 9, 302, 303, 304
    electronic messages, 302-304
    InBox (see InBox)
    LAN, 303, 304
    security with, 318
    WAN, 304
EMS architecture, 363
encapsulated PostScript files, 279
enhanced graphics adapter (EGA), 266

error messages, TOPS, 381-398
EtherLink, FlashCard and, 414
Ethernet, 13, 14, 28, 29, 39, 50, 320, 330, 414
    coaxial cable and, 48
    Macintosh cards, 400
    PC cards, 401
    thick and thin, 49-50
    TOPS/Macintosh, installation and, 54
    twisted pair topology and, 49-50
EtherPort, 331
Excel spreadsheet, 24, 92, 232-246, 379
    1-2-3 conversion factors, 239-240, 241-243, 244, 246
    comma separated values (CSV) and, 248
    dBASE and, 235-237, 244
    exporting from, 237-239
    file sharing with, 256
    Filemaker and, 248-255
    financial negatives (Lotus 1-2-3), 241
    IBM PC display, 233
    IBM/Mac connection, 234
    Mac dBASE and, 248
    Macintosh display, 233
    Multiplan translation, 243-244
    NetPrint and, 258
    odd names in 1-2-3, 240
    PC dBASE II or III, 248
    reading 1-2-3 files into, 239
    running across TOPS, 255
    running Excel, 255
    symbolic link format, 234
    TOPS-Excel scenario, 256-258
    unlisted programs, translation of, 245
expanded memory, 363
expanded memory manager (EMM), 363
extended memory specification (XMS), 363
Quarterdeck, 367-370
extended memory specification (XMS), 363

F

Farallon Computing, 14, 38
Fastpath, 49, 50, 320, 330, 332
FAX, 302, 303, 337, 338
fiberoptic cables, 40
Fiberoptic LAN, 14
file access, 30, 33, 375
File Clients command, TOPS/DOS, 105
file format, personal computer, 7
file servers, 10
File Servers command, TOPS/DOS, 106
FileMaker, 248-255
    BASIC file (commas), 250, 253

communications with, 262
confidential layouts, 260
host and guest files, 259
input to, 252-253
output from, 249
passwords and access control, 260-261
performing an output with, 251
running on TOPS, 259
security, 260
SYLK file, 250, 253
text file (tabs), 250, 253
TOPS and, tips for use, 262
files, 30, 35, 36
    compatibility, cross-system, 34
    naming conventions for, 35, 36
    read-only, 33
    translation of, 35
filters, 160, 161
Finder, TOPS/Macintosh, 87
FlashBox, 22, 38, 39
FlashCard, 22, 26, 38, 39, 59
    device driver for, 413
    direct memory access (DMA) channels and, 411
    EtherLink Card for, 414
    hardware for, 410
    installation and configuration of, 410-417
    interrupt request lines and, 410
    software changes and, 415
    software for, 413
    switch adjustment for, 412
FlashTalk, 16, 42, 45, 46, 50
flat telco wire, 328
floppy disk drives, TOPS/Macintosh and, 93-95
forks, 35, 36, 284-296
FoxBASE+, 263
FreeHand, 296

G

gateways, 4, 320, 339-341
    configurations for, 341
    installation of, 339-340
    local area network (LAN), 3
    TOPS settings for, 342
    TOPS/NOVELL, 3Com Etherlink card and, 344
    TOPS/NOVELL, ARCnet card and, 344
    TOPS/NOVELL, IBM token ring PC adapter and, 345
    TOPS/PC-NFS, 345
Getting the Most From Your Hardware With Microsoft Excel, 255
Glue, 277
Goldhaber, Nat, 15

Gookin, Dan, 187
graphics, 264-297
   Canvas for, 293, 295
   CGA for, 266
   converters and translators for, 282
   Desk-Paint for, 271
   draw formats for, 277-278
   drawing vs. painting in, 275-277
   EGA for, 266
   encapsulated PostScript files, 279
   enhanced images, 294
   file forks and, 284-297
   FreeHand for, 296
   Graphics Link converter, 282
   gray-scale images, 271
   HIJAAK, 282-283
   Metafile converter, 282
   painted pictures, 269-271
   resource forks, 286, 289, 290-297
   scanning images in, 271, 291
   sharing, 280-282
   TIFF for, 297
   TOPS translator, 282
   VGA for, 266
   Windows Draw Plus, 276
Graphics Link converter, 282
gray scale images, 271, 274

H
half-bridged networks, 337
halftone images, 272, 273
hardware
   advanced memory specification, 365
   memory and, 365
Hayes Interbridge connection, 334, 335
hidden files, 172
Hide Name command, TOPS/DOS, 105
hierarchical file structure (HFS), 28 91
HIJAAK, 282-283, 403
host files, 259, 333
HP-GL, 278

I
IBM, 10, 13, 26, 27
   AppleTalk cards, 400
   crosstraining with Macintosh, 405-409
   Ethernet cards, 401
   Excel display on, 233
   file organization, 32
   Macintosh and, TOPS networks using, 27-28
   token ring PC adapter, TOPS/NOVELL gateway and, 345
   TOPS and, 20, 39-40
IBM networks, 13

InBox, 22, 304, 306-310, 316, 318, 379
   broadcast news options, 317
   enclosures with, 312-315
   Message Center in, 304-306
   network of, 305
   passwords and security with, 316
   personal connection installation for, 305
   phone messages with, 315
   receiving end of, 310-312
   routing list messages, 318
installation, 52-80
   clients and dedicated servers, 77, 78
   software versions and, 52
   TOPS software modules, 53
   TOPS/DOS, 58-71
   TOPS/DOS, 360K floppy, 70-71
   TOPS/DOS, 720K installation, 68-69
   TOPS/DOS, automated installation, 61-63
   TOPS/DOS, backup copies, 60, 61
   TOPS/DOS, CONFIG and AUTOEXEC files, 63, 66
   TOPS/DOS, fine-tuning, 72
   TOPS/DOS, floppy booting and added drives, 76-77
   TOPS/DOS, floppy disks, 67-68
   TOPS/DOS, hard disk, 63-67
   TOPS/DOS, high density, 68-69
   TOPS/DOS, Installer program, 62
   TOPS/DOS, loading, 60
   TOPS/DOS, nonstandard configurations, 71
   TOPS/DOS, running start, 59-61
   TOPS/DOS, setup menu, 64
   TOPS/DOS, software loading, 71
   TOPS/DOS, software transfer menu, 65
   TOPS/DOS, TOPSKRNL.DAT file, 73-75
   TOPS/DOS, TOPSPRTR.DAT file, 76
   TOPS/Macintosh, 53-58
   TOPS/Macintosh, connections for, 54
   TOPS/Macintosh, Ethernet, 54
   TOPS/Macintosh, Installer program, 57-58
   TOPS/Macintosh, LocalTalk, 54
   TOPS/Macintosh, TOPS Spool, 56, 58
   TOPS/Macintosh, TOPS Translator, 58
   upgrades and, 78-80
Intel Corp, 13
intelligent devices, 19
interrupt request lines, FlashCard and, 410
interrupt vector tables, 349

J
JKL files, NetPrint and, 156
jumper blocks, 410
junction boxes, 324

L
Lattice Net, 49
Liaison, 335
LOADTOPS, 98
local area network (LAN), 1-16
   Apple networks, 14
   ARCnet, 13
   bridges and gateways in, 3, 4
   description of, 2
   electronic mail and, 303
   Ethernet, 13
   extending size of, 3
   IBM networks, 13
   protocols for, 3, 13
   ring and star configurations in, 2
   speed in, 14
   TOPS and PC-LAN compatibility, 341
   wide area network (WAN) vs., 3
local devices, 19-20, 112
local printer, 112
   TPRINT and, printers, DOS, 138-139
local zone, 47
LocalTalk, 14, 16, 28, 29, 48, 49, 54, 318, 335
locking, 34
LOGOUT command, TOPS/DOS, 170
Lotus 1-2-3, 92
   conversion factors, Excel, 239-240, 242-243
   Excel unsupported functions, 246
   exporting from Excel to, 242-242, 244
Lotus PIC, 278

M
MacDraw PICT, 277
Mace Utilities, 403
Macintosh, 9, 13, 14, 15, 16, 27
   computer and peripheral requirements, TOPS use, 29
   Ethernet cards, 400
   Excel display on, 233
   file forks in, 35, 36
   file organization, 32
   Hierarchical File System (HFS), 28
   Macintosh File System (MFS), 28
   PCs and, TOPS networks using, 27-28
   printer drivers, 402
   TOPS connectors for, 37-39
   TOPS/Macintosh, 20

Macintosh File System
(MFS), Macintosh, 28
MacPaint, 270, 284
MacWrite II, 192
mainframe computers, 5
 personal computers vs., 6
memory, 359-366, 370-372
 architecture of, 360-363
 CONFIG.SYS slimming to improve, 364
 EMS architecture, 363
 hardware solutions to increase, 365
 loading and unloading TOPS, 373
 mapping, 365
 problems with, 358
 requirements of, 359
 software applications decisions and, 370-372
 software solutions, 366
 TOPSKRNL.DAT reduction, 372
memory-resident software, TOPS/DOS, 99, 170
Metafile converter, 282
Micrografx PIC and DRW, 278
Microsoft, 35
 Rich Text format, translator, TOPS-type and, 222-223
Microsoft Word, NetPrint and, 351-355
minicomputers, connections for, 329
modems, 14, 49, 333, 337
mount command, 30, 31
 TOPS/DOS, 106, 171
 TOPS/Macintosh, 85
 TOPS/Macintosh, options for, 86-87
MS-DOS computers, TOPS/Macintosh, server use of, 90-92
MSP, 271
multi-user applications, 33-34
MultiFinder, 53
Multimate, 21, 209-211
Multiplan, Excel translation, 243-244
multiplexing, 336

N

NETBIOS, 13
NetPrint, 21, 128, 140-158
 configuration for, 142, 143-146, 146-147
 CONFIGURE batch file for, 153
 DIP switch settings and, 157-158
 DOS command line use of, 154-155
 Excel and, 258
 installation and setup of, 140-142
 JKL files and, 156
 Microsoft Word and, 351-355
 PRINT command syntax, 155
 printing with, 140-158
 problems with, 155-156
 queue management with, 150-151
 running, 149-150
 TOPS emulation tips for, 151-154
 Windows/286 and, 355-356
NetWare, 10
network devices, 18-19
network file system (NFS), 345
network management software, 402
network printers, 112
 AppleTalk, 402
 TPRINT and printers, 135-136, 138
networks, 7-8, 9, 10-12, 30
 Apple-type, 14
 client/server, 12
 clients to, 10, 11
 communications, limitations in, 323
 distributed network architecture, 12
 file server, 10
 half-bridged, 337
 InBox, 305
 NETBIOS protocol in, 13
 network devices, 18-19
 PC and Macintosh, TOPS use and, 27-28
 PC-only, TOPS use and, 26
 scanning and, 225
 speed in, 14
 systems network architecture in, 13
 token-ring standard for, 13
 troubleshooting, 328-329
NFS protocol, 329, 345
nodes, 17, 18, 43, 45, 320
Norton Utilities, 403
Novell, 10

O

Okyto, 336
Omninet, 7, 10
open command, TOPS/Macintosh, 84
open network computing (ONC), 345
Open Systems Interconnect (OSI), 14
operating systems, TOPS, mixing of, 23-24, 23
optical character recognition (OCR) (see scanning)
Oracle, 263
output devices, 18

P

PageMaker, 298-300, 379
 AppleTalk and, 357
 Run-Time Windows and, 357
 Windows 2.03 and, 356
 Windows/286 and, 356
paging, 363
painted pictures, 269-271
 MacPaint for, 270
 MSP for, 271
 PCX for, 271
 PIC for, 271
 PIX for, 271
 SuperPaint for, 270
 TIFF for, 271
parameter passing, batch file for, 186
passive star topology, 51, 322
passwords, 376
 Filemaker, 260-261
PATH, DOS commands and, 160
pause, 160, 161
PC Network, 10, 13, 14
PC-only networks, 26
PC Tools Deluxe, 403
PCX, 271, 403
peer-to-peer communications, 14
peripherals, 9
personal computers, 5-8
 central processing unit (CPU), 12
 data storage in, 10, 11
 disk and file format on, 7
 local area network (LAN) development and, 5
 PC-only networks, TOPS use and, 26
 standards for, 9
PhoneNet, 14, 44, 48, 51
PIC, 271, 278
pipes, 160, 161
PIX, 271
PostScript, 9, 21, 110-111, 128, 279
PRINT command, syntax of, NetPrint, 155
printer drivers, Apple Macintosh, 402
printer ports, AppleTalk, 54
printers, 9
printers, DOS, 128-158
 local printers and TPRINT, 138-139
 Macintosh printers and, 128
 mounting printers from TOPS menu, 133-134
 naming printers, 132
 parallel printers and, 129
 printing screens to remote printer, 134
 publishing printers in, 129-132
 publishing serial printers, 132-133
 remote printer, TPRINT for, 136-137
 TPRINT, 134-140
 using mounted printers, 134
printing with TOPS, 110-127
 changing print job order in, 123-125
 Macintosh, spooling on, 116-117
 network printing procedures, 111-116
 network vs. remote printers, 111, 112
 optional Spool techniques in, 126-127
 PostScript factors in, 110-111
 remote printer procedure, 112-115
 Spool difficulties, 127
 spooler information explained, 122

spooling mounted volumes, 123
  turning off Spool, 125-126
product directory, 399-404
protected mode, 363
protocols
  Apple, 14
  local area network (LAN), 3, 13
  NETBIOS, 13
  NFS, 345
  ONC, 345
PSTACK, 21, 78, 98
PSTAT command, 169
publish command, 30, 31
  TOPS/DOS, 102-104, 167, 168
  TOPS/Macintosh, 84, 86-87

Q

Quarterdeck, 367-370
Quattro, 371
QuickDOS II, 403

R

RAM, 359, 363
read only memory (ROM), 359
read-only files, 33
real mode, 363
rebooting system batch file, 187, 377
Red Ryder, 336
Remember option, TOPS/DOS, 107-109
remote access, 333-334
remote devices, 19-20
remote printer, 112, 134
  TPRINT and printers, DOS for, 136-137
repeaters, 22, 39, 44, 46, 319
  AppleTalk, 401
  bus expansion and, 45
ResEdit, 403
resistors, placement of, 324
resource fork, 35, 36, 286, 289, 290
Rich Text format, Microsoft, translator, TOPS-type and, 222-223
ring configuration, local area network (LAN), 2
RJ-11 plugs, 43
ROM, 359
round telco wire, 328
routing lists, InBox, 318
Run-Time Windows, PageMaker and, 357

S

scanned images, 271
scanning, 223, 225-228, 291, 292
Scrapbook, 277
screen fonts, server, 94
screening, 272

security, 33-34, 376
  electronic mail, 318
  Filemaker, 260
  passwords for, 376
  Spool and, 374-375
  TOPS/DOS, 105
server network, decentralized, 16
servers, 30-31, 77-78
  commands for, TOPS/DOS, 168-170
  dedicated, 77-78
  MS-DOS computers, TOPS/Macintosh use of, 90-92
  screen fonts, 94
  TOPS software, 332
shadow RAM, 363
Shiva, 337
SHUTDOWN command,TOPS/DOS, 169, 171
sign-on procedure, 11
SneakerNet, 7
software, 22-23
  communications server, 332
  memory and, 366
  memory-resident, TOPS/DOS and, 99
  memory-saving applications decisions, 370-372
  multiple versions, installation and, 52
  multiple versions, TOPS and, 35
  network management, 402
  TOPS modules, 53
speed of transmission, 14, 16
Spool, 20, 21, 56, 116-127
  changing print job order with, 123-125
  explanation of information from, 122
  Macintosh operating systems and, 116-117
  mounted volumes and, 123
  optional techniques, 126-127
  problems, 127, 374
  security and, 374-375
  testing, 118-122
  tips for operation, 373-379
  TOPS/Macintosh, 58, 81
  turning off, 125-126
spreadsheets and databases, 231-263
  restrictions, 231-232
  running other databases across TOPS, 262
  running other spreadsheets across TOPS, 259
  TOPS translators and, 247
SQL, 263
standardization 9, 13, 191
star controller, 51
star topology, 2, 42-43, 50-51
stations, 17, 18
storage devices, 18

Suitcase, 53, 56, 94
Sun Microsystems, 14, 18, 345
Sun/TOPS, printing on, 333
SuperPaint, 270
switch, 160, 161
Switcher, 53
symbolic link, 234
Synoptics, 49
Systems Network Architecture, 13

T

3COM, 13, 341,344
Tandy, 15
tasks, background, 116
TCOPY utility, 178
TDEL utility, 178
TDIR utility, 177-178
telco wire, 328
TeleConnector, 22, 37-39, 40, 44, 48, 319, 323
Telefinder, 336
TIFF, 271, 284, 297, 403
Timbuktu Remote, 335
token-ring standard, 13
topologies
  active star, 322
  bus, 321, 42, 43
  daisy chain, 325-328
  passive star, 322
  star, 42, 43, 50-51
  twisted pair, 42
TOPS, 1, 10, 13, 14-16, 17-20, 23-26
  3COM and, 341-344
  AppleShare compatibility and, 350
  clients in, 30, 31
  connection of (see connection)
  decentralized servers, 16
  dedicated server for, 77-78
  distributed services in, 25
  error messages, 381-398
  etiquette for, 34
  file access, 30
  file compatibility, 34, 35, 36
  FileMaker and, tips for use, 262
  FlashBox, 22
  FlashCard, 22
  future developments in, 379-380
  general printing with (see printing with TOPS)
  InBox, 22
  interoperability in, 15
  Macintosh and PC networks, 27
  multi-user applications on, 33
  multiple versions, 35
  NetPrint, 21
  network actions of, 30
  operating systems, 23-24, 26
  operation of, 15, 16, 24

428 Index

PC-only networks, 26
procedural considerations for, 31-33
products in, 20
Repeater, 22
requirements for, 29
security on, 33
server in, 30, 31
server software, 332
software for, 22-23
spreadsheets and databases with, 231-263
TeleConnector, 22
TOPS Spool, 20
TOPS Translators, 21
TOPS/DOS, 21, 29
TOPS/Macintosh, 20, 29
TOPS/Sun, 22
transmission speed of, 16
TWINDOW problems, 349
Unix-based computers and, 28, 346-348
Windows and, printing with, 357-358
wiring for, 16
word processing and translation, 189-230
TOPS Spool (see Spool)
TOPS Translators (see translation)
TOPS/DOS, 21, 97-109
  AUTOEXEC.BAT factor, 162
  batch files, 163-164, 179-188
  client commands, 171
  client utilities in, 105-107
  command list, 165, 166, 167
  command parameters, 168
  commanding TOPS from, 159-188
  CONFIG and AUTOEXEC files in, 97-98
  DOS commands, 159-164
  error messages for, 381-391
  file clients command, 105
  File Servers command, 106
  fine-tuning, 72
  help for PUBLISH, 167
  hidden files, 172
  hide name command, 105
  installation of, 58-71
  loading, 97-99, 100-101
  LOGOUT command, 170
  making batch files, 180
  memory-resident software and, 99
  menu in, 99-100
  Mount command, 171
  mounting server volume via TOPSMENU, 106
  parameter passing batch file, 186
  PATH factor in, 160-162
  post-installation operation, 97
  PSTAT command, 169

Publish command, 102-104, 168
  rebooting system batch file, 187
  Remember option in, 107-109
  requirements for, 29
  server commands, 168-170
  server rules, 101-102
  server utilities for, 101-105
  shutdown command, 169
  TOPS command format for, 164-171
  TOPSTART.BAT, 108
  UNLOAD command, 170
  unloading problems, 170
  Unmount command, 171
  upgrading, 80
  using batch files, 181-184
  utilities, 172-179
  XSYNC command, 168, 173
TOPS/Macintosh, 20, 29, 81-96
  automated actions, 88
  browsing files, 90
  commands for, 84-86, 88-90
  DA Window in, 82-84
  Desk Accessory in, 82
  DOS servers, file management on, 92
  error messages with, 391-398
  file structures and, 91
  filtering ASCII files in, 89
  Finder and Desktop file, 87
  floppy disk only systems, 93-95
  hierarchical file structure (HFS) and, 91
  icons in, 95
  installation of, 53-58
  launching TOPS from floppy disk, 93
  mount and publish options, 86-87
  MS-DOS computer as server, 90-92
  multiple network access to published volume, 86
  networking with, 82
  optional commands, 86-90
  server screen fonts, 94
  single floppy systems, 93
  Suitcase utility, 94
  upgrading, 79-80
TOPS/NOVELL, 344-345
TOPS/PC-NFS gateway, 345
TOPS/Sun, 22
TOPSEXEC.COM, 98
TOPSKRNL, 21, 29, 73-7578, 98
TOPSPRTR, 129
  TOPS/DOS installation and, 76
TOPSTALK, 21, 98
TOPSTART, 108
TPRINT, 128
  local printers and, printers, DOS, 138-139
  network printers, printers, DOS and, 135-136

print queue management with printers, DOS, 137
printers, DOS, use of, 134-135
remote printers, TOPS and, 136-137
setting saving, printers, DOS, 139-140
Transcendental Operating System (see TOPS)
translator programs, 21, 24
translator, TOPS-type, 21, 195-230, 247
  Apple File Exchange and, 215-220
  available formats for, 209
  DisplayWrite translation, 211-213
  error messages in, 398
  file control preferences menu, 208-209
  For New File Names option, 208
  Foreign Format selection, 198
  graphics and, 282
  In Case of File Name Conflict option, 208
  installation of, TOPS/Macintosh, 58
  intracultural transfers and, 221
  log menu, 203
  Macintosh Format selection, 198
  Microsoft Rich Text format, 222-223
  Multimate translation, 209-211
  multiple file translation, 203
  optical character recognition (OCR) devices and, 223
  other formats and, 220
  other sources for, 214-220
  scanner test and, 225-228
  scanning, 223
  Select Files window for, 199
  settings for, 204-205
  Show All Applications option, 205
  Show All Files option, 206
  Show New Files option, 207
  source file selection, 200
  special preferences menu for, 205-208
  startup of, 196
  status messages for, 208
  TOPS/Macintosh, 81
  transaction log in, 202
  translation error option, 209
  translation process in, 197
  word processing strategy for, 228-230
  WordPerfect CONVERT and, 221-222
  WordStar translation, 213-214
  WriteNow to save, 223
trunks, 45, 321
TWINDOW, problems with, 349
twisted pair cabling, 40, 42-45, 59-50

U

universal symbols, 265

Unix, 13, 24, 27, 28, 194, 346-348
UNLOAD command, TOPS/DOS, 170
unmount command, 34, 171
uploading, 304, 333
utilities, TOPS/DOS, 172-179
   hidden files, 172
   TCOPY, 178
   TDEL, 178
   TDIR, 177-178
   XDEL, 176-177
   XDIR, 174-176
   XSYNC, 173

V
video graphics adapter (VGA), 266
Videoshow PIC, 278
voice mail, 302
volumes, 30
Volumes Published command, TOPS/DOS, 104
VROOM (virtual real-time object oriented memory manager), 371

W
warm boot, 377
Web, The, TOPS development from, 14, 15
wide area networks (WAN), 3, 304
Windows, printing with, TOPS considerations for, 357-358
Windows 2.03
   AppleTalk and, 356
   PageMaker and, 356
Windows Draw Plus, 276
Windows GDI Metafiles WMF, 278
Windows/286
   AppleTalk and, 356
   NetPrint and, 355-356
   PageMaker and, 356
wiring, 323-325
   junction boxes, 324
   resistor placement, 324
word processing
   present situation in, 189-190
   reading vs. translating, 193-195
   standardization in, 191
   TOPS and, 191-192
   TOPS translators for, 195-228
WordPerfect, 21, 24, 35, 192, 193, 194, 221-222
WordStar, 21, 213-214
workstations, 17, 18
write access, 33
write protection, 33

X
XCOPY command, problems with, 374
XDEL utility, 176-177
XDIR utility, 174-176
Xerox Corp, 13
XMS (extended memory specification), 363
XSYNC command, 168, 173

Z
Zenographics IMA, 278
zones, 47, 48, 83

Other Bestsellers of Related Interest

THE PRINT SHOP PROJECT BOOK: Business Cards, Banners, and Beyond—Deborah Homan and Philip Seyer Associates

Design business cards and letterheads! Create greeting cards and banners! Make your own advertisements and signs! You can learn to do all this—AND MORE—simply and easily. Here is your guide to Print Shop, the #1 bestselling product on Softsel "Home and Education" bestseller list! Offering simple instructions without sacrificing detail, the authors provide over 150 sample projects. 224 pages, 171 illustrations Book No. 3218, $15.95 paperback only

IBM® DESKTOP PUBLISHING—Gabriel Lanyi and Jon Barrett

Put together the desktop publishing system that most effectively and affordably meets your personal and professional needs. *IBM Desktop Publishing* covers every aspect of producing printed material with your IBM PC or compatible computer. This definitive sourcebook provides the information you need to put together a DTP system that not only fills your needs but that takes into consideration your budget, technical abilities, and equipment you may already own. 256 pages, 90 illustrations. Book No. 3109, $19.95 paperback, $28.95 hardcover

ELECTRONIC PUBLISHING: Evaluation, Procurement and Management—D.W. "Dave" Gater; Bill Ferguson, Illustrator

Attention high-end users! Help is on the way! Now there are answers to your questions and solutions for all those frustrating problems! *Electronic Publishing: Evaluation, Procurement and Management* brings sorely needed information to anyone who wants to, or is responsible for, improving production rates and enhancing the attractiveness of the final product, yet must do so within the restrictions of a limited budget. If you are a professional manager or practitioner who must put together an "industrial strength" system with many terminals and operators, then this book is for you! 320 pages, 118 illustrations. Book No. 3114, $29.95 hardcover only

DESKTOP TYPOGRAPHY WITH QUARKXPRESS™—Frank J. Romano

"I highly recommend it." **Fred Ebrahami, President of Quark Inc.**

Here's where you'll find a model for using QuarkXPress as a page design and typesetting tool. This book explains and illustrates basic typographic principles within the context of pages actually produced with QuarkXPress for the MacIntosh™. Using many example documents to demonstrate concepts, the author carefully examines: text, levels of text, and first lines of text; lists, tables and captions; balance and asymmetry; and more. 209 pages, 73 illustrations. Book No. 3023, $19.95 paperback, $29.95 hardcover

---

Look for These and Other TAB Books at Your Local Bookstore

To Order Call Toll Free 1-800-822-8158
(in PA and AK call 717-794-2191)

or write to TAB BOOKS Inc., Blue Ridge Summit, PA 17294-0840.

For a catalog describing more than 1300 titles, write to TAB BOOKS Inc., Blue Ridge Summit, PA 17294-0840. Catalog is free with purchase; otherwise send $1.00 in check or money order made payable to TAB BOOKS Inc. (and receive $1.00 credit on your next purchase).

BYLINE: AN INTRODUCTION—Leo Scanlon
Endorsed by Ashton-Tate, publisher of BYLINE!

This book provides a practical, step-by-step pproach to learning BYLINE, the popular desktop publishing package from Ashton-Tate. Whether you are producing letters, reports, articles, newsletters, brochures, or financial summaries, this guide will show you how to use BYLINE's powerful features to make them more professional and eye-catching! 190 pages, 54 illustrations, Book No. 2977, $17.95 paperback only

SUPERCHARGED GRAPHICS: A Programmer's Source Code Toolbox—Lee Adams

This advanced graphics learning resource provides programs from which you can create your own graphics. Complete source code and user documentation are given for four major programs: drafting, paintbrush, 3D CAD, and animation. Covering hardware, software, and graphic management aspects, this computer-graphics tutorial demonstrates keyboard control techniques, mouse control techniques, and more! 496 pages, 180 illustrations. Book No. 2959, $19.95 paperback, $29.95 hardcover

Look for These and Other TAB Books at Your Local Bookstore

To Order Call Toll Free 1-800-822-8158
(in PA and AK call 717-794-2191)

or write to TAB BOOKS Inc., Blue Ridge Summit, PA 17294-0840.

Title	Product No.	Quantity	Price

☐ Check or money order made payable to TAB BOOKS Inc.

Charge my ☐ VISA ☐ MasterCard ☐ American Express

Acct. No. _____ Exp. _____

Signature: _____

Name: _____

City: _____

State: _____ Zip: _____

Subtotal $ _____
Postage and Handling
($3.00 in U.S., $5.00 outside U.S.) $ _____
In PA, NY, & ME add applicable sales tax $ _____
TOTAL $ _____

TAB BOOKS catalog free with purchase; otherwise send $1.00 in check or money order and receive $1.00 credit on your next purchase.

Orders outside U.S. must pay with international money order in U.S. dollars.

TAB Guarantee: If for any reason you are not satisfied with the book(s) you order, simply return it (them) within 15 days and receive a full refund.　　　　　　　　　　　　　　　　　　　　　　　　　　　BC